THE
INSTITUTIONAL
INVESTOR
SERIES IN FINANCE

The Institutional Investor Focus on Investment Management

The Institutional Investor Series in Finance

Implementing Capital Budgeting Techniques, Revised Edition
Harold Bierman, Jr.

The Institutional Investor Focus on Investment Management
Frank Fabozzi, editor

The Financial Manager's Guide to Bond Refunding Opportunities
John D. Finnerty, Andrew J. Kalotay, and Francis X. Farrell, Jr.

The Debt/Equity Choice
Ronald W. Masulis

International Corporate Finance, Second Edition
Alan Shapiro

Corporate Restructuring and Executive Compensation
Joel M. Stern, G. Bennett Stewart III, and Donald H. Chew, Jr.,
editors

Marketing Financial Services
David Zenoff, editor

The Institutional Investor Focus on Investment Management

EDITED BY

Frank J. Fabozzi

Managing Editor
The Journal of Portfolio Management
and

Visiting Professor of Finance
Sloan School of Management
Massachusetts Institute of Technology

Ballinger Publishing Company

Cambridge, Massachusetts
A Subsidiary of Harper & Row, Publishers, Inc.

International Standard Book Number: 0-88730-275-0

Library of Congress Catalog Card Number: 88-38947

Printed in the United States of America

Library of Congress Cataloging-in-Publication Data

The Institutional investor focus on investment management / edited by Frank J. Fabozzi.
    p. cm. — (The Institutional investor series in finance)

    Bibliography: p.
    Includes index.
    ISBN 0-88730-275-0
    1. Portfolio management. 2. Investment analysis. I. Fabozzi, Frank J. II. Series.
    HG4529.5.I57   1988   88-38947
    332.6—dc19   CIP

Contributing Authors

Robert D. Arnott   First Quadrant Corp.
Lawrence N. Bader   Salomon Brothers Inc
Peter L. Bernstein   Peter L. Bernstein, Inc.
Fischer Black   Goldman Sachs & Co.
Stephen G. Bodurtha   Kidder, Peabody & Co., Inc.
Richard Bookstaber   Morgan Stanley & Co., Inc.
Peter M. Brackman   Prudential-Bache Capital Funding
Richard A. Brealey   London Business School
Edward A. Brill   Bankers Trust Company
Gary P. Brinson   First Chicago Investment Advisors
Steven J. Carlson   Shearson Lehman Mortgage Securities
Andrew S. Carron   First Boston Corporation
Raj Daryanani   Citicorp North American Investment Bank
Ravi E. Dattatreya   Prudential-Bache Capital Funding
Tony Estep   New Amsterdam Partners
Frank J. Fabozzi   Massachusetts Institute of Technology
Nimrod Fachler   First Chicago Investment Advisors
John D. Finnerty   College Savings Bank
H. Gifford Fong   Gifford Fong Associates
Russell J. Fuller   Washington State University
William J. Gartland   Drexel Burnham Lambert
Gary L. Gastineau   Salomon Brothers Inc
Bennett W. Golub   First Boston Corporation
Laurie S. Goodman   Goldman Sachs & Co.
Floyd J. Gould   Investment Research Company and
  University of Chicago
Mark Grinblatt   University of California–Los Angeles
Steven Guterman   Salomon Brothers Inc
Erol Hakanoglu   Goldman Sachs & Co.
Nick Hanson   Salomon Brothers Inc
David J. Hartzell   Salomon Brothers Inc

Eric I. Hemel First Boston Corporation
Joanne M. Hill PaineWebber
Anshuman Jain Kidder, Peabody & Co., Inc.
Frank J. Jones Kidder, Peabody & Co., Inc.
Timothy B. Kiggins Drexel Burnham Lambert
Mark Kritzman New Amsterdam Partners
Beth A. Krumholz Kidder, Peabody & Co., Inc.
Andrew D. Langerman Drexel Burnham Lambert
Dean LeBaron Batterymarch
Martin L. Leibowitz Salomon Brothers Inc
Donald L. Luskin Wells Fargo Investment Advisors
Richard W. McEnally University of North Carolina–Chapel Hill
Llewellyn Miller Drexel Burnham Lambert
Sharmin Mossavar-Rahmani Fidelity Management Trust Co.
Uday Rajan Drexel Burnham Lambert
Aruna S. Ramamurti Triangle Portfolio Associates
Marc R. Reinganum University of Iowa
Edgar A. Robie, Jr. Western Asset Management Co.
Ramine Rouhani Goldman Sachs & Co.
Prakash A. Shimpi Drexel Burnham Lambert
Evan Schulman Batterymach
David Shulman Salomon Brothers Inc
Joseph Snailer Citicorp North American Investment Bank
Janet Spratlin
James A. Sprow Washington State University
Kenneth H. Sullivan Drexel Burnham Lambert
Ronald J. Surz Becker, Burke Associates Inc.
Eric M. P. Tang Gifford Fong Associates
Sheridan Titman University of California–Los Angeles
Francis H. Trainer, Jr. Sanford C. Bernstein & Co., Inc.
Paul Vianna Salomon Brothers Inc
Gudmundur Vigfusson Prudential-Bache Capital Funding
Richard A. Wood, Jr. Kidder, Peabody & Co., Inc.
Jess B. Yawitz Goldman Sachs & Co.
Mark Zurack Goldman Sachs & Co.

Contents

PART II ■ Fixed Income Management ■ 259

PART IV ▪ Asset Allocation ▪ 659

Foreword

Peter L. Bernstein

Can another book of readings be worth the effort? Yes.

Readers look at introductions to books like this for one of two reasons. On the one hand, they hope that the introduction will reveal whether the book is going to justify their time and effort — resources that all readers consider to be in extremely short supply. On the other hand, they hope that the introduction will provide a summary so useful that it will hold the necessary expenditure of time and effort to a bare minimum.

As this volume offers forty-five separate chapters, I am afraid that I cannot oblige with a summary that will suffice to minimize time and effort. The reader who did actually plow through such a summary would be too exhausted when done to look at even two or three of the chapters with any care.

This foreword, therefore, provides the one hand rather than the other. And on that hand — whether the material here justifies the expenditure of valuable time and effort — I have no hesitation in declaring that the papers in this book justify whatever time and effort they require.

I make this statement so confidently because of the critical importance of the common theme that runs through these contributions, a theme that no serious practitioner or academic can afford to ignore. The focus of all these authors is on the array of dazzling innovations that has burst upon the process of investing institutional portfolios in the past few years. Indeed, the whole purpose of the book is to help the reader to understand, measure, and profit from those innovations.

Change has sliced through every aspect of investing. The very definition of acceptable assets has broadened. New kinds of assets, both actual and synthetic, have come into use. Accepted wisdom in portfolio theory has gone through a major transformation. Few people even suspected the complexities that were imbedded in the character of fixed income vehicles and that are now an integral part of fixed income portfolio management. New instruments and new strategies have blurred the distinctions among asset classes while permitting the construction of portfolios with payoff functions tailor-made to a client's needs. These developments, in turn, have stimulated more systematic methods for defining client needs, responding in part to prods from new accounting standards and reporting requirements. As a by-product, the strategies of transacting buys and sells have been raised from a secondary role to a central part of the portfolio management process.

Drawing on an unusual degree of familiarity with both the literature and the requirements of the world of investors, Frank Fabozzi has selected these forty-five contributions precisely because they deal with what is new rather than with what is familiar. The book is not easy reading, therefore, but its reward:effort ratio is unusually high.

Convention requires a book of readings to have subdivisions. This one has three: Equity Management, Fixed Income Management, and Asset Allocation. While useful, these divisions are also misleading. Investing is an exercise in dealing with uncertainty, and the nature of uncertainty is invariant, regardless of the asset involved. In other words, risk is a many-headed monster, but the faces on those heads look much the same regardless of the perspective from which you see them.

This means that equity investors can learn from studying the problems of fixed income investors, and vice versa. Both can benefit from insights into the new techniques of asset allocation, and asset allocation will fail if the allocator fails to grasp the essential character of the underlying assets. In short, do not confine your reading to your favored subdivision, or you will miss much of what this book has to offer.

Investment management is a field in which the need to keep learning is inexhaustible. Even the most expert among us are involved in the endless task of education. Perhaps that is what makes them so expert. The aim of *The Institutional Investor Focus on Investment Management* is to keep its readers in that select subset of the investment world.

PART I

Equity Management

1

How Did We Get Here and Where Are We Going?*

Peter L. Bernstein
Peter L. Bernstein, Inc.
  and
Editor, *The Journal of Portfolio Management*

The theme of the conference from which this article is based was Tradition and Innovation. In the spirit of that theme, my observations concentrate first, and briefly, on which innovations from the past are still having an influence on our work and on the markets. Second, and at greater length, I will explore what these past innovations portend for the future.

We know that we cannot predict the future. On the other hand, we can predict the nature of risk with some degree of confidence. The essence of this analysis, therefore, is an assessment of the risks that the future holds in store for us.

The risks are big. A more curious conclusion is that many of the changes and innovations I describe, which appear benign and positive at first glance, have in fact added to those risks and are likely to lead to a bumpier rather than a smoother path in the future.

I. The Past: Longer Term Influences

I find a bewildering pattern of changes over the 35 years since I first entered the investment management profession. Furthermore, the pace of these

---

*This article is adapted from the author's address to the opening session of the Financial Analysts' Federation Annual Conference, Philadelphia, May 11, 1987.

changes seems to be accelerating rather than stabilizing. A lot may have happened between the early 1950s and the early 1980s, but those changes seem almost to have been dwarfed by the changes of the past five years or so.

I shall look first at two of the longer term changes and then turn to the manner in which they have galvanized innovation in the present.

The single most overwhelming influence out of the past has nothing directly to do with portfolio management, security analysis, or financial markets. Rather, it was a gigantic technological innovation: the computer, or, more particularly, the PC.

It seems only yesterday — and in fact, it was only about ten years ago — that I held my first hand-held calculator in hand. Until then, I did most of my calculations on a slide rule or a pad of paper, with only an occasional pass at the cumbersome mechanical calculator.

The first hand-held calculator was a $35 Bowmar that added, subtracted, multiplied, and divided, but it could not do square roots. About two years later, I acquired an HP-41 programmable calculator, and life began to quicken. Without that HP, I doubt if I would have been so nimble with my first Apple II+ — not even with an Apple IIe — and Visicalc, but then we were off and running.

Without the computer there would be no money market funds, no globalized markets, no active trading in derivative securities, no 100-million, or even 50-million-share days on the stock exchange, no multibillion dollar trading days in foreign exchanges, no talk of duration or convexity or synthetics or caps or swaps.

In our work the computer has made possible the practical use of the ideas of the efficient market and modern portfolio theory. Without the computer Harry Markowitz's 1952 article on mean/variance would be languishing in the dust, Bill Sharpe and Steve Ross would be obscure assistant professors in equally obscure business schools, and how many of us would ever have heard of Black or Scholes?

Without the computer the dividend discount model would be an intellectual curiosity discovered by John Burr Williams 50 years ago, rather than the essence of most valuation models in use today. Furthermore, the dividend discount model and the introduction of the "riskless rate" in the capital asset pricing model combined to integrate interest sensitivity into equity analysis, contributing to a dramatic increase in the covariance between equity returns and interest rates since about 1980.

In fact, the other major event of the longer term past was the huge rise in interest rates that began in the late 1960s and that has never again subsided to pre-1970 levels. Quite aside from the enormous economic and financial consequences associated with that development, the elevated levels of interest rates brought fixed-income management into prominence as a profession of its own. This development led in turn to the demise of the balanced manager and the growth of a coterie of specialized managers — much to my sorrow, I must say, even though few people seem to share my concerns about the disappearance of balanced management.

II. But Just in the Past Five Years...

Let me list briefly the more recent major changes in investment management and financial analysis. Each of these developments is worth an article on its own, but the sheer number of these innovations and the sense of their extraordinary magnitude will suffice for my purposes here.

Here they are, in no particular order:

- Globalization of investment management
- Systematic asset allocation techniques
- Portfolio insurance
- The sophisticated integration of real estate into portfolios of financial assets
- An explosion in the variety of quantitative techniques and applications
- The proliferation of derivative instruments that are traded at unprecedented levels of activity: options, futures, options on futures, synthetics of all types, swaps, junk bonds, and other fixed-income securities that I do not even begin to understand but seem to have even the kitchen sink itself attached to them
- The takeover game and the aggressive growth of the investment banking arm of the traditional brokerage house
- Associated with all this, a stupendous increase in portfolio turnover rates, adding to brokerage profitability and encouraging a serious brain drain from academe to Wall Street. What happens when the best minds in finance are no longer there to each the young?
- Securitization of an increasing variety of assets that were never marketable in the past
- Indexing in new forms and new applications
- With FASB (Financial Accounting Standards Board) 87, the rediscovery of the old idea that assets exist to fund liabilities, *and for no other reason,* and that the liabilities must therefore define the character of the asset mix. Will this development, perhaps, bring back my missing balanced manager in a new incarnation?
- Finally, the most intriguing of the new developments, the development of techniques to trade composite assets, or entire portfolios — index options and futures, industry-oriented mutual funds, program trading, Instinet, POSIT, and other experiments that are still being researched

III. What Does All This Portend?

Many of these changes appear positive, in the sense that they enable us to do things that we could never do before. An increased variety of instruments means more efficient financing arrangements and the opening up of new opportunities for finance. Better techniques for hedging risk should make more types of investment possible. More active markets and new areas for diversification should reduce risk and may also increase expected returns.

On the other hand, as I suggested at the outset, these forces are having a profound effect on the investment environment itself, beyond their impact on the way in which we manage our clients' money. That effect is far from benign in many instances. The consequence is that the environment is becoming riskier, more uncertain, less amenable to systematic measurement and prediction.

In the turbulent world in which we live today, the careful calibrations of the capital asset pricing model, arbitrage pricing theory, and the dividend discount model may simply be the deck chairs on the Titanic. I am reminded of the excellent title to an article in *The Journal of Portfolio Management:* "Better Betas Didn't Help The Boat People!"

I find four aspects of these trends especially troubling.

1. New Players   For many years, the markets were dominated by pension fund investors, with erratic but diminishing activity on the part of individuals and trust accounts. Now we see a growing number of new players (a word to be used advisedly) with unknown value structures and new instruments but with a growing influence on security prices.

There are four major groups of new players.

The first is the foreigner, whose ownership of U.S. assets is growing at an annual rate of well over $100 billion. The foreign investor values U.S. assets in nondollar currencies that fluctuate versus the dollar, giving different value perspectives from our own. Furthermore, the foreign investor has time horizons and investment objectives that may be entirely different from the horizons and objectives of the traditionally dominant investors in our markets.

The second new player is the corporation itself, suddenly a buyer rather than an issuer of equity securities and a much more aggressive and varied issuer of debt securities — and all of this in huge amounts. Like the foreigner the corporation has unorthodox time horizons and investment goals.

Third, brokers have become big traders for their own accounts, with the agency role diminishing relative to the use of their own capital. This process has assumed orders of magnitude that would boggle the minds of the Gus Levys and Sy Lewises of the past. In addition, the brokers have been the ones who corralled the best minds in finance to design, create, promote, and then issue and trade the potpourri of new instruments that characterize today's marketplace.

Finally, look at what has been happening in the market for mutual funds. Not only are mutual fund assets growing at a stunning rate; they are growing in areas that hardly existed in the past. International funds are now over $7 billion, up from only $1 billion in 1985. More important, fixed-income funds are approaching $200 billion in assets, up from only $30 billion at the end of 1984.

These new funds and their first-time owners will have sale and redemption patterns that we do not yet understand but that can have a meaningful effect on the pattern of security prices. We had a vivid example of this in April 1987, when we discovered that the public, suffering from sticker shock on low rates on short-term money, had started to use long-term municipal bond funds as parking places for idle cash. Sudden withdrawals to pay taxes and in response to a sharp jump in taxable interest rates socked a naturally illiquid market with a mighty blow.

2. Dynamic Hedging Portfolio insurance, other dynamic hedging strategies, and the rapid expansion in the use of synthetic as well as actual hedging instruments raises the question of who will fund the risks that others choose to avoid. How much can we rely on the willingness of those "others" to fund those risks? The process is most important at the extremes, but the extremes are precisely the moment when no one wants to fund the other person's hedge. We will not know whether the whole thing is a house of cards until too late.

Portfolio insurance has another disturbing consequence. The best reason for equity portfolio insurance is to increase the equity share of total assets. Portfolio insurance is most effective, in other words, as a substitute for bonds. *Stated another way, the users of portfolio insurance eschew diversification.*

All hedging strategies ultimately lead to less diversification, because they appear to have less downside than diversification. You hold just one asset and hedge its downside risks, while a diversified portfolio can always hold one or another asset that is declining in value. On the other hand, hedging strategies reduce the attractions of buy-and-hold and bring more concentrated buying and selling into the market. This development can only make the markets riskier.

3. Efficiency versus Liquidity It is a bromide to observe that information is traveling faster and more vividly every day. This process is accelerating with the advent of longer trading hours and the internationalization of the marketplace.

Thus, in an information sense, the markets are becoming increasingly efficient. Although we should welcome the idea that more people have more knowledge about more things, the other side of that coin is less attractive.

The rapid dissemination of good news and bad news and just plain more news means a greater tendency toward the homogeneous expectations that theoreticians like to tell us about. Homogeneous expectations are a mixed blessing, however, because they lead to discontinuous price movements as prices move rapidly to their new equilibrium values.

Liquidity, on the other hand, depends upon heterogeneous expectations and inefficient markets. The ability to trade at a price close to the last price means either that little information has become available to change equilibrium prices or that traders hold differing opinions about the available information. Liquid markets are much noisier than efficient markets.

This tension between greater information efficiency and the need for liquidity is leading to increased volatility in all markets, at least in terms of short-term price changes. This is not a passing phenomenon: it is here to stay. What does that mean for required rates of return?

4. What of the Market Portfolio?   All of these trends, quite aside from major developments that I have not even mentioned, are making the market portfolio itself incredibly risky. The character of the underlying assets in the market portfolio are becoming riskier and the covariances among their returns are becoming more obscure.

Let me name just a few examples of this development. Debt quality is low, even among governments. Equities are leveraged far beyond anything seen in the past. Values of all assets in globalized markets are made more volatile by fluctuating exchange rates. Stock markets are at record highs in most countries, both absolutely and in terms of conventional valuation parameters.

If this is the way the traditional pieces look, remember that we now have a host of new pieces in the market portfolio. We have little reliable experience with these new pieces, especially in the area of synthetics, swaps, other hedging devices, and securitized illiquid assets. How do they act in relation to one another and to the traditional pieces? Have they lives of their own? No one knows the answers to these questions, except on the basis of experience so limited that it does not deserve the label of statistical significance.

Indeed, the covariances among the different parts of the market portfolio — and even among the subsegments of each part — are fluid and dynamic. They defy systematic prediction.

Finally, to cite an obvious but painful truth, the ability of policymakers to contain financial volatility and crisis is limited, even if the policymakers had a clear idea of what kind of action is warranted. I need not elaborate on the disillusionment with fiscal policy, the inflationary anxieties associated with monetary policy, the threat of protectionism, the dubious effectiveness of exchange rate stabilization, and the political obstacles to coordination of fiscal, monetary, and trade policies.

This leads me to conclude by recalling one of Bob Kirby's many wise and succinct observations. "The S&P 500? That's such an imprudent portfolio, I wouldn't even buy it for my mother-in-law."

2

The Collapse of the Efficient Market Hypothesis
A Look at the Empirical Anomalies of the 1980s*

Marc R. Reinganum
Phillips Professor of Finance
College of Business
University of Iowa

I. Introduction

The last decade witnessed an explosion in research that demolished widely held beliefs about the price behaviors of stock market securities. As a group this research comprises the "market anomaly" literature. Of course, an anomaly can exist only relative to a given benchmark, and by the mid-1970s such a benchmark clearly existed: the efficient market hypothesis. By the mid-1970s a preponderance of academic research suggested that capital markets were informationally efficient, so that stock prices fully reflected all available information. Operationally, this meant that changes in stock prices were unpredictable from one day to the next and that returns earned by stocks over time were commensurate with their levels of risk. Thus stock returns were characterized as being independently and identically distributed over time, and differences in expected or mean returns among stocks were attributed to their risks as measured by beta, a covariance measure of risk with the market. This view seemed reasonable and much empirical work supported it.[1]

By the mid-1980s this efficient markets view of stock price movements came under serious seige on two fronts. First, a body of research emerged

---

*The title for this paper was selected prior to the stock market crash of October 19, 1987.
1. For example, see Eugene F. Fama, *Foundations of Finance: Portfolio Decisions and Securities Prices* (New York: Basic Books, Inc., 1976).

that documented that differences in average rates of returns among securities are not completely explained by their betas. A striking finding in this literature is that a firm's stock market capitalization seems to be a better predictor of future returns than a firm's estimated beta. On the second front, another group of papers revealed that stock returns are *not* identically distributed over time. In particular, this research uncovered systematic patterns in stock returns that vary with certain calendar periods. The purpose of this article is to survey the major research findings in these two areas.

II. The Failure of Beta

In the 1960s two articles by Nicholson suggested that firms with low price/ earnings (P/E) ratios outperform firms with high P/E ratios.[2] Among his findings, Nicholson in 1960 reported that the three-year appreciation of the five stocks with the lowest P/E ratios averaged 56 percent, whereas the equivalent appreciation for the five stocks with the highest P/E ratios equaled only 21 percent. At that time Nicholson's results were surprising since most financial analysts assumed high P/E stocks were bought for growth.

Modern portfolio theory, and the capital asset pricing model (CAPM) in particular, would offer an alternative interpretation of Nicholson's findings. According to the CAPM, the reason that low P/E stocks could experience average rates of return greater than those of high P/E stocks is that low P/E stocks may be riskier than their high P/E counterparts. Since the risk of a security within the CAPM is measured by its beta, the CAPM could explain Nicholson's findings as long as the betas of low P/E companies were sufficiently greater than the betas of high P/E companies.

Nearly 10 years after Nicholson's second article, Basu resurrected the P/E effect in a way that seriously challenged the efficient market hypothesis.[3] Unlike Nicholson, Basu had at his disposal the paradigm of the CAPM, and the CAPM dictated how to measure risk using beta. In addition, Basu had the advantage of computerized data files from COMPUSTAT and CRSP, so that he could analyze 1,400 industrial firms that traded on the New York Stock Exchange between September 1956 and August 1971. Thus Basu's effort represented a large-scale study of the potential P/E effect which carefully controlled for risk as measured by beta. Figure 1 plots the average annual abnormal returns for Basu's five P/E portfolios. On a risk-adjusted basis, Basu reported that the difference in average annual returns between

---

2. See S. Francis Nicholson, "Price-Earnings Ratios," *Financial Analysts' Journal 16* (July-August 1960): 43–45. Also see S. Francis Nicholson, "Price Ratios in Relation to Investment Results," *Financial Analysts' Journal 24* (January-February 1968): 105–109.
3. See S. Basu, "Investment Performance of Common Stocks in Relation to Their Price-Earnings Ratios: A Test of the Efficient Market Hypothesis," *Journal of Finance 32* (June 1977): 663–82.

FIGURE 1. Basu's Computation of Annual Average Abnormal Portfolio Returns Based on Jensen's Differential.

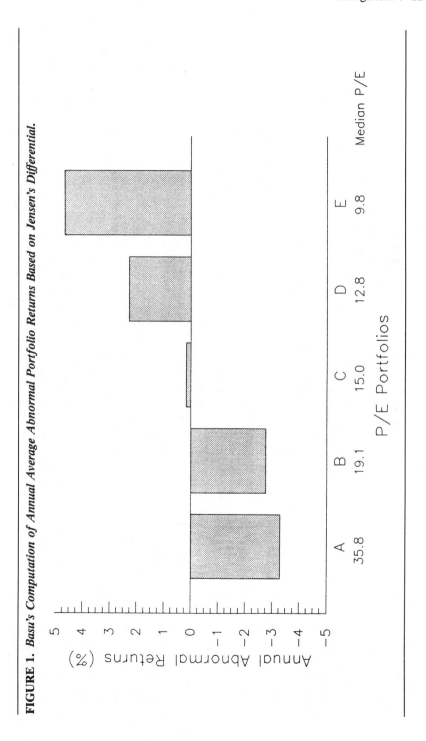

low and high P/E securities exceeded 7 percent. Furthermore, this return differential seemed to be stable between the two seven-year periods of Basu's study. Basu looked at potential factors other than beta risk differentials (for example, differential taxes and transaction costs) that might explain the return differential between low and high P/E stocks but still concluded that both tax-exempt and tax-paying investors could profit by acquiring low P/E stocks. Beta failed in the sense that, on an annual basis, low P/E portfolios earned superior rates of return after controlling for risk.

The real deluge of evidence reporting major deficiencies in the CAPM did not begin until 1981. In March of that year, papers by Banz and Reinganum, appearing in the *Journal of Financial Economics,* suggested that economically and statistically significant abnormal returns could be earned by grouping securities on the basis of their stock market capitalizations (price per share times number of shares outstanding).[4] In particular, both authors reported that the average returns of small capitalization stocks significantly exceeded the average returns of large capitalization stocks, even after adjusting returns for beta risk.[5]

Banz analyzed the monthly returns of New York Stock Exchange (NYSE) stocks over the period 1931–1975. During this period Banz found that the 50 smallest NYSE stocks outperformed the 50 largest companies by 1.01 percent per month on average. Banz also presented evidence that suggest the so-called size effect was not linear; that is, the large, positive abnormal returns were clustered among the very smallest NYSE companies.

Reinganum studied the size effect over a shorter interval of time, 1963–1977, but included all the firms that traded on the American as well as New York stock exchanges. He reported a median capitalization for his small firm portfolio of only $8.3 million. As might be expected, the magnitude of the effect increased as one dipped further down the capitalization scale. Reinganum's evidence indicated that the smallest firm portfolio earned a mean

---

4. See Rolf W. Banz, "The Relationship between Return and Market Value of Common Stocks," *Journal of Financial Economics 9* (March 1981): 3–18. Also see Marc R. Reinganum, "Misspecification of Capital Asset Pricing: Empirical Anomalies Based on Earnings' Yields and Market Values," *Journal of Financial Economics 9* (March 1981): 19–46.

5. An offshoot of the research on the size effect concerned the question of whether the size effect and the P/E effect were two, independent phenomena or manifestations of just one effect. Reinganum's 1981 article presented evidence that suggested the size effect subsumed the P/E effect. Basu ["The Relation between Earnings' Yield, Market Value and Return," *Journal of Financial Economics 12* (June 1983): 129–56] later disputed Reinganum's claim. Thomas Cook and Michael Rozeff ["Size and Earnings/Price Ratio Anomalies: One Effect or Two?" *Journal of Financial and Quantitative Analysis 19* (December 1984): 449–66] replicated Reinganum's findings using his methods but were unable to corroborate Basu's assertion that the P/E effect subsumed the size effect. Cook and Rozeff argued for both a P/E and a size effect. Regardless of the outcome of this debate, the evidence clearly points out the inability of beta to explain cross-sectional differences in average returns.

excess return of 0.05 percent per trading day whereas the largest firm group experienced a mean excess return of −0.034 percent per trading day. Furthermore, Reinganum's evidence displayed a virtually monotonic relationship between the market capitalization and mean excess returns (see Figure 2). Based on annual data, Reinganum calculated the difference in unadjusted returns between small and large firms to be 23.3 percent on average.[6] Of course, both Banz and Reinganum recognized that the size effect varied from subperiod to subperiod and in fact, in some subperiods, was negative. The variability of the size effect was emphasized in a subsequent paper by Brown, Kleidon, and Marsh.[7]

The importance of the research by Banz and Reinganum is that it clearly establishes differences in average returns cannot be explained by differences in estimated betas. The discrepancies between what small stocks actually earn and what small stocks are predicted to earn, based on their level of beta risk, are significant both statistically and economically. Naturally, other researchers attempted to explain these anomalous findings using a variety of arguments. Some researchers questioned whether beta risk was appropriately estimated.[8] Others investigated whether transaction costs might eliminate profitable exploitation of the size effect.[9] More recent research attempts to reconcile the size effect with measures of risk alluded to in the arbitrage price theory, but this evidence is mixed. In any event the empirical evidence from the 1980s clearly shows that estimated betas fail to explain important differences in average returns between small and large companies. The failure of beta to account for cross-sectional differences in average returns opened up the door to devise simple trading strategies that systematically beat well-accepted investment benchmarks. This research constitutes one branch of the empirical anomalies.[10]

---

6. See Marc R. Reinganum, "Portfolio Strategies Based on Market Capitalization," *The Journal of Portfolio Management 9* (Winter 1983): 29–36.

7. See Philip Brown, Allan W. Kleidon, and Terry A. Marsh, "New Evidence on the Nature of Size-related Anomalies in Stock Prices," *Journal of Financial Economics 12* (June 1983): 33–56.

8. For example, see Richard Roll, "A Possible Explanation of the Small Firm Effect," *Journal of Finance 36* (September 1981): 879–88. Also see Marc R. Reinganum, "A Direct Test of Roll's Conjecture on the Firm Size Effect," *Journal of Finance 37* (March 1982): 27–35.

9. For example, see Hans R. Stoll and Richard E. Whaley, "Transaction Costs and the Small Firm Effect," *Journal of Financial Economics 12* (June 1983): 57–80. Also see Paul Schultz, "Transaction Costs and the Small Firm Effect: A Comment," *Journal of Financial Economics 12* (June 1983): 81–88.

10. Other research also explores potential deficiencies in beta, such as studies of the Value Line ranking system [for example, Fisher Black, "Yes, Virginia There Is Hope: Tests of the Value Line Ranking System," *Financial Analysts Journal 29* (September-October 1973): 10–14] and studies of a dividend yield effect [for example, Robert H. Litzenberger and Krishna Ramaswamy, "The Effects of Personal Taxes and Dividends on Capital Asset Prices: Theory and Market Equilibrium," *Journal of Financial Economics 7* (June 1979): 163–95]. However, the magnitude of the size effect seems much larger than either of these two effects.

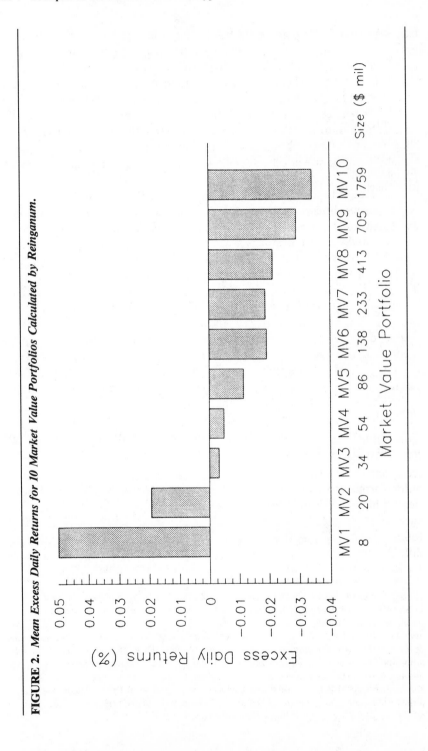

FIGURE 2. *Mean Excess Daily Returns for 10 Market Value Portfolios Calculated by Reinganum.*

III. Systematic Patterns in Stock Returns

The second set of research papers that drive a stake into the heart of the classical interpretation of the efficient market hypothesis analyze predictable changes in expected returns. Through the mid-1970s, most academic researchers probably accepted the proposition that stock returns are independently and identically distributed, at least as a very good first approximation. This view of stock returns grew out of research that suggested stock prices follow a random walk. By the mid-1980s this view of stock price movements imploded. As researchers scrutinized the data more and more closely, four fascinating patterns in stock emerged:

1. A month-of-the-year effect
2. A week-of-the-month effect
3. A day-of-the-week effect
4. An hour-of-the-day effect

Perhaps with the next several years "minute-of-the-hour" and "second-of-the-minute" papers will be written!

The month-of-the-year effect is commonly referred to as the January effect. As early as 1976, Rozeff and Kinney documented that the mean returns in January exceed the mean returns of the other months for a market index of NYSE stocks over the period 1904–1974.[11] However, it was not until seven years later that research returned to this topic with a vengeance. In 1983 Keim, investigating the size effect earlier documented by Banz and Reinganum, discovered that this effect is not uniform throughout the calendar year.[12] That is, although small firms outperform large ones on average, the return differential varies by calendar month. Keim reported that, over the 1963–1979 period, nearly 50 percent of the average magnitude of the size effect occurs in January. Furthermore, Keim found that small firms *always* outperformed large ones in January, even in years in which large firms experienced higher average returns than small ones. Figure 3 displays the differences in average daily excess returns between the smallest and largest portfolios by calendar month. The pattern of January returns is unmistakably different from those of the other months. In January the returns of small

---

11. See Michael S. Rozeff and William R. Kinney, Jr., "Capital Market Seasonality: The Case of Stock Returns," *Journal of Financial Economics 3* (October 1976): 379–402. Following up on the research of Rozeff and Kinney, Seha Tinic and Richard West ["Risk and Return: January vs. the Rest of the Year," *Journal of Financial Economics 13* (December 1984): 561–74] discover that January is the *only* month in which a consistently positive, statistically significant relationship between risk and return exists. At least within the framework of the CAPM, they find investors are compensated for bearing risk only in January.
12. See Donald B. Keim, "Size-Related Anomalies and Stock Return Seasonality: Further Empirical Evidence," *Journal of Financial Economics 12* (June 1983): 13–32.

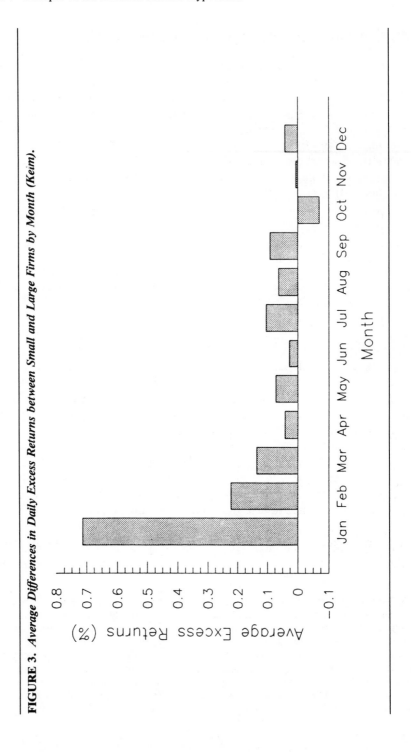

FIGURE 3. *Average Differences in Daily Excess Returns between Small and Large Firms by Month (Keim).*

firms surge ahead of those of their larger brethren. Thus the January effect is primarily a phenomenon found among smaller capitalization stocks. The dramatic shifts in mean returns are not observed among the very largest stocks.

Keim's research begged an explanation, and the "tax-loss selling hypothesis" emerged as the leading contender. The folklore behind the tax-loss selling hypothesis is that individuals sell their losers, which reduces their tax liability. This selling pressure, according to this reasoning, lowers the price of the stock at the end of December. In January the motive for tax selling is eliminated, the selling pressure is relieved, and stock prices rebound resulting in a high January return. While this argument does not seem to be an equilibrium one, some earlier empirical work supported it. For example, Branch reported that abnormal profits could be earned if one bought the stock of companies whose prices reach yearly lows in the last week of December and sold these stocks in January.[13]

Reinganum in 1983 investigated the tax-loss selling hypothesis as it applied to small and large firms.[14] Based on a measure of potential tax-loss selling, he classified firms into four groups ranging from the previous year's losers to the previous year's winners. Reinganum concluded that the abnormally high returns witnessed during the first few days in January appeared to be consistent with the tax-loss selling hypothesis. However, tax-loss selling could not explain the entire January effect, because the small firms least likely to be sold for tax reasons also experienced large average January returns relative to other months.[15] After eliminating a list of possible spurious causes of the turn-of-the-year effect, Roll reported a negative relationship between the turn-of-the-year return and the return during the preceding year. While such evidence is consistent with a tax-loss selling story, Roll concludes that transaction costs and low liquidity probably prevents the elimination of the return seasonality. Schultz enhanced the credibility of the tax-loss selling hypothesis. He detected no evidence of a January effect in small stock returns prior to the War Revenue Act of 1917.[16]

The search for an explanation of the January effect led to investigations of the returns of stocks traded on international markets. Gultekin and Gultekin survey stock return indexes from most major industrial countries and

13. See Ben Branch, "A Tax Loss Trading Rule," *Journal of Business 50* (April 1977): 198–207.
14. See Marc R. Reinganum, "The Anomalous Stock Market Behavior of Small Firms in January: Empirical Tests for Tax-Loss Selling Effects," *Journal of Financial Economics 12* (June 1983): 89–104.
15. See Richard Roll, "Vas ist das?" *The Journal of Portfolio Management 9* (Winter 1983): 18–28.
16. See Paul Schultz, "Personal Income Taxes and the January Effect: Small Firm Stock Returns before the War Revenue Act of 1917: A Note," *Journal of Finance 40* (March 1985): 333–43.

find evidence of seasonality that is manifested at the turn of the tax year, usually January.[17] They also report that the stock return seasonality does not seem to be related to size. Brown, Keim, Kleidon, and Marsh studied the returns of securities listed on the Australian stock exchange.[18] They discover a January seasonal in returns among Australian stocks. Their smallest portfolio earned 8.86 percent on average during January. Unlike the United States, however, the Australian tax year ends on June 30. Thus Brown et al. challenge the assertion that the January effect is tax driven, although they do recognize the possibility that some of the effect may be caused by the integration of capital markets worldwide (that is, with the United States). Interestingly, Brown et al. also find large average returns in July for the Australian stock. In fact, among the smaller portfolios, the July average returns tend to be slightly larger than the January returns.

Berges, McConnell, and Schlarbaum analyze returns of Canadian stocks over the period 1951–1980.[19] The Canadian data also exhibit a strong seasonal in January. However, the Canadian returns display a strong January effect even during the period in which there were no capital gains taxes. Berges et al. conclude that this evidence does not support the tax-loss selling hypothesis as the sole explanation of the January effect. Kato and Schallheim study returns of securities that trade on the Tokyo Stock Exchange.[20] They detect the presence of both the January and size effects. Their data also reveal somewhat larger returns in June. Reinganum and Shapiro examine seasonality in the London Stock Exchange.[21] Prior to the introduction of a capital gains tax in England, the authors could not reject the hypothesis that the mean monthly returns for all months are identical. After the introduction of a tax, the authors report two months stand apart from the rest, January and April. Reinganum and Shapiro conclude that the April evidence is consistent with the tax-loss selling hypothesis (since the tax-year end is April 5), but the January returns are not.

The January effect or month-of-the-year effect has been extensively examined using stock return data from the United States as well as a host of other industrialized countries. Overwhelmingly the evidence indicates that

---

17. See Mustafa N. Gultekin and N. Bulent Gultekin, "Stock Market Seasonality: International Evidence," *Journal of Financial Economics 12* (December 1983): 469–82.

18. See Philip Brown, Donald B. Keim, Allan W. Kleidon, and Terry A. Marsh, "Stock Return Seasonalities and the Tax-Loss Selling Hypothesis: Analysis of the Arguments and Australian Evidence," *Journal of Financial Economics 12* (June 1983): 105–28.

19. See Angel Berges, John J. McConnell, and Gary G. Schlarbaum, "The Turn-of-the-Year in Canada," *Journal of Finance 39* (March 1984): 185–92.

20. See Kato Kiyoshi and James S. Schallheim, "Seasonal and Size Anomalies in the Japanese Stock Market," *Journal of Financial and Quantitative Analysis 20* (June 1985): 243–60.

21. See Marc R. Reinganum and Alan C. Shapiro, "Taxes and Stock Return Seasonality: Evidence for the London Stock Exchange," *Journal of Business 60* (April 1987): 281–95.

the mean monthly return in January is substantially different than the mean returns of most other months. In particular the January returns are the largest. The reasons for the exceptional performance of stocks in January, especially small ones, is still debated. Some evidence suggests that the pattern of stock returns in January may be tax induced, but the evidence is mixed. In any case the January effect marks a real departure from the view that stock returns are independently and identically distributed. The mean returns in January are significantly different from those of other months, both in a statistical and economic sense.

The next anomalous pattern might be termed the week-of-the-month effect. Actually this anomaly refers to the pattern of returns earned by firms within a trading month. Over the period from 1963 through 1981, Ariel divided trading months into two, equal periods.[22] A trading month starts on the last trading day (inclusive) of a calendar month and extends to the last trading day (exclusive) of the following calendar month. Ariel reports that, using an equal-weighted market index, the 19-year cumulative returns attributable to the first half of a trading month are 2552.40 percent. In contrast, the 19-year cumulative returns earned during the last half of the trading month are a paltry −0.25 percent. The results are truly astounding. Perhaps Ariel's own summation is the most dramatic: "During the nineteen years studied, all of the market's cumulative advance occurred during the first half of the trading months, with the last half of the trading months contributing nothing" (p. 173). Furthermore, Ariel rules out the possibility that this effect is just another manifestation of the January effect. Even when Januaries are removed from the sample, Ariel calculates a statistically significant difference between the mean returns from the first and second halves of a month. Ariel's finding of a week-of-the-month effect in stock returns is still unexplained.

A much larger body of evidence investigates the day-of-the-week effect. This effect refers to the unusual behavior of stock prices from the close of trading on Friday to the close on Monday. Under the calendar time hypothesis, one might expect the return from Friday close to Monday close to be three times as large as the returns for any other one trading day. But, based on the daily returns of the S&P 500 composite portfolio over the period from 1953 through 1977, French finds that Monday's returns are actually negative on average.[23] In fact the mean returns on Monday were negative in 20 of the 25 years. Ignoring transaction costs, French calculates that a trading rule that sold on Friday afternoon, held cash over the weekend, and repurchased

---

22. See Robert A. Ariel, "A Monthly Effect in Stock Returns," *Journal of Financial Economics 18* (March 1987): 161–74.

23. See Kenneth R. French, "Stock Returns for the Weekend Effect," *Journal of Financial Economics 8* (March 1980): 55–69.

on Monday afternoon would net an investor an average annual return of 13.4 percent. Independently Gibbons and Hess reached similar conclusions.[24] Gibbons and Hess studied not only various market indices, but the 30 individual securities that comprise the Dow Jones 30. From the period July 1962–December 1978, they report a negative Monday return for their various indexes as well as for each of the 30 individual securities. Gibbons and Hess also find below average returns for T-bills on Mondays. Keim and Stambaugh document average negative Monday returns back through 1928.[25] Jaffe and Westerfield extend the study of this phenomenon to the United Kingdom, Japan, Canada, and Australia.[26] They detect a weekend effect in each country, although the lowest mean returns in Japan and Australia occur on Tuesday.

The initial studies of the day-of-the-week effect confined themselves to an analysis of the returns from the close of trading on Friday to the close on Monday. These studies prompted inquiry into another question: Exactly when do these negative returns develop? From the Friday close to the Monday open? From the Monday open to the Monday close? Rogalski decomposes daily close to close returns into trading day (open to close) and nontrading day (close to open) returns.[27] For the Dow Jones Industrial Average and the Standard and Poor's 500 Composite Index, Rogalski finds that the negative component of the Friday close to Monday close return actually occurs between the Friday close and the Monday open. He attributes the entire phenomenon to the nontrading period. Rogalski also reports that the Monday returns are positive on average in January, particularly so for small firms.

Smirlock and Starks dispute Rogalski's conclusion using data on the DJIA over the 21-year period 1963–1983.[28] In the period that overlaps with Rogalski's study (1974–1983), the results reported by Smirlock and Starks concur with those of Rogalski: the weekend effect occurs entirely during the nontrading period. But in the prior sample periods, the results are reversed; the entire effect is observed during the active trading time on Monday. For the overall period Smirlock and Starks find that part of the negative Monday return occurs during trading hours and part happens during nontrading. Figure 4 displays the mean daily returns that Smirlock and Starks calculate.

24. See Michael Gibbons and Patrick Hess, "Day of the Week Effects and Asset Returns," *Journal of Business 54* (October 1981): 579–96.
25. See Donald B. Keim and Robert F. Stambaugh, "A Further Investigation of the Weekend Effect in Stock Returns," *Journal of Finance 39* (July 1984): 819–35.
26. See Jeffrey Jaffe and Randolph Westerfield, "The Week-End Effect in Common Stock Returns: The International Evidence," *Journal of Finance 40* (June 1985): 433–54.
27. See Richard J. Rogalski, "New Findings Regarding Day-of-the-Week Returns over Trading and Non-Trading Periods: A Note," *Journal of Finance 39* (December 1984): 1603–14.
28. See Michael Smirlock and Laura Starks, "Day-of-the-Week and Intraday Effects in Stock Returns," *Journal of Financial Economics 17* (September 1986): 197–210.

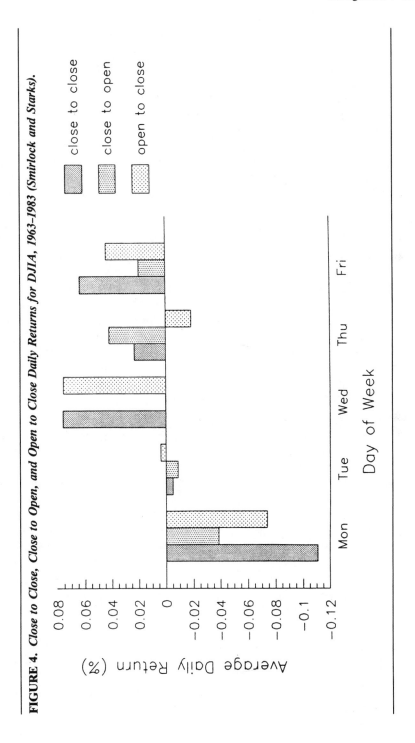

FIGURE 4. *Close to Close, Close to Open, and Open to Close Daily Returns for DJIA, 1963–1983 (Smirlock and Starks).*

Despite the debate about precisely when the negative returns occur, one fact remains undisputed: the average daily return from Friday close to Monday close is negative whereas for all other trading days it is positive.

Research did not stop after daily returns were broken up into close-to-open and open-to-close components. Rather, the level of time disaggregation continued and investigation into a potential hour-of-the-day effect developed. Smirlock and Starks collected hourly observations on the Dow Jones Industrial Average over the 1963–1983 period. They report that during the first hour of trading the Monday returns are negative on average, but for the other days of the week the average returns in that first hour are positive. Harris, using transactions data for NYSE companies for the 14-month period between December 1981 and January 1983, calculates returns for 15-minute intervals during the trading day.[29] He finds that during the first 45 minutes of trading on Mondays prices tend to drop. In contrast, on the other weekday mornings, they tend to rise. Yet, perhaps the most intriguing result described by Harris is one that all days share in common: during the last 15 minutes of trading, prices tend to jump up dramatically. Harris reports that this end-of-day phenomenon is not unduly influenced by just a couple of observations. Rather, it occurs in more than 90 percent of the cases. The evidence from Smirlock and Starks and from Harris clearly reveals intraday patterns in stock returns.

IV. Conclusion

During the 1960s and 1970s, the efficient markets hypothesis marshalled much evidence in its favor. Stock prices seemed to fluctuate randomly and differences in mean returns between stocks were attributed to their riskiness as measured by beta. But the research of the past decade challenged both of these fundamental tenets. One branch of research documented that stock prices did not change in a manner that could be described as statistically independent and identical. Predictable patterns in stock prices emerged. The mean returns in January stood apart from those of other months. Small firms in particular experienced unusually large January returns especially at the beginning of that month. Other research unearthed the fact that the positive advances made by the market over long periods of time occur almost exclusively in the first part of the month and almost never in the second part of the month. Stated differently, the average returns in the first half of a month are positive and in the second half are zero.

Patterns of price changes by trading day also surfaced. On Mondays, returns tend to be negative. In contrast, the other weekdays possess positive

---

29. See Lawrence Harris, "A Transaction Data Study of Weekly and Intraday Patterns in Stock Returns," *Journal of Financial Economics 16* (May 1986): 99–117.

returns as one might expect. The dissection of intraday returns also began. Indeed the tendency for stock prices to rise during the last 15 minutes of trading is one of the most fascinating discoveries from this nascent research.

The failure of beta to explain differences in average returns over long periods also manifested itself in research during the past decade. Several different investment strategies seem to earn unusually high rates of return even after adjustments for beta risk are taken into account. The two strategies that have garnered most of the attention are those based on price/earnings ratios and those based on stock market capitalizations. On average, low P/E stocks significantly outperform high P/E securities. Similarly, small capitalization stocks experience much higher average returns than large capitalization stocks. Some research suggests that the P/E and size effects may not be independent of each other. In any case the empirical evidence reveals that beta-based benchmarks can be beaten.

Why has the classical view of efficient classical markets begun to collapse at this time? The answer does not lie in the quality or caliber of earlier research. Indeed, much of the earlier work on random walks and the capital asset pricing model unveiled important insights into the behavior of stock market prices. Rather, the answer lies, at least in part, in technological change; the tools available to researchers in the late 1980s are much more powerful than those available just 20 years earlier. For example, the mainframe computing capabilities of the 1960s now fit on desktops. Similar advances have been made with respect to databases. In the 1960s hand-collecting data for 30 securities was a major undertaking. By the 1980s researchers culled computer tapes filled with transactions data for all listed securities. As technology advances so will the discoveries in capital markets.

The collapse of the classical efficient market hypothesis does not mean that information is ignored in the pricing of assets. Indeed a myriad of event studies shows just the opposite. But the collapse, caused by the mountain of empirical anomalies, does mean that the modeling efforts must become more sophisticated. No longer can stock prices be viewed as following a random walk, even approximately. The predictable patterns in stock returns cry out for a coherent, unified explanation. Perhaps that is what the next decade will reveal.

3

What Hath MPT Wrought:
Which Risks Reap Rewards?*

Robert D. Arnott
President and Chief Investment Officer
First Quadrant Corp.

I. Introduction

The theories upon which Modern Portfolio Theory (MPT) is based have been under increasing attack of late. We have seen demonstrations that beta has little to do with return. This is further corroborated in this article. Many studies have suggested that the markets do not follow a random walk. Such factors as size, stock price variability, and P/E seem related to return, suggesting that security price behavior is not explained by the Random Walk Hypothesis. These results also are corroborated in this article.

Do we discard the theories that underly MPT? If so, do we throw out the tools that MPT has generated? The first of these two questions will be debated in the academic journals for years to come. To the second question, an emphatic "No" is appropriate. MPT tools can be of value whether or not the theories are accurate.

In fact, the purpose of this article is to examine precisely which elements of security risk the investment markets use in security pricing. This issue can be phrased another way: While no one disputes the idea that the

---

*This article is reprinted from the Fall 1983 issue of *The Journal of Portfolio Management*.
**This article was written when the author was Vice President of The Boston Company.

investment markets generally provide higher returns for higher risks, for which risks do investors require compensation? Furthermore, are these risks systematic or do they represent inefficiencies that savvy participants in the marketplace can exploit?

The following analysis systematically examines these questions, using several measures of risks to accomplish this. The methodology will compare ex ante risk measures with subsequent security returns.[1] Two measures will evaluate the extent to which a given risk measure is associated with subsequent return. The first of these is the average annual information coefficient (IC);[2] the second is a measure of consistency, which we term the "stability t-statistic."[3]

II. Is Beta Dead?

Beta is the most widely recognized risk measure in use in the investment community. Past studies support the market beta as the single most significant contributor to stock price comovement.[4] In short, beta has withstood all scrutiny to date as a legitimate measure of security behavior and risk and as an even more significant descriptor of portfolio behavior and risk.

---

1. The test universe for this study consists of some 700 issues on the Boston Company database, including all S&P 500 stocks and stocks on the Boston Company list of closely followed stocks. These tests were partially cross-checked against the full 4000-stock database (including dead stocks), to test for survivor bias. These tests revealed no meaningful differences vis-à-vis the 700-stock test.
2. The information coefficient (IC) is simply the correlation between a selected return predictor and the subsequent total return. In most instances, a rank correlation is used. We use a simple correlation, since a simple correlation captures performance extremes better than a rank correlation. In practice, there is rarely any significant difference between these two correlation measures. The IC is widely used in the investment community in preference to an R^2 measure. One reason for this is the simplicity of the concept. A second reason is that an IC is directly and linearly related to the excess returns that a security selection strategy can achieve, while an R^2 is related to the potential value of a model in a more subtle way.
3. We determine the "stability t-statistic" by computing annual ICs for each year in the study. A standard deviation of these annual IC measures is determined, and we then calculate the "stability t-statistic" by dividing the mean IC by the standard error in the estimate of mean IC. Clearly, a return forecasting model with an IC averaging 0.1 and a standard deviation of 0.1 is more consistent and useful than a model with an average IC of 0.1 and a standard deviation of 0.3. This "stability t-statistic" provides a simple measure of return forecasting model consistency and, one can assume, the likelihood of a security selection model continuing to add value.
4. See the following articles: James L. Farrell, Jr., "Analyzing Covariation of Returns to Determine Homogeneous Stock Groupings," *Journal of Business* (April 1974): 186–207; Robert D. Arnott, "Cluster Analysis and Stock Price Comovement," *Financial Analysts Journal* (November/December 1980): 56–62; Barr Rosenberg, "Extra-Market Components of Covariance in Security Returns," *Journal of Financial and Quantitative Analysis* 9: 263–74.

Why, then, has there been so much controversy regarding the merits of beta? Logic dictates that investors will be risk averse and will expect more return for higher risk investments. Furthermore, logic suggests that rational investors will largely ignore elements of risk that they can eliminate through diversification.

These two ideas form the basis of the Capital Assets Pricing Model (CAPM). The CAPM suggests that the investor will be compensated for non-diversifiable risk and will not be compensated for diversifiable risk. This makes sense theoretically, but has failed to pass a blizzard of empirical tests.

Therein lies the problem. If investors are not compensated for accepting significant non-diversifiable risk, and if investors demand higher return for higher risk investments, then beta must not be the risk for which investors demand compensation! Indeed, it is not surprising that investors may focus on a risk other than beta. Investors will expect greater returns for those issues with greater perceived risk. This *perceived* risk need not bear any meaningful relationship with beta.

Table 1 summarizes the 1-year Information Coefficients for a number of potential risk measures. The first of these is "true beta."[5] Each information coefficient represents the correlation between true beta in a given year and total return for that year. In any given year there is typically a strong relationship between beta and return. This is only natural: High beta stocks should outperform low beta stocks in an up market, leading to a strong positive IC, and should underperform low beta stocks in a down market, leading to a strong negative IC.

The important item to note is that the mean IC is only 0.07, with a standard deviation of 0.26. This means that the estimated mean IC of 0.07 has a standard error of 0.07.[6] In other words, while beta is a significant descriptor of stock price behavior, we cannot assume with any confidence that the investor is compensated for this risk in the long run. The mean IC is not significantly different from zero.

In any case, no investor can know, ex ante, the true beta for a given year. We have nevertheless constructed an "expected beta," derived from historical data, that represent a good estimator for "true beta." This expected beta is derived from exponentially-weighted historical price behavior and is

---

5. "True beta" is determined by measuring the 52-week or 156-week regression coefficient of stock behavior relative to the S&P 500 Stock Index, over the same 1-year or 3-year span that is used for the total return calculation.

6. The standard deviation of a series of data can be used to estimate the likely error in the mean; this likely error in the mean, or standard error, is simply:

$$\sqrt{\frac{\Sigma(x_i - \bar{x})^2}{n-1}},$$

where n is the number of data samples.

TABLE 1a. *1-Year Information Coefficients — Annual Summary.*

	1964	1965	1966	1967	1968	1969	1970	1971
True beta					+.17	−.09	−.29	+.25
Exp. Beta					+.17	+.02	−.31	+.21
True risk					+.24	−.16	−.47	+.11
Exp. risk					+.20	−.15	−.25	+.22
EPS uncer.	+.22	+.25	+.16	+.21	+.16	−.28	+.14	−.11
Capitalization	+.19	+.29	+.08	+.43	+.34	−.08	+.07	+.15
Total sales	−.02	+.18	+.16	+.33	+.23	+.12	−.01	+.17
Book/price	+.16	+.09	−.20	+.05	+.19	−.32	+.14	−.20
Earnings yield	+.24	+.11	−.10	+.15	+.23	−.23	+.21	−.03
Ret. EPS yield	+.16	+.24	−.03	+.21	+.23	−.13	+.15	+.08

adjusted towards a beta of 1.0 using a Vasicek adjustment.[7] Table 2 shows that the expected beta has a correlation with the "true beta" of 0.53.

If, however, we assume that this expected beta is typical of the ex ante estimates of beta that may have existed prior to each year (in fact, it is a better estimate than many beta estimates), we find more disappointing results. The mean IC of this expected beta measure is just 0.04, with a standard error of 0.05. These figures lack statistical significance and suggest that expected beta has a strikingly weak relationship with subsequent stock performance.

We might speculate that the long-term relationship between beta and return is stronger. This hypothesis is tested in Table 3, which shows the annual Information Coefficient for these same beta measures vis-à-vis 3-year total return results. The mean ICs are 0.03 and 0.06 for true beta (measured over the 3-year span) and expected beta (measured as before), respectively. Neither IC is very significant, although the figure for expected beta is marginally significant at the 90% level. In short, the relationship between beta and long-term returns hardly differs from the shorter term results.

Is beta dead? As a predictor of stock returns, we (and many others) have demonstrated that beta is of limited value at best. But beta is not dead. Beta's value is as a predictor of risk for the individual security and, more importantly, for portfolios.

---

7. The expected beta is determined by regressing all available weekly behavior *prior to* the time span used for return measurement of a stock against the S&P 500 index, using an exponential weighting function of $e^{-0.99t}$ to emphasize more recent data. This historical beta is then adjusted toward 1.00, using a Vasicek adjustment, with the formula:

$$\text{expected beta} = 0.3 + 0.7 \times \text{historical beta}.$$

1972	1973	1974	1975	1976	1977	1978	1979	1980	1981
+.22	−.28	−.32	+.38	+.19	−.13	+.23	+.36	+.47	−.15
.00	−.16	−.15	+.27	+.11	+.14	+.08	+.18	+.30	−.30
−.05	−.30	−.42	+.39	+.24	+.19	+.26	+.43	+.38	−.25
−.06	−.16	−.15	+.24	+.16	+.21	+.22	+.34	+.28	−.27
−.10	+.01	+.27	+.25	+.42	+.19	+.09	+.19	−.20	+.11
+.05	−.02	+.16	+.35	+.40	+.44	+.24	+.24	−.01	+.22
+.20	+.02	−.03	+.15	+.19	+.40	+.25	+.28	+.17	+.12
−.19	+.05	+.26	+.26	+.37	+.14	−.06	+.06	−.18	+.16
−.08	+.03	+.26	+.16	+.29	+.16	−.01	−.12	−.14	+.13
+.07	+.03	+.20	+.14	+.29	+.19	+.09	−.03	−.12	+.11

III. Stock Price Risk

If investors do not demand compensation for systematic risk, or beta, perhaps total price volatility is the perceived risk. We can test this hypothesis in the same way as the beta was tested.

The performance of "true risk" as a return measure also appears in Table 1. "True risk" is simply the standard deviation of stock price activity

TABLE 1b. *1-Year Information Coefficients — Overall Summary.*

	Mean IC	Std Dev	Std Err	Stab "t"
True beta	+.07	.26	.07	1.0
Exp. beta	+.04	.19	.05	0.7
True risk	+.04	.30	.08	0.5
Exp. risk	+.06	.23	.06	1.0
EPS uncer.	+.11	.19	.04	2.6**
Capitalization	+.20	.18	.04	5.2***
Total sales	+.16	.12	.03	5.5***
Book/price	+.04	.19	.04	1.0
Earnings yield	+.07	.16	.04	1.9*
Ret. EPS yield	+.10	.12	.03	3.6***

* — Significant at the 90% level.
** — Significant at the 99% level.
*** — Significant at the 99.9% level.

TABLE 2. *Correlations.*

	True Beta	Exp. Beta	True Risk	Exp. Risk	EPS Uncer.	Cap.	Total Sales	Book/ Price	EPS Yield
Exp. beta	0.53								
True risk	0.61	0.54							
Exp. risk	0.50	0.67	0.73						
EPS uncer.	−0.01	0.00	0.19	0.18					
Capitalization	−0.02	0.00	0.35	0.37	0.36				
Total sales	0.00	0.01	0.31	0.31	−0.03	0.70			
Book/price	0.01	−0.03	0.07	0.06	0.58	0.29	−0.14		
Earnings yield	0.02	−0.06	−0.09	−0.11	0.44	0.11	−0.17	0.32	
Ret. EPS yield	0.01	−0.01	0.03	0.03	0.52	0.19	−0.06	0.27	0.77

during the year in which return is tested. As is noted in Table 1B, the mean IC for "true risk" is only 0.04. With a standard error of 0.08, this IC is utterly insignificant. An examination of ex ante expected risk reveals marginally better results. This "expected risk" is determined by exponentially weighting past stock price volatility.[8] The mean IC is 0.06, with a standard error of 0.06.

Once again, it is appropriate to examine the relationship between volatility and longer term returns. As shown on Table 3, the 3-year performance of stocks is more strongly related to stock volatility than is the 1-year performance. The 3-year ICs relative to true risk (measured over the same 3-year span as return) and relative to "expected risk" (as defined before) are 0.08 and 0.13, respectively. The IC for the "true risk" measure is not significant, but the IC for "expected risk" is significant at the 95% level.

All of the ICs associated with beta or risk measures are positive. This is consistent with the idea that the investment community demands greater return for greater stock price risk, both non-diversifiable and total. Only two of the ICs are significant, however; hence, this relationship must be considered as a relatively weak one.

Note that the investment community appears more averse to the expected total stock price risk, demanding more return, than to the expected non-diversifiable portion of risk, or beta, which the CAPM would suggest is more important. It is also interesting that "expected risk" is apparently more strongly related to return than "true risk."

We would speculate that, if volatility exceeds expectations, investors would increase their required return and drop the price for a stock. This would reduce actual return and would weaken the relationship between true volatility and return.

Finally, it is interesting to note that the correlation between expected volatility and expected beta is 0.67, and that expected beta has ICs that are approximately two-thirds as strong as the ICs for expected volatility. This would suggest that any relationship between beta and return is predicated solely on volatility, and that the investment community requires no additional return for systematic risk except to the extent that systematic risk is related to stock volatility. Since none of these phenomena is statistically significant, however, a more detailed examination is not warranted without more extensive testing.

In short, the investment markets are remarkably insensitive to stock price risk. Yet, investors are almost universally risk averse. It is a rare investor or portfolio manager who would knowingly choose a "risky" investment

---

8. The "expected risk" is determined by measuring the historical weekly standard deviation of stock price behavior, using all available weekly data *prior to* the time span used for return measurement, using an exponential weighting function of $e^{-0.98t}$ to emphasize more recent data.

TABLE 3a. *3-Year Information Coefficients — Annual Summary.*

	1964	1965	1966	1967	1968	1969	1970
True beta					+.07	−.10	−.10
Exp. beta					+.02	+.02	−.04
True risk					+.04	−.10	−.15
Exp. risk					+.02	−.06	−.04
EPS uncer.	+.24	+.28	+.26	+.11	+.05	−.11	−.01
Capitalization	+.25	+.34	+.42	+.36	+.25	+.09	+.12
Total sales	+.19	+.30	+.31	+.29	+.22	+.15	+.18
Book/price	+.02	+.01	+.04	+.05	+.05	−.21	−.16
Earnings yield	−.02	+.02	+.18	+.10	+.18	−.07	−.05
Ret. EPS yield	+.03	+.14	+.12	+.14	+.17	−.01	.00

over a "safe" investment without a substantial increase in expected return. But Tables 1 and 3 demonstrate that volatile or high beta issues do not generate appreciably more return than stable or low beta issues. Since it is clear that investors do not demand substantially more return for more price risk, price risk must differ sharply from *perceived* risk. In order to determine what constitutes perceived risk, let us now examine which investment characteristics *are* related to return.

IV. Earnings Uncertainty

Earnings do matter. Studies have demonstrated that, when earnings expectations change, the stock price responds, usually simultaneously,[9] that earnings surprises significantly affect prices even for some time after the surprise earnings have been announced,[10] and that uncertain earnings growth prospects leds to uncertain returns and stock volatility.[11] Since much investment community attention is focused on earnings, earnings uncertainty might be an element of *perceived* risk. In other words, investors may demand greater return on a stock with uncertain earnings than on a predictable "safe" stock.

For this test, we define earnings uncertainty by dividing the 7-year standard deviation in earnings per share by the stock price.[12] By taking a simple

---

9. See the following articles: Edwin J. Elton, Martin J. Gruber, and Mustafa Gultekin, "Earnings Expectations and Share Prices," *Management Science* (September 1981): 975–87; Edwin J. Elton, Martin J. Gruber, and Sak Mo Koo, "Expectational Data: The Effect of Quarterly Reports," Working Paper, New York University.

10. Henry A. Latané and Charles P. Jones, "Standardized Unexpected Earnings — 1971–77," *Journal of Finance* (June 1979): 717–24.

11. Tony Estep, Nick Hanson, and Cal Johnson, "Sources of Value and Risk in Common Stocks," *The Journal of Portfolio Management* (Summer 1983): 5–13.

12. A one-quarter lag was introduced to the ex ante test data to allow for reporting lags.

1971	1972	1973	1974	1975	1976	1977	1978	1979
−.02	−.05	−.19	−.20	+.28	+.11	−.03	+.23	+.31
−.05	−.10	−.13	+.15	+.23	+.15	+.12	+.14	+.19
−.06	−.15	−.20	−.14	+.38	+.36	+.33	+.36	+.30
−.04	−.12	−.05	+.23	+.28	+.33	+.33	+.36	+.32
−.01	+.16	+.25	+.45	+.36	+.32	+.26	+.16	+.09
+.08	+.10	+.18	+.38	+.48	+.43	+.40	+.30	+.27
+.15	+.07	+.04	+.11	+.30	+.32	+.37	+.31	+.33
−.05	+.16	+.21	+.37	+.34	+.29	+.12	−.07	−.07
−.02	−.01	+.14	+.37	+.20	+.20	+.06	−.07	−.15
+.07	+.03	+.09	+.38	+.23	+.24	+.15	+.04	−.04

standard deviation, rather than a percent standard deviation around a trend, we eliminate any mathematical problems associated with negative earnings data. This approach does require some normalization to correct for discrepancies between high-price, high-earnings companies and low-price, low-earnings companies. We normalize by dividing by stock price, which once again avoids mathematical problems with companies with negative earnings data, while introducing a slight P/E effect.

Table 1 shows that ex ante earnings uncertainty does indeed correlate with return. The annual IC averages 0.11, with a standard error of just 0.04.

TABLE 3b. *3-Year Information Coefficients — Overall Summary.*

	Mean IC	Std Dev	Std Err	Stab "t"
True beta	+.03	.17	.05	0.6
Exp. beta	+.06	.12	.03	1.7*
True risk	+.08	.24	.06	1.2
Exp. risk	+.13	.19	.05	2.3*
EPS uncer.	+.18	.15	.04	4.7***
Capitalization	+.28	.13	.03	8.4***
Total sales	+.23	.10	.03	8.9***
Book/price	+.07	.17	.04	1.6*
Earnings yield	+.07	.14	.03	1.9*
Ret. EPS yield	+.11	.11	.03	4.1***

*—Significant at the 90% level.
**—Significant at the 99% level.
***—Significant at the 99.9% level.

Unlike the results for beta or price volatility, this result is mathematically significant at the 99% level. The longer term relationship between earnings uncertainty with subsequent 3-year total return is 0.18, which is significant at the 99.9% level.

Thus, we can confidently assert that earnings uncertainty is a major component of the *perceived* stock risk, for which greater return is required. Earnings uncertainty is related to stock price volatility with a correlation of 0.18–0.19, so stocks with high earnings uncertainty will be more volatile than stocks with stable earnings. Much of this risk is not systematic, however, and can be eliminated through diversification: Table 2 shows that there is essentially no correlation between earnings uncertainty and expected or actual beta.

V. The Size Effect

A growing body of evidence supports the idea that small-capitalization stocks significantly outperform large-capitalization stocks.[13] This effect is so strong and so consistent that even advocates of the Efficient Markets Hypothesis have found no refutation of this effect. On the other hand, any non-systematic or diversifiable effect that exhibits a significant ex ante relationship with return clearly violates both the Efficient Markets Hypothesis and the CAPM.

The results presented in Tables 1 and 3 support the small stock effect,[14] even though our 700-stock test universe is heavily weighted toward larger issues and others have found this effect to be strongest for the very small issues that are absent from our study. Nonetheless, even in this universe of larger issues, the smaller stocks generate superior returns to a striking extent. The 1-year IC averages 0.20, with a standard error of only 0.04, while the 3-year IC averages a startling 0.28, with a standard error of just 0.03; both are significant at the 99.9% level. This small stock effect was evident in 15 of the last 18 years and never failed for any 3-year span.

Capitalization actually combines a size effect with a value effect. If we use total sales, net income, or book value as a measure of size, we find a size effect that is mathematically significant but not quite as great as the capitalization size effect. Tables 1 and 3 show the results for a size effect based on total sales.[15] The results for such a model are just as significant as the capi-

---

13. See the following articles: R. W. Banz, "The Relationship Between Return and Market Value of Common Stocks," *Journal of Financial Economics* 9: 1–18; A. F. Ehrbar, "Giant Payoffs from Midget Stocks," *Fortune* (June 30, 1980): 111–13.

14. Our test is based on log-capitalization, or log (price × shares outstanding), at year-end immediately before the period over which returns are measured.

15. Our test is based on log (total sales), using sales in the year preceding the period over which returns are measured. A one-quarter "reporting lag" is introduced to prevent the inclusion of data that might have been unavailable at the time.

talization effect, but the ICs are lower. This occurs because a capitalization model can be viewed as a sales effect combined with a value effect based on the ratio of sales per share to stock price, or as a net income effect combined with an earnings yield effect, or a book value effect combined with a book to price ratio effect. Thus, if small companies generate better total returns than large companies, and if value measures such as an earnings yield are also correlated with subsequent total returns, then it is not surprising that capitalization is a stronger indicator of return than the internal measures of company size. Several value effects will be further reviewed in the next section.

If there is a size effect, why do we not see institutions stampede into smaller stocks and obliterate the size effect? The problem, once again, is one of perceived risk. Few investment practitioners would consider Maine Public Service to be safer than General Telephone, for example. Maine Public Service has hardly any institutional following, it is not widely understood, and it is illiquid (the stock moved almost 10% on just 10,000 shares of trading in three days in April 1982). Perhaps most important, a big loss in General Telephone is more likely to be forgiven by most clients than a big loss in Maine Public Service. Nonetheless, Maine Public Service is less volatile, has far less systematic risk (beta), and has generated more than 5% per annum more total return from 1975 through mid-1982 than General Telephone.

A second possible source of the small stock effect, which is related to perceived risk, is constituency: Who owns the stock, and what risks matter to them? The constituency of large stocks is usually dominated by institutional investors with well diversified portfolios. Institutional investors like to understand a company, so they want stocks covered by analysts; they like liquidity, so they favor the large companies on which block trades are easy; they are penalized by their clients for losing money on obscure bets, so they are encouraged to focus on large, good-quality, respectable stocks; their broad diversification means that only a modest expected return premium vis-à-vis potential non-stock investments is necessary to justify an investment, and, finally, the small size of the small issues precludes large investments, so there is a sense that these issues are "too small" to be worth the trouble. The constituency of small stocks is often individuals whose portfolios display little diversification; this includes small investors who cannot afford diversification and insiders with substantial undiversified holdings in their own company. These undiversified investors could be expected to require a larger expected return premium to justify their holdings in these small stocks.

This size effect, like the earnings uncertainty effect, is not meaningfully related to systematic risk. The correlation between size and either true beta or expected beta is effectively zero. As with the earnings uncertainty effect, however, the size effect is related to volatility. The correlation between size and volatility is 0.35, so small stocks are more volatile than large stocks. But, once again, this appears to be largely specific risk, which we can eliminate through diversification.

VI. Fundamental Risk

Fundamental ratios, such as P/E and the price to book ratio, are based on the consensus assessment by the investment community of the *fundamental* risk in a company. While P/E is not as tangible a measure of risk as beta, volatility, or even earnings uncertainty, it implies a judgment of the fundamental risk of a company. A high P/E suggests that the investment community believes that the company will grow quickly and predictably and that the risk of failing to achieve this growth is slight; a low P/E suggests an expectation of slow growth with substantial risk that growth will not be achieved. Thus, fundamental ratios of this sort can be viewed as quantitative measures of qualitative consensus risk judgments.

Tables 1 and 3 summarize the results for three value measures:[16] the ratio of book value per share to stock price, the ratio of earnings per share to price (or earnings yield), and the retained earnings yield (earnings yield — dividend yield). Each shows positive correlation with subsequent returns, over both a 1-year and a 3-year span, with various levels of significance. The book to price ratio is not much better than the beta or volatility measures, with a 1-year IC averaging only 0.04 and a 3-year IC averaging only 0.07, and is sufficiently inconsistent that the 1-year results are not significant and the 3-year results are barely significant at the 90% level. Earnings yield is somewhat better than book-to-price, with 1-year and 3-year ICs both averaging 0.07. While these figures are similar to the ICs for beta and volatility, earnings yield is more consistently related to subsequent return than beta or volatility, so these results are both significant at the 90% level. Finally, retained earnings yield is substantially better than either of these, with 1-year and 3-year ICs of 0.10 and 0.11, respectively. These are consistent enough results that they are both significant at a 99.9% level.

It is reasonable to speculate that this retained earnings yield measures investor confidence that retained earnings will ultimately accrue to the shareholder. A high retained earnings yield suggests a lack of confidence in the likelihood that shareholders will ultimately benefit from the retained earnings, hence, a *risk* that the earnings are not meaningful or sustainable.

This evidence tells us that traditional value measures many be quantitative evidence of perceived qualitative risks. Many of these value measures are not particularly strong or consistent, but some are significant. For the

---

16. Many measures and strategies other than the ones shown here have been tested, particularly value-oriented approaches. These are representative of the kind of results we observe in our tests.

most part, these value measures are not strongly correlated with systematic risk nor, surprisingly, with total volatility. Thus, once again, we find potential avenues for diversifiable risk, which may lead to superior returns.

VII. Yes, Virginia, There Is a Santa Claus

The market prices securities to reward risk. Investors willing to accept higher risk will reap greater returns. This idea is not new and has never been challenged. The key question is: Which risks are factored into the pricing mechanism of the market?

If the market were perfectly rational and efficient, some version of the CAPM would hold true, and returns would be directly related to non-diversifiable risk. But the market *is people,* and people are not perfectly rational. People expect greater return for greater *perceived* risk: They price securities in accordance with the consensus *perceived* risk. If the market is rational, this consesus perceived risk for a security will match the non-diversifiable risk of that security. *There is substantial evidence that this is not the case.*

Any of several strategies can be developed by exploiting the discrepancies between *perceived* risk and expected non-diversifiable risk. These strategies can lead to superior long-term performance without increased risk: Those elements of perceived risk that are diversifiable can, by definition, be eliminated through diversification.

What does any such strategy imply? To achieve superior results in the long run, one must invest in areas that are perceived by the consensus to be high-risk. By definition, this is a contrarian strategy. This implies the sale of "wonderful, safe" stocks and the purchase of the unloved "dogs," which are viewed as risky investments. Since such issues are demonstrated to have greater price volatility, this strategy will result in some spectacular flops that will typically be more than offset by spectacular gains. Finally, it is often more comfortable to fail conventionally than to succeed unconventionally; no portfolio manager was ever fired for buying IBM. This strategy, of necessity, forces the uncomfortable and unconventional decisions.

Can a strategy based on buying perceived risk that is not systematic risk backfire? Yes, two conditions can cause inferior performance. First, the perceived risk measure used in a strategy must be diversifiable. If the risk subsequently is found to be systematic, so that diversification does not reduce the risk for the portfolio, the exploitation of that risk may not result in superior performance. Second, if the aversion to some element of perceived risk increases over time (if there is a "flight to safety"), a strategy based on that element of perceived risk will fail. This second type of failure will be temporary but can cover an uncomfortable span of time. The two-tier market of 1969–1972 was an unpleasant time for managers using a value-oriented price to book strategy for this very reason. The use of a multidisciplinary strategy, focusing on several aspects of perceived risk, can avert both of these potential problems most of the time.

In short, there is a Santa Claus in the investment business who hands out superior performance without increased risk. This present is given only to those with the courage to ignore conventional wisdom and to buy the "risky" issues that do not add to true portfolio risk.

4

Efficient Markets, Investment Management Selection, and the Loser's Game

Floyd J. Gould
Principal
Investment Research Company
    and
Hobart W. Williams Professor of
    Applied Mathematics and Management Science
Graduate School of Business
University of Chicago

I. Introduction

All of what follows is expository. Some of it is distilled from a lecture I have had the opportunity to give to MBA students for 15 years, and some of it is distilled from recent research from many sources.[1] The lecture material is from a quantitative models course — one of those courses that the faculty at Chicago decided was good gristle for the students. It is also a course that most of the students decide is neither palatable nor in their interest, and so they tolerate it only with monumental impatience. They don't like math, the course is too hard, they don't see its relevance, they will hire others to do it for them, etc., etc.

---

1. K. French and R. Roll, "Stock Return Variances: The Arrival of Information and the Reaction of Traders," *Journal of Financial Economics* (September 1986): 5–26; F. J. Gould, "The Re-Emergence of Relative Strength Tactics in Active Asset Allocation — New Evidence," invited address, Portfolio Risk Management Course — Alternative Strategies for Capital Preservation, Executive Enterprises, New York, October 5, 1987; C. P. Jones and B. Bublitz, "The CAPM and Equity Return Regularities: An Extension," *Financial Analysts' Journal* (May–June 1987): 77–80; D. B. Keim, "The CAPM and Equity Return Regularities," *Financial Analysts' Journal* (May–June 1986): 19–34; A. W. Lo and A. C. MacKinlay, "Stock Market Prices Do Not Follow Random Walks: Evidence from a Simple Specification Test," *Review of Financial Studies* (Spring 1988): 3–40; and B. Rosenberg, K. Reed, and R. Lanstein, "Persuasive Evidence of Market Inefficiency," *The Journal of Portfolio Management* (Spring 1985): 9–16.

This lecture material is rephrased here for those involved with various aspects of financial markets. The discourse points out the importance to the community of having an educated understanding of the role played by quantitative models, and in particular the efficient market model, along with what we call inefficiencies, also referred to as distortions, or anomalies.

Following some general reflections, I show some relevance of these conceptual topics to the concrete and difficult job of the pension plan sponsor in his or her role as a selector of investment managers. This will involve a comparison of real-world track records (of a manager's trading strategy) versus the importance of simulations and backtesting. I will demonstrate that many if not most plan sponsors — in the process of selecting managers — pursue what is basically, for the organization they work for, a self-destruct strategy. I then conclude with several conjectures as to why a sponsor would adopt such a strategy.

II. Models and Distortions

In order to describe observed phenomena in the physical and biological world, scholars devise models. Scholars also devise models to describe economic phenomena. In this spirit we have the efficient market theory of equity prices, which implies that past price behavior can provide no information about future prices or future rates of return. An efficient market is one in which the prices behave in accordance with this model.

An *anomaly* is defined to be a departure from a model. The history of all models is such that, initially, a wide body of research produces evidence that tends to support (and indeed leads to the formulation of) the model. A model is a haven for those seeking refuge from chaos. It provides an orderly focus for thought, for discussion, for further research, and what is most interesting to the scholar, a model is a context for the discovery of counterexamples, meaning exceptions to the model. As the state of knowledge matures, these exceptions, or anomalies, are discovered. Those discoveries are then challenged, debated, and finally some of those discoveries will be accepted as facts. Eventually, continued maturation producing more and more in the way of counterexamples leads to the articulation of new models that incorporate and formally extend the previous models and theories.[2]

Of course, some models (such as the flat-earth hypothesis) are eventually rejected totally. But more typically we find that models are generalized or extended (e.g., Newtonian physics, extended to general relativity, extended to unified field theory, extended most recently to superstring theory).

---

2. For a detailed discussion, see T. Kuhn, *The Structure of Scientific Revolutions* (Chicago: University of Chicago Press, 1970), pp. 52–53.

This points out that a model is a *limited,* or *selective,* representation of reality. In this sense, *no model is more than an approximation of reality.*[3] Since no model is reality itself, it is a logical necessity that anomalies will be found in all models. The question should not be whether or not a model is correct—for, as I repeat, no model is reality. The question is merely *how long* it will take for the discovery of valid anomalies, and the subsequent extension of the old model into a new, "updated" one that explains whatever is known up the present, including those anomalous observations.

In the context of efficient market models, the anomalies are called *distortions,* or *inefficiencies.* What I have just said is that inefficiencies must always exist. Traders seek to exploit inefficiencies systematically. In so doing, it is one of the properties of markets that they make those inefficiencies disappear (though new ones may appear). Thus inefficiencies are temporary and it is the traders who drive them away and make the markets efficient. From the real-world point of view, an efficient market is not one that is in every respect efficient in the sense of the theoretic model. It is one with many keen competing investors, exploiting perceived inefficiencies, and it is therefore a market that is dynamically *in the process* of eliminating some inefficiencies while others appear. The concept of efficiency is approximated via this process.

Traders seek to find inefficiencies because it is a way to obtain systematic (risk adjusted) excess returns. Any trader who claims to produce systematic (as opposed to haphazardly lucky) excess returns must at least implicitly be claiming to be exploiting an inefficiency.

The problem for the investment manager's client (for example, the pension plan sponsor) is that those wonderful potentially profitable inefficiencies cannot be absolutely proven until they have been exploited away. In other words, by the time convincing objective evidence has been compiled on the existence of some particular inefficiency it is likely that traders have already taken most of the profit out of it. Hence, of necessity, there must be an element of uncertainty, ex ante, in the attempt to identify and exploit inefficiency.

III. Inefficiencies, the Selection of Managers, and the "Track Record" as the Ultimate Bane to Future Success

I have just said that traders, or portfolio managers, who are really "onto something" have in fact discovered an inefficiency. What I have also said is

---

3. For an elaboration, see F. J. Gould and G. D. Eppen, *Quantitative Concepts for Management* (Englewood Cliffs, N.J.: Prentice-Hall, 1985), Chap. 1.

that by the time an inefficiency can be clearly proven to exist it is too late, for by then it is almost certain that clever traders will have exploited those inefficiencies to the point of their disappearance (and I have stated that these traders' activities cause that disappearance).

But ironically many plan sponsors self-destruct by seeking the very proof that guarantees extinction. This contributes to the creation of what Charles Ellis describes as a "Losers Game."[4] Typically the "prudent (meaning conservative) sponsor" seeks as a prerequisite to employing a particular strategy a three- to five-year live track record documenting the past success of that strategy. But by the time such a record is available those inefficiencies that were exploited as the cause of that success have probably vanished, and it is too late for the sponsor.

A typical scenario is this. An inefficiency is discovered. A small amount of capital is raised and a new investment counseling firm is established to exploit the discovery. Early results are extraordinary. The small amount of money under management, initially, becomes a bundle as accounts grow and new clients come to the window. By the time the track record is three to five years, everyone is signing and the success of the strategy is essentially history. From here on it is doomed to languish in stastical mediocrity, and the best intentions are the source of built-in failure.

This seemingly hopeless picture is consistent with the fact that most of the dollars that plan sponsors invest just happen to earn returns quite short of the performance of the index. And of course this is why so many sponsors have turned to indexing.

Is indexing the only alternative? It may be possible for some plan sponsors to consistently earn more than the index. But such sponsors must be willing to develop their own skills beyond what is required to line up columns of numbers and compare five-year track records on a spreadsheet. They will need to make sound judgments and intrinsic evaluations concerning potentially profitable strategies. The thesis here is that in order to find enhancement, such evaluations will need to be performed *before* the real-world record is established.

IV. What about Simulation?

An important tool in such evaluation might well be historical simulation, often referred to as "back-testing." Simulation is a powerful tool made possible only by the processing capability of the high-speed computer. That fact in itself should suggest there is something here worth looking at. But in spite of the technology, the process of back-testing is, among plan sponsors, in

---

4. C. D. Ellis, *Investment Policy* (Homewood, Ill.: Dow-Jones Irwin, 1985).

fairly wide disrepute. The reason is that this powerful tool can be so easily misused to produce results that mislead. I do not believe or mean to suggest that this misuse is widely intentional, though certainly it could be and surely in some instances that is what happens. For the most part, however, the majority of those who use simulation simply and unknowingly do not do so properly.

The proper implementation of this tool requires substantial technical background, methodological depth, and good clean and realistic data that may be expensive if not impossible to obtain. It also requires something else —extensive experience and judgment about the actual real-world phenomena being simulated, including in particular realistic assessments of quantities that may well be unknowable, such as the costs that would have been incurred in trading in a world in which the simulated strategy did not exist. The truth is that most back-testers simply do not have the required combination of skills, knowledge, prescience, and data to do the job properly. And some of the most egregious offenders have been academics with only a casual and superficial experience of the world they purport to study.

Unfortunately even the most technically trained plan sponsor is rather helpless in this situation. It is essentially impossible for him or her to verify the validity of someone else's back-tested study. With my academic nitpicking mentality I can say that for certain. There is no practical way you can verify the simulations of others, and that is certainly an excellent reason for, if not rejecting such studies, at least not placing heavy reliance on them.

This is unfortunate because a careful and honest 10- or 15-year simulation is worth more than a five-year track record. The latter, as I've pointed out, is merely good evidence that an inefficiency has been discovered, exploited, and probably is no longer present. On the other hand, I doubt that back-testing has itself ever been responsible for the disappearance of an inefficiency.

V. Evaluating the Manager

The bottom line, it seems to me, is rather personal. If the plan sponsor has respect for the skill and intellectual honesty of the manager he or she may legitimately indulge in the luxury of giving some attention to simulated results (and of course this is only a special case of the credibility that he may wish to invest in the manager and his strategies). In this respect, if the plan sponsor is to win the loser's game, an important part of his job is to *evaluate the manager per se as well as the manager's strategy*. The bottom line is that as much as strategies, the sponsor is a selector of persons. In markets, distorted asset prices are moved toward their risk-adjusted equilibrium values through the process of trading and the existence of competition. And so prices are recidivistic, tending to achieve, in the long run, no more than their appropriate lackluster values. To the contrary, when we scrutinize the patterns of achievement of individuals, it seems that outliers exist and persist. That is, individuals who have been top performers for the past five years in their chosen endeavors, whatever they may be, tend to be top performers in the next five years, whether the endeavors be the same or different (and politics notwithstanding).

And so, in summary, I believe the correct prescription is to focus the bet on the track record of individuals, rather than on the proven record of any particular strategy. This is not to say that one should race out to place the whole farm in the hands of bright achievers with novel and appealing trading strategies. Perhaps a well-conceived strategy goes something like this. "Most of our equity portfolio is indexed, because history tells us that this passive approach is very powerful, very hard to beat. But we do recognize the possibility, if not the probability, of finding inefficiency and doing better. And consequently some appropriate portion has been set aside for allocation to active managers." I know of several plan sponsors who do in fact adhere to a policy similar to this, within the guidelines of their particular asset-allocation constraints.

Since none of the above is particularly startling or profound, one wonders why the community at large behaves in what seems to be a less than rational fashion. In spite of the self-destruct feature, many plan sponsors select money managers to employ strategies that have outstanding five-year live track records and consequently little hope of continued outperformance. Why does such selection occur? Is the plan sponsor irrational?

VI. The Principal Agent Problem and the Concept of Regret

Economists have studied and are continuing to study scenarios where the representative of a firm has self-interest that is by some measures detrimental, or in conflict with, the overall interest of the firm. In other words, the incentives of the individual differ from the best-interests of the firm. This is related to what is called "the principal agent problem."[5] The problem I have been discussing is a variation of this principal agent phenomenon.

One interesting explanation of seemingly irrational behavior is the concept of "regret."[6] In the context of this discussion, regret can be explained as follows. Consider two scenarios:

---

5. See, for example, E. F. Fama, "Agency Problems and the Theory of the Firm," *Journal of Political of Political Economy 88*, no. 2 (1980): 288–307.
6. See M. Statman, "Investor Psychology and Market Inefficiencies," Preprint, Leavey School of Business Administration, Santa Clara University, Santa Clara, Calif.

Scenario 1   Use conventional and traditional standards and procedures to hire a money manager. Suppose the results are quite disappointing. The manager underperforms the market by 15 percent.

Scenario 2   You are innovative and somewhat unconventional in your selection. You say, "This makes sense to me," and explain why, to your board. You convince them that the choice makes sense, even though the manager has no substantial proven track record with this particular strategy. Now, as in Scenario 1, suppose results are disappointing.

What happens in these two cases? It is asserted that in Scenario 2 you experience more pain, due to *regret,* than in Scenario 1. The gist of the argument is that the outcome in Scenario 1 was essentially an act of God. You did things the way they are always done! You can't be blamed. You were prudent. In Scenario 2 you went out on a limb. You bore *responsibility*. If only you had not tried to be so smart! If only you had done things the usual way, you wouldn't have been in nearly so much trouble.

The model is that the individual has an aversion to regret (as well as risk) built into his utility function. In markets, people hire money managers to play the role of scapegoats, meaning to bear the pain of regret. Plan sponsors who use the traditional self-destruct criteria are acting in a way that reduces potential regret, even though the results of their behavior may not be consistent with organizational objectives (that is, to maximize returns).

These behavioral (and organizational) issues will surely be the focus of continuing research. In concluding I will simply suggest one additional implication of the "regret model." Managers whose selection involves much responsibility will produce higher returns than those whose selection involves little responsibility. In an asset pricing model where regret is a factor, the preference for low-regret managers should drive down their expected return. This provides another argument for serious reconsideration of traditional selection procedures.

5

Timing versus Selection Revisited*

Russell J. Fuller
Professor of Finance
Washington State University

James A. Sprow
Doctoral Candidate
Washington State University

This article deals with the question of market timing and security analysis by presenting a range of possible rates of return that can hypothetically be achieved based on market timing versus stock selection. We make no attempt to assess the probabilities of achieving the various rates of return; readers may assess their own chances of success using either strategy. However, by knowing what the range of possible outcomes is for each approach to investing the investor will be better able to determine how to allocate his or her efforts and resources in the investment process.

Timing strategies basically consist of two decisions — when to buy and when to sell. Stock selection, for the purposes of this article, was considered to be based on the determination of the growth rate of common stock dividends. While for individual stocks there is obviously more to security analysis than just the security's dividend growth rate, capital market theory suggests that investors should hold well-diversified portfolios; the dividend growth rate for such portfolios is clearly a distinguishing characteristic for security analysis purposes. Thus, for analyzing timing strategies, the purchase price and sale price are considered; for stock selection purposes, the

---

* The original article by Professor Fuller ("Timing vs. Selection: Which Holds the Key?") was published in the Winter 1977 issue of *The Journal of Portfolio Management*. The new article updates the study with respect to the historical data concerning the S&P 500.

dividend growth rate is considered. Using this simplified approach, we can use the dividend discount model to determine the range of possible rates of return that can hypothetically be achieved from market timing versus stock selection.

I. The Dividend Discount Model

The dividend discount model proposed by Williams[1] in his classic book and elaborated on by Gordon[2] and others suggests the following formula for determining the price of common stocks:

$$P_o = \frac{D_1}{1+R} + \frac{D_2}{(1+R)^2} + \cdots + \frac{D_n}{(1+R)^n}, \tag{1}$$

where

P_o = current stock price,
D_t = dividend received in the tth year,
R = return required by investors.

Thus R is the rate of return investors require to justify the purchase price (P_o) of a common stock given its expected dividend stream over the life of the company. (D_n includes any liquidating dividend in the last year of the company's existence.)

If the dividend is expected to grow at a constant rate (G) for a reasonably long period of time, the following equation[3] is a reasonable approximation of equation (1):

$$P_o = \frac{D_1}{R_o - G_o} \quad \text{or more generally} \quad P_n = \frac{D_{n+1}}{R_n - G_n}. \tag{2}$$

Equation (2) is a particularly useful formula, because it allows one to estimate the price of a stock at some point in the future (P_n). Since most investors do not intend to hold a stock for the life of the company, they must estimate a future sale price in order to determine the return on the purchase price (P_o), given the holding period (n years), the dividends received during the holding period

$$\left(\sum_{t=1}^{n} D_t \right),$$

---

1. John Burr Williams, *The Theory of Investment Value* (Cambridge: Mass.: Harvard University Press, 1938).
2. M.J. Gordon, "Dividends, Earnings and Stock Prices," *Review of Economics and Statistics* (May 1959): 96–105.
3. For a proof of this equation, see most college textbooks on finance or investments. For example, see Russell J. Fuller and James L. Farrell, Jr., *Modern Investments and Security Analysis* (New York: McGraw-Hill, 1987), p. 277.

and the sale price at the end of the holding period (P_n). In equation form:

$$P_o = \sum_{t=1}^{n} \frac{D_t}{(1+R)^t} + \frac{P_n}{(1+R)^n}. \tag{3}$$

By solving for R in equation (3), one can determine the compound annual rate of return on a common stock investment.

II. The Discount Factor ($R - G$)

Equation (2) is a powerful tool for analyzing the factors that influence stock prices. In a more simplified form, equation (2) becomes

$$P = \frac{D}{R-G}. \tag{4}$$

According to this equation, stock prices are determined by two factors: (1) the current dividend, and (2) the difference or spread between the rate of return required by investors and the expected growth rate of dividends. This spread ($R - G$) will be referred to as the discount factor. By transposing equation (4), the discount factor can be shown to be equal to the dividend yield:

$$R - G = \frac{D}{P}. \tag{5}$$

Thus the dividend yield provides a handy yardstick for measuring the discount factor. For example, dividend yields for the Standard and Poor's 500 have averaged approximately 4.3 percent over the past 40 years.

With respect to market timing, it is the discount factor or dividend yield for the S&P 500 at market tops and market bottoms that is of most interest. Table 1 lists the dividend yield for the S&P 500 at market tops and bottoms over the post World War II period. Note that the discount factor (dividend yield) ranged from a low of 2.5 percent at the recent 1987 market top to a high of 6.7 percent at the 1982 market bottom.

For the purposes of this article, three possible discount factors were used to determine purchase and sale prices: a high price discount factor of 2.6 percent; an average discount factor of 4.0 percent; and a low price discount factor of 6.0 percent. The high-price and low-price discount factors conservatively represent the extremes reached at market tops and bottoms since 1946, and 4 percent is about the average dividend yield or discount factor for the same period.

III. The Dividend Growth Rate (G)

Three possible dividend growth rates are considered for this article: a high dividend growth rate of 9 percent; an average dividend growth rate of 6 per-

TABLE 1. *Discount Factors* $(R-G)$ *at Market Tops and Bottoms.*

Date	Discount Factor $(R-G)$ (%)	S&P 500 Price	Annual Dividend
1946 top	3.5	19.25	0.68
1948 bottom	6.1	13.84	0.84
1952 top	5.3	26.59	1.40
1953 bottom	6.3	22.71	1.44
1956 top	3.7	49.74	1.84
1957 bottom	4.6	38.98	1.80
1961 top	2.8	72.64	2.04
1962 bottom	4.0	52.32	2.08
1966 top	3.0	94.06	2.80
1966 bottom	3.9	73.20	2.88
1968 top	2.8	108.37	3.08
1970 bottom	4.6	69.29	3.20
1973 top	2.6	120.24	3.16
1974 bottom	5.8	62.28	3.60
1976 top	3.6	107.83	3.84
1978 bottom	5.5	86.90	4.80
1980 top	4.4	140.52	6.16
1982 bottom	6.7	102.40	6.84
1987 top	2.5	336.77	8.50
1987 low (to date)	3.8	224.84	8.50
Minimum	2.5		
Maximum	6.7		
Average	4.0		

Source: Standard and Poor's.

cent; and a low growth rate of 3 percent. Examining overlapping 10-year periods of dividends for the S&P 500, we found that dividend growth averaged 5.6 percent during the period 1936–1986 with a range of 2.7–9.7 percent. Thus our hypothetical range of 3–9 percent dividend growth fairly well encompasses the actual experience of the S&P 500, and 6 percent is reasonably close to the average growth rate. Obviously for individual stocks, the dividend growth rates will cover a considerably wider range, but for well-diversified portfolios, a 3–9 percent range appears reasonable.

Table 2 illustrates the stream of future dividends, assuming growth rates (G_o) of 3 percent, 6 percent, and 9 percent. As a starting point for D_i, $8.50

TABLE 2. *Dividend Streams Assuming Various Levels of Constant Growth Rates.*

Year (n)	$G_o = 3\%$	$G_o = 6\%$	$G_o = 9\%$
0	$8.50	$8.50	$8.50
1	8.76	9.01	9.27
2	9.02	9.55	10.10
3	9.29	10.12	11.01
4	9.57	10.73	12.00
5	9.85	11.37	13.08
6	10.15	12.06	14.26
7	10.45	12.78	15.54
8	10.77	13.55	16.94
9	11.09	14.36	18.46
10	11.42	15.22	20.12
11	11.77	16.14	21.93
12	12.12	17.10	23.91
13	12.48	18.13	26.06
14	12.86	19.22	28.40
15	13.24	20.37	30.96
16	13.64	21.59	33.75
17	14.05	22.89	36.78
18	14.47	24.26	40.10
19	14.90	25.72	43.70
20	15.35	27.26	47.64
21	15.81	28.90	51.92
22	16.29	30.63	56.60
23	16.78	32.47	61.69
24	17.28	34.42	67.24
25	17.80	36.48	73.30
26	18.33	38.67	79.89
27	18.88	40.99	87.08
28	19.45	43.45	94.92
29	20.03	46.06	103.46
30	20.63	48.82	112.78
31	21.25	51.75	122.93
32	21.89	54.85	133.99
33	22.54	58.15	146.05
34	23.22	61.63	159.19
35	23.92	65.33	173.52
36	24.64	69.25	189.14
37	25.37	73.41	206.16
38	26.14	77.81	224.71
39	26.92	82.48	244.94
40	27.73	87.43	266.98
41	28.56	92.67	291.01

was used because this is reasonably close to the 1987 annual rate of dividends for the S&P 500 Composite index.

IV. The Range of Possible Returns

Given the assumptions of three possible discount factors for both the purchase and the sale price (2.6 percent = high; 4.0 percent = average; 6.0 percent = low), and three possible dividend growth rates (3 percent, 6 percent, 9 percent), a range of possible compound annual rates of return can be calculated using equation (3). The starting point is the dividend to be received in the first year (D_1), which was assumed to be $8.50. Assuming G_o to be constant over the entire holding period of n years, the stream of dividends

$$\left(\sum_{t=1}^{n} D_t\right)$$

can be calculated, as was done in Table 2.

Using equation (2), the purchase price (P_o) is determined by dividing D_1 by the discount factor $(R_o - G_o)$. Given a dividend of $8.50, P_o could vary from $141.67 to $326.92 using a range of 2.6–6 percent for the discount factor; an average discount factor of 4 percent gives a purchase price of $212.50. Table 3 lists the possible purchase prices given excellent timing (Bi-Lo), average timing, (Bi-Avg), and poor timing (Bi-Hi).

Compound annual rates of return were calculated for holding periods of 1, 5, 10, 25, and 40 years. A one-year holding period would normally be considered too short a time horizon for serious investors. Forty years is probably too long, since it might stretch past the life expectancy of an investor in his 30s. However, the one-year and 40-year periods were included in order to demonstrate the effect time has on investment returns. Whether 5, 10, or 25 years is the more appropriate holding period depends on each investor's personal situation.

TABLE 3. *Possible Purchase Prices.*

Timing	Discount Factor $(R_o - G_o)$	Purchase Price (P_o)[a]
Bi-Lo	6.0%	$141.67
Bi-Avg	4.0%	$212.50
Bi-Hi	2.6%	$326.92

a. Solving equation (2), where $P_o = D_1/(R_o - G_o)$ and $D_1 = $8.50.

TABLE 4. *Possible Sale Prices.*

Sales Price (P_n) ($)[a]

Timing	Discount Factor $(R_n - G_n)$	Year 1 Dividend Growth			Year 5 Dividend Growth			Year 10 Dividend Growth			Year 25 Dividend Growth			Year 40 Dividend Growth		
		3%	6%	9%	3%	6%	9%	3%	6%	9%	3%	6%	9%	3%	6%	9%
Sell-Lo	6.0%	146	150	154	164	190	218	190	254	335	297	608	1,222	462	1,457	4,450
Sell-Avg	4.0%	219	225	232	246	284	327	286	381	503	445	912	1,832	693	2,186	6,675
Sell-Hi	2.6%	337	347	356	379	437	503	439	585	774	685	1,403	2,819	1,066	3,363	10,268

a. Solving equation (2), where $P_n = D_{n+1}/(R_n - G_n)$ with D_{n+1} taken from the appropriate column in Table 2.

TABLE 5. *The Hypothetical Range of Compound Annual Rates of Return.*

	Discount Factor for		Compound Annual Rates of Return (%)					
			1 Year			5 Years		
	Purchase Price	Sale Price	Dividend Growth			Dividend Growth		
Timing	$(R_o - G_o)$	$(R_n - G_n)$	3%	6%	9%	3%	6%	9%
Bi-Lo, Sell-Hi	6.0%	2.6%	143.9	150.4	157.4	26.2	29.8	33.3
Bi-Lo, Sell-Avg	6.0%	4.0%	60.6	64.9	69.5	16.9	20.1	23.4
Bi-Lo, Sell-Lo	6.0%	6.0%	9.0	12.0	15.0	9.0	12.0	15.0
Bi-Avg, Sell-Hi	4.0%	2.6%	62.6	66.9	71.7	15.7	18.9	22.2
Bi-Avg, Sell-Avg	4.0%	4.0%	7.0	10.0	13.0	7.0	10.0	13.0
Bi-Avg, Sell-Lo	4.0%	6.0%	−27.3	−25.4	−23.4	−0.3	2.4	5.2
Bi-Hi, Sell-Hi	2.6%	2.6%	5.6	8.6	11.6	5.6	8.6	11.6
Bi-Hi, Sell-Avg	2.6%	4.0%	−30.4	−28.6	−26.6	−2.4	0.3	3.1
Bi-Hi, Sell-Lo	2.6%	6.0%	−52.7	−51.5	−50.1	−9.2	−6.6	−4.1

a. Solving for R in equation (3), where $P_o = \sum_{t=1}^{n}[D_t/(1+R)^t + P_n/(1+R)^n]$.

The sale price for poor timing (Sell-Lo), average timing (Sell-Avg), and excellent timing (Sell-Hi) at the end of each holding period (year n) is calculated by dividing D_{n+1} by the three discount factors $(R_n - G_n)$, once again using 6 percent, 4 percent, and 2.6 percent as the possible discount factors. Table 4 lists the possible sale prices for 1-, 5-, 10-, 25-, and 40-year holding periods and dividend growth rates of 3 percent, 6 percent, and 9 percent.

Having determined the dividend stream under assumptions of 3 percent, 6 percent, and 9 percent dividend growth rates, as well as purchase prices and sale prices under assumptions of 6 percent, 4 percent, and 2.6 percent discount factors, the compound annual rates of return for various holding periods can be calculated by solving for r in equation (3). Table 5 lists the compound annual rates of return for all possible combinations of assumed purchase prices, sale prices, and dividend growth rates for 1-, 5-, 10-, 25-, and 40-year holding periods.

Using Table 5, one can examine the impact that above average or below average success with respect to timing of the purchase and sale decisions and stock selection can have on investment returns for various holding periods. Note that the specific assumptions underlying the construction of Table 5 are not particularly crucial to the general conclusions drawn from the analysis that follows. As long as the assumptions used to construct the table are a reasonable approximation of realized investor experience, the reader will probably reach conclusions similar to those that follow.

for Various Holding Periods.[a]

10 Years			25 Years			40 Years		
Dividend Growth			Dividend Growth			Dividend Growth		
3%	6%	9%	3%	6%	9%	3%	6%	9%
16.3	19.6	22.8	10.9	14.0	17.1	9.8	12.8	15.9
12.4	15.5	18.6	9.9	12.9	15.9	9.4	12.3	15.4
9.0	12.0	15.0	9.0	12.0	15.0	9.0	12.0	15.0
10.9	14.0	17.1	8.2	11.2	14.3	7.5	10.6	13.6
7.0	10.0	13.0	7.0	10.0	13.0	7.0	10.0	13.0
3.7	6.5	9.4	6.1	9.0	12.0	6.6	9.6	12.5
5.6	8.6	11.6	5.6	8.6	11.6	5.6	8.6	11.6
1.8	4.7	7.5	4.3	7.3	10.3	5.0	8.0	10.9
-2.0	0.9	4.0	3.4	6.3	9.2	4.5	7.5	10.4

V. Timing of the Purchase Decision

Figure 1 illustrates the impact that the timing of the purchase decision can have on investor returns if the dividend growth rate is held constant by assuming an average discount factor of 4 percent. It is obvious that the timing of the purchase decision has a tremendous impact on the rate of return if the holding period is relatively short. But even assuming a 25-year holding period, there is still a 5.6 percent difference in the compound annual rate of return for exceptional purchase timing versus very poor purchase timing (Bi-Lo return at 25 years = 12.9 percent; Bi-Hi = 7.3 percent). To illustrate the magnitude of the impact of the purchase decision timing, $1,000 invested at 12.9 percent compounds to $20,776 over a 25-year holding period versus only $5,821 if the rate of return is 7.3 percent. (For the Bi-Avg return of 10 percent, $1,000 compounds to $10,835 in 25 years.)

At 40 years, the Bi-Lo and Bi-Hi curves appear to "flatten out" and, in fact, if the holding period is extended further the Bi-Lo curve would approach a constant 12 percent and the Bi-Hi curve a constant 8 percent. Thus no matter how long the holding period, time will not "bail out" poor timing of the purchase decision, relative to good timing.

Note that the Bi-Avg return in Figure 1 is a constant 10 percent. Referring back to equation (4) where

$$P = \frac{D}{R - G},$$

FIGURE 1. *Compound Annual Rates of Return Holding Constant the Sale Price and Dividend Growth Rate while Varying the Purchase Price.*

Assumptions

Dividend Growth Rate = 6.0%
Discount Factor for Sale Price $(R_n - G_n)$ = Avg = 4.0%
Discount Factor for Purchase Price $(R_0 - G_0)$ = Lo = 6.0%
Avg = 4.0%
Hi = 2.6%

Results (from Table 5)
Compound Annual Rates of Return (%)

Timing	1 Year	5 Years	10 Years	25 Years	40 Years
Bi-Lo, Sell-Avg	64.9	20.1	15.5	12.9	12.3
Bi-Avg, Sell-Avg	10.0	10.0	10.0	10.0	10.0
Bi-Hi, Sell-Avg	−28.6	0.3	4.7	7.3	8.0

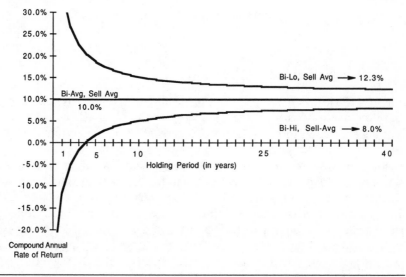

a simple algebraic transformation will reveal that the investor's rate of return is equal to the dividend yield at the time of purchase plus the growth rate of dividends:

$$R = \frac{D}{P} + G. \qquad (6)$$

This relationship assumes that the discount factor $(R - G)$ is the same on the date of purchase and the date of sale, which was the case in Figure 1 for Bi-Avg, Sell-Avg. Equation (6) may help put historical rates of return into perspective. In the postwar era the average growth rate of dividends for stocks as a group has been slightly less than 6 percent and dividend yields have averaged a little over 4 percent, resulting in an average return to common stock investors of approximately 10 percent, which is verified by the studies of Ibbotson Associates.[4]

VI. Timing of the Sale Decision

Figure 2 illustrates the impact that the sale decision can have on investment return if the dividend growth rate is held constant at 6 percent and the purchase price is held constant by assuming an average discount factor of 4 percent. In a fashion somewhat similar to the purchase decision, the impact of the timing of the sale decision on investment returns is quite large if the holding period is relatively short and the impact tends to diminish as the holding period lengthens. However, a poor sale decision will not have near the impact of a poor purchase decision if the holding period is relatively long. For a 25-year holding period, there is only a 2.2 percent difference in the annual rate of return for exceptional sale timing (Sell-Hi = 11.2 percent) versus very poor timing (Sell-Lo = 9.0 percent). If $1,000 were invested at 11.2 percent for 25 years, it would compound to $14,211; invested at 9.0 percent for 25 years, $1,000 would compound to $8,623.

VII. Combinations of Timing for the Purchase and Sale Decisions

In Figure 3 the rates of return for the combinations of Bi-Lo with Sell-Hi, Sell-Avg, and Sell-Lo are compared with the combinations of Bi-Hi with Sell-Hi, Sell-Avg, and Sell-Lo, holding the dividend growth rate constant at 6 percent. (The other possible timing combinations of Bi-Avg with Sell-Hi, Sell-Avg, and Sell-Lo are not illustrated in order to simplify the graph. The Bi-Avg group would lie between the Bi-Lo and Bi-Hi groups and trend toward 10 percent.)

From Figure 3 it is apparent that, given enough time, the Bi-Lo group trends toward 12 percent while the Bi-Hi group trends toward 8 percent. Using equation (6), where

$$R = \frac{D}{P} + G,$$

as a rough guide to analyze the results of the two groups, the initial dividend yield of the Bi-Lo group is 6.0 percent versus 2.6 percent for the Bi-Hi group. Assuming the same growth in dividends (G) for both groups, Bi-Lo

---

4. *Stocks, Bonds, Bills and Inflation: 1987 Yearbook* (Chicago: Ibbotson Associates, 1987).

FIGURE 2. *Compound Annual Rates of Return Holding Constant the Purchase Price and Dividend Growth Rate while Varying the Sale Price.*

Assumptions

Dividend Growth Rate = 6.0%

Discount Factor for Purchase Price $(R_0 - G_0)$ = Avg = 4.0%

Discount Factor for Sale Price $(R_n - G_n)$ = Lo = 6.0%

Avg = 4.0%

Hi = 2.6%

Results (from Table 5)
Compound Annual Rates of Return (%)

Timing	1 Year	5 Years	10 Years	25 Years	40 Years
Bi-Avg, Sell-Hi	66.9	18.9	14.0	11.2	10.6
Bi-Avg, Sell-Avg	10.0	10.0	10.0	10.0	10.0
Bi-Avg, Sell-Lo	−25.4	2.4	6.5	9.0	9.6

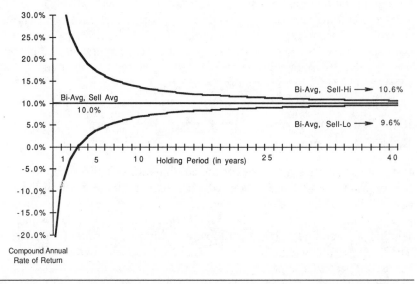

will always have *at least* a 3.4 percent greater compound annual rate of return than Bi-Hi, regardless of the sale price and the length of the holding period. Thus, the timing of the purchase decision is far more important than the timing of the sale decision.

VIII. The Dividend Growth Rate

Figure 4 illustrates the effect changes in the dividend growth rate have on rates of return, while holding constant the discount factor at 4.0 percent (Bi-

FIGURE 3. *Compound Annual Rates of Return Holding Constant the Purchase Price and Dividend Growth Rate while Varying the Sale Price.*

Assumptions

Dividend Growth Rate = 6.0%

Discount Factor for Purchase Price $(R_0 - G_0)$ and for Sale Price $(R_n - G_n)$:

Lo = 6.0%   Avg = 4.0%   Hi = 2.6%

Results (from Table 5)
Compound Annual Rates of Return (%)

Timing	1 Year	5 Years	10 Years	25 Years	40 Years
Bi-Lo, Sell-Hi	150.4	29.8	19.6	14.0	12.8
Bi-Lo, Sell-Avg	64.9	20.1	15.5	12.9	12.3
Bi-Lo, Sell-Lo	12.0	12.0	12.0	12.0	12.0
Bi-Hi, Sell-Hi	8.6	8.6	8.6	8.6	8.6
Bi-Hi, Sell-Avg	−28.6	0.3	4.7	7.3	8.0
Bi-Hi, Sell-Lo	−51.5	−6.6	0.9	6.3	7.5

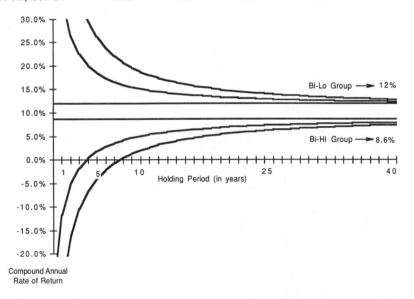

Avg, Sell-Avg). When it is assumed that the discount factor is constant, then the difference in rates of return is simply the difference in dividend growth rates, regardless of the holding period. Because Figure 4 is not as dramatic as the previous illustrations with their curves and so forth, one might tend to underestimate the importance of the dividend growth rate. If so, consider that $1,000 invested at the 13 percent rate indicated for G_o = Hi compounds to $21,231 in 25 years; at the 7 percent rate indicated for G_o = Lo, $1,000

FIGURE 4. *Compound Annual Rates of Return Holding Constant the Discount Factor while Varying the Dividend Growth Rate.*

Assumptions

Dividend Growth Rate: Lo = 3.0%, Avg = 6%, Hi = 9%
Discount Factor for Purchase Price $(R_0 - G_0)$ = Avg = 4.0%
Discount Factor for Sale Price $(R_n - G_n)$ = Avg = 4.0%

Results (from Table 5)
Compound Annual Rates of Return (%)

Timing	G_0	1 Year	5 Years	10 Years	25 Years	40 Years
Bi-Avg, Sell-Avg	3.0%	7.0	7.0	7.0	7.0	7.0
Bi-Avg, Sell-Avg	6.0%	10.0	10.0	10.0	10.0	10.0
Bi-Avg, Sell-Avg	9.0%	13.0	13.0	13.0	13.0	13.0

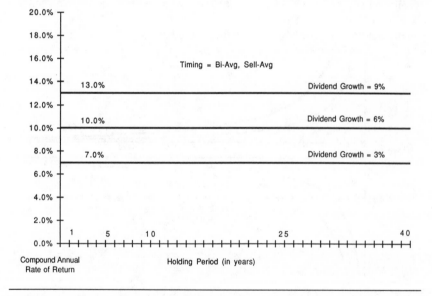

only compounds to $5,427 in the same period. And, as the following section will demonstrate, superior stock selection can offset poor market timing — but only if the holding period is extremely long.

IX. Market Timing versus Stock Selection

In order to illustrate the impact market timing can have on rates of return versus the impact of stock selection, Figure 5 graphs the combination of the best possible timing with the worst dividend growth (Bi-Lo, Sell-Hi, G_o = Lo)

FIGURE 5. *Best Timing and Worst Dividend Growth versus Worst Timing and Best Dividend Growth.*

Assumptions

Best Timing and Worst Dividend Growth: $R_0 - G_0 = $ Bi-Lo $= 6.0\%$
$R_n - G_n = $ Sell-Hi $= 2.6\%$
$G_0 = $ Lo $= 3.0\%$

Worst Timing and Best Dividend Growth: $R_0 - G_0 = $ Bi-Hi $= 2.6\%$
$R_n - G_n = $ Sell-Lo $= 6.0\%$
$G_0 = $ Hi $= 9.0\%$

Results (from Table 5)
Compound Annual Rates of Return (%)

Timing	G_0	1 Year	5 Years	10 Years	25 Years	40 Years
Bi-Lo, Sell-Hi	Lo	143.9	26.2	16.3	10.9	9.8
Bi-Hi, Sell-Lo	Hi	−50.1	−4.1	4.0	9.2	10.4

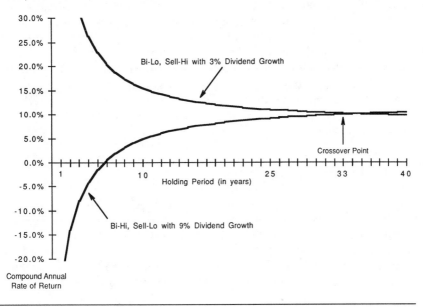

versus the combination of the worst possible timing with the best possible dividend growth (Bi-Hi, Sell-Lo, $G_o = $ Hi).

It is obvious to most stock market participants that timing dominates dividends in determining the investor's return when the holding period is relatively short. Notice, however, that in Figure 5, it is 33 years before the combination of an excellent growth rate in dividends and poor timing results in a higher return than the combination of excellent timing and poor dividend growth. Therefore, given the assumptions underlying Figure 5, it is clear that the value of perfect information with respect to timing is far greater than the value of perfect information with respect to future dividend growth rates, given any reasonable holding period. The question is not whether the game of timing is worth playing — it is, and it is worth more than the game of trying to forecast future earnings and dividends. The real question is what are the probabilities of success for either game.

X. The Random Walk versus Higgledy-Piggledy Growth

The weak form of the efficient market hypothesis[5] suggests that stock prices follow a random walk with no significant correlation between past price changes and future price changes. Academicians have tested a great number of trading techniques to see if they can produce above normal profits. Given a long enough time horizon, most trading strategies have been shown to do no better, and generally worse, than a simple buy-and-hold strategy.[6]

Unfortunately the evidence presented by Lintner and Glauber[7] and others[8] suggests that the chances of forecasting superior earnings and dividend growth are not much better than the chances of achieving superior timing. Thus the literature suggests that the market is reasonably efficient. Given enough chances, most investors will get average results, which in the case of Bi-Avg, Sell-Avg, $G_o =$ Avg, would be a compound annual return of approximately 10 percent.

XI. To Try or Not to Try?

One conclusion that is frequently drawn from the efficient market hypothesis is that the best investment strategy is a passive strategy — that is, buy and hold a well-diversified portfolio and keep costs at a minimum by not expending resources in trying to outperform the market by either security selection or market timing. Obviously there are many market participants who do not accept this conclusion, and this article should aid them in determining where

---

5. Most recent investment textbooks will have discussion of the efficient market hypothesis: for example, see Fuller and Farrell, *Modern Investments and Security Analysis,* Chap. 5.
6. For example, a recent study tested over 2,000 technical trading strategies and found that not one produced above normal returns. See J.O. Hanlon and C.W. Ward, "How to Lose at Winning Strategies," *The Journal of Portfolio Management* (Spring 1986): 20–23.
7. John Lintner and Robert Glauber, "Higgledy Piggledy Growth," reprinted in J. Lorie and R.A. Brealey, *Modern Developments in Investment Management* (New York: Praeger, 1972).
8. For a discussion of earnings as a random walk, see Richard A. Brealey, *An Introduction to Risk and Return from Common Stocks,* 2nd ed. (Cambridge, Mass.: MIT Press, 1983), pp. 83–100.

the potential rewards lie in trying to outperform the market. Figure 5 suggests that the greatest benefits lie in improving the timing aspect of the total return equation. And of the two timing decisions, the purchase decision is by far the more important. (Investors who can Bi-Lo, have it made.) However, each market participant will have to evaluate their personal skills in deciding whether to allocate their time and resources on market timing, security analysis, or some combination of both.

6

Manager Style and the Sources of Equity Returns*

Tony Estep
General Partner
New Amsterdam Partners

I. Introduction

Pension sponsors, endowment treasurers, and others who hire investment managers are always trying to analyze the value added by their managers. Clients want to be certain that each manager's stock selection efforts produce a list of holdings that has higher returns, net of fees and transaction costs, than some passive alternative that mimics the manager's "style." And they want to choose a group of managers with complementary approaches, or "styles," so that the overall portfolio does not have any risk that is not assumed deliberately in the hope of compensation. Typically, a manager of managers tries to reach these goals by analyzing the historical return patterns of the present managers, and other candidates, using a statistical model that tries to define each manager's active return and the sources of that return.

These goals are laudable and rational, yet the results have not always been satisfactory. Expectations of both active return and risk have proven overoptimistic. It is tempting to blame this on changing market patterns, market efficiency, or bad luck, but manager selections are influenced heavily by possible errors and weaknesses in the present models of active return.

---

*This article is reprinted from the Winter 1987 issue of *The Journal of Portfolio Management*.

These models are statistical, rather than fundamental; their explanatory power is low, in the neighborhood of 10%, and they contain many components that, although totally insignificant, are often given weight in manager selection. A better model, based on fundamental financial concepts, can improve this process substantially.

Stock returns consist of three components: growth of shareholders' equity, cash flow yield (dividends plus share repurchase minus dilution from share issuance), and a change in valuation (measured by change in price/book ratio). This view of stock returns is not econometric conjecture, but a mathematical identity.

When we analyze the returns of various managers or management techniques in this way, we derive a picture of historical results that is easier to interpret, more informative, and frequently different from statistical models. We see right away that no matter how managers pick stocks, their returns can be viewed as the sum of growth, cash flow yield, and valuation change.

When we analyze how much of each manager's return has come from each source, we discover that:

- It is much easier to compare a manager's returns to an appropriate passive alternative.
- It is much easier to find out whether a group of managers really has complementary "styles."
- It is much easier to tell the difference between value added by active selection and by luck.

When our financial model of return is substituted for statistical models, we realize that the sum of growth plus cash flow yield is the dominant source of true, repeatable active returns, even though most measurement and strategic planning effort is directed toward the valuation change component. The result may be to tempt a sponsor to use too many managers; to select managers with low probabilities of future success; to build a portfolio with considerable uncompensated risk, and to have the wrong mix of managers.

II. The Three Sources of Stock Returns

Over any period, past or future, we know that the return from a stock is, by definition:

$$T = \text{Chg } P + \frac{CF}{P},$$

where:

T = total return over any single period,

CF = cash flow received,

P = price paid, and

Chg P = (ending price − beginning price)/beginning price.

By some algebraic tricks, we can write this equation in terms of familiar accounting variables, so that we can divide the returns from a common stock into three components: growth, cash flow yield, and valuation change. Thus:

$$T = g + \frac{ROE - g}{PB} + \text{Chg } PB(1 + g),$$

where:

g = growth of shareholders' equity during the period,
ROE = return on equity (net income/equity),
PB = price/book ratio, and
$\text{Chg } PB$ = (ending PB − beginning PB)/beginning PB.

Note that the middle term in this equation is called "cash flow yield" (CFY), because it is an estimate of all cash received by shareholders from dividends plus share repurchase minus share issuance. This equation is known as the T-Model[1] because its dependent variable is T, total return including appreciation, dividends, and share repurchase or dilution (for a detailed explanation of the adaptation of this model to the purposes of this article, see the Appendix).

Unlike statistical models, this equation has its origins in a mathematical identity. Even though in practical application it contains some approximation, the model does an excellent job of estimating return when its governing variables are known. Its cross-sectional R^2 (estimated versus actual return) for the stocks in the Dow Jones Average in 1985 was 0.94. In other words, the after-the-fact return estimates made by the T-Model explained 94% of the differences in returns among those thirty stocks. The details appear in Table 1. By contrast, the statistical model described by William Sharpe[2] explains only 10.4% of individual security returns, again with after-the-fact knowledge of the "returns to factors" that are the model's independent variables. Sharpe points out that no factor "explains" as much as 4% of stock returns.

III. Management Style and Sources of Return

Different investment management organizations emphsize different criteria in picking stocks. A few firms make explicit estimates of expected returns. More typical, however, are portfolio managers who select stocks because of one or more "attributes" that they believe will be associated with future returns.

---

1. Tony Estep, "A New Method for Valuing Common Stocks," *Financial Analysts Journal* (November-December 1985).
2. William Sharpe, "Factors in New York Stock Exchange Security Returns 1931–1979," *Journal of Portfolio Management* (Summer 1982).

TABLE 1. *Actual 1985 Returns and Their Components for the Thirty Stocks in the Dow Jones Average (%) (R^2 estimated versus actual ret. = 0.94).*[a]

Ticker	Growth of Equity g	Valuation Change $\dfrac{\text{Chg } PB}{PB}(1+g)$	Cash Flow Yield $\dfrac{ROE-g}{PB}$	Estimated Return T	Actual Return
UK	−18.4	103.5	12.5	97.6	102.0
WX	−13.5	63.4	24.3	74.2	74.7
ALD	112.3	73.6	−117.5	68.5	42.4
Z	16.4	48.7	0.4	65.6	67.7
MCD	12.6	41.0	4.2	57.7	58.3
MRK	3.5	38.3	6.6	48.5	49.2
AXP	15.7	28.6	1.5	45.8	44.4
DD	3.6	34.2	5.8	43.5	43.2
T	6.3	25.8	3.4	35.5	34.5
OI	9.7	23.6	1.5	34.8	35.4
GE	10.6	18.2	3.9	32.7	32.4
CHV	5.4	16.6	7.1	29.1	29.7
IBM	20.8	6.1	1.4	28.3	29.9
XON	0.8	13.5	13.1	27.5	29.9
PG	3.8	18.9	4.7	27.3	26.9
S	8.3	15.4	3.7	27.3	28.4
AC	21.0	11.9	−5.8	27.1	24.8
GT	10.6	11.4	2.8	24.8	26.4
UTX	5.6	16.6	2.5	24.7	24.6
MMM	5.1	7.4	5.1	17.6	18.6
MO	15.7	−8.0	6.2	14.0	14.5
X	11.2	6.2	−4.8	12.5	6.3
EK	−8.1	10.2	8.1	10.3	10.6
N	8.0	3.4	−1.7	9.7	8.7
AA	−1.1	5.4	0.6	5.0	7.3
IP	−3.1	−6.5	8.8	−0.9	−1.4
TX	4.0	−15.6	8.8	−2.8	−3.3
BS	−15.6	15.3	−6.2	−6.5	−8.9
NAV	39.7	−25.7	−24.6	−10.7	4.6
GM	22.2	−32.2	−5.3	−15.3	−3.7

a. Reading from the left, the columns in this table show the values for growth of equity, valuation change, and cash flow yield actually realized in 1985 for the companies in the Dow Jones Average; the return estimated by summing those three numbers; and the actual return to an owner of the company's stock in 1985. It is clear from casual inspection that the values of T are close approximations to the actual returns. In fact, regressing the T column on actual return gives a fit (R^2) of 0.94.

Examples include: low exposure to foreign earnings, proprietary market position for products, and a strong balance sheet. These attributes have no direct connection with return, but they tend to "tilt" the sources of return, giving the portfolio a character that causes its returns to differ from a passive portfolio. Another common approach is to emphasize high expected earnings growth. Still another seeks low price/earnings or low price/book ratios.

In light of what we have just learned about the sources of return, it is easy to recognize that these selection tools are incomplete models of expected return. When growth is high, expected return may be high if *ROE* and price/book happen to have the right values. Similarly, low price/earnings or price/book will raise cash flow yield and may signal high expected return, if growth and *ROE* are not too low. Nevertheless, the success enjoyed by these naive models seems to come in spite of, rather than because of, the level of understanding of their users—even though portfolios will be active in the sense that their returns will have a pattern different from a passive portfolio.

The existence of these characteristic return patterns, and the difficulty of understanding their sources, has spawned a resigned, not to say cynical, approach among those who hire multiple managers. A school of thought has grown up that no longer views return as the product of financial fundamentals like growth and cash flow but, rather, as the result of "exposure" to attributes such as foreign income or labor intensity.

Hoping to impose order on things, sponsors use statistical programs to analyze the differences between their managed portfolios and some index. Managers whose non-market returns act similarly are said to have the same "style," presumably due to similar "exposures" to the statistical attributes that are asserted to "generate" returns. As styles come into and out of market fashion in an unpredictable way, the argument goes, it is best to have some of each—thus diversifying away overall style risk while getting active stock-picking.

We can increase the merit of this general idea by replacing a statistical analysis of active returns with the more powerful and informative analysis of the T-Model. The insights gained in this way can help us to find managers whose styles complement each other, and who have achieved returns by skill rather than luck.

Tables 2 and 3 compare the sources of return for five portfolios, each selected and rebalanced at January 1 for each of the four years 1982–1985. The portfolios are: the S&P 500, a portfolio of the largest one hundred companies ranked by market value at January 1 of each year, a portfolio of companies chosen by our growth model to have the highest expected growth rates in the coming year, a "value" portfolio of fifty stocks chosen by the T-Model to have the highest expected returns in the coming year, and a "small-cap" portfolio representative of companies with small market capitalizations.

A few conclusions are striking:

- In a given year, valuation change is the largest source of return.
- Over a longer period of time, valuation change is by far the most volatile and unreliable source of return; in fact, this single component is more volatile than total return, the sum of all three components!

TABLE 2. *Sources of Return for Portfolios Representing Various Styles, 1982–1985 (%).*[a]

	g	Chg Val	*CFY*	Estimated Return	Actual Return
		1985			
S&P	10.1	18.8	3.8	32.7	31.2
BIG	5.8	20.5	6.7	32.3	32.1
Growth	26.2	5.7	−4.3	27.6	25.1
T-Model	12.4	26.7	6.0	45.1	42.3
Small-Cap	11.6	24.7	−1.0	35.3	32.7
		1984			
S&P	9.0	−9.9	4.8	3.8	1.3
BIG	8.4	−12.2	9.7	5.8	1.2
Growth	43.5	−54.9	−4.5	−16.0	−16.7
T-Model	14.4	−0.5	4.3	18.3	18.3
Small-Cap	13.9	−10.3	1.5	5.1	3.1
		1983			
S&P	14.2	16.5	1.2	31.8	29.0
BIG	11.4	5.3	4.4	21.2	19.0
Growth	45.5	11.4	−7.4	49.0	45.0
T-Model	13.0	7.0	4.2	24.3	21.2
Small-Cap	19.4	26.5	−0.2	45.6	42.3
		1982			
S&P	8.9	23.7	5.2	37.8	34.3
BIG	10.2	6.9	5.5	22.3	19.6
Growth	19.0	26.7	−1.2	44.4	40.6
T-Model	16.9	36.5	11.3	64.6	51.0
Small-Cap	15.8	26.0	−1.4	40.4	40.3

a. Each block shows the components of estimated return for a single portfolio representing a "style." For example, the top line of the top block shows the components of return estimated in 1985 for the S&P 500 (equal weighted). Growth of shareholders' equity was 10.1%, cash flow yield was 3.8%, and valuation change contributed 18.8% to a total return estimate of 32.7%. The actual return for that year was 31.2%.

■ The overall volatility of growth and cash flow yield put together is less than that of valuation change.
■ Growth of shareholders' equity was never negative for any of the portfolios.

TABLE 3. *Grand Averages and Volatility (%).*[a]

	g	Chg Val	CFY	Estimated Return	Actual Return
Overall Average	16.5	9.8	2.4	28.6	25.6
Standard Deviation	10.4	20.1	4.7	18.3	17.1

Data Grouped by Source of Return (%)				
	1982	1983	1984	1985
Growth				
S&P	10.1	9.0	14.2	8.9
BIG	5.8	8.4	11.4	10.2
Growth	26.2	43.5	45.5	19.0
T-Model	12.4	14.4	13.0	16.9
Small-Cap	11.6	13.9	19.4	15.8
Cash Flow Yield				
S&P	3.8	4.8	1.2	5.2
BIG	6.7	9.7	4.4	5.5
Growth	−4.3	−4.5	−7.4	−1.2
T-Model	6.0	4.3	4.2	11.3
Small-Cap	−1.0	1.5	−0.2	−1.4
Valuation Change				
S&P	18.8	−9.9	16.5	23.7
BIG	20.5	−12.2	5.3	6.9
Growth	5.7	−54.9	11.4	26.7
T-Model	26.7	−0.5	7.0	36.5
Small-Cap	24.7	−10.3	26.5	26.0

a. The Grand Averages show the average growth, *CFY*, and valuation change for all universes averaged over all years: Standard Deviation is the standard deviation of the whole sample. Data Grouped by Sources of Return allows convenient comparison of the growth, *CFY*, and valuation change components across portfolios and time. The top line shows that the growth component was 10.1%, 9.0%, 14.2%, and 8.9% for the S&P for the years 1982–1985, respectively, while the "Growth" portfolio exhibited growth rates of between 19.0% and 45.5%.

- Cash flow yield was negative only for the high-growth portfolio, and then it was small relative to growth; the sum of cash flow yield and growth was never negative for any portfolio in any year.
- This means that *stock market losses over this period were in every case due to adverse valuation change.*

Table 4 gives the average values for the data in Tables 2 and 3. When the data are averaged, more patterns emerge. In particular, note that:

TABLE 4. *Arithmetic Averages of Data in Tables 2 and 3 (%).*

	g	Chg Val	CFY	Estimated Return	Actual Return
S&P					
Average	10.6	12.3	3.8	26.5	24.0
Std. dev.	2.2	13.1	1.6	13.3	13.2
BIG					
Average	9.0	5.1	6.6	20.4	18.0
Std. dev.	2.1	11.6	2.0	9.5	11.0
Growth					
Average	33.6	−2.8	−4.4	26.3	23.5
Std. dev.	11.3	31.1	2.2	25.7	24.4
T-Model					
Average	14.2	17.4	6.5	38.1	33.2
Std. dev.	1.7	14.8	2.9	18.3	13.8
Small-Cap					
Average	15.2	16.7	−0.3	31.6	29.6
St. dev.	2.9	15.6	1.1	15.7	15.7

- The "small-cap effect" is partly due to higher-than-average growth and partly due to a favorable valuation shift enjoyed by small companies in the past five years.
- The portfolio including the companies with the highest growth rate did not always have the highest yearly returns; it had the lowest yearly return on one occasion.
- Over the period, the high-growth portfolio did not have the highest average return, because, over the whole five-year period, high-growth stocks suffered a slight downward revaluation while other segments of the market were market up.
- The volatility of valuation shifts is much higher for the growth strategy than for any other.
- The "value" style of total-return investing was successful because its "cheapness and growth" selections beat the market in all three sources of return.

IV. Style Diversification and Overall Expected Return

Cash flow yield is the smallest source of return, although it is relatively stable. For the S&P, for example, the mean cash flow yield was more than twice its standard deviation, implying that *CFY* is a source of return that a manager can predict with some confidence. Unfortunately, it is not large enough to swamp out the large fluctuations in the other components.

Growth is the largest source of long-term return, and is not as unstable as one might expect. For some portfolios, growth had a standard deviation about the same as that of *CFY*, with a much higher mean. The relationship of growth to valuation change is interesting. Up to a certain point, we can identify growth opportunities that are cheap (that is, may increase in value). When growth is too high, however, it is overpriced by the market so that future evaluation shifts prove to be negative. Inspecting the data, one is tempted to conclude that accurate, conservative estimates of growth are the key to investment success.

Valuation change is the largest component of returns in the short term — that is, one and sometimes even two years — but it is very unpredictable. Furthermore, even weak assumptions about market efficiency suggest that valuation change cannot be a reliable, repeatable source of return. Unless a manager is consistent at getting valuation shifts that beat the market's, past successes in this component should almost be discounted as a measure of management skill.

There is a key realization that, once understood, greatly clarifies this issue. *Over the long run, the mean expected return from valuation shifts must be zero for any truly passive strategy. The price/book ratio of stocks in the aggregate will not go to infinity, nor will it go to zero. No strategy that does not involve turnover can generate repeatable returns from this source.*

Sponsors who do this type of analysis will often find that managers with good recent track records have received most or all of their returns from favorable valuation shifts. The common practice of attempting to build a portfolio of complementary managers from a group who all fit this description will result in a pool of managers whose expected return and expected style covariance is probably much different, and much worse, than the sponsor thinks.

What does the evidence say about the practice of "style diversification"? It would seem that this idea might offer less than meets the eye. We have seen that our growth model did an excellent job at selecting stocks with high growth, but those stocks did not have particularly good performance because of adverse value shifts. Similarly, the BIG portfolio had cash flow yield well above that of the S&P, but underperformed it.

This illustrates a fundamental pitfall in the notion of style diversification. Suppose you hire one manager who is good at finding the stocks with highest growth, another who finds stocks with highest cash flow yields, and another "rotating" manager who tries to find those that will experience favorable revaluation. It is possible that all three of these managers will build portfolios that excel in their single specialty but will still underperform the market individually and as a group. That is, the return contribution to each manager's portfolio from the component that identifies a particular "style" may be superior, as was the case with the BIG and Growth portfolios, but

TABLE 5. *Choosing Two Managers with Complementary Styles: Returns (%).*

	g	Chg Val	CFY	Estimated Return	Actual Return
S&P	10.6	12.3	3.8	26.5	<u>24.0</u>
BIG	9.0	5.1	<u>6.6</u>	20.4	18.0
Growth	<u>33.6</u>	−2.8	−4.4	26.3	23.5
Growth + BIG	21.3	1.2	1.1	23.4	20.8

the return contribution from the "style" may not be enough to offset a bad result in another component.

Imagine that you had selected a management strategy from Table 5 in 1981. Would you pick Growth as your growth manager and BIG as your value manager? That would certainly give the desired style offset — but, as it turned out, the portfolios underperformed the S&P individually and together. A portfolio evenly divided between these two styles would have had good stylistic balance, but an average return over the period of only 20.8% — far below the index. Return comes from the sum of all columns!

Another illustration of this is shown in Figures 1, 2, and 3. Using just the S&P 500 stocks as our selection universe, we created three portfolios. One was a list of fifty growth companies, chosen by our growth model as shown in Tables 2 and 4 but confined to stocks within the S&P. One was a list of fifty companies with the highest expected cash flow yield. The third

FIGURE 1. *Sometimes Growth Performs Best.*[a]

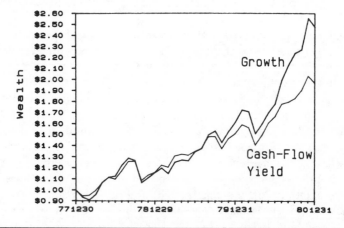

a. To illustrate the idea of style diversity, we created two portfolios of fifty stocks chosen from within the S&P 500 companies. One group had the highest cash flow yield at the beginning of each year since 1978, and another had the highest historical growth rate.

FIGURE 2. *Sometimes Cash Flow Yield Performs Best.*[a]

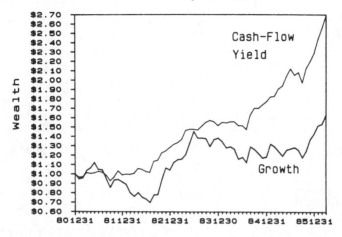

a. Although the growth list performed much better through 1980, it failed to perform as well as Treasury bills over the 1981–1985 period, while cash flow yield stocks did very well.

FIGURE 3. *The T-Model Selects Highest Returns with Greatest Consistency.*[a]

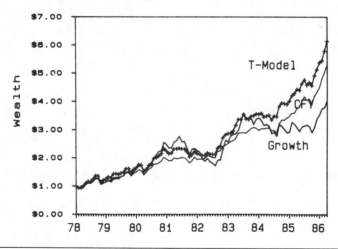

a. A third portfolio, consisting of the fifty stocks with the highest expected return as estimated by the T-Model, did better than either the "growth" or "value" portfolios.

was a list of fifty companies with the highest expected returns as estimated by the T-Model at the beginning of the year. We divided the 1977–1985 period in half. In the first half, the growth portfolio outperformed cash flow yield, but this was sharply reversed in the second half. The T-Model portfolio, relying neither on *CFY* nor on growth for all its returns, gradually built an insurmountable lead over both of them.

There is no clear-cut answer to the question of style mix, but it should be obvious that sponsors should demand a total return emphasis from every manager, no matter what the manager's predilection. That is, a sponsor should insist that the growth and small-cap managers be value-conscious and that the value manager analyze companies for profitability and growth. In short, one-dimensional management probably will not add value. An overall portfolio consisting of a portion managed by a seeker of growth plus another portion managed by a seeker of cheapness is not the same as a portfolio of cheap, fast-growing stocks.

V. Conclusion

The technique presented here can be used for manager evaluation and strategic planning in a multi-manager fund. The analysis is applicable to any investment portfolio. It becomes more complex when there is a lot of portfolio turnover, so this paper applied it only to portfolios that were held unchanged for a year at a time.

Nonetheless, with appropriate effort, we can separate the returns from any portfolio into three components: growth in shareholders' equity, cash flow yield, and change in valuation. This procedure explains over 90% of the variance of individual stock returns, in terms of three components—as contrasted to statistical models that explain about 10% in terms of many components. (It is possible that a statistical model might be used to explain further the returns due to valuation shift.)

We know that these three components make up every manager's return, and we know something about the behavior of the components. Therefore, we can draw some other conclusions. Growth and cash flow yield are much more forecastable than valuation change. At the same time, they are complementary to some extent: high growth usually makes *CFY* lower, and vice versa. Real managerial skill is required to beat the benchmark in both categories.

Valuation change has the highest variance, and a low expected value. For an index portfolio, the long-run expected mean return from this source is zero. Active management will affect this term's variance considerably without necessarily adding value. This term is the hardest to forecast; it has much less connection with company fundamentals and much more with market fads and fashions.

Consequently, outstanding short-term performance almost always comes from valuation shifts, because that is the source of greatest variance—but it is also the least repeatable and reliable source. Attributes that "explain" valuation change have variance associated with them, but it is *uncompensated* variance. Thus, models that identify managers as being "good" because they give the portfolio "exposure" to certain "factors" may be injurious to the portfolio in two ways: The manager may have zero or negative true selection capability when we analyze it properly, and the "factors" in valuation change that the manager is trying to play probably have no long-term positive return associated with them.

Risk control means control of valuation risk. Aversion to downside risk means avoidance of large volatility of valuation, because negative returns are almost entirely the outcome of bad results from this single component. A growth strategy is by far the most likely to have negative returns. Over time, valuation shifts cannot be counted on to provide any return unless the manager's selection process explicitly seeks them and has a good record of finding them.

Style diversification is not as simple, and possibly not as beneficial, as is widely believed. Returns earned by devotees of small stocks, or growth stocks, or some other market segment, may be partly or mostly due to non-repeatable valuation shifts. Moreover, adding several one-dimensional managers cannot produce a portfolio of stocks with the multidimensional qualities that make up high expected returns.

The best kind of manager is certainly one who can beat a chosen benchmark in all three sources of return. To achieve that, the manager must use a selection technique that focuses directly on an estimate of future total return.

Appendix

The T-Model, as originally developed, is intended to be a tool for analysts to estimate future expected returns so that they can select stocks. The model can also explain returns after the fact, something that other valuation models do poorly. This appendix does not present a rigorous derivation but, rather, explains the T-Model by example.

Where IBM Shareholders Earned Their Returns in 1985

In 1985, International Business Machines Corporation reported the financial results shown below. Also shown are some market valuation data.

Financial Data for IBM, 1985

Net income	$6,555 mil
Dividends paid	2,703
Beginning equity	26,489
Ending equity	31,990
Change in equity	20.8%
Return on beginning equity	24.7%

(continued)

Financial Data for IBM, 1985 (cont.)

Dividend yield	3.59%
Beginning shares out	612.9 mil
Ending shares out	615.4
Change in shares out	0.41%
Price at beginning of year	123.125
Price at end of year	155.5
Price/Book at beginning	2.85
Price/Book at end	2.99
Change in price/book	5.0%

The T-Model relies on the mathematical equality between return and some of these reported results.

The change in the market value of a company's outstanding common stock is:

$$\text{Chg } Cap = g + (\text{Chg } PB)(1+g), \tag{1}$$

where:

$\text{Chg } Cap = $ change in market capitalization,

$g = $ change in common equity, and

$\text{Chg } PB = $ change in price/book ratio.

$$\text{"Change" in } X = \frac{\text{Ending } X - \text{Beginning } X}{\text{Beginning } X}$$

The change in share price is:

$$\text{Chg } Px = (1 + \text{Chg } Cap)\left(\frac{\text{Beginning Shares}}{\text{Ending Shares}}\right) - 1, \tag{2}$$

where:

$\text{Chg } Px = $ change in share price.

Substituting the values for IBM into Equation (2), we get:

$$\begin{aligned} \text{Chg } Cap &= g + (\text{Chg } PB)(1+g) \\ &= 0.2077 + (0.05)(1.2077) \\ &= 0.268; \end{aligned}$$

$$\begin{aligned} \text{Chg } Px &= 1.268(612.9/615.4) - 1 \\ &= 0.263, \text{ or } 26.3\%. \end{aligned}$$

This equals IBM's price change of 26.3% (from 123⅛ to 155½). Thus, IBM's shareholders received their 26.3% price appreciation from three sources: a 20.8% increase in shareholders' equity, a 5.0% increase in price/book valuation, and a slight reduction in return due to share issuance of 0.4%. *This is not a coincidence or a neatly chosen example. It always works. It is a mathematical identity.*

But, one may object, an identity is uninformative — more or less self-evident. How can this tell us anything about stock selection or portfolio management? Besides, this formulation has two imponderable elements: change in price/book, and change in shares outstanding. We beg the reader's indulgence for a little longer.

The return received by a shareholder is of course identical to:

$$\text{Total Return} = \text{Chg } Px + \frac{Divs}{\text{Begin } Px} \tag{3a}$$

$$= (1 + \text{Chg } Cap)\left(\frac{\text{Beginning Shares}}{\text{Ending Shares}}\right) - 1$$

$$+ \frac{Divs}{\text{Begin } Px} \tag{3b}$$

where:

$Divs$ = dividends per share collected during the year, and
Begin Px = share price at beginning of year.

To calculate total return, we add the dividend yield to the price change.

Now, by adding a little bit of economic assumption we can rid ourselves of one of the two imponderable terms mentioned above. The change in shares outstanding is presumably due to the company's issuance of shares to finance growth or its repurchase of shares if it has retained more earnings than it needs to grow. If this is true, then:

Dividend Yield + Effect of Share Repurchase or Issuance

$$= \frac{ROE - g}{PB}, \tag{4}$$

where:

ROE = return on equity = net income/equity, and
PB = price/book ratio.

We call the term on the right of Equation (4) the cash flow yield, because it is intended to approximate dividend yield plus share repurchase or minus the effect of share issuance. This eliminates the need to identify changes in shares outstanding.

This might not matter if we wanted only to have an after-the-fact explanatory formula, but we have grander goals in mind that would be frustrated if elaborate models of share issuance were required. So now we can say:

$$\text{Total Return} = \text{Chg } Cap + \frac{ROE - g}{PB}, \tag{5a}$$

or fully written out as:

$$\text{Total Return} = g + \text{Chg } PB(1+g) + \frac{ROE - g}{PB}. \tag{5b}$$

Equation (5b) is known as the T-Model.

The T-Model equation is not absolutely exact, as is Equation (3b). The inexactitude arises because Equation (4) only approximates share transactions. However, the T-Model gives a good approximation of total return. Again using IBM as our example:

$$\text{Total Return} = 0.208 + 0.05(1.208) + \frac{0.247 - 0.208}{2.85}$$

$$= 0.282, \text{ or } 28.2\%.$$

This is not quite equal to the actual return of 29.9%. The difference is the error introduced by the assumptions behind Equation (4). Our equation estimates that IBM shareholders got their total return from three sources:

20.8% from growth in shareholders' equity;
5.9% from change in valuation;
1.4% from yield net of share issuance (cash flow yield).

In general, this technique for partitioning produces excellent results. Table 1 in the main body of this paper shows results for the stocks in the Dow Jones Average, which in 1985 included some cases that were very hard for the T-Model to handle because of massive reorganizations. Nonetheless, the estimates are generally useful.

7

How to Combine Active Management with Index Funds*

Richard A. Brealey
Deputy Principal
London Business School

I. Introduction

In an influential article written in 1973, Jack Treynor and Fischer Black suggested that it was conceptually useful to separate the selection of the common stock portfolio into two stages.[1] First, the manager should place bets on specific stocks by taking long positions in those stocks that the manager expects to provide positive abnormal returns and by taking short positions in stocks that the manager expects to give negative abnormal returns. Second, the manager should adjust the fund's exposure to market-wide movements by buying or selling an index fund. Treynor–Black referred to the first step as the construction of the active portfolio and the second step as that of blending in the passive portfolio.

Since the publication of the Treynor–Black article, many pension schemes have invested part of their money in an index fund while putting the remainder in one or more actively managed funds, but the practice of active-passive management is linked only tenuously to the original theory. Of course, Treynor–Black assumed that the manager could freely sell short those stocks with negative expected abnormal returns.

---

*This article is reprinted from the Winter 1986 issue of *The Journal of Portfolio Management*.
1. See J.L. Treynor and F. Black, "How to Use Security Analysis to Improve Portfolio Selection," *Journal of Business* 46 (January 1973): 66–86.

I shall argue that if managers are in fact unable to sell stocks short, a pension scheme would be justified in dividing its portfolio between an active and a passive fund only in very special circumstances. Indeed, if managers cannot sell short individual stocks, they may wish to *reduce* their market exposure by selling index futures.

II. The Role of Index Funds

Limitations on Short Selling

A short seller is not free to use the proceeds from a short sale and this acts as a deterrent to the short sale of individual stocks. This problem has been alleviated by the establishment of the traded options market, since an investor can largely replicate a short sale by simultaneously buying the put, selling the call, and borrowing the present value of the exercise price.[2] Nevertheless, it is costly to arrange three separate contracts simply to sell one stock short. In addition, traded options are available only on a limited number of stocks.

In this article, I shall assume that investors are effectively prohibited from selling short individual stocks. I shall then look at the circumstances in which it would be inadvisable to invest any part of the portfolio in an index fund.[3]

Suppose that an active manager is pessimistic about the outlook for a particular stock and would like to sell it short. In principle, he could borrow and sell the passive portfolio's holding in that stock. In practice, if the portfolios are managed by different firms, this is difficult to arrange and rarely done. Also, if the stocks analysed by the active manager constitute only a small proportion of the market portfolio, then it would be of little help to borrow stock from the passive portfolio. For these reasons, I shall assume that the active manager and the pension fund as a whole are both prohibited from taking any short positions.

Apart from considering the effect of a prohibition on the short sale of individual stocks, I shall retain all the other assumptions of the Treynor-Black article. In particular, I shall assume that investors choose a mean-variance efficient portfolio, that they are free to borrow and lend at a single interest rate, that stocks are related only through their common relationship with the market, and that there are no transactions costs. The last of these assumptions is crucial: high transactions costs would increase the incentive for a manager to invest part of the portfolio in an index fund.

2. Strictly, the two strategies are equivalent only for European options.
3. I shall loosely use the term index fund to denote any fund whose returns are highly correlated with those on the market portfolio.

Forecast Returns

The active manager needs to forecast the abnormal return from each stock. The average abnormal return is zero, but in any period there is a wide spread between the best- and worst-performing stocks. I assume that the abnormal returns on each stock are normally distributed with a variance of s^2.

The forecasts of an investor who could predict these abnormal returns perfectly would also have a variance of s^2. At the other extreme, if an investor could not distinguish at all among the prospects for different stocks, the forecasts would have zero variance. Thus, the spread among forecasts depends on (a) the spread among the actual abnormal returns, and (b) the investor's ability to distinguish the prospects for different stocks.

Suppose the manager could forecast the abnormal returns with a correlation of R. Then the average forecast abnormal return would be zero and the variance of the forecasts would be $(Rs)^2$.

Figure 1 shows a picture of these forecast abnormal returns. Half the stocks that the active portfolio manager analyzes will appear overvalued and therefore have negative expected abnormal returns. The manager would sell these stocks short if short sales were permitted. On the other hand, if short sales are prohibited, the best that the manager can do is to have zero holdings in the overvalued stocks. In other words, the manager will behave as if these stocks had zero expected abnormal returns.

The other half of the stocks that the manager analyzes will appear undervalued and will be included in the active portfolio. The average expected abnormal return on this group of stocks is $.8Rs$, and the uncertainty surrounding each forecast is described by the variance $(1 - R^2)s^2$.

Step 1: Choosing the Active Portfolio

We can now ask, "What sort of active portfolio should the manager plan to hold if half the stocks are expected to have a forecast abnormal return of zero and the remainder have an average forecast abnormal return of $.8Rs$?"

In choosing the active portfolio, the manager should ensure that the last dollar invested in each stock is working equally hard. Treynor–Black show that this condition implies that holdings in the active portfolio should be proportional to the ratio of expected abnormal reward to variance. If all the stocks analyzed have the same variance, then a stock with the average positive forecast return will also have an average holding in the active portfolio. Thus, the ratio of expected reward to variance for the average holding is $.8Rs/(1 - R^2)s^2$.

Step 2: Blending in the Passive Portfolio

In deciding how heavily to bet on the market, the manager should use the same rule employed when placing bets on individual stocks. In other words,

FIGURE 1.

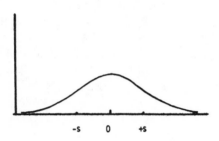

(a) Distribution of actual abnormal returns

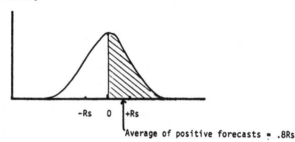

(b) Distribution of forecast abnormal returns

the manager should buy or sell an index fund until the total investment in the market is proportional to the ratio of expected market reward to variance. We can write this ratio as $(r_m - r_f)/s_m^2$, where:

r_m = expected market return,
r_f = risk-free interest rate, and
s_m^2 = variance of forecast market return.

The optimal investment in the market portfolio as a proportion of the average holding in the active portfolio is:

$$\frac{r_m - r_f}{s_m^2} \cdot \frac{(1 - R^2)s^2}{.8Rs}.$$

Suppose the manager analyzes N stocks. Since half of these stocks are likely to provide positive expected abnormal returns, the expected investment in the market portfolio as a proportion of the *total* investment in the active portfolio is:

$$\frac{r_m - r_f}{s_m^2} \cdot \frac{(1 - R^2)s}{.4NR}.$$

When Should the Portfolio be Invested in an Index Fund?

Since the active portfolio contains only long positions, the manager cannot place bets on specific stocks without simultaneously placing bets on the market. The manager will, therefore, want to invest in an index fund only if the active portfolio does not give sufficient exposure to market movements.

If the mean beta of the stocks analyzed is $\bar{\beta}$, the active portfolio will be expected to provide exactly the desired investment in the market if:

$$\frac{r_m - r_f}{s_m^2} \cdot \frac{(1 - R^2)s}{.4NR} = \bar{\beta}.$$

Equally, we can say that an investor can expect the active portfolio to provide the desired investment in the market if the number of stocks analyzed is:

$$N = \frac{r_m - r_f}{s_m^2} \cdot \frac{(1 - R^2)s}{.4R\beta}.$$

Table 1 shows the critical values of N assuming $r_m - r_f = .09$, $s_m = .22$ and $\bar{\beta} = 1.0$. Notice, for example, that if $R = .15$ and $s = .4$, the active portfolio is likely to provide a sufficient stake in the market as long as the manager analyzes 12 stocks. If analysis covers less than this number, a positive stake in an index fund will probably be necessary. On the other hand, if

TABLE 1.[a]

Forecasting Correlation (R)	Specific Risk of Stocks Analyzed (s)		
	.2	.3	.4
.01	93	139	186
.05	19	28	37
.10	9	15	18
.15	6	9	12
.20	5	7	8

a. If the number of stocks analyzed (N) is more than the critical value, the optimal stock portfolio is not expected to include a positive investment in an index fund.

analysis covers more than 12 stocks, the manager will on average wish to sell the market short. Notice that this decision is appropriate even though the market offers an expected reward of $r_m - r_f = 9\%$.[4] The motivation is simply because the manager acquires a large stake in the market through the bets on individual stocks.

Table 1 implies that the active portfolio may well provide a more than adequate investment in the market when investors are limited in the short positions that they can take. The common practice of dividing the portfolio between an index fund and one or more active funds makes sense only if few stocks are analyzed or the manager's forecasting correlation is low. If more than 100 stocks are analyzed, then the forecasting correlation would typically need to be less than .01 to justify a separate holding in an index fund! It is difficult to imagine how the plan sponsor could hope to detect such a low level of forecasting skill.

III. Short Selling Constraints, Portfolio Performance and Index Futures

In the last section, I argued that, when there are limitations on the short sale of individual stocks, investors with any worthwhile forecasting ability are likely to pick up a larger investment in the market than they would like. In contrast to wanting to hold an index fund, these investors would actively wish to sell the market portfolio short. The introduction of index futures has made this strategy possible. Therefore, in this section, I consider the extent to which a manager might wish to sell index futures and the effect of such sales on portfolio performance.[5]

A Simulation Model

As long as the active manager cannot sell stocks short and as long as the passive manager does not *want* to sell the index short, Treynor–Black's two stages of portfolio management are still valid. In other words, the active manager simply ignores overvalued stocks and constructs the active portfolio from those stocks with positive forecast abnormal returns. At the second stage, the passive manager purchases an index fund to give the appropriate market exposure.

---

4. If the forecast reward on the market is less than 9%, the critical values of N would also be less than those shown in Table 1. Obviously, in the extreme case where the forecast reward was zero or negative, the manager would never wish to invest in an index fund regardless of the number of stocks analyzed.

5. Notice that a position in index futures is simply like a bet on the market. As long as the investor can provide margin in the form of bills, margin requirements make no difference to the composition of the efficient equity portfolio.

In this section, however, we are interested in circumstances in which the passive manager does want to sell the index short. In these cases, it is not possible to construct the active portfolio without simultaneously taking into account the forecast market return and market variance. For example, if the index cannot be sold short, the manager might want to invest less in high beta stocks when the forecast market return is low or the uncertainty surrounding the forecast is high.

Because the separation of function no longer holds, I employ simulation to assess the effect on performance of market short sales. More specifically, I assume that an investor selects an active portfolio from a group of N stocks and *either* a long position in a market index fund *or* a short position in index futures.[6] I calculate the portfolio that offers the highest rate of expected reward to risk under each of the three assumptions:

(a) a complete prohibition on short sales,
(b) a restriction on the short sale of individual stocks, and
(c) no restrictions on short selling.[7]

The Gains from Short Selling

Table 2 shows the difference between the ratio of reward to risk on the optimal portfolio and the ratio of reward to risk on an index fund, averaged over 100 iterations. If short sales of individual stocks are prohibited, the manager derives no benefit from spotting overvalued stocks. Indeed, such a prohibition is equivalent to halving the number of stocks analyzed. Since the ratio of expected reward to risk should increase in proportion to the number of stocks analyzed, the gains from security analysis are twice as large when there are no constraints on short sales as when there is a complete prohibition. This is apparent from Table 2.

For example, a manager with a forecasting correlation of .10 can achieve a similar improvement in the ratio of expected reward to risk (.109) by analyzing 10 stocks when there are no restrictions on short sales as by analyzing 20 stocks when short sales are banned. To put it another way, suppose the manager analyzes 10 stocks with a correlation of .1. If short sales are not allowed, the result of this security analysis is to increase the expected reward-to-risk ratio by .057. But, if short sales are unrestricted, the investor realizes roughly twice the benefit from security analysis—a gain of .109 in the expected reward-to-risk ratio.

---

6. I assume that the dividend payments on the index are known, so that an investor can replicate the purchase of index futures by a levered investment in an index fund.
7. Notice that, by the underlying assumption of the diagonal model, the investor cannot replicate the short sale of an individual stock by selling the market index and repurchasing all stocks but one.

TABLE 2.

Number of Stocks Analyzed (N)	No Short Sales			Short Sales of Market Only			Unrestricted Short Sales		
	R = .05	R = .10	R = .15	R = .05	R = .10	R = .15	R = .05	R = .10	R = .15
10	.015	.057	.117	.015	.058	.119	.030	.109	.217
20	.029	.103	.193	.029	.106	.212	.057	.195	.373
50	.065	.177	.295	.069	.229	.430	.129	.402	.718

Ratio of reward to variability of market portfolio = 9/22 = .409.

As one would expect, when the investor is allowed to sell only the market short, the gains from security analysis lie between the two extremes. When few stocks are analyzed and the manager has little forecasting ability, the investor is unlikely to want to sell the market short. In this case, the availability of market index futures would make almost no difference to the investor's performance. By contrast, when the manager analyzes a large number of stocks or has considerable forecasting ability, then that manager is likely to pick up a much larger holding in the market than is necessary, and there are significant gains from being able to sell index futures short. For example, if $N = 50$ and $R = .15$, then the gain from security analysis is .295 in the absence of index futures and .430 with index futures. For a fund that has the same risk as the market, this is equivalent to an improvement of 3% in the fund's annual return.

Portfolio Sales of Index Futures

Table 3 shows the proportion of occasions that an investor would want to sell index futures. Notice that, even if there are no restrictions on the short sale of individual stocks, the investor will want to sell index futures when the stocks under analysis happen by chance to appear predominantly undervalued. On the other hand, the motivation to sell the market index is much stronger when there is a restriction on the short sale of individual stocks. In this case, the investor — who has only modest forecasting abilty but who analyzes a large number of stocks — is likely to sell index futures in most years.

Table 4 shows the average net investment in the market index and Table 5 averages only the short positions in the index. If the manager is free to sell individual stocks short, the active portfolio will contain short positions in overvalued stocks and long positions in undervalued stocks. Since stocks are as likely to be overvalued as undervalued, the average net investment in the active portfolio is zero. Thus, the amount invested in the index fund is on average equal to the total value of the portfolio.

TABLE 3. *The Percentage of Occasions on which the Optimal Portfolio Contains a Short Position in the Market Index.*

Number of Stocks Analyzed (N)	Short Sales of Market			Unrestricted Short Sales		
	$R = .05$	$R = .10$	$R = .15$	$R = .05$	$R = .10$	$R = .15$
10	0	4	32	0	0	4
20	1	56	90	0	6	12
50	87	100	100	4	16	28

TABLE 4. *The Average Net Investment in the Market Index as a Percentage of Fund Value.*

Number of Stocks Analyzed (N)	No Short Sales			Short Sales of Market			Unrestricted Short Sales		
	$R=.05$	$R=.10$	$R=.15$	$R=.05$	$R=.10$	$R=.15$	$R=.05$	$R=.10$	$R=.15$
10	72	45	25	72	45	21	99	98	98
20	46	10	2	45	0	-22	99	99	98
50	2	0	0	-16	-37	-42	97	98	98

TABLE 5. *The Average of the Short Positions in the Market Index as a Percentage of Fund Value.*

Number of Stocks Analyzed (N)	Short Sales of Market			Unrestricted Short Sales		
	$R = .05$	$R = .10$	$R = .15$	$R = .05$	$R = .10$	$R = .15$
10	0	0	4	0	0	0
20	0	10	24	0	2	7
50	18	37	42	2	11	27

I have already noted that if by chance the stocks analyzed appear to be predominantly undervalued, the investor may wish to reduce market exposure by selling index futures. Nevertheless, Table 5 shows that, as long as individual stocks can be sold short, then sales of index futures will be fairly small.

When there is a complete prohibition on short sales, the active portfolio contains only long positions. If N and R are small, the manager will not want to place large bets on individual stocks and will on average invest positive amounts in an index fund. We have seen, however, that higher values of N and R would make the manager want to sell the market short most of the time. Tables 4 and 5 suggest that, in these cases, managers are justified in taking substantial short positions in the index.

In summary, if managers are not free to sell individual stocks short, then only managers with negligible forecasting ability should hold an index fund as part of their total portfolio. The remainder should not only have zero holdings in the index fund but, in most years, should reduce their market exposure significantly by the sale of index futures.

IV. Index Futures and Prices

Because index futures allow investors to reduce their market exposure, the price of index futures need not be the same as that of an equivalent portfolio of stocks, and the prices of the stocks themselves may be affected by the introduction of futures. This section, therefore, discusses briefly the possible price effects of index futures.

If investors are not free to sell short individual stocks, then the value of index futures must be less than or equal to the value of an equivalent levered position in the underlying stocks. Since the net supply of index futures is zero, the sale of futures by investors with non-consensus forecasts must be matched by purchases from investors who were previously prepared to hold at least part of their wealth in the form of an index fund. If this results in a potential excess supply of index futures, then there will be zero outstanding supply of index funds and the futures will sell at a discount on the index.

Because the introduction of index futures makes some investors better off in their own eyes and leaves none worse off, it should result in an increase in the value of the market portfolio.

If the disagreement about returns is symmetric, there will be no change in relative stock prices and the introduction of index futures will induce an identical rise in the price of each stock. For example, assume that the market is composed of just two stocks and three representative investors. Investors A and B have equal sums invested in the two common stocks, whereas the consensus investor C has a much larger amount invested. The characteristics of the two stocks and each investor's forecasts are as follows:

Stock	Capitalization As % of Market	Expected Reward % $(\bar{r}_j - r_f)$		
		A	B	C
1	50	20	−10	5
2	50	−10	20	5

I assume that the variance of returns on each stock is 200 and the correlation between the returns is 0.5.

If no short sales are permitted, A and B will invest only in the stock that has a positive forecast reward, and C will invest in an index fund composed of equal amounts in each stock.

If investors are now permitted to trade index futures, A's investment in Stock 1 will be 9 times greater, offset by selling index futures. B will likewise with Stock 2. The additional supply of these stocks will be provided by C, who will substitute index futures for the holding in the index fund. Since the aggregate portfolio of the non-consensus investors is unaffected by the introduction of index futures, there will be no change in relative prices. A and B are now in their own eyes better off and C is unaffected, so that prices of both stocks must rise to prevent excess demand.

If the disagreement between investors is not symmetric, then there will be a rise in the price of stocks on which they agree and a relative fall in the price of stocks on which they disagree.[8] This can be illustrated by a further simple example. Assume that the market is expanded to three stocks with the following characteristics:

---

8. This result was first suggested by E. Miller, "Risk, Uncertainty, and Divergence of Opinion," *Journal of Finance* 32 (September 1977): 1151–68.

Stock	Capitalization As % of Market	Expected Reward $(\bar{r}_j - r_f)$		
		A	B	C
1	33	20	−10	16
2	33	−10	20	16
3	33	16	16	16

As in the previous example, the variance of returns on each stock is 200 and the correlation between the returns is in each case 0.5.

When short sales are prohibited, A's portfolio will hold 67% in Stock 1 and the balance in Stock 3. B will hold equivalent proportions of Stocks 2 and 3, and C will invest in an index fund composed of equal holdings in each stock.

If each investor is now permitted to trade index futures, A will wish to invest 4.6 times his aggregate stock investment in Stock 1 and 4 times his aggregate stock investment in Stock 3 and will seek to offset these purchases by the sale of index futures. B will likewise wish to hold similar proportions of Stocks 2 and 3 and to sell index futures. C will be willing to purchase futures, offsetting that purchase by the sale of equal amounts of each stock. As a result, there will be a relative deficiency of demand for Stocks 1 and 2 and an excess demand for Stock 3. This imbalance will result in a rise in the price of Stock 3 relative to that of Stocks 1 and 2.

Notice that these two simple examples assumed that the index futures simply provided an average of the returns on the individual stocks. Thus, each investor was able to replicate exactly the short sale of an individual stock by selling the index future and repurchasing all other stocks. In practice, not only would such a strategy be very costly but any changes in the construction of the index or uncertainty about dividends would make it impossible to replicate the short sale of an individual stock. This would reduce the incentive for A and B to sell index futures. Nevertheless, as long as this incentive did not disappear entirely, the effect would be a relative rise in the price of those stocks on which investors are agreed.

V. Summary and Conclusion

In the first section of this article I suggested that the practice of active-passive portfolio management finds little support in the original theory. One reason for this is that separation of the management task into an active and passive component is generally only feasible when the investor can sell individual stocks short. If this is not the case, the portfolio should not hold an investment in both an active portfolio and an index fund except in a very limited range of circumstances.

In the second section, I argued that managers who have more than a negligible degree of forecasting ability should generally aim to *reduce* exposure to the market index. This they can now do by the sale of index futures.

If there existed an unsatisfied demand by some investors to reduce their market exposure, then the introduction of index futures should have resulted in a shift in security prices. In particular, the extra choice available to investors should have had the effect of increasing overall market values, but this would have been accompanied by a relative fall in the price of stocks that some investors regarded as overpriced. Finally, if the incentive to reduce market exposure is sufficiently great, the price of index futures can remain below that of the equivalent stocks.

8

The Revolution in Composite Assets

Donald L. Luskin
Senior Vice President
Wells Fargo Investment Advisors

I. Introduction

There is a subtle but pervasive revolution going on in the theory and practice of investment — a revolution in the most fundamental assumptions with which investors frame their notions of their investment assets. The old regime of security analysis emphasized individual assets, but over the last quarter century it has been gradually replaced by a new regime of portfolio management, with corresponding emphasis on composite assets. The new emphasis on composite assets is as revolutionary in relation to traditional investment perspectives as an Apollo astronaut's photograph of the whole Earth rising above the Sea of Tranquility is to a map of the New York City subway system.

By "composite assets" I mean diversified investment aggregates, such as portfolios of stocks or bonds, that are themselves made up of individual assets, but are nonetheless thought of globally, as indivisible units. The composite asset perspective operates on the macrocosmic, whole-portfolio level, relegating individual assets to the role of mere building blocks.

II. Investment Strategies with Composite Assets

As of this writing, approximately $200 billion is invested on behalf of America's largest and most sophisticated corporate and public pension plans and endowments in various equity and fixed-income index funds. The phenomenal growth of index funds is only partially attributable to frustration with traditional active management. Perhaps it is just as well explained by a preference for systematic diversification, rigid investment discipline and tight cost control made possible by a perspective that treats the benchmark index as a single composite asset.

The impact of these enormous funds, and the attitude that has made them so popular, can be seen when a new stock is added to Standard and Poor's 500, the most widely followed benchmark index. In the weeks following addition, new stocks can be observed to appreciably outperform the market, reflecting not only buying pressure from index funds but also the enhancement of the stock's credibility and prestige resulting from membership in this exclusive composite asset club.

Many index funds now seek not simply to mimic or reproduce published indexes but instead to offer what amount to competing alternative composite assets. Some such funds offer biases, or "tilts," in index composition or weighting in favor of particular investment attributes, such as yield or size, while still maintaining diversification and broad market exposure. Others use quantitative models to select securities thought to be underpriced, combining them into portfolios designed to track, yet still outperform, a published index. In both cases investors are still pursuing the holy grail of better-than-market performance, but they are doing so in a new composite asset framework.

Asset allocation strategies are born not only of the recognition that it is difficult or impossible to beat the market through stock selection but also of the belief that such a pursuit is essentially trivial. Allocation decisions between broad investment classes—that is, composite assets—are now understood to be the prime contributor to risks and returns. On the strategic level pension plans now typically retain specialized consultants to help structure asset allocation to meet long-term obligations while maximizing expected return. On the tactical level investment managers recommend short-term shifts between composite assets in response to models of the relative risk-adjusted attractiveness of asset classes.

Stock index futures are arguably the most successful new products in the history of the securities industry, trading a daily value far in excess of the underlying stock market. They are used by institutions as generic proxies for composite assets—units for transferring systematic risk in all manner of hedging, positioning and restructuring activities at the whole-portfolio level. Arbitrage between index futures and their underlying physical indexes treats the stock and futures exchanges as competing marketplaces for equivalent and interchangeable composite assets.

III. Trading in Terms of Composite Assets

Unfortunately, the futures market remains the closest current approximation to a composite assets exchange, leaving a gross mismatch between the way investors think about their investment goals and the way they must carry them out. For investors who customarily think in terms of composite assets, a preference to trade in the same composite terms flows inevitably from important functional requirements of their investment strategies. Transactions must be made proportionately and simultaneously across all the assets comprising a composite asset, yet institutions like the New York Stock Exchange and the over-the-counter network of government bond dealers still only trade individual assets, one at a time.

To redress this deficiency, the securities brokerage industry has improvised several ex officio exchange mechanisms of its own. In "package" trading a broker acts as an off-floor dealer/specialist to facilitate simultaneous trading of a list of assets. In equities it has been estimated that package trading now accounts for upward of 25 percent of daily New York Stock Exchange volume.

In the increasingly popular "crossing networks," brokers provide a central computerized bulletin board facility on which investors may confidentially post lists of assets to be traded. Executions are consummated when lists, or combinations of lists, are able to be paired off in the computer. Although these networks are still in their infancy, they have already begun to attract significant interest from investors; their trading volume is now reported in the millions of shares on many days.

The revolution in composite assets has caught the New York Stock Exchange in an uncomfortable competitive position. On the one hand, in the wake of the October 1987 crash, the NYSE is seeking to strengthen its infrastructure to handle orders motivated by composite asset strategies. Though it recently put in place rules to prohibit use of its computerized order entry systems for index futures arbitrage on days when the market experiences large price changes, at the same time, it would like to take a leadership role in the inevitable growth of trading of composite assets. For example, it has advocated the creation of a specialist post for trading entire standardized portfolios of stocks all at once.

The revolution in composite assets will be complete when exchange mechanisms allow investors to trade and clear composite assets entirely in composite terms. For instance, someday investors will be able to place an order to buy a $10 million composite asset comprising a specified number of individual assets, with a specified theoretical tracking error versus a specified index, and specified levels of biases toward specified economic and risk factors. Ultimately, clearing institutions may have to evolve to accommodate transfers of wealth in units subtler than share certificates.

IV. Roots of the Composite Asset Revolution

Like most revolutions, the revolution in composite assets has been gradual, progressing inevitably out of a complex of economic, conceptual, regulatory, and technological factors. Most fundamentally, it was necessitated by the sweeping institutionalization of markets that has occurred over the last 25 years. The vast magnitude of institutional investment funds, and the complexities of accommodating their astonishing rate of growth, are grossly out of scale with the notion of traditional analysis of individual assets. Diversification of institutional holdings into composite assets is virtually automatic, and a matching conceptual framework is functionally unavoidable.

Beyond this simple argument of necessity, there are a number of other, subtler reasons why institutional investors have come to prefer to think and act in terms of composite assets. First, the regulatory environment has developed in ways that increasingly mandate it. For example, the Employee Retirement Income Security Act of 1974 (ERISA) judges the prudence of individual investment opportunities in their whole-portfolio context, explicitly acknowledging the axiom that uncorrelated risky individual assets can be combined into less risky composite assets. Thus traditional investment decisions on the individual asset level take a back seat to considerations of how they will affect the overall composite assets of which they are but components. As another example, Financial Accounting Standards Board (FASB) Statement 87 is forcing corporations to account for the values of their pension plans as the surplus of assets over liabilities. FASB 87 mandates that the surplus itself be thought of as a single asset (or liability) owned by the corporation, a supercomposite asset perspective not only beyond individual assets but even beyond individual asset classes as well.

Second, institutional investors have increasingly come to be measured by unforgiving standards of performance, denominated by indexes that are themselves composite assets. There has even evolved a new consulting business in designing custom measurement indexes, called normals, geared to benchmarking particular management styles. When the measure of success — and thus compensation, as well — is denominated in composite terms, even traditional investors whose thinking is dominated by individual asset analysis are subtly induced to adopt the composite assets perspective.

Third, institutional investors are drawn to perceived cost benefits of the composite asset perspective. Management fees for computer-driven composite asset strategies such as indexing are generally much lower than those for human-labor intensive strategies dependent on active individual asset analysis. And many believe that composite asset trading techniques such as package trading reduce the explicit and implicit costs of transacting. Because a composite asset can be thought of as a single trade, much larger than any of its components taken individually, by packaging the transaction in a single conceptual unit the trader should be entitled to a quantity discount resulting in lower unit commissions. Potentially more significant, the percentage bid/offer spread is thought to be lower for relatively informationless composite assets than it would be for individual assets, because they are presumably less risky for the marketplace to facilitate.

Whatever the economic or regulatory stimuli, the revolution in composite assets would not have been possible without the development of a constellation of new concepts and processes of quantitative analysis. As Graham and Dodd's *Security Analysis* drew for a generation of investors a map of the world dominated by individual assets, Markowitz's *Portfolio Selection* introduced a new generation to "Modern Portfolio Theory," the language of composite assets. In the 25 years since Markowitz's theoretical work was first published, his basic insights have been extended to a complex of implementation-oriented tools that give portfolio managers the conceptual framework in which assets can be described, measured, and manipulated as composites.

Modern Portfolio Theory (MPT) might have remained nothing more than an academic artifact had it not been for the parallel development of inexpensive high-speed computers capable of putting MPT's insights at the practical disposal of portfolio managers. With the data-processing tools available 25 years ago, merely constructing a census index fund was a prohibitively laborious exercise. Today's microcomputers, on the other hand, have allowed MPT to be brought to a point of refinement in which huge portfolios can be constructed and optimized instantaneously, creating the capability to make and implement the most complex portfolio-level decisions in a micro-timing framework appropriate even for day-trading.

V. Afterword

Like the mountaineer who scales the peak one step at a time, only to be startled when he looks back down his path and realizes just how high he has climbed, many observers are made uncomfortable by the revolution in composite assets. Have today's computer-driven, composite asset oriented investment processes somehow grown too far and too fast, forgetting that the individual assets that make them possible are the life blood of real corporations and governments?

For some, the stock market crash of October 1987 was the long-awaited proof that the composite assets revolution has spun out of control. The truth is exactly the opposite. Thinking and trading in composite assets has, in fact, given investors an unprecedented degree of control over their investments. It was this very control that allowed investors to effect almost instantly a drastic negative revaluation of equities that, in the past, would have taken months to accomplish. As technologies of all types, from the automobile to the telephone, have accelerated almost every aspect of contemporary life, thinking and trading in terms of composite assets has similarly accelerated the investment process. If markets are, primarily, mechanisms for the expression of opinions in the form of prices, our society should endorse technologies that make such expressions more efficient and more free.

9

Arbitrage, Program Trading, and the Tail of the Dog

Gary L. Gastineau
Vice President
Salomon Brothers Inc.

I. Introduction

Since stock index options and futures have become active trading vehicles, investors and regulators who had come to accept stock options have questioned the desirability of the newer instruments. Even a casual reader of the business press must be impressed with reports that we are in a "new era" of highly volatile securities markets and ever growing transaction volume. The media report domination and distortion of the markets by a small group of investors characterized in a broad sense as arbitrageurs. Arbitrageurs fall into two distinct camps. The *risk arbitrageur* attempts to profit by speculating on mergers, acquisitions, and other corporate restructuring. Risk arbitrage flourished in the merger markets of the early and mid-1980s, peaking at about the time of the Levine and Boesky scandals. The focus of this discussion, however, is on the other kind of arbitrageur, commonly known as *the program trader* or the *stock index arbitrageur*.

The term *program trading* originally included many large-scale portfolio adjustments by institutional investors. As a result of media attention focused on index arbitrage, the original meaning is less commonly used. The earlier definition remains a source of occasional confusion, however. Program trading in the form of index options and futures arbitrage is not primarily an option phenomenon, but its expiration effect is much like the impact attributed to stock options a few years ago. Furthermore, option-related phenomena like portfolio insurance are so closely tied to the effects attributed to program trading that any regulation of index options and futures markets has broad implications.

II. Arbitrage

The classic definition of arbitrage describes the simultaneous purchase in one market and sale in another of virtually identical securities or commodities. The arbitrageur profits by exploiting the difference in price between the two markets. The arbitrage process makes the market operate more effectively by eliminating price differences. Pure arbitrage, where the items purchased and sold are identical, is rare and opportunities are infrequent. In many cases, however, similar securities or commodities either exist or can be constructed in two different markets and a pricing discrepancy can be detected and exploited. Much of the detection and exploitation turns on the availability of high-speed, on-line electronic computation and communications capability. The presence of so much sophisticated silicon and the absence of any detailed knowledge on the part of the average investor as to how and why this kind of arbitrage works, has led to the widespread view that this is a largely autonomous sector of the market which serves as the tail that wags the dog. Program trading is credited or blamed for dramatic movements in stock prices, particularly on days when stock index options and futures expire. The true relationships between stock price behavior and index options and futures trading are complex, but they are not beyond the understanding of the investor who is willing to spend some time thinking about how markets work.

III. What Has Happened to the Securities Markets?

As Figures 1–3 illustrate, the securities markets have been characterized by rapidly growing volume and declining transaction costs. The volume on the New York Stock Exchange, Figure 1, has grown from 1.5 billion shares in 1965 to 27.5 billion shares in 1985, a compound growth rate of nearly 15 percent. The number of companies listed for trading has grown from 1,273 to 1,541 over the same period, a much more modest growth rate of less than 1 percent annually. Figure 2 shows that trading volume in the average company grew from less than 5,000 shares per day in 1965 to more than 70,000 shares per day in 1985.

Most participants in the securities markets will agree that anything that increases the trading volume of a security tends to reduce the average transaction cost because greater volume tends to narrow the spread between the bid price and the asked price. The bid-asked spread, though frequently ignored in transaction cost analysis in favor of a focus entirely on commissions, is an extremely important cost of doing business. Opportunities to

FIGURE 1. *New York Stock Exchange Reported Share Volume, 1965–1986.*

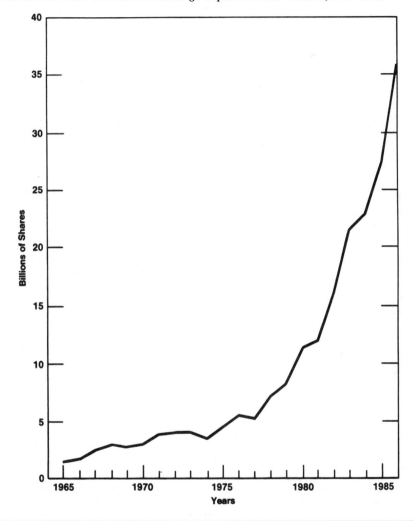

lower transaction costs by eliminating the bid-asked spread are sometimes available to institutional investors, but most market participants must buy at the asked price and sell at the bid price.

The growth in volume and the corresponding decline in the average bid-asked spread has been accompanied by a dramatic decline in institutional brokerage commissions from fixed rates 20 years ago to fully negotiated rates today. As illustrated in Figure 3, the securities industry under competitive ("third market") and Securities and Exchange Commission pressure

FIGURE 2. *New York Stock Exchange Reported Share Volume, Average Listed Company, 1965–1986.*

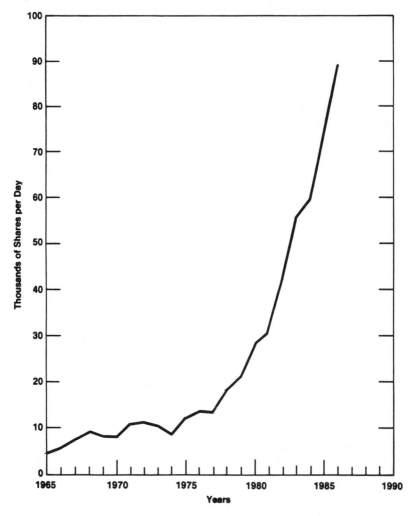

adopted the first quantity discounts in 1968. In May 1975 fully negotiable commission rates were adopted. Because the services provided in exchange for commission dollars vary so widely, an unequivocal graph of commission declines since the mid-1960s would be virtually impossible to construct. It is no secret that unbundled, pure execution commissions on listed stocks for large institutional traders can be less than five cents per share today. The pre-1968 fixed rate worked out to $.39 per share on a $40 stock.

FIGURE 3. *Commissions (cents per share).*

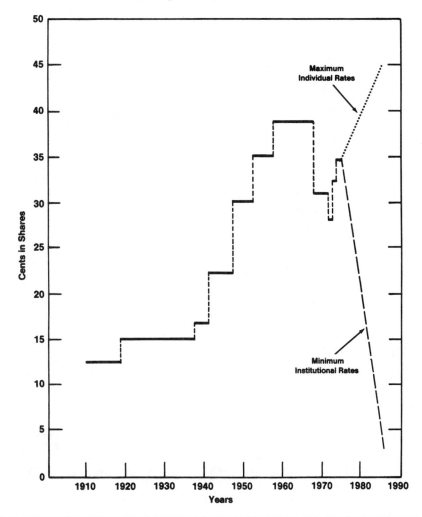

Just as the volume of common stock trading and the cost of trading that volume have changed dramatically, there have been equally significant developments in markets for derivative securities. The growth in derivative securities markets combined with increased trading volume and declining trading costs have led to many of the phenomena that are now perceived as shaking the foundations of an efficient securities market. Figure 4 illustrates the growth in derivative markets superimposed upon the growth chart for New York Stock Exchange common stock trading.

FIGURE 4. *Volume of Common Stocks and Derivative Securities, 1965–1986.*

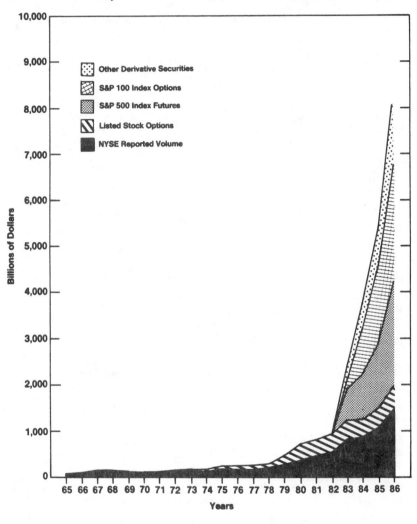

Figure 4 may exaggerate the importance of equity derivative instruments relative to trading in the underlying stocks. First, the options are related to the underlying market by assuming that each option contract is equal in "value" to the face value of the underlying security or index. In addition both options and futures contracts are outstanding for a relatively short period of time while the common stocks are outstanding throughout the period. Even if we mentally reduce the apparent impact by half to compensate for these factors, the growth of the derivative markets cannot be ignored.

The dramatic growth in derivative markets, particularly the growth in index options and index futures options, suggests several things:

1. If these markets are responsible for destabilizing the equity markets, we should expect a great deal more destabilization than we have seen.
2. Even a casual examination of bid-asked spreads and commission costs in the index futures and options markets suggests that transaction costs in these markets are *even lower than in the underlying securities markets after the cost reductions of recent years.*
3. Lower transaction costs have probably been partly responsible for the fact that institutional portfolio turnover (reflected in the growing volume figures) is much higher today than 20 years ago. Even the most conservative investor can make portfolio changes at low cost today.
4. With the very dramatic increase in volume illustrated, a great deal more must be going on than meets the untutored eye.

Before anyone goes too far in accusing the derivative markets of creating instability, it seems appropriate to examine recent patterns of stock price fluctuations. Primarily for historic reasons the press and the public tend to focus on movements in the Dow Jones Industrial Average as the primary indicator of what is going on in the stock market. Because the Dow and the broader averages have moved up sharply since fall of 1982, there has been a tendency to lose perspective on what a given point move in the Dow means. A 20-point move in the Dow was better than a two percentage point change when the Dow was at 900. A 20-point move is less than a one percentage point change with the Dow over 2000. The tendency to report a 10- or 20-point change as a major market move persists. The press reports dramatic swings measured in points for the Dow and rarely notes that these dramatic swings pale in comparison with earlier price changes measured in percentage terms.[1] When the Dow Jones Industrials dropped 41.91 on April 30, 1986, that was the largest one-day *point* decline on record at the time. However, that 2.3 percent decline had been exceeded at least 362 times over the preceding 60 years for an average of *once every two months.* Even the 4.61 percent decline (86.61 Dow points) of September 11, 1986 had been exceeded four times in the postwar period and numerous times before. We will have more to say about this decline in a moment.

By any standard, the extraordinarily volatile markets of October, 1987 are in a class by themselves. As this is written, these events are still surrounded by controversy. A preliminary judgment suggests that the decline was initiated by portfolio managers reacting to investment fundamentals in a time-honored manner: concern about the federal budget and trade deficits, inflation, recession, currency relationships, and interest rates led to a number of individual decisions to sell common stocks. What would have been a

---

1. *Newsweek* did make this point when calling for a 10-for-1 split in the Dow (March 2, 1987, p. 55).

moderate decline was turned into a rout when portfolio insurance sell orders were triggered. Too many investors tried, like the biblical camel, to pass through the eye of a needle. Index arbitrage was impractical during much of this period. The absence of index arbitrage may have contributed to panic, particularly on what is now known as Black Monday.

Serious studies of market volatility, most notably one by Laslow Birinyi and Nicholas Hanson of Salomon Brothers, correctly pointed out that volatility in the stock market had *declined,* not increased prior to the decline of late 1987.[2] Our own study of option premiums and stock price volatility confirms this conclusion for the period since listed stock option trading began.[3] The net effect of somewhat lower volatility when combined with rising volume and falling transaction costs had been an environment in which investors could make changes in their portfolios more easily and at less cost than ever before. Ironically, it was the ease and cheapness with which portfolio transactions could be made that led to the program trading or stock index arbitrage phenomenon. The efficient futures markets which index arbitrage helped create in turn made portfolio insurance feasible.

IV. Portfolio Adjustments Using Derivative Markets

Suppose a large institutional investor decides on the basis of a consultation with his fortune teller or other guru to move from a 10 percent cash position to 25 percent cash in equity portfolios. This may seem like a relatively modest change, but for many institutions this move can require the sale of several billion dollars worth of securities. To put that number in perspective, the average value of securities traded daily on the New York Stock Exchange in 1985 was barely over $4 billion. Obviously the exchange can handle this investor's volume; but there may be a few other people who want to sell stocks at about the same time. This investor's decision may have a perceptible impact on the market.

The investor can accomplish this portfolio change in several ways. If the actual positions in the portfolio are liquidated on the exchange, the impact on the market is direct. Less costly ways to make this change would be to sell stock index futures, sell index call option contracts, or buy index put options. Some institutional managers will use futures or options, but others lack the authority to trade in the derivative (options or futures) markets. These managers will do what institutional portfolio managers have done for years. They will call one of the major block trading firms and solicit bids for the securities they would like to sell to raise cash in their portfolios. At some

---

2. Laszlo Birinyi and H. Nicholas Hanson, *Market Volatility: Perception and Reality* (New York: Salomon Brothers, December 1985).

3. See Gary Gastineau, *The Options Manual* (New York: McGraw-Hill, 1988), chap. 10.

risk of oversimplification, the securities firm asked to make a bid will usually lay off some risk in the index futures or options market or in the market for options on individual stocks. The methods used to arrive at a price for the securities to be sold by the institution to the block positioning firm are frequently complex. The block positioning firm may lay off only part of the risk in the derivative securities markets, or it may place some or all of the securities directly with a buyer. The securities firm is in business to make a profit, and it is safe to assume that, on average, it does so. Also given the volume in the derivative markets, it is safe to assume that many transactions initiated by someone who wants to change the market exposure of a portfolio will give rise to a series of transactions. Apart from the market impact, declining transaction costs and growing derivative markets make this kind of portfolio adjustment far less costly than it was even a few years ago. *Dramatic changes in market risk exposure are possible at modest cost.*

An effort by one or several institutional portfolio managers to reduce equity market exposure either simultaneously or in sequence will put downward pressure on the stock market and the derivative markets. The prices of stocks, index futures, and index call options will decline until some market participant finds it attractive to buy them.

If the primary impact of the original sale implementation is on the derivative markets, a program trader, index fund manager, or index arbitrageur will find it attractive to buy index futures or index call options and sell (long or short) some common stocks. Thus, even if the decision by the institutional manager to reduce equity market exposure is originally implemented in the derivative markets, it eventually leads to actual selling of stocks. The uptick rule on short sales often inhibits index arbitrage transactions, but the distortions it causes were not a problem prior to Black Monday. Index funds switching from stocks to underpriced futures and arbitrageurs closing long stock–short futures positions help mitigate the effect of the uptick restriction. Proposals to eliminate the uptick rule entirely or for index arbitrage transactions may eliminate this problem.

Obviously the same mechanism works in reverse when one or several portfolio managers decide to increase their exposure to the equity markets. Because these markets are related, a decision by one large participant to sell (or to buy) will lead to subsequent movement in the pricing of both the underlying securities and the derivative securities. The important point is that *it was the investment decision by the portfolio manager that created the opportunity for the program trader.* The program trader does not operate in a vacuum. His actions are not calculated to move the market. The reason the market moves is the original portfolio decision that only incidentally created an opportunity for the arbitrage oriented program trader. The September 11, 1986 decline and the October 1987 decline were initiated by portfolio managers concerned about the economic outlook and anxious to reduce their commitment to equities. This initial decision to sell was amplified by another group, the *portfolio insurers*.

V. Portfolio Insurance

Portfolio insurance is another phenomenon that has been growing quietly but rapidly. Portfolio insurance is a technique whereby an institutional portfolio manager purchases an actual or synthetic put option. The synthetic put option is usually created in the index futures market. The "insurance" provides a high degree of assurance that the performance of the portfolio will not fall below a certain standard over a period that can range up to several years.

There is no organized reporting of insured portfolios, but one reasonable estimate is that approximately $10 billion of institutional equity portfolios was managed under a commitment to portfolio insurance at the end of 1985. This had grown to more than $40 billion by the end of 1986, and continued growth was probably measured in billions of dollars of new commitments per month in early 1987.

More often than not synthetic puts for insured portfolios are created or actual puts are purchased when there has been a prior decline in the underlying equities. The idea behind portfolio insurance may seem like locking the barn door after the horse has been stolen. A better way to phrase it might be: Accept risks early in a period as long as you are sure that a very-low-risk portfolio can earn your minimum required return over the balance of the period. If early returns are good, little of the low-risk asset need be purchased. If early returns are poor, the risk of the portfolio will have to be very low later in the period. Portfolio insurers will be major participants in the derivative securities markets only *after* a market move has occurred. If the Dow were to drop several hundred points, even over a period of three to six months, the effect on existing insurance programs plus the growth of new insurance programs would lead to systematic sales of index futures or purchases of index puts. At various times during a subsequent market rise the derivative contracts would be closed, providing the portfolios with increased exposure to the market on the upside. By the nature of portfolio insurance, puts usually will be created — that is, index futures positions will be *sold* — during and subsequent to market declines; and futures positions will be *purchased* during and subsequent to market advances. The decision to take a position in the derivative markets is determined in advance by the ground rules of the portfolio insurance program. The general pattern used by all portfolio insurance programs is similar: Insurance puts are purchased *after* a decline. Actual or synthetic puts are liquidated *after* an advance. The insurance is purchased or sold without much regard for any overpricing or underpricing of the derivative instrument.

Because insurance programs trigger automatic or semiautomatic futures or options transactions, there will be occasions when portfolio insurance will have an impact on *relative values* in the derivative securities markets. Through the activities of program traders, the change in relative valuation of the derivative markets will have a significant impact on the value of the underlying equity securities. In other words *portfolio insurance will tend to accentuate market advances and declines.* While insurance transactions operate directly in the derivative markets, they create the same kind of opportunities for program traders that *anyone* using the stock market or the derivative markets creates.

VI. Program Trading: A Mechanism for Market Equilibrium

As a variety of articles and books on index options and futures have noted, there is a band of prices within which index futures and options can trade relative to the value of the underlying index without giving rise to an arbitrage opportunity. The uncertainty associated with using a basket of securities rather than the entire index, the cost of undertaking a variety of transactions, and several other factors combine to make program trading a sometime rather than an all-the-time thing. Program traders exist to take advantage of pricing discrepancies. They iron out the discrepancies that other market participants create between the derivative markets and the underlying equities markets. Some index funds also act as program traders, switching between stocks and index futures to take advantage of pricing discrepancies. Whereas the typical program trader is trying to create a synthetic Treasury bill with a greater yield than a Treasury bill, the index fund arbitrageur is trying to create an index fund with a better return than the index.

It is useful to divide the major participants in the equity derivative markets into two categories. The division is based upon the effect their market participation has on the equilibrium between the derivative markets and the underlying securities markets. It is difficult to come up with a name for each category without implying that either or both are somehow doing something inappropriate. Investors who use these derivative markets to adjust the overall equity exposure of a portfolio have found a quick way to increase or reduce equity market exposure in a short period of time. They might be called "price acceptors." They accept the price the market offers. The portfolio insurer is also a price acceptor. The portfolio insurance operational algorithm calls for a futures or options market transaction in response to certain behavior in the portfolio or in the index. Many of these price acceptors are aware of valuation issues and valuation discrepancies, but in the overall context of the business they are trying to run, they cannot afford to let valuation discrepancies keep them from avoiding greater risks, such as the risks associated with having too much or too little stock market exposure. Other things being equal, they tend to push prices out of equilibrium.

The term "price setters" might suggest something illegal, so let us call the program traders, arbitrageurs, index funds, and valuation enthusiasts, "equilibrators." Equilibrators take advantage of the opportunities created by the price acceptors and bring the underlying equities and their derivative markets back into equilibrium. They are, in effect, setting the prices of the derivative securities. They make possible participation of price acceptors without undue market disruption, and they keep total transaction costs modest.

VII. Some Thoughts on Regulation

A number of proposals have been made to reduce or eliminate the occasionally unsettling effects of options and futures transactions, especially close to expiration dates. The so-called triple witching hours, when a variety of contracts expire at the same time, have been the focus of considerable debate.

The nature of the factors leading to this expiration day phenomenon suggest that this is a problem that may not go away by itself. Looked at another way, however, it is not necessarily a problem. As the Stoll and Whaley study of the expiration phenomenon correctly pointed out, the price distorting effect of program trading seems to be concentrated in a period of a few minutes immediately before expiration on the last day of the life of an option or futures contract.[4] One is led to the suspicion that more information on market orders will help reduce even this temporary instability induced by program traders. The plan to use opening rather than closing prices to arrive at option and futures settlement prices might also be helpful, but I suspect disclosure will prove more important than timing.

Theoretical analysis and empirical studies have generally concluded that the growth of derivative securities markets and falling transaction costs reduce volatility as well as increase market efficiency. The action of the market on September 11, 1986 and in October 1987 calls this conclusion into question. It is entirely possible that the ease, speed, and economy with which a market timing decision or a portfolio insurance transaction can be implemented will lead to market instability. Here too, however, other market participants have an incentive to take offsetting actions once they understand how and why the market timers and portfolio insurers are operating.

The only reasonable conclusion is that no unequivocal answer is possible until we have had more experience. One can only hope that regulators' initial efforts will focus on dissemination of information to give the market

---

4. Hans R. Stoll and Robert Whaley, "Expiration Day Effects of Index Options and Futures," New York University Graduate School of Business, 1986.

mechanism a chance to work before artificial limitations are imposed on investors' freedom of action. The history of markets is full of examples where the basic market mechanism itself has provided admirable regulation. All too often the rush to regulate has destroyed a market without providing any added protection to market participants.

It is too soon after the crash of 1987, and this author's perspective is too limited, to provide perfect solutions to all the problems that have come to light. Nonetheless, an options-oriented perspective and an admitted free-market bias suggest that revisions in the market mechanism should include the following at a minimum:

1. The capacity of automatic order entry and execution systems must be far larger than anyone would have thought necessary a few years ago.
2. Information on customer limit orders and order flow now available only to exchange specialists must be totally computerized and readily available to all interested parties.
3. Option position limits must be eliminated. If position limits had been scrapped before October, 1987, and long-term puts had been available, the crash might have been much less severe.
4. The requirement that short sales be made only on price upticks should be scrapped. It delays price equilibrium and contributes to the chaos of a selling panic.

Hopefully, these revisions will be included among the inevitable structural changes which the crash has initiated. If these changes are included, the market's capacity to provide portfolio insurance will equal the demand. The price of index puts will reflect the risk of relying on dynamic hedging. Market forces will balance supply and demand; and Adam Smith will have been proved right once again.

10

Establishing an Arbitrage Program
Stock Index Arbitrage

Mark Zurack
Vice President
Goldman, Sachs & Co.

I. Introduction

Imagine a quiet Thursday in the market with the Dow Jones Industrial Average down 5.20 for the day. It is 3 P.M., and most institutional trading desks with buy orders to fill are looking for opportunities to purchase stock without affecting the market. At 3:10 P.M., the trading desk receives a flurry of calls all for the same reason. With no news of significance on the tape, why is the market suddenly up 8.40 for the day? In unison, the traders reply, "index arbitrage."

In stock index arbitrage programs, a portfolio of stocks is combined with stock index futures or options contracts to achieve a higher return than that available in other investment strategies of comparable risk. To understand why stock index arbitrage programs occur, it is important to know the basics of the stock index options and futures market.

This article focuses on the stock index futures and options markets as they relate to index arbitrage. Our objectives are twofold: to explain how an arbitrage strategy is brought to market and how to create and monitor stock index arbitrage programs for clients.

Preface to the Updated Study

In June 1985, when this article was written, cash managers were the largest players in the index arbitrage business. They enjoyed a steady stream of profits by purchasing stocks and selling stock index contracts. Back then the spread between the stock and futures was consistently overvalued. But since then market conditions have changed, and so have the players who trade stocks against futures.

To be specific, the stock index market has passed through four pricing periods. Up until mid-1985, mispricings well in excess of 1% were common. From that time through September 1987, the market grew more efficient. Figures 1 and 2 highlight the difference in pricing during these two periods; they show the largest premium and discount to fair value as well as the average premium or discount to fair value for the nearby S&P 500 futures contract. Note that during the first nine months of 1987, the S&P 500 contract almost never traded more than 0.7% from fair value. Then came October.

Beginning late in the afternoon of October 16, 1987, and for about 4 weeks thereafter, S&P 500 futures contracts traded at mispricings as high as 20% (see Figure 3). Throughout this period index arbitrage virtually came to a halt for three main reasons: temporary program trading bans; technical difficulties in trading and processing market baskets; and the fact that prices displayed on trading "screens" were no longer reliable indicators of prices at which stocks could be traded. On November 12, the ban on program trading was lifted and the relationship between actual prices and theoretical values returned to pre-crash levels. Whether it will stay there in 1988 and beyond depends on regulation changes, market volatility and market liquidity.

Although the cash/futures spread is now trading close to fair value, its volatility as measured by the monthly range between the largest premium and discount is close to its 1985 range. To profit in this environment, index arbitrageurs trade more often to capture smaller mispricings over shorter investment horizons. Typically, these arbitrageurs are not cash managers trying to lock in a spread over some time period; instead they are aggressive investors who are betting that they can profit from volatility in the cash/futures spread.

II. Options and Futures: The Basic Concepts

A first step toward greater understanding of these new markets is to clarify the difference between stock index options and stock index futures. Options and futures are often perceived as being similar because both are "derivative" instruments — one step removed from the underlying security or commodity to which they relate — and because both create leverage relative to cash flow. In fact the relationship of an option to the underlying index is quite different from that of a futures contract to its underlying index, resulting in very different risk/reward characteristics.

An option is simply a *right,* which may or may not be exercised, to buy or sell something. A futures is an *obligation* to buy or sell. The purchase or

FIGURE 1. *Percent Premium from Fair Value for the Nearby S&P 500 Futures Contract.*

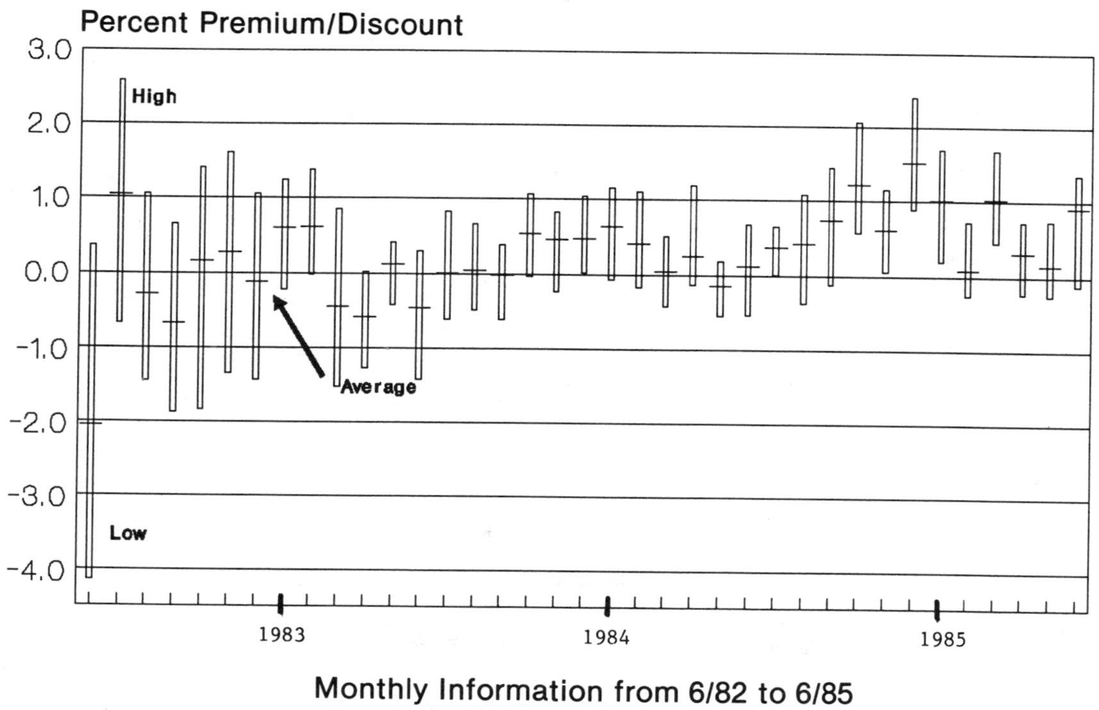
Percent Premium/Discount
3.0
2.0
1.0
0.0
-1.0
-2.0
-3.0
-4.0
High
Low
Average
1983
1984
1985
Monthly Information from 6/82 to 6/85

FIGURE 2. *Percent Premium from Fair Value for the Nearby S&P 500 Futures Contract.*

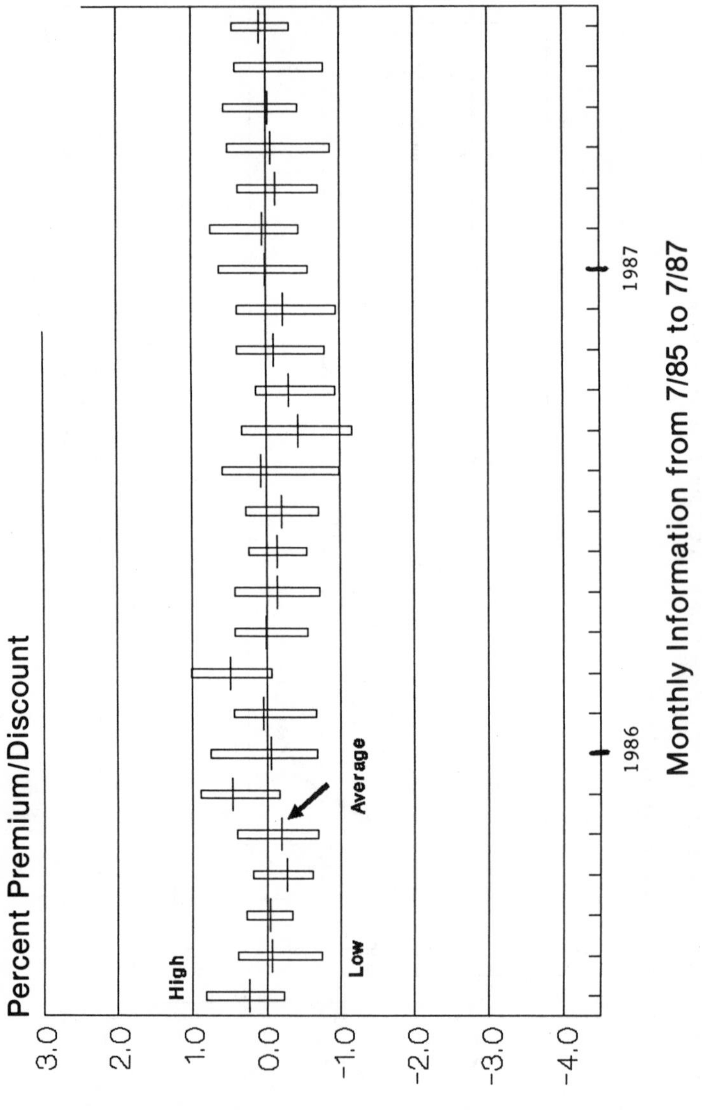

FIGURE 3. *Percent Premium/Discount from Fair Value for the Nearby S&P 500 Contract.*

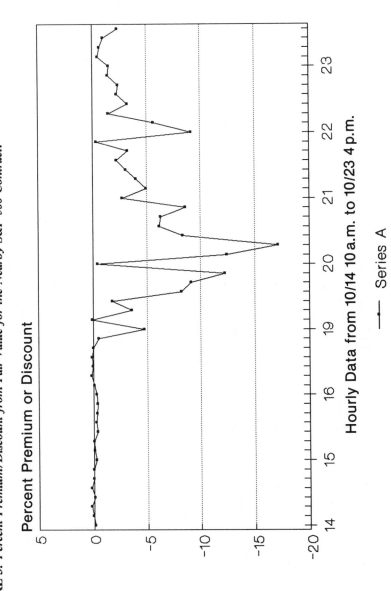

sale of a futures contract is tantamount to the purchase or sale of the underlying item itself, except that transfer of ownership is delayed in time. Therefore futures are exposed to the same broad price changes as the underlying item. Options, on the other hand, have significantly different risk characteristics because they limit loss from adverse movement. The call option purchaser, for example, can lose only the amount paid for the option, not the value of the stock itself.

Both options and futures can be used in conjunction with the underlying security or commodity to hedge or leverage an investor's holdings. With options, investors can create a wide range of risk and reward patterns. For example, a stock portfolio manager who buys puts on an index pays a certain premium to have limited downside risk while still maintaining almost full upside potential. With futures, however, the investor can own only more or less of a given item, and adjust the timing of when he will own it. The key concept is that an option is a *right* while a futures contract is an *obligation*. Being long or short futures is equivalent to being long or short the underlying commodity, with time (and cash flow leverage) being the only difference.

Unlike most other futures or options contracts, the owner of a stock index future or option does not close the contract by taking possession of (or delivering) the underlying commodity (the stocks in the index). At expiration, the obligation is settled by receiving or paying the cash difference between the closing value of the index and the previous day's futures price or strike price of the option. Stated differently, the ending value of an index futures or options contract is based totally on the value of the index at the contract's expiration. Thus, in all markets, at expiration, there is convergence between the cash and futures and options markets.

III. Stock Index Futures and Options

Trading and Market Value of Futures Contracts

Table 1 shows the characteristics of four stock index futures contracts that trade on four separate exchanges. The dollar value of a stock index futures contract generally equals 500 times its price; the exception is the Major Market contract (valued at 250 times the price).

Handling Margin on Futures Contracts

An investor entering a stock index futures contract faces two types of margin requirements, neither of which involves the borrowing of funds. The *initial margin* demanded by an exchange for each contract opened can be thought of as good faith money, or a performance bond. It must be posted

TABLE 1. *Listed Stock Index Futures Contracts.*

Quotron Symbol	Contract Name	Exchange	Number of Stocks	Weighting
SP	S&P 500	Chicago Mercantile Exchange	500	Market capitalization
YX	NYSE	New York Stock Exchange	1,560	Market capitalization
MX	Major Market	Chicago Board of Trade	20	Price
KV	Value Line	Kansas City Board of Trade	1,700	Approximately equal dollar (geometrically)

in cash or Treasury bills. The second form of margin, *variation margin,* is required to ensure that holders of futures contracts can cover their liabilities at the time of final settlement. Variation margin is calculated daily by measuring the change in the value of the index futures from the previous day. Variation margin must be settled in cash, meaning that each day money flows in and out of the contract holder's commodity futures account if the futures contract changes in price.

Trading and Market Value of Options Contracts

Although five exchanges list options on many different major and submarket indexes, few contracts are consistently liquid. The most liquid, and most frequently used in arbitrage, is the S&P 100 (OEX) index option, which is based on a capitalization-weighted index of 100 stocks. More than 80 percent of all volume in stock index options is in S&P 100 contracts.

Margin and Early Exercise Risk on Options Contracts

Index options are not marked to the market each day. Additional collateral is required to cover positions in cases where the market goes against the seller. Because index options are settled in cash, there is the risk of early exercise for the seller of index options. When a buyer of index options exercises his position prior to expiration, he receives the cash difference between the index's closing value that day and the option's strike price. The seller is not informed of the early exercise notice until the following morning and is exposed to stock market risk between the previous night's close and the time the short position can be reestablished.

IV. Economic Motivation of an Index Futures Arbitrage Program

Pricing of Stock Index Futures

The initiation of an arbitrage program between stocks and index futures is dependent on the price of the futures contract deviating from a specified value. Therefore index futures arbitrage decisions revolve around the pricing of futures contracts. To understand the pricing of a stock index futures contract, remember that a futures contract is an agreement to buy or sell a commodity at some point in the future. The only differences between making the transaction immediately and agreeing to a futures transaction are the time delay in transfer of ownership and cash flow effects. The impact of the time delay on the price of the underlying commodity is the next consideration.

Many futures markets are cost-of-carry markets, where the difference between spot and futures prices, known as the basis, relates very closely to the cost of holding the commodity from the present to the settlement date. This cost of carry primarily includes the time value of money, plus storage costs, insurance charges, and so on. A good example is the futures market in gold (for convenience, the costs of storage, insurance, and delivery are ignored). Assume that the spot price of gold is $300 per ounce and that an arbitrageur can borrow or lend at 8 percent per annum. The price for a delivery date six months out would be $300 plus the cost of carry of $12 ($300 times 0.5 years times 0.08) for a total of $312. Thus the basis—$312 minus $300, or $12—equals the cost of carry.

To extend the example to stock index futures, we assume the value of the S&P 500 spot index at 180, the cost of money at 8 percent per year, and the futures contract expiration at three months. One additional variable must be introduced. Unlike the case of gold, which provides no income, the investor who purchases all the stocks in the S&P 500 receives dividends on them while they are held. Thus the opportunity cost for investors who buy the market using stock index futures contracts is the dividend income forgone, which, in this example, we assume to be 4 percent per year. Using the above methodology, we calculate the *basis* or *spread* between the index and the futures at 1.80 and the *fair value* of the futures contract at 181.80 based on the difference between the financing cost of the index ($180 \times .08 \times .25$ years = 3.60) and the dividend income forgone by not owning the stocks in the index ($180 \times .04 \times .25$ years = 1.80). Implicit in both calculations is the condition that the price of the futures contract will converge to equal the value of the index on the contract expiration date.

Arbitraging the Spread

When the actual price of the futures contract differs from its cost-of-carry value, arbitrageurs will step in and take advantage of the mispricing in the

TABLE 2. *Arbitrage Return versus the S&P 500 Index.*

	S&P 500 Index				
	160	170	180	190	200
Gain (loss) on stocks purchased	(20)	(10)	0	10	20
Ending value of the futures contract	160	170	180	190	200
Gain (loss) on futures contracts	23	13	3	(7)	(17)
Dividends received	1.80	1.80	1.80	1.80	1.80
Annual total return	10.68%	10.68%	10.68%	10.68%	10.68%

market. In a stock index futures program, the arbitrageur will capture the spread between the index and the futures by purchasing a portfolio of all or some of the stocks in the index and selling the futures contract. For example, if the three-month futures contract noted above sold at 183, or 1.20 above its fair value of 181.80, an arbitrageur would buy the index at 180 (assuming no transaction costs — an assumption that will be relaxed later) and sell the futures contract at 183. Three months later, upon convergence, the arbitrageur would capture the three-point spread between the index and the futures plus the dividend yield of 1.80; as shown in Table 2, this indicates a 10.68 percent annual return independent of the movement of the stock market:

Index arbitrage return (no transaction costs)

$$= \frac{\text{Futures} - \text{Index}}{\text{Index}} \times \frac{365}{\text{No. of days until expiration}} + \frac{\text{Annual}}{\text{dividend yield}}$$

$$= \frac{183 - 180}{180} \times \frac{365}{91} + 4\%$$

$$= \frac{3}{180} \times 4.01 + 4\%$$

$$= 10.68\%.$$

Most arbitrageurs employing this stratgegy try to achieve a return of 200–400 basis points above the rate on Treasury bills.

The Impact of Transaction Costs

In the example we assumed no transaction costs in projecting returns. Actually transaction costs have a strong impact on total return and must be taken out of the spread to calculate the true rate of return:

$$\begin{array}{c}\text{Index}\\\text{arbitrage} =\\\text{return}\end{array} \frac{\text{Futures} - \text{Index} - \begin{array}{c}\text{Transaction costs ex-}\\\text{pressed in index terms}\end{array}}{\begin{array}{c}\text{Index} + \text{Transaction costs going}\\\text{into the position}\end{array}} \times \frac{365}{\begin{array}{c}\text{No. of days until}\\\text{expiration}\end{array}}$$

$$+ \text{ Annual dividend return.}$$

The total cost of creating an index arbitrage varies betweeen 0.6 percent and 1 percent of the index's value and is a function of three factors:

1. The market impact of buying stocks on the offered and selling stocks on the bid sides of the market rather than the last sale
2. Stock commissions going into and out of a trade
3. Futures commissions going into and out of a trade

In our example, with the S&P index at 180, if transaction costs are assumed to equal 0.75 percent or 1.35 (.0075 × 180) in index terms, the return to the arbitrageur who bought the index and sold futures would equal 7.66 percent, as shown:

FIGURE 4. *Percent Premium Over Fair Value for the Nearby S&P 500 Futures Contract.*

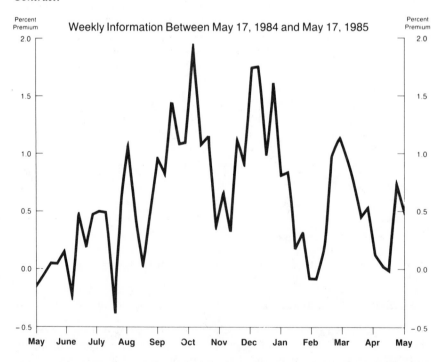

FIGURE 5. *Implied Return after Transaction Costs for the Strategy of Purchasing Stocks and Selling S&P 500 Futures Versus the Near Term Treasury Bill Rate.*

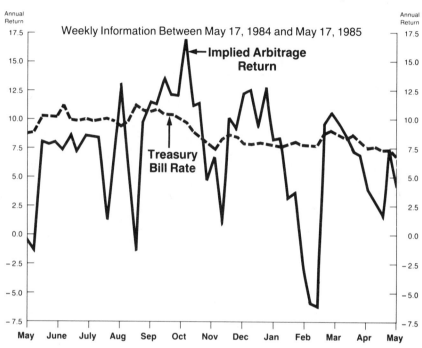

$$\frac{(183-180)-1.35}{180+.68} \times \frac{365}{91} +4\% = 7.66\%.$$

This is less than the risk-free interest rate. The trade looks attractive before transaction costs, but it falls apart when trading costs are considered. Figures 4 and 5 show that although the futures become overvalued quite frequently, trading costs make the arbitrage uneconomical in most cases. Therefore index arbitrage programs do not come into the market continually, and when the opportunity exists to execute a program successfully, there is a great deal of competition among arbitrageurs.

Stock Index Options Arbitrage, Synthetic Futures, and Forward Conversions

In some cases index options are used in index arbitrage because it is easier to work with the 100 stocks in the S&P 100 index rather than the 500 stocks in the S&P 500 index and index options do not involve variation margin calls.

TABLE 3. *Comparison of the NYSE Futures and NYSE Call/Put Combination at Different Expiring Index Values.*

	Index Value at Expiration				
	85.00	90.00	95.00	100.00	105.00
NYSE futures contract value	85.00	90.00	95.00	100.00	105.00
Purchased at	96.75	96.75	96.75	96.75	96.75
Profit (loss) on futures	(11.75)	(6.75)	(1.74)	3.25	8.25
NYSE 95 call value	0	0	0	5.00	10.00
Purchased at	3.50	3.50	3.50	3.50	3.50
Profit (loss) on call	(3.50)	(3.50)	(3.50)	1.50	6.50
NYSE 95 put value	(10.00)	(5.00)	0	0	0
Sold at	(1.75)	(1.75)	(1.75)	(1.75)	(1.75)
Profit (loss) on put	(8.25)	(3.25)	1.75	1.75	1.75
Total option profit and loss[a]	(11.75)	(6.75)	(1.75)	3.25	8.25

a. Before taxes and commissions.

When options are used, the arbitrageur will combine the purchase of an index with the sale of calls and purchase of puts on that index. This strategy is frequently referred to as a *forward conversion*. The option combination is called a *synthetic futures* because it has the same economic properties as a short futures position.

We can show the similarities of a futures contract and a synthetic futures through an example. Assume that with the New York Stock Exchange Composite at 95, a call on the NYSE with a strike price of 95 is purchased for $3.50 and a put with a strike price of 95 is sold short for $1.75, resulting in a debit of $175 [($3.50 − $1.75) × 100]. At that time the NYSE futures is trading at 96.75; the spread of 1.75 between the index and its futures thus equals the spread of the NYSE 95 call and put. On the day of expiration the futures contract converges to equal the index. Table 3 shows that the change in the call/put combination at expiration will equal the change in the value of the futures position under all market scenarios; therefore, the profit and loss on the option combination and the actual futures contract is the same in all markets.[1]

To illustrate an index forward conversion, we assume that the S&P 100 index is trading at 175; three-month calls and puts with a strike price of 175

1. This assumes that the option positions are not exercised before expiration and that they are established at a spread equaling the cost of carrying the position to expiration. It also assumes that the NYSE index options and futures expire on the same day.

are selling at $6 and $3, respectively; and the annual dividend yield for the index equals 4 percent. If the arbitrageur were to buy the index at 175 and sell the call and buy the put, the total package would cost 172. In three months, the package will be worth 175 under all market scenarios. The return to the arbitrageur would be 11 percent based on a combination of option premium and dividend income (before transaction costs):[2]

Index option arbitrage return

$$= \frac{\begin{array}{c}\text{Option's} \\ \text{strike price}\end{array} - \begin{array}{c}\text{Index} \\ \text{value}\end{array} + \begin{array}{c}\text{Call} \\ \text{price}\end{array} - \begin{array}{c}\text{Put} \\ \text{price}\end{array}}{\text{Index value} - \text{Call price} + \text{Put price}} \times \frac{365}{\begin{array}{c}\text{No. of days until} \\ \text{expiration}\end{array}} + \begin{array}{c}\text{Dividend} \\ \text{yield}\end{array}$$

$$= \frac{175 - 172}{172} \times \frac{365}{91} + 4\% = 11\%.$$

The transaction costs for an index options arbitrage program are very similar to those for a futures program and affect the return accordingly.

Risks of an Arbitrage Program

We have identified four risks that can negatively affect the return of an arbitrage program:

1. Yield Risk Dividend yield will be less than expected. We project dividends by extrapolating the last payment and ex-date and reinvesting dividends at the Treasury-bill yield. For any given arbitrage program, the realized dividend yield will differ somewhat from its expected yield due to changing dividend policy by the companies comprising the index.

2. Early Exercise Risk The short call in index options arbitrage is exercised prematurely, and the market moves against the position before it is reestablished.

3. Tracking Risk The portfolio purchased underperforms the index it is trying to match. This risk, known as tracking error, is a function of the number of stocks in the portfolio and can reduce total annual return significantly over short periods of time. However, the likelihood is just as great that tracking error will improve return as that it will reduce it. In addition, annual tracking error declines if the position is held for more than three months or the trades are repeated over time (see Table 4).

4. Variation Margin Risk In futures arbitrage the cost of financing variation margin will reduce the return of the trade. This risk can be reduced by

---

2. Assuming the call is not exercised prior to expiration.

TABLE 4. *Annual Tracking Error.*

Number of Stocks	Possible Reduction of Annualized Expected Return
Three-Month Arbitrage versus the S&P 500 Index[a]	
100	3.5%
150	2.8
200	2.0
500	0.1–0.2
One-Year Arbitrage or Four Three-Month Arbitrages[a]	
100	1.75%
150	1.40
200	1.00
500	0.05–0.1

a. One standard deviation estimate.
Source: Barr Rosenberg Associates.

adjusting the futures position at the beginning of the trade using the formula below:

$$\text{Adjusted futures position} = \frac{\text{Original futures position}}{1 + (\text{Daily risk-free rate} \times \text{No. of days until expiration})}.$$

V. What to Do After a Position Is Created: When to Reverse and Roll Over the Position

Once an arbitrage transaction is made, the investor must decide whether to (1) reverse the position before expiration, (2) extend it by buying back the existing futures contracts and selling contracts expiring in a later month, or (3) close the position at expiration. If reversal is desired, the stock/options/futures position should be thought of as a short-term money market security whose total return depends on the yields at which the arbitrage is created and reversed. For example, the realized return for a 90-day arbitrage trade created at 12 percent and reversed 30 days later at 9 percent is 18 percent annually, as shown below (note that this does not assume compounded interest):

$$(\text{Portfolio return} \times 30 \text{ days}) + (9\% \times 60 \text{ days}) = (12\% \times 90 \text{ days}).$$

$$\text{Portfolio return} = 18\% \text{ per annum}.$$

Three factors should be considered before an arbitrage position is reversed:

1. The impact of selling stocks at the bid side of the market
2. The opportunity cost of not being invested between the time the trade is reversed and a new position is reestablished

3. The extra cost of reestablishing a position in a later contract month versus rolling over existing futures contracts without touching the stocks

In our example, if the arbitrageur reinvested the proceeds of his 30-day, 18 percent trade at 9 percent for the next 60 days, then recreated the position at 11 percent for the next 90 days, his total realized return over 180 days would be 11.5 percent annually:

$$(18\% \times 30 \text{ days}) + (9\% \times 60 \text{ days}) + (11\% \times 90 \text{ days}) = 11.5\% \text{ per annum.}$$

In contrast, had the investor held his stocks for 180 days, his 180-day return would equal the average of the original 12 percent trade and the yield achieved by extending the position for an additional 90 days. Under most market scenarios, the return of extending a position should exceed that of reestablishing the arbitrage. We generally favor extending the futures position into a later contract month over reversing it because the investor who rolls forward his contracts saves the transaction costs of having to trade in and out of stock positions.

To extend the life of the arbitrage position, we determine the spread required to meet the arbitrageur's return objective and place an order on the floor to roll over the futures/options contracts at that spread. The spread is determined from the investor's required return using the following calculation:

For index futures

$$= \frac{\substack{\text{Far-month} \\ \text{contract} \\ \text{price}} - \substack{\text{Near-month} \\ \text{contract} \\ \text{price}} - \substack{\text{Futures contract} \\ \text{commissions in} \\ \text{index terms}}}{\text{Index value}} \times \frac{365}{\substack{\text{No. of days between} \\ \text{expirations of the} \\ \text{two contracts}}}$$

+ Annualized dividend yield between the expiration of the two contracts.

For index options (assuming unchanged strike price)

$$= \frac{\substack{\text{Far-month} \\ \text{put-call} \\ \text{spread}} - \substack{\text{Near-month} \\ \text{put-call} \\ \text{spread}} - \substack{\text{Options contract} \\ \text{commissions in} \\ \text{index terms}}}{\text{Index value}} \times \frac{365}{\substack{\text{No. of days between} \\ \text{expirations of the} \\ \text{two contracts}}}$$

+ Annualized dividend yield between the expiration of the two contracts.

For example, if the near-month S&P futures contract is selling at 183, the index is at 180, the far-month contract expiring in 91 days is at 187, the annual dividend yield between the expiration dates of both contracts is 4.0 percent, and the futures commission is 0.05 ($25 per contract), the return in a roll-over trade would equal

$$\frac{187 - 183 - 0.05}{180} \times \frac{365}{91} + 4.0\% = 12.80\%.$$

VI. The Impact of Stock Index Arbitrage Programs on the Market

At the outset, we referred to a quiet Thursday in which the market increased 13 points in 10 minutes for no apparent fundamental reason other than index arbitrage programs. Because of the increased popularity of index arbitrage, many traders watch the spread between each index and its appropriate futures or options contract with the hope of buying the index as soon as the spread widens to the point where the trade makes sense. In addition, to assure the arbitrage is traded properly, the market portfolio must be on the floor of the NYSE ready to be executed as soon as the spread widens. Since arbitrage orders tend to be similar across the board, the road to success in this transaction is to be the first trader to reach the specialist with the portfolio when the spread reaches its desired level. Here's what really happened that Thursday: At 3:05 P.M., the spread between the S&P 500 index and its nearby futures contract widened, inducing arbitrageurs to go into the market to buy stocks. Since timing is everything, a broker will try to buy each stock immediately and will pay whatever the market will bear to do so. When more than one broker goes in with a market portfolio at one point in time, the sudden inflow of buyers causes momentum that, on average, temporarily moves the Dow Jones Industrial Average three to four points per program.

Index arbitrage works both ways. Consider a different situation. One Tuesday morning both the bond and stock markets open strongly, and by 11:30 A.M. the DJIA is up six points. Suddenly the spread between the index and its nearby futures contract moves to a discount to fair value. Arbitrageurs who reverse their positions by selling stocks and buying futures put a great deal of selling pressure on the market and cause it to decline quickly and sharply.

Many wonder why the spread is so volatile given the widespread knowledge of stock index arbitrage. The answer lies in the composition of the trading community using index options and futures. As mentioned earlier, most participants in these markets are short-term speculators, unconcerned about premiums and cost-of-carry valuations. They are generally taking short-term positions on the market and, as they say in the futures pit, "The trend is their friend." Arbitrage activity may reverse the trend temporarily but in most cases will not change the direction of an $8–10 billion market. Over time we expect this market to become more efficient, and the incremental return over interest rates in arbitrage programs should not return to the peak levels experienced in late 1984. However, we believe that the spread will fluctuate around fair value in the foreseeable future and that arbitrage programs will continue to occur.

VII. Peak Periods of Arbitrage Activity: Expiration Days

Index arbitrageurs require that the spread between the index and the futures and options contracts deviate significantly from its cost-of-carry value, due to the impact of transaction costs on total return. The main cost of trading a market portfolio is the specialist's spread in the stock at the time of the trade. Therefore it is in the arbitrageur's best interest to minimize the impact of the bid-ask spread. One way of doing this is to trade at the close of the NYSE on the expiration date of a contract. All index futures and options contracts close at the value of the index expiration, which is the third Friday of the month. The arbitrageur with short futures contracts who closes his positions on expiration is indifferent to the market impact of selling all of the stocks in the index at the NYSE close, because that impact is offset by a profit in the short futures position, which settles at the closing index value on that date.[3] Thus many arbitrageurs frequently look to unwind their long stock–short futures position at the NYSE close on expiration.

This activity concerns many institutional investors who worry about the impact of having billions of dollars of stocks being sold in the market at one point in time. However, not all investors sell stocks at expiration. Some buy stocks at expiration because they think arbitrage activity is artificially lowering share prices. In addition some investors participate in a strategy at expiration called "selling the spread," which is accomplished by purchasing a futures contract expiring soon and simultaneously selling another contract expiring a few months later. This is initiated when the spread between the near- and far-term contracts is greater than its cost-of-carry value. When the first contract expires, the arbitrageur will buy all the stocks in the index on the close, netting him a long stock–short futures position. In this situation all market impact incurred in the purchase of stocks will be offset by profits taken in the long futures contract, which closes at the value of the index at expiration.

VIII. Summary

To help summarize this article, here are four questions to consider when setting up a stock index arbitrage program:

---

3. Assuming the arbitrageur owns the entire index and all stocks are trading at the time of execution.

What stock index should be arbitraged? If the program is designed to improve cash returns, the index providing the most opportunities for excess returns should be selected. However, enough capital should be committed to the program so that the index can be purchased; that is, the stocks in the index should be purchased in their correct proportions.

Should the entire index or a basket (subset of the index) be purchased? A basket is easier to manage and requires less capital. However, more risk is assumed when a subset of the index is purchased.

Should options or futures contracts be used in the program? Both. By considering arbitrage trades in both options and futures contracts there are more opportunities to profit from mispricings in the markets. If the program uses stock index options, daily variation margin calls are of no concern. But if trades include short American options (S&P 100, SMI, and others), there is the risk of early exercise.

What level of return should be sought? A level that compensates for time, trouble, and risk should be sought. If the level is set too low, the opportunity to lock in a higher return is lost; if too high, the trade will never be executed.

11

A Systematic Approach to Generating Excess Returns Using a Multiple Variable Model*

Aruna S. Ramamurti
President
Triangle Portfolio Associates

I. Introduction

There is little doubt that positive risk-adjusted excess returns (residual returns) to fundamental variables, such as size and earnings yield, exist in the market.[1] A careful investigation of the historical data reveals that for significant periods of time the residual returns to size and earnings yield have been positive and persistent. Nevertheless there are periods when the returns to size and earnings yield are negative. Other researchers have analyzed methods of creating portfolios with the attributes of small size and high earnings yield that have provided superior returns over historical periods.[2]

In this article a multiple regression technique is used to generate monthly returns to size, earnings yield (E/P), and return on equity (ROE) on a sample of about 900 securities for the period April 1977 through March 1986.[3]

*The author thanks T. Daniel Coggin for his helpful comments and suggestions.

1. See Donald B. Keim, "The CAPM and Equity Return Regularities," *Financial Analysts' Journal* (May-June 1986): 19–33.
2. See Richard J. Dowen and W. Scott Bauman, "A Fundamental Multifactor Asset Pricing Model," *Financial Analysts' Journal* (July-August 1986): 45–51.
3. Return on equity was included as a variable in the model because several valuation models use historical return on equity to compute changes in price to book ratio and the implied return to shareholders. See Jarrod W. Wilcox, "The P/B – ROE Valuation Model," *Financial Analysts' Journal* (January-February 1984): 58–66.

The returns to the variables are generated after the return to the stock is adjusted for its systematic risk relative to the market. Additionally the variables are standardized so that the returns to the variables are generated on a comparable scale. The returns to the three variables contributed significant amounts to securities returns over many time periods, although the direction and magnitude of the effects often varied over time. The time series of returns to the variables generated are analyzed to determine if there are long- or short-term trends that could be used to forecast the future returns. The autocorrelation functions of the returns to size and ROE did not show a significant relationship to 12 lags. Although the autocorrelations of the returns to E/P are significant to the first and eighth lag, the process that generated the returns is not easily identifiable.

In order to determine if the returns could be utilized to identify securities that would contribute residual returns, a naive predictive model is used. The one-month-ahead returns to size, E/P, and ROE are forecast as the average of the prior 12 months of estimated returns. The expected residual returns to the securities in the sample are then computed from the exposure to the variable and its forecast expected return. The sample of securities is ranked by expected residual return and grouped into portfolios. It was found that the portfolios with the highest expected returns also had the highest realized returns, in most of the time periods. Furthermore, the top ranked portfolios consistently outperformed the Standard and Poor's market index.

II. Data and Methodology

The sample of stocks used in the study consists of approximately 900 of the largest market capitalization companies in the Standard and Poor's Compustat Price-Dividend-Earnings primary and secondary security files for quarterly and annual periods. In order to reduce survivorship bias, the primary and secondary data files are merged with the Compustat Research file before screening for the largest 900 companies. The variables studied are computed as of the end of the prior month, starting with March 1977 and ending with February 1986. A firm is included in the sample in any month if 12 months of returns and prior annual earnings data were available as of that month-end date. Annual and quarterly accounting data was not presumed to be available for public use until 30 days after the end of the fiscal period. This procedure is meant to assure than an investor could have actually computed and used the variables studied here in order to obtain superior returns. As a result of the requirements on the admissibility of firms into the sample, the number of firms used varied between 600 and 900 during the period of the study. For example, in April 1977 there are 664 observations for ROE, 718 observations for E/P, and 817 observations available for beta, market capitalization, and total returns respectively. At the end of the period in March

1986, there are 828 observations for E/P ratio, 865 observations for ROE, and 881 observations for beta, market capitalization, and total return.

The variable for size (market capitalization) is computed as the product of the number of shares outstanding times the month end price of the security. Since many prior studies have found that the size effect is log-linear on returns, the variable used to proxy size is the natural logarithm of the market capitalization:

$$K_i = \log(\text{market capitalization}).$$

The variable for earnings yield is computed as the ratio of the latest 12 months reported primary earnings to month end price:

$$E_i = \text{trailing 12 month earnings/month-end price}.$$

The variable for return on equity is computed as the ratio of the latest 12 months reported primary earnings to book equity:

$$O_i = (\text{Net income})/(\text{Book equity}).$$

Tables 1 and 2 summarize the variable data, the sample beta and market capitalization. Table 1 gives the range of means and standard deviations of the independent variables used in each month of the study. The median market capitalization of the sample in each month and the mean beta of the

TABLE 1. *Range in Sample Means of Monthly Independent Variables.*[a]

Value	Market Cap[b] ($ billions)	Beta	K_t Size	E_t E/P (%)	O_t ROE (%)
Low	0.295	1.08	19.47	0.05	10.96
	(2.212)	(0.29)	(0.92)	(8.12)	(8.67)
High	1.019	1.19	20.81	15.3	16.43
	(4.474)	(0.37)	(1.16)	(60.40)	(71.93)

a. Standard deviations are shown in parentheses below the means.
b. Median.

TABLE 2. *Range in Correlation Coefficients of Independent Variables.*

Value	Size-E/P	Size-ROE	E/P-ROE
Low	−0.14	−0.03	−0.63
High	0.30	0.15	0.89

TABLE 3. *Summary Statistics.*

	Arithmetic Mean	Geometric Mean	Standard Deviation	Correlation of Returns Size	E/P	ROE
Size	−0.53[a]	−0.53	1.09	1.00	0.19	−0.03
E/P	0.26[b]	0.26	1.28		1.00	−0.68
ROE	0.01	0.01	1.29			1.00
Intercept	0.48[c]	0.47	1.66			

a. Significant at 0.05 percent level.
b. Significant at 2.50 percent level.
c. Significant at 0.25 percent level.

sample of securities is also displayed. The *median* market capitalization increased from $295 million in April 1977 to $1,019 million in March 1986. In contrast the size variable, the natural logarithm of the market capitalization, increased from a *mean* of 19.47 in April 1977 to a *mean* of 20.81 in March 1986. The *mean* beta of the sample varied from a low of 1.08 in May 1985 to a high of 1.19 in October 1979 during the period. The *mean E/P* ratio sample ranged from a low of 0.05 percent in March 1986 to a high of 15.3 percent in April 1980. The *mean* return on equity for the sample varied from a low of 10.96 percent in August 1983 to a high of 16.43 percent in June 1980.

The lowest standard deviation occurred in April 1978 for market capitalization, in June 1981 for beta, in August 1983 for the size variable, in July 1977 for *E/P*, and October 1977 for ROE respectively. The largest values for standard deviation occurred in March 1986 for market capitalization and *E/P*, in June 1984 for beta, in April 1977 for size, and July 1985 for ROE respectively.

The ranges in the correlation coefficients are displayed in Table 3. The smallest correlation of −0.14 between size and *E/P* occurred in April 1977, and the largest correlation of 0.30 occurred in March 1986. The lowest correlation between size and ROE occurred in July 1985, while the largest value of 0.15 belonged to January 1982. The correlation between *E/P* and ROE varied from significant negative to positive values, with −0.63 in July 1985 and 0.89 in March 1981. A meta-analysis of the monthly seies of correlations shows that this observed variation is real and not entirely attributable to sampling error.[4]

---

4. See T. Daniel Coggin and John E. Hunter, "Problems in Measuring the Quality of Investment Information: The Perils of the Information Coefficient," *Financial Analysts' Journal* (May-June 1983): 25–33. Using the meta-analysis approach suggested by the authors, the chisquares for each monthly series of observed correlations between size-*E/P*, size-ROE, and *E/P*-ROE are 1,047, 2,468, and 311 respectively. The chi square necessary to imply real vari-

The relationship between size and E/P is insignificant for most of the time period, as also that between size and ROE. However, the correlation between E/P and ROE is significant at the 1 percent level in all except 24 months of the period.[5] This would imply that the impact of E/P and ROE cannot be independently assessed in most time periods, due to multicollinearity. However, since our primary goal is the *prediction* of residual return, multicollinearity is not a problem, and all three variables are used in the specification of residual return.

The sample of securities changes over time based on availability of data. Additionally the units of each of the variables differs, according to the formulas used to define them. Hence, in order to obtain parameter estimates that are comparable, both cross-sectionally and across time, the variables size, E/P and ROE are standardized across the sample each month by subtracting the mean of each variable, respectively, and dividing by the sample standard deviation for that variable.

The coefficient to such a standard independent variable in a regression can then be interpreted as the result of a one standard deviation change in the variable from its sample mean. The slope and the intercept of a regression in which X_i is the independent variable differs from that in which X_{zi} is the independent variable. However, it can be shown that the expected value of the dependent variable is the same in both the regressions.[6]

---

ation in the observed correlations is 124 at the 5 percent confidence level with 100 degrees of freedom.

5. An appendix containing the monthly values of the means and standard deviations of the regression variables, along with the correlation coefficients of the variables with one another for each month of the study is available from the author upon request. The median market capitalization values and mean of the betas, and the standard deviations of market capitalization and beta are also available upon request.

6. Let a regression of the dependent variable Y_i on the standardized independent variable X_{zi} be of the form

$$Y_i = a_s + b_s X_{zi} + e_i,$$

where $X_{zi} = (X_i - \bar{X})/S_x$, and $E(Y) = a_s$. Substituting for X_{zi} we get

$$Y_i = a_s + b_s (X_i - \bar{X})/S_x + e_i,$$
$$Y_i = (a_s - b_s \bar{X}/S_x) + b_s (X_i/S_x) + e_i.$$

This results in

$$Y_i = a_n + b_n X_i + e_i,$$

where, by substitution:

$$a_n = (a_s - b_s \bar{X}/S_x),$$
$$b_n X_i = b_s X_i/S_x \Rightarrow b_n = b_s/S_x.$$

(See A. Goldberger, *Econometric Theory* (New York: John Wiley, 1963), p. 197.) Additionally

$$E(Y) = a_n + b_n \bar{X}.$$

Substituting for a_n and b_n,

$$E(Y) = (a_s - b_s \bar{X}/S_x) + b_s \bar{X}/S_x$$
$$= a_s.$$

Thus the standardization process does not change the expected value of the dependent variable.

The monthly total returns on the S&P 500 stock index is used as the proxy for returns on the market. The proxy for the risk-free rate is the return on the one-month Treasury bill. The total return on the security is computed as the sum of dividend and capital change. A fundamental beta was obtained for each security in the sample each month from BARRA.[7] Assuming that the capital asset pricing model is a valid return-generating model, the risk-adjusted residual return (R_i) is created as the dependent variable in the regression using

$$R_i = (R_{si} - R_f) - b_i(R_m - R_f),$$

where

R_{si} = the total return on the ith security.
R_m = the total return on the market.
R_f = the risk free return.
b_i = the beta on the ith security.

III. Historical Analysis and Results

The cross-sectional regression equation used to estimate the parameters is of the form:

$$R_i = a + K_i R_K + E_i R_E + O_i R_O + e_i,$$

where the dependent variable R_i is the nonstandardized residual return of the security, a is the intercept of the regression, R_K, R_E, and R_O are the estimated returns to the standardized independent variables size (K), $E/P(E)$, and ROE(O) respectively, and e_i is the error term.[8]

The parameters in the regression, namely the returns to the variables, can be interpreted as the return to a measure of one standard deviation above the mean value of the variable in the sample of securities. The intercept in this regression stands for the effect of an overall exogeneous variable, such as an industry variable, that has a different impact in each of the time periods. Since the independent variables in the regression are standardized, the intercept is the mean of the dependent variable, namely the mean residual return of the sample in each month.

---

7. See Barr Rosenberg and Vinay Marathe, "The Prediction of Investment Risk: Systematic and Residual Risk," *Proceedings of the Seminar on the Analysis of Security Prices* (University of Chicago, 1975), pp. 85–150. The authors discuss the computation of the fundamental beta in this article. BARRA is an investment consulting organization in Orinda, California, that provides betas and other investment research products.
8. The expected residual return to a security is assumed to be a linear function of the returns to size, E/P and ROE, respectively, of the form:

$$E(R_i) = E(K_i)R_K + E(E_i)R_E + E(O_i)R_O.$$

The F values indicate that the hypothesis that the coefficients were not different from zero can be discarded at the 5 percent level of significance in 65 of the 108 months of regressions. The size effect was significant at better than the 1 percent level in 65 of 108 months; the E/P effect and ROE effects were significant at better than 1 percent level in 47 of 108 months.[9]

The summary results of the regression are reported in Table 3. For each of the three variables the arithmetic means, the geometric means, the standard deviations, and the correlation of the time series of monthly returns to the variables is reported. Although the return to ROE was significant in many of the individual time periods, for the entire period the average returns to size and E/P alone were significant. We can attribute this to the fact that, during a part of the period lower ROE securities had superior returns relative to higher ROE securities, contrary to expectations. On the other hand, while the return to small securities became negative relative to larger securities during the last two years of the study, the magnitude of the returns was considerably less compared to the size effect during the earlier period.

Although the variables E/P and ROE were positively correlated in most of the months of the study, the returns to the variables were negatively correlated. The correlation between the return to size and return to E/P was positive, while the correlation between the return to size and the return to ROE was insignificant. A meta-analysis of the monthly series of the return to the variables enables a test of the hypothesis that there is no real variation in the estimated coefficients. The chi-square test reveals that the observed variation in the coefficients was no more than that attributable to sampling error.[10] Hence there is no real variation around the estimated mean values of the estimated coefficients in Table 3.

Figure 1 displays the cumulative risk-adjusted returns to a one standard deviation exposure to the variable through the period. This return would have been earned by a security in excess of the risk premium and the risk-free return. Assuming a normal distribution of exposures to the variables in the sample, $100 invested in a security with an exposure to E/P greater than that of 84 percent of the securities in the sample (that is, one standard deviation away from the mean) would have resulted in $132 at the end of the period, in addition to the compounded amount provided by the market return adjusted for the beta of the sample. The interpretation would be similar for size and ROE.

---

9. The table containing the complete month by month results of the cross-sectional multiple regression is available from the author upon request.

10. See T. Daniel Coggin and John E. Hunter, "A Meta-Analysis of the Pricing of the 'Risk' Factors of Arbitrage Pricing Theory," *The Journal of Portfolio Management* (Fall 1987): 35–38. The chi-square for the return to size is 8.1; the chi-square for the return to E/P is 8.5; the chi-square for the return to ROE is 8.5; and the chi-square for the intercept is 3.3. The chi-square value necessary to imply real variation in the observed correlations is 124 at the 5 percent confidence level with 100 degrees of freedom.

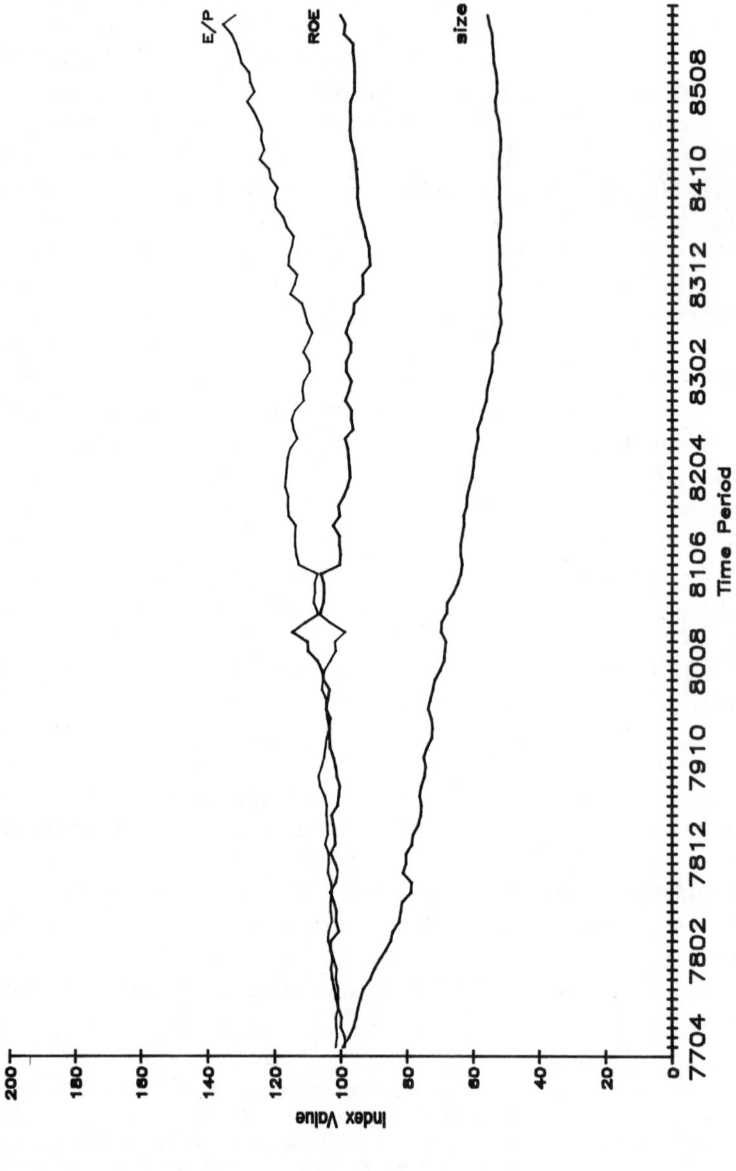

FIGURE 1. *Cumulative Returns to Regression Variables, April 1977–March 1986.*

IV. Forecast Methodology and Results

In order to determine whether there were trends in the returns to variables, the autocorrelation structure of the returns were analyzed. Figures 2–4 show the autocorrelations for each factor to 12 lags. The autocorrelations are bounded by the standard errors of the values. The bounds are plotted to test the hypothesis that the autocorrelations are not significantly different from zero at any of the lags. In the case of the E/P variable, the first and eighth order correlations were significant. Further analysis might be successful in determining the type of process that could have generated these factor returns. On the other hand the autocorrelation patterns clearly demonstrate that an autoregressive process did not generate the factor returns for size and ROE. Although several studies have substantiated the presence of seasonality in the size parameter, there was no evidence of the January effect in the returns to the size variable in this study.

In the absence of a stochastic process that would forecast the returns to the variables, the one-period-ahead expected returns are formulated as the average of the previous 12 months of estimated returns:

$$R_{vt+1}^{f} = \left(\sum_{j=t-11}^{t} R_{vj} \right) \Big/ 12,$$

where f stands for the forecast return, and v stands for the variables size, E/P, and ROE, respectively.

Starting in April 1978, a set of returns is computed accordingly for each of the variables. The expected residual return for each security was then forecast using

$$R_{it+1}^{f} = R_{Kt+1}^{f} K_{it} + R_{Et+1}^{f} E_{it} + R_{Ot+1}^{f} O_{it}.$$

This equation simply multiplies the month-end exposure of the security to each variable with the forecast return to that variable for the next month and adds the terms to generate the forecast return to the security. The securities are then ranked in deciles of roughly 90 stocks each based on the expected residual returns. The realized returns on each of these portfolios are computed for the next month. The returns are forecast again the following month, the securities are ranked, portfolios formed, and the realized returns are computed, and so on until the end of the period March 1986.[11]

A rank order correlation is calculated each month between the ranking obtained from the forecast residual returns and that obtained each month from the actual residual returns. The mean correlation coefficient of 0.08 for

---

11. The results of this analysis displaying the actual total returns on each of the decile portfolios and the comparable total return on the S&P 500 common stock index for each month that security residual returns were forecast is available from the author upon request.

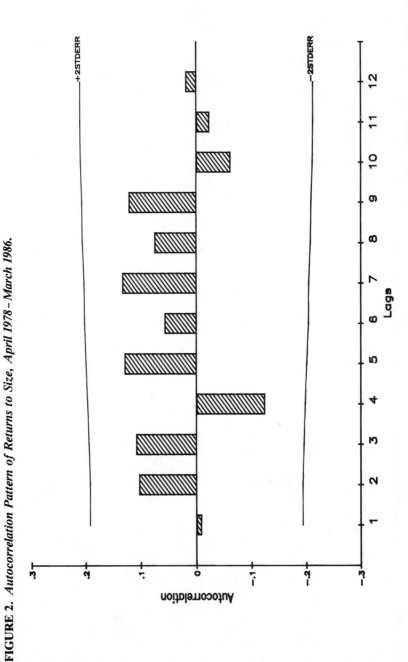

FIGURE 2. *Autocorrelation Pattern of Returns to Size, April 1978 – March 1986.*

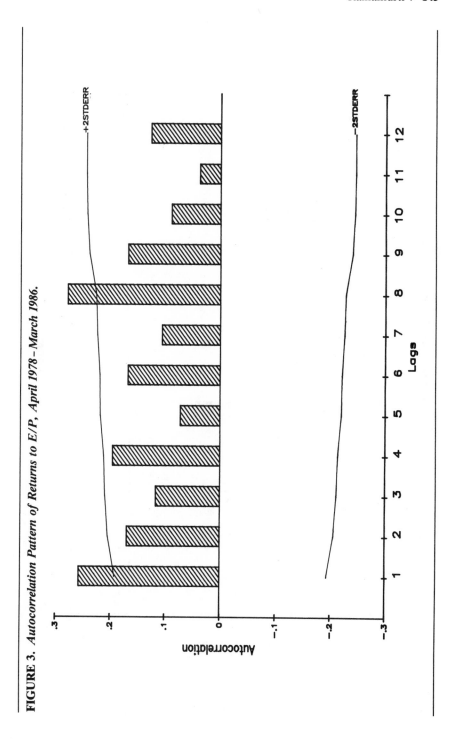

FIGURE 3. *Autocorrelation Pattern of Returns to E/P, April 1978 – March 1986.*

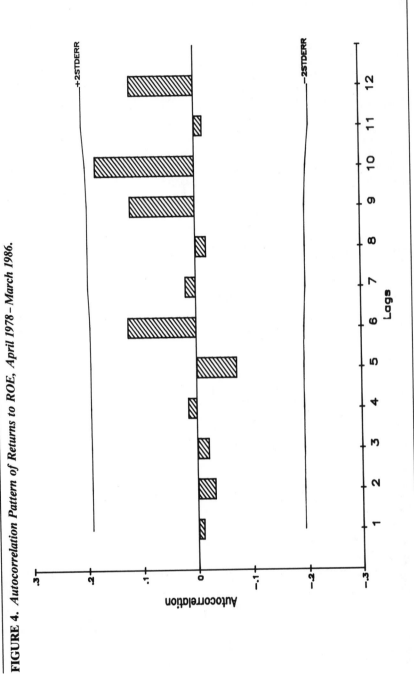

FIGURE 4. *Autocorrelation Pattern of Returns to ROE, April 1978 – March 1986.*

the period, ranged between a high value of 0.37 and a low value of −0.41, with a standard deviation of 0.14.

In order to test the hypothesis that there is no real variation in the observed rank order correlations (information coefficients), a meta-analysis was performed on the rank correlation coefficients.[12] The chi-square statistic is found to be 1,632, denoting that the observed variation in the rank correlations is real and not entirely attributable to sampling error. However, as we shall see, the *mean* correlation of 0.08 is still sufficient to generate superior residual returns.

Table 4 summarizes the mean monthly arithmetic and geometric returns, the standard deviation of the returns, average beta, the realized alpha, the average forecast alpha, the residual risk (variance), diversification, and turnover in the 10 decile portfolios. The arithmetic mean, the geometric mean, and the standard deviations are obtained from the total portfolio returns for the deciles. The beta and forecast alphas are the average monthly values over the period. The realized alpha, residual risk, and R^2 are generated from a regression of decile portfolio excess returns over the risk-free rate relative to excess returns of the S&P 500 over the risk-free rate.

The mean of the returns on the top six deciles ranked higher than the return of the S&P 500 index. Although the turnover in the decile portfolios was high, the return earned was sufficiently superior to compensate for the transaction costs incurred. For example, the average monthly turnover in the first decile of 63 percent, with an imputed round trip transaction cost of 1 percent would reduce the geometric mean monthly return to 2.73 percent.

Figure 5 displays the cumulative value of $100 invested in the top four deciles, compared to the same amount invested in the S&P 500 index over the time period of study. At the end of March 1986, the first decile portfolio would have grown to $2,398.60, the second decile portfolio would have grown to $1,136.41, the third decile portfolio would have grown to $707.94 and the fourth decile portfolio would have grown to $572.66, relative to $398.33 from the S&P 500 index.

V. Conclusions

This article explains the risk-adjusted excess returns to securities using a multiple variable model. The resulting returns to the variables are used to forecast future returns to the variables. Although the forecast methodology is a naive one, the method has been used successfully to rank securities using

---

12. The variance due to sampling error was computed to be 0.0011, while the observed variance was 0.0187, resulting in a chi-square value of 1,632, with 100 degrees of freedom. This value is significant well beyond the 5 percent level.

TABLE 4. *Average Statistics on Decile Portfolios, April 1978–March 1986.*

	Dec. 1	Dec. 2	Dec. 3	Dec. 4	Dec. 5	Dec. 6	Dec. 7	Dec. 8	Dec. 9	Dec. 10	S&P 500
Geometric mean* (%)	3.36	2.56	2.06	1.83	1.89	1.56	1.35	1.31	1.05	0.84	1.45
Arithmetic mean* (%)	3.58	2.71	2.19	1.96	2.02	1.68	1.46	1.42	1.16	0.95	1.53
Standard deviation (%)	6.72	5.37	5.07	5.07	5.20	4.94	4.76	4.70	4.84	4.74	4.22
Beta	1.33	1.13	1.09	1.10	1.16	1.08	1.06	1.03	1.07	1.02	1.00
Actual alpha (%)	1.84	1.10	0.61	0.38	0.40	0.10	−0.09	−0.11	−0.40	−0.58	NA
Forecast alpha (%)	1.20	0.72	0.51	0.33	0.16	−0.02	−0.20	−0.41	−0.69	−1.35	NA
Residual risk	13.57	6.22	4.87	4.39	3.28	3.62	2.58	3.24	3.15	3.86	NA
R square	0.70	0.79	0.81	0.83	0.88	0.85	0.89	0.86	0.87	0.83	NA
Turnover	0.63	0.72	0.73	0.75	0.75	0.76	0.75	0.77	0.67	0.61	NA

*Arithmetic and geometric means computed on portfolio total returns.

FIGURE 5. *Cumulative Returns on Decile Portfolios versus S&P 500, April 1978 – March 1986.*

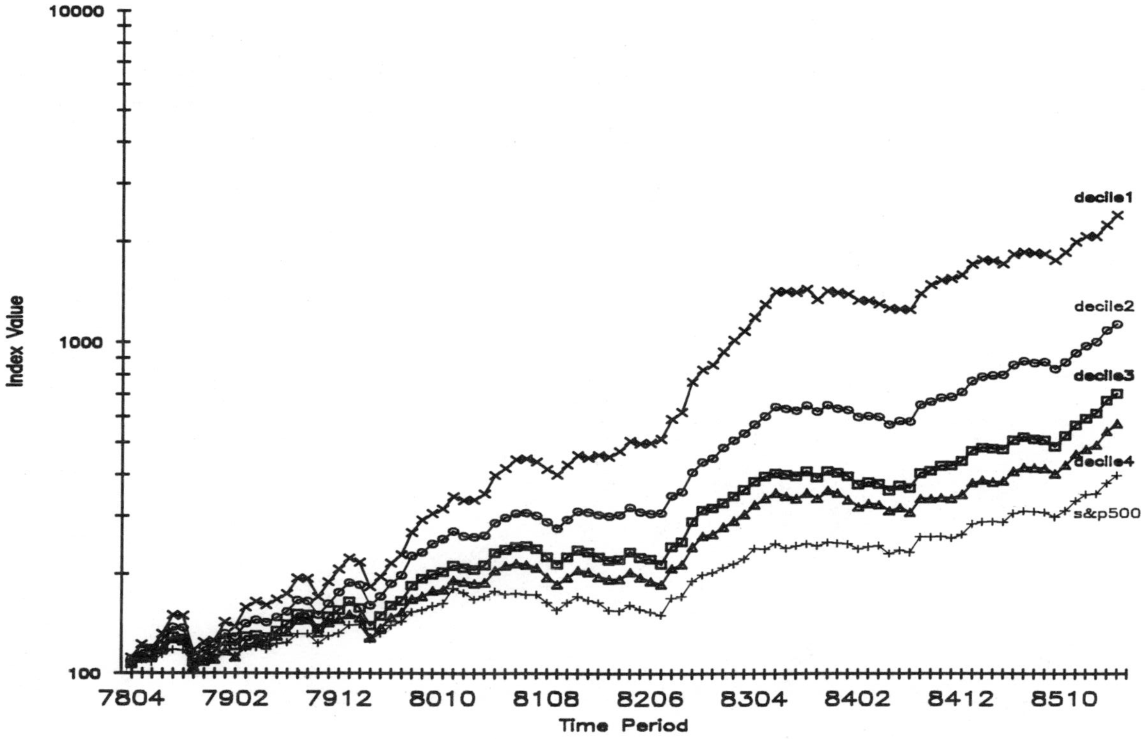

forecast excess returns and to form portfolios that consistently outperformed the market during the period studied.

The explanatory power of the regression would improve if industry or economic sector variables were included as dependent variables. Additionally, there may be other variables of interest that could improve the specification of the returns on securities. Informational variables and analysts' earnings expectations related variables could be used to improve the model.[13] The forecast methodology might be improved by attempting to forecast the returns to the variables as a function of both historic returns and exogeneous variables, such as interest rates or inflation rates.

---

13. Firms neglected by institutions were shown to provide superior risk adjusted returns in "Giraffes, Institutions and Neglected Firms," by Avner Arbel, Steven Carvell, and Paul Strebel, *Financial Analysts' Journal* (May-June 1983): 57–63. Analysts' earnings expectations were shown to have a significant impact on stock price performance in "Earnings Expectations and Security Prices," by Eugene H. Hawkins, Stanley C. Chamberlin, and Wayne E. Daniel, *Financial Analysts' Journal* (September-October 1984).

12

The Valuation of Financial Assets in Inflation

Tony Estep*
Principal
New Amsterdam Partners

Nick Hanson
Vice President
Salomon Brothers Inc

I. Introduction

In free capital markets, both buyer and seller would like to know the purchasing power of future payments promised to the investor. This would enable both to strike a well-reasoned bargain whose value in future goods and services was understood by both. In recent years, rapidly changing inflation has altered the terms of many financial transactions after the transactions were made. Since such transactions are denominated in currencies, and since the exchange rate between currencies and goods and services has declined sharply, the effect has been to enable users of funds to pay back less in goods and services than they bargained for.

As a result, financial markets have been disrupted and are likely to be disrupted again in the future. This paper analyzes the returns on financial assets stated in their equivalent value in goods and services. Investors are painfully aware that "nominal" returns are meaningless; the real value of returns, that is their purchasing value, is clearly the determinant of investment value. The paper describes some methods of estimating the purchasing power of investment returns; indicates the benefits which the investor may hope to gain from these methods; and shows that financial markets are remarkably

* When this article was written, Mr. Estep was employed by Salomon Brothers Inc.

consistent and efficient in pricing real returns, no matter how inconsistent they seem to those who view markets in terms of nominal returns.

We present a simple analysis of asset valuation which rests on two fundamental assumptions: *investors want real returns;* and *investors regard an asset's price as the present worth of the future payments* it will return to its owners.

Investors who want real returns will include an inflation premium in the expected return they demand from an investment. Thus, other things equal, yields will rise when inflation expectations rise, and vice versa.

In the case of common stocks, the growth rate of future dividend payments will be affected to some extent by changes in inflation. We define a measure of this flowthrough, and show how it can affect stock values. Stocks of companies which exhibit low flowthrough will be "interest sensitive," and those with high flowthrough will be (to some extent) "inflation hedges." We also show how changes in inflation expectations, flowthrough, and market prices are related to the volatility of asset values.

II. Real Expected Returns

The analysis presented here is applicable to any financial asset: bonds, taxable or tax-exempt, annuities, mortgages, or stocks. The discussion will be presented in terms of common stocks, but the reader should have no difficulty making analogous arguments for any other asset. The expected return on an asset is calculated from the following well-known relationship:

$$P = \frac{D_1}{1+k} + \frac{D_2}{(1+k)^2} + \cdots + \frac{D_n}{(1+k)^n}, \tag{1}$$

where n is the number of payments.

This equation says simply that the price P of an asset is the present worth of all the future payments D_i expected from the asset. Since the price is set by the market, and the future payments are set by the issuer, the two sides of the equation will be made equal by adjusting the term "rate" in the denominator. The rate k which makes the two sides equal is the Internal Rate of Return, and is referred to by various other names. Yield to Maturity, Discount Rate, and Expected Return are some of the aliases of this useful number.

Although this return is the rate expected by an investor who pays no taxes and who denominates returns in nominal terms, it is not the purchasing power return in the real world with inflation and taxes. This paper details the effects of inflation, but taxes will have to be left for a future date. Equation (1) above is the full expression of the concept of expected internal rate of return. Some simplifying assumptions may be made, if desired, without loss of generality, so that we may consider the effect of real and nominal growth in the payment stream. These assumptions are convenient but are not essential to the correctness of the following arguments.

If the payments are expected to grow in perpetuity at a constant rate, g, then the nth payment is:

$$D_n = (1+g)^n D_o, \tag{2}$$

where D_o is the current payment.

In this case it may be shown that the valuation equation (1) above simplifies to:

$$P = \frac{D_o(1+g)}{k-g}. \tag{3}$$

The derivation is well-known and will not be repeated here.[1]

Since we are interested in an expression for real returns, let us suppose that the expected growth of payments from corporate dividends is related to inflation expectations. Specifically, suppose that the growth of corporate dividends has two components: real growth, and growth due to inflation in the selling price of the corporation's products, flowing through to profits.

That portion of the growth of dividends that comes from inflation is not real—in the sense that it does not enhance the purchasing power of the corporation nor the investor. However, it is essential to the investor that the corporation achieves this illusory growth, since otherwise the purchasing power of both will decline. What is needed, then, is an expression to relate the change in value of an investment to changes in inflation. *The key to this relationship is the "flowthrough constant."*

III. Real Returns When Inflation is Expected

Suppose that a corporation's stock is priced as shown in equation (3) above. All investors agree on the expected growth rate, inflation rate, dividend expectation, and the discounting rate that is appropriate to payments offered by the stock of the corporation. In other words, the market is in equilibrium. Then:

$$(1+k) = (1+R)(1+I), \tag{4}$$

where R is the real return from the stock (the discount rate in the absence of inflation), and I is the anticipated inflation.

But suppose further that the expectation for future profits for the company is also affected by inflation; specifically, suppose that the growth rate of profits is expected to be influenced such that:

$$(1+g) = (1+G)(1+fI), \tag{5}$$

where G is the real growth rate and f is the flowthrough constant: the fraction of inflation which flows through to profit (and dividend) growth.

---

1. Note that here and throughout this article the formulas assume periodic compounding, as opposed to continuous compounding.

Now the value of the stock is given by:

$$P = \frac{D_o(1+G)(1+fI)}{(1+R)(1+I)-(1+G)(1+fI)}. \tag{6}$$

This equation is general. The only simplifying assumption is that growth, inflation, and flowthrough must be represented by long-term average rates. When we are attempting to value stocks in the aggregate (for example, the S&P 500), this is not a problem.

This valuation equation enables us to assess the effect of real growth, inflation, and flowthrough on the value of stocks to an investor. For example, it is apparent that a reduction in flowthrough will reduce the numerator and increase the denominator; this reduces the value of the fraction (and thus the price of the asset) if inflation expectations rise.

IV. Effects of Flowthrough on Investment Values

Consider a company which is able to capture all inflation in future growth; we would say that flowthrough = 1.0. Then equation (6) becomes:

$$P = \frac{D_o(1+G)(1+I)}{(1+R(1+I)-(1+G)(1+I)} = \frac{D_o(1+G)}{R-G}. \tag{7}$$

This tells us that the value of the company's future payments in terms of goods and services does not change when inflation expectations change. Note that this is the substance of the Modigliani–Cohn argument.[2] The authors argue that if the S&P 500 had an inflation flowthrough of 1.0, it should sell at almost 3 times its current level. But, alas, it has not (see below).

At the other end of the spectrum is a company with a flowthrough of zero; the return on equity (ROE) and thus the growth rate of this company are fixed, perhaps by regulatory fiat (or perhaps because we are looking at a preferred stock). Then g stays the same no matter what happens to inflation, and changes in nominal return will have to come from changes in price. This is easy to see if we consider expected return to equal yield plus growth. Solving equation (1) for k gives:

$$k = \underbrace{\frac{D_o(1+g)}{P}}_{\text{Yield}} + \underbrace{g}_{\text{Growth}}. \tag{8}$$

Growth is fixed if flowthrough = 0. If we have an increase in inflation expectations which dictates a corresponding rise in nominal return (to keep real

2. Franco Modigliani and William Cohn, "Inflation, Rational Valuation, and the Market," *Financial Analysts Journal* (March/April 1979).

FIGURE 1. *AAA Utilities vs. Utility Stock Yields vs. S&P Forest Products Yield.*

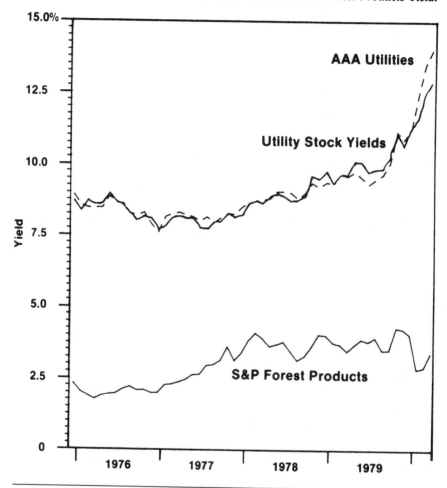

return the same), the increase must come from a gain in yield. The starting dividend has not changed, so the only source of increase in yield is a decrease in price.

This illustrates one of the principal characteristics of a company with low flowthrough. Investors expect little from the growth component of return, so the stock "sells on a yield basis"—that is, it is sensitive to changes in interest rates. Figure 1 presents a striking picture of this. The yield of utility stocks tracks bond yields with remarkable fidelity during the period shown. This suggests that investors did not expect utility growth rates to capture much, if any, of inflation expectations which influenced their interest rate preferences over the period.

For comparison, the figure also presents a picture of the yields of a high flowthrough group (the forest products industry), illustrating that they are lower than, and unrelated to, yields on low flowthrough assets.

It might seem counter to intuition that a stable payment stream, such as the expected dividends from a utility company, would be viewed as risky. Yet, *if the value of expected payments is fixed in nominal terms, their purchasing power is exactly as volatile as the rate of inflation.*

V. Historical Flowthrough for Certain Industries

Table 1 provides a perspective on the flowthrough achieved by various industries over certain periods in the past. The data in the table were derived as follows: the least-squares compound growth rate of earnings, g, for each industry was determined, as was the least-squares compound growth rate of unit output for each industry, G. Then using equation (5) the inflation component of earnings growth was found by:

$$g - G = (1 + G)fI. \tag{9}$$

Then the flowthrough constant may be obtained from:

$$f = \frac{g - G}{(1 + G)I}. \tag{10}$$

The same deflator was used for all calculations, since presumably the investor is interested in the spending power of the investment returns; this is reasonably well estimated by changes in the Consumer Price Index.

VI. Relative Price/Earnings and Relative Yields

If two companies have different flowthroughs, it is not possible to determine their relative valuation by considering their comparative price/earnings (P/E) ratios at different times. This is made clear by considering what would happen to the companies in our previous example, one with a flowthrough of 1.0 and the other with a flowthrough of 0. Since the price of the first stayed the same while the price of the other declined, it is clear that the relationships between the P/E ratios must change, even though the returns to investors, in real terms, did not alter. The same is true of relative yields. Any time that changing inflation expectations are elements in determining investment value, relative P/E or relative yield will be useless for making valuation comparisons in a world in which companies exhibit different flowthroughs.

TABLE 1. *Inflation Flowthrough Characteristics of Selected Market Groups.*

Industry	1965–79	1970–79	1970–75	1975–79
400 Industrials	0.56	0.98	1.27	0.92
Aluminum	0.25	1.81	–	4.67
Beverages soft drink	0.73	0.68	0.72	0.51
Chemicals	0.12	0.83	1.90	0.32
Cigarettes	1.31	1.08	0.97	1.52
Cosmetics	0.83	0.61	0.56	0.95
Drugs	0.31	0.55	0.62	0.38
Electrical equipment	0.37	0.70	0.21	1.08
Electric utilities	0.39	0.08	–	0.15
Electronic instruments	NA	2.33	3.00	1.53
Semiconductors	NA	1.66	2.29	1.77
Food	0.62	0.83	0.88	0.61
Forest products	1.56	2.20	2.18	2.58
Machinery	1.08	1.98	1.95	0.88
Office equipment	0.99	1.11	1.09	1.02
Offshore drilling	1.17	1.21	1.35	–
Oil composite	1.09	1.37	2.42	1.78
Domestic oils	1.37	2.19	3.03	1.97
International oils	0.98	1.05	2.17	1.74
Oil equipment	2.96	3.58	4.00	1.06
Paper	0.95	2.04	–	0.58
Restaurants	1.71	2.45	2.77	2.14
Retail stores	0.43	0.58	0.10	0.92

The numbers here represent the historical inflation flowthrough coefficients obtained for the industry groups. The numbers were derived by solving the following equation:

$$(1 + g_i) = (1 + G)(1 + f_i I),$$

where g_i = the growth in nominal corporate profits for industry i,

   G = the growth of real output for industry i,

   I = the inflation rate (taken here to be the growth rate in the Consumer Price Index), and

   f_i = the flowthrough effect for industry i.

The profit growth rates were obtained by regressing the earnings of the S&P industry groups against time to obtain a compound growth rate for each period. The real output growth rates were arrived at by regressing the relevant industrial production indices against time. A common deflator, the Consumer Price Index, was used, since the value of earnings in terms of real spending power was sought.

Thirty-four industry groups were tested for significant inflation flowthrough effects. Data for 21 of these industries were obtained which were statistically significant. A dash in the table indicates a period for which a statistically significant relationship could not be found. Data for the electronic instruments and semiconductors groups commence in 1970, and therefore meaningful flowthroughs are unobtainable for the whole 1965–79 period.

It is important to note that these numbers represent historical flowthrough effects and although they may contain indicators for future flowthroughs, there is no certainty that the future will repeat the patterns of the past.

Carrying this point further, one observation is that *it will not be possible to draw conclusions about the relative attractiveness of stocks and bonds by comparing their yields, or the "earnings yield" of stocks with the yields of bonds, unless we restrict the analysis to stocks with flowthrough very near zero.* Stocks with flowthrough near 1.0 could confound this type of analysis by seeming to move independently of bond rates. (This is true of other assets as well; consider the prices of hard assets and commodities in recent and past inflationary periods.) This effect makes analyses based upon an "equity risk premium" rather suspect.

VII. The Volatility of Asset Prices

Changes in the price of an asset which is valued by investors on the basis of expected return will be determined by changes in expected growth rate, changes in inflation expectations, flowthrough, and the sensitivity of the asset's price to these factors. In periods during which inflation expectations are changing rapidly and significantly, assets with low flowthrough will experience large price changes. This is not a consequence of some change in the nature of financial markets, as has been asserted recently by some observers; it has always been true, and is the consequence of the arithmetic of price changes versus yield changes. If investors decide to demand higher nominal returns from assets with low flowthrough (in order to keep real returns the same in light of higher expected inflation) they will price the asset so that the yield rises enough to compensate. The price change required will depend upon the change in yield per unit change in price. Just what is the sensitivity of an asset's price to changes in inflation? To answer that question, we must again adopt the assumption that investors want real returns. Then for small changes in inflation expectations, it can be shown from equation (6) that the relative price change will be:

$$\frac{\Delta P}{P} \approx T\left[\frac{f-1}{(1+I)(1+fI)}\right]\Delta I \text{ where } T = \frac{(1+R)(1+I)}{(1+R)(1+I)-(1+G)(1+fI)}.$$

(11)

T is equal to the "duration" of the asset as that term is commonly understood by bond investors (see, for example, "Bond Immunization, Part I" by Martin Leibowitz, available from Salomon Brothers). Duration is defined as the average time required to receive a payment, each payment having been weighted by its present value. It follows from this definition that, for the case of discrete compounding, duration is equal to the percentage change in price per small change in expected return, multiplied by one plus the expected return. Duration is thus a measure of price sensitivity to changes in discount rate; the longer the duration, the more price volatility. For the case where the price of the asset is given by equation (3), it can be shown that:

TABLE 2. *Price Changes in Inflation (%).*

Flowthrough	Duration 5	10	15	20	25	30
0.0	−2.3	−4.6	−6.8	−9.1	−11.4	−13.6
0.3	−1.7	−3.3	−5.0	−6.7	−8.3	−10.0
0.5	−1.0	−2.2	−3.3	−4.3	−5.4	−6.5
0.8	−0.5	−1.0	−1.6	−2.1	−2.6	−3.2
1.0	0.0	0.0	0.0	0.0	0.0	0.0

This table displays the approximate expected percentage price changes calculated from equation (11), for various levels of flowthrough and duration when inflation expectations increase from 10% to 10½%. A decline in expectations from 10% to 9½% will cause changes of the same magnitude as those shown, but of opposite sign.

$$T = \frac{1+k}{k-g} = \frac{1+k}{\text{Yield}} . \tag{12}$$

Thus, for two assets with the same expected return, the higher-yielding asset will have a shorter duration, and vice versa.

The sensitivity of prices to small changes in future growth is given by:

$$\frac{\Delta P}{P} \approx \frac{T}{1+g} \Delta g. \tag{13}$$

If growth is very uncertain, investors will naturally price the asset so that most of the expected return comes from yield, so assets with uncertain growth rates tend to have short duration (since duration is inversely related to yield; see above). See Table 2 for an example of the effect of inflation, flowthrough, and duration on stock prices.

This brings up a striking corollary observation. *Free markets seem to price stocks in such a manner that stocks with very short durations have very uncertain growth rates (a current example: Ford Motor), or low inflation flowthrough (Virginia Electric).* One could well argue that these are the sort of investments which offer the highest true risk when investing in an uncertain world. Then a portfolio selected to maximize yield (and minimize duration) would simply be a portfolio of stocks with low flowthrough or unpredictable growth. Thus one would demand higher returns from such a portfolio, because it would be very risky in the sense properly considered by investors.

Empirical evidence strongly corroborates this expectation (see papers by Elton & Gruber, Blume, Ramaswamy & Litzenberger, and a number of others). In most cases, those who have examined this evidence, observing that such portfolios exhibit betas similar to portfolios of average yield, have interpreted the results as implying that the market exhibits a systematic in-efficiency or have attributed these results to tax effects, rather than consid-ering that beta might not be a measure of the risk in the portfolios. One or more future papers will discuss in detail the estimation of economic and in-vestment risk.

VIII. Sources of Inflation Forecasts

In studying this topic, it is useful to have a source of inflation forecasts that reflects some sort of consensus view of long-term expectations for inflation. Fortunately, there is such a source in the term structure of forward Govern-ment rates.

Over the period 1926–1978, the average real rate on short Government paper has been about zero; that is, risk-free investments have had an aver-age return equal to the inflation rate. Therefore, estimates of future short rates contain in them an estimate of future inflation expectations. The struc-ture of long rates may always be viewed, by a simple mathematical transfor-mation, as a series of future short-term rates.

Let us pause to observe that this process sounds rather farfetched, even though it has a certain undeniable logic. A complete description of one way to go about this is given in Ibbotson and Sinquefield's classic monograph "Stocks, Bonds, Bills and Inflation." In it, the authors offer this comment: "Yield curve forecasts have not been very accurate in the past. However. . . the interest rate forecasts have been unbiased. . .the inflation forecasts have also been unbiased. Furthermore, we know of no way to make more accur-ate forecasts."

For the purposes we propose here, the term structure method is ideal, because we are not trying to make forecasts of inflation so much as trying to discover what inflation rate the financial markets are impounding. This is just what the term structure method accomplishes.

The technique is based on the notion that an investor who wants to buy a long bond with a maturity N years can either buy a bond with a maturity of N years, or buy a bond with a maturity of $N-1$ years and roll over the proceeds at the then prevailing 1-year rate when his bond matures. If we can observe the yields offered by bonds of N and $N-1$ years, we may solve for the implicit 1-year rate $N-1$ years from now. After subtracting the maturity premium (Ibbotson & Sinquefield place this at 170 basis points), we have an estimate of the expected inflation rate in year N.

Table 3 shows these rates for the years 1959 to the present. Note that the forecasts seem plausible in the sense that if one had taken a poll at the time, the results of the poll would likely have been about the same as those shown. In an economic sense, financial markets serve that purpose, with the added advantage that participants back their opinions with money. Of

TABLE 3. *Expected Long-Term Inflation Rates (%).*

Year	1Q	2Q	3Q	4Q
1959	2.2	2.0	1.9	1.8
1960	2.1	2.2	2.2	2.3
1961	2.3	2.1	2.3	2.5
1962	2.5	2.4	2.4	2.3
1963	2.4	2.4	2.4	2.5
1964	2.5	2.5	2.5	2.5
1965	2.5	2.5	2.6	2.6
1966	2.7	2.8	2.7	2.7
1967	2.8	3.2	3.1	3.6
1968	3.4	3.2	3.2	3.6
1969	4.3	4.0	3.6	3.8
1970	3.8	4.2	4.2	4.3
1971	4.5	4.5	4.0	4.3
1972	4.4	4.2	3.7	3.3
1973	5.7	5.6	6.1	6.6
1974	6.9	7.5	7.9	7.3
1975	6.8	6.9	6.9	7.1
1976	6.8	6.8	6.6	6.6
1977	6.5	6.7	6.4	6.5
1978	6.9	7.0	7.0	7.0
1979	7.2	7.3	7.2	8.0

These expected long-term inflation rates were obtained from term structure of U.S. Treasury securities (quarterly average rates, calculated at the end of the quarter).

course, the forecasts made in previous years, of inflation actually experienced in the late 1970s, were very wrong. Inflation turned out to be much higher than expected. *It is for precisely that reason that inflation flowthrough is a key element of investment risk and value.*

13

Measuring the Risk Premium on the Market Portfolio

John D. Finnerty
Executive Vice President
College Savings Bank
and
Adjunct Professor
Fordham University

I. Introduction

There are at least three crucial analytical issues encountered by money managers who apply the capital asset pricing model (CAPM) to value an asset. First, what value should be used for beta? An extensive literature exists that tests the stationarity of beta and that develops procedures for estimating beta.[1] Second, what time period is most appropriate for measuring the risk premium on the market portfolio? There seems to be general (although not universal) agreement that it is appropriate to use historical market risk premiums observed over an extended period to infer expected future risk premiums on the market portfolio. In particular, Ibbotson and Sinquefield's study,[2] recently updated by Siegel,[3] which provides return data for years

1. On the first point, see for example Frank J. Fabozzi and Jack Clark Francis, "Beta as a Random Coefficient," *Journal of Financial and Quantitative Analysis 13* (March 1978): 101–16; and Shyam Sunder, "Stationarity of Market Risk: Random Coefficients Tests for Individual Stocks," *Journal of Finance 35* (September 1980): 883–96. On the second point, see for example Barr Rosenberg, "Prediction of Common Stock Betas," *The Journal of Portfolio Management 11* (Winter 1985): 5–14.
2. Roger G. Ibbotson and Rex A. Sinquefield, *Stocks, Bonds, Bills, and Inflation: The Past and the Future* (Charlottesville, Va.: Financial Analysts Research Foundation, 1982).
3. Laurence B. Siegel, ed., *Stocks, Bonds, Bills, and Inflation, 1987 Yearbook* (Chicago: Ibbotson Associates, 1987).

beginning in 1926, is the source most frequently cited in finance textbooks for the average historical market risk premium. Most textbooks recommend using the estimate based on the full period spanning 1926 to the present. However, that procedure is correct only if the process generating the market risk premiums is stationary.

The third issue, which is the subject of this article, concerns the correct measure of the "average" market risk premium to use: the arithmetic mean or the geometric mean.[4] There is disagreement over this issue. Brealey and Myers,[5] Brigham,[6] Franks, Broyles, and Carleton,[7] and Siegel[8] state that the arithmetic mean is the appropriate measure to use. Jacob and Pettit,[9] Levy and Sarnat,[10] Moyer, McGuigan, and Kretlow,[11] Reilly,[12] Schall and Haley,[13] and Weston and Copeland[14] either state that the geometric mean is the correct measure or else cite Ibbotson and Sinquefield's historical study of arithmetic and geometric risk premiums and quote a range for the market risk premium that is only consistent with the geometric mean.[15] Others, such as

---

4. In addition to these three issues, there is the more fundamental issue as to whether the CAPM is the correct model to use or whether there is some alternative to the CAPM, such as a model based on arbitrage pricing theory (APT), that might be superior to CAPM. Among the earliest papers to raise this question were Richard Roll, "A Critique of the Asset Pricing Theory's Tests," *Journal of Financial Economics 4* (March 1977): 129–76; Richard Roll and Stephen A. Ross, "An Empirical Investigation of the Arbitrage Pricing Theory," *Journal of Finance 35* (December 1980): 1073–1103; and Stephen A. Ross, "The Arbitrage Theory of Capital Asset Pricing," *Journal of Economic Theory 13* (December 1976): 341–60. Sharpe analyzes the principal differences between CAPM, APT, and other asset pricing models and explains how these competing models might be reconciled. See William F. Sharpe, "Factor Models, CAPMs, and the APT," *The Journal of Portfolio Management 11* (Fall 1984): 21–25.
5. Richard Brealey and Stewart Myers, *Principles of Corporate Finance,* 2nd ed. (New York: McGraw-Hill, 1984).
6. Eugene F. Brigham, *Financial Management: Theory and Practice,* 3rd ed. (Chicago: Dryden, 1982).
7. Julian R. Franks, John E. Broyles, and Willard T. Carleton, *Corporate Finance* (Boston: Kent, 1985).
8. Siegel, *Stocks, Bonds, Bills, and Inflation, 1987 Yearbook.*
9. Nancy L. Jacob and R. Richardson Pettit, *Investments* (Homewood, Ill.: Richard D. Irwin, 1984).
10. Haim Levy and Marshall Sarnat, *Capital Investment and Financial Decisions,* 3rd ed. (Englewood Cliffs, N.J.: Prentice-Hall, 1986).
11. R. Charles Moyer, James R. McGuigan, and William J. Kretlow, *Contemporary Financial Management,* 2nd ed. (St. Paul, Minn.: West, 1984).
12. Frank K. Reilly, *Investments,* 2nd ed. (Chicago: Dryden, 1986).
13. Lawrence D. Schall and Charles W. Haley, *Introduction to Financial Management,* 4th ed. (New York: McGraw-Hill, 1986).
14. J. Fred Weston and Thomas E. Copeland, *Managerial Finance,* 8th ed. (Chicago: Dryden, 1986).
15. For example, Moyer et al. (*Contemporary Financial Management,* p. 363) state that "the average market risk premium should be in the 5 to 7 percent range." Schall and Haley (*Introduction to Financial Management,* p. 190) calculate a 6.1 percent risk premium on the market

Francis,[16] Harrington,[17] Sharpe,[18] and Van Horne,[19] make no attempt to resolve the issue.[20]

This article demonstrates that the arithmetic mean, rather than the geometric mean, should be used to measure the expected risk premium on the market portfolio.

II. Why the Choice of Mean Matters

In the two-factor CAPM, the one-period expected rate of return is

$$E[\tilde{R}] = r_f + B \cdot (E[\tilde{R}_m] - r_f) = r_f + B \cdot E[\tilde{r}_m], \tag{1}$$

where the tilde denotes a random variable and where $E[\tilde{R}]$ denotes the expected rate of return, r_f denotes the risk-free rate, B denotes the security's beta, $E[\tilde{R}_m]$ denotes the expected rate of return on the market portfolio, and $E[\tilde{r}_m]$ denotes the expected risk premium on the market portfolio. For the market portfolio, $B = 1$.

Siegel[21] reports that the arithmetic mean of the annual risk premiums on the market portfolio was 8.6 percent over the 61-year period 1926–1986 and that the geometric mean of the annual risk premiums was 6.3 percent over the same period. Consider a stock for which $B = 1$ and suppose $r_f = 8$ percent. Using the arithmetic mean as the measure of the market risk premium implies a required rate of return, R, of

---

portfolio. Weston and Copeland (*Managerial Finance,* p. 433) state that "returns on the market for long periods have been shown...to be at the 9 to 11 percent level. The level of [the risk-free rate] has been characteristically at the 4 to 6 percent level." This implies a market risk premium of 5 to 7 percent. Ibbotson and Sinquefield (*Stocks, Bonds, Bills, and Inflation,* p. 71) report a geometric mean of 5.9 percent and an arithmetic mean of 8.3 percent for the risk premium on the market portfolio. Siegel (*Stocks, Bonds, Bills, and Inflation, 1987 Yearbook,* p. 46) reports a geometric mean of 6.3 percent and an arithmetic mean of 8.6 percent.

16. Jack Clark Francis, *Investments,* 4th ed. (New York: McGraw-Hill, 1986).

17. Diana R. Harrington, *Modern Portfolio Theory and the Capital Asset Pricing Model* (Englewood Cliffs, N.J.: Prentice-Hall, 1983).

18. William F. Sharpe, *Investments,* 3rd ed. (Englewood Cliffs, N.J.: Prentice-Hall, 1985).

19. James C. Van Horne, *Financial Management and Policy,* 7th ed. (Englewood Cliffs, N.J.: Prentice-Hall, 1986).

20. Francis (*Investments,* pp. 924–29) devotes an entire appendix to a discussion of the geometric mean versus the arithmetic mean without ever addressing this particular issue. Harrington (*Modern Portfolio Theory and the Capital Asset Pricing Model,* p. 125) says simply that "analysts using history to project market returns must choose between arithmetic and geometric methods." Van Horne (*Financial Management and Policy,* p. 213) states that "the expected return on the market portfolio has exceeded the risk-free rate by anywhere from 3 to 7 percent in recent years." This seems more consistent with the geometric mean than with the arithmetic mean although the qualifying phrase "in recent years" clouds the meaning of Van Horne's statement.

21. Siegel, *Stocks, Bonds, Bills, and Inflation, 1987 Yearbook,* p. 46.

$$R = 8\% + (1 \times 8.6\%) = 16.6\%.$$

Using the geometric mean implies a required rate of return of

$$R = 8\% + (1 \times 6.3\%) = 14.3\%.$$

The two estimates differ by 230 basis points. A value for beta greater than 1 would, of course, magnify the effect on the required rate of return of the difference between the arithmetic mean and the geometric mean. In any case a difference of 230 basis points is large enough to affect an investment decision.

Consider a block of common stock that is expected to yield a stream of cash dividends amounting to $10 million per year for 10 years and to be worth $75 million (based on the current price earnings multiple applied to projected future earnings) at the end of 10 years. Discounting this stream at the 16.6 percent rate gives a present value of $63.4 million. Discounting instead at the 14.3 percent rate gives a present value of $71.3 million, which is $7.9 million or 12 percent greater than the $63.4 million value. Which value is correct? The difference is large enough to affect an investor's willingness to purchase the block. Suppose the block were offered at an aggregate price of $67 million. Using the geometric mean as the measure of the market risk premium would favor making the investment, but using the arithmetic mean as the market risk premium would favor not making the investment.

III. Justification for the Arithmetic Mean

For a sample consisting of N returns $\{r_1, r_2, \ldots, r_N\}$, each $r_n > -1$, the arithmetic mean is defined as

$$A = (1/N) \sum_{n=1}^{N} r_n, \tag{2}$$

and the geometric mean is defined as

$$G = \left[\prod_{n=1}^{N} (1+r_n) \right]^{1/N} - 1. \tag{3}$$

$G < A$ unless $r_n = r$ for all n, in which case $G = A$.[22]

Assume that in each future period there are K possible annual risk premiums on the market portfolio, which are denoted r_k, $k = 1, \ldots, K$, and that the distributions of the $r_k(t)$ are independent and identical for all years with

---

22. Franco Modigliani and Gerald A. Pogue, "An Introduction to Risk and Return: Concepts and Evidence, Part I," *Financial Analysts Journal* 30 (March-April 1974): 68–80.

common mean μ. Also assume, for the sake of convenience only, that all the r_k are equally likely in any year and that r_f is constant over time.[23]

Let $E[\tilde{r}_m]$ denote the expected risk premium on the market portfolio for a T-period investment holding period. $E[\tilde{r}_m]$ equals the expected total rate of return on the market portfolio over T periods per dollar invested minus one (to get the expected risk-adjusted rate of return) minus also the risk-free rate (to get the expected risk premium). The expected total rate of return over T periods equals the Tth root of the expected compound amount after T periods.

First consider the case in which there are two periods ($T=2$) and two possible values for the market risk premium in each period, $r_1 = .3083$ and $r_2 = -.1363$. Suppose the risk-free rate is 8 percent. There are four possible compound amounts as of the end of the second period per dollar of initial wealth:

$$\$1 \begin{cases} (1+.08+.3083)\cdot(1+.08+.3083) \\ (1+.08+.3083)\cdot(1+.08-.1363) \\ (1+.08-.1363)\cdot(1+.08+.3083) \\ (1+.08-.1363)\cdot(1+.08-.1363) \end{cases}$$

all of which are equally likely. The expected future risk premium on the market portfolio is

$$\begin{aligned} E[\tilde{r}_m] &= [(1/4)(1.3883)^2 + (1/2)(1.3883)(0.9437) \\ &\quad + (1/4)(0.9437)^2]^{1/2} - 1 - .08 \\ &= ([(1/2)(1.3883) + (1/2)(0.9437)]^2)^{1/2} - 1.08 \\ &= (1/2)(1.3883) + (1/2)(0.9437) - 1.08 \\ &= .086, \text{ or } 8.6\%. \end{aligned} \tag{4}$$

Note that the arithmetic mean of the historical risk premiums is also 8.6 percent:

$$\mu = \frac{.3083 + (-.1363)}{2} = .086.$$

Under the assumption that the process generating the risk premiums on the market portfolio remains stationary over time, the maximum likelihood estimator for the expected future risk premium on the market portfolio is the arithmetic mean of the historical risk premiums.

---

23. The results developed below could also be derived for the more general case in which the probability of each r_k is p_k, where $0 < p_k < 1$ for all k and

$$\sum_{k=1}^{K} p_k = 1.$$

Generalizing to $T > 2$ periods, the terminal portfolio wealth at the end of T periods per dollar of initial wealth is the compound amount

$$W(T) = \prod_{t=1}^{T} (1 + r_f + \tilde{r}_k(t)). \tag{5}$$

There are K^T possible realizations of equation (5), not all of which are different from one another. The expected risk premium on the market portfolio is

$$E[\tilde{r}_m] = \left[\sum_{j=1}^{K^T} \left\{ (1/K^T) \prod_{t=1}^{T} (1 + r_f + r_k(t)) \right\} \right]^{1/T} - 1 - r_f$$

$$= (1/K) \left[\sum_{j=1}^{K^T} \prod_{t=1}^{T} (1 + r_f + r_k(t)) \right]^{1/T} - 1 - r_f. \tag{6}$$

By applying the binomial theorem, equation (6) can be rewritten as

$$E[\tilde{r}_m] = (1/K) \left[\left\{ \sum_{k=1}^{K} (1 + r_f + r_k) \right\}^{T} \right]^{1/T} - 1 - r_f$$

$$= (1/K) \sum_{k=1}^{K} r_k = \mu, \tag{7}$$

the arithmetic mean of the historical risk premiums.

IV. Interpretation of the Geometric Mean

Suppose the market risk premiums are not identically distributed but instead are generated by a process that will never generate any historical market risk premium a second time until each of them has occurred once. Consider again the two-period example discussed earlier. Suppose that either $r_1 = .3083$ or $r_2 = -.1363$ can occur the first period. Under the foregoing assumption, whichever one does not occur the first period must occur the second. What is the expected risk premium on the market portfolio in that case?

Denote the expected risk premium on the market portfolio $E[\tilde{r}_m(2)]$ to distinguish it from $E[\tilde{r}_m]$ in equation (4). There are two possible realizations of the two-period compound amount per dollar of initial wealth. These are equally likely and of the form $(1 + .08 + .3083)(1 + .08 - .1363)$. Thus the expected risk premium is

$$E[\tilde{r}_m(2)] = [(1/2)(1.3883)(0.9437) + (1/2)(1.3883)(0.9437)]^{1/2}$$
$$- 1 - .08$$
$$= [(1.3883)(0.9437)]^{1/2} - 1 - .08$$
$$= .065, \text{ or } 6.5\%.$$

The geometric mean of the historical risk premiums $r_1 = .3083$ and $r_2 = -.1363$ is

$$G = [(1+.3083)(1-.1363)]^{1/2} - 1 = .063, \text{ or } 6.3\%.$$

The geometric mean of the historical risk premiums, 6.3 percent, closely approximates the expected risk premium on the market portfolio under the assumption that the historical risk premiums are regenerated in the future in such a way that each historical risk premium incorporated in the calculation of the geometric mean cannot occur a second time until all the others incorporated in that calculation have occurred. Such an assumption seems unusually restrictive.

V. Conclusion

There has been disagreement regarding the correct procedure for calculating the risk premium on the market portfolio in the CAPM. This article demonstrates that the arithmetic mean, rather than the geometric mean, is the correct measure of the expected market risk premium. Resolution of this disagreement is important. Using the wrong value for the market risk premium leads to asset valuation errors, which can lead to incorrect investment decisions.

14

The Uses of Options in Performance Structuring*

Richard Bookstaber
Principal
Morgan Stanley & Co., Inc.

I. Introduction

During the first ten years of listed option trading, options were viewed as tactical, if not outright speculative, instruments. Investors purchased calls to gain leverage, bought puts to lock in gains or speculate on declines, and used covered writes to enhance yields on sluggish issues. The implications of options positions for the return characteristics of the overall portfolio were rarely a consideration; the concern in option trading was trade-by-trade profitability, not cumulative portfolio effects. As option markets have matured, however, and as new instruments, such as index and interest rate options and futures, have been introduced to address the major sources of financial risk, the emphasis has shifted toward using options strategically in portfolio management.

The purpose of this article is to address the role of options in portfolio management; to explain the concepts behind option-related techniques for structuring portfolio returns and controlling financial risks, and to lay out both the opportunities and difficulties these techniques present.

The topic of options we will address is more general than it might at first seem. Broadly speaking, options are instruments with a payoff that is

---

*Reprinted from the Summer 1985 issue of *The Journal of Portfolio Management*.

contingent on the value of another, underlying security. Listed options are traded on a number of exchanges, but options can also be traded over the counter and, most important, can be created synthetically through the proper set of transactions in other securities. Listed options, while the most visible option contracts, are only a small part of the picture.

When dealing with option strategies, the topic of portfolio management also covers a broad area. We can think of portfolio management as the management of overall investment or financial risk. Besides the management of equity and bond investment portfolios, portfolio management includes balancing asset and liability risk in banks and in savings and loans, creating payment streams to match obligations in insurance companies and pension funds, and constructing securities to satisfy the financing patterns required by corporations.

Portfolio management is typically approached as a two-dimensional tradeoff between the mean and variance of returns. The mix of risky assets and cash is the only tool that managers have at their disposal in adjusting the portfolio. The mix dictates the mean-variance tradeoff the portfolio will face.

Figures 1a and 1b illustrate this tradeoff. These figures depict portfolio returns with the familiar bell-shaped curve of the normal distribution. In

FIGURE 1a.

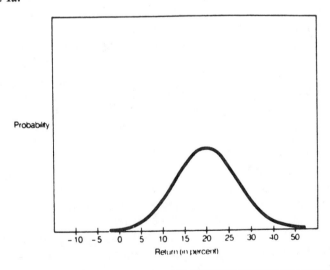

Return distribution of a stock portfolio. Mean return is 20 percent, with a standard deviation of 30 percent.

FIGURE 1b.

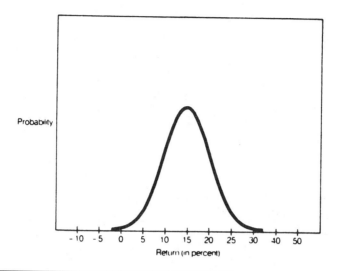

Return distribution of a stock portfolio. Mean return is 15 percent, with a standard deviation of 20 percent. Compared to the return portfolio of Figure 1a, the investor has both lower expected return and lower risk. The returns continue to be normally distributed, however.

this setting, a two-dimensional mean-variance tradeoff is a natural way of looking at returns, since the mean and variance completely describe the normal distribution. A more conservative manager will move funds from risky assets into cash, ending up with a return distribution such as Figure 1b, with less variance and a lower expected return. A more aggressive manager will go in the opposite direction, levering to achieve a higher expected return at the cost of higher variance. In either case, the manager can measure the alterations in the structure of returns simply in terms of mean and variance.

Comfortable and intuitive though it is, this two-dimensional tradeoff will not always result in a return distribution that meets portfolio objectives. A manager might prefer to control some other aspect of returns. For example, a manager may wish to achieve some guaranteed minimum return while retaining a portion of the upward return potential.[1] This objective would

1. The desirability of this type of insured portfolio is discussed in H. Leland, "Who Should Buy Portfolio Insurance?" *Journal of Finance* 35 (May 1980): 581–94 and M. Brennan and R. Solanki, "Optimal Portfolio Insurance," *Journal of Financial and Quantitative Analysis* 16 (September 1981): 279–300. Skewness preference, i.e., a preference for a return distribution characterized by a degree of skewness as well as mean and variance, is discussed in A. Kraus and R. Litzenberger, "Skewness Preference and the Valuation of Risky Assets," *Journal of Finance* 31 (September 1976): 1085–1100.

FIGURE 1c.

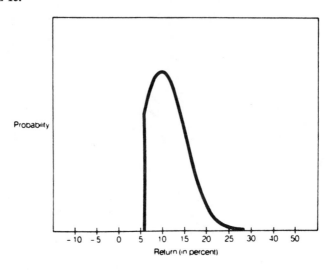

The return distribution that might be preferred by the portfolio manager. The probability of a large loss is eliminated.

imply a non-symmetric return distribution such as that shown in Figure 1c. This distribution truncates the downside risk while the right-hand tail still maintains some of the upside potential. Forming this return distribution requires more than mean-variance tradeoffs — it cannot be constructed using the conventional procedures of portfolio management.

The ability to form distributions of this type may have a value far beyond simply meeting subjective preferences. For example, the very pattern of liabilities may lead to a need for non-symmetric, non-normal returns. The obligation of a pension fund to meet a minimum actuarial payoff would lead to a return distribution like that shown in Figure 1c. Other complex payoffs, such as those generated by the carefully tailored annuity products of the life insurance industry or the variable rate liabilities of many corporations and thrift institutions, will lead to return objectives that cannot be met by simple mean-variance adjustments.

Options are the building blocks for constructing the payoffs to meet these complex return objectives. We can use options to create the portfolio insurance depicted in Figure 1c, or to mold returns to conform with virtually any other feasible distribution. This capacity for options to expand the set of contingencies has been established theoretically.[2] Here we will deal with the practical issues of how managers can implement these strategies.

2. See S. Ross, "Options and Efficiency," *Quarterly Journal of Economics* 90 (February 1987):

II. The Insurance Feature of Option Contracts

Let us begin by looking at an option as an insurance contract. The premium for the insurance is part of the option price. The variety of payoffs from option strategies comes from taking selective positions in the insurance — buying some insurance protection over one range of security prices, selling some insurance over another.

We can see the essential insurance feature of an option contract by constructing an option through an insurance-motivated transaction. Suppose an investor buys a security worth $1200 by investing $200 directly and borrowing the remaining $1000. The security is retained as collateral by the lender, to be released to the investor in one year upon repayment of the $1000 loan. Further, suppose the investor wishes to have protection should the security decline in value before the loan comes due and therefore arranges for the loan on a no-recourse basis. Then, if the investor fails to make the $1000 payment in one year, the lender will receive ownership of the security and will have no further recourse to the investor. This no-recourse feature amounts to giving the investor an insurance contract on the investment, with a deductible equal to the $200 initial investment.

At the end of the year, what will be the best strategy for the investor to pursue? Obviously, the investor will pay back the loan if the security value at the end of the year is at least as great as the $1000 necessary to gain clear ownership. The investor's profit in doing so will be the security value, S^*, less the loan payment, or $S^* - 1000$. If the security is worth less than the loan payment, the investor will be better off simply to walk away from the loan and let the lender take ownership, since the $1000 payment to claim the security will net the investor a loss. The payoff pattern from this insured loan is identical to that of a call option on the security with an exercise price of $1000. The call option gives the right to buy the security for $1000 and has a payoff that is the security price minus the exercise price, $S^* - 1000$, or zero, whichever is greater.

Using this no-recourse loan as a vehicle for analyzing a call option, we see the price of the call option can be broken up into three parts. First, there is the initial payment of $200. This payment, the difference between the security price and the $1000 exercise price, is called the *intrinsic value* of the option. Second, there is an interest carrying cost from holding the security in escrow. The investor pays the exercise price at the end of the year, but the lender has the $1000 tied up in the security over the loan period. Given an interest rate of r, this interest cost will be $(r/(1+r))1000$. The third part of the

75–89; D. Breeden and R. Litzenberger, "Prices of State-Contingent Claims Implicit in Option Prices," *Journal of Business* 52 (October 1978): 621–51; and F. Arditti and K. John, "Spanning the State Space with Options," *Journal of Financial and Quantitative Analysis* 15 (March 1980): 1–19.

option price is the insurance cost of the downside protection. Since the lender is absorbing the loss, there will be an insurance premium, P, implicit in the price of the call option.

Combining these three terms, and denoting the exercise price by E, we can express the call option as

$$C = (S-E) + E(r/(1+r)) + P.$$

This expression shows the option price consists of intrinsic value, prepaid interest, and insurance against loss.

To gain more insight into the nature of the insurance premium, P, consider the contract the lender would need in order to overcome the risk from the loan's no-recourse feature. If the security is worth more than the exercise price at the end of the year, the lender will receive the $1000 payment and no other compensation will be necessary. If the value is less than the exercise price, the lender will have paid $1000 for a security that is now worth less than that; the lender will have lost $1000 - S^*$. The compensating contract, then, must give a payout equal to the difference between the exercise price and security price when the security price is less than the exercise price; it must give no payout when the security price is equal to or greater than the exercise price. This is exactly the payout given by a *put option*. A put option gives the right to sell the underlying security at the exercise price; its payout is the maximum of zero and $(E-S)$, the exercise price minus the security price.

Put and Call Options Redefined

The insurance premium for the no-recourse loan, P, is thus equal to a put option with one year to maturity and an exercise price of $1000. In this context, then, we can define a call option and a put option as follows:

Call option: A contract giving the holder the underlying security at maturity while insuring against any loss during the term of the contract beyond a deductible equal to the intrinsic value of the option.

Put option: An insurance contract that pays off to cover fully any security price decline below the face value of the contract, which is the put option's exercise price.

Some of the characteristics of option pricing are evident from viewing options in this insurance context. First, just as insurance premiums increase with an increase in riskiness, so option prices increase with an increase in the price volatility of the security. Second, call prices are an increasing function of interest rates, since higher interest rates increase the interest carrying cost. Third, just as insurance premiums decline as the amount of the deductible increases, so the insurance cost, P, drops as the intrinsic value of the call option increases. Fourth, the longer the term of the coverage,

TABLE 1.

Security Price	Value of Option with Exercise Price of $49	Value of Option with Exercise Price of $50	Value of Option with Exercise Price of $51	Total Strategy Value
—	—	—	—	—
—	—	—	—	—
—	—	—	—	—
46	0	0	0	0
47	0	0	0	0
48	0	0	0	0
49	0	0	0	0
50	1	0	0	1
51	2	−2	0	0
52	3	−4	1	0
53	4	−6	2	0
—	—	—	—	—
—	—	—	—	—
—	—	—	—	—

i.e., the longer the time to expiration of the option, the more the option will cost.[3]

Different patterns of returns are possible by properly selecting the option coverage. Indeed, given options at all exercise prices and all times to expiration, we could construct the entire range of attainable return structures.

To see this more concretely, consider a strategy of buying one option with an exercise price of $100, writing two options each with an exercise price of $101, and buying one option with an exercise price of $102. This position, called a butterfly spread, will lead to a payoff of $1 if the underlying security is at $100 at the time of option expiration, and a payoff of zero otherwise. Such a binary payoff can be used as the basic building block from any payoff schedule (see Table 1).[4]

Obviously, only a small part of this set of options are actually traded on the listed exchanges. These institutional limitations would seem to be a serious constraint for turning the great theoretical potential of performance

---

3. These characteristics, and a readable presentation of the nature of option pricing, can be found in R. Bookstaber, *Option Pricing and Investment Strategies* (Chicago: Probus Publishing, 1987). A more rigorous and detailed treatment can be found in J. Cox and M. Rubinstein, *Option Markets* (Englewood Cliffs, N.J.: Prentice-Hall, 1985).
4. The creation of these binary payoffs, called primitive securities, through the use of option positions is covered in Breeden and Litzenberger, "Skewness Preference."

structuring into a real opportunity. As we will see in the next section, however, we are not restricted to listed options. We can construct synthetic options of any exercise price and any time to expiration through the use of dynamic trading strategies.

III. The Creation of Option Positions Using Dynamic Trading Techniques

The key difficulty in employing option methods is that the appropriate option contracts often do not exist in the market place. While a growing number of markets and securities are covered by option instruments, these may not match the terms of the option contract required for the portfolio strategy. For example, the maturity of the traded options may not match the manager's time horizon, or the security underlying the option contract may not match the asset mix of the portfolio. Fortunately, the principles of option theory can be applied to create the option contract synthetically even when the required option does not exist in the market. This is done by a dynamic reallocation of funds across sets of assets, or by a dynamic readjustment of positions in listed options and futures contracts.

To develop the dynamic strategy, we will concentrate on the creation of insurance provided by the protective put option. We can apply the same principles in forming other option positions and creating other return structures.

Dynamic Strategies as Multi-Point Stop-Loss Strategies

The simplest and most widely known technique for achieving downside protection is the stop-loss order. An investor can assure a $100 floor on a security price by stopping out of the security at a price equal to the present value of $100, $100(1/(1+r))^T$ and putting the funds in the risk-free asset for the remaining time period, T. Once stopped out, the funds will accrue interest at the rate r and will be worth $100 at the end of the time period.

For example, if there is a year left in the holding period for the strategy and if r is 10%, then the security would be stopped out at $91. Putting the $91 in the risk-free asset at 10% would give the desired $100 return by the end of the year.

Figure 2 illustrates this stop-loss order. The figure overlays the security price with the percentage of the portfolio invested in the security. Note that the level of the stop approaches the floor as the end of the holding period approaches, because the funds have less and less time to accrue interest. Once the security price drops below the stop, all funds are taken out of the security.

This insurance method is effective, but is also costly. It fails to take into account the possibility that the security may rebound from the decline, eliminating any possibility of sharing in later increases in the security price.

FIGURE 2. *Investment Pattern for a One-Point Stop-Loss Strategy.*

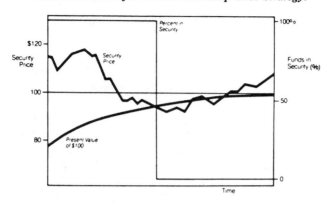

We can remedy this deficiency to a limited degree by allowing the stop to be reversible. Rather than pursuing this one-point stop-loss strategy, suppose we employ a two-point strategy where the investment is stopped out of the security when the price drops below the stop, and the security is bought when the price moves back through the stop-loss point. This will allow the required downside protection while no longer shutting the investor completely out of possible appreciation. This strategy is illustrated in Figure 3.

This two-point strategy, while superior to the simple stop-loss strategy, still imposes its own costs. In addition to imposing greater transaction costs, every reversal leads to a loss equal to the distance between the selling and buying point. Setting the points close together will not eliminate these costs.

FIGURE 3. *Investment Pattern for a Two-Point Stop-Loss Strategy.*

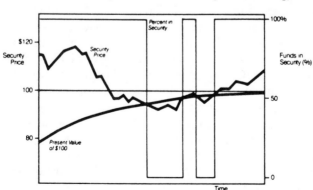

The closer these two points, the smaller the cost per reversal but the more frequently such reversals will occur. This cost will be greatest if the security vibrates around the breakeven point and will be smallest if the breakeven point is never hit.

Both the nonreversible one-point stop-loss strategy and the two-point stop-loss strategy will thus lead to a reduction in the expected return. This risk-return tradeoff is as expected, since the strategies provide a reduction of downside risk. The two-point stop-loss strategy will have the higher return, since it gives the opportunity to gain from price appreciation.

Given the results of the two-point strategy, we should logically consider the effects of extending the flexibility further. If we are confident the security in question will remain risky over the holding period—that is, if we believe the security will continue to be volatile—then there is no need to sell off completely when the security reaches the breakeven point of $100(1/(1+r))^T$. Instead, we might move in or out of the security gradually as the security moves away from the breakeven point. This will lessen the chance of being whipsawed by repeated reversals.

Given the time left in the holding period, security volatility will make periodic moves around the breakeven point likely. Such moves will be more likely the longer the time left, the greater the volatility, and the closer the security price is to the breakeven point. Accordingly, the proportion of the security we stop out should take all of these factors into account. Furthermore, the breakeven point for the stop will change over time and with interest rates.

Thus, the rule we use for moving in and out of the security should be a function of the security price, the insured price, the holding period of the strategy, the interest rate, and the volatility of the security. Since these stop-loss strategies all mimic the sort of non-linearities common to options, it is not surprising these are the same factors we discussed above as determining the price of an option.

Obviously, an unlimited number of stop-loss adjustments are available to use with these factors in mind. Figure 4 shows the return to one particular strategy. With this alternative, we hold 50% of the funds in the security and 50% in the risk-free asset when we hit the breakeven point; we move completely in or out of the security only when the price has moved a significant distance away from the breakeven point. We let this strategy stop out completely at a point with twice the time factor as the breakeven point, $100 \times (1/(1+r))^{2T}$, stop out one half at the breakeven point, $100(1/(1+r))^2$, and fully invest at $100(1+r)^T$. This three-point stop-loss strategy continues to give the required protection. Furthermore, by making finer adjustments and by retaining a partial holding over more of the range of the security price, the strategy will provide the protection for the least cost of the three strategies considered so far.

FIGURE 4. *Investment Pattern for a Three-Point Stop-Loss Strategy.*

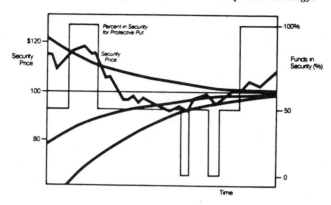

A Put Option as the Least-Cost Insurance Strategy

A cost is imposed by the insurance protection because the dynamic adjustments gradually pull funds out of the security as it declines and only gradually put funds back into the security as it appreciates. Hence, the insured position cannot fully participate in the appreciation.

Our objective is to find the lowest-cost insurance contract. The best adjustment strategy will be the strategy that provides the downside protection for a predetermined cost while allowing the greatest sharing of security appreciation on the upside. We already know that the put option represents such an insurance contract for protecting against downside risk. If we could find a dynamic stopless strategy that replicated the behavior of a put option with a time to expiration equal to the investor's time horizon, and an exercise price of $100, we would have protection that precisely meets the insurance objectives, and, given efficient markets, that gives the protection at the lowest defined price.

All three stop-loss strategies considered above approximate a put option. They all give downside protection similar to that of a put option. And, like a put option, the two-point and three-point stop-loss strategies share in some of the upward potential of the security as well. On the other hand, they are not perfect replicas of a put option; they move in jumps as the security price changes, rather than in the smooth, continuous fashion of a put option. Nevertheless, they do suggest that an extension of the dynamic stop-loss strategy will move us closer to the pure option protection desired.

Option pricing theory has shown this is in fact the case; we can create an option position by pursuing a strategy that dynamically adjusts the proportion of the underlying security and the risk-free asset.[5] Since an option can be replicated by such a strategy, this further implies the option price must always equal the cost of this replicating portfolio.

We can write the call option and put option equations as:

$$C = a_c - b_c B$$

and

$$P = -a_p S + b_p B,$$

where S is the security price, B is the price of the risk-free bond, and where the values of a_c, a_p, b_c, and b_p are proportionality factors that take on values between zero and one.[6]

The call option is created by borrowing money at the risk-free rate (borrowing is implied by a negative value for b_c) and using it to purchase an amount a_c of the security. The borrowing leads to the leverage that is characteristic of a call option. The put is created by shorting the security (shorting is implied by a negative value for a_p) and putting an amount equal to b_p into the risk-free asset. When the put option position is combined with a long position in the security to form an insured position, the net effect of combining the initial long position in the security with the short position required to replicate the put option is a positive, but less than full, investment in the security.[7]

---

5. The procedure for replicating an option through a dynamically adjusted position in the underlying security and risk-free asset is implied in the original work on option pricing in F. Black and M. Scholes, "The Pricing of Options and Corporate Liabilities," *Journal of Political Economy* 81 (May 1973): 637–54 and R. Merton, "Theory of Rational Option Pricing," *Bell Journal of Economics and Management Science* 4 (Spring 1973): 141–83. This procedure is discussed in simpler terms in Chapter 4 of Bookstaber, *Option Strategies* and M. Rubinstein and H. Leland, "Replicating Options with Positions in Stock and Cash," *Financial Analysts Journal* 37 (July 1981): 63–72. Other hedging strategies can be constructed that give the same protection as this put option and may even do so for a lower expected cost. The cost of these alternatives would be uncertain and would depend on the path of price, so we do not pursue them further here.

6. The exact functional form these factors take on depends on the assumptions of the model being used, particularly the distributional assumptions. If stock prices are assumed to be described by a lognormal distribution, the well-known Black–Scholes model will be appropriate.

7. The portfolio for replicating a put option is directly related to the replicating portfolio for a call option. This relationship can be expressed by the put-call parity formula presented in the first section of this article:

$$C = (S - E) + E(r/(1 + r)) + P,$$

or

$$C = S - E(1/(1 + r)) + P.$$

As this formula shows, a call option can be created by holding the security, S, borrowing $E(1/(1 + r))$, and thus repaying E at expiration, and holding a put option. This creates a pro-

FIGURE 5. *Investment Pattern for a Protective Put Option Strategy, Compared with the Three-Point Stop-Loss of Figure 4.*

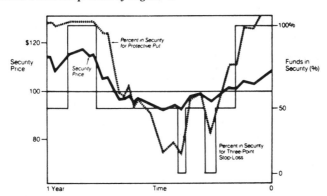

As was suggested by the three-point stop-loss strategy, the proportion of stocks and bonds in the option replication varies both over time and as the security price changes. The replicating portfolio must be continuously adjusted; hence, the dynamic nature of the strategy. The proportion terms a_c, a_p, b_c and b_p are not constants; rather, they are variables that will change with the time to the maturity of the holding period and with changes in the security price. As the three-point strategy further suggests, these terms will also be a function of the volatility of the security and the riskless interest rate.

Figure 5 illustrates the proportion of investment in the security when the investor follows the dynamic stop-loss adjustment of the protective put option strategy. This strategy provides the complete downside protection at the lowest defined cost. The strategy is overlaid on the three-point strategy described in Figure 4.

The naive one-point stop-loss strategy has been proposed in a number of insurance settings. For example, the original construction of the contingent immunization strategy for bond portfolios involves stopping out of an interest-sensitive bond position once a critical portfolio price or interest rate level is passed.[8] It should be clear from this discussion that such strategies,

---

tective put on a portfolio that is similar to holding a call option on the portfolio. In fact, the only difference between the two is that a call option is levered through borrowing while the protective put position is not.

8. For example, see M. Leibowitz and A. Weinberger, "Contingent Immunization, Part I: Risk Control Procedures," *Financial Analysts Journal* 38 (November/December 1982): 17–31.

while providing the desired protection, are a more costly means of securing that protection than a strategy that more closely approximates the return structure of a put option.

IV. Variations on the Dynamic Strategy Using Listed Futures and Option Contracts

As with any strategy, the dynamic strategy presents practical difficulties. These include:

1. *The need for continuous adjustment.* Theoretically, the option position requires continuous portfolio adjustments. The appropriate mix of the security and riskless asset changes over time and with changes in the security price. Discrete adjustments, by failing to account for the continuous nature of the movement of the security price and of time, will lead to a margin of error in the payoff of the option, as well as in its cost.
2. *The accurate estimation of security price volatility.* The appropriate portfolio mix will also depend on the volatility of the security. A highly volatile security will be more costly to insure, since the adjustments will catch less of each price swing. If the volatility of the security is forecast incorrectly, the result may lead to a higher cost or to less than complete protection.
3. *The specification of the stochastic process driving security prices.* The functional form of the proportionality terms in the option model depends on the nature of security price movements. The direction of the price movements has no bearing on the option model, but the way price movements tend to evolve does matter. For example, a security price that is typified by large periodic jumps will lead to a model specification, and hence to a different dynamic strategy, than a security whose price never experiences discrete jumps. Accuracy in the specification of the stochastic process is as important as accuracy in the estimation of the security price volatility emerging from that process.[9]

Just how critical these factors are to the successful implementation of the dynamic option strategies is an empirical question that cannot be answered here. Some of these problems are mitigated by using listed futures and option contracts in forming the dynamic strategy. We will discuss these variations on the dynamic strategy next.

---

9. In particular, if there are sudden jumps in the underlying security while the Black–Scholes model is being used, the position will be subject to unexpected losses. The strategy will be unsuccessful in replicating an option position.

Using Futures in Dynamic Strategies

The essential feature of the dynamic strategy is that the position in the security varies as the time to maturity and the security price vary. Obviously, one way to vary the size of the position is by transacting directly in the security itself. When there are futures on the security, we can also vary the position by leaving the actual security holdings unchanged and transacting in the futures contract instead.

For example, a put option on a well-diversified stock portfolio can be replicated by using a short position in an index future. As the portfolio value declines, requiring a smaller position in the portfolio, the short position will be increased. The short position will react in a direction opposite the portfolio position, leaving a net return to market movements that is essentially the same as if a portion of the portfolio itself had been sold off and transferred to the risk-free asset. The futures act as a damper on the effective portfolio position. The futures position is an alternative for the construction of dynamic strategies for any position that is highly correlated with the movement of traded futures, be they stocks, stock portfolios, bonds, foreign exchange, metals, or commodities.

Futures have a number of attractive features. First, because they combine a position in the asset with borrowing, they can lead to less costly transactions than the investor would incur with transfers between the security and cash. Second, execution is often better in the futures than in the cash market. This is particularly true when a single futures contract can be substituted for a portfolio-wide transaction, as in the case of stock or bond portfolios. Third, since futures are levered instruments, less cash is necessary to carry out the dynamic strategy.

The third point is especially important when the dynamic strategy is pursued separately from the portfolio holdings. For example, consider a pension sponsor with a number of outside managers, each managing a fraction of the fund. If the sponsor decides to pursue a dynamic strategy, the sponsor could conceivably have each manager restructure its management methods to incorporate the dynamic strategy.

There are obvious practical and administrative difficulties in doing this. And even if it were done successfully, the end result of having options on each of the individual portfolios would be an inefficient means of attaining the desired option on the overall pension fund investment.[10] On the other hand, the alternative of having the sponsor retain enough of the fund to

---

10. This happens because an option on a portfolio of securities will not behave in the same way as a portfolio of options on each of the individual securities. The portfolio of options will be more expensive than the option on the portfolio. This is discussed in Merton, "Theory of Rational Option Pricing."

make the market/cash adjustments itself would greatly reduce the amount retained under the outside managers, and would therefore change the character of the fund.

We can overcome these difficulties by using futures as the vehicle for making the dynamic adjustments. The pension fund sponsor, pursuing a dynamic strategy with futures, would need only retain enough cash to meet margin requirements. The sponsor could monitor its overall fund value, and, assuming its holdings are closely correlated with the overall market, use index futures to create a position that would be equivalent to selling off the necessary proportion of its holdings. The sponsor could do this without making any alteration in the managers' roles, without significant changes in the amount under management, even without the knowledge of the managers. With protection against poor performance, any superior management performance will still lead to relative performance gains under the dynamic strategy.

Strictly speaking, the replication of a put or call option requires a proper balancing of positions in the riskless asset as well as risky security. The position in the riskless asset serves to make the position self-financing, i.e., the position neither requires further funding nor gives out payments from the time it is initiated until the expiration of the option contract. The self-financing feature is critical to the theoretical development of option pricing. Options are, after all, self-financing instruments: Once an option is purchased, no cash flow takes place until its exercise or expiration. Shifting between the risky security and the riskless asset maintains an economy in the development of the theoretical pricing argument since no other assets or transactions need to be tracked.

Nevertheless, when our attention moves from option pricing to hedging, and from theoretical development to practical implementation, the stringent requirements of maintaining a self-financing portfolio no longer apply. In practice, our concern is only with maintaining a position that gives a security payoff equal to that of an option. Failure to hold the proper proportion of funds in the riskless asset will not affect this essential return structure. It will affect only the ex post cost of the protection.

For example, if the manager chooses to place funds made available from the strategy into another risky asset rather than into the riskless asset, the overall cost of the dynamic strategy may now be thought to depend on the performance of that risky asset. But clearly that facet of the strategy can easily be separated from the insurance service the strategy is delivering.[11]

---

11. The role of the riskless asset in creating a synthetic option is similar to its role in creating a synthetic forward contract for foreign exchange. The textbook method for creating a synthetic forward contract involves borrowing in one currency and converting it in the spot market into

It is important to recognize this role of the riskless asset when using futures contracts in constructing dynamic hedges, because the most efficient use of futures may not maintain the theoretically correct position in the risk-free asset. Because they are levered, futures implicitly contain a short position in the risk-free asset, but this position will not necessarily equal that required for the strategy to be self-financing.

The most efficient use of futures may lead to periodic payments or cash requirements. When properly treated, these cause no difficulties for the construction or evaluation of the strategy. On the contrary, they may lead to important advantages over transactions in the security itself.

Using Options to Create Options

A second variation on dynamic strategies is the use of listed options. As with futures, listed options may exist on indexes and securities that are closely correlated with the security of interest. Obviously, if there is a listed option that is fairly priced and that exactly meets the time and contract specifications for hedging, then it will be preferred to constructing the option synthetically. Frequently, however, there is a listed option that only partially fits the hedging requirements. For example, the listed option may be on a slightly different underlying asset, perhaps on a Treasury bond futures contract when the underlying asset is a corporate bond portfolio, or on a stock index that does not exactly match the construction of the underlying stock portfolio, or the listed option may have too short a time to maturity or be at the wrong exercise price.

The first of these problems will not be unique to the use of the listed options. It will exist for futures and may also exist when a dynamic strategy is pursued directly through the underlying asset. Dynamic adjustments of stock or bond portfolios must be done piecemeal. The subset of securities to be adjusted will not exactly match the overall portfolio. As a result, it is possible the discrete adjustment of the dynamic strategy may induce more basis risk than the use of listed options that, although not perfectly correlated with the underlying asset, overcome the problems related to discrete adjustments.

---

a second currency where the funds are then loaned out at the risk-free rate until the maturity of the contract. The result of these transactions is an obligation to deliver the first currency (to pay off the loan) and to receive the second currency. In practice, the funds need not actually be borrowed nor do they need to be loaned out as a riskless asset in the second currency. For example, the firm's own funds could be converted and the converted funds could be used for working capital needs. The end result of creating a forward contract will still be met, although the contract would be entangled with other transactions, and it would be more difficult to distinguish the nature of the forward contract. However, it is clear that creating the forward contract in this fashion might be more useful to the firm.

The second problem of listed options is that the time to expiration is shorter than the time horizon demanded for the option protection. Listed options often cannot be found more than three months out, while the time horizon for dynamic strategies is typically one year or more. On the other hand, these short-term listed options can themselves be employed in a dynamic strategy for creating synthetic longer-term options. This strategy is similar to rolling over short-term futures contracts to create longer-term protection.

For example, suppose an investor were interested in a $100 floor for a security price for one year, and put options existed with three months to maturity. The investor might buy a three-month put with an exercise price of $100, and upon expiration of that put buy another three-month put with the same exercise price. The position would be liquidated at the end of six months, a new three-month option purchased, and the procedure would be repeated again at the end of nine months.

If the option expired out of the money, there would be no proceeds from the strategy, and more funds would be necessary to roll over the strategy. If the security dropped below the floor, the put option would return the difference between the floor price and the security price, covering the loss and providing the intrinsic value for buying the next contract.[12]

The actual cost of this particular technique depends on the path the security price takes. To see this, consider a security currently priced at $100 together with a call option purchased on the security with an exercise price of $100. Suppose a six-month option cost $10 while a three-month option cost $6. If the security is again at $100 when the three-month option expires, a second $6 option will have to be purchased, and the total cost of the rolling over strategy will be $12, or $2 more than the cost of the six-month option. If, on the other hand, the stock drops to $80 in three months, the price of the call option for the next three months will be far less, since the option is now $20 out of the money. The next option may cost only $1, leading the rolling over strategy to be less costly. The same will be true if the security rises substantially, to, say, $120. The first of the three-month options will then pay off $20 at expiration, and the second option, being in the money, will have a small premium above their intrinsic value, selling for, say, $21. The total cost of the rolling over strategy will then be $7, compared to the $10 cost for the straight six-month option.

---

12. If the exercise price of the synthetic option could not be matched by the listed options, it could still be constructed using the rolling over of listed options by following the proper hedge ratio. For example, if the hedge ratio or delta of the listed option is .5 while the hedge ratio of the desired synthetic option is .75, then .75/.5 − 1.5 of the listed option would be held for each of the synthetic options to be constructed.

This path dependence can be eliminated, and options can realize their full potential in the hedge, by using fractional option positions rather than a one-for-one option position in the hedge.[13]

The use of listed options does have a number of particularly attractive features not shared by the other dynamic methods. First, the transaction costs and the timing of the transaction are known in advance. Second, like futures, the options are already levered, requiring less of a cash commitment than the straight security/bond strategy. And third, the option contract is protected against unforeseen jumps in the security price or changes in the security price volatility.

In a perfect market setting, the standard dynamic return structuring techniques using reallocations between the security and the riskless asset will replicate the desired option contract exactly. In practice, however, transaction costs, basis risk, capital constraints, and fundamental uncertainty about the return process and return volatility of the security make the proper choice of return structuring techniques more difficult.

We can, however, overcome some of the difficulties by making dynamic adjustments with the futures rather than the cash instrument, or by constructing the return structuring by rolling over listed options. Furthermore, having a number of alternative routes to achieving the desired return structuring permits the exploitation of mispricing in the various instruments. For example, if listed options are considered to be underpriced, they may be preferred to the dynamic strategy on that basis alone. These methods are not always a practical alternative, however. Since listed options and futures may not exist on the underlying security itself, the problems of basis risk may be accentuated. These aspects of return-structuring techniques should be the subject of further empirical testing and comparison.

V. Applications of Performance Structuring

The flexibility of dynamic strategies allows the return distribution to be molded in a wide variety of ways. We can also apply such strategies beyond the creation of the portfolio insurance we have dealt with here to more complex and specialized applications ranging from hedging single-premium deferred

---

13. In any case, this problem of path dependence has occasionally been overstated. While path dependence does lead to uncertainty, in practice, any strategy, including the straight dynamic approach, will face uncertainty, because the market and security price movement will not fit the assumptions of any model precisely. The key issue is whether the risk imposed by this uncertainty, and the cost of employing the strategies, is large in proportion to the benefit derived from being able to form a return that comes closer to meeting the portfolio objectives. Furthermore, rolling over positions can enhance returns if the investor has expertise in execution.

annuities in the life insurance industry to asset-liability management for thrift institutions. In this section, I will present three examples intended to be more or less generic and to cover a range of possible strategies.

Cutting Losses: Protective Portfolio with Options

Protective puts are the best known and most widely used option-type strategy. There are a number of variations on portfolio insurance designed to adapt the basic concept of the protective put to particular markets and risks. For example, protective puts can be extended beyond the bond and equity markets to insure floor prices for commodities or foreign exchange, can be set to assure returns equal to a pension plan's actuarial interest rate assumptions, or can be modified to express the floor return as a fixed differential off the Treasry bill rate or other interest rates.[14]

Table 2 presents the results of creating the simple dynamic put option on an equity portfolio. The objective here is to achieve a floor return of 0% from the portfolio, while maximizing the share of any increase in the equity position. The strategy used here is repeated each year with an end-of-year horizon each year. That is, a new protective put with one year to expiration is constructed each January. Hence, we can look at the performance as a series of independent trials.

The table shows the annual results of this strategy for the years 1973–83. The first column of the table gives the returns to equity (the S&P 500 Composite). The next two columns relate to the performance of the synthetic option strategy. The first of these columns gives the annual return to the strategy, the second gives the capture of the strategy.

The capture is the return to the synthetic option strategy as a percent of the equity portfolio. Since replicating an option position involves a gradual shift into equity as the equity increases in value, only part of the equity performance will be shared by the option position. The incomplete capture is a direct implication of option price behavior; option prices move less than one-to-one with changes in the price of the underlying asset. The incomplete capture of potential gains can be thought of as a cost of pursuing the option strategy. This serves to emphasize that option-related strategies have trade-offs consistent with market efficiency. Changes in return structure are met with commensurate costs. The cost for the repeated one-year protective put positions used in this example is greater than a single longer-term put option

---

14. Applications can be found in *Winning the Interest Rate Game,* edited by F. Fabozzi (Chicago: Probus Publishing, 1985); J. Tilley and D. Jacob, *Asset/Liability Management for Insurance Companies* (New York: Morgan Stanley Fixed Income Research, 1983); and J. Tilley, *Hedging Interest Rate Risk for Interest Sensitive Products* (New York: Morgan Stanley Fixed Income Research, 1984).

TABLE 2. *Protective Put Strategy Simulation Comparison of Annual Returns.*

		Dynamic Strategy			
Year	Equity	With Floor Exercise Price	Capture	With Variable Exercise Price	Capture
1973	−14.9%	−0.52%	Floor	−0.99%	Floor
1974	−25.2	−0.71	Floor	−0.99	Floor
1975	34.1	20.68	61%	31.20	91%
1976	23.0	14.99	65	22.42	98
1977	−7.2	−0.38	Floor	−1.02	Floor
1978	6.5	4.55	70	0.35	5
1979	18.5	16.62	90	18.48	100
1980	33.4	26.89	81	30.00	90
1981	−5.6	−0.38	Floor	−1.13	Floor
1982	20.8	11.30	54	1.96	9
1983	22.2	18.94	85	22.17	100

Cumulative Returns for 11 Years Compounded:

    7.80%   9.76%   10.40%

- 52-week periods were used instead of exact calendar years.
- EQUITY: S&P 500 Stock Index adjusted for dividends.
- Capture is the dynamic strategy return as a percent of the return to the equity portfolio when the equity portfolio return exceeds the 0% floor.
- Includes transactions costs of $25 per contract round trip.
- Assets are reallocated once every week.

would be. The capture can be increased by taking a longer investment horizon in the performance structure.

It is evident from Table 2 that the portfolio performed as expected in providing the 0% floor return. In the four years that the equity market saw negative returns, the return to the structured portfolio was 0%. In the years of positive return, the structured portfolio shared to varying degrees in that return. In most cases, the protective put returned over 75% of the return to the equity portfolio. The capture was higher in years of higher equity return and was also higher the longer the equity sustained a high rate of return. This is an attractive and natural feature of option prices. The proportion of funds in equity is the average of proportions held over the annual period. In the simulation, these proportions were readjusted weekly.[15]

---

15. In practice, it is unlikely that weekly adjustments will actually be necessary. Depending on market conditions, in particular the degree of price movement, as few as four adjustments a year may be sufficient.

Going With the Winners: Strategies for Accentuating Gains

How much would it be worth to be able to receive a perfect stock-bond market timing service, a service that could always pick when holding stocks would do better than holding bonds? It is possible to create and price such a service through the simple option strategy of buying an index call option and placing the remainder of the portfolio in bonds.

To see this, select the call option to have an exercise price that equals the return possible through a bond investment. Then, if the option pays off, it will give a return equal to the stock market return less the bond price, while if the option expires worthless, the overall portfolio return will still equal the bond return. The net effect of this strategy will be to give a return equal to the equity or the bond, whichever is greater. This is the return that would be generated by following the advice of a perfect market timer. The cost of this strategy is the cost of the call option on the market.[16]

As this perfect market-timing example illustrates, options can perform a strategic as well as defensive role in portfolio management. The proper dynamic allocation between equities and bonds will replicate a call option on the market and provide a return equal to the greater of the two. Added onto an actively managed stock portfolio, such an allocation strategy can accentuate gains by increasing market participation during upswings while moving out of the market during downturns.[17] Table 3 shows the annual results of pursuing this strategy over the 1973–1983 period.

The gradual adjustments that constitute the dynamic technique lead the structure market-timing strategy to capture only a portion of the return of the better performing asset. As we discussed in the last example, this is a result of the core feature of option returns of reacting less than one-to-one with price changes in the underlying security.

In two instances, however, the option return actually is lower than either the bond or equity return. In 1976 the structured return was 16.6%, compared to 18.4% for bonds and 23% for equity; in 1981 it was −10.6%, compared to −1% for bonds and −5.6% for equity. The failure in the strategy is the result of employing only weekly adjustments in the historical simula-

---

16. The relationship between market timing and option valuation was first pointed out by Merton. [See R. Merton, "On Market Timing and Investment Performance. I. An Equilibrium Theory of Value for Market Forecasts," *Journal of Business* 54 (July 1981): 363–406.] As put-call parity suggests, this relationship can also be looked at through a put option strategy. The market timing service can be created with a put option by holding the equity and buying a put option with an exercise price equal to the bond return.

17. A variation of this strategy can be used to form a variable beta portfolio, a portfolio with a high beta, and thus high leverage, in strong markets, and with a low beta, and thus little reaction to the market, when the market declines. The variable beta strategy is presented in Chapter 6 of R. Bookstaber and R. Clarke, *Option Strategies for Institutional Investment Management* (Reading, Mass.: Addison-Wesley, 1983).

TABLE 3. *Market Timing Strategy Simulation Comparison of Annual Total Returns.*

Year	Bond	Equity	Dynamic Strategy	Capture
1973	0.83%	−14.86%	−5.96%	57%
1974	2.77	−25.25	−6.23	68
1975	6.96	34.15	26.34	71
1976	18.39	22.07	17.78	Floor
1977	−0.64	−7.20	−4.44	42
1978	−1.19	6.48	1.64	37
1979	−1.58	18.48	14.21	79
1980	−2.95	33.38	21.68	68
1981	−0.98	−5.58	−7.74	Floor
1982	44.99	20.79	34.93	58
1983	1.03	22.17	16.32	75

Cumulative Returns for 11 Years Compounded:

5.41%   7.80%   8.94%

- 52-week periods were used instead of exact calendar years.
- For purposes of this study, the asset classes are defined as follows:
  BOND: 20-year Treasury Bonds;
  EQUITY: S&P 500 Stock Index adjusted for dividends.
- Capture is the absolute difference of the dynamic strategy return and the lower of the bond or equity return, divided by the absolute difference of the bond and equity return.
- Includes transactions costs of $25 per contract round trip.
- Assets are reallocated once every week.

tion. While generally adjustments in the proportions of security holdings need to be made only infrequently, adjustments in the times of dramatic price movements may need to be made more than once a week to replicate the option position. These two years were marked by such price movements, and the inability of the simulation to make immediate allocation changes led to the inferior performance. This serves to emphasize the need for good monitoring and execution facilities in following dynamic strategies.

This market-timing strategy can be adapted to other portfolio management settings. For example, it can be used to accentuate the performance of a number of managers by creating an option that will lead to a return equal to the largest of the managers' returns. The same method could be used to focus in on the best of a number of investment themes. A manager who, for example, is interested in both energy-intensive industries and recreation-related industries could create options on each area to increase the leverage of the better performing area.

Combined Strategies: Extensions to Multiple Risky Assets

Having presented examples both for cutting losses through portfolio insurance and for accentuating gains through call option positions, the next logical step is to combine the two.[18] The resulting strategy will give the greater of the bond or equity return with a floor return equal to the short-term rate.

Table 4 presents the result of combining the two previous strategies in this way. Over the eleven-year period from 1973 to 1983, all three assets in

18. Strategy is presented in J. Tilley and G. Latainer, "A Synthetic Framework for Asset Allocation," *Financial Analysts Journal* (May-June 1985): 32–43. A theoretical discussion of this concept is presented in the following two papers: R. M. Stulz, "Options on the Minimum or the Maximum of Two Risky Assets," *Journal of Financial Economics* 10 (July 1982): 161–85 and R. C. Stapleton and M. G. Subrahamanyan, "The Valuation of Multivariate Contingent Claims in Discrete Time Models," *Journal of Finance* 39 (March 1984): 207–28.

TABLE 4. *Multiple Risky Asset Strategy Simulation Comparison of Annual Total Returns.*

| | Asset Class | | Dynamic Strategy | |
| | | | Floor Ex- | |
Year	Bond	Equity	ercise Price	Capture
1973	0.83%	−14.86%	0.44%	53%
1974	2.77	−25.25	0.11	4
1975	6.96	34.15	16.39	48
1976	18.39	22.97	11.67	51
1977	−0.64	−7.20	0.01	Floor
1978	−1.19	6.48	3.84	59
1979	−1.58	18.48	13.20	71
1980	−2.95	33.38	16.59	50
1981	−0.98	−5.58	−0.04	Floor
1982	44.99	20.79	24.38	54
1983	1.03	22.17	13.74	62

Cumulative Returns for 11 Years Compounded:

 5.41%   7.80%   8.81%

- 52-week periods were used instead of exact calendar years.
- For purposes of this study, the asset classes are defined as follows:
  BOND: 20-year Treasury Bonds;
  EQUITY: S&P 500 Stock Index adjusted for dividends.
- Capture is the dynamic strategy return as a percent of the return to the equity portfolio when the equity portfolio return exceeds the 0% floor.
- Includes transactions costs of $25 per contract round trip.
- Assets are reallocated once every week.

the strategy came into use at some point. From 1973 to 1980, returns shifted between the floor of 0% and some capture of the equity rate. The capture was almost 100% in 1976 and 1979, and roughly two-thirds in 1975 and 1979. In 1982 the bond market had twice the return of equity and over three times the return of cash, and the dynamic strategy shifted toward bonds. The stock-bond option in this strategy, which represents the market-timing aspect of the strategy, was sensitive enough to capture 81% of this return.

This strategy is easily extended to other risk-return considerations, and to more than two risky assets. One way to look at the combined strategy is as a call option on the best performing of the risky assets with a residual position in cash. The call option gives the leverage on the upside while giving out protection on the downside. Furthermore, the call option can be selected before the fact to act like a call option only on the asset that turns out to be the best performer. If one of the areas does well, the options will pay off for that area; if they all do poorly and the option expires out of the money, the cash position will still guarantee a floor return.

VI. The Implications of Performance Structuring for Portfolio Evaluation

Care must be taken in evaluating portfolios with return distributions altered by option strategies. Methods of performance evaluation that depend on mean and variance measures of returns — as all of the common methods do — cannot be applied to portfolios resulting from dynamic strategies for the simple reason that those portfolios depend on more than mean and variance.[19] These strategies mold the return distributions, bringing the higher moments, such as skewness and kurtosis, into play.

For example, the protective put leads to a truncation of the left tail of the portfolio return distribution and a leftward shift of the distribution. The truncation reflects the cost of the insurance. Figure 6 shows the distribution of the underlying portfolio, with the familiar normal distribution and the distribution that results when a put option is purchased on that portfolio.

In contrast to this strategy, consider the distributional effect of writing a covered-call option on the same underlying portfolio. The covered call has the opposite effect of the put option. It truncates the right tail of the distribution while shifting the distribution to the right. The truncation is the result of selling off the upward potential to the call buyer, and the shift reflects the premium received from that sale. Figure 7 compares the distribution of covered-call writing with that of the underlying portfolio.

---

19. Further discussion of the problems addressed in this section is provided in R. Bookstaber and R. Clarke, "Option Portfolio Strategies: Measurement and Evaluation," *Journal of Business* 57 (October 1984): 469–92.

FIGURE 6. *Return Distributions for Protective Put Options.*

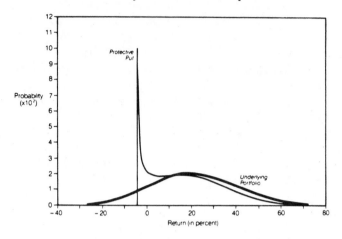

FIGURE 7. *Return Distribution for Writing Covered Call Options.*

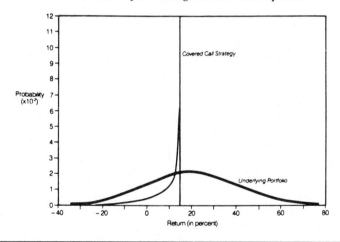

Even a cursory reference to Figures 6 and 7 demonstrates that distributions resulting from option strategies cannot be understood by looking at the mean and variance alone. Indeed, in this particular case, an analysis based solely on expected return and variance of return will make call writing appear superior to put buying. The two strategies have much the same effect on expected return. The expected return drops from 18% for the underlying stock portfolio to 13.6% for the portfolio fully covered by a call option, and to 14.5% for the portfolio fully covered by the protective put. But the standard deviation of returns drops from 20% for the underlying portfolio to only 16.7% for the put strategy, while it is cut to 5.8% for the covered call strategy. The put strategy has a standard deviation that is nearly three times higher than for call writing. If standard deviation or variance is used as a proxy for risk, writing a covered call will be preferred to buying a protective put.[20]

Variance is not a suitable proxy for risk, however, since the option strategies reduce risk *asymmetrically*. The call truncates the right-hand side of the distribution and thereby reduces the desirable upside variance. The put, on the other hand, reduces the variance on the undesirable left-hand portion of the return distribution. It is natural, then, for a reduction in variance to be compensated differently for the two strategies.

This example illustrates the shortcomings of evaluation methods that rely on summary statistics such as mean and variance in dealing with option-related strategies. By trading off between the mean and the higher moments of the distribution, many unusual mean-variance relationships are possible.

For example, it is possible to construct a covered call strategy with both a higher expected return *and* a lower variance than the underlying portfolio. Or, by using far-out-of-the-money call options, it is possible to construct a portfolio insurance strategy that yields the same return floor as a protective put but with a higher expected return. (This strategy will give a high probability of achieving only the floor return and a small chance of receiving a very high return.) Such a strategy may not, in fact, lead to a desirable return structure. Strictly on a mean-variance basis, however, it certainly appears superior to the conventional insurance strategy of using a protective put.[21]

These two examples show the potential for misleading statements and inaccurate evaluations of alternative strategies. The incomplete state of performance evaluation may foster conflict between portfolio and management objectives. The strategies that lead to good measures of management success

---

20. This bias will appear for the Sharpe measure (which measures performance as the difference between the portfolio return and the risk-free rate, divided by the standard deviation of portfolio returns), the Treynor index (which measures performance as the difference between the portfolio return and the risk-free rate, divided by the portfolio beta), and the Jensen measure (which measures performance by the "alpha" of the security market line regression, i.e. by the vertical distance between the portfolio return and the capital market line).

21. For this reason, care must be taken in using the expected return as the sole criterion for selecting the best portfolio insurance strategy. The protective put option may be the least-cost strategy in that it provides the desired protection for the lowest drop in expected return *while preserving the features of the underlying security return distribution*. But it will not be the least-cost strategy if no constraints are placed on alteration of the security return structure above the point of protection. The same is true of other option strategies. Unless the return structure is specified over the entire range of possible outcomes, there will be some strategies that fulfill the stated objectives at an apparently low cost but do so only by making unfavorable tradeoffs in other regions of the return distribution.

may not be those which best address the portfolio objectives. Given techniques that extend performance structuring beyond the two-dimensional plane of mean and variance, it is natural to expect that evaluation methods for these techniques must also break out of the mean-variance framework. We need a new set of performance techniques for the quantitative evaluation of portfolios engaged in these strategies.

Misinterpretations are also likely in the qualitative review of the performance of dynamically structured portfolios. For example, the portfolio insurance strategy requires selling off the security as the price declines and gradually buying it back as the price rises. Viewed outside the context of dynamic management, such a pattern of trading does not lead to favorable conclusions as to the manager's trading skills. Furthermore, most managers are evaluated by rankings based on realized return performance rather than on meeting distributional objectives. In these rankings, a manager's successful pursuit of a strategy for meeting a specified return objective may be overshadowed if a drop in realized return was a necessary cost of meeting that objective.[22] As with the misinterpretations inherent in applying the quantitative evaluation methods, the possibility of the manager pursuing a dynamic strategy may convey a mistaken impression that could keep these strategies from being correctly selected or effectively implemented.

VII. Conclusion

The opportunities that option strategies present for molding the return distributions to meet investment objectives apply to a wide number of portfolio management and risk control problems. In their most general form, option strategies allow the manager to expand the set of insurable contingencies far beyond those available with static hedging methods. The use of dynamic hedging strategies to create the desired option-type payoffs allows returns to be structured even further than is possible with listed options; risks can be defined according to the specific asset/liability mix and risk preferences of management. The tools of option theory provide the technology for expanding the dimensions of risk management to meet the specialized demands of business.

---

22. The potential conflict of the manager between meeting the sponsor's objectives and maximizing relative performance suggests that the sponsor of the investment program might be better suited to the performance structuring role. We have discussed above how futures can facilitate this.

Morgan Stanley's approaches to product design take these differences into account at the outset. For example, strategies in the insurance area include hedging single-premium deferred annuities and universal life policies. For savings and loans, these techniques have been applied to asset-liability management and cash management. Other applications range from protecting investments in foreign currencies from adverse currency price movements to hedging the credit risk of high-yield bond portfolios.

We can summarize the technology of option theory as a payoff processor which reshapes return distributions. The set of return distributions for the assets enter the processor, where the dynamic hedging technology remolds them to specification. The payoffs exit the processor with distributions of the desired shape.

Naturally, the benefits of dynamic return structuring are not gained without a cost. The protection of portfolio insurance is not free. Its cost, explicit in the price of a put option, is implicit in the dynamic strategy for replicating a put option, since, as we have seen, such a strategy leads only to partial participation in price increases. To state without qualification that a protective put strategy, or any other dynamic strategy, is superior to holding the uninsured portfolio ignores the risk-return tradeoffs that form the basis of asset pricing. While it is no doubt true that ex post the insured strategy will do better over some particular time period, ex ante the insurance will impose a cost. The same point applies to other strategies as well.[23]

The major issue we have addressed in this paper is how to minimize the cost of performance structuring, that is, how to find the dynamic strategy that best fulfills a given objective while still preserving the other features of the portfolio distribution. The least-cost dynamic strategy for meeting the objective of portfolio insurance will be the strategy which best replicates a put option. This conclusion flows over into a wide range of other portfolio objectives. In general, the least-cost means of return structuring can be represented through the appropriate set of put and call options on the underlying asset. This leads the goal of minimizing costs one step further, to finding the dynamic strategy which best replicates the required set of put and call options.

We have dealt with this and with the related issue of finding the most effective strategy, the strategy that gives the greatest chance of meeting the investment objectives under all possible market scenarios. We have addressed only indirectly a second vital issue of performance structuring: finding the strategy that meets the needs and objectives of the investor. Poorly written insurance policies can be formed just as easily with dynamic strategies as with more conventional insurance techniques. A strategy must not only meet its objectives, and do so at the least cost; the objectives themselves must also be intelligently conceived.

Like creating policies in insurance or contracts in law, creating the proper performance structure in finance is possible only when the nature of the risks and the objectives of the client are known. This requires more than an understanding of the tools of performance structuring. It requires a knowledge of

---

23. For other patterns of return structuring, the strategy may initially lead to positive inflows rather than costs as, for example, does the writing of covered call options. But in this case the cost balancing the initial inflow will be a reduction in the potential return from the later price movements.

the business being analyzed. The investment needs of the pension fund differ in scope and complexity from those of the insurance company, which in turn differ from those of the thrift institution. This is an area that is part art and part science, where judgment and experience are of key importance.

15

Measuring and Interpreting Volatility

Joanne M. Hill
Vice President
PaineWebber

I. Introduction

The measurement of historical volatility is an important component in the evaluation of options and option strategies. Historical volatility is commonly compared to the volatility implied in option prices to assess whether options are trading "cheap" or "rich." Volatility measured over different historical time periods also often serves as a basis for developing forecasts of volatility for option valuation or strategy analysis. Applications of option valuation include determining the cost of portfolio insurance and the value of options attached to or embedded in fixed income instruments such as callable bonds, putable bonds, and mortgage-backed securities.

The estimation of volatility from a series of price data is not as straightforward as it may seem. It is not unusual to see different annualized historical volatility estimates for the same time period from different sources. In most instances, different "acceptable" calculation methods explain these discrepancies in the measurements of historical volatility. This article reviews several methodological issues in the calculation of an annualized volatility estimate from historical price data. These issues include the measure used for the rate of return, the number of degrees of freedom and mean (sample or population) used in the calculation, and the method for annualizing the "periodic" standard deviation estimate. Specific recommendations are made with regard to the appropriate methodology for the volatility estimation, depending on the circumstances at hand. A method for converting volatility measures to expected price ranges is also suggested. These price ranges, which are anticipated with a given probability over a specific time interval, can be useful benchmarks for comparison with actual changes in price over the same time interval.

The statistic, standard deviation, is used to measure historical volatility. The formula for the standard deviation or volatility measures over a sample of N observations of a variable R is calculated as follows:

$$\text{Volatility} = SD = \left[\sum_{i=1}^{N} \left(\frac{(R_i - \bar{R})^2}{N-1} \right) \right]^{1/2}, \tag{1}$$

where

$R_i = $ observation i on variable R;
$\bar{R} = $ the average of R_i, $i = 1, 2, ..., N$; and
$N = $ the number of observations in the sample.

This article evaluates some alternative methods for applying this formula in calculating the historical volatility from a time series of prices. The method chosen can significantly influence the level of the historical volatility measure.

II. Return Calculation and Return Distribution Assumptions

Two measures of return are commonly used:

1. Percentage changes in daily prices
2. Natural logarithm of price relatives

Both percentage price changes and the natural logarithm of price relatives are acceptable as return measures. Percentage price changes are often used with daily price data. These returns are typically assumed to follow a normal probability distribution (see Figure 1a).

Another acceptable return measure is the natural logarithm (ln) of price relatives (P_t / P_{t-1}) between date t and $t-1$, that is $\ln(P_t / P_{t-1})$. This term is equivalent to $1 + R$ where R is the continuously compounded return over interval t or e^{Rt}; that is $\ln(P_t / P_{t-1})$ is equivalent to $1 + e^{Rt}$. When the return interval is short, such as a day in length, the difference in terms of the annualized measure between continuous compounding of gains and losses and daily compounding is very small. (The use of daily percentage price changes is consistent with a process of daily compounding.)

Both percentage price changes and the natural logarithms of price relatives are normally distributed variables if price changes are independent of

FIGURE 1. *Normal and Lognormal Density Functions.*

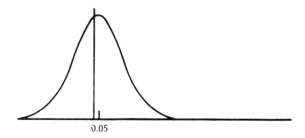

a) **Normal Density Function**
(Mean: .05 or 5%, Standard Deviation: .30 or 30%)

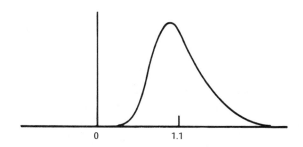

b) **Lognormal Density Function**
(Mean: 1.10, Standard Deviation: ;34)

Source: J.C. Cox and M. Rubinstein, *Options Markets* (New York: Prentice Hall, Inc., 1985), p. 202.

one another.[1] The standard deviation formula in equation (1) can be used as a measure of the volatility of a distribution when the underlying variable is distributed normally. Note that the Black–Scholes model assumes that prices are lognormally distributed as shown in Figure 1b. A lognormal distribution

---

1. This conclusion follows from the central limit theorem of probability theory assuming price changes are independent of one another and distributed identically. This assumption has an interesting implication. If price changes are independent of one another, there should be no pattern in the sequence of price changes, that is price changes should follow a random walk. The use of historical volatility measures determined by equation (1) is, therefore, inconsistent

of prices is the equivalent of a normal distribution of the logarithm of those prices. Since the logarithm of a variable is a measure of its continuous rate of change, the assumption that continuous (or directly measured) rates of change (return) are normally distributed is consistent with lognormality in prices. Note also that assuming price relatives or P_t/P_{t-1} are lognormally distributed is identical to assuming $\ln(P_t/P_{t-1})$ or $\ln(1+R)$ is normally distributed. Therefore, either measure of return can be used in volatility calculation depending on convenience.

III. The Calculation of Daily Standard Deviation from Daily Return Data

Divisor or Degrees of Freedom

When using sample data including the sample mean to calculate a variance or standard deviation, the sum of the squared deviations about the sample mean should be divided by the number of those observations (N) minus 1 that is, by $N-1$. The divisor of $N-1$ rather than N is appropriate because the mean is calculated from a sample, thereby reducing the degrees of freedom by 1.

The @ STD function in LOTUS 123 divides by N and therefore understates the sample volatility estimate.[2] The effect of using N rather than $N-1$ is a decreasing function of N; that is, for very large N, the difference is trivial; however, for small N, for example twenty observations or less, the effect can be significant. Table 1 contains historical volatility estimates for the March '86 Treasury bond futures contract using 10, 20, and 30 days of price data. These volatility estimates are calculated using both N and $N-1$ to illustrate the effect of calculating a population volatility measure where a sample measure is appropriate. Note that the 10-day annualized volatility estimates based on N versus $N-1$ differ by .50%. The 20-day volatility estimates differ by .35% and the 30-day volatility estimates by .20%.

---

with the validity of technical analysis based on a pattern or trend in price changes. Any pattern or trend in prices would produce serially related price changes. In the presence of serial correlation, the formula for standard deviation should be adjusted to take into account the dependence (or serial correlation) of price changes on one another. The adjustment required is to multiply the standard deviation by the square root of $(1+S)/(1-S)$, where $S=$ the serial correlation between daily returns. See also note 5.

2. On page 292 of the LOTUS 123 manual, the following formula for a sample standard deviation is provided:

Sample STD = @ SQRT (@ COUNT (list)/(@ COUNT (list) − 1)) *@STD (list)

where (list) = the range of cells over which the calculation is to be done.

TABLE 1. *Historical Volatility Estimates Using Different Calculation Methods.*[a]

	Basis for Annualizing Volatility		
	250 days	260 days	365 days
10-day Volatility Estimates			
% price changes			
$N=10$	8.61%	8.78%	10.41%
$N=9$	9.08	9.26	10.97
Ln(price relatives)			
$N=10$	8.59	8.76	10.38
$N=9$	9.05	9.23	10.94
20-day Volatility Estimates			
% price changes			
$N=20$	13.54%	13.81%	16.36%
$N=19$	13.89	14.16	16.78
Ln(price relatives)			
$N=20$	13.57	13.84	16.40
$N=19$	13.93	14.20	16.83
30-day Volatility Estimates			
% price change			
$N=30$	12.12%	12.36%	14.65%
$N=29$	12.33	12.57	14.90
Ln(price relatives)			
$N=30$	12.15	12.39	14.68
$N=29$	12.36	12.60	14.93

a. Based on the closing prices of the March '86 Treasury Bond futures contract over the period from December 13, 1985, through January 27, 1986.

Use of Sample or Population Mean

It is, in fact, correct to use the population mean instead of the sample mean for calculating volatility when a theoretical basis exists for the mean of the distribution or when the mean of the population is either given by assumption or known with certainty. In most cases, however, the population mean is unknown and the sample mean is used as the "best estimate" of this unknown value. Therefore, most volatility measurement appropriately uses $N-1$ as the divisor in equation (1). If the population mean is known or fixed by assumption, it is acceptable to divide by N.

An example of the use of a population mean is in the calculation of the standard deviation of the residual errors in a regression. These errors are by definition distributed normally with a mean of 0. Therefore, many residual standard deviations are calculated as the mean of the squared residual errors. This represents the standard deviation of residual errors around a mean of 0.

Another application of the use of a population mean would be in the circumstance in which a return or price change series is expected to have a mean significantly different from the sample mean. This expected mean may have been derived as an average of a series of returns measured over a very long period. That is, the best prediction of next period's price is the current period's price multiplied by one plus the expected rate of price appreciation. For example, the sample mean over very short time periods, say less than 30 days, may be unsustainably high or low given the range of returns typically observed for the instrument. Therefore, the standard deviation can be measured with respect to the expected return or population mean. To reiterate, in the rare circumstance when a population mean assumption is used rather than the sample mean, it is correct to use N as a divisor.

IV. The Calculation of Annualized Standard Deviation

The annualization of historical volatility from weekly or monthly percentage price changes or from price relative data is straightforward. The formula converting weekly or monthly volatility to an annualized volatility number is thus:

$$\text{Annualized Volatility} = \text{Monthly Volatility} \times \sqrt{12}; \qquad (2)$$
$$= \text{Weekly Volatility} \times \sqrt{52}. \qquad (3)$$

When the sample consists of daily data, however, the situation becomes more complicated. There are 365 days in a non-leap year and 366 in a leap year. Annualizing using a 365 day basis implicitly assumes that volatility on non-trading days is equal to that on trading days. Most academic evidence, on the other hand, suggests that returns are generated from a process that is closer to one based on trading days than one based on calendar days. If returns followed a calendar time process, volatility on Mondays would be three times that of other weekdays. However, empirical tests have shown Monday volatility is only modestly (10 to 20%) above that of other weekdays, which supports the trading time model.[3]

Therefore, the number of trading days in a typical year is the appropriate number for annualization. Since the typical year is 52 weeks and 1 day, there should be at least 110 (52 × 2) weekend days, leaving 255 trading days. The stock and commodity exchanges usually observe 7 additional holidays

---

3. See, for example, D.W. French, "The Weekend Effect on the Distribution of Stock Prices," *Journal of Financial Economics* 13 (1984): 547–59 or other references cited therein.

or have 247 trading days per year.[4] Banks and U.S. government bond dealers may also have several (3 or 4) additional holidays.

Multipliers of 250 or 260 are often used for annualizing trading-day volatility calculated from daily data.[5] The volatility estimates based on a 260, trading-day year as shown in Table 1, are roughly 0.25% higher than those found using a 250 day year. Using a 365 day calendar basis for annualizing volatility produces estimates between 1% and 3% higher than does a 260 day basis. Obviously, the higher the level of daily volatility, the larger the difference between trading and calendar-day volatility estimates. We recommend using a 250 trading day year:

$$\text{Annualized Volatility} = \text{Daily Volatility} \times \sqrt{250}. \qquad (4)$$

V. Interpretation of Volatility Estimates

When observing price changes in the instrument underlying an option, the question arises of whether an observed price move is consistent with the volatility implied in the option price or with a historical volatility estimate. For example, after selling a call option at a price reflecting an implied volatility of 15%, would a change in price of 2 points in 10 days be consistent with the 15% implied volatility?

One approach is to measure historical volatility over the time frame of the price move, comparing it to the implied volatility at the time the option position was opened. This method is imperfect, however, because the level of volatility over 10 days will reflect the extent of price movement on days within that period as well as the movement from the beginning to end point. A more useful approach is to find the range of prices around the initial price that is consistent with the original volatility estimate. If price movement is regularly at the extremes of this range or outside of the range, it is a positive

---

4. Stock Exchange holidays include New Year's Day, Washington's Birthday, Good Friday, Memorial Day, Independence Day, Thanksgiving, and Christmas. Banking holidays also include Martin Luther King Day (in some states), Columbus Day, and Veteran's Day, but exclude Good Friday. If Christmas and New Year's fall on a weekend day, exchange officials decide whether a holiday is given.

5. These volatility annualization formulas implicitly assume return observations are independent of one another; that is, there is no serial correlation in the return series. Results are not significantly affected by minor violations of this assumption. However, there are circumstances in which serial return correlation can be a problem. For example, a broad-based index may require two trading periods to react completely to economic information with actively trading securities responding first and others later. Therefore, one may wish to adjust the historic volatility for the level of serial correlation in the returns when estimating volatilities of very broad indexes such as the NYSE or the Value Line Index or bond indexes. An adjustment of this type would involve applying a first order auto-regressive correction such as described in note 1 to the return or price relative series.

indication that volatility is rising. If price movements are well within the price range based on one unit of volatility, chances are that volatility is declining.

The interpretation of historical volatility as estimated by the standard deviation is the range of daily returns (or daily price relatives) around the mean in which approximately two-thirds (68.3%) of the possible future outcomes are expected to fall. In other words, for the case of 10% volatility based on percentage price changes, there is a 68.3% probability (or roughly two chances out of three) that the next day's price will be within a plus or minus 10% annualized percentage change of today's price. In terms of price relatives, this would mean there are two out of three chances that the next day's price will be between 99.37 and 100.63% of today's price or between 90 and 110% of today's price on an annualized basis; 10% annualized volatility converted to a daily volatility equals .63% or $(10\%/\sqrt{250})$. Therefore, in this situation, one would expect a range of 99.37 to 100.63 on a security priced at 100 with a probability of .683 or 68.3%. Two standard deviations encompass roughly 95% of all possible values or a range of 98.74 [100 − (2 × .63)] to 101.26 [100 + (2 × .63)]. The probabilities associated with different units of volatility for a normal distribution are shown in Table 2.

The annualized volatility measure can, therefore, easily be converted into a price range expected with a given probability over a particular time interval. First, the annualized volatility is transformed to a number applicable to the time interval involved. Second, the current price is multiplied by 1 plus or minus the periodic volatility times the units of volatility associated with the probability.

For example, the price range expected with a 95.4% probability over the next week, consistent with a 15% annualized probability and assuming the current price is equal to 100, would be given as:

Weekly Volatility $.0208 = .15/\sqrt{52}$
95.4% = 2 units of volatility
Price Range: $100 \times (1 + (.0208 \times 2)) = 104.16$;
$100 \times (1 - (.0208 \times 2)) = 95.84$.

TABLE 2.

Units of Volatility (Standard Deviation)	Probability of Observing Price in the Range of Units × Volatility
−½ to +½	.3830
−1 to +1	.6826
−1½ to +1½	.8664
−2 to +2	.9544
−2½ to +2½	.9876
−3 to +3	.9974

TABLE 3.

| | Initial Price = 100 | Annualized Volatility = 15% |
| | Time = 1 Month | Monthly Volatility = 4.33% |

Units of Volatility (Standard Deviation)	Price Range	Chance of Observing Price Outside of Range
$-\frac{1}{2}$ to $+\frac{1}{2}$	97.83–102.16	.617
-1 to $+1$	95.67–104.33	.317
$-1\frac{1}{2}$ to $+1\frac{1}{2}$	93.50–106.49	.134
-2 to $+2$	91.34–108.66	.045

Therefore, a price range of from 95.84 to 104.10 over a period of one week can be expected with a 95.4% probability consistent with our annualized volatility estimate of 15%.

For a given volatility, it is also possible to calculate a range of prices outside of which a price is expected to fall with a given probability. As an example, consider the case above in which a security (or future) is priced at 100 with a 15% annualized volatility. The probabilities associated with different price ranges over a period of one month, that is the chance of observing a price outside that range, given the 15% volatility are shown in Table 3.

It is also possible to construct a table of price ranges for varying time periods that are associated with a particular number of volatility units. Assume one wants to know the range of prices beginning today for each of the next 8 weeks that are consistent with a 15% annualized volatility and a chance of .317 of being outside the range (.683 of being within the range). Since these probabilities represent one standard deviation, simply find the appropriate standard deviation for 1, 2, ..., 8 weeks of time and multiply 1 plus this number and 1 minus this number by the current price of 100 as shown in Table 4.

TABLE 4.

Beginning Price = 100   Annualized Volatility = 15%
Initial Volatility = Annual Volatility/$\sqrt{52N}$ (N = Number of weeks)
Chance of Observing Prices Outside of Range = .317

Time In Weeks	Price Range
1	97.92–102.08
2	97.06–102.94
3	96.39–103.60
4	95.84–104.16
5	95.35–104.65
6	94.90–105.09
7	94.48–105.50
8	94.11–105.88

Note that the range expands at a much greater rate in the first four weeks than in the second four weeks. The potential upside range for one standard deviation increases by 2.08 points from 102.08 to 104.16 between the end of the first and fourth weeks. However, the upside range increases by only 1.23 points from 104.65 to 105.88 between the end of the fifth and eighth weeks. This is the effect of the nonlinearity of the function that converts short-term to longer-term volatility.

Intuitively, these results imply that volatility increases over time, but at a decreasing rate such that monthly volatility is considerably less than four times weekly volatility. A large price move over a short period does not necessarily mean that volatility is increasing. The price move should be evaluated in the context of this type of analysis to see whether it lies significantly outside the range of likely prices for this short period.

VI. Overview

The differences in volatility estimates for 10, 20, and 30 observations as shown in Table 1 confirm the methodological impacts suggested by the above discussion. In summary: (1) there is little difference between volatility estimates based on the natural logarithm of price relatives vs. percentage price changes over periods as short as a day, both of which should satisfy the normal distribution assumption; (2) when using a sample mean in the standard deviation formula, it is important to use the number of observations minus 1 as the divisor, especially for small return samples; (3) the annualization of a daily volatility estimate should take into account the number of trading days rather than calendar days in a year; that is the annual volatility is estimated by multiplying the daily volatility by the square root of 250; and (4) it is possible to convert volatility measures to expected price ranges. These price ranges can be very useful as reference points for detecting changes in volatility from short-term price moves.

16

Balancing Tracking Risk versus Trading Costs in Broad-based Index Funds
An Analysis Using the Russell 2000 As an Example

Stephen G. Bodurtha*
Assistant Vice President
Kidder, Peabody & Co.

I. Introduction

The emergence of equity funds linked to broad-based stock indexes such as the Russell 2000 raises new opportunities and challenges in passive money management. For pension sponsors, these broader index funds open the door to the universe of small capitalization stocks that is regarded by many experts to offer the best risk/return profile in the equity markets, but which has traditionally generated the highest management and trading costs. In the go-slow, cost-conscious world created by Black Monday, a relatively low-cost, passive index product emphasizing the long-term growth characteristics of "small cap" issues would appear to be a natural component of any pension fund's asset mix.

But for these potential rewards to be tapped, some formidable logistical issues must be addressed. Foremost among these challenges is the task of constructing portfolios that will mimic the performance of the actual Russell indexes.

II. A Fundamental Trade-off: Tracking Error versus Transaction Costs

Of course, it is theoretically possible to track an index perfectly by trading all the stocks in that index. However, the pursuit of lower (or zero) tracking

*The author wishes to thank Geoffrey Luce for his assistance in the analysis.

FIGURE 1. *A Key Trade-off: Transaction Costs versus Tracking Error.*

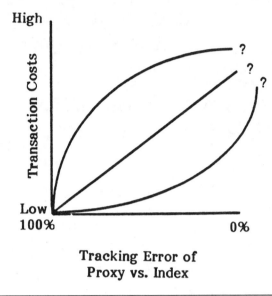

error may lead to higher transaction costs, since the asset manager will need to trade more of the stocks in the index that are relatively costly to buy and sell (by virtue, for instance, of lower liquidity or wider bid-ask spreads). This trade-off between tracking error and transaction costs is illustrated in Figure 1.

For asset managers who are interested in setting up an index portfolio, there are two key questions regarding this trade-off: (1) What is the shape and position of the trade-off curve for the chosen index? And (2) where should asset managers be positioned on the trade-off curve? In other words, asset managers need to assess both the marginal costs of reducing tracking error (at each point on the curve), as well as their own preference for trading off transaction costs versus tracking error. If a manager is very sensitive to accurate tracking, then he or she may be willing to incur higher transaction costs. Alternatively, an asset manager whose priority is to reduce trading costs may be content to trade only the more liquid issues in the index, at the risk of underperforming (or outperforming) the index.

With broader-based indexes such as the Russell 2000, managing the trade-off between tracking error and transaction costs could become a profound challenge. For example, Figure 2 shows how even a small to medium sized Russell 2000 portfolio ($25 million) would generate many large individual trades (relative to average daily volume). These large trades would tend to generate high transaction costs.

FIGURE 2. *The Russell 2000: Trade Size Implied by a $25 Million Program versus Market Cap.*

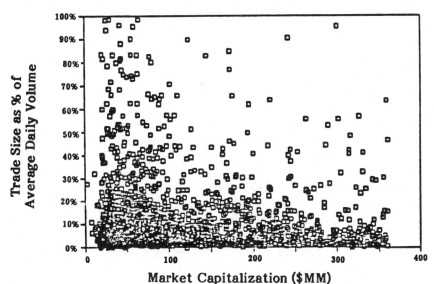

In fact, this figure probably understates the problem somewhat, since the Y-axis has been truncated at 100 percent. Hidden from view in this chart are numerous trades that would amount to several hundred percent of the stock's average daily volume. Moreover, it is interesting to note that the large capitalization stocks (that is, those that have the greatest weight in the Russell 2000) are not necessarily the most liquid. For example, many of the stocks above $100 million in market capitalization would, in a $25 million program, need to be traded in amounts greater than 20 percent of their average daily volume. Thus, creating a proxy portfolio simply by picking the largest capitalization issues might not produce a good solution.

III. Strategies for Constructing Index Proxies

Of course, the trade-off between tracking error and transaction costs is not unique to the Russell 2000. Investment managers have already developed approaches for constructing index portfolios. Some of these are discussed in the following sections, using the Russell 2000 as an example.

Choose the Stocks That Minimize Expected Tracking Error

One strategy is to choose, say, 250 stocks that minimize the expected tracking error of the portfolio versus the target index. There are now a variety of models (some available from commercial services) that will optimize a list of stocks to produce a basket that is expected to track a desired index most closely. The major benefit of this strategy is that investors can track the performance of a target index reasonably well with a manageable number of stocks. A potential shortcoming is that the trades that fall out of an optimization may generate heavy transaction costs.

Trade Only Stocks That Are Listed on the New York Stock Exchange

For the purposes of building proxy portfolios, New York Stock Exchange stocks (or, more generally, exchange-listed issues) have some unique appeal. First, the NYSE represents, in general, a liquid universe of stocks, on which the trading costs could be expected to be tolerable. Second, and perhaps even more important, NYSE stocks can generally be bought and sold at closing prices on the days that futures contracts expire. Through the so-called market-on-close (MOC) mechanism, investors may submit orders to buy or sell at the close and be assured of getting the closing price. This option is valuable to an investor who relies on an index futures contract, since the expiration value of the futures is based on the closing prices of the stocks in the associated index. Virtually all users of stock index futures depend to some degree on being able to trade the issues in the index at the same price as their futures positions at expiration.[1]

As much as MOC orders might help, however, obviously not all of the stocks in the Russell 2000 are NYSE-listed. In fact, NYSE issues account for about 500 of the total number of stocks in the Russell 2000, and for about 40 percent of the aggregate market capitalization of that index. In addition, there are a good number of liquid OTC stocks in the Russell 2000, so choosing only NYSE issues is probably not equivalent to selecting the least expensive equities to trade.

Trade Stocks That Meet Certain Liquidity or Size Requirements

Another simple approach is to trade only those stocks that meet a minimum standard for liquidity or market capitalization. For instance, relying on Figure 3, an asset manager might decide to trade stocks in amounts that would not exceed 20 percent of their average daily trading volume. Or, the manager might select the stocks whose market capitalizations exceed $100 million.

The primary virtue of this approach is its simplicity. However, a real drawback is that simple selection criteria (such as 20 percent average volume)

---

1. Trading in Russell 2000 and Russell 3000 stock index futures began on the New York Futures Exchange in September 1987. At the time of this writing, the Russell futures had not been able to sustain meaningful trading volume.

FIGURE 3. *The Russell 2000: Trade Size Implied by A $25 Million Program versus Market Cap.*

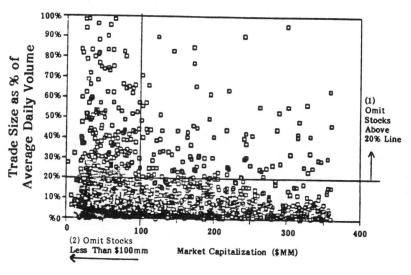

may provide an incomplete or flawed reflection of transaction costs. In Figure 4, we can see how a "20 percent cutoff" still leaves plenty of expensive stocks, with bid-ask spreads in excess of 2 percent of market value.

IV. Estimating the Cost of Trading Different Proxy Portfolios

This last example begs the question of how one can distinguish between an expensive and a cheap trade. With the Russell 2000, or any broad-based stock index, we need to be able to make some assessment of how costly it will be to trade different proxy portfolios. Asset managers may want to rely on their own assumptions or experience in estimating transaction costs. But for simplicity's sake, we will assume for now that, on a given trade:

% Transaction costs = 1/2 the bid-ask spread (in % terms)

+ (% bid-ask spread × trade size divided by
average daily volume).

This equation suggests that investors pay (on a buy or a sell order) one-half of the bid-ask spread plus a variable charge for trading a greater volume of shares as a percentage of the average day's volume. For instance, if the prevailing bid and ask quotes on a stock were $40 and $41, respectively, and an investor wanted to buy a quantity of shares equal to 100 percent of the

FIGURE 4. *Bid–Ask Spreads versus Trade Size for a $25 Million Russell 2000 Program.*

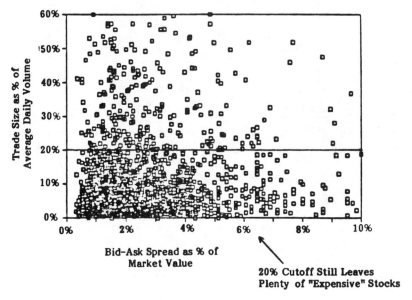

20% Cutoff Still Leaves
Plenty of "Expensive" Stocks

average daily volume in the stock, then that investor would incur transaction costs equal to $0.50 (one-half of the bid-ask spread) plus $1.00, for a total of $1.50, or 3.7 percent (using the midpoint of the bid-ask spread — $40.50 — as the market value of the stock). This formula does not account for commission costs.

V. Comparing Different Proxy Portfolios on the Basis of Predicted Tracking Error and Expected Transaction Costs

Using the aforementioned formula for transaction costs, and relying on tracking error projections from the BARRA risk model,[2] we can now compare the proxy portfolios that result from some of the simple strategies outlined previously. The first portfolio shown in Table 1 is the one containing all stocks in the Russell 2000 index. The predicted tracking error of this portfolio is, of course, zero, and the estimated trading costs are quite high, as expected. The proxy portfolio containing the 250 largest cap stocks in the

2. BARRA is a commercial provider of portfolio risk measurement services.

TABLE 1. *Comparison of Russell 2000 Proxies Using Various Selection Criteria.*

Selection Criteria	Predicted Tracking Error (%)	Estimated Trading Costs on a $25 Million Program (%)
All stocks in the Russell 2000	0	1.71
250 largest cap stocks in the Russell 2000	2.59	1.23
NYSE stocks in the Russell 2000	2.22	1.05
Optimized portfolio of 250 stocks that minimizes predicted tracking error	1.59	2.37
Optimized 250 stock portfolio adjusted to reduce trading costs	2.06	1.54

Russell 2000 (the second basket) fares slightly better in terms of expected transaction costs, but at the expense of substantial tracking error.[3]

The NYSE stock portfolio represents an improvement over the "250 large-cap" basket on both standards. However, the NYSE portfolio has been tailored somewhat (not optimized) to reduce tracking error. In contrast, the large-cap basket was not optimized at all. For each stock in the large-cap portfolio, shares were purchased in exact proportion to the market capitalization of the company.

The fourth portfolio shown is an optimized, 250-stock basket. These results show that the lowest tracking error that the risk model could produce with a limit of 250 stocks was 1.59%. The universe of stocks from which the model picked the 250-stock portfolio was the 1,000 largest cap stocks in the Russell 2000. In this case, 1,000 stocks represented the full capacity of the risk model supplying the tracking error projections.

What is most interesting about this optimized portfolio is the exceptionally high transaction costs it would be expected to incur in a $25 million program. In fact, it is projected to be even more expensive than trading all the stocks in the Russell 2000 index. This result might seem counter-intuitive at first. But it seems to suggest that, when dealing with a relatively illiquid universe of stocks, it is better to spread a given amount of dollars over a lot of issues, rather than to focus all the trading activity in fewer illiquid securities.

The final basket shown is the result of some simple changes in the optimized portfolio. Specifically, each of the stocks in the optimized basket was

---

3. Tracking error is defined as the standard deviation of the difference in performance between the proxy portfolio's return and the target index. For example, a tracking error of 2.00 percent would imply that, two-thirds of the time, the annual return on the proxy portfolio being analyzed is expected to differ (either positively or negatively) from the target index by 2.00 percent or less in absolute terms.

ranked by its marginal contribution to transaction costs (from highest to lowest). The five "most expensive" stocks were eliminated from the portfolio, and the funds that had been invested in those issues were reallocated to the five least expensive stocks. What is intriguing here is that a very quick-and-dirty adjustment could produce a highly favorable shift in transaction costs, while not sacrificing all that much in terms of tracking error. With more elaborate refinement, it seems clear that a more attractive proxy basket could be created by this method than by following any one simple decision rule.

VI. Implications of the Analysis

The foregoing analysis has several important implications for asset managers:

1. In the context of a broad-based index such as the Russell 2000, it is very important to consider transaction costs as well as tracking error.
2. It seems clear that trading Russell baskets can be an expensive proposition. Even if one assumes that transaction costs are limited to just one-half the bid-ask spread, the one-way costs of trading a Russell 2000 basket are still about 1.00 percent. In contrast, the transaction costs generated by trading an S&P 500 basket are often 0.30 percent or less.
3. This relatively high level of transaction costs suggests that the Russell futures (at least the Russell 2000) could become quite mispriced before arbitrage forces them back into line with their fair value. The reason for this is that arbitrageurs would have to pay these transaction costs before they could profit from mispriced futures.
4. Proxy portfolios based on simple, one-dimensional criteria (such as minimizing tracking error) can produce unsatisfactory results.
5. At least in the case of the Russell 2000, trading fewer stocks does not necessarily provide a good solution, both in terms of transaction costs and tracking error. As the amount of dollars to be invested increases, it seems desirable to spread those dollars over a greater number of stocks so as to avoid very large trades in individual issues.

17

Trading:
The Fixable Leak*

Dean LeBaron
Trustee
Batterymarch Financial
 Management

Evan Schulman
Partner
Batterymarch Canada

I. Introduction

Studies periodically jolt investors with new evidence that they rarely "beat the market." Somehow, dart board techniques confound the typical investment manager most of the time. In too many years, capitalization-weighted portfolios that are managed underperform the capitalization-weighted index by about a percentage point. The cost of the trading system partially explains this intuitively jarring underperformance by skilled professionals. While there may be differences of opinion about how to measure trading costs, investment managers are realizing that trading costs are related to investment returns.

We can measure trading costs in several ways. One way is to calculate the difference between the price of the stock immediately before entering the order and the net cost or proceeds. Another is to figure the difference between the net costs or proceeds and the price of the security shortly after trading it. To do either rather than both is like trying to measure the height of a house above ground by looking at only one side of it. If the house sits on a slope, we will get different answers depending on which side we approach.

---

*This article is reprinted from the Fall 1981 issue of *The Journal of Portfolio Management*.

In the case of buying a stock, if favorable information reaches the market before execution, the transaction cost may appear high when in reality the price adjustment had nothing to do with trading, but with security valuation instead. A similar analysis applies to measuring after the trade. A truer picture of the cost may be to measure both ways and take either the average or smaller of the two. This will approximate 1% per side for most institutions. Multiplied by portfolio turnover and added to management fees, the total shortfall is approximately 1%.

One percent seems small in comparison to the typical equity volatility of 22% annually, but 1% less return each year leads to 20% less accumulated wealth in 25 years and 36% less in 50 years. Very few investment strategies can overcome this sort of penalty. One percent per year of managed institutionalized assets is billions of dollars.

II. Bid/Ask Chasms

Jack Treynor, former editor of the *Financial Analysts Journal,* believes that trading costs approximate 10% per dollar traded.[1] He bases this estimate on a comparison of performance between actual portfolios and paper portfolios. We believe this transaction tariff is overstated, because nobody reports the results of paper portfolios that underperform. Treynor's view of investor behavior, however, is important.

He divides the world into two classes, traders and investors. Eager traders, driven by recent and readily discountable company information, try to feed on the wealth of value-oriented investors who establish bid/ask spreads or chasms for their protection. If the trader leaps the chasm, but his information didn't warrant the leap, his portfolio will underperform. If the trader has valuable information and the value-oriented investor stands too close to the edge of the bid/ask spread, the investor's portfolio will underperform. In either case, there is a transfer of wealth from one to another, but not a leak from the system as a whole. It is a zero sum game—small comfort, of course, to the client who is watching his wealth being transferred.

As long as there are traders and investors with differing opinions, these transfers will go on. What need not continue, however, is the small but constant leak that extracts a price from all who use the system, in proportion to their use. Part of this trading loss or leak is payment for an antiquated labor-intensive system and another is a monopoly rent to the specialist. The latter need not be paid; the former could be rendered almost insignificant. If this were done, the game of "traders and chasms" would be played using far less

---

1. Jack L. Treynor, "What Does it Take to Win the Trading Game?" *Financial Analysts Journal* (January/February 1981).

of our scarce resources. It is important to measure trading costs and to seek improvements. Trading costs count.

Visualize the scene from the visitors' gallery of the New York Stock Exchange. There are hundreds of people shouting, scribbling notes on pieces of paper, and waving their hands. Overhead, vacuum tubes whoosh their capsules into the bowels of the building.[2] There is a pervading machine shop din that most unions would claim is damaging to the mental state of its workers. This is the heart of western capitalism, where capital moves away from unproductive confines to its highest and best use. Out on the street, runners carry pieces of paper worth millions of dollars in little black bags, making deliveries of securities all over lower Manhattan. They wait to pick up their receipts and then hustle along to the next delivery. This system remains true to its time-honored practice. Senior investment executives brought up in this tradition have worked for decades to preserve it.

III. Plugging the Leak

For a while the Securities and Exchange Commission seemed to be advancing a National Open Market System over the opposition of entrenched industry interests, but discussions about it have resulted only in transient fanfare for an experiment by Merrill Lynch in automated trading on the Cincinnati Stock Exchange, and in the advent of Instinet as a computer exchange linking some eighty institutions and forty brokers. Yet, an automated electronic market would bring all financial participants together in a computerized environment, with rules governing who goes first and at what price. The function of the specialist — with privileged trading information — would become redundant. Even the real estate at Wall and Broad Street wouldn't be necessary for transactions requiring only wire connections.

Computers can execute and confirm orders based on programmed trading decisions 24 hours a day, seven days a week. Delivery and settlement can also be automated. Depository Trust Company immobilizes stock certificates and allows them to be treated as computerized bytes. This process is comparable to check clearing, which leads to a deposit entry instead of cash for each customer's account at a bank. Paper delivery is virtually eliminated. There are procedures for machine-to-machine reconciliation of settlements among the transaction participants: managers, brokers, and custodian banks. This process could accelerate next-day settlement of all transactions, surpassing the Japanese, who normally have a two-day system, and our own practice of five-day settlement.

---

2. The authors, in their efforts not to embarass themselves and the NYSE, decided to see if this statement had been corrected by modernization. An Exchange member confirmed that the vacuum tubes were still in use.

Nothing in the streamlining of settlement procedures requires a technological leap. The technology has been available for a decade. Brokerage firms and stock exchange members should examine the modern trading procedures pioneered by index funds and subsequently applied to active management. Those involved learned that machines could improve the quality and lower the costs of participating in the trading process, just as mass production improved the quality and lowered the costs of automobile manufacturing. While computers have been reducing the cost per unit of computation by 20% annually, individuals engaged in the conventional trading process have become more expensive at a 10% rate, resulting in an enormous gap in favor of machines.

IV. Why Does the Leak Persist?

The case for lower costs through computerized trading seems compelling. Why does the old system live on? In the days of fixed commission rates, services were provided to increase a brokerage firm's market share. Now some of these services are available at an extra cost within a lower, but essentially noncompetitive commission structure.[3] This feature allows investment managers to pay indirectly for services that they might otherwise have to provide themselves. It is still customary to use client brokerage for services unrelated to investment research. For example, performance measurement statistics used in marketing can usually be bought with commissions, even though the mandate of ERISA suggests fiduciaries should strive for the "best possible execution."

The leak persists because the direct participants in the trading process have a vested interest in the soft-dollar (payment via commission) to hard-dollar conversion procedure. The general resistance to change is not surprising, since almost all the participants prefer things the way they are. Implementing an efficient transaction system would be useful in reducing the fixable leak. Tampering with the system raises questions and poses the threat of other changes.

Investment managers who want to work on the leak now don't have to wait for the National Open Market System. Three steps are available to them. The first is to start measuring their transaction costs. The second is to factor out that part of the transaction cost that is simply a wealth transfer to other investors: This measurement will tell institutions just how much investment information they have. If institutions aren't shaken into inactivity

---

3. How is it possible to negotiate the commission rate *after* the trade? Without alternative bids, the only way to solve this problem is to refer to a price list.

by confronting their information content, the appropriate third step is to design and use an efficient trading system that will quickly and cheaply find and match the other side of their desired transactions. The result will be improved return for clients with no increase in investment risk.

18

Customized Performance Standards

Ronald J. Surz
Principal
Becker, Burke Associates Inc.

I. Introduction

The art of measuring and evaluating investment performance has come a long way. During its infancy in the 1960s, the fledgling performance measurement industry discovered "truth" in the time-weighted return as the performance standard. During the 1970s the industry evolved toward assessment of the time-weighted return as it relates to the risks. And the Information Age of the 1980s has brought us new insights into attribution of who and how value is added within the risk-return matrix.

Attribution explains performance by identifying areas where the manager has succeeded or failed, such as timing, security selection, rotation. The sponsor's role in this attribution is obvious: The sponsor hires the managers and allocates monies to them. Sponsor attribution is achieved by contrasting the total plan's results to other plans with similar structures and risks. Manager attribution is achieved by contrasting a manager's results to the results of other managers with similar portfolio characteristics. The collection of these portfolio characteristics is said to define the manager's "style."

However, many equity managers have objected to such style categorizations, claiming to be unique. These unique managers assert that there is no universe of comparable funds to compare them against. This dilemma has been addressed by creating a customized index that attempts to capture the pure essence of the manager. These customized indexes are commonly known as normal portfolios or reference portfolios. The manager's essence is captured by identifying the portfolio that would be held if the manager had no market insights; it is his information-neutral position.

In practice this information-neutral portfolio is constructed by identifying the securities that might be held in the manager's portfolio, and the probability of holding each individual issue; the normal portfolio is the probability-weighted average of these securities. Any deviation from the neutral position described by the normal portfolio embodies all of the manager's judgments, so that the difference between actual performance and reference portfolio performance is attributable to manager decisions.

There are several problems with the current normal portfolio approach. Some providers of normal portfolios use exotic formulas and complex methodologies that are impossible to understand and verify. There is no reliable means for ascertaining the degree of skill that is reflected in actual performance. Normal portfolios offer a benchmark for estimating information-neutral performance but offer virtually no basis for evaluating performance above or below this benchmark. That is, the industry needs a means for converting performance differentials into skill assessments.

A new technology, called Customized Performance Standards (CPS), measures the probability that a manager's performance differential is due to skill. This technology applies the fundamental laws of statistical inference to measure the chance of achieving the manager's result at random. It does this by extending the normal portfolio concept to a reference distribution. A computer emulates the manager's opportunity set by forming all portfolios (actually, a very good sample of all portfolios) that could be held by the manager, while still maintaining his or her "essence." These simulated portfolios form a background distribution for evaluating the manager. The median of the distribution is a heuristic normal portfolio; the other fractiles are the probabilities that skill is actually a factor.

The primary application of CPS is for performance evaluation and attribution. A natural outgrowth of CPS's capacity in these areas is to use CPS for performance-related fees. This article describes the CPS methodology in more detail and presents some of its applications.

II. Methodology

CPS begins with the money manager's description of his essence, or style. This description can be supplied at the security level or at the portfolio level. At the security level the manager identifies the universe of stocks that could be held in his portfolio and the typical (or information-neutral) commitment to each stock. This is totally analogous to the identification of a single normal portfolio. At the portfolio level the manager identifies the typical characteristics of his portfolio with regard to such fundamentals as dividend yield, capitalization, price/book, and so on. Of course, the manager can describe his style at both the security and the portfolio level; in most cases it is best to have both descriptions. In addition the manager can describe any rules that he applies to portfolio construction, such as number of names, minimum and maximum positions, and so forth. The sponsor verifies that these descriptions and rules are consistent with his best interests or modifies them to coincide with his interests.

CPS uses this information to emulate the manager's decision set. A random sample of portfolios is drawn from the manager's stock universe, using his construction rules. On average the simulated portfolios have the information-neutral commitment to each stock; this assures that the median of the reference distribution is the manager's reference portfolio. In other words the median of the opportunity set distribution represents a heuristic normal portfolio; it is the expected result that would fall out from following the manager's rules. A stratified sampling technique improves computer efficiency by enabling 1,000 random portfolios to replicate the characteristics of a much larger sample. If the manager has not described his style at the security level, the portfolio construction stage of the methodology is an unconstrained sampling of random securities from approximately 6,000 stocks on New York Stock Exchange, over the counter, and on regional exchanges. This unconstrained sampling is described in Section V.

The next step is to apply the manager's portfolio characteristics. A subset of the random portfolios described above is created. This subset consists of all random portfolios that conform to the characteristics provided by the manager, such as high yield and low capitalization.

Finally, performance results are calculated for the portfolio subset, and the reference distributions are created. Typically this reference distribution comprises at least 300 random portfolios. Performance results are calculated quarterly, and up to five years of history are typically reviewed. Cumulative performance allows for portfolio turnover over time. That is, changes in portfolio composition are simulated on a quarterly basis, without transaction costs. Transaction costs are omitted to reflect the lack of information in the simulations; actual transactions should be information motivated, and the value of the information should exceed transaction costs. Disappointing results stay in the distributions, thus eliminating survivorship bias; the computer doesn't fire anybody. In effect each cumulative portfolio simulation represents a decision path that could have been taken by the manager over time. The sampling technique minimizes bias and assures reproducibility; in other words, reruns of the computer system produce very similar results, even if the number of trials is increased. The distributions of these random portfolios form the basis for performance measurement and attribution, as discussed in the next section.

III. Performance Evaluation

Evaluation and attribution of a manager's performance is accomplished by measuring style and skill effects. The style effect is measured by comparing the manager's reference distribution to a total distribution; each quarter an unconstrained total distribution is created to measure the opportunity set available to the investing public as a whole. Skill effects are measured in two ways. If the manager has changed style, the wisdom of this decision can be evaluated by contrasting the manager's dynamic reference distribution to a control distribution that ignores the style changes. The second measure of skill is the manager's customized ranking within his or her reference distribution; this is primarily the manager's selection skill. The manager's customized performance ranking measures the probability that the performance result is merely a matter of chance. Ideally, you would like to be at least 90 percent confident that the manager has skill before accolades and fee increases are bestowed, or vice versa for poor performance.

The primary purpose of performance evaluation is to decide whether a manager should be terminated or entrusted with additional funds. This is a difficult decision because there is always the fear that a manager will be terminated unjustly, or that he will be terminated just before he vindicates himself. Contributing to this concern is the ready availability of consultants to conduct a manager search. A customized performance ranking alleviates the problem of unjust termination by quantifying the probability that the manager has made errors in judgment. If the probability of poor decision making is high, and if the manager appears unable to correct his or her problems, then termination is the appropriate course of action.

In many situations the decision is not that evident. A reasonable course of action in such situations would be partial termination. For example, some investments could be withdrawn from the manager, and the withdrawals could be invested in a shadow portfolio, which would be a passively managed portfolio tracking the manager's normal portfolio. The collection of such shadow portfolios across several managers comprises a completeness fund. This reduces the manager's fee, insulates the total portfolio from future disappointments, and maintains diversification. Of course money would flow to the manager if results were good.

Customized performance rankings could be used to determine the balance between active management and the shadow portfolio. The mechanics would be similar to those described in the following section. The idea of partial termination, and the use of shadow portfolios, has not been tried in practice. A similar concept that *has* is performance-related fees. The next section describes the application of CPS for using performance-related fees.

IV. Performance-Related Fees

The issue of managers' compensation has become very topical recently. In a free enterprise economy, it seems natural that the investment community will embrace performance-related fees. The client favors such fees because it seems logical to compensate well for good performance and to pay less for poor performance. Since many investment management firms are prospering, there is a general feeling that fees are probably too high. ("Where are the clients' yachts?") Managers favor these fees because they believe that they will be the good performers who will be well compensated.

The regulatory environment is evolving toward greater acceptance of performance-related fees. The Securities and Exchange Commission authorized performance-based fees in November 1985, making it possible for non-ERISA plans to enter into such agreements.[1] Then in September 1986 the U.S. Department of Labor approved performance-based fees for two managers, paving the way for broader authorizations in the future for ERISA plans.

Most performance-related fee arrangements have been structured along the lines depicted in Figure 1. Essentially the manager earns his current fee only if he outperforms a benchmark portfolio by an agreed-upon amount. Performance below the benchmark-plus target results in reduced fees, but there is usually some floor fee, called a base fee. Performance above the benchmark-plus target results in increased fees, and there is normally some ceiling placed on this.

To establish this relationship, the following items must be negotiated between sponsor and manager:

1. Benchmark portfolio
2. Base fee
3. Target excess return
4. Maximum fee
5. Fee rate—change in fee per performance unit
6. Time period

There is consensus that the benchmark portfolio should reflect the manager's investment style. Accordingly the most sensible arrangements incorporate a customized benchmark that is similar to a normal portfolio. However,

---

1. ERISA is the Employee Retirement Income Security Act of 1974. It established standards of fair practice for nongovernmental retirement plans.

FIGURE 1. *Typical Approach to Performance-Related Fees.*

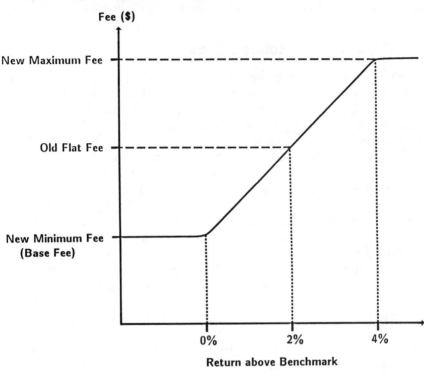

many performance-related fee agreements use the Standard and Poor's 500 as the benchmark regardless of the manager's style; this appears to be easier for many sponsors to agree to because it is easier to understand.

The next four negotiable items—base fee, target excess return, maximum fee, and fee rate—deal with tying relative performance to fees. Generally speaking, these items are established on a somewhat arbitrary basis. It is common to set the base fee near a passive management fee and to fix the target at 2 percent above the benchmark. The rationale for a passive-management base fee is that the benchmark result could have been achieved with certainty for a passive fee. The rationale for the 2 percent target rests primarily in custom; convention would have it that a good manager should outperform the S&P by 2 percent, although the data generally does not bear out this convention.

These rationalizations do not stand up to scrutiny. Performance below the benchmark is still compensated at the base fee, even though real losses have been sustained relative to the passive alternative. Similarly the 2 percent bogey is probably going to be as tough to beat in the future as it has been in the past. Some remedies to these problems can be found through the use of CPS. An alternative approach to performance-related fees would begin by establishing the manager's confidence in his ability to outperform his customized benchmark portfolio. If the manager states the odds of this outperformance at 50-50, the optimal sponsor decision is passive management. Most managers would state the chances of outperformance at 2-in-3, or better. This expression of confidence can be used to structure a more rational performance-related fee arrangement. Fees can be structured such that the manager receives his current fees if his confidence is borne out in experience. To accomplish this, the manager is compensated in relation to his customized performance ranking. A ranking at the confidence level (for example, the thirty-third percentile for the manager who has 2-in-3 confidence) results in the old fee being paid. Rankings above and below the confidence level result in fee increases and reductions. Figure 2 shows how this agreement can be structured. The appeal of this arrangement is that it compensates the

FIGURE 2. *Customized Performance Standards Approach.*

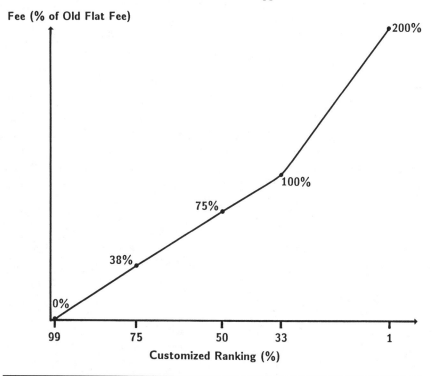

manager in accordance with the likelihood that value has actually been added, or subtracted. Also, it eliminates much of the arbitrariness that is inherent in most of the current deals. Some have argued that since the manager cannot know the composition of this thirty-third percentile portfolio, he cannot compete against it. This is precisely the beauty of CPS; since the manager can't know, the bogey can't be gamed. The manager should know his normal portfolio, so he overweights some securities and underweights others to add value; the question is whether or not these weightings are skillful.

The last item for negotiation is time period. The minimum time period that has been contemplated is one year, and one year seems appropriate. This opinion is based on the following observations:

- Multiple-year contracts are usually "rolling," which means that a good-performing manager can ride out one good year for an extended period. If a poor-performing manager is fired before the contract period lapses, he will probably not be asked to rebate overpayments. That is, the cumulative arrangement is "cancellable with penalty."
- With a one-year arrangement the manager can stay in the game. One bad year will not result in several years of reduced fees.
- With annual fees manager and sponsor get to start fresh each year. Tensions should be lower, and incentives for gaming should be reduced.
- Long-run fees should be fairer with annual settlements.
- The custom of paying fees on an annual basis is preserved.
- Being a Chicagoan, I'm accustomed to saying "Wait until next year."

V. The Results

Does the technique work? To test the methodology, we have applied CPS without customization to a large data base of stocks. If the methodology works, this unconstrained portfolio construction should produce return distributions that are similar to those of performance evaluators with huge data bases. Table 1 shows how the CPS results compare to those of the Wilshire Cooperative (WILCOP)[2] Data Base for equity returns. The WILCOP data base consists of approximately 1,000 funds, with total assets in excess of $100 billion. It is constructed by collecting client data from more than 15 pension consulting firms across the country. As can be seen from the table, the results to date are quite comparable. This is true in spite of the fact that the CPS distributions do not suffer from the "survivorship basis" that results when managers are removed from accounts in evaluators' data bases. CPS never "fires a manager."

Two other tests of CPS have also been performed. To test security-specific customizations, distributions of industry-specific portfolios have been

---

2. WILCOP is a registered trademark of Wilshire Associates, Santa Monica, California.

TABLE 1. CPS History, 1986 and 1987.

	3/86			6/86			9/86			12/86		
	WILCOP	CPS	S&P	WILCOP	CPS	S&P	WILCOP	CPS	S&P	WILCOP	CPS	S&P
1 Quarter												
25	18.4	16.6		6.7	7.8		−5.3	−5.9		6.3	6.7	
50	16.1	14.3	14.1	4.5	5.7	5.9	−7.7	−7.8	−7.0	4.8	5.0	5.4
75	13.9	11.8		3.0	3.5		−10.5	−9.7		3.4	3.3	
2 Quarters												
25	40.4	37.4		24.9	24.0		−0.6	0.6		−0.8	−0.4	
50	36.5	33.8	33.8	21.3	20.7	20.9	−3.2	−2.5	−1.4	−3.3	−3.2	−2.0
75	32.8	30.1		18.5	17.3		−6.3	−5.3		−6.5	−5.6	
3 Quarters												
25	33.5	31.3		47.6	45.4		15.0	15.4		4.5	6.2	
50	29.9	27.3	28.3	42.6	40.8	41.8	12.1	11.4	12.5	1.2	2.4	3.9
75	25.6	23.4		38.0	36.1		8.3	7.3		−2.2	−0.9	
1 Year												
25	44.5	41.6		40.8	39.0		35.5	35.2		21.0	22.0	
50	40.1	36.4	37.8	35.9	33.9	35.9	31.6	29.6	31.9	17.3	16.8	18.6
75	35.3	31.1		30.9	29.1		27.7	24.9		13.5	12.2	
2 Years												
25	33.4	31.0		37.5	32.9		25.3	24.5		27.4	26.8	
50	30.6	27.5	28.0	34.5	29.8	33.5	22.7	21.5	22.9	24.6	23.5	25.0
75	26.5	23.6		30.7	27.1		20.1	18.4		21.7	20.2	
3 Years												
25	23.1	22.3		20.8	17.8		17.9	16.0		19.8	18.3	
50	20.7	19.6	21.1	18.1	15.6	19.2	15.1	13.5	16.5	17.8	16.0	18.4
75	17.4	16.4		14.3	13.6		12.7	11.4		14.2	13.6	
5 Years												
25	19.5	19.9		21.9	18.5		21.7	20.0		22.0	19.8	
50	17.7	17.2	17.3	19.4	16.9	19.2	19.9	18.5	20.1	19.7	18.1	19.7
75	15.1	14.4		17.4	15.0		17.6	16.6		17.0	16.0	

TABLE 1 *Continued*

	3/87			6/87			9/87			12/87		
	WILCOP	CPS	S&P	WILCOP	CPS	S&P	WILCOP	CPS	S&P	WILCOP	CPS	S&P
1 Quarter												
25	23.9	23.1		5.2	5.7		8.1	8.5		−20.6	−20.9	
50	21.5	20.6	21.3	3.5	4.1	5.1	6.6	6.6	6.6	−23.0	−22.4	−22.6
75	19.4	18.2		1.9	2.4		5.1	4.6		−24.8	−24.2	
2 Quarters												
25	30.8	30.0		28.4	28.9		12.8	13.6		−14.9	−15.4	
50	27.4	26.7	27.8	25.2	25.6	27.6	10.2	11.0	12.1	−17.6	−17.3	−17.5
75	24.2	23.1		21.7	22.2		7.5	8.0		−20.0	−19.6	
3 Quarters												
25	20.9	21.0		35.9	36.0		38.0	38.3		−11.3	−11.3	
50	17.5	16.9	18.9	31.4	31.8	34.5	33.3	33.7	36.0	−14.5	−14.0	−13.2
75	13.9	12.8		26.7	27.9		28.1	29.6		−18.1	−16.8	
1 Year												
25	26.9	28.9		26.3	26.7		45.1	45.5		7.1	7.8	
50	22.9	23.6	26.0	21.4	21.7	25.1	40.2	40.4	43.3	2.6	3.8	5.2
75	18.4	18.5		16.7	17.0		34.5	35.2		−1.7	0.5	
2 Years												
25	34.3	32.7		31.0	31.1		39.5	38.7		12.5	13.3	
50	31.3	29.4	31.8	28.4	27.6	30.4	36.5	35.0	37.5	10.1	9.9	11.7
75	28.3	21.0		25.6	24.1		33.1	31.4		8.0	6.8	
3 Years												
25	30.4	27.9		32.7	31.2		31.4	30.3		19.1	19.2	
50	27.8	25.6	27.3	30.1	28.6	30.6	28.6	27.5	29.4	16.9	16.4	17.1
75	24.7	22.9		27.4	25.8		26.1	24.8		15.1	13.9	
5 Years												
25	28.4	26.5		29.5	27.8		28.1	26.7		18.0	16.3	
50	26.4	24.5	26.4	27.5	25.0	27.8	25.9	24.8	26.7	15.6	14.5	16.5
75	18.6	19.9		25.2	23.8		23.5	22.7		13.6	12.7	

formed; these distributions can be used to identify a manager's or analyst's proficiency at forming portfolios within a given industry. To test portfolio-specific customizations, distributions by "manager style" have been formed. Figure 3 shows how managers' styles are defined. For example, "defensive" portfolios are those portfolios with above-median capitalization and below-median aggressiveness; aggressiveness is a composite of portfolio yield and P/E.

Table 2 summarizes these distributions for the year ending December 31, 1987. The industry distributions are close to those provided by WILCOP and have been for all periods tested. The manager's style distributions are not directly comparable to published distributions because they are defined differently by the various service providers; however, the CPS manager's style distributions seem reasonable in relation to other published distributions. These tests were initiated in the first quarter of 1986 and are repeated every quarter.

Finally, the methodology has been applied to live managers. Tables 3a and 3b exemplify one such application. As can be seen from the table, this manager's style moved in and out of favor during periods ending June 30, 1987, but there is a high probability that the manager made mistakes during

TABLE 2. *Industry and Style Distributions for the Year Ending December 31, 1987.*

Industry Distributions (%)

	Non-durables	Durables	Materials and Services	Capital Goods	Technology
25	7.2	17.2	19.2	15.7	10.6
50	0.7	13.3	14.3	12.4	5.1
75	−0.7	7.4	9.5	7.6	1.1

	Energy	Transportation	Utility	Finance
25	13.4	2.3	0.0	−9.1
50	10.4	−0.8	−1.8	−13.4
75	7.4	−6.1	−4.2	−16.7

Style Distributions (%)

	Defensive	Aggressive	Cautious	Venturesome	Core
25	8.3	6.7	8.7	5.9	7.9
50	4.7	3.1	4.5	2.4	4.8
75	0.4	−0.6	−0.4	−1.9	0.6

FIGURE 3. *Investment Manager Style Matrix.*

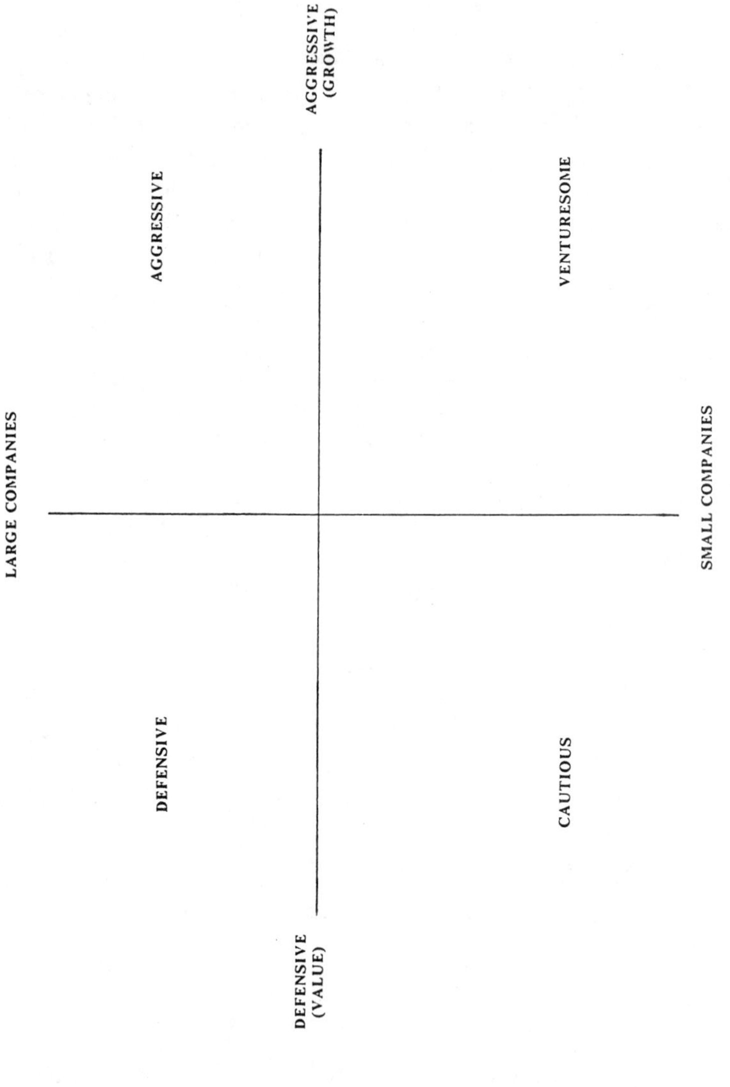

LARGE COMPANIES

DEFENSIVE

AGGRESSIVE

DEFENSIVE
(VALUE)

AGGRESSIVE
(GROWTH)

CAUTIOUS

VENTURESOME

SMALL COMPANIES

TABLE 3a. *Portfolio Characteristics Rankings.*

Quarter	Capitalization		Price/Earnings		Yield		Earnings Growth	
	Total	Custom	Total	Custom	Total	Custom	Total	Custom
86/4								
Median	9.3	7.6	14.6	18.6	3.3	2.1	5.1	10.9
Manager	7.3		16.7		2.1		4.6	
Manager rank	68	54	31	71	98	53	55	97
87/1								
Median	9.5	6.3	14.8	18.7	3.2	2.0	5.1	10.2
Manager	7.7		18.9		1.7		6.7	
Manager rank	69	30	19	48	99	88	34	88
87/2								
Median	12.2	7.9	18.8	24.8	2.7	1.6	5.6	9.8
Manager	9.7		23.8		1.4		10.8	
Manager rank	64	30	13	59	99	81	9	34

TABLE 3b. *Performance Rankings.*

Quarter	3 Years		2 Years		1 Year		3 Quarters		2 Quarters		1 Quarter	
	Total	Custom	Total	Custom	Total	Custom	Total	Custom	Total	Custom	Total	Custom
86/4												
Median	16.0	13.9	23.5	23.0	16.8	14.5	2.4	−1.8	−3.2	−7.2	5.0	5.4
Manager	15.4		26.9		19.1		−1.7		−9.8		5.7	
Manager rank	56	35	25	22	38	24	79	49	95	76	41	45
87/1												
Median	25.6	26.0	29.4	31.0	23.6	23.3	16.9	16.1	26.7	32.1	20.6	25.2
Manager	27.0		35.4		20.2		10.3		29.3		22.3	
Manager rank	35	38	13	18	68	65	87	87	30	70	32	78
87/2												
Median	28.6	27.9	27.8	28.3	21.8	19.5	31.8	36.0	25.4	28.9	4.1	2.8
Manager	28.5		28.7		9.6		28.5		21.6		−0.6	
Manager rank	52	44	42	45	95	93	71	88	78	92	95	91

the year ending June 30, 1987. That is, the chances are high that the poor relative one-year performance result is due to bad judgment rather than bad luck. By contrast, earlier manager results are quite satisfactory.

VI. Conclusion

The use of normal portfolios for performance evaluation and performance-based fees has become widely accepted. Properly constructed, a normal portfolio is the best benchmark against which a manager's performance can be compared. However, a problem still remains in determining whether performance above the benchmark is due to skill, and whether performance below the benchmark is due to lack of skill. Some have asserted that this skill assessment is achievable by forecasting the standard deviation of the normal portfolio. Unfortunately this forecast is subject to error since it is based on history and since the standard deviation of a normal portfolio changes over time. A better way to detect a manager's skill is to create a reference distribution of the manager's opportunity set. The median of the reference distribution is a heuristic normal portfolio, and the fractiles are the probabilities that skill was actually a factor. Customized Performance Standards extend the normal portfolio concept to a reference distribution framework that can be used to ascertain managers' skill.

19

How Clients Can Win the Gaming Game*

Mark Grinblatt
Associate Professor
Graduate School of Management
UCLA

Sheridan Titman
Associate Professor
Graduate School of Management
UCLA

I. Introduction

How enlightened was the decision of the Department of Labor and the Securities and Exchange Commission to approve performance-based fee arrangements for managers of pension funds? A recent *Institutional Investor* article states, "Pension officers are turning to performance-based systems because they are fed up with shelling out millions of dollars in fees year after year for money management strategies that can't even seem to keep up with the market."[1] Many observers also believe that performance-based fees may create greater incentives for portfolio managers to use their talents for the benefit of the pension fund.

This article demonstrates that incentive fee contracts could lead to results that are quite the opposite of these perceptions. Many performance contracts can create incentives for the portfolio manager to game the contract at the expense of the pension fund. For example, the archetypical performance contract provides an incentive to the portfolio manager to increase the unsystematic volatility of the portfolio and/or target a portfolio beta

*This article is reprinted from the Summer 1987 issue of *The Journal of Portfolio Management*. The authors would like to thank Michael Brennen, Richard Roll, Eduardo Schwartz, and Meir Statman for their helpful comments.
1. Fran Hawthorne, "The Dawning of Performance Fees," *Institutional Investor* (September 1986): 139–46.

that substantially deviates from one. Such contracts offer the portfolio manager a riskless arbitrage opportunity that is easy to implement.

The client does not have to provide a manager with this opportunity. By appropriately altering the contracts, adding a cap on the maximum performance fee, and instituting a penalty for negative performance, clients can overcome the adverse incentives problem.

II. Performance-Based Contracts and Options

The simplest performance contract has two features: a base fee and a bonus based on the degree to which the managed portfolio's return exceeds the return of some benchmark, typically the Standard & Poor's 500. The article in *Institutional Investor,* for instance, notes that Chicago Corp. will get 10% of the difference between the performance of its managed portfolio and that of the S&P 500.

Note that the Chicago Corp. contract has many of the features of a call option. Figure 1 illustrates the performance-based contract's percentage reward to the manager as a function of the return of the portfolio in excess of the return of the S&P 500. The flat portion of the figure, the base fee, corresponds to the value of an option when it is out-of-the-money; the positively sloped portion corresponds to the value of an in-the-money option. The bonus trigger point of the Chicago Corp. contract is at zero, implying that the kink in the graph is at its intersection with the vertical axis.

More general performance fee contracts could have positive or negative bonus trigger points, which would shift the graph to the right or to the left. They could have caps on the fee and/or several trigger points at which the bonus rate increases. They might also be represented as a series of escalating steps.

Although we cannot analyze all the contracts that currently are being considered, we can approximate most of them by a few representative contracts. The insights gained from examining a few representative contracts generalize to most situations.

Consider a manager whose portfolio holds the equity securities in the S&P 500 (properly proportioned). In this case, the manager's reward will be the vertical intercept of the performance graph, which normally will be the base fee. On the other hand, suppose that a manger holds a leveraged position in the S&P 500. To make the example simple, suppose that this manager borrows $1 million at a rate of 9% and invests $2 million in the S&P 500. Figure 2 plots the return of this levered S&P 500 position in excess of the S&P 500 return as a function of the S&P 500 return. R_f is the cost of the borrowed money. The S&P 500 portfolio (i.e., the unlevered position) lies on the horizontal axis in this diagram. The levered position in the S&P 500 described above is a 45-degree line. In general, the slope of this line increases and the intercept decreases as the leverage increases.

FIGURE 1. *Management Fee as a Function of the Return of the Portfolio in Excess of the Return of the S&P 500.*

Panel A: Simple Fee Structure

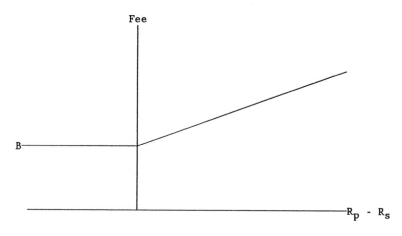

Panel B: Complex Fee Structure

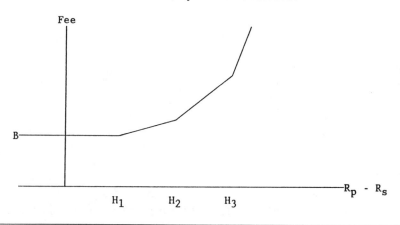

III. Algebraic Analysis of the Value of Performance-Based Fees

Figure 2 allows us to plot the performance fee of a levered position in the S&P 500 as a function of the S&P 500 return. For simplicity, let us assume that the fee structure is similar to the Chicago Corp. example, namely:

$$F = \max[B, B + Vm(\tilde{R}_p - \tilde{R}_s)]$$
$$= B + Vm[\max(0, \tilde{R}_p - \tilde{R}_s)], \tag{1}$$

FIGURE 2. *Return in Excess of the S&P 500 Return of a 50% Levered Portfolio as a Function of the Return of the S&P 500.*

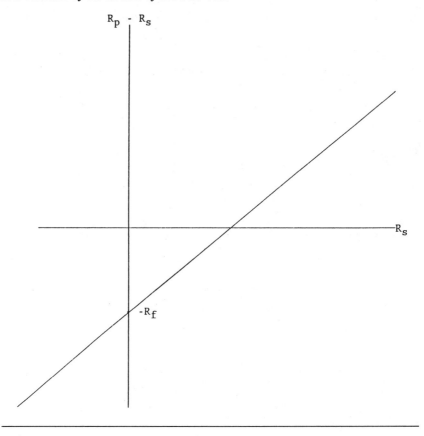

where:

B = base fee,

V = net asset value of the fund at the beginning of the evaluation period,

m = fraction of the return of the fund in excess of the S&P return awarded to the manager as a bonus for good performance,

$\tilde{R}_p$ = return of the managed portfolio, and

$\tilde{R}_s$ = return of the S&P 500 portfolio.

In the case described above, we assumed that $\tilde{R}_p = 2\tilde{R}_s - 0.09$ and V = 1,000,000. If we also assume that m = 0.10, as is true for Chicago Corp., we can write the fee in equation (1) as

$$F = B + 100{,}000 \max(0, \tilde{R}_s - 0.09). \tag{2}$$

FIGURE 3. *Management Fee for a 50% Levered Portfolio as a Function of the Return of the S&P 500.*

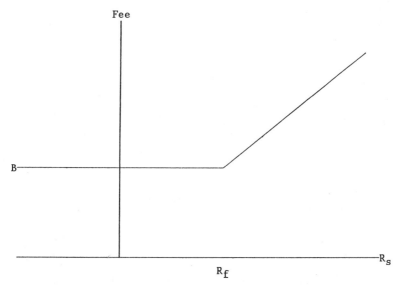

Figure 3 plots this equation, which represents the fee as a function of the return of the S&P 500. This still has the shape of a call option payoff. Note, however, what happens if the leverage of the position changes. If the fraction f of V, with $f > 1$, is invested in the S&P 500, and $V(f-1)$ is borrowed to finance this purchase, equation (2) becomes

$$F = B + 100{,}000(f-1) \max(0, \tilde{R}_s - 0.09), \tag{3}$$

and for $f < 1$ (i.e., the fund is long in the risk-free asset), equation (2) becomes

$$F = B + 100{,}000(1-f) \max(0, 0.09 - \tilde{R}_s). \tag{4}$$

Equations (3) and (4) are plotted in Figure 4 for various values of f. Panel A illustrates that, as f increases above one (i.e., becomes more levered), the slope of the payoff changes — it becomes steeper to the right of the kink. Alternatively, as we know from equation (3), increasing the leverage of the position implies that the fee structure has more call options implicit in the payoff. Call options always have positive value. Therefore, as the manager levers up the portfolio, the present (and expected) value of the fee contract increases. Similarly, as we can see in Panel B, decreases in f below one (i.e., placing a portion of the portfolio in a risk-free asset) make the slope of the payoff steeper to the left of the kink. This represents an increase in the number of put options awarded to the manager. Note that any increase in

FIGURE 4. *Management Fee for Various Portfolios of the Risk-Free Asset and the S&P 500 as a Function of the Return of the S&P 500.*

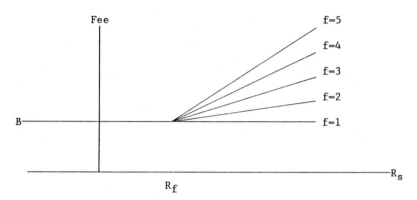

Panel A: Leverage Positions in the S&P 500

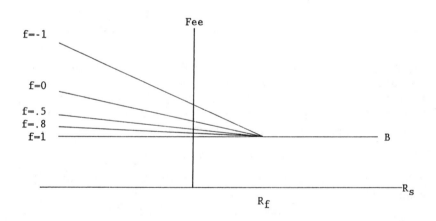

Panel B: Portfolios with Long Positions in the Risk-Free Asset

fees as a result of leverage changes is offset by a decrease in the expected return of the fund, because leverage changes per se cannot benefit the fund.

The portfolio manager has the opportunity to capture the present value of these fees risklessly. For a levered portfolio, call options can be written on a $1 investment in the S&P 500 in the personal portfolio with striking prices equal to one plus the risk-free rate. In years where the S&P 500 does poorly, the manager will be compensated by the decline in the value of the options shorted for the personal portfolio. In years where the S&P 500 does well, the manager will be compensated through the management fee for the liability incurred by the option short positons. In either event, the manager's profit is equal to the sum of the base fee and the proceeds from the sale of the options in the personal portfolio. The number of options the manager writes is the product of V, m, and $f-1$.

To hedge the fees for a portfolio with a positive net position in the risk-free asset (i.e., $f < 1$), the manager merely needs to write comparable put options. The number of options written is the product of V, m, and $1 - f$. Note that this hedging need never be known to the pension fund officers.

More general fee contracts might impose caps on the fee structure (e.g., 2% of net asset value) or may have many trigger points. These fee structures, as currently implemented, generally provide incentives to employ risk-free borrowing or lending to create a risk position that substantially differs from the risk of the S&P 500 portfolio alone. The fee, in this case, can be hedged with portfolios of call (or put) options. The striking prices of the options depend on the trigger points, the proportion of the managed portfolio invested in the risk-free asset, and the cap.

For example, the contract with a cap and a single trigger point for a manager who follows a buy-and-hold strategy in the S&P 500 and a risk-free asset can be hedged by (1) purchasing options on the S&P 500 with striking prices that are related to the trigger point for the bonus, and (2) writing options with striking prices that are related to the cap. The striking prices of these options also vary as the amount of leverage in the portfolio varies.[2]

IV. A Numerical Example of Contract Valuation

We used the Black–Scholes[3] model as a simple exercise to calculate the value of the performance-based fee for various portfolios of S&P 500 equities and a risk-free asset. Under the assumption that the manager is compensated annually, we estimated the value of the one-year European calls on the S&P 500 required to create a perfect hedge on the fee contract arranged for Chicago Corp. The numbers are expressed as a percentage of net asset value.

In this example, $m = 0.1$, and we assumed that the volatility of the S&P portfolio is 0.20, which yields a call option value equal to 7.97% of the value of the underlying asset.[4] The parameters of the option contract give the relevant put option an identical value. For risk-free investments, short or long, amounting to 10% of the net asset value of the managed fund, and

---

2. Technical analysis of many of these more general contracts may be found in Mark Grinblatt and Sheridan Titman, "Adverse Risk Incentives and the Design of Performance-Based Contracts," Working Paper, UCLA, 1987.

3. Fischer Black and Myron Scholes, "The Pricing of Options and Corporate Liabilities," *Journal of Political Economy* (May/June 1973): 637–54.

4. The borrowing rate of interest does not affect the calculation of the call and put option values, because the present value of the striking price is not affected by the interest rate.

hence portfolio betas (relative to the benchmark) of 1.1 and 0.9, respectively, this performance-based fee can, without risk, be guaranteed to offer 79.7 basis points of net asset value per year in excess of the base fee. For betas of 0.8 or 1.2, the bonus fee is equivalent to paying the manager an additional 159.4 basis points per year.

Even though the European option valued above is not traded, performance-based fees still can be almost perfectly hedged with publicly traded American index options. Alternatively, we could hedge with dynamic trading strategies that mimic options—employing futures contracts, index funds, or individual securities. The hedge ratios for these trading strategies are more complicated to calculate, and they change over time, but the European option values still represent the market value of the performance-based contract that should be used for comparison with standard fixed management fees. The example above indicates that a leveraged portfolio or a portfolio with a beta (relative to the benchmark) that is substantially less than one would make the Chicago Corp. performance contract significantly more lucrative than most standard fixed management fees.

V. Designing Contracts without Adverse Risk Incentives

We have demonstrated that managers with performance-based contracts can increase the value of their fees by increasing leverage or investing in a risk-free asset. This tendency to alter the risk of the managed portfolio is similar to the incentives that equityholders have to expropriate wealth from existing bondholders by such techniques as increasing their leverage, choosing riskier projects, or paying dividends. Bondholders, aware of the adverse incentives of value-maximizing equityholders, include covenants that limit these forms of expropriation.

Pension funds could place similar restrictions on the behavior of their performance-compensated portfolio managers. For instance, a contract could prohibit the manager from borrowing or holding short or long positions in a risk-free asset or equivalent positions in futures or option contracts.

The manager could, however, still achieve higher fees by choosing to hold securities with either very high betas or very low betas. The client could try to counter this behavior by basing the fee on a measure of performance that is adjusted for beta,[5] but there is a vast literature in finance on classes of securities that outperform beta-based benchmarks as traditionally computed. Moreover, in this case, the manager can gain by choosing stocks with large amounts of unsystematic risk. This action could be even worse from the pension fund's perspective, because it might increase the fund's riskiness

---

5. For a review of these techniques, see Mark Grinblatt, "How to Evaluate a Portfolio Manager," *Financial Markets and Portfolio Management* 1, no. 2 (March 1987): 9–20.

without increasing its expected return. Indeed, contractual limitations on the manager could be counterproductive if they limit the manager's flexibility, and hence, the opportunity to achieve abnormal returns.

A pension fund officer could also try to eliminate the incentive to increase risk by changing the performance contract. In the absence of a cap, a manager whose penalties from losses are as large as the benefits from gains earns a fee that is perfectly correlated with pension fund performance. Nevertheless, unlimited penalties against the portfolio manager are probably impossible.

A cap on the fee does not eliminate the incentive to increase or decrease risk if the bonus is triggered when the return of the portfolio is greater than that of the S&P 500, as in Figure 5, Panel A. If the bonus is triggered for portfolio returns that are less than the S&P return, as in Panel B of Figure 5, the contract may eliminate the incentive. These types of contracts provide a reward for performance above that of the S&P, a penalty for performance below that of the S&P 500, and caps on both rewards and penalties.

If the maximum gain in compensation that the manager can achieve from beating the S&P (above what would be achievable by matching the S&P) is no greater than the maximum loss in compensation from doing worse than the S&P, the adverse risk incentive is eliminated for certain types of portfolio managers. These are managers who follow strategies that allow only small changes in the risk of the portfolio over time, such as buy-and-hold and many balancing strategies.

Contracts with penalties that exceed rewards may not preclude gaming if the portfolio manager can aggressively alter the portfolio's risk within the evaluation period. Some strategies, for instance, can virtually guarantee that the manager will receive the maximum fee, irrespective of the severity of the penalty. These strategies dramatically alter the risk of the managed portfolio over time in response to past movements in stock prices.[6]

Although the changes in risk required to guarantee the maximum fee are too drastic to be realistic, in that they generate large transaction costs and can be easily detected, the incentive to aggressively alter risk still exists. Evidence of this form of gaming was found in a recent *Wall Street Journal* article[7] which recalled "a couple of managers who stated their objectives as investing in blue-chip stocks with market capitalizations over $500 million. But when the managers' performance numbers sagged, they began to 'stretch for performance by going for takeover candidates and high-flying over-the-counter stocks.'"

---

6. These strategies are described in Grinblatt and Titman, "Adverse Risk Incentives and the Design of Performance-Based Contracts."

7. John Dorfman, "Paying a Pro to Help Find a Money Manager," *Wall Street Journal,* 24 December 1986.

FIGURE 5. *Management Fees wth Caps as a Function of the Return of the Portfolio in Excess of the Return of the S&P 500.*

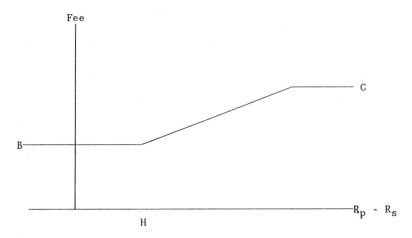

Panel A: Positive Bonus Trigger Point

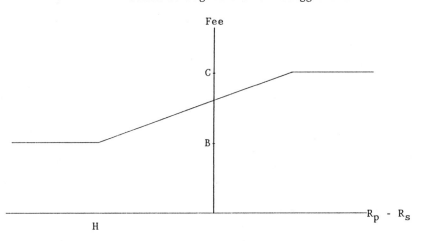

Panel B: Negative Bonus Trigger Point

B = base fee.
H = hurdle point at which a bonus to the base fee is first received.
C = cap or maximum fee.

Although we believe that contracts should have maximum penalties for poor performance that exceed the maximum reward for good performance (relative to purchasing the S&P), penalties that are too severe are not desirable. Such penalties will not only eliminate the manager's incentive to alter risk, but will reduce the incentives of the manager to improve the true performance of the fund as well. Superior stock selection requires non-zero unsystematic risk in the portfolio, which reduces the present values of contracts with sufficiently large penalties relative to the rewards. For this reason, careful design of the performance-based contract is important.

VI. Long-Term Reputation Considerations

The model we have described oversimplifies the rewards and penalties that actual portfolio managers face. The model also assumes a one-period horizon for managers. In reality, these managers may be more concerned about the renewal of lucrative contracts and about their long-term reputations than about the additional amounts they can earn by altering risk in the manner outlined above.

If the risk of the portfolio is easily observed by the pension fund officers, these reputation considerations will tend to mitigate the adverse incentive effects discussed here. The true risk of an actively managed portfolio is difficult to measure, however, so our simple model may capture incentive problems that are present in more complicated settings.[8] Moreover, reputation considerations may reinforce our arguments about adverse risk incentives.

Regardless of the type of compensation contract, there is a maximum amount that the portfolio manager can lose by performing very poorly. The manager cannot do worse than lose all existing and present and future business. On the other hand, the upside potential associated with significantly outperforming the benchmark is considerable, particularly if the manager is a newcomer to the profession and is still managing small amounts of money. This asymmetry suggests that, even for a manager with a fixed percentage fee contract, the long-run payout may be similar to a contract with a very generous cap. The need to offset the increased adverse risk incentives created by these reputational issues may necessitate larger penalties or lower caps on the performance contract as compared with the levels specified in the previous section.

On the other hand, an established manager with an illustrious track record may already be managing a great deal of money. The potential loss for such a manager from performing poorly may outweigh the gains from

---

8. The pension fund officer expects the returns of an actively mnaged portfolio to differ from the return of the S&P 500. For such an actively managed portfolio, volatility is measured imprecisely, except in very long time series. For this and other theoretical reasons, it would be impossible to determine on the basis of a few observed ex post returns whether a difference between the two returns is due to a deliberate attempt to game the contract or to active management based on superior investment talent.

performing well. In this case, reputational considerations may imply that the fee appears to have a very tight cap, in which case the contract should decrease the penalties or increase the cap from the levels specified in the previous section.

VII. Conclusion

We have shown that pension fund officers could inadvertently agree to performance-based fees that are substantially more lucrative to the manager than standard fixed management fees. The fee structure might also encourage the fund's portfolio manager to assume unnecessary unsystematic risk and to select a target beta that substantially differs from one. Although we demonstrate this possibility in a single-period model, we argue that reputation considerations do not fundamentally alter these conclusions.

Our analysis also demonstrates that a client can mitigate these adverse incentives with appropriately designed contracts. Caps on fees, as well as sizable penalties for poor performance, can eliminate incentives to alter the risk of the fund.

Numerical estimates of the value of these contracts suggest that the issues raised here are not trivial. For instance, a portfolio manager with a contract that lacks a cap can substantially increase the fee, on average, by small additions of unsystematic risk or by inducing small deviations in the portfolio's beta from one.

Our analysis has assumed that the appropriate benchmark is the return of the S&P 500. A pension fund that requires a more conservative investment strategy should select a less risky benchmark, such as a weighted average of the S&P 500 return and the Treasury bill return. With an appropriate cap and base fee, contracts with such a benchmark would induce a target beta that is approximately equal to the weight on the S&P 500. Alternatively, funds desiring riskier strategies might consider leveraged positions in the S&P 500 or a riskier portfolio (such as an equally weighted portfolio of all NYSE stocks) as a benchmark.

This paper has not discussed a number of issues that may affect the risk incentives of the portfolio manager. These include the optimal length of the evaluation period, restrictions on the portfolio manager's personal portfolio, the extent to which the investment choices of the portfolio manager are monitored, and the choice between using inside portfolio managers and hiring outsiders. For example, inside managers might be less tempted to alter the risk of the portfolio to game the fee, because the rewards for successful performance relative to the penalties for poor performance are probably smaller for inside managers than for outside managers, especially when issues such as job security and public exposure are considered.

Future research that examines these issues may provide additional insights that are relevant to the design of performance-based contracts.

20

Measuring Non-U.S. Equity Portfolio Performance*

Gary P. Brinson
President and
  Chief Investment Officer
First Chicago Investment Advisors

Nimrod Fachler
Investment Officer
First Chicago Investment Advisors

I. Introduction

This article has two aims. First, we establish the correct benchmark index for measuring the performance of non-U.S. equity portfolios. Second, we propose an analytical framework for analyzing and evaluating the portfolio's performance.

II. The Capital International Indexes

The most widely used international return indexes are the Capital International Perspective (CIP) Indexes published in Geneva, Switzerland by Capital International S.A.[1] The advantages of the CIP indexes are:

1. The uniformity of the calculation method and the base date allow easy and accurate comparison among the various indexes.
2. The indexes date back, in most cases, to 1959, creating an extensive database for research and analysis.

---

*Reprinted from the Spring 1985 issue of *The Journal of Portfolio Management*.
1. For a comprehensive description of the coverage and methodology the reader can refer to the quarterly edition of CIP. Also see an expanded explanation in N. Sikorsky, "The Origin and Construction of the Capital International Indices," *Columbia Journal of World Business* (Summer 1982): 24–29.

TABLE 1. *Statistics Summary—Five Years Ending 12/31/83 (monthly data, local currency, price change only).*

Market	Domestic Index	CIP Annual Return (%)	Domestic Annual Return (%)	CIP Annual Std. DV. (%)	Domestic Annual Std. DV. (%)	R^2 Domestic/ CIP
Australia	All ordinary	15.95	16.19	24.03	22.14	.983
Belgium	Belgian S.E.	6.43	6.80	16.62	15.28	.972
Canada	Toronto S.E.	14.16	14.27	22.85	21.42	.973
France	CAC	11.31	10.50	20.30	18.26	.898
Germany	Commerz Bank	5.65	4.97	13.07	12.99	.989
Hong Kong	Hang Seng Bank	13.23	12.04	36.72	35.65	.990
Italy	Banca Comm.	23.41	22.71	27.57	28.51	.978
Japan	Tokyo S.E.	12.44	10.24	10.64	8.80	.933
Netherlands	ANPCBS	15.61	11.62	15.19	17.07	.738
Singapore	Straits Times	19.04	23.47	24.30	24.49	.917
Switzerland	Swiss Bank Co.	6.05	5.20	11.16	11.24	.879
UK	FT All Share	15.77	16.40	17.81	17.38	.979

3. CIP provides industry indexes allowing for a comparison of industrial trends across national stock markets.
4. The separation into local currency and dollar-adjusted returns allows an explicit evaluation of the impact of the currency movements on the returns and risk of the non-U.S. markets.

The main drawback of the CIP data is the limited and varied quality and depth of the market coverage. As of December 31, 1983, the companies included in the "World Index" accounted for 59.9% of world capitalization. For the individual markets, the percentage coverage varied from lows of 53% for Australia and 55% for Denmark to a high of 81.4% for the Netherlands.[2]

Table 1 examines the representativeness of the national market CIP indexes. Note, in particular, the results for the Netherlands, Switzerland, and France, where the movements of the domestic indexes explain only 74%, 88%, and 90%, respectively, of the movements of the relevant CIP index. The domestic indexes we chose for this analysis were, by our judgment, the most comprehensive and well constructed indexes available.

Table 2 shows the results of a regression analysis for 12 markets covered where, in each case, the CIP index return is the dependent variable and the domestic index is the independent variable (the same domestic indexes as in Table 1). All the constants are insignificantly different from zero. The betas,

---

2. For a full description of the market coverage, refer to CIP Quarterly Edition, 4th quarter 1983.

TABLE 2. *Regression Summary—Five Years Ending 12/31/83 (monthly data, local currency, price change only).*

Market	Constant	T-Stat Constant	Beta	T-Stat Beta	Durbin-Watson
Australia	−.093	−0.77	1.076	57.94	1.83
Belgium	−.058	−0.54	1.072	44.49	2.53
Canada	−.051	−0.36	1.052	45.86	1.72
France	.008	0.03	1.055	22.20	1.64
Germany	.054	1.04	1.001	72.23	2.62
Hong Kong	.083	0.59	1.025	74.30	2.18
Italy	.116	0.73	0.956	50.42	2.21
Japan	.039	0.35	1.168	28.40	1.66
Netherlands	.356	1.06	0.965	12.78	1.64
Singapore	−.216	−0.79	0.950	25.32	2.25
Switzerland	.099	0.67	0.931	20.52	2.89
UK	−.059	−0.60	1.014	52.49	1.78

however, show some significant deviations from 1.0. That is the case for Japan, Australia, Italy, Belgium, and Canada, where the betas are 1.168, 1.076, 0.956, 1.072, and 1.052, respectively. In the Japanese case, the high beta of the CIP index versus the domestic index can be a significant factor, as the Japanese market will be the largest single-country holding in most non-U.S. equity portfolios. Regardless of the weaknesses revealed in Tables 1 and 2, CIP is the most widely used international index and, like its U.S. counterpart (S&P 500), is *generally* suitable for *general* measures of investment performance.

III. The Selection of the Benchmark Index

Nevertheless, the correct aggregate index to be used for performance analysis depends on the objectives and policy constraints of the portfolios being evaluated. Global portfolios, for example, should benchmark off the World Index. This index includes the U.S. and all non-U.S. markets. The proportions are based on the relative market capitalization of the individual markets.

For non-U.S. portfolios, most people use CIP's Europe, Australia, and Far East (EAFE) Index. We suggest below that this index does not properly cover the non-U.S. universe. Specifically, it excludes Canada, South-African Gold Mines, and Mexico. To overcome that weakness, we have constructed a more meaningful non-U.S. index. The information we use for constructing the index is taken directly from the CIP monthly publication.

Let us define:

$P_{U.S.}$ = Proportion of total capitalization represented by the U.S. in the World Index,

$(1 - P_{U.S.})$ = Proportion represented by non-U.S. in the World Index,

$R_{U.S.}$ = Total return of the U.S. index,

R_W = Total return of the World Index, and

R_X = Total return of the non-U.S. Index.

Then:

$$R_W = R_{U.S.} \cdot P_{U.S.} + R_X \cdot (1 - P_{U.S.}), \tag{1}$$

and

$$R_X = \frac{R_W - (R_{U.S.} \cdot P_{U.S.})}{(1 - P_{U.S.})}. \tag{2}$$

The difference between the returns on the non-U.S. and EAFE indexes can be significant. The difference in the returns and standard deviations of the two indexes during 1983 are shown in Table 3.

IV. Performance Attribution Systems

Once we have the appropriate index for performance comparison, we can define results in the following context:

TABLE 3. *Annualized Total Returns and Standard Deviations, Periods Ending 12/30/83 (net yield, monthly data).*

	EAFE Index	Non-U.S. Index
10 years' total return	10.5	10.8
10 years' standard deviation	15.9	16.4
5 years' total return	9.5	10.5
5 years' standard deviation	14.9	15.5
3 years' total return	6.5	6.4
3 years' standard deviation	15.2	15.2

Performance Differential =

Return on active Portfolio − Return on the Index.

The remainder of this paper deals directly with the analysis and evaluation of the performance differential arising from active management.

Let us define our terms as follows:

$W_{x,i}$ = Proportion of market x in the index where $\sum W_{x,i} = 1$.
$W_{x,p}$ = Proportion of market x in the portfolio where $\sum W_{x,p} = 1$.
$R_{x,i}$ = Return on market x in the index in U.S. dollar terms.
$R_{x,p}$ = Return on market x in the portfolio in U.S. dollar terms.
R_I = Return on non-U.S. index in U.S. dollar terms.
R_p = Return on the active portfolio in U.S. dollar terms.

We present here a two-dimensional model. It considers two decisions: market selection across countries and security selection within markets.

Market Selection

This component measures the effect of a decision to be active on market selection—that is, to overweight or underweight a certain market vis-à-vis its normal position as defined by the weight of that market in the non-U.S. Index. We define the impact of market selection as:

$$\text{Market Selection}_{(x)} = (W_{x,p} - W_{x,i}) \cdot (R_{x,i} - R_I). \tag{3}$$

Four cases are possible:

	Overweight (Wx,p > Wx,i)	Underweight (Wx,p < Wx,i)
Rx,i > R₁	(+) Market selection > 0	(−) Market selection < 0
Rx,i < R₁	(−) Market selection < 0	(+) Market selection > 0

A positive market selection is associated with being overweight in an above-average peformance country or underweight in a below-average performance country. Negative market selection occurs when the portfolio is overweighted in a below-average performance country or underweighted in an above-average performance country. A neutral market selection is associated with taking a passive stance on market weight, $W_{x,p} = W_{x,i}$, or is implied when the performance of market x is the same as the overall index, $R_{x,i} = R_I$.

Stock Selection

This component measures the effect of having an active selection of stocks within each country market that is different from the market portfolio. We define the stock selection component as:

$$\text{Stock Selection}_{(x)} = (R_{x,p} - R_{x,i}) \cdot W_{x,i}. \tag{4}$$

Two points require explicit discussion. First, if we were to index our holdings in market X and thus cause the performance to exactly match that of the index, that is $R_{x,p} = R_{x,i}$, then by definition the stock selection component will equal zero. Second, it is important to notice that the return differential is being multiplied by the passive weight, $W_{x,i}$, so that the two return components of market selection and stock selection are totally independent of each other.

It can be difficult to evaluate the stock selection ability of the investment manager simply by looking at the stock selection component, because we have multiplied the return differential by the weight to properly identify the sum of stock selection across all markets. Small performance in a large market can result in a larger stock selection component to total performance differential than a substantial overperformance in a small capitalization market.

We can, however, isolate the stock selection capability by constructing a time series of the return differential $R_{x,p} - R_{x,i}$. This differential is neutral of market size biases and can be examined for its statistical significance.

Cross Product

A cross product between two phenomena or two decisions can occur each time that the two occur simultaneously. We define the cross product in our case as:

$$\text{Cross Product}_{(x)} = (W_{x,p} - W_{x,i}) \cdot (R_{x,p} - R_{x,i}). \tag{5}$$

In order for the cross product to be different from zero, both the market selection *and* the stock selection components should be different from zero.

To put it all together on one market level, using equations (3), (4), and (5), we find:

Total Performance Differential$_{(x)}$

$$= (W_{x,p} - W_{x,i}) \cdot (R_{x,i} - R_I)$$
(Market selection)
$$+ (R_{x,p} - R_{x,i}) \cdot (W_{x,i})$$
(Stock selection)
$$+ (W_{x,p} - W_{x,i}) \cdot (R_{x,p} - R_{x,i}).$$
(Cross product) (6)

Therefore:

Total Performance Differential$_{(x)}$

$$= W_{x,p} \cdot (R_{x,p} - R_I) - W_{x,i} \cdot (R_{x,i} - R_I). \quad (7)$$

On a portfolio level, equation (7) reduces to:

Total Portfolio Performance Differential

$$= \sum (W_{x,p} \cdot R_{x,p}) - \sum (W_{x,i} \cdot R_{x,i}). \quad (8)$$

This is an intuitively appealing result, as it states that the total performance differential is equal to the total return on the portfolio minus the total return on the benchmark index.

V. Example

Let us assume that we have a non-U.S. portfolio currently invested in Japan, U.K., and Germany. The portfolio is being measured against its Index. The relevant data during the period were:

Market	% in Portfolio ($W_{x,p}$)	Return in Portfolio ($R_{x,p}$)	% in Index ($W_{x,i}$)	Return in Index ($R_{x,i}$)
Japan	55	6	45	4
U.K.	30	−2	35	4
Germany	15	4	20	6

Total Return Portfolio = $6 \cdot 0.55 + (-2) \cdot 0.30 + 6 \cdot 0.15 = 3.3$
Total Return Index $= 4 \cdot 0.45 + 4 \cdot 0.35 + 6 \cdot 0.20 = 4.4$
Total Differential $= 3.3 - 4.4 = -1.1$

The component breakdown table looks like this in basis points:

Market	Market Selection Equation (3)	Stock Selection Equation (4)	Cross Product Equation (5)	Total Equation (7)
Japan	−4	+90	+20	+106
U.K.	+2	−210	+30	−178
Germany	−8	−40	+10	−38
Total	−10	−160	+60	−110

VI. Extensions

The model described here assumes a portfolio that is fully invested in equities and has no direct currency strategies. Extensions are possible for investors who use cash or active currency strategies in their portfolios.

Investors who use cash in their portfolio can introduce an element of market timing. The component will measure the effect of not being fully invested in equities in each market. All the variables necessary for the analysis, i.e., return on equities, return on cash, and proportion of cash out of total holding, are readily available for a normal accounting system supporting the portfolio.

Investors who use active currency strategies can introduce a currency selection component. All the previously discussed components would then be analyzed in local currency terms. The data we need for this analysis are the change of each currency rate against the U.S. dollar during the period, the index weight in each currency (equal $W_{x,i}$), and the portfolio weight in each currency. The analysis of the currency component is relatively complicated because of the number of cross products that have to be introduced. The exact specification of the currency factor is beyond the scope of this study, but it should provide a useful topic for further research.

VII. Summary

A performance measurement system similar to the one described in this paper can be beneficial for both the international investor and the international investment manager. For the investor, it can provide a better understanding of the risks and returns associated with the different types of decisions taken by the money manager and with the different equity markets outside the U.S.A. For the investment manager, the system can help in understanding the consequences of each major portfolio decision; it can also simplify and improve the articulation and communication of performance results and their attribution.

Since most international active management results will be discussed relative to a benchmark, with references to the respective contribution of market selection and stock selection effects, the analytical benchmark suggested in this article should provide a timely and useful set of performance measurement techniques.

PART II

Fixed Income
Management

21

The Effective Yield
A Basic Analysis

Ravi E. Dattatreya
Director, Financial Strategies Group
Prudential-Bache Capital Funding

Peter M. Brackman
Financial Strategies Group
Prudential-Bache Capital Funding

Gudmundur Vigfusson
Financial Strategies Group
Prudential-Bache Capital Funding

I. Introduction

Current yield, yield-to-maturity and effective yield are useful parameters in the comparative analysis of fixed-income securities. In this article, these terms are defined and their values in fixed-income analysis explained. In addition, the concept of break-even analysis is introduced.

The total return from a bond is determined by three factors: the size and frequency of the interest payments, i.e., the coupon rate of the bond and how often it is paid; the salvage value resulting from the sale or maturity of the bond; and the interest rate at which the coupon payments will be reinvested. Current yield, yield-to-maturity and effective yield incorporate these factors to varying degrees.

II. Yield Measures

Current yield is simply the rate at which coupon income is earned. Mathematically, it is equal to the annualized coupon rate divided by the market price of the bond. Therefore, for discount bonds, current yield is greater than the coupon rate; for premium bonds, it is less than the coupon rate. Current yield is a simple measure—it considers neither the return from reinvestment of cash flows, nor the capital gain or loss due to price appreciation or depreciation.

The current yield calculation can be improved by considering the capital gain or loss from a security. *Modified current yield* is defined to be equal to the current yield of a security plus or minus the annual discount or premium amount (difference from par per year). This measure is an improvement over current yield, but it does not consider the time value of money.

Yield-to-maturity (or simply *yield*) is an internal rate of return. If all cash flows generated by a security are discounted at this rate, the market price is achieved. Thus yield-to-maturity takes the time value of money into account. Unlike current yield, this measure incorporates both the reinvestment of coupon payments and any capital gain or loss. However, it assumes that all coupon flows are reinvested at a rate equal to the yield. As a result, yield may not be satisfactory for all circumstances, but it does serve as a market-wide standard for relating the cash flows of a bond to its market value.

Interest-on-interest is an important component in determining the true return to maturity of a security. Given the recent volatility of interest rates, it would be naive to assume that all coupon flows throughout the life of a bond are reinvested at a specific and constant rate. If interest rates drop, thus lowering reinvestment rates, true return will be less than the yield. The opposite will be true if interest rates climb. This factor is not incorporated in the yield calculation.

Effective yield[1] is a measure for which the constraint of reinvesting cash flows at a security's yield is relaxed. This measure is the rate of return of a security achieved by reinvesting all coupon cash flows at a given reinvestment rate. The concept of effective yield also allows one to determine returns from a security to any chosen point in time known as the *horizon date,* which may or may not be equal to the maturity date.

To understand how effective yield is computed, the concept of *future value* must be understood. The future value of a security is the total cash flow that the security will generate assuming a particular reinvestment rate to the specified future point in time, i.e., the horizon date. If the horizon date is equal to the maturity date, the future value of the investment is simply the sum of each cash flow reinvested at the given rate to maturity.

Because the horizon date is not always equal to the maturity date, a mechanism is required to evaluate the bond's salvage value at horizon.[2] If

---

1. Also known as realized rate of return, total rate of return or realized compound yield.
2. In order to compute the effective yield, a set of assumptions must be made to determine reinvestment rates and salvage values. Caution must be exercised in making these assumptions. The various theoretical and practical issues involved in the proper selection of these assumptions are beyond the scope of this article but are discussed in Ravi Dattatreya and Frank Fabozzi, *Active Total Return Management of Fixed Income Portfolios* (Chicago: Probus Publishing, 1989). However, even a simple analysis can provide valuable insight into the behavior of effective yield, and this simple approach is taken here.

the horizon date occurs prior to the maturity date, the future value of the investment has two components: (1) the sum of each cash flow due before the horizon, reinvested at a given rate to horizon, plus (2) the present value at horizon of all cash flows scheduled to occur after the horizon, discounted at another given rate (known as the *horizon rate*[3]). If the horizon date is beyond the maturity date, the future value of the investment is the sum of each cash flow reinvested at the given rate to maturity, then reinvested over the remaining investment periods to the horizon date. The effective yield is then computed by relating the future value of the security to the term of horizon.

III. Sensitivity Analysis

In calculating effective yield, the reinvestment of all coupons at a single, constant rate is still assumed. However, the constant rate of reinvestment can be chosen to reflect the cumulative effect of expected future interest rates. Also, sensitivity analysis can be performed by examining the trends and characteristics of effective yields computed over a range of reinvestment rates and horizon periods.

As discussed above, effective yield has two components: reinvestment income and salvage value. Keeping salvage value constant, a security's rate of return increases as the reinvestment rate increases. This effect is greater for high-coupon bonds, since their sizeable cash flows, which are reinvested at the higher reinvestment rates, cause the bond's return to move upward by a larger extent than would the return of current-coupon bonds. The larger the coupon of the bond, the greater is the positive effect of a higher reinvestment rate. For low-coupon, discount bonds, a substantial portion of a security's return is locked into the salvage value. In this case, the reinvestment component still increases as rates increase, but does so more slowly. However, the reinvestment component for a zero-coupon bond is immune to the effects of reinvestment rates because it does not make any coupon payments and thus there is nothing to reinvest.[4] If horizon equals maturity, the salvage value is par. Thus, the total return itself is independent of reinvestment rate levels for the zero-coupon bond.

In Figure 1, four bonds are compared, each of five-year maturity, but with coupons of 0%, 5%, 10%, and 15%. A horizon period of five years is assumed and the initial prices are chosen such that all bonds yield 10% to maturity. By choosing horizon equal to maturity, we have eliminated the impact of changes in salvage value on the effective yield. The graph illustrates that the reinvestment component and hence the effective yields rise as

---

3. It is common practice to choose a security's yield as the horizon rate.

4. This effect holds true only if the horizon date is less than or equal to the maturity date. If horizon is longer than maturity, the principal payment at maturity has to be reinvested, and therefore, reinvestment risk enters the picture.

FIGURE 1. *Effective Yields for Five-Year Bonds with Various Coupons.*

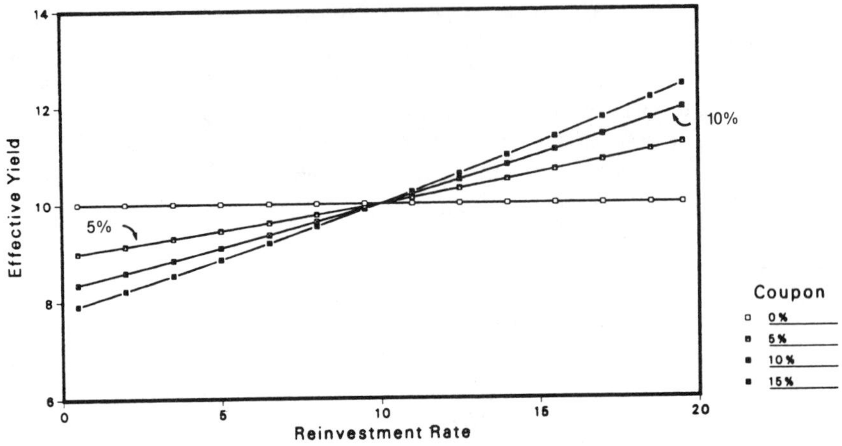

Note: The initial prices are chosen such that all bonds yield 10% to maturity. The horizon period is assumed to be five years (the maturity of the bonds).

reinvestment-rate assumptions increase and that yields increase more dramatically for higher-coupon securities. The zero-coupon bond has a perfectly horizontal line, showing its immunity to reinvestment rates.

The time to horizon also impacts effect yield. In Figure 2, the effective yield for a 10% coupon, five-year bond priced at par is examined. The reinvestment rate is varied from 0% to 20% and the effective yield is plotted for one, five and ten-year horizons. The salvage value, or the price of the bond at horizon, is assumed to be the initial price of par, i.e., the bond is priced at the original yield of 10%. Figure 2 illustrates that the reinvestment rate has a greater impact on effective yield at longer horizons.

The assumptions made in the determination of a bond's salvage value can significantly influence effective yield. An interesting phenomenon occurs if, for each scenario, a single interest rate is used to determine both the horizon yield for the bond and the reinvestment rate, instead of setting the horizon yield to the initial yield of the bond. Figure 3 shows the effective yield for the same 10%, five-year bond with this new assumption for salvage value. The horizons used are three, four and five years. This example shows that for shorter horizons, the effective yield is greater at lower reinvestment rates because the impact of reinvestment is small, while that of the salvage value is large. For longer horizons, the reinvestment rate dominates the impact of salvage value and therefore effective yield increases with interest-rate levels.

FIGURE 2. *Effective Yields for a Five-Year, 10% Bond at Various Horizons.*

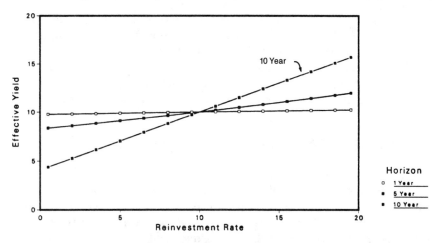

Note: The bonds are initially priced at par and yield 10%. The salvage values (the prices of the bonds at horizon) are assumed to be the prices at the initial yields of 10%, i.e., par.

FIGURE 3. *Effective Yields for a Five-Year, 10% Bond at Various Horizons.*

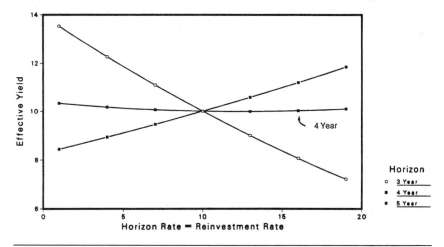

Note: The bonds are initially priced at par and yield 10%. The salvage values (the prices of the bonds at horizon) are assumed to be the prices at the horizon yields, which are set equal to the assumed reinvestment rates.

IV. Immunization

For some particular horizon — approximately four years for the bond in Figure 3 — effective yield is almost constant, independent of the interest rate. This horizon, known as the *duration* of the bond, is the point at which the negative effect of a higher interest rate on salvage value is exactly balanced by its positive effect on reinvestment returns. The technique of equating duration to horizon to obtain more stable returns is called *immunization*.

V. Break-Even Reinvestment Rate Analysis

Choosing a reasonable horizon and then comparing expected horizon returns is a frequently used methodology in managing fixed-income portfolios.[5] The effective yield concept provides a way to determine relative attractiveness of different bonds. In this context, determining the *break-even reinvestment rate* between two bonds is a useful technique.

A break-even reinvestment rate is the rate at which the effective yields for two bonds over a given horizon are equal. Depending on the two bonds' maturities, coupons and prices, the effective yield of one of the bonds is expected to be greater than that of the other if the reinvestment rate is below the break-even rate, and smaller if it is above the break-even rate. Therefore, depending on the expectation of where interest rates are likely to be, it is possible to conclude whether one bond is relatively more attractive than another. This is especially so if the break-even rate is extreme, i.e., much higher or much lower than current or expected interest rates. Sometimes the break-even rate is within the expected interest-rate band, in which case the analysis may be inconclusive as to the determination of the more attractive bond.

Figure 4 compares Bond 1, a five-year 15% bond that is priced at 120, and Bond 2, a five-year 5% bond that is priced at 80, for a horizon of five years (the same as the maturity of the bonds). The effective yields for the bonds at various reinvestment rates from 8% to 16% are shown. Bond 2 has a greater effective yield if an 8% reinvestment rate is assumed. On the other hand, if a 16% reinvestment rate is assumed, Bond 1 would have a higher effective yield. Both bonds have higher returns as reinvestment-rate assumptions climb, yet they do not increase at the same rate. Figure 5 shows a graph of this relationship, which is a sloping curve for each bond, but the curve for Bond 1 is steeper.

---

5. In fact, this is the preferred method in portfolio management. See Dattatreya and Fabozzi, *Active Total Return Management of Fixed-Income Portfolios.*

FIGURE 4. *Break-Even Reinvestment Rate Analysis between Two Five-Year Bonds.*

Settlement 10/01/1987
Horizon 10/01/1992

	BOND 1	BOND 2
Calendar	Treasury	Treasury
Coupon	15.000	5.000
Maturity	10/01/1992	10/01/1992
Price	120	80
Yield	9.84	10.21

Reinvestment Rate

	8	9	10	11	12	13	14	15	16

Effective Yield

	8	9	10	11	12	13	14	15	16
BOND 1	9.41	9.64	9.88	10.12	10.36	10.61	10.86	11.12	11.37
BOND 2	9.95	10.07	10.18	10.30	10.42	10.55	10.67	10.80	10.93

Breakeven Rate: 12.49

Note: The horizon is five years, the same as the maturity of the bonds.

FIGURE 5. *Break-Even Reinvestment Rate Analysis between Two Five-Year Bonds.*

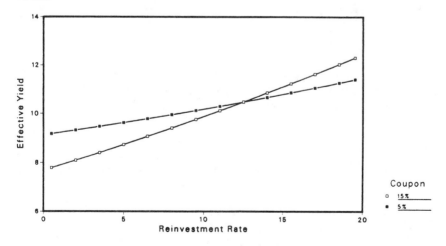

Note: The 15% bond is priced at 120, while the 5% bond is priced at 80. The horizon is five years, the same as the maturity of the bonds.

Figure 5 illustrates the point at which the two curves intersect. This point is called the break-even point, and the reinvestment rate that produces this intersection of the two curves is the *break-even reinvestment rate*. If the bonds' expected cash flows are reinvested at this rate, both bonds would generate the same effective yield.

By examining the location of the break-even reinvestment rate between two bonds, one can determine which bond is more attractive. If an investor's expectation of future rates is higher than the break-even reinvestment rate, then the 15% bond will achieve a greater effective yield than the 5% bond, as shown by Figure 5. Conversely, if an investor's expectation of future rates is lower than the break-even reinvestment rate, then the 5% bond will achieve a greater effective yield.

A break-even reinvestment rate does not always exist for any two bonds. It may be that one bond will always have a higher effective yield than another for any assumed reinvestment rate. Figure 6 shows a comparison between the same five-year bonds as in Figure 4; however, Bond 2 is now priced at 90. Over any range of selected reinvestment rates, Bond 1 will always generate higher effective yields than Bond 2, and therefore no break-even point exists between them. At these prices, Bond 1 is inherently cheaper, i.e., the better investment.

FIGURE 6. *Break-Even Reinvestment Rate Analysis between Two Five-Year Bonds.*

Settlement 10/01/1987
Horizon 10/01/1992

	BOND 1	BOND 2
Calendar	Treasury	Treasury
Coupon	15.000	5.000
Maturity	10/01/1992	10/01/1992
Price	120	90
Yield	9.84	7.43

Reinvestment Rate

6	7	8	9	10	11	12	13	14

Effective Yield

	6	7	8	9	10	11	12	13	14
BOND 1	8.96	9.18	9.41	9.64	9.88	10.12	10.36	10.61	10.86
BOND 2	7.28	7.38	7.49	7.61	7.72	7.84	7.96	8.08	8.21

Breakeven Rate: None

Note: The horizon is five years, the same as the maturity of the bonds.

VI. Summary

Effective yield — a rate of return achieved by reinvesting all coupon cash flows from a security at a reinvestment rate selected by the investor — is a more accurate parameter for evaluating fixed-income securities than is yield-to-maturity. Effective yield relaxes the constraints imposed by yield-to-maturity by allowing the investor to reinvest cash flows at a rate other than the security's yield. Effective yield employs such concepts as future value, horizon date, salvage value and horizon rate. Even a simple-minded analysis provides valuable insight into the behavior of effective yield. Break-even reinvestment analysis employs all of the concepts developed here to compare two securities or portfolios and to determine which is a better investment for a given horizon. A break-even point does not always exist between two securities or portfolios, in which case one bond is always cheaper than the other. An understanding of the tools described in this article and the roles that they play can lead to more intelligent investment management.

22

Convexity:
An Introduction

Jess B. Yawitz
Vice President
Fixed Income Division
Goldman Sachs & Co.

One of the most striking developments of the last decade is the extensive use of duration by the fixed income community. Duration analysis has been integrated successfully into a wide range of hedging and asset management techniques. Many of the new approaches to structured or passive bond management are extensions of the original duration-based concept of immunization.

Just when the fixed income community is beginning to feel comfortable with duration, we are asked to consider yet another characteristic of a fixed income instrument, its *convexity*. The purpose of this article is to present a non-technical discussion of convexity, emphasizing the following points:

(i) What is convexity and why does it matter?
(ii) What is the basic shape of the price-rate relationship for securities with positive convexity, negative convexity, and zero convexity?
(iii) What determines a security's convexity?
(iv) For equal maturity or equal duration, what determines which securities possess relatively more or less convexity?
(v) What are the implications of convexity for pricing and hedging fixed income securities?
(vi) How is convexity measured?

FIGURE 1. *Convexity.*

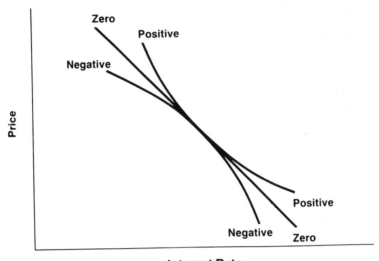

I. What is Convexity?

The Price-Rate Relationship

An understanding of convexity is critical to the accurate pricing and hedging of fixed income instruments.

Convexity is a measure of the changing price response of a fixed-income security as rates rise or fall.[1] As such, it can be represented by the curvature exhibited in a price-rate diagram (Figure 1).

A curve is said to be "convex" or to possess positive convexity when it is rounded like a segment of a circle viewed from the outside. It is "concave," or displays negative convexity, when it is rounded like a segment of a circle viewed from the inside. Convexity is zero for a straight line.

Convexity, either positive or negative, is present when a security's price-rate relationship is non-linear (Figure 1). A fixed income security has positive convexity if a 100-basis-point rate reduction leads to a price increase that is larger than the corresponding price decrease if rates rise 100 basis points.

---

1. We measure convexity under the assumption of an equal change in rates on bonds without options. For a non-option security, we can measure convexity using the price-yield relationship on the bond itself. This is not, however, appropriate for bonds with options because the convexity effect from the option is reflected in a relatively larger or smaller yield change.

We can illustrate the concept of convexity with a simple game. The return distribution offered by each of the three different versions of the game should provide a numerical, a graphical, and most of all an intuitive demonstration of convexity. Once these are under our belts, we can consider convexity in fixed income instruments. By attaching these simple games to a one-year bond, we show how convexity affects both the return distribution and the yield on the security. While the analysis is quite simple, we can nevertheless draw several important implications from this straightforward illustration.

A Simple Convexity Game

What would you pay, or require in payment, to play each of the following games?

> Game #1: I have a bag containing one red, one black, and two white marbles. If you draw the red one, you pay me $10. If you draw the black one, I pay you $10. No money is exchanged if a white marble is drawn.
>
> Game #2: You pay me $10 if red; I pay you $20 if black; no payment if white.
>
> Game #3: You pay me $20 if red; I pay you $10 if black; no payment if white.

The expected return from playing Game #1 is, of course, zero. There is a 25% chance of winning $10, a 25% chance of losing $10, and a 50% chance that no money changes hands. The outcomes of this game display *symmetry*. So long as you don't mind a small wager, it is reasonable to assume that you would neither pay me nor require me to pay you in order to play this game. The outcomes of this game have *zero convexity*.

You would be delighted if you could play Game #2 without being required to make an initial payment to me, since you receive twice the payment from me if a black marble is drawn than you would pay to me for a red one. But unless I'm irrational, I will require an up-front payment from you if I am to play this game. Since this game offers you a favorable *asymmetric* outcome distribution, the initial payment I would insist on receiving is the expected value to you of playing the game.

Expected Gain = Probability of Black × $20 − Probability of Red × $10
= 1/4($20) − 1/4($10) = $2.50

Your fair payment for playing Game #2 is $2.50. Your return outcomes will evidence *positive convexity*.

Similarly, you would not play Game #3 without an up-front payment from me. This game has *negative convexity* to you, positive convexity to me. In the same way as I computed the fair initial payment in Game #2, I should pay you $2.50 to play Game #3.

FIGURE 2. *A 10% Bond and Game #1: Zero Convexity.*

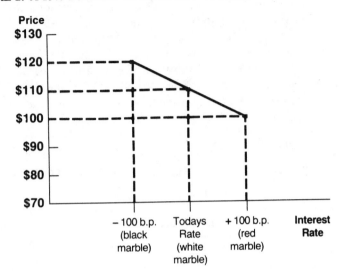

Drawing	Interest Rate Change	Final Value of $100 Investment
Black Marble	–100 b.p.	$120
White Marble	No Change	$110
Red Marble	+ 100 b.p.	$100

An Extension to Bond Pricing

Suppose one-year maturity bonds yield 10% and pay a single coupon at maturity. You could invest $100 to receive a $10 coupon and return of your $100 in one year. Now, consider the effect of adding each of the three games to this one-year bond.

(i) Zero Convexity Suppose Game #1 is attached to this one-year bond, and the bondholder plays the game at the end of the year: a marble is drawn when the bond matures. Remember, neither party requires compensation in order to play. It follows that if Game #1 is attached to a security, its price should not be affected. In the case of the one-year bond, its yield will remain at 10%.

Now, suppose a red marble corresponds to a 100-basis-point rise in interest rates, a black marble means rates fall 100 basis points, and a white marble means rates remain unchanged. Figure 2 portrays the price-rate relationship (connecting the points with a straight line) after the bond matures and the game is played. The fact that all three price outcomes fall on the same straight line segment is evidence of the zero convexity of this security. The price increase for a 100-basis-point decline in interest rates equals the price decrease for a 100-basis-point interest rate rise.

(ii) Positive Convexity   Suppose a new security is formed by combining the 10% bond and Game #2. Since the buyer of the bond should be willing to pay $2.50 to play this game, it follows that the fair price of the hybrid security is $100 plus the present value of $2.50, or $102.27.[2]

In order to price the combination of a bond and Game #2 at par, the coupon payment on the bond must be reduced by an amount that has the effect of reducing the current value (present value) of the bond by $2.27. This coupon reduction is $2.50 (remember, the game is played in one year when the bond matures), implying that the revised coupon is $7.50. Notice that the *yield* on the $100 investment is only 7.50% even though its *expected return* remains 10%. Here is the distribution of cash returns in one year that the bondholder has purchased for $100:

- $107.50 if rates are unchanged.
- $97.50 if rates rise 100 basis points.
- $127.50 if rates fall 100 basis points.

Figure 3 portrays the price-rate relationship for the security composed of Game #2 and a bond yielding 7.50%. After Game #2, the original $100 investment is worth either $127.50, $107.50, or $97.50. Connecting these three prices, one can readily see that this security offers positive convexity. The price increase for a 100-basis-point decline in interest rates exceeds the price decrease for a 100-basis-point interest rate rise.

In our simple examples, the expected return offered by the combination of a one-year bond and one of the games can be divided into the instrument's yield plus the expected return from convexity.

(iii) Negative Convexity   Having demonstrated that the combination of Game #2 with a bond creates a positively convex instrument, I will briefly describe the negatively convex security composed of Game #3 and a one-year bond. One requires $2.50 to play Game #3. If this game is added to the par bond ($10 coupon), the new security is worth $97.73. In order to sell at par, the coupon on the bond must be increased by an amount that has a present value of $2.27, or $2.50. The revised coupon must be $12.50, and the instrument would be priced to yield 12.50%, with the *expected return* remaining at 10%.

After the bond matures and Game #3 is played, the original $100 investment is worth:

---

2. Using a 10% interest rate for discounting, the fair price of the security is $100 + $2.50/1.10 = $102.27.

FIGURE 3. *A 7.50% Bond and Game #2: Positive Convexity.*

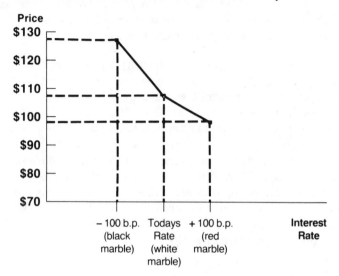

Drawing	Interest Rate Change	Final Value of $100 Investment
Black Marble	−100 b.p.	$127.50
White Marble	No Change	$107.50
Red Marble	+ 100 b.p.	$ 97.50

- $112.50 if rates are unchanged.
- $122.50 if rates fall 100 basis points.
- $92.50 if rates rise 100 basis points.

As portrayed in Figure 4, the price-rate relationship for this instrument displays negative convexity. The price increase for a 100-basis-point decline in interest rates is smaller than the price decrease for a 100-basis-point interest rate rise.

Implications of These Simple Examples

Although it is quite simple, the previous discussion has important implications for understanding convexity in more complex securities. The distribution of outcomes from Game #2 looks very much like the price behavior of a call option on a bond. If nothing happens to rates, the owner of the option loses a portion of its time value. This is the $2.27 paid today to play Game #2 in one year. If rates rise, the value of the option falls, but by less than the increase in value that would accompany an equal-sized fall in rates.

FIGURE 4. *A 12.50% Bond and Game #3: Negative Convexity.*

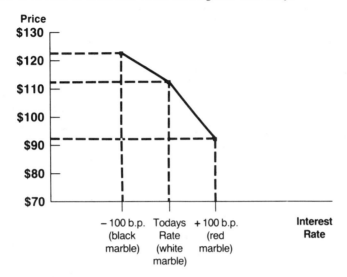

Drawing	Interest Rate Change	Final Value of $100 Investment
Black Marble	−100 b.p.	$122.50
White Marble	No Change	$112.50
Red Marble	+100 b.p.	$ 92.50

If we reversed the red and black marble payoffs in Game #3, its returns would look very similar to a strategy of *writing* a call option on a bond. This revised version of Game #3 is simply the mirror image of Game #2, with negative convexity.

The earlier discussion illustrates the effect of convexity on the yields of equal-maturity instruments. In our examples, the security with no convexity had a 10% yield while the positively and negatively convex securities were priced to yield 7.50% and 12.50%, respectively. Failure to account for the effect of convexity would mistakenly lead one to conclude that the security with positive convexity is *overpriced* while the negatively convex security is *cheap*.

II. What Determines a Bond's Convexity?

We are just about ready to extend our discussion to consider how convexity is determined and how it affects the returns and the pricing of actual fixed-income securities. Before proceeding with these topics, however, let us take a moment to briefly review the concept of duration, which is closely related to convexity.

A Digression on Duration

Duration is a measure of the life of a bond, a weighted average of the time intervals to each expected payment — coupon and principal — with each interval weighted by the discounted present value of the associated payment. Two different duration measures are in common use: Macaulay's duration (named for its originator, Frederick Macaulay) and a variant of it known as Modified duration. The difference between the two duration concepts is most easily demonstrated by an example.

Macaulay's duration converts any series of cash flows into its single payment equivalent for the purposes of measuring price sensitivity to interest rate changes.

A five-year maturity zero coupon bond has a Macaulay's duration of five years, since all proceeds will be paid at maturity. Assuming semi-annual discounting, with the rate of return (R) denominated in decimal form, we can express the percentage price change of this instrument as:

$$\% \, \Delta P = -5\frac{(\Delta R)}{1+R/2} \times 100. \tag{1}$$

If R increases from 10% to 11%, equation (1) would approximate the percentage price change in the five-year zero as:

$$\% \, \Delta P = -5\frac{(.01)}{1.05} \times 100 = 4.76\%. $$

In general, we can express any bond's percentage price change using Macaulay's duration (D):

$$\% \, \Delta P = -D\frac{(\Delta R)}{1+R/2} \times 100. \tag{2}$$

The interest rate change is expressed in terms of the change in the annualized rate as a percentage of the semi-annual discount factor.

Modified duration (D_m) is Macaulay's duration divided by $1+R/2$:

$$D_m = \frac{D}{1+R/2}. \tag{3}$$

Making the appropriate substitution into equation (2), we can express a bond's percentage price change using D_m:

$$\% \, \Delta P = -D_m \Delta R \times 100. \tag{4}$$

Equation (4) provides an easy method of approximating a bond's percentage price change for a given basis-point change in rates. Returning to the earlier

example of the five-year zero, its Modified duration when evaluated at a 10%
yield is:

$$D_m = \frac{5}{1.05} = 4.76 \text{ years.}$$

Modified duration would lead one to estimate that a rise in rates from
10% to 11% would lead to a 4.76% fall in price.

The choice of Macaulay's or Modified duration as the appropriate measure of a bond's relative price volatility depends on the circumstances. As
the previous example indicates, both measures allow one to easily estimate
price change for a given level and change in rates. Modified duration already
takes account of the effect of the level of rates on the price-change-per-basis-
point relationship. As such, it provides an easy shorthand approach to relate
price change to a particular basis point change in rates.

We may now proceed to our discussion of the determinants of convexity.

Bonds with Options

Figure 5 portrays the actual price-interest rate graph of a five-year maturity
call option on a 9% coupon, five-year maturity bond.[3] Its price-interest rate

---

3. This is a European-type option with a par strike price.

FIGURE 5. *The Value of a Five-Year Maturity European Call Option on a
9%, Five-Year Bond.*

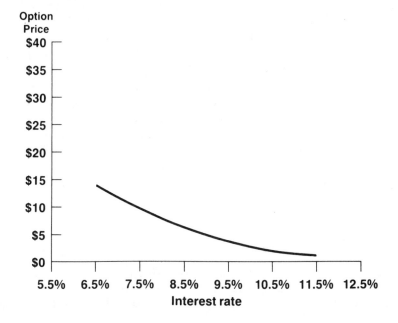

FIGURE 6. *Combining a Long and Short Option Position with a 10-Year Bond.*

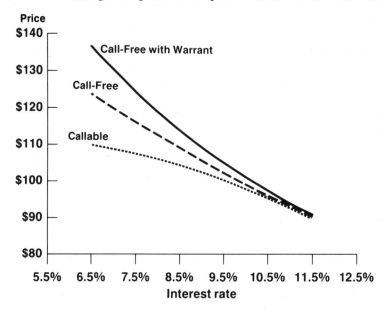

relationship evidences positive convexity. We graph the price-rate relationship for a 9% coupon, 10-year maturity bond in Figure 6. The price graph of a conventional callable (borrower has the option) 10-year maturity bond can be generated by simply subtracting the option's price from the price of the non-callable bond. As plotted in Figure 6, the callable bond evidences *negative convexity* over most of the range of interest rates. When rates are relatively high and the call is nearly worthless, the price behavior of the callable bond approximates that of the non-callable.

Suppose this same call option is attached to the non-callable bond, in the form of a warrant that allows the investor to purchase a 9% coupon, five-year maturity bond, five years from today. The price-yield relationship for this bond is constructed by adding the option value to the price of the non-callable bond. As indicated in Figure 6, this instrument possesses positive convexity.

Bonds Without Options

Understanding the basic convexity characteristics of bonds with options is relatively easy when the option dominates the convexity of the entire instrument. The convexity of options is intuitive and straightforward. An option possesses positive convexity because its hedge ratio[4] increases as it becomes closer to the money or more deeply in the money. It is a bit more difficult to evaluate the convexity of bonds without options. Nevertheless, I will attempt to develop intuition into the validity of the following statements about the convexity of such bonds:

> Statement One: For equal *duration* bonds, zeros have the least convexity, high coupon bonds the most convexity.
>
> Statement Two: For equal *maturity* bonds, zeros have the most convexity.
>
> Statement Three: Doubling duration more than doubles convexity.

Rather than prove these statements rigorously, I will use a series of arithmetic examples to demonstrate their validity.

Statement One: For equal duration bonds, zeros have the least convexity, high coupon bonds the most convexity.

Suppose I have $100 to invest, and I desire a portfolio with a five-year Macaulay's duration. Assume the yield curve is *flat* at an 8% level. Consider the following three portfolios, each of which has a five-year duration:

> Portfolio #1: Invest $100 in a five-year zero.
> Portfolio #2: Invest $50 each in a three-year and a seven-year zero.
> Portfolio #3: Invest $50 in cash and $50 in a ten-year zero.

Table 1 presents data for the value and duration of each portfolio at various interest rate levels. Several points are noteworthy. In a rising-rate environment, Portfolio #1 experiences the largest price decrease while Portfolio #3 has the smallest decrease. If rates fall, Portfolio #3 again does best (largest price increase) and Portfolio #1 performs the worst. As evidenced by the price-rate relationships graphed in Figure 7, all three portfolios possess positive convexity, with Portfolio #3 showing the most convexity and Portfolio #1 the least. Returning to Table 1, notice that as rates rise, the duration of Portfolio #3 falls significantly, the duration of Portfolio #2 falls somewhat, and the duration of Portfolio #1 remains at five years.

The stronger the (Macaulay's) duration-reducing effect of rising interest rates, the greater the positive convexity of the portfolio.

The reason for the relationship between duration and interest rates for our three portfolios is straightforward. Regardless of the level of rates, Portfolio #1 is always 100% invested in a five-year duration instrument. This portfolio, however, does possess some positive convexity, since as rates rise the dollar investment decreases, leading to a smaller price decline if rates continue to rise further.

---

4. The hedge ratio is the change in the option price divided by the change in the price of the underlying asset.

TABLE 1.

Port-folio #	Initial Value	Initial Duration	Value When Rates Rise 200 b.p.[a]	Duration When Rates Rise 200 b.p.	Value When Rates Fall 200 b.p.	Duration When Rates Fall 200 b.p.
1	$100.00	5	$90.88	5	$110.15	5
2	100.00	5	90.94	4.92	110.23	5.08
3	100.00	5	91.29	4.52	110.66	5.48

		Weights in	
		Shorter Zero	Longer Zero
	Initial	50%	50%
Portfolio 2	Rates rise 200 b.p.	52	48
	Rates fall 200 b.p.	48	52
Portfolio 3	Rates rise 200 b.p.	55	45
	Rates fall 200 b.p.	45	55

Portfolio 1 = $100 in a five-year zero coupon bond

Portfolio 2 = $50 in a three-year zero coupon bond and $50 in a seven-year coupon bond

Portfolio 3 = $50 in a ten-year zero coupon bond and $50 in cash

a. A 200-basis point rate change is used in order to amplify the effects of convexity.

For Portfolios #2 and #3, rate changes have the added effect of altering duration. As we know, the Macaulay's duration of a portfolio composed of two zeros is simply a present-value weighted average of each zero's maturity. For our two dumbbell portfolios, the initial weights are 50% in cash or the shorter zero and 50% in the longer zero. The second section of Table 1 indicates the effect on the present value weights of various changes in interest rate levels. As rates rise, the present value contribution from the shorter zero rises above 50%, since its value decreases less than that of the longer zero. The result is to reduce portfolio duration, which reduces the adverse price effect if rates continue to increase.

This discussion has important implications for coupon-bearing bonds. In order to maintain a given duration, say five years, it is necessary to lengthen maturity as the coupon increases. This has the effect of moving the par payment farther out, and generally increasing the *dispersion* of the cash flows around the bond's duration. This increased dispersion is just like the effect of moving from Portfolio #1 to #2 to #3.

FIGURE 7. *Price-Rate Behavior for Three 5-Year Duration Portfolios.*

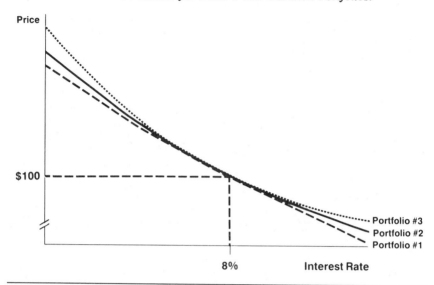

A coupon bond can, of course, be viewed as a portfolio of zeros with the appropriate maturities. As rates rise, the highest coupon bonds (for equal duration) experience the greatest reduction in duration since they have the most positive convexity. But as Portfolio #1 illustrates, a zero coupon bond experiences no duration reduction and has the least positive convexity.

Statement Two: For equal maturity bonds, zeros have the most convexity.

Demonstrating the validity of this statement is really an exercise in comparing apples with oranges. Nevertheless, I will try to provide an intuitive explanation.

In this case, let us compare a five-year zero and a five-year coupon bond. Since the coupon bond is a series of zeros — each having some convexity — the convexity of the bond is simply an average of the convexity of each of its component zeros. But for zeros, convexity increases with maturity. (In fact, as Statement Three indicates, for zeros and coupon bonds alike, convexity actually increases more than in proportion to maturity). Thus, the final payment has the most convexity and the zero is composed entirely of the bond's final payment. It therefore follows that the coupon bond has less convexity than an equal-maturity zero. More generally, for equal-maturity bonds, convexity is reduced when the coupon is increased, since a smaller portion of the bond's value is represented by the most convex component, the final payment.

FIGURE 8. *Convexity and Duration.*

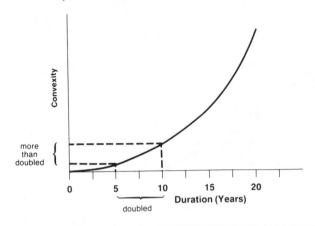

Statement Three: Doubling duration *more* than doubles convexity.

We have already demonstrated the validity of this statement in the example portrayed in Table 1. As Figure 7 indicates, Portfolio #3 has more convexity than Portfolio #1. The convexity in Portfolio #3 (cash and a 10-year zero) is due entirely to the investment in the 10-year zero, since cash has zero convexity. It must follow that since a $50 investment in a 10-year zero has more convexity than a $100 investment in a five-year zero, doubling duration more than doubles convexity. Figure 8 presents a graph of the duration-convexity relationship.

III. Implications of Convexity

Hedging and Convexity

Understanding convexity is essential for effective hedging. Suppose I wish to hedge a long position in a 10-year note, for which the price-rate relationship is graphed in Figure 9 (denoted by the solid black line). The note, now priced at $100, displays some positive convexity.

Two hedge vehicles are available. Assume each is priced at $100 and has the duration of the 10-year note. Hedge vehicle one has zero convexity while hedge vehicle two possesses significant positive convexity.

If the hedge could be implemented by short-selling hedge vehicle one, the net position will show a gain regardless of the direction of the interest rate movement. In Figure 10, the upper curve indicates the relationship between the rate change and gains to the net position by hedging with instrument one.

FIGURE 9.

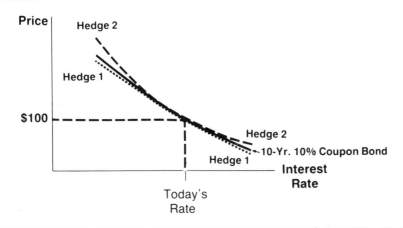

FIGURE 10.

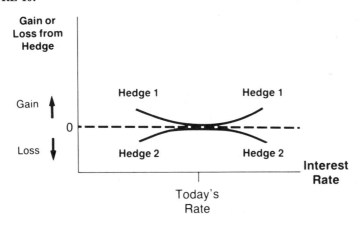

If the hedge is implemented with the second instrument, a loss will be incurred regardless of the direction of the change in rates. This results from the net negative convexity in the portfolio. In Figure 10, the lower curve shows the relationship between rates and the loss incurred by hedging with vehicle two.

Volatility and Convexity

A simple modification of one of the earlier examples demonstrates the relationship between volatility and convexity, and the resultant effect on a security's yield. Returning to Game #2, we can double the volatility of returns by doubling the size of each outcome, to form the following game:

> Game #2a: If you draw the red marble, you pay me $20. If you draw the black marble, I pay you $40. No money is exchanged if a white marble is drawn.

Your expected gain from playing this game is computed as:

$$\text{Expected Gain} = \text{Probability of Black} \times \$40 - \text{Probability of Red} \times \$20$$
$$= 1/4(\$40) - 1/4(\$20) = \$5.00$$

Again, the game is played when the bond matures. Consistent with our earlier discussion, attaching Game #2a to a 10% coupon, one-year bond would imply a dollar price of $100 plus $5/1.10 = $104.55 for the unit. In order to price the combination at par, the coupon payment on the bond must be reduced by $5.00. This implies a revised coupon of $5.00, with the entire $100 investment then offering only a 5% yield. Doubling volatility doubles the value of the game, thereby doubling the coupon reduction (and the yield reduction) necessary to price the combination at par. As in the earlier examples, the expected return on the investment remains 10%.

Convexity as a Measure of "Acceleration"

There is a useful analogy that can be drawn between the price-rate behavior of a convex bond and the physical sciences. Specifically, duration and convexity can be related to speed and acceleration.

Figure 11 contains the price-rate relationship for a prototypical positively convex bond. The slope of this curve from geometry—the rise over the run—is the product of price times Modified duration. Since, from equation (4),

$$\frac{\Delta P}{P} \times 100 = \% \, \Delta P = -D_m \Delta R \times 100, \quad \text{then}$$

$$\text{Slope} = \frac{\Delta P}{\Delta R} = -P(D_m).$$

This product of price times Modified duration is also commonly referred to as dollar-duration.

The slope expresses the change in price with respect to rate changes at a given point on the curve. A zero convexity bond would evidence a price-rate relationship along the straight line that is drawn tangent to the curve in Figure 11. For the positively convex bond, a fall in rates increases its dollar-duration, thereby increasing the absolute price change as rates fall further. By analogy, Figure 11 can relate to acceleration of a moving body by depicting distance traveled on the vertical axis and time span on the horizontal, starting from the point of tangency. On the convex curve, speed accelerates moving

FIGURE 11. *Positive Convexity: Acceleration of the Price-Yield Relationship.*

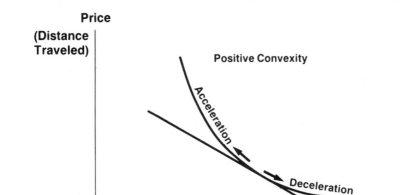

to the left and decelerates moving to the right. On the tangent line, speed remains constant throughout. In the same sense, positive convexity leads to an *acceleration* of the price response when rates fall and a *deceleration* when rates rise. The price-rate relationship for a positively convex bond is preferable to that of an otherwise identical non-convex or negatively convex bond, which does not offer this favorable "acceleration" characteristic.

IV. Measuring Convexity

A popular convention for expressing the convexity of a bond makes use of the duration concept. You will recall that a 100-basis-point increase in rates would cause an anticipated 5% decrease in price for a bond with a Modified duration of five years. But we know that if this bond has no option provisions, its price-rate relationship will display positive convexity, and its price will fall by less than 5%. If the bond experiences an actual price decrease of 4.85%, we would say that its "gain from convexity" is 0.15%.

Similarly, we can measure the convexity of a portfolio with reference to duration. The duration of a portfolio can be obtained by computing the present-value weighted average of the duration of the individual bonds. The convexity of a portfolio can be computed in an analogous way. Suppose we wish to form various portfolios composed of the following two bonds:

Bond #1
    Price   = $100
    Duration   = 5 years
    Gain from convexity = 0.16%
Bond #2
    Price   = $100
    Duration   = 10 years
    Gain from convexity = 0.64%

(i) Portfolio One A portfolio composed of Bond #1 and Bond #2 has the following characteristics:

$$\text{Net price} = \$200$$

$$\text{Duration} = \frac{\$100}{\$200}(5) + \frac{\$100}{\$200}(10) = 7.5 \text{ years}$$

$$\text{Gain from convexity} = \frac{\$100}{\$200}(.16\%) + \frac{\$100}{\$200}(.64) = .40\%$$

(ii) Portfolio Two Suppose you want to hedge Bond #2, and hedge by undertaking a short position in Bond #1. Since the dollar price of each bond is $100, a zero-duration portfolio can be obtained by short selling two of Bond #1. (Assume the $200 proceeds from the short sale are invested in cash.) The net convexity position, however, it not zero but rather is positive. The portfolio has the following characteristics:

$$\text{Net price} = \$100$$

$$\text{Duration} = \frac{\$100}{\$100}(10) + \frac{\$200}{\$100}(0) - \frac{\$200}{\$100}(5) = 0$$

$$\text{Gain from convexity} = \frac{\$100}{\$100}(.64\%) + \frac{\$200}{\$100}(0\%) - \frac{\$200}{\$100}(.16\%) = .32\%$$

Similar to the calculation of duration, the computation of the convexity of a portfolio is a straightforward present-value weighted average of each bond's convexity.

V. Summary

- Convexity is a measure of the shape of the price-interest rate relationship of a fixed income security. A bond possesses positive convexity if its price increase associated with a given fall in rates is greater than its price decrease for the same-sized rise in rates.
- Convexity is "priced out" in a bond's yield. Bonds with positive convexity may appear overpriced when compared on a yield basis with less convex bonds.

- Zero coupon bonds have the least positive convexity for their *duration* and the most convexity for their *maturity*.
- High coupon bonds have the most convexity for their *duration* and the least convexity for their *maturity*.
- The convexity of a portfolio of bonds can be calculated using the same weighted average approach as used to compute portfolio duration.

23

Convexity:
The Name is New but You Always Knew What It Was

Kenneth H. Sullivan
Managing Director
Drexel Burnham Lambert

Timothy B. Kiggins
Associate
Drexel Burnham Lambert

I. Introduction

Convexity is a term that has begun to dominate discussions of portfolio strategy. The popularization of the word convexity has caused investors and investment bankers alike to scramble to assemble computerized mathematical models based on differential equations so that they too can maximize their convexity. What's more, frightened investors are learning that they own negative convexity.

Let's not move too fast, folks. Convexity is not available for free; you have to pay for it even if you can't calculate it. When you get past the jargon currently in fashion, though, you'll see that you always knew what convexity was and what it cost to buy it.

You always knew that cushion bonds (bonds callable in the future which are trading substantially over the first call price) would trade at yields much higher than their noncallable or underwater counterparts. You also knew that even on a yield-to-first-call basis the spreads were attractive relative to the aforementioned counterparts. Of course, the reasons were that the cushion bonds would underperform noncallables in a rally and that they would similarly underperform a noncallable bond of maturity equal to the first call date in the event of a significant market decline. The case in which you would win was the case in which yields remained relatively stable, since the higher initial yield would dominate the lesser price performance. If you understand that trade-off, you understand how to make use of convexity.

In this article, we review the background on how one measure of the price performance potential of a bond (or other security) came to be quantified as convexity. We then characterize several familiar types of fixed income investments by their inherent convexities. We go on to describe the process of estimating the convexity of individual securities and then combinations of securities, which leads to the design and construction of portfolios. Convexity is not symmetrical. That is, the gain from convexity as rates change in one direction is not necessarily the same as the gain from a rate change in the other direction. Finally, we propose a framework for deciding what price to pay for incremental convexity, which is based on relative returns and one's estimate of volatility. You might be surprised to find that securities with "negative convexity" are often superior values.

II. Background

Just when you mastered duration to the point where you could explain it to your client or boss, the word "convexity" started to make the rounds. When you asked for an explanation from your research department or your investment adviser, you were told: "Convexity? That's simple. That's just the rate of change of duration." Or you got a reply like: "That's an important parameter that you calculate by taking the second derivative of the price with respect to yield." That kind of explanation wasn't very helpful. Meanwhile, you're being told that you have some negative convexity in your portfolio. Don't sell just yet.

Before presenting price vs. yield graphs and drawing tangents to curves, let's take an example from real life. You are at Belmont Park watching the feature event. You've placed a bet that would pay $100 on a horse which has been in second place by 5 lengths but has just started gaining on the horse in first place as they near the finish. I offer to buy your bet from you for $50. Should you sell? What are the considerations behind your decision?

Intuitively, you know that your horse might win because it is closing the gap on its competitor. The rate at which it is closing the gap and the distance (or alternatively, the time) left to cross the finish line are the factors you are considering. Visually, you can probably make this kind of decision reasonably well. Mathematically, you could be even more precise if you knew: (i) the "acceleration" of the second place horse relative to the first, (ii) the "velocity" of the first horse and (iii) the distance to the finish line. You would calculate which horse reaches the line first and then sell your bet or hold it on the basis of the calculation. In doing so, you would be applying the same principles as in duration (velocity), convexity (acceleration), yield change (distance to the finish line) and yield spread (the 5-length lead). The problem is: you can't visually evaluate the relative performance of two bonds starting from two different yields. You have to run the numbers to compare the two bonds, or you have to know someone else who can.

Convexity sounds intimidating but it is more easily understood if you visualize two bonds that begin with the same dollar value. As market yields fall, one bond seems to appreciate faster than the other. It seems to accelerate since its advantage keeps getting larger as yields continue to fall. The price advantage produced by this tendency to accelerate past or outperform the other bond is the gain from its convexity, or acceleration. All other things being equal (which is seldom the case), convexity is helpful when yields rise, too. The bond that gained more when yields fell will also fall less when yields rise.

To apply convexity to fixed income investment analysis, it is important to understand the application of duration (or the modified version thereof).

Duration

Duration had its origins as the "weighted average time to receipt of the payments on an obligation, with the weights determined by the present value of each cash flow." It was found that assets and liabilities of equal duration appreciated or declined in value by approximately equal percentages, even if their market values, maturities or cash flow patterns were mismatched. Further refinements produced the measure called modified duration. While not significantly different from duration (Macaulay duration), modified duration more accurately measures the change in price one can expect from a given change in yield. The example in Table 1 illustrates the point.

Note that the dollar changes in market values are approximately the same for the assets and liabilities. In effect, the assets are hedged by the liability. Modified duration was designed to quickly produce hedge ratios. The interpretation of modified duration is the following. For a bond with a modified duration of 7.56, the price of the bond should change by 7.56% for every 100 basis point change in yields. Our example in Table 1 was based on 10 basis point yield changes, and the market values changed by approximately one-tenth of the respective durations. So far, so good.

In Table 2, we have taken the same securities and calculated the percentage change in market value of each for the case in which yields change by 100 basis points. If duration is the only characteristic you need to monitor to manage bonds, then it should predict the price changes with accuracy comparable to the case in which we varied yields by 10 basis points.

Discrepancies between the calculated percentage change in price and the estimate of change indicated by the modified duration begin to appear. Our hedge, which looked very good over the range defined by ±10 basis points, failed at ±100 basis points. If the assets and liabilities are left as they are, and the change in rates is made larger, the difference in their percentage changes in value increases further. It accelerates in the same way that our

TABLE 1.

	Principal Amount ($000)	Yield	Current Price ($)	Market Value ($000)	Modified Duration	% Change in Value after a Change in Rates		Dollar Value of Change after a Change in Rates ($000)	
						−10 bp	+10 bp	−10 bp	+10 bp
Assets									
10% 2-year note	100	11%	98.25	98.25	1.76	+.173%	−.173%	.17	.17
12% 30-yr. bond	100	13	92.48	92.48	7.56	+.757	−.746	.70	.69
Total or wtd. avg.	200		95.38	190.8	4.57			.87	.86
Liability									
11% 10-yr. note	156	11.80%	95.40	148.8	5.87	+.591%	−.585%	.88	.87

TABLE 2.

	Principal Amount ($000)	Yield	Current Price ($)	Market Value ($000)	Modified Duration	% Change in Value after a Change in Rates		Dollar Value of Change after a Change in Rates ($000)	
						−100 bp	+100 bp	−100 bp	+100 bp
Assets									
10% 2-year note	100	11%	98.25	98.25	1.76	+1.78%	−1.74%	+1.75	−1.71
12% 30-yr. bond	100	13	92.48	92.48	7.56	+8.13	−7.05	+7.52	−6.52
Total or wtd. avg.	200		95.38	190.8	4.57			+9.27	−8.23
Liability									
11% 10-yr. note	156	11.80%	95.40	148.8	5.87	+6.11%	−5.63%	+9.08	−8.37
						Gain from hedge		+.19	+.14

TABLE 3.

Change in Rates (basis points)	Price: Initial Case of 12% Yield	% Change in Value of 30-Year Bond	% Change Estimated by Using Modified Duration of 8.1	Difference between Actual and Estimated Change
+300	$80.261	−19.7%	−24.3%	4.6%
+250	83.017	−17.0	−20.2	2.3
+200	85.961	−14.0	−16.2	2.2
+150	89.110	−10.9	−12.1	1.2
+100	92.484	−7.5	−8.1	0.6
+50	96.105	−3.9	−4.0	0.1
No change	100.000	NC	NC	0.0
−50	104.200	+4.2	+4.0	0.2
−100	108.725	+8.7	+8.1	0.6
−150	113.623	+13.6	+12.1	1.5
−200	118.929	+18.9	+16.2	2.7
−250	124.690	+24.7	+20.2	4.5
−300	130.957	+31.0	+24.3	6.7

horse accelerated as it neared the finish line. Table 3 illustrates the growing difference between the actual value of the 12%, 30-year bond and the value that would have been predicted by using the modified duration.

Table 3 makes the point that modified duration works quite well for hedgers who can adjust their positions frequently (perhaps every 10 basis points as in Table 1). What about a portfolio investor, however, who would incur significant transaction costs if he kept adjusting his portfolio every time market rates changed? Given that interest rate volatility recently has been in excess of 100 basis points per year, it would seem advisable to examine the effects of large (greater than 100 basis points) yield changes on various fixed income investments. Returning to Table 3, the column labeled "Difference between Actual and Estimated Change" is the amount by which duration erred in predicting the value for a given yield change. Most of this amount is attributable to the convexity of the bond.

Convexity

It was discussed earlier that modified duration is an estimate of the percentage change in the price of a security per 100 basis points change in market yield. Convexity is defined as the change in duration per 100 basis points change in market yield. Why 100 basis points? It's convenient to express it that way. It gives you a number such as a convexity of .5, which means that a change in yield in either direction will produce a gain approximately .5%

above that which one could expect based on the percentage change indicated by the duration.

Convexity has its roots in options. The price curves for options are upward sloping and upward sloping at an increasing rate. Figure 1a is a graph of a call option on a bond expressed the way we normally think about options. Figure 1b re-casts the same curve in terms of yield on the bond underlying the option. Note how the option prices curve upward. This curvature, when it increases upward, is and always has been described as convex in the world of mathematics.

In Figure 2 we apply the same type of graphic analysis to a bond, using the 12%, 30-year bond from Table 3. The graph has curvature and that curvature is upward. This means that a 30-year noncallable bond is convex. Conceptually, the vertical distances between the curve and the line at the 100 basis point marks left and right of the current yield on Figure 3 represent the convexity, or simply put, the degree to which the graph is curved. The more curved is the graph, the higher the convexity.

Actually, the difference between the curve and the line is not all attributable to what has been defined as convexity. Convexity accounts for most of the difference, though, and virtually all of it for reasonable yield changes.

Look back to Table 3. The increasing differences between actual values and those that would have been predicted by duration assume a pattern identical to the vertical differences between the curve and the "duration line" drawn in Figure 3. For small yield changes, the differences are small, but the differences accelerate as the yield change increases.

There it is. Convexity. It's just a curved line that curves upward. But what about negative convexity? It's really concavity downward. As shown below, it's a curve that has its curvature downward.

The curve is always below the "duration line," a line drawn at a tangent to the point representing today's yield and price. Not many fixed income investments possess price characteristics like those in Figure 4, that is, a constant downward curve over the range of probable rates. One class of security that fits this case is high coupon mortgage pass-throughs, often called premium pass-throughs. It's no wonder that premiums sell at very attractive yields; they have to offer a higher return at the outset since they will underperform bonds with a "normal" convexity if yields shift.

Convexity is neither good nor bad. It's simply another feature inherent in a security. Whether the investment is good or bad depends on how much was paid for the convexity. Figure 5 makes the point for an extreme case. If market yields do not drift from the initial yield, Y_0, past Y_t in either direction then the concave bond (negative convexity bond) outperforms the convex bond. If the two bonds started from the same initial yield, you would always take the convex bond over the negatively convex bond. But they seldom start that way. As in our example of cushion bonds, the bond with less

FIGURE 1a.

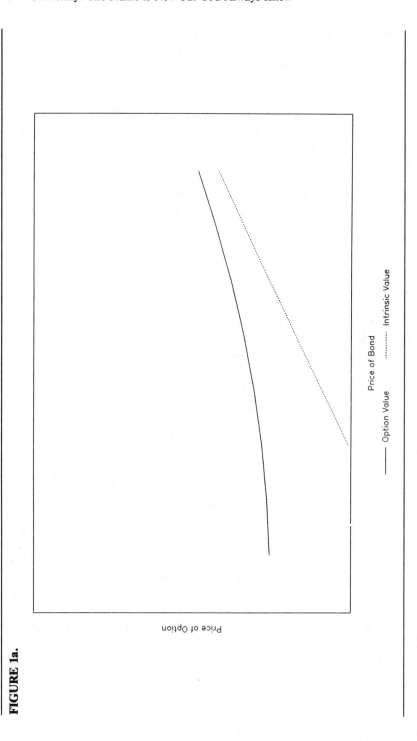

Price of Option

Price of Bond

——— Option Value   ·········· Intrinsic Value

FIGURE 1b.

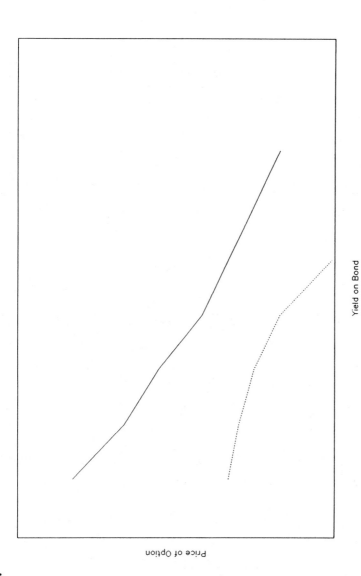

Price of Option

Yield on Bond

——— Option Value ·········· Intrinsic Value

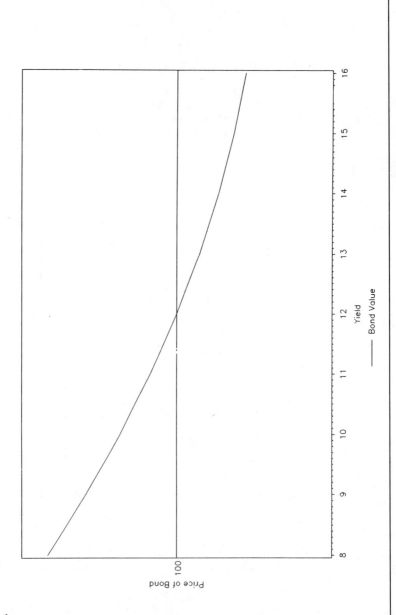

FIGURE 2.

FIGURE 3.

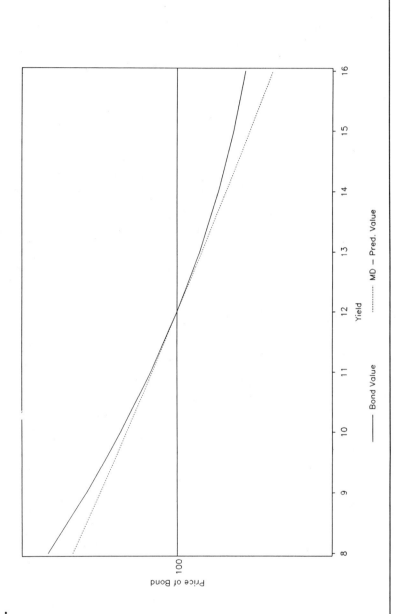

FIGURE 4.

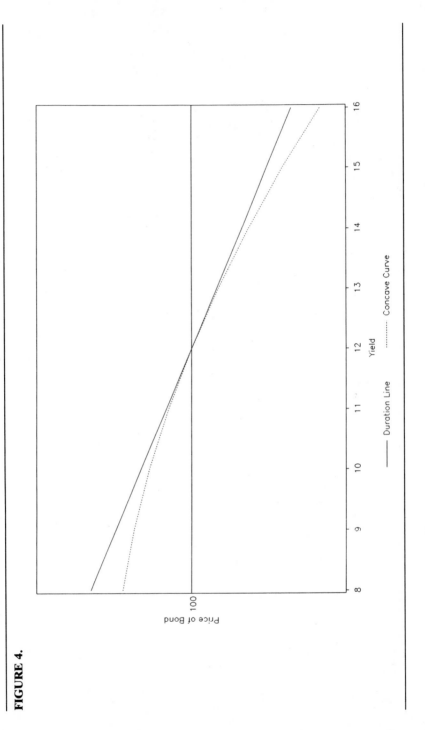

FIGURE 5.

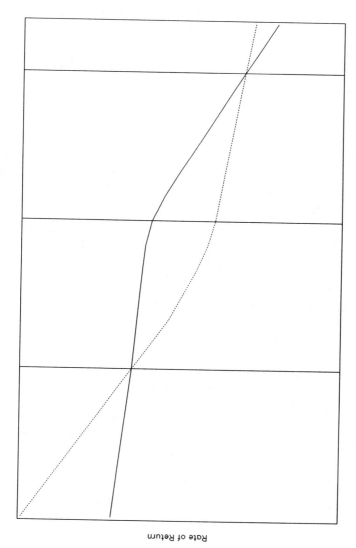

Rate of Return

Market Yields

—— Concave Bond .... Convex Bond

convexity almost always starts out with a lead in the race, often a substantial one. Further, most bonds with negative convexity exhibit it over only a portion of probable yields.

III. Convexity of Certain Familiar Bond Types

For those who have no desire to deal with convexity numerically, this section is designed to provide a qualitative look at how convex one bond might be relative to another. We use this section to illustrate some basic relationships between the terms of certain bonds and the resulting convexity or lack thereof.

Discounts versus Currents

Upon examination, we find that there is little difference in price performance between discount bonds and current coupon bonds of equal duration. The following example illustrates the relationship. Take three Treasury or stripped Treasury securities of approximately equal duration — a current coupon issue such as the 10⅞ of '93, a discount issue such as the 7¼ of '92 and a zero coupon receipt due in July 1990. For purposes of comparing their price performance over a range of yields we have constructed Table 4 assuming that $100 was invested in each security, and then market yields changed in the 100 basis point increments shown.

All three bonds display convexity since the incremental gains for each 100 basis point decline in yields are greater than the durations. Under a microscope you will find that the zero of '90 has less convexity than either of the coupon bonds. A zero will always have less convexity than a noncallable bond of equal duration. As the table shows, that knowledge is not worth much. The important lesson from Table 4 is that there is no significant difference in convexity between discounts and current coupons as long as (i) the durations are matched and (ii) there are no call features that come into play in the relevant yield range. Let's examine the first of these factors in greater detail.

Long Durations versus Short Durations

All of the bonds analyzed in the previous section had durations of 5 years. In this section, the relationship between convexity and duration is examined. First, we look at the price-yield curve for coupon bonds with 11% coupons and initial yields of 11%, and vary the maturities. The result is presented in Figure 6.

Two characteristics stand out in Figure 6. The first notable feature is the relative slope of the curves. The curve for the 30-year bond is much steeper than the curve for the one-year note. The steepness is the "duration effect."

TABLE 4. *Relative Performance/Price Gain or Loss.*

Security				Yield Changes (in basis points)					
	−400	−300	−200	−100	N.C.	+100	+200	+300	+400
10⅞ of '93 (Dur. = 5.01)	+24.3	+17.6	+11.3	+5.4	—	−5.0	−9.8	−14.2	−18.3
7¼ of '92 (Dur. = 5.24)	+25.1	+18.2	+11.7	+5.6	—	−5.2	−10.2	−14.8	−19.1
Zero of 7/1/90 (Dur. = 5.16)	+23.2	+16.9	+10.9	+5.3	—	−5.0	−9.7	−14.2	−18.5

FIGURE 6.

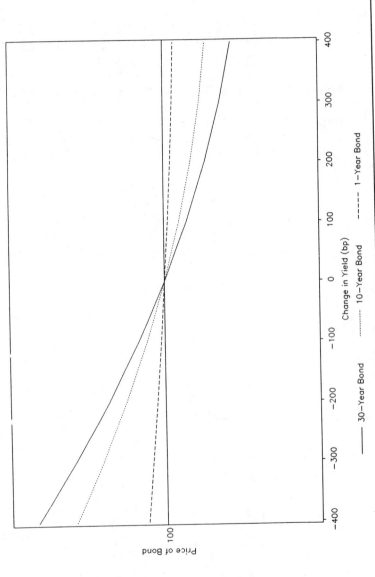

In other words, the steeper curve, which represents a greater sensitivity to changes in yields, is the result of the longer duration of the long bond.

The second notable feature in Figure 6 is the degree of curvature of each of the price-yield curves. The one-year note has nearly a straight line, while the long bond curves upward. The degree of curvature is estimated by the parameter called convexity. From the graph it is obvious that the long bond has more curvature and therefore more convexity. This effect is more easily seen in Figure 7.

The gains shown for the notes and bonds in Figure 7 represent the amounts by which each bond outperforms its straight duration line. It is clear that long duration bonds have more convexity than short duration bonds. A final look at the relationship between duration and convexity is presented in Figure 8. In Figure 8 the degree to which duration contributes to additional convexity is plotted for the 11% coupon notes and bonds to which we referred earlier.

There are two important pieces of insight in Figure 8. The first is that a bond with a duration of 8.0 is more than twice as convex as two bonds each with a duration of 4.0. From Figure 8 we can see that the price gain for any given yield change rises at an increasing rate, making the convexity of individual bonds and combinations of bonds an important concept to understand if you are putting together a portfolio. We'll cover this in more detail below.

The second insight to be drawn from Figure 8 is the importance of making the connection between convexity and volatility. We cannot overemphasize the fact that more convexity is not necessarily better than less convexity. It depends on the incremental price paid for the more convex bond *and* on the subsequent market volatility. If you pay up two points for a more convex bond with a duration of 8.0 instead of buying two 4.0-duration bonds, you will lose money unless market rates move by more than 220 basis points. This relationship between the value of convexity and the market's perception of volatility is essential to developing bond investment strategies which make use of convexity. Basically, if convexity costs too much, you should be selling it, not buying it.

Noncallables versus Callables

Callable bonds may be repurchased from investors by the original issuer, usually at a premium over par value, beginning on a specified date prior to maturity. Because of the call feature, callable bonds will exhibit different price behavior than noncallable bonds. When market yields approach or reach lower levels than the coupon on a callable bond, the nature of the bond begins to change. (We aren't going to get into a deep theoretical discussion of the valuation of call features on bonds here.)

FIGURE 7.

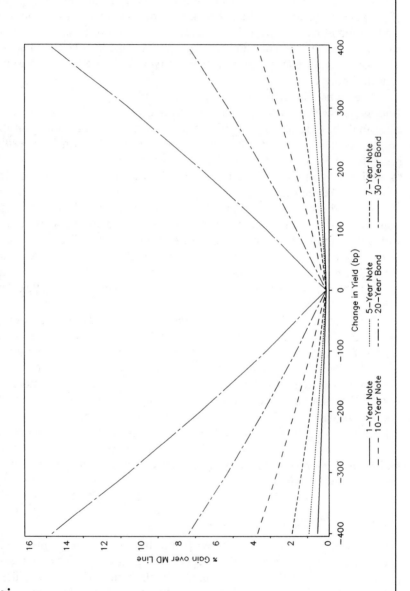

FIGURE 8.

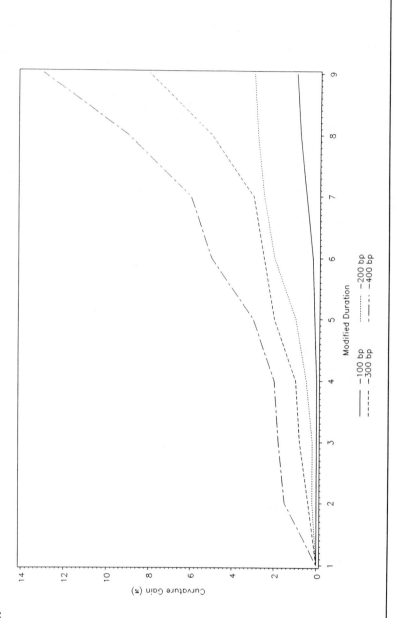

Think about how you would view a 12% 20-year bond that is callable or refundable after 10 years, typical of the terms of many corporate issues. When rates are high, say 16%, you would view it as a 20-year bond since the likelihood of, and penalty from, an early call at par is negligible. A bond trading at 76⅛ isn't materially hurt by an early call. If rates decline from 12% to 8%, however, how does your view of the bond change? If it were noncallable, it would trade at about 139⅝. The existence of the call feature prevents the bond from reaching 139⅞ when rates drop to 8%. This unhappy result is called negative convexity.

When the 12% bond traded at a 16% yield it had a duration of 6.15. As yields decline the duration rose; at a 15% yield, the duration is 6.47. That's normal convexity. Somewhere along the curve, though, this bond started to trade more like a 10-year bond (first call date) than a 20-year bond. This probabilistic assessment of likely call date causes the perception of the duration to shorten. When the probable duration declines at the same time yields decline, that is negative convexity. This bond would have a duration of 9.20 at 8% yields if it were noncallable. Instead it has the price action of a 10-year bond with a duration of 4.29. We'll spend more time on probable duration when we get to mortgage pass-throughs.

Figure 9 shows a simulation of the probable price performance of two 12% 20-year bonds, one noncallable and the other callable after five years. In the critical zone near par the spread between the two bonds changes from time to time as market conditions change. This variation over time is not an accident *and* there is no one spread that is correct at all times. The magnitude of the spread depends on market volatility. Changing volatilities cause changing perceptions as to whether our 12% callable bond is a five-year bond, a 20-year bond, or something in between. Higher volatilities will cause the spread between the two lines to widen.

The trick once again is trading off incremental price against convexity. For bonds that are trading near par, the price difference between a callable bond and a noncallable bond will be relatively small, perhaps a couple of points or less. The most difficult of corporate bonds from an analytical point of view are the cushion bonds, callable bonds whose coupons exceed market yields and therefore are probable candidates for early call. While it is not our intent to present a pricing model for cushion bonds, the principles involved in analyzing them provide a useful introduction to the derivation of the price-duration-convexity relationships for mortgage securities.

Cushion Bonds versus Noncallables

The greatest difficulty with callable bonds trading at a premium is projecting the ultimate maturity. If market rates stay below the coupon rate, the bond

FIGURE 9.

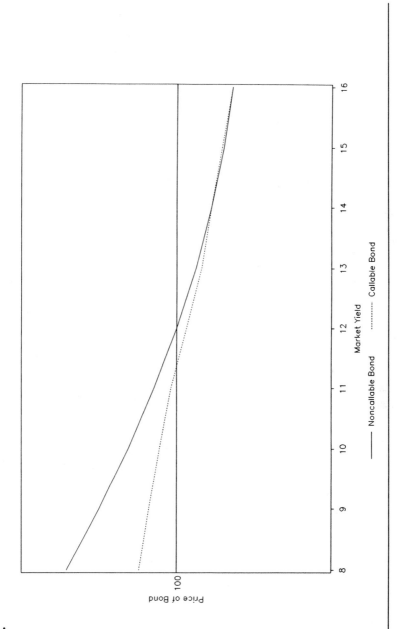

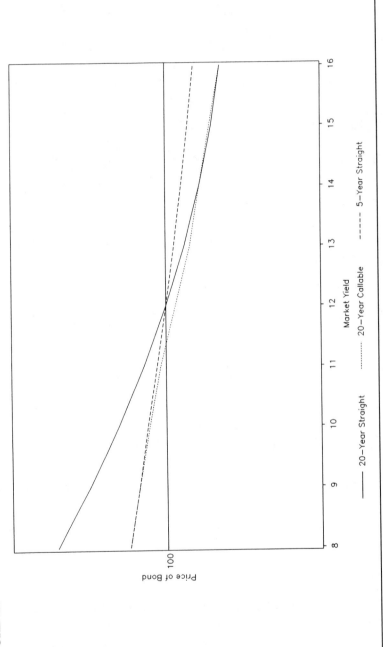

FIGURE 10.

will be repaid at the first call date. If rates rise to levels at or above the coupon rate, the bond will continue outstanding. As Figure 9 shows the cushion bond will underperform the noncallable 20-year bond in a market rally. Figure 10 adds a 12% coupon noncallable 5-year bond, which shows that for a significant market decline, the 5-year bond is the preferred issue. The point made by these graphs is that if you expect rates to fall, the long duration issue with the greatest amount of duration and convexity should be chosen to maximize the effect of falling yields. On the other hand, if you feel rates are likely to rise, the defensive issue should be purchased, that is, a fixed income security with a short duration—the 5-year which will minimize price losses.

Tables 5 and 6 illustrate the effect of different levels of interest rate volatility on cushion and noncallable bonds. For a 200 basis point rise, the noncallable, short duration, 5-year bond minimizes the percentage decline in price. For a 200 basis point fall, the long duration noncallable 20-year bond maximizes the percentage increase in price. Table 6 demonstrates the interesting property of cushion bonds. Not only do they ordinarily provide a premium yield at purchase, they also outperform noncallables on a price-performance basis for small yield changes.

TABLE 5. *Initial Yield Level—11%, 12% Coupons.*

+200 bp	Price Loss (%)
Noncallable bond—20-year	(13.97)
Callable bond—20-year, 5 years to call	(12.08)
Noncallable—5-year bond	(7.09)
−200 bp	**Price Gain (%)**
Noncallable bond—20-year	18.13
Callable bond—20-year, 5 years to call	8.12
Noncallable bond—5-year bond	7.81

TABLE 6. *Initial Yield Level—11%, 12% Coupons.*

+25 bp	Price Loss (%)
Noncallable bond—20-year	(1.9)
Callable bond—20-year, 5 years to call	(.7)
Noncallable—5-year bond	(.9)
−25 bp	**Price Gain (%)**
Noncallable bond—20-year	2.0
Callable bond—20-year, 5 years to call	2.2
Noncallable bond—5-year bond	.9

Depending on the direction of interest rates, either the 5-year noncallable bond or the 20-year noncallable bond will outperform the cushion bond. The initial premium on the noncallable bond is more than compensated for by its superior duration-based price performance over the cushion bond. Suppose you feel the fixed income markets will be relatively stable and yields will stay within a range of 25 basis points in either direction. In Table 6, for either a 25 basis point rise or fall, the cushion bond outperforms the noncallables. Yields did not fall enough for the 20-year bond to overcome the cushion bond's initial price advantage. For the rising yield case, the 5-year noncallable bond's low duration makes its price less vulnerable to rising yields than the 20-year callable bond. However, again, yields did not rise enough to compensate for the initial premium (.27 points) on the 5-year bond.

Since cushion bonds have either shorter durations (compared to the 20-year noncallable) or longer durations (compared to the 5-year noncallable), for a sizeable market rally or decline, the cushion bond's initial price discount will be overcome by the noncallable bond's duration-based superior price performance. For minor market moves, the superior price performance of the noncallable bond will not compensate for its initial premium over the cushion bond. Basically, it all comes down to the investors' judgment about market volatility. In a high volatility environment, the price gains (savings) on the long (short) duration noncallable bonds will offset the initial price premium. In a low volatility market, these price gains (savings) from long (short) duration bonds will not occur, so the cushion bonds will be undervalued.

The time to first call date (seasoning) is important to consider when evaluating cushion bonds. The closer the proximity of the first call date on a cushion bond to the current date, the greater the chance the bond will be called. As the probability of the bond being called increases, the cushion bond trades at an increasingly greater discount to the noncallable bond. Figure 11 illustrates this effect. The bond callable in 3 years trades at a discount to the bonds callable in 5 and 10 years.

Preference for the noncallable bond or the 10-, 5-, or 3-year callable bond depends on the investor's estimate of prospective volatility. By specifying yield volatilities, and pricing the bond accordingly, the investor can see whether the duration-based price effect exceeds the bond's initial premium. If it does not, the cheaper cushion bond should be purchased. If it does, the initially higher priced noncallable bond should be bought.

Another way to view and price a cushion is to consider it a buy-and-write strategy. Basically, a bond is being bought and a deeply-in-the-money call is written resulting in a portfolio consisting of a long bond and a short call option. If yields fall substantially, the bond's price increases; however, the short call option value also rises. The increase in the call option's value causes the portfolio to lag behind a noncallable bond in a market rally.

FIGURE 11.

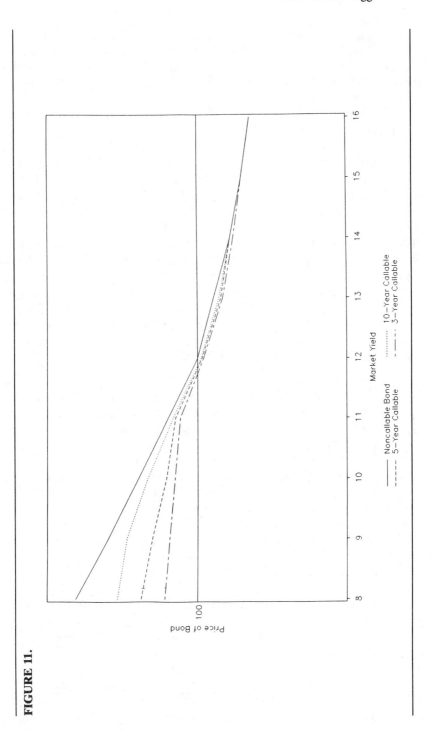

Conversely, for a substantial rise in yields, the call option declines in value and the bond price also falls. The cushion bond will outperform a noncallable bond of equivalent stated maturity because of the fee income from the short call option. (The fee is implied by the lower price and higher yield at which callable bonds can be acquired.) The portfolio will underperform a bond where the maturity date equals the call date because of the price duration effect discussed earlier.

If an investor has access to a call option pricing model for fixed income securities, the implicit call option in a cushion bond can be valued. The model must incorporate an assumption about yield volatility and consider exercise on any day on or after the call date. Once the option is priced, if the price of the noncallable bond minus the price of the option is greater than the cushion bond, the cushion bond is undervalued. If the price of the noncallable minus the call is less than the cushion, the cushion bond is overvalued. Again, the price of the call option is primarily influenced by the expected volatility of the underlying asset. So, like the earlier example, depending on whether one expects high (low) volatility in the market, the call option will be under (over) valued, and the cushion bond will be over (under) priced relative to noncallable issues or issues callable at a later date.

Mortgages versus Noncallable Bonds

Mortgage-related securities are similar to callable bonds in that the borrower has the right to prepay the lender or investor prior to maturity. The principal difference, and the factor that makes mortgages difficult to analyze, is the characteristic of partial prepayment experienced by investors in pools of mortgages. Instead of the whole issue being prepaid at a certain time, perhaps only one out of fifty loans in the pool will be prepaid. Also, while corporations will typically act rationally with respect to refinancing decisions, individual borrowers may not always respond immediately to refinancing opportunities. Finally, mortgagors often prepay mortgages even if new mortgage rates are above the old coupon rate in order to move to a new dwelling. Due-on-sale clauses have resulted in many prepayments that would not have been made otherwise, but not all mortgages are due on sale.

The level of detail required to properly assess the probable life of specific pass-throughs is too great to examine here. The principles, however, can be applied generally to most pass-throughs. The most important relationship is the sensitivity of prepayment rates to changes in yields. Intuitively we know that a decline in yields should produce an increase in prepayment rates. More loans can be economically refinanced, and even for loans that cannot be refinanced, the probability that the occupant moves (and repays the mortgage) increases as yields fall. Figure 12 illustrates the general form of this relationship, which can be quantified for specific groups of pass-throughs with rigorous statistical analysis. Note that the curve is

FIGURE 12. *Sensitivity of CPR to Yield Changes.*

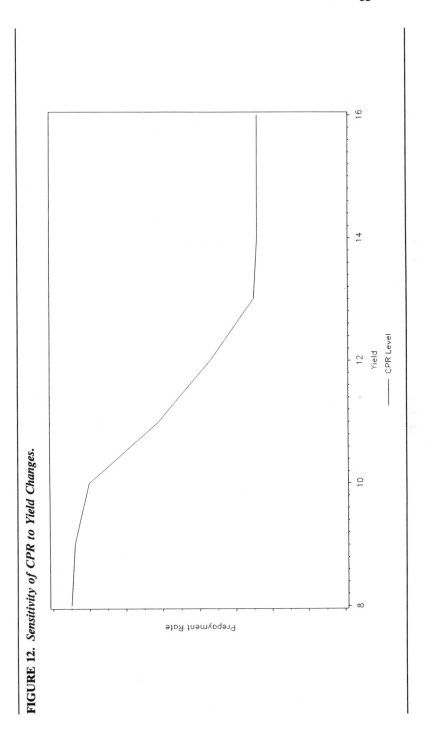

FIGURE 13.

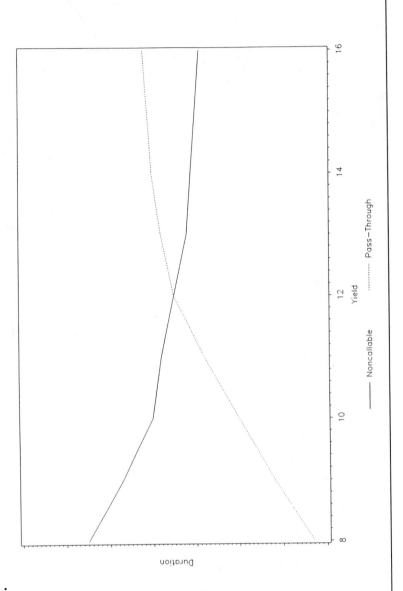

kinked in the middle. Analysis has shown that the conditional prepayment rate (CPR) accelerates as yields decline and approach the coupon rate on the mortgage. While refinancings are not yet occurring, the "penalty" or lost value by prepaying has diminished to the point where the old low rate is no longer a deterrent to moving. As yields decline more and more below the coupon, the number of refinancings accelerates and then stabilizes at a high level. While it would seem logical if all the loans were prepaid if rates fell two or three percentage points below the coupon, in real life this doesn't always happen.

What does all this have to do with convexity? The duration of noncallable bonds increases as yields fall. That was the feature that produced the positive attributes of convexity. With mortgages, however, if CPR's rise as yields fall, the duration shortens. Figure 13 demonstrates this effect for two 12% securities, one a noncallable bond and the other a pass-through.

The effect of the changing duration on the price of the pass-through is shown in Figure 14. The tendency of the duration to shorten as a result of higher prepayments causes the price performance of pass-throughs with coupons higher than market yields to appear similar to that of cushion bonds.

The relatively flat price-yield curve for mortgages has some attractive characteristics for devising defensive strategies. Mortgages will generally outperform noncallables for stable to moderately declining markets. A forthcoming report examines the relationship between prepayment rates and market yields and other factors, which enables us to determine the price sensitivity of mortgages with greater precision.

Discount Mortgages versus Current Mortgages

Many investors observe the higher yields available on current coupon mortgages relative to those of discount mortgages and are tempted to conclude that the currents are cheap relative to the discounts. In order to make the determination of relative value, a number of factors must be analyzed.

First, a holding period must be decided upon. Discounts and currents have distinctly different prepayment patterns. Also, the longer the holding period, the greater the chance that prepayment rates change to levels quite different from those at the initial purchase. This relationship must be estimated.

Finally, the likely variation of yields from the current level is best estimated by examining market volatility. If there were no volatility, the selection process would be easy — currents would outperform discounts because they had a higher initial yield and neither experienced a price change. We all know that yields will change. Studying price volatility can help us determine the chance that rates will change, either up or down, by enough to cause currents to underperform.

Figure 15 compares the price-yield curves of an 8% pass-through and a 12% pass-through. Because they are both pass-throughs, the shape of the

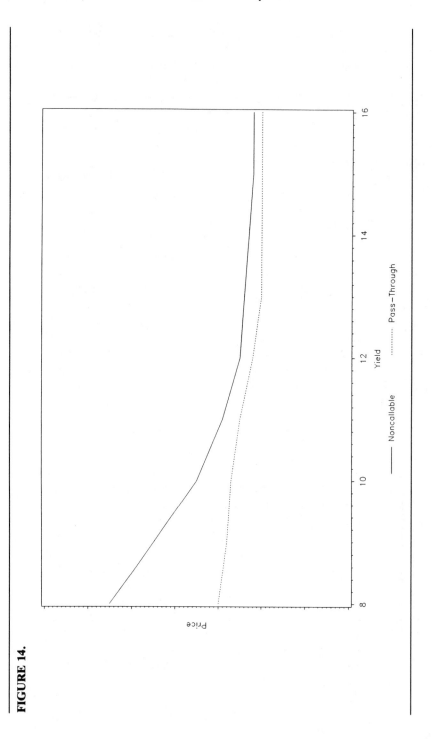

FIGURE 14.

FIGURE 15. *Discount and Current Mortgages.*

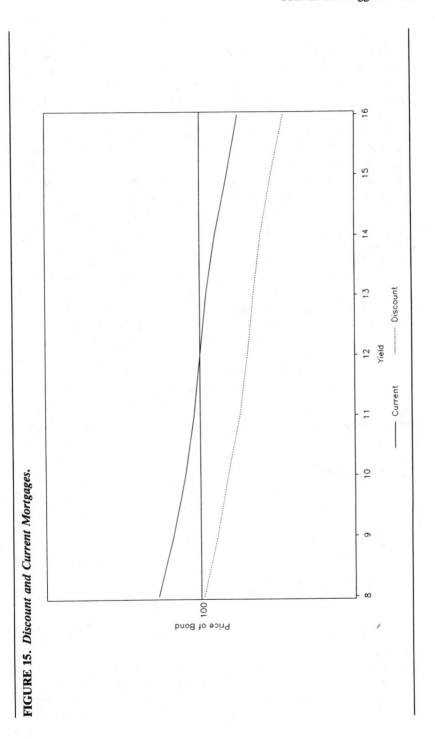

two curves is similar (although not exactly the same) but shifted sideways and down. Each generic mortgage group will have its own curve across this range of yields. Assume that: (i) current market yields are about 12% for discounts and 12¼% for currents, (ii) volatility is about 120 basis points per year, and (iii) a holding period or horizon of three years is desired for comparative purposes. Which is the better value?

To avoid developing complex distributions of prices and returns, we've simplified the analysis to illustrate the point about the importance of volatility. We have placed dashed lines, 200 basis points, to the left and right of the initial yields, 12 and 12¼%. For a normal distribution with a volatility of 120 basis points per year, the odds of rates going outside these dashed lines are about one in three. Further, the odds of rates shifting between 100 and 200 basis points away from the starting yield are also about one in three. This leaves the chance of rates ending within 100 basis points of the starting yield at about one-third. Table 7 summarizes the outcomes.

The estimated price relationships in Table 7 translate into the total returns shown in Table 8. The initial advantage of the current over the discount is erased by the superior price performance of the discount for larger yield changes, particularly when yields decline. Their durations were not

---

TABLE 7. *Effect of Volatility on Prices.*

	Discount Mortgage	Current Mortgage
Coupon	8%	12½%
Beginning yield/CPR	12%–6% per year	12¼%–8% per year
Remaining term	300 months	330 months
Price	$79.30	$99.65
Duration (modified)	5.1 years	4.8 years
CPR assumed if yield changes by		
−200 bp	7.0% per year	18.0% per year
−100 bp	6.5	12.0
NC	6.0	8.0
+100 bp	5.5	7.0
+200 bp	5.0	6.0
Probable price and price change based on yield change over 3 years and assumed CPR		
−200 bp	$89.10 (+12.4%)	$105.91 (+6.2%)
−100 bp	84.45 (+7.1)	103.51 (+3.9)
NC	80.00 (+0.9)	99.63 (NC)
+100 bp	75.75 (−4.5)	95.02 (−4.6)
+200 bp	71.66 (−9.6)	90.41 (−9.3)

TABLE 8. *Effect of Volatility on Total Return (Reinvestment Rate of 12%).*

	Total Return Given Changes in Markets Yields of				
	−200 bp	−100 bp	NC	+100 bp	+200 bp
Discount	14.11%	13.07%	12.00%	10.91%	9.79%
Current	12.85%	12.73%	12.19%	11.36%	10.47%
Approx. probability	1/6	1/6	1/3	1/6	1/6

drastically different, but their convexities were. The discount is convex over the range of yields used in this analysis, while the current coupon exhibits negative convexity on the low-rate side of this zone and no convexity at all on the upper end.

The final step in this simplified version of volatility-adjusted rate of return analysis is to weight the returns in Table 8 by the approximate probabilities of each scenario. The result is shown below:

	Volatility-Adjusted Rate of Return
Discount mortgage	11.98%
Current coupon mortgage	11.97%

Note how close the adjusted returns are. Market participants intuitively priced the current coupons to levels that made them comfortable with lower call protection. It appears that the market has appropriately priced the incremental convexity of the discounts.

This analysis can be extended to include both callable and noncallable bonds. Breakeven volatility is another measure that can be derived to compare two securities with different convexities. In this case, the breakeven volatility is 120 basis points per year, quite close to current levels. The relative attractiveness of any of the possible bond investments should be tested against probable changes in rates over the relevant time horizon for the comparison.

In effect this volatility adjustment is a much-simplified method of pricing into the rate of return the option-like characteristics of some bonds, as well as the convexity inherent in bonds that have no call options, and of combining the two factors into the same analytical framework.

Hyperconvex Bonds (Bonds with Long Options)

In recent years, a new type of bond has become available in the marketplace. The bonds in this group have option-like characteristics which are

FIGURE 16.

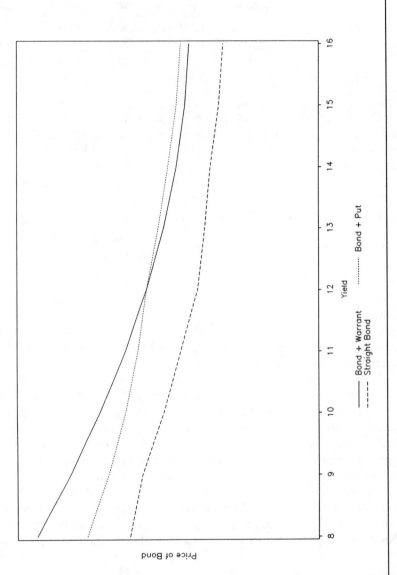

Price of Bond

Yield

Bond + Warrant
Straight Bond

Bond + Put

effectively "long" positions in options as opposed to the short position implied by an optional call by an issuer. We have dubbed these bonds "hyperconvex" bonds because the increasing value of the bond is extremely sensitive to declines in rates while the declining value is less sensitive to rate declines than a noncallable bond. The most frequently encountered bonds of this type are:

- Bonds with puts prior to maturity
- Bonds with bond purchase warrants attached
- Bonds with contingent takedown options

Because the value of the option purchased with each type of bond increases faster than the value of the bond itself, but decreases at a slower rate, the bond has more convexity than a noncallable bond of similar maturity. Figure 16 compares the price-yield curve of a 20-year bond with a put after five years with the curve of a 20-year noncallable bond.

Investors pay a higher price (lower initial yield) for hyperconvex bonds but can recover this premium over normal bonds if market yields move significantly in one direction. We demonstrated the analysis in the last section —if prospective volatility is low, don't pay a premium for bonds with more convexity. It takes highly volatile markets to make hyperconvex bonds a good value.

In the past six months, over $2 billion of hyperconvex bonds were issued in the public markets, mostly bonds with puts. Considerable doubt was raised at the time as to whether purchasing such bonds was a wise idea. The subsequent sharp decline in rates (however, consistent with the volatility experience of the Volcker years) resulted in large profits for all bonds including bonds with puts. Interestingly, though, bonds with warrants would have been substantially better investments than bonds with puts. Look back at Figure 16, and you can see that the additional convexity in hyperconvex bonds is not symmetrical. This means that in order to get the most bang for your buck, you have to guess which way rates are going as well as estimate the volatility.

Another strategy is suggested by the lack of symmetry in hyperconvex bonds. This is the ability to combine a hyperconvex bond with a negatively convex bond and thereby produce a combination that has the same price sensitivity as a noncallable bond, but has a higher return over the range of probable yields. Figure 17 suggests the strategy and the following section provides additional detail.

The dashed line representing the combination of a mortgage (current coupon variety) and a bond with a bond purchase warrant (the hyperconvex bond) could represent a superior investment strategy over a vast range of probable interest rates.

FIGURE 17. *Combining Bonds with Different Convexities.*

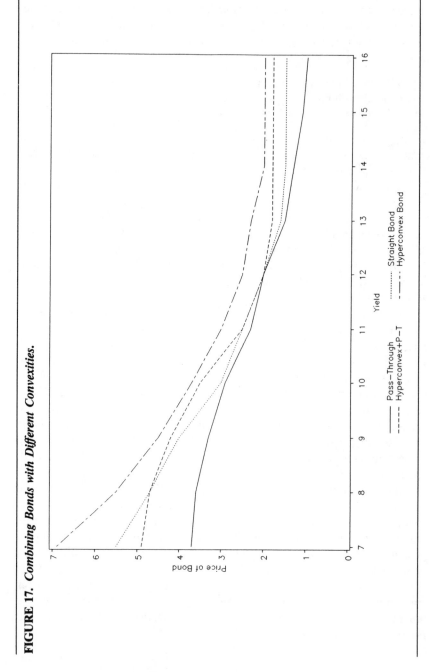

IV. Framework for Evaluating the Convexity of Securities or Portfolios

Combinations of Long and Short Duration Bonds

Identifying the characteristics of individual bonds is an important beginning to portfolio structuring and analysis, but only a beginning. Each of the thousands of bonds has its own characteristics. In addition to other features, each bond can be described in terms of a yield, a duration and a convexity.

A fortunate aspect of portfolio analysis is that durations are additive, i.e., the duration of a combination of two bonds is the weighed average of the two durations. Thus, if a portfolio manager wishes to create a $100 pool with a duration of 5.0 years, there are a great many ways that this can be accomplished. A few examples are presented below.

	Bonds		Portfolio	
Alternative	$ Value	Duration	$ Value	Duration
I.	50	2.0 yrs.	100	5.0 yrs.
	50	8.0		
II.	25	1.0	100	5.0
	50	4.0		
	25	11.0		
III.	10	10.0	100	5.0
	20	2.0		
	30	4.0		
	40	6.0		

The alternative portfolios can also include short positions either in the cash or futures market or in options on the cash or futures market. There are an unlimited number of ways to produce a target duration.

The problem of selecting among the alternatives can be narrowed down by examining what happens to the alternatives if yields change, not by a small amount in which case the portfolios all perform similarly, but by an amount large enough for the different convexities to come into play. All other things equal, we would select the portfolio that had the greatest positive convexity.

Before moving on, let's provide two cautionary notes. First, one of the "all other things equal" assumptions we have made implicitly so far is that when yields change, they change by equal amounts across the entire yield curve. If the yields do not change by equal amounts, the three portfolios will change by different amounts. A second cautionary note is that convexity is not symmetrical, particularly for securities laden with option-like features. The gain resulting from a decline in rates may not be equal to the loss from rising rates.

Combinations of Positive and Negative Convexity Bonds

Like duration, convexity for combinations of securities can be aggregated by weighting consistent measures of convexity by the investment in or value of each type of security. By consistent measure we mean expressing the convexity "per 100 basis points of change" or some other consistent basis point interval.

Since duration is expressed and interpreted "per 100 basis points of change," it is tempting to express convexity the same way. Before jumping on the bandwagon, however, refer back to Figures 7 and 8. The whole point of measuring convexity is to secure gains and avoid unexpected losses. Figure 8 shows that convexity just isn't that big a factor until yield changes reach 200 basis points. Of course, you could rebalance every 100 basis points, but that doesn't mean you shouldn't have planned beyond the first 100 basis points.

To complete the example we started earlier, let's make the following assumptions (which are realistic for Treasury securities):

Bond	Duration (% per 100 bp)	Convexity Gain (% of Value)	
		100 bp Chg.	200 bp Chg.
A	1.0%	.02%	.08%
B	2.0	.04	.16
C	4.0	.15	.52
D	6.0	.23	1.01
E	8.0	.60	2.40
F	10.0	.97	4.29
G	11.0	1.16	5.15

The gains from convexity shown are the gains for a decline in rates. The gains for rising rates are yet another set of numbers.

The effect on the hypothetical portfolios, each with a duration of 5.0, is set forth in Table 9.

The three portfolios all consist of Treasury notes and stripped coupons, and all have identical durations of 5.0 years. The convexity of each portfolio, as measured by gain per 100 basis points change in rates, differs only slightly. The range from high to low of .24 to .37 does not indicate any significant difference. As the measure of convexity shifts to the 200 basis point change in rates, the differences are not trivial. A half-point difference in performance is important, especially when you thought there was no difference. Further, we are dealing with grossly simplified portfolios of noncallable securities. Introducing complex bonds forces closer scrutiny of portfolio performance.

The nature of the cash flows of the aggregate portfolio is the principal determinant of its convexity. Portfolio III from Table 9 had the cash flow

TABLE 9. *Profile of Three Portfolios.*

Portfolio	Bond	$ Value	Duration	Convexity −100 bp	Convexity −200 bp	Duration (% per 100 bp)	Convexity −100 bp	Convexity −200 bp
				Bond Characteristics		**$100 Portfolio Characteristics**		
I.	B	50	2.0	.04%	.16%	5.0%	.32%	1.28%
	E	50	8.0	.60	2.40			
II.	A	25	1.0	.02	.08	5.0	.37	1.57
	C	50	4.0	.15	.52			
	G	25	11.0	1.16	5.15			
III.	F	10	10.0	.97	4.29	5.0	.24	1.02
	B	20	2.0	.04	.16			
	C	30	4.0	.15	.52			
	D	40	6.0	.23	1.01			

pattern that was most level, that is, minimum variance from the mean. Portfolio II had the largest variance, largely because Bond G is a "stripped" Treasury with a high contribution to the overall convexity. We could have constructed a bizarre portfolio, one containing equal parts of Bond A and Bond G, to make the point about barbells and dumbbells being more convex than bullets, but the case is simply not realistic. Most investors have a more diverse selection of securities with a more balanced cash flow pattern. Extreme barbells are extraordinarily susceptible to changes in the shape of the yield curve.

The Yield–Convexity Trade-Off

On pages 319 through 323, we worked out a simple version of a trade-off of yield and convexity. The conclusion was reached that a yield spread of 25 basis points between current coupon mortgages and discount mortgages of approximately equal duration based on the use of conditional prepayment rates was appropriate compensation for lack of convexity if volatility is 120 basis points a year. If volatility increases, the spread is not wide enough because the value of the incremental convexity of the discount is more than 25 basis points in expected yield. You don't have to have an opinion on direction, just an opinion on the level of volatility.

The same framework can be applied to our hypothetical portfolios, or any portfolio. In effect, for a given horizon (which can differ from the portfolio duration) and volatility, a distribution of scenarios is generated. The expected return and the appropriate measures of upward and downward convexity of each component of the portfolio can be quantified, and the aggregate volatility-adjusted return can be determined. By identifying the same parameters for securities that are not in the portfolio, expected performance can be maximized.

V. Methods of Estimating Convexity

The objective in calculating convexity is to estimate the degree to which a price will change in addition to the change that can be predicted by the duration. Several mathematical techniques can be applied to the task of estimating the effect of the curvature above or below the initial duration line. Considerable work has been done in the use of calculus to represent the price-yield curve of bonds in terms of parameters. The most notable of these parameters are duration and convexity. For yield changes of 100 basis points or less, the use of duration and convexity probably suffices. The measure of convexity is defined by the rate of change of duration given a 100 basis points change in yield. To estimate the effects on a portfolio of changes in yields of 200 basis points or more, additional parameters would be required to accurately predict the change in values. The residual error grows rapidly as the yield change increases. In effect, the skewness of the curvature, particularly for bonds with option-like features, forces a higher level of sensitivity analysis, particularly in volatile markets where the probability of substantial changes in yields is high.

Most investors do not wish to get involved in differential equations. In fact, since all convexity estimates are saddled with the simplifying assumption of constant yield curve shape (which has never been true for long), there is the question of whether parametric analysis is mathematical overkill. We subscribe to its value as a tool, but for those who do not wish to brush up on their calculus, we offer the following method as means of quantifying curvature, which employs readily available calculations.

Estimating Convexity for Bonds and Mortgage-Backed Securities

The convexity of a bond for a given yield change can be quickly approximated by performing the calculations indicated below.

- An 11% coupon noncallable bond with a ten-year maturity initially selling at par is the subject of the analysis.
- Calculate the modified duration of the bond 5.98.
- Calculate the actual bond price based on your interest rate scenario. Assume rates will either rise or fall by 100 basis points.

Actual price for 12% YTM (+100 bp)	94.27
Initial price for 11% YTM	100.00
Actual price for 10% YTM (−100 bp)	106.23

- Calculate the predicted bond prices based on the bond's modified duration.

  | Predicted price for 12% YTM (+100 bp) | 94.02 |
  | Predicted price for 10% YTM (−100 bp) | 105.98 |

- The predicted price is determined by:

$$\text{Predicted Price} = \text{Initial Price} \times \left(1 - \frac{\text{Modified Duration}}{100} \times \frac{\pm \text{bp Chg}}{100}\right).$$

- Calculate convexity per 100 basis points.

	−100 bp	+100 bp
Actual price	106.23	94.27
Predicted price	105.98	94.02
Initial price	100.00	100.00
Actual change from initial price	6.23	−5.73
Predicted price change based on modified duration	5.98	−5.98
Convexity	.25	.25

The interpretation of the .25 convexity calculated above is that the subject bond will outperform equal duration bonds with no convexity by .25% The convexity of a mortgage-backed security for a given yield change can also be quickly estimated using the above method. However, an additional assumption is required, the change in the mortgage-backed security's prepayment rate must be considered for a given shift in yield.

The above example used a bond initially selling at par. The actual price change resulting for a given basis point shift in yields requires an adjustment to percentage terms if the bond initially sold at a discount or a premium to par. The following example illustrates the procedure for a premium bond.

Example for a Premium Bond

- Assume the 11% coupon bond was initially priced at 105.00 to yield 10.19%.
- The volatility scenario calls for a 200 basis point rate change in either direction.
- Modified duration equals 6.09

	−200 bp	+200 bp
Actual price	118.93	93.23
Predicted price[a]	117.79	92.21
Initial price	105.00	105.00
Actual price change[b]	13.92	−11.78
Due to duration	12.79	−12.79
Gain[c]	1.13	1.01
Convexity (% chg.)	1.08	.96

a. Note that

$$[(\text{Actual Price} - \text{Predicted Price}) \div \text{Initial Price}] \times 100 = \text{Convexity}$$

$$[(93.23 - 92.21) \div 105.00] \times 100 = .96$$

b. General solution:

$$\text{Total Price Change} = 100 \times \frac{\text{Actual Price} - \text{Initial Price}}{\text{Initial Price}}$$

c. [Actual Price − Predicted Price] and [Actual Price Change − Due to Duration] may differ slightly due to rounding error.

Example for Mortgage Securities

The convexity of a mortgage-backed security for a given yield change can also be quickly estimated using the above method. However, an additional assumption is required, the change in the mortgage-backed security's prepayment rate must be considered for a given shift in yield.

- Assume a 11.25% FHLMC Conventional: Regular PC with an age of 4 years, a prepayment rate of .55% per month, and a price of 99.97.
- The volatility scenario calls for a ±200 basis point change.
- Modified duration equals 5.34

−200 Basis Points

Prepayment rate	1.01
Actual price	108.43
Predicted price	110.65
Total price change	8.46
Change from predicted price modified duration	10.68
Convexity	−2.22

+200 Basis Points

Prepayment rate	.37
Actual price	89.85
Predicted Price	89.29
Total price change	−10.12
Change from predicted price modified duration	−10.68
Convexity	.56

We discussed earlier in this article the lack of symmetry in convexity of certain securities. The example above illustrates one case. The FHLMC exhibits negative convexity for declining rates and positive convexity for rising rates. This changing convexity is not unique to mortgages although they are a prominent example, often cited in the press.

For portfolio design purposes, there is no single convexity number that adequately describes sensitivity to yield changes if the portfolio contains complex bonds. High levels of volatility may make bonds with long options attractive; however, one must still have an opinion on the direction of rates since you could buy either bonds with warrants or bonds with puts. Both may be good values if volatility is high, but their performance thereafter depends on the direction of movement in rates.

Parametric Analysis

The method illustrated above provides a quick way to calculate the difference between the actual price of a bond and the predicted price based on modified duration. We have termed this value convexity; however, strictly speaking, this statement is incorrect. The amount a bond changes in price for a given change in yield can be represented by a Taylor Series (basically a set of differential equations). The first term in the Taylor Series is modified duration (the first derivative of price with respect to yield). This value accounts for most of the price change in a straight bond. The second term is convexity (the second derivative of price with respect to yield) which usually accounts for the small portion of the price change not explained by modified duration. The remaining terms in the Taylor Series generally account for a negligible amount of the bond's price change, as long as the yield change is small. This amount that is ignored is generally referred to as the residual.

In the above examples the residual and the true convexity were combined and termed convexity. Essentially, the amount of the price change explained by modified duration was calculated directly and the remaining unexplained component was termed convexity. For trade evaluation purposes, combining the residual component and the convexity component of the bond's price change will generally provide a reliable estimate of a bond's convexity. If an investor is engaged in parametric analysis (explaining how the change in one variable affects another variable, such as how a change in yield affects a bond's price) of a dedicated portfolio with a long horizon and low turnover objectives, then isolating the price change due to modified duration, convexity and the remaining terms (the residual) in the Taylor Series becomes more important.

24

Callable Corporate Bonds:
Pricing and Portfolio Considerations

Andrew D. Langerman
Vice President
Drexel Burnham Lambert

William J. Gartland
Associate
Drexel Burnham Lambert

I. Introduction

Selecting corporate bonds is a more complicated task than ever. Credit analysis, the fundamental evaluation of the incremental spread over Treasuries required to lend money in today's rapidly changing environment has never been more difficult. Beyond this, the nominal spread received by the investor when he purchases a new issue callable bond at say +175 to the 30-year pays not just for credit risk, but must also compensate for the risk of early call. The investor has explicitly given the issuer certain valuable options and he must be compensated for these with extra yield.

In the low volatility interest rate environment of the 1970s (before 1979), these options were of relatively little value to the corporate issuer. Today, when rates can move down 350 basis points in a year and up 100 basis points in 6 months, these options can be worth in excess of 80 basis points on long bonds. We have developed an option pricing model to value explicitly the options embedded in corporate bonds and to separate the yield spread into the fundamental credit spread and the spread attributable to the options. Our call adjusted spreads and call adjusted yields allow direct comparison of bonds with different call features or different coupons.

The calls in bonds not only affect the pricing, they also strongly affect the performance of bonds when rates change. Bonds lengthen in a decline and shorten in a rally. Call adjusted duration measures the price sensitivity of callable bonds. This measure will be of primary importance to the portfolio or asset/liability manager who wishes to target a given duration.

Some callable bonds are overvalued given their lack of call protection. Yet with spreads at historically wide levels, many callable bonds represent excellent value. When properly analyzed, the corporate sector can significantly contribute to portfolio performance.

There is a darker side to the rally experienced in the credit markets. The sustained surge of corporate bond tenders and redemptions is forcing portfolio managers to reinvest millions of dollars far sooner than planned to rebalance their holdings. But before we jump back into the market with this windfall, let's examine the lessons we have learned.

Lesson 1: When Rates Go Up, You Lose

In June of 1980, AT&T brought to market a ten year issue with a coupon of 10⅜%. At +75 basis points to the 10-year Treasury, these bonds were aggressively bought by investors. However, the run-up in interest rates did not peak until mid-to-late 1981.

When AT&T issued another 10-year note in March 1981, the current coupon had risen to 13¼%, and the market value of the 10⅜'s had fallen to 84.919%. Holders of the 10⅜'s would be forced to realize a 15 point loss to swap into the new issue and participate in the higher yields.

Lesson 2: When Rates Go Down, You Lose

Five years after missing the opportunity to buy the 13¼'s, the holders of the 10⅜'s had quite a different problem. By March of 1986, comparable maturity Treasury yields had fallen to about 7.35%, and the issuer's right to redeem the bonds was threatening the holders' high current income. On June 1, AT&T ended all speculation and redeemed the bonds at par, leaving the holders to reinvest at the lower market rates.

Lesson 3: When Rates Are Stable, You Win

Part of the compensation callable corporate bondholders receive is in payment for the issuer's right to redeem the bonds prior to maturity. In a stable rate environment, this right will not be exercised, and the callable bondholder will receive the premium in his coupon payments through the stated maturity of the bond. (In practice, premium call prices and to a lesser extent underwriting costs provide some tolerance for rate movements before bonds will be retired prior to maturity.)

Before you get the wrong idea, callable corporate bonds are still wise investments, provided you are aware of all the risks you have taken and you receive adequate compensation for these risks. In this article, we will first examine the features which impact pricing characteristics of bonds traded in the public markets, and present a method for assessing the relative value of callable corporate bonds. Once the determination of value can be made, our attention will shift to the performance characteristics of the bonds which should be considered prior to placing bonds in a portfolio.

II. Value of Corporate Bonds

In its purest form, the value of a bond is exactly equal to the present value of all its future cash flows. In this case, the cash flow schedule can be laid out with certainty (except for the risk of default), so the calculation of the bond's price is straightforward.

Cash Flow Uncertainty

While corporations do occasionally issue bonds of this type, the more general bond structures have features which introduce uncertainty in the timing of the cash flows. The issuers often reserve the right to call the bond from the bondholders at some time prior to maturity. As a result, the repayment of principal may occur sooner than anticipated if interest rates fall.

Typically, intermediates issued for 10 years are callable at par after seven years. Seven year issues are callable at par in five years, and five year issues are callable at par in three years. Telephone company issues are generally forty years to maturity, callable after five years at par plus a premium which declines to zero after thirty-five years. Industrial and utility companies generally issue thirty year bonds which are callable at the time of issue at par plus a premium. This premium declines to zero in 25 or 29 years. These bonds are usually refunding restricted for the first five or ten years.

The refunding restriction prohibits the issuer from replacing the outstanding bonds with bonds sold at a lower interest cost. However, the company may redeem the bonds using cash generated from on-going operations, the sale of an asset or portion of the business, or the issuance of common stock. For this reason, these bonds are said to be cash callable during the refunding restricted period.

The second major source of cash flow uncertainty is the sinking fund provisions that exist in most long industrial and utility bonds. Sinking funds provide a schedule for the orderly retirement of principal, usually at par. But the issuers often have the option to double or triple their sinking fund payments and accumulate credits which may be used to satisfy future obligations.

In the case of electric utilities, the issuers usually have an obligation to retire a fixed percentage (1%–2%) of all their outstanding debt each year at par but they are given the option to choose the issue they retire (called a funnel sinker), or use certain credits to satisfy their obligation. As a result, holders of high coupon issues stand to lose large portions of their positions if the company funnels to that issue, or no bonds at all may be taken if the company chooses to pledge additional property in lieu of sinking bonds.

Bondholders' Risks and Rewards

The holder of a callable bond has accepted two forms of risk because of the uncertain timing of cash flows from his security. The first of these is credit risk; the incremental chance that interest and principal will not be received as scheduled due to default. The other risk is interest rate risk. At one extreme, interest rate risk is the chance that the issuer will exercise his call option when it is to the holders' economic disadvantage. At the other extreme it is the chance that the bondholder will be forced to hold a low coupon bond in a rising rate environment.

Fortunately, neither of these risks is borne without compensation. To lure investors to buy corporate bonds, the issuers offer yields which exceed the yields on comparable Treasury securities. The price paid for a bond is fair when the gross spread to the Treasury yield curve adequately reflects the risks being assumed by the bondholder.

The question of creditworthiness is a complicated one based upon many subjective forecasts and opinions (e.g., cash flow and profitability projections, the ability and goals of management, opinions of accountants and analysts). For the purposes of this discussion, let us assume that the spread required for a given credit can be found. We will focus our attention on the valuation of the interest rate risk component of the gross spread. A callable bond will be deemed fairly valued if the residual spread is adequate for the issuer's credit.

III. Determining Relative Value for Callable Bonds

There are many ways to determine the relative value of corporate bonds with embedded call options. For example, one might propose a specific interest rate scenario for the future and evaluate a selected security at several points in the future. If the bond would be called away at any of these points, a yield to that call date can be calculated and value determined. The shortcoming of this method is that it requires a fairly accurate prediction of the level of future interest rates. If one knew what rates would do in the future, there would be no uncertainty in the timing of the cash flows and the valuation process would be identical to that of the bullet mentioned earlier.

We have chosen a volatility based options pricing model which explicitly calculates the value of the options. This approach subjects the callable bond to a range of interest rate scenarios determined by the perceived level of market interest rate volatility. The bond is valued at regular intervals through its stated maturity under all prevailing interest rate profiles. The results are weighted to reflect the probability of actually experiencing a particular environment.

This method does not depend upon an accurate prediction of future interest rates, but merely an assessment of the variability of the rates. On the contrary, the probabilistic approach recognizes the random nature of rate movements (sometimes up, sometimes down). The value assigned to the bond is, in a sense, a weighted average of the value for each rate scenario.

While it is useful to know how much the issuer has implicitly paid for the right to redeem his bonds, we find it most useful to express value in terms of the call-adjusted spread to the Treasury yield curve. The technique allows us to rank bonds based solely on the credit of the issuer. More importantly, if the call-adjusted spread for a particular bond exceeds the credit spread determined by the traditional analysis of creditworthiness, the bond is relatively cheap and should be an attractive buy candidate. On the other hand, if the call-adjusted spread is less than the traditionally derived credit spread, one concludes the price does not reflect the full value of the embedded calls and the bond should be sold/not bought.

IV. What is Volatility and Why Is It Important?

Volatility in the present context is the magnitude of variation in market interest rates, and is measured by the standard deviation of changes in absolute yields. Just as changes in yields cause corresponding changes in bond prices, increases in interest rate volatility cause the value of the embedded options to increase, leaving less of the quoted spread to pay for the credit risk. Put simply, volatility gives time value to the options.

Throughout the 1960s and early 1970s volatility was a relatively stable 50–65 basis points per year, as shown in Figure 1. At this level of volatility, the value of the options embedded in the 30-year bonds is only about 25 basis points depending upon the specific structure (see Table 1) and the failure to recognize the options was of little consequence.

However, when the Federal Reserve stopped regulating interest rates and began focusing on the money supply in October, 1979, volatility shot up to over 200 basis points per year. It has once again stabilized somewhat. However, the new level is about 150 basis points per year. This makes the calls on long bonds worth about 120–150 basis points at this volatility. As you can see, the call premium is now a much more significant portion of the quoted yield.

FIGURE 1.

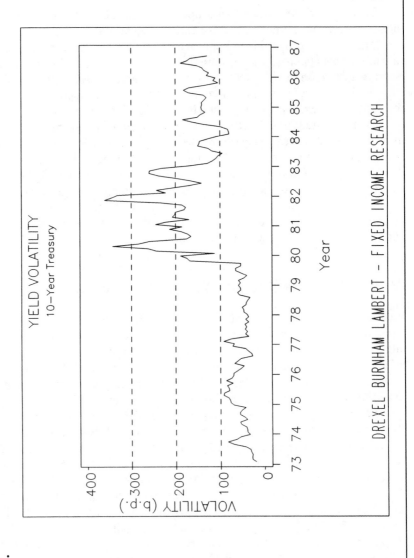

TABLE 1. *Allocation of Quoted Spread Current Coupon Bonds at Various Volatilities.*[a]

	Yrs. to Mat.	Yrs. to Call	Quoted[a] Sprd. (bp)	Volatility					
				150		100		50	
				Adj. Sprd.	Opt. Prem.	Adj. Sprd.	Opt. Prem.	Adj. Sprd.	Opt. Prem.
Aa intermediate industrials	10	7	79	41	38	57	22	72	7
	7	5	86	60	26	73	13	83	3
	5	3	84	43	40	60	23	76	8
Aa intermediate utilities	10	5	84	40	44	63	20	80	3
	7	5	86	60	26	73	13	83	3
	5	3	94	53	40	70	23	86	8
Aa intermediate finance	10	7	74	36	38	52	22	66	7
	7	5	76	50	26	63	12	73	3
	5	3	84	43	40	60	23	76	8
Aa long industrials	30	10	120–125	2	119	56	65	100	21
Aa long utilities	30	5	155–165	16	147	85	78	139	23
Aa long phones	40	5	158	−12	167	68	88	129	26

a. As of October 1, 1986.

V. Portfolio Considerations

Once a bond has been identified as a buy candidate, its performance characteristics must be evaluated against the portfolio's goals. The traditional portfolio manager has always been faced with the choice of evaluating the bond to its stated maturity, or recognizing that the bond may be redeemed and evaluating to the redemption date. This means choosing between radically different measures of such quantities as yield, average life, and modified duration (see Table 2).

Intuitively it would seem that the callable bond is really a hybrid of a bond with the stated maturity and one which "matures" on the first redemption date. Then it would follow that the effective modified duration and expected life of the bond would be somewhere between these limiting cases.

The effective modified duration is computed by evaluating the price of the callable bond after a small parallel shift in the yield curve. The percentage change in the price for this small yield change is then explicitly calculated. Expected life is the weighted average time to redemption of the bonds. The weights used are the probability of being called at each evaluation point. Table 3 shows these relationships for several bonds.

The question remains, how are callable bonds perceived in the market? If the market totally ignores the embedded options, then the traditional modified duration should predict the percentage change in the bond's price for a change in market yields. The truth is that the call-adjusted modified duration is a better predictor of the price sensitivity of a callable bond.

Table 4 compares the percentage price change predicted by the two measures of modified duration with the observed change in the price of the R. J. Reynolds 11¾'s of August 15, 2015. Observations were made at roughly one week intervals during the three month period from November 1, 1985 to January 31, 1986. The average magnitude of deviation from the observed change was 1.78% for the traditional MD compared with just 0.65% for the call-adjusted MD. Thus portfolios matched on the basis of traditional duration are in reality mismatched to their corresponding liabilities and the portfolio manager remains exposed to the interest rate risk he sought to eliminate. In addition, such portfolios require more frequent rematching.

VI. Conclusions

A well balanced portfolio should contain some securities which do well when rates go down, others which are best when rates rise, and still others which excel when rates fluctuate moderately around a stable level. Callable corporates will not perform as well as non-callable bonds in a significant rally, and they will lose considerable market value when rates rise significantly (unlike floating rate instruments). Yet when rates move randomly in some

TABLE 2. Bond Performance Parameters: Maturity versus Redemption.[a]

Company	Bond Description			Redemption		Measured to Maturity			Measured to Redemption		
	Coupon	Maturity	Price	Date	Price	YTM	Avg. Life	Mod. Dur.	YTC	Avg. Life	Mod. Dur.
ALUMINUM CO AMER	13.875	01/15/11	112.250	01/15/91	106.938[b]	12.28	16.04	7.39	11.46	4.27	3.16
ALABAMA PWR CO	9.375	05/01/16	98.375	05/01/91	106.380[b]	9.54	29.57	9.45	11.03	4.56	3.48
AMOCO CORP	9.875	02/01/16	104.750	02/01/96	104.387	9.39	23.62	9.70	9.40	9.31	6.01
ATLANTIC RICHFIELD	10.500	10/15/95	111.418	10/15/92	100.000	8.65	9.02	5.70	8.07	6.02	4.32
ATLANTIC RICHFIELD	11.000	04/15/13	106.792	04/15/93	106.600[b]	10.25	17.53	8.57	10.28	6.52	4.45
AMERICAN TEL & TELE	8.625	04/01/26	93.000	04/01/91	106.210	9.29	39.48	10.51	11.77	4.48	3.58
AMERICAN EXPRESS CR	10.875	05/15/13	106.606	05/15/93	105.440	10.15	26.60	8.72	10.08	6.61	4.54
BORDEN INC	8.375	04/15/16	94.250	04/15/06	100.000	8.93	28.72	10.04	9.01	19.52	8.88
BURLINGTON NORTHERN	11.625	08/15/15	111.250	08/15/95	105.760[b]	10.39	19.35	8.87	10.09	8.86	5.59
BURLINGTON NORTHERN	9.000	04/01/16	93.750	04/01/96	104.500[b]	9.64	29.48	9.79	10.34	9.48	6.16
BELL TELEPHONE CORP	8.750	04/01/26	94.500	04/01/91	107.500	9.27	39.48	10.51	11.68	4.48	3.58
CHEVRON CORP	8.750	03/01/96	100.250	03/01/93	100.000	8.71	9.40	6.27	8.70	6.40	4.79
CHEVRON CORP	9.375	06/01/16	100.250	06/01/96	104.000	9.35	22.05	9.67	9.59	9.65	6.08
CHESAPEAKE&POTO TEL	9.125	07/01/26	98.250	07/01/91	107.140	9.29	39.73	10.24	10.80	4.73	3.66
DU PONT E I DE NEMO	8.450	11/15/04	95.000	NOW	104.740	9.01	11.09	8.66	110.45	0.10	0.06
FORD MTR CO DEL	10.750	07/01/95	108.875	07/01/92	100.000	9.24	8.73	5.59	8.74	5.73	4.19
GENERAL MTRS ACCEP	10.250	06/01/90	104.640	06/01/88	100.000	8.73	3.65	2.92	7.20	1.65	1.46
GENERAL MTRS ACCEP	8.250	04/01/16	90.866	04/01/96	103.600	9.15	29.48	10.27	10.00	9.48	6.30
GENERAL MTRS CORP	7.500	08/15/93	96.363	08/15/91	100.000	8.20	6.86	5.18	8.42	4.85	3.93
HOSPITAL CORP AMER	9.000	03/15/16	94.000	03/15/96	108.250[b]	9.61	27.44	9.77	10.28	9.44	6.12

TABLE 2 *Continued*

Company	Bond Description			Redemption		Measured to Maturity			Measured to Redemption		
	Coupon	Maturity	Price	Date	Price	YTM	Avg. Life	Mod. Dur.	YTC	Avg. Life	Mod. Dur.
PENNEY J C INC	12.125	02/01/93	111.468	02/01/90	100.000	9.66	6.31	4.46	8.11	3.48	2.74
PENNEY J C INC	9.375	03/01/16	96.500	03/01/96	104.688^b	9.74	21.33	9.60	10.27	9.40	6.04
K MART CORP	12.750	03/01/15	112.500	03/01/95	106.250^b	11.27	18.90	8.29	10.91	8.40	5.26
MOUNTAIN STS TEL &	9.000	04/01/26	96.375	04/01/91	107.170	9.35	39.48	10.42	11.33	4.48	3.57
MARATHON OIL CO	12.500	03/01/94	100.000	03/01/87	100.000	12.49	7.40	4.68	12.35	0.40	0.38
NEW YORK TEL CO	8.625	05/15/24	93.000	05/15/91	104.520	9.30	37.61	10.10	11.39	4.60	3.54
PACIFIC BELL	11.375	08/15/24	117.500	08/15/90	108.710	9.64	37.85	9.83	7.98	3.86	3.13
PACIFIC BELL	9.250	03/01/26	97.375	03/01/91	106.060	9.50	39.40	10.18	11.12	4.40	3.48
PUBLIC SVC ELEC & G	7.500	04/01/96	94.189	04/01/91	101.700^b	8.40	9.48	6.58	9.43	4.48	3.69
PUBLIC SVC ELEC & G	8.750	04/01/16	92.616	04/01/91	106.200^b	9.50	29.48	9.93	12.01	4.48	3.56
REYNOLDS R J INDS I	11.350	11/01/15	110.250	11/01/95	105.675^b	10.24	19.56	8.74	10.00	9.07	5.55
SOUTHWESTERN BELL T	11.875	10/18/21	120.375	10/18/90	109.960	9.80	35.03	9.27	8.00	4.03	3.13
TENNECO INC	12.125	05/01/05	106.331	05/01/90	105.750^b	11.30	11.59	7.25	11.27	3.57	2.73
TENNECO INC	11.125	05/15/13	103.697	05/15/94	104.620^b	10.70	17.11	8.37	10.80	7.60	4.91
UNION ELEC CO	8.875	05/01/96	99.750	05/01/91	108.880	8.91	9.57	6.15	9.40	4.56	3.56

a. Prices as of October 1, 1986.
b. Bond is currently cash callable.

moderate range, the premium paid by the issuer for the embedded options gives the callable bond a considerable advantage over alternative investments. However, the investor must recognize that by accepting the additional yield, he has taken a bet on interest rate volatility.

So the callable bond investor is left with three choices:

1. Ignore the options and treat all corporate bonds alike.
2. Use a rule of thumb to value the options.
3. Use an options based method to value the options in each individual bond.

Ignorance of the options is excusable when volatility and the corresponding option values are low. But given the current level of volatility, bondholders are implicitly writing calls worth several points every time they purchase a callable bond. Ignoring the options today has a significant impact on current income. The "Rule of Thumb" approach is better, but with the multitude of corporate bond structures in existence, it is hard to believe that a few general rules will adequately cover all cases.

Systematic use of a probabilistic valuation method in the bond selection process will produce portfolios which on average provide better results than other methods. The same law of averages has made millionaires of many Las Vegas casino operators (the house always has slightly better odds). Bond valuation methods like the one discussed in this article let the investor see the true credit spread of an issue after netting out the value of the options. Inadequate compensation for credit quality cannot be hidden behind a large nominal spread which barely pays for all the calls.

Choosing callable bonds for a portfolio is however a two step process. Determining that sufficient compensation is being provided for all contingent risks is one part. But equally important is the need to evaluate the bond's performance characteristics in light of the embedded options. Callable bonds are viewed in the market to be securities which are shorter than their stated maturities. The purchaser of a new 40-year phone bond owns a security which trades more like a 10-year Treasury in terms of its price volatility and effective modified duration. The decision to include such a bond in a portfolio should consciously reflect this fact, or the portfolio performance will not meet the expectations. Finally, investors must train themselves not to be fooled by the seemingly large spreads of some callables. The issuer's right to redeem the bonds limits their potential to appreciate during a rally. The call price becomes a ceiling. No matter how much further rates fall, the bond's price will not rise.[1]

---

1. Did someone say "negative convexity"? See Kenneth H. Sullivan and Timothy B. Kiggins, "Convexity: The Name Is New but You Always Knew What It Was," the previous article in this book.

TABLE 3. *Bond Performance Parameters: Traditional versus Call-Adjusted Approach.*[a]

		Bond Description			
				Redemption	
Company	Coupon	Maturity	Price	Date	Price
ALUMINUM CO AMER	13.875	01/15/11	112.250	01/15/91	106.938[b]
ALABAMA PWR CO	9.375	05/01/16	98.375	05/01/91	106.380[b]
AMOCO CORP	9.875	02/01/16	104.750	02/01/96	104.387
ATLANTIC RICHFIELD	10.500	10/15/95	111.418	10/15/92	100.000
ATLANTIC RICHFIELD	11.000	04/15/13	106.792	04/15/93	106.600[b]
AMERICAN TEL & TELE	8.625	04/01/26	93.000	04/01/91	106.210
AMERICAN EXPRESS CR	10.875	05/15/13	106.606	05/15/93	105.440
BORDEN INC	8.375	04/15/16	94.250	04/15/06	100.000
BURLINGTON NORTHERN	11.625	08/15/15	111.250	08/15/95	105.760[b]
BURLINGTON NORTHERN	9.000	04/01/16	93.750	04/01/96	104.500[b]
BELL TELEPHONE CORP	8.750	04/01/26	94.500	04/01/91	107.500
CHEVRON CORP	8.750	03/01/96	100.250	03/01/93	100.000
CHEVRON CORP	9.375	06/01/16	100.250	06/01/96	104.000
CHESAPEAKE&POTO TEL	9.125	07/01/26	98.250	07/01/91	107.140
DU PONT E I DE NEMO	8.450	11/15/04	95.000	NOW	104.740
FORD MTR CO DEL	10.750	07/01/95	108.875	07/01/92	100.000
GENERAL MTRS ACCEP	10.250	06/01/90	104.640	06/01/88	100.000
GENERAL MTRS ACCEP	8.250	04/01/16	90.866	04/01/96	103.600
GENERAL MTRS CORP	7.500	08/15/93	96.363	08/15/91	100.000
HOSPITAL CORP AMER	9.000	03/15/16	94.000	03/15/96	108.250[b]
PENNEY J C INC	12.125	02/01/93	111.468	02/01/90	100.000
PENNEY J C INC	9.375	03/01/16	96.500	03/01/96	104.688[b]
K MART CORP	12.750	03/01/15	112.500	03/01/95	106.250[b]
MOUNTAIN STS TEL &	9.000	04/01/26	96.375	04/01/91	107.170
MARATHON OIL CO	12.500	03/01/94	100.000	03/01/87	100.000
NEW YORK TEL CO	8.625	05/15/24	93.000	05/15/91	104.520
PACIFIC BELL	11.375	08/15/24	117.500	08/15/90	108.710
PACIFIC BELL	9.250	03/01/26	97.375	03/01/91	106.060
PUBLIC SVC ELEC & G	7.500	04/01/96	94.189	04/01/91	101.700[b]
PUBLIC SVC ELEC & G	8.750	04/01/16	92.616	04/01/91	106.200[b]
REYNOLDS R J INDS I	11.350	11/01/15	110.250	11/01/95	105.675[b]
SOUTHWESTERN BELL T	11.875	10/18/21	120.375	10/18/90	109.960
TENNECO INC	12.125	05/01/05	106.331	05/01/90	105.750[b]
TENNECO INC	11.125	05/15/13	103.697	05/15/94	104.620[b]
UNION ELEC CO	8.875	05/01/96	99.750	05/01/91	108.880[b]

a. Prices as of October 1, 1986.

b. Bond is currently cash callable.

c. Traditional measurements calculated to refunding date.

Traditional Measures				Call-Adjusted Measures			
Yield	Avg. Life	Mod. Dur.	Spread to Dur. Matched Treas.	Call-Adj. Yield	Exp. Life	Call-Adj. Mod. Dur.	Call-Adj. Spread
11.46	4.27	3.163	468c	10.36	8.70	4.286	342
9.54	29.57	9.450	204	7.95	19.74	6.438	56
9.39	23.62	9.702	188	8.25	17.32	6.938	83
8.07	6.02	4.317	112c	7.78	7.15	4.954	63
10.25	17.53	8.568	277	9.06	12.37	5.740	176
9.29	39.48	10.505	175	7.70	27.77	6.875	28
10.08	6.61	4.542	206c	8.55	16.64	6.096	120
8.93	28.72	10.035	141	8.37	25.85	9.147	87
10.09	8.86	5.591	281c	9.29	14.37	6.321	191
9.64	29.48	9.792	212	8.54	22.68	7.456	110
9.27	39.48	10.512	173	7.66	27.55	6.850	24
8.70	6.40	4.787	160c	8.22	8.13	5.550	95
9.35	22.05	9.670	184	8.42	17.24	7.164	99
9.29	39.73	10.236	176	7.49	26.30	6.557	9
9.01	11.09	8.659	153	8.09	7.62	4.265	115
8.74	5.73	4.193	181c	8.41	6.86	4.748	132
7.20	1.65	1.458	109c	7.06	2.08	1.827	74
9.15	29.48	10.273	162	8.02	23.10	7.807	57
8.20	6.86	5.183	97	7.87	6.29	4.808	77
9.61	27.44	9.770	209	8.57	21.19	7.423	113
8.11	3.48	2.739	145c	8.07	4.13	3.174	129
9.74	21.33	9.597	223	9.00	16.94	6.977	158
10.91	8.40	5.256	367c	10.15	13.54	5.918	283
9.35	39.48	10.421	181	7.68	26.76	6.692	27
12.35	0.40	0.377	685c	10.23	2.67	1.816	391
9.30	37.61	10.104	177	7.60	25.78	6.719	19
7.98	3.86	3.129	121c	6.61	13.72	4.702	−47
9.50	39.40	10.177	197	7.75	25.40	6.297	38
8.40	9.48	6.579	99	7.87	7.77	5.407	61
9.50	29.48	9.931	198	8.18	21.09	6.846	76
10.00	9.07	5.547	272c	9.17	14.66	6.434	178
8.00	4.03	3.130	123c	6.69	13.58	4.656	−37
11.27	3.57	2.734	461c	9.80	7.66	4.285	286
10.70	17.11	8.373	323	9.79	13.06	5.990	245
8.91	9.57	6.151	156	8.25	7.93	5.318	100

TABLE 4. Modified Duration Predicted Percentage Price Change: Traditional versus Call-Adjusted Approach.
ISSUER: R J REYNOLDS   COUPON: 11.75   MATURITY: 08/15/15
FIRST REFUNDING DATE: 08/15/95 AT 105.875

| Date | Price | YTM | YTC | Yield on Duration Matched Treasury | | Modified Duration | | Percentage Price Change | | |
| | | | | | | | | Predicted | | Actual |
				Trad.	Call-Adj.	Trad.	Call-Adj.	Trad.	Call-Adj.	
11/01/85	101.629	11.55		10.38	10.06	8.09	6.38	—	—	—
11/08/85	102.484	11.45		10.29	9.95	8.13	6.40	0.73	0.70	0.84
11/22/85	102.918	11.40		10.16	9.85	8.13	6.40	1.06	0.64	0.42
12/13/85	105.588	11.10	10.77	9.72	9.26	8.25	6.47	3.58	3.78	2.59
12/20/85	107.907	10.85	10.69	9.01	9.12	5.62	6.50	5.86	0.91	2.20
12/27/85	108.384	10.80		8.92	9.03	5.61	6.53	0.51	0.59	0.44
01/10/86	106.059	11.05		9.83	9.46	8.21	6.46	-5.11	-2.81	-2.15
01/17/86	106.986	10.95	10.92	9.16	9.28	5.53	6.43	5.50	1.16	0.87
01/24/86	105.613	11.10		9.51	9.23	8.14	6.43	-1.94	0.32	-1.28
01/31/86	107.451	10.90	10.84	9.01	9.11	5.80	6.43	4.07	0.77	1.74

25

Interest Rate Anticipation Strategies*

Gifford Fong
President
Gifford Fong Associates

Frank J. Fabozzi
Visiting Professor of Finance
Sloan School of Management
Massachusetts Institute of
Technology

I. Introduction

The philosophy in rate anticipation is to take advantage of the return implication of expected interest rate change through bond portfolio management. Interest rate change is the dominant source of marginal total return — marginal in relation to the return if no rate change had occurred. As long as there is volatility in rates, this problem will exist. If one is to pursue an active management strategy, there must be an explicit recognition of the effect of interest rate change.

As an active management technique, interest rate anticipation should be concerned with three dimensions: direction of the change in rates, magnitude of the change across maturities, and the timing of the change. If interest rates drop, the price of the bond will rise to reflect the new yield level. Conversely, if rates increase, the price of the bond will decline. The increase or decrease will be directly related to the security's duration. Therefore, the maturity should be lengthened and the coupon decreased — or, equivalently, duration should be increased — when rates are expected to drop, and the opposite action taken when rates are expected to rise. Where along the maturity

---

*This article is an update derived from "Active Strategies," *Fixed Income Portfolio Management,* by H. Gifford Fong and Frank J. Fabozzi (Homewood, Ill.: Dow Jones-Irwin, 1985), chap. 7.

spectrum the portfolio is positioned should be guided by the shape of the expected yield curve change. Finally, the timing of the expected rate change will be important in evaluating the relative importance of rate change, coupon return, and reinvestment return.

Interest rate anticipation strategies seek to recognize and assess the role of interest rate changes on the total return of a portfolio over a specified time horizon. For purposes of discussion the generation of the required interest rate forecast itself will not be covered. It is, at best, extremely difficult to forecast the future direction of rates, much less their magnitude. There are some who would assert that it is impossible. The emphasis here is on how the portfolio manager can harness the forecast once it is determined. To assess the impact and implications of interest rate change, it is useful to apply the forecasts of interest rate change to a portfolio.

II. Input for Interest Rate Anticipation Strategies

Table 1 summarizes inputs suitable for simulating the effect of interest rate change for a portfolio of 86 bonds shown in the table. A framework of one year has been chosen for this illustration, but this would vary according to the portfolio manager's expectations and desires.

Three scenarios of interest rate change are shown. These have been derived from historical interest rate change tendencies over the 10 years prior to the analysis. There is a bullish scenario, a market-implicit forecast scenario, and a bearish scenario. The market-implicit forecast is based on term structure analysis.

Multiscenario approaches recognize the uncertainty associated with interest rate forecasting and, accordingly, allow a form of sensitivity analysis. In the illustration, these forecasts take the form of the most likely (market-implicit), optimistic (declining rates), and pessimistic (rising rates) cases. The manager's own forecast would be, of course, an alternative. Each scenario is described along with a specified probability. Figures in Table 1 reflect the forecast yield for each scenario as well as the present yield to maturity for each scenario.

To reflect the effect of quality, issuing, or coupon sectors, additional factors can be imposed which will modify the basic shift represented by the forecast Treasury yield curves in Table 1. For example, a single A rated bond may be expected to shift by 10 percent less than the anticipated shift of a Treasury bond of the same maturity. Assuming the Treasury bond yield was to shift 100 basis points, the modified shift for the single A bond would be 90 basis points. The additional factors of issuing sector and coupon group could further modify the primary shift. All of these factors can be termed *volatility factors*. They modify, on the margin, the anticipated change due to overall interest rates, and allow the fine tuning of the anticipated reaction to interest rate changes based on the unique characteristics of the bond.

TABLE 1. *Interest Rate Projection and Sample Bond Portfolio.*

Interest Rate Projection: October 30, 1987–October 30, 1988

Scenario 1 (33.33% probability): Falling rates, 10-year historical volatility basis (10-77–10-87); reinvestment rate is calculated for each bond.

Scenario 2 (33.33% probability): Market implicit forecast; reinvestment rate is calculated for each bond.

Scenario 3 (33.33% probability): Rising rates, 10-year historical volatility basis (10-77–10-87); reinvestment rate is calculated for each bond.

Maturity (years)	Present YTM (%)	Forecast Yield (%)			Maturity Date	Roll	Forecast Yield Shifts (B.P.)		
		Scenario					Scenario		
		1	2	3			1	2	3
.250	5.848	4.424	8.125	8.137	01-29-88	.0	−142.4	227.7	228.9
.500	6.742	5.128	8.245	9.144	04-30-88	.0	−161.4	150.3	240.2
1.000	7.137	5.441	8.262	9.364	10-29-88	.0	−169.6	112.5	222.7
2.000	7.678	5.945	8.517	9.750	10-30-89	−54.3	−223.9	58.4	168.5
3.000	8.021	6.229	8.723	9.938	10-30-90	−34.4	−207.7	49.5	172.8
4.000	8.278	6.442	8.877	10.135	10-30-91	−25.8	−205.0	44.4	165.9
5.000	8.471	6.604	9.002	10.305	10-29-92	−19.4	−203.0	40.6	166.3
10.000	8.956	7.069	9.274	10.658	10-30-97	−9.7	−198.0	26.3	163.1
20.000	9.083	7.381	9.305	10.711	10-30-07	−1.3	−173.3	21.9	162.3
30.000	9.142	7.429	9.340	10.754	10-30-17	−.6	−171.8	19.4	160.8

TABLE 1 *Continued*

Bond No.	Par Value	% of Total	CUSIP	Issuer Name	Quality	Type	Coupon	Stated Maturity Date	Effective Maturity Date	Price	YTM (%)	Duration (years)
1	1000.	1.3	313586MU	FEDERAL NATL MTG ASSN	AAA	1	11.000	11/10/88	11/10/88	103.313	7.58	0.95
2	1000.	1.1	744567AP	PUBLIC SVC ELEC & GAS CO	AA1	1	5.125	06/01/89	06/01/89	95.081	8.50	1.51
3	1000.	1.2	449220AM	IBM CR CORP	AAA	1	7.125	07/15/89	07/15/89	98.223	8.25	1.61
4	1000.	1.2	313311CS	FEDERAL FARM CR BKS FDG CORP	AAA	1	10.600	10/23/89	10/23/89	104.000	8.36	1.84
5	1000.	1.2	370424DQ	GENERAL MTRS ACCEP CORP	AA1	1	9.500	12/01/89	12/01/89	101.388	8.75	1.87
6	1000.	1.2	345370AB	FORD MTR CO DEL	AA1	1	8.125	01/15/90	01/15/90	99.042	8.60	2.02
7	1000.	1.3	313311DW	FEDERAL FARM CR BKS FDG CORP	AAA	1	10.950	01/22/90	01/22/90	105.031	8.41	1.99
8	1000.	1.2	046003AU	ASSOCIATES CORP NORTH AMER	AA1	1	14.500	02/01/90	02/01/88	101.250	9.05	0.26
9	1000.	1.3	313311EE	FEDERAL FARM CR BKS FDG CORP	AAA	1	10.400	07/23/90	07/23/90	104.344	8.57	2.39
10	1000.	1.3	313311EE	FEDERAL FARM CR BKS FDG CORP	AAA	1	10.400	07/23/90	07/23/90	104.344	8.57	2.39
11	1000.	1.3	313388KL	FEDERAL HOME LN BKS	AAA	1	12.500	09/25/90	09/25/90	110.125	8.48	2.52
12	1000.	1.2	842400BX	SOUTHERN CALIF EDISON CO	AA1	1	10.000	10/01/90	10/01/88	102.250	7.41	0.90
13	1000.	0.9	450680AL	ITT FINL CORP	BAA1	1	.000	11/01/90	11/01/90	75.569	9.54	3.01
14	1000.	1.3	313586MY	FEDERAL NATL MTG ASSN	AAA	1	10.900	11/12/90	11/12/90	106.563	8.40	2.56
15	1000.	1.2	025818AJ	AMERICAN EXPRESS CR CORP	AA1	1	12.875	01/15/91	01/15/88	100.875	8.29	0.81
16	1000.	1.3	067900AA	BARCLAYS NORTH AMERN CAP CORP	AAA	1	14.625	06/15/91	06/15/88	104.000	7.90	0.59
17	1000.	1.2	345397AG	FORD MTR CR CO	AA1	1	7.500	11/15/91	11/15/91	94.682	9.10	3.42
18	1000.	1.1	122781AD	BURROUGHS CORP	A1	1	6.000	06/01/92	06/01/92	90.444	8.56	3.94
19	1000.	1.1	345397AL	FORD MTR CR CO	AA1	1	7.500	10/15/92	10/15/92	92.785	9.35	4.19
20	1000.	1.3	749285AG	RCA CORP	AAA	1	12.750	10/15/92	10/15/92	107.875	8.30	1.79
21	1000.	1.1	814823AY	SECURITY PAC CORP	AA1	1	8.250	07/01/93	07/01/93	92.948	9.90	4.47
22	1000.	1.1	345397AQ	FORD MTR CR CO	AA1	1	7.875	07/15/93	07/15/93	93.150	9.45	4.55
23	1000.	1.3	761753AK	REYNOLDS R J INDS INC	A1	1	10.750	08/01/93	08/01/91	104.500	9.29	3.12
24	1000.	1.1	313388DR	FEDERAL HOME LN BKS	AAA	1	7.375	11/26/93	11/26/93	91.781	9.17	4.78
25	1000.	1.1	313388DR	FEDERAL HOME LN BKS	AAA	1	7.375	11/26/93	11/26/93	91.781	9.17	4.78
26	1000.	1.4	449220AC	IBM CR CORP	AAA	1	13.750	03/15/94	03/15/94	114.345	10.59	4.52
27	1000.	1.5	313311HQ	FEDERAL FARM CR BKS FDG CORP	AAA	1	14.250	04/20/94	04/20/94	123.031	9.42	4.64
28	1000.	1.4	783549AL	RYDER SYS INC	A1	1	13.375	09/01/94	09/01/91	112.500	9.41	3.11
29	1000.	1.4	423326AN	HELLER FINANCIAL INC	BAA1	1	13.000	09/15/94	09/15/94	114.632	10.00	4.83

TABLE 1 *Continued*

Bond No.	Par Value	% of Total	CUSIP	Issuer Name	Quality	Type	Coupon	Stated Maturity Date	Effective Maturity Date	Price	YTM (%)	Duration (years)
30	1000.	1.2	125569AP	CIT GROUP HOLDINGS INC	AA1	1	9.500	06/01/95	06/01/95	97.112	10.05	5.33
31	1000.	1.1	264399BR	DUKE POWER CO	AA1	1	8.500	07/01/95	07/01/95	94.617	9.50	5.57
32	1000.	1.2	708160AB	PENNEY J C INC	A1	1	8.875	07/15/95	07/15/95	95.827	9.65	5.55
33	1000.	1.2	459200AE	INTERNATIONAL BUSINESS MACHS	AAA	1	10.250	10/15/95	10/15/92	104.500	9.10	4.02
34	1000.	0.9	341099AN	FLORIDA POWER CORP	A1	1	4.875	11/01/95	11/01/95	74.304	9.54	6.26
35	1000.	1.1	842400BC	SOUTHERN CALIF EDISON CO	AA1	1	7.875	12/01/95	12/01/95	89.980	9.69	5.80
36	1000.	1.1	842400BC	SOUTHERN CALIF EDISON CO	AA1	1	7.875	12/01/95	12/01/95	89.980	9.69	5.80
37	1000.	1.1	345370AN	FORD MTR CO DEL	AA1	1	8.500	04/01/96	04/01/96	92.918	9.75	6.04
38	1000.	1.1	717265AB	PHELPS DODGE CORP	BAA1	1	8.100	06/15/96	06/15/96	88.307	10.16	6.00
39	1000.	1.1	370424BF	GENERAL MTRS ACCEP CORP	AA1	1	8.125	10/15/96	10/15/96	88.796	10.05	6.34
40	1000.	1.1	313400MK	FEDERAL HOME LN MTG CORP	AAA	1	8.600	10/30/96	10/30/96	93.531	9.69	6.35
41	1000.	0.9	845743AH	SOUTHWESTERN PUB SVC CO	AA1	1	5.700	02/01/97	02/01/97	77.172	9.45	6.88
42	1000.	1.1	053528AS	AVCO FINL SVCS INC	A1	1	9.125	03/01/98	03/01/98	93.808	10.10	6.68
43	1000.	1.1	713448AE	PEPSICO INC	AA1	1	7.625	12/18/98	12/18/98	86.347	9.65	7.18
44	1000.	1.1	345397AM	FORD MTR CR CO	AA1	1	8.700	04/01/99	04/01/99	90.623	10.10	7.19
45	1000.	0.9	718167AQ	PHILIP MORRIS INC	A1	1	6.000	11/15/99	11/15/99	72.069	10.05	7.77
46	1000.	1.2	852245AC	SQUIBB CORP	AA2	1	11.500	11/15/99	11/15/87	100.125	7.81	0.04
47	1000.	1.4	450680AM	ITT FINL CORP	A1	1	11.850	12/01/99	12/01/89	115.250	5.79	1.85
48	1000.	1.3	046003AQ	ASSOCIATES CORP NORTH AMER	AA1	1	12.125	02/01/00	02/01/90	107.750	10.35	2.00
49	1000.	1.1	264399AN	DUKE POWER CO	AA1	1	8.500	03/01/00	03/01/00	90.130	9.90	7.51
50	1000.	1.1	406216AE	HALLIBURTON CO	AA1	1	9.250	04/01/00	04/01/00	94.380	10.05	7.43
51	1000.	1.4	046003AR	ASSOCIATES CORP NORTH AMER	AA1	1	13.125	05/15/00	05/15/90	110.750	10.27	2.15
52	1000.	1.2	022249AH	ALUMINUM CO AMER	A1	1	9.450	05/15/00	05/15/00	93.417	10.40	7.10
53	1000.	1.3	370424CC	GENERAL MTRS ACCEP CORP	AA1	1	11.750	07/15/00	07/15/90	106.000	9.82	2.34
54	1000.	0.9	031177AV	AMERICAN TEL & TELEG CO	A1	1	6.000	08/01/00	08/01/00	72.653	9.80	8.20
55	1000.	1.1	260543AF	DOW CHEM CO	A1	1	8.900	11/01/00	11/01/00	92.092	10.00	7.38
56	1000.	1.0	744465AL	PUBLIC SVC CO IND INC	BAA1	1	7.625	01/01/01	01/01/01	78.579	10.69	7.65
57	1000.	1.1	302292AE	EXXON PIPELINE COMPANY	AAA	1	8.250	03/01/01	03/01/01	87.906	9.90	7.86
58	1000.	1.0	264399AQ	DUKE POWER CO	AA1	1	7.500	03/01/01	03/01/01	81.784	10.00	8.00

TABLE 1 *Continued*

Bond No.	Par Value	% of Total	CUSIP	Issuer Name	Quality	Type	Coupon	Stated Maturity Date	Effective Maturity Date	Price	YTM (%)	Duration (years)
59	1000.	1.1	345397BE	FORD MTR CR CO	AA1	1	8.375	11/01/01	11/01/01	86.883	10.15	7.71
60	1000.	1.0	744567BK	PUBLIC SVC ELEC & GAS CO	AA1	1	7.500	04/01/02	04/01/02	80.462	10.10	8.33
61	1000.	1.1	313586GJ	FEDERAL NATL MTG ASSN	AAA	1	8.200	07/10/02	07/10/02	88.500	9.68	8.19
62	1000.	1.2	370424BU	GENERAL MTRS ACCEP CORP	AA1	1	9.750	05/01/03	05/01/03	95.047	10.40	7.72
63	1000.	1.2	842400BM	SOUTHERN CALIF EDISON CO	AA1	1	9.625	11/01/03	11/01/03	94.759	10.30	7.87
64	1000.	1.1	125569AV	CIT GROUP HOLDINGS INC	A1	1	9.850	08/15/04	08/15/04	93.405	10.70	8.09
65	1000.	1.2	459200AB	INTERNATIONAL BUSINESS MACHS	AAA	1	9.375	10/01/04	10/01/04	97.375	9.69	8.63
66	1000.	1.2	081721AW	BENEFICIAL CORP	BAA1	1	9.000	01/15/05	01/15/05	99.250	9.08	8.80
67	1000.	1.1	030177BE	AMERICAN TEL & TELEG CO	A1	1	8.800	05/15/05	05/15/05	90.538	9.95	8.46
68	1000.	1.2	406216AF	HALLIBURTON CO	AA1	1	10.200	06/01/05	06/01/05	96.055	9.70	8.00
69	1000.	0.8	708160AH	PENNEY J C INC	A1	1	6.000	05/01/06	05/01/06	65.659	10.15	9.25
70	1000.	1.1	030177BG	AMERICAN TEL & TELEG CO	A1	1	8.625	02/01/07	02/01/07	87.560	10.10	8.89
71	1000.	1.2	373334BS	GEORGIA POWER CO	BAA1	1	11.000	04/01/09	04/01/09	98.000	11.25	8.45
72	1000.	1.2	14141AW	CAROLINA PWR & LT CO	A1	1	10.500	05/15/09	05/15/09	99.567	10.55	8.49
73	1000.	1.3	341081BR	FLORIDA PWR & LT CO	AA1	1	11.300	05/01/10	05/01/10	103.762	10.85	8.31
74	1000.	1.3	048825AF	ATLANTIC RICHFIELD CO	A1	1	11.375	05/01/10	05/01/10	103.102	11.00	8.24
75	1000.	1.3	260543AN	DOW CHEM CO	A1	1	11.250	07/15/10	07/15/10	103.316	10.85	8.53
76	1000.	1.1	694886BM	PACIFIC TEL & TELEG CO	AA1	1	9.875	02/15/16	02/15/16	94.775	10.45	9.37
77	1000.	1.0	842332AX	SOUTHERN BELL TEL & TELEG CO	AA1	1	8.250	04/15/16	04/15/16	82.785	10.10	9.98
78	1000.	1.0	451794AN	ILLINOIS BELL TEL CO	AA1	1	8.250	08/18/16	08/18/16	83.129	10.05	9.88
79	1000.	1.1	694886BN	PACIFIC TEL & TELEG CO	AA1	1	9.750	07/01/19	07/01/19	93.540	10.45	9.41
80	1000.	1.3	843486AK	SOUTHERN NEW ENGLAND TEL CO	AA1	1	11.500	08/15/25	08/15/25	107.049	10.73	9.39
81	1000.	1.3	912827JQ	NTS	AAA	1	9.250	05/15/89	05/15/89	102.469	7.52	1.42
82	1000.	1.2	912827VF	NTS	AAA	1	7.750	08/31/89	08/31/89	100.125	7.65	1.72
83	1000.	1.3	912827QA	NTS	AAA	1	11.500	10/15/90	10/15/90	108.688	8.13	2.60
84	1000.	1.3	912827NV	NTS	AAA	1	10.500	11/15/92	11/15/92	107.969	8.52	3.91
85	1000.	1.3	912827PM	NTS	AAA	1	10.125	05/15/93	05/15/93	106.500	8.62	4.23
86	1000.	1.1	912827UT	NTS	AAA	1	7.000	04/15/94	04/15/94	91.469	8.76	5.23

TABLE 1 *Continued*

Portfolio Totals

Average duration (years)	5.137
Average yield (%)	9.427
Dur. wtd. avg. yield (%)	9.857
Average coupon (%)	9.605
Average effective maturity	4-11-97
Avg. time to maturity (years)	9.455
Average quality	AA2
Total par value ($000)	86,000.000
Total market value ($000)	84,868.450
Number of issues	86
Number of issues held	86

Current Maturity Sector Concentrations

Sector	Sector range (years)	Concen- tration (%)
Short	Less than 3.00	31.16
Intermediate	3.00 to 12.00	35.73
Long	Greater than 12.00	33.11

The volatility factor for an issuing sector can be estimated from historical data using the following simple linear regression:

$$\Delta S_t = a + (1+b)\Delta T_t + e_t, \qquad (1)$$

where

ΔS_t = change in interest rate for the issuing sector in month t (in basis points)

ΔT_t = change in interest rate for the Treasury issue in month t (in basis points)

e_t = error term in month t

and a and b are the parameters of the model to be estimated. The parameter b is the issuing sector volatility and the parameter a is the issuing sector spread change.

Table 2 shows the estimate of a and b for 30 issuing sectors based on 10 years of monthly data. For example, if Treasuries increase by 100 basis points, AAA Industrials will, on average, increase by only 61.02 basis points, as shown below:

$$\Delta S = 5.02 + [1 + (-0.440)]\Delta T$$
$$= 61.02$$

For AA Financials, a 100 basis point increase in Treasuries would increase the interest rate on obligations in this issuing sector by 60.75 basis points, on average, as shown below:

TABLE 2. *Issuing Sector Spread Changes and Issuing Sector Volatility.*

Sector ID	Issuing Sector	Issuing Sector Spread Changes (basis points)	Issuing Sector Volatility (%)
TR,	U.S. Treasury	.00	0.00
AG,	U.S. agency	−.72	−9.00
I1,	AAA industrial	5.02	−44.00
I2,	AA industrial	−7.17	−41.80
I3,	A industrial	−3.58	−42.00
I4,	BAA industrial	−10.75	−58.20
O1,	AAA oil	−52.31	−64.20
O2,	AA oil	−33.68	−60.00
O3,	A oil	−50.16	−51.50
O4,	BAA oil	−91.72	−61.80
T1,	AAA telephone	−.72	−28.80
T2,	AA telephone	3.58	−27.60
T3,	A telephone	−13.61	−38.80
T4,	BAA telephone	−25.08	−57.70
E1,	AAA electric utility	−5.02	−39.90
E2,	AA electric utility	−8.60	−31.00
E3,	A electric utility	−5.73	−35.30
E4,	BAA electric utility	.72	−33.00
G1,	AAA gas utility	8.60	−31.00
G2,	AA gas utility	7.17	−45.20
G3,	A gas utility	−12.90	−55.40
G4,	BAA gas utility	−10.75	−33.50
F1,	AAA finance	−23.65	−42.80
F2,	AA finance	−5.73	−33.50
F3,	A finance	−12.18	−42.90
F4,	BAA finance	−8.60	−36.00
U1,	AAA utility	−.72	−33.30
U2,	AA utility	−.72	−29.40
U3,	A utility	−7.17	−37.90
U4,	BAA utility	−4.30	−36.00

$$\Delta S = -5.73 + [1 + (-0.335)]\Delta T$$
$$= 60.77$$

As noted previously, it is also possible to refine the procedure further by estimating different sector spreads by an issuing sector for different maturities and/or quality classifications.

Table 3 exemplifies the results of translating interest rate change into expected (composite) rates of return for four individual securities in the portfolio. The returns are also presented for each of the three scenarios. Returns are based on maturity unless indicated that the issue would be called under the particular scenario. The columns are largely self-explanatory, but those of particular importance are described below:

TABLE 3. *Analysis of Five Issues of the 86-Issue Portfolio for Each of the Three Interest Rate Forecasts and the Composite (Current Date 10-30-87; Projection Date 10-30-88).*

Face Value ($000)	Bond Description		Price (%)	Yield to Effective Maturity	Components of Return (%)						Total Return (%)	Effective Maturity Date	Duration (years)
					Yield Curve	Time	Spread Change	Earned Interest	Mat/Call	Reinvestment			
1000	41 845743AH SOUTHWESTERN PUB SVC CO 5.7000% 02-01-97 E2 AA1	Current:	77.172	9.45MAT								02-01-97	7.00
		Scenario 1:	86.331	7.99MAT	12.8	2.8	-3.8	7.4	.0	.2	19.4	02-01-97	6.56
		Scenario 2:	78.290	9.56MAT	-2.5	2.8	1.1	7.4	.0	.2	9.0	02-01-97	6.46
		Scenario 3:	73.947	10.49MAT	-10.4	2.8	3.4	7.4	.0	.2	3.4	02-01-97	6.40
		Composite:	79.523	9.35	.0	2.8	.2	7.4	.0	.2	10.6	02-01-97	6.47
1000	42 053528AS AVCO FINL SVCS INC 9.1250% 03-01-98 F3 A1	Current:	93.808	10.10MAT								03-01-98	6.78
		Scenario 1:	101.711	8.85MAT	9.9	1.0	-2.4	9.8	.0	.2	18.4	03-01-98	6.51
		Scenario 2:	94.036	10.13MAT	-2.2	1.0	1.4	9.8	.0	.2	10.2	03-01-98	6.38
		Scenario 3:	89.710	10.91MAT	-9.9	1.0	4.5	9.8	.0	.2	5.6	03-01-98	6.30
		Composite:	95.152	9.96	-.7	1.0	1.2	9.8	.0	.2	11.4	03-01-98	6.40
1000	43 713448AE PEPSICO INC 7.6250% 12-18-98 I2 AA1	Current:	86.347	9.65MAT								12-18-98	7.41
		Scenario 1:	94.513	8.44MAT	13.8	1.5	-5.8	8.9	.0	.2	18.5	12-18-98	7.15
		Scenario 2:	86.636	9.73MAT	-2.3	1.5	1.2	8.9	.0	.2	9.4	12-18-98	7.00
		Scenario 3:	82.179	10.53MAT	-10.8	1.5	4.5	8.9	.0	.2	4.8	12-18-98	6.90
		Composite:	87.776	9.56	.2	1.5	.0	8.9	.0	.2	10.7	12-18-98	7.01

TABLE 3 *Continued*

Face Value ($000)	Bond Description		Price (%)	Yield to Effective Maturity	Components of Return (%)						Total Return (%)	Effective Maturity Date	Duration (years)
					Yield Curve	Time	Spread Change	Earned Interest	Mat/ Call	Rein- vest- ment			
1000	44 345397AM FORD MTR CR CO 8.7000% 04-01-99 F2 AA1	Current:	90.623	10.10MAT									7.25
		Scenario 1:	99.671	8.75MAT	10.5	1.1	-1.6	9.6	.0	.2	19.8	04-01-99	7.05
		Scenario 2:	90.429	10.21MAT	-2.2	1.1	.9	9.6	.0	.2	9.6	04-01-99	6.87
		Scenario 3:	85.247	11.13MAT	-10.6	1.1	3.5	9.6	.0	.2	3.9	04-01-99	6.75
		Composite:	91.782	10.03	-.8	1.1	1.0	9.6	.0	.2	11.1	04-01-99	6.89
1000	45 718167 AQ PHILIP MORRIS INC 6.0000% 11-15-99 13 A1	Current:	72.069	10.05MAT									8.07
		Scenario 1:	79.909	8.89MAT	15.2	2.4	-6.7	8.3	.0	.2	19.4	11-15-99	7.84
		Scenario 2:	72.756	10.16MAT	-2.5	2.4	1.0	8.3	.0	.2	9.5	11-15-99	7.67
		Scenario 3:	68.680	10.96MAT	-11.8	2.4	4.8	8.3	.0	.2	3.9	11-15-99	7.55
		Composite:	73.781	10.00	.3	2.4	-.3	8.3	.0	.2	10.9	11-15-99	7.69

Yield curve	Return due to changes in the nominal yield curve
Time	Return assuming the initial yield curve remains constant over the projection horizon (i.e., rolling down the yield curve)
Spread change	Return attributable to spread change and volatility effects
Earned interest	Interest accrued over the projection period
Maturity/call	Change in principal value for securities projected to be called or to mature. (The price change is separate from that caused by the interest rate effects.)
Reinvestment	Interest on interest earned over the projection period, as well as reinvestment from maturities, calls, puts, sinking fund payments and any other prepayments
Total return	The sum of all components of return
Duration	The first figure in the column is current duration; remaining figures are the duration at the end of the assumed holding period for the particular scenario.

Table 4 summarizes the portfolio return for each scenario and the composite return for the 86-issue portfolio for which the return simulation was performed. The foregoing analysis can be extremely helpful in executing an effective active management strategy. Analytical insights are achieved by partitioning a set of expected interest rate changes into implied rates of return. Each graduation provides further insight into the sources and, hence, the causes of performance. Analysis beyond the total return permits both the establishment and monitoring of policy. For example, a manager stressing rate anticipation should have the return due from overall changes in interest rates dominate the return from spread relationships. Conversely, a manager with an emphasis on spread relationship exploitation should have this component dominate.

In terms of a portfolio perspective, comparing total returns of securities in the portfolio can be the first step in screening the most desirable portfolio holdings.

III. Relative Return Value Analysis

Relative return analysis is a tool that allows a manager to compare alternative securities systematically. It recognizes that choosing the highest expected return security may be inappropriate, since either it may not be the security with the highest realized return, or the level of associated risk may be undesirable. The objective here is to identify the highest expected return security for a given level of risk.

This technique is illustrated in Figure 1. Duration is on the horizontal axis and on the vertical axis is the composite expected return, which is the probability-weighted return of each of the three scenario returns from the return simulation process; however, any other alternative that a manager

TABLE 4. *Summary of Portfolio Return for Each of the Three Interest Rate Scenarios and the Composite (Portfolio Return on Beginning Market Value — 10-30-87–10-30-88).*

	Yield Change Impact	Time (Roll) Impact	Spread Change Impact	Earned Interest	Coupon Rein-vestment	Matured/ Called	Mat/Call Rein-vestment	Total	Annual Total
Scenario 1 (10-30-88)	6.65	.37	-1.73	9.07	.21	.35	.55	15.47	14.91
Scenario 2 (10-30-88)	-1.74	.40	.60	9.33	.22	-.10	.32	9.03	8.84
Scenario 3 (10-30-88)	-7.42	.40	2.36	9.33	.23	-.10	.32	5.12	5.06
Composite (10-30-88)	-.84	.39	.41	9.24	.22	.05	.40	9.88	9.64

FIGURE 1. *Composite Total Return versus Duration.*

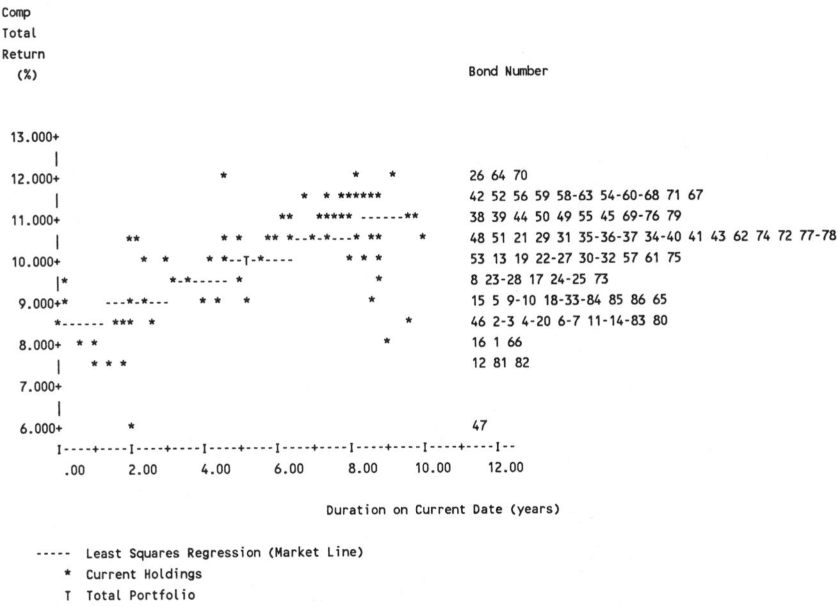

```
Comp
Total
Return
  (%)                                                            Bond Number


 13.000+
     |
 12.000+                         *                  *     *      26 64 70
     |                                   *   *  ******         42 52 56 59 58-63 54-60-68 71 67
 11.000+                               **    *****  ------**    38 39 44 50 49 55 45 69-76 79
     |              **          *  *   ** *--*-*---* **    *    48 51 21 29 31 35-36-37 34-40 41 43 62 74 72 77-78
 10.000+        *  *      * *--T-*----     * * *              53 13 19 22-27 30-32 57 61 75
     |*                  *-*----- *              *            8 23-28 17 24-25 73
  9.000+*      ---*-*---   * *   *              *             15 5 9-10 18-33-84 85 86 65
     *------ ***  *                         *                 46 2-3 4-20 6-7 11-14-83 80
  8.000+ * *                              *                   16 1 66
     |     * * *                                              12 81 82
  7.000+
     |
  6.000+        *                                             47
     I----+----I----+----I----+----I----+----I----+----I----+----I--
       .00    2.00    4.00    6.00    8.00   10.00   12.00

                          Duration on Current Date (years)


   -----  Least Squares Regression (Market Line)
     *    Current Holdings
     T    Total Portfolio
```

employs for defining expected return can be used. Within the diagram is a regression line (dashed line), individual security representation (asterisks), portfolio average return/duration (letter T) and bond identification number (far right-hand margin). The regression line represents the average relationship between return and duration exhibited by the individual securities making up the portfolio. Using the regression line as fair value, we can conclude that bonds above the line are those with greater expected return per unit of duration than the average relationship; bonds below the line have less return per unit of duration.

For example, the best bond for the total expected return and duration optimizer appears to be bond 26, which has a duration of about 4.58 years and composite return of about 11.8 percent.

Table 5 indicates the individual securities from the 86-issue sample bond portfolio that lie one standard error (in this case an excess return of .9137 percent) above the market line. As can be seen from the table, bond 26, IBM CR Corp, 13.7500 of 1994, had an excess return of 2.2 percent at the time of the analysis. The worst bond, as indicated in Figure 1, is bond 47. An analysis similar to that in Table 3 would explain why bonds 26 and 47 would be expected to perform in this manner.

TABLE 5. *Composite Total Return versus Duration on Current Date for Bonds More than One Standard Error above the Market Line.*

Total Return (%) vs. Duration on Current Date for Bonds More than
1.0000 Standard Errors = .913% above the Market Line

Bond No.	Bond Name	Coupon Rate (%)	Stated Maturity	Quality	Comp (%)	Duration (years)	Return Minus Market Line
26	IBM CR CORP	13.7500	03-15-94	AAA	11.8	4.58	2.2
51	ASSOCIATES CORP NORTH AMER	13.1250	05-15-00	AA1	10.7	2.26	1.6
48	ASSOCIATES CORP NORTH AMER	12.1250	02-01-00	AA1	10.4	2.06	1.5
64	CIT GROUP HOLDINGS INC	9.8500	08-15-04	A1	12.1	8.27	1.3
8	ASSOCIATES CORP NORTH AMER	14.5000	02-01-90	AA1	9.7	.26	1.2
53	GENERAL MTRS ACCEP CORP	11.7500	07-15-00	AA1	10.2	2.41	1.1
42	AVCO FINL SVCS INC	9.1250	03-01-98	A1	11.4	6.78	1.1
38	PHELPS DODGE CORP	8.1000	06-15-96	BAA1	11.2	6.21	1.0
29	HELLER FINANCIAL INC	13.0000	09-15-94	BAA1	10.7	4.90	.9
	Mean	11.8543	08-12-97	AA3	10.9	4.08	1.3

Note: Bonds are listed in descending order with respect to the arithmetic value of (Return − Market Line).

FIGURE 2. *Scenario 1: Total Return versus Duration.*

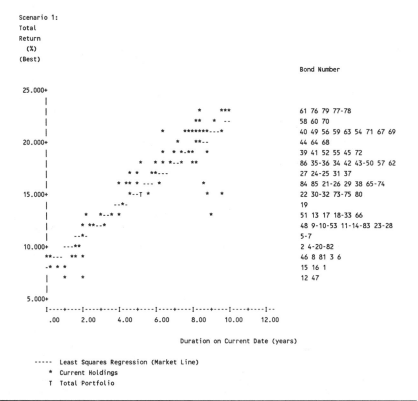

```
Scenario 1:
Total
Return
 (%)
(Best)
                                                              Bond Number

25.000+
     |
     |                                   *     ***            61 76 79 77-78
     |                                  **   *  --            58 60 70
     |                           *    *******---*             40 49 56 59 63 54 71 67 69
20.000+                             *    **--                 44 64 68
     |                           * * *-**   *                 39 41 52 55 45 72
     |                      *   * * *--* **                   86 35-36 34 42 43-50 57 62
     |                * *   **---                             27 24-25 31 37
     |              * ** * --- *           *                  84 85 21-26 29 38 65-74
15.000+              *--T *           *  *                    22 30-32 73-75 80
     |                --*-                                    19
     |            *  *--* *                    *              51 13 17 18-33 66
     |          * **--*                                       48 9-10-53 11-14-83 23-28
     |            --*-                                        5-7
10.000+      ---**                                           2 4-20-82
       **--- ** *                                            46 8 81 3 6
      -* * *                                                 15 16 1
     |   *  *                                                12 47
     |
 5.000+
     I----+----I----+----I----+----I----+----I----+----I----+----I--
      .00    2.00    4.00    6.00    8.00   10.00   12.00

                   Duration on Current Date (years)

     -----  Least Squares Regression (Market Line)
        *   Current Holdings
        T   Total Portfolio
```

The analysis should also be performed for each scenario. Figures 2 and 3 are the results for the best case (scenario 1), and worst case (scenario 3), respectively.

Given this kind of two-dimensional framework, a manager has the ability (at least a first cut) to differentiate the return characteristics of the securities in a portfolio. This form of analysis is very similar to the security market line approach, which is used fairly widely in the analysis of equity securities.

It should be noted that in the fixed-income market, there is no measure of risk comparable to the equity measure of market risk or beta. What is used in the analysis is duration, which is not necessarily a risk measure. It is a measure of volatility. Although volatility is not the best measure of risk, duration does quantify risk to the extent that the volatility is a risk surrogate. Duration is also a measure of the length of the security—a better measure, in many situations, than maturity. So, duration is a measure for differentiating

FIGURE 3. *Scenario 3: Total Return versus Duration.*

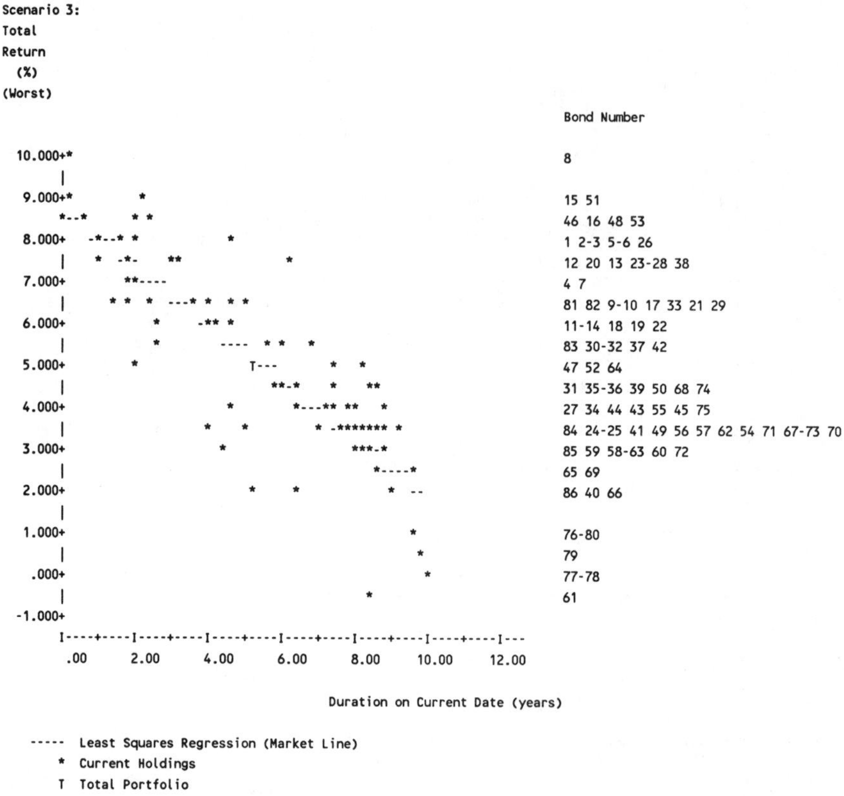

```
Scenario 3:
Total
Return
  (%)
(Worst)
                                                    Bond Number

  10.000+*                                          8
        I
   9.000+*        *                                 15 51
        *--*        * *                             46 16 48 53
   8.000+    -*--* *          *                     1 2-3 5-6 26
        I    * -*-   **          *                  12 20 13 23-28 38
   7.000+      **----                               4 7
        I    * *  * ---* * * *                      81 82 9-10 17 33 21 29
   6.000+      *      -** *                          11-14 18 19 22
        I        *     ---- * *  *                  83 30-32 37 42
   5.000+    *          T---    *  *                47 52 64
        I              **-*   *   **                31 35-36 39 50 68 74
   4.000+        *      *---** ** *                 27 34 44 43 55 45 75
        I          *   *      * -******** *         84 24-25 41 49 56 57 62 54 71 67-73 70
   3.000+        *            ***-*                 85 59 58-63 60 72
        I                         *----*            65 69
   2.000+          *   *        *  --                86 40 66
        I
   1.000+                          *                76-80
        I                          *                79
    .000+                          *                77-78
        I                        *                  61
  -1.000+
        I----+----I----+----I----+----I----+----I----+----I----+----I---
          .00    2.00    4.00    6.00    8.00    10.00   12.00

                        Duration on Current Date (years)

     -----  Least Squares Regression (Market Line)
        *   Current Holdings
        T   Total Portfolio
```

securities. If, lacking a better summary risk measure, we can use duration (like beta is used on the equity side), we might consider the horizontal axis to be a normalization for volatility, so we can make judgments about any two securities that lie along the same vertical line projecting upward from any given duration level.

IV. Strategic Frontier Analysis

Strategic frontier analysis is a tool for evaluating both the upside and the downside return characteristics of a security. It is a procedure for analyzing the return behavior of securities under alternative interest rate scenarios.

Figure 4 provides the display that is employed in strategic frontier analysis. Again we have a two-dimensional framework. The total expected return

FIGURE 4. *Hypothetical Upside/Downside Trade-off.*

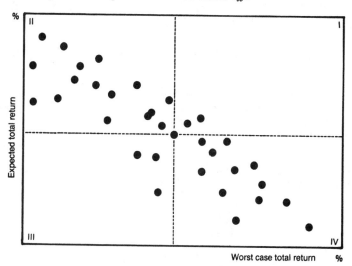

is shown on the vertical axis. This could be the total expected return of the most likely scenario of interest rate change, or perhaps the return of the most optimistic scenario of interest rate change. On the horizontal axis is the return of the worst case scenario. Again, these scenarios are those used in the return simulation process.

In Figure 4, the dots represent the individual security holdings in the portfolio we are analyzing as well as the securities on the potential purchase list. The intersection of the dashed lines in this diagram indicates the portfolio average return, and we can see that this represents a particular position within this framework. Any particular position is defined by the return under either the optimistic scenario or the most likely scenario along one axis, and the returns from the worse case scenario along the other axis.

Once we have this type of framework, we can actually partition the diagram into quadrants as displayed in Figure 4. The portfolio average is at the origin, or center, of the quadrants. Partitioning the diagram into the four quadrants allows a manager to draw conclusions about the return behavior of the securities that fall into each of these quadrants. Let's discuss each of these quadrants.

Securities within quadrant II might be considered *aggressive* securities. They are aggressive from the standpoint that, if the most likely scenario prevails, a manager would do extremely well. If the worst case scenario were to prevail, however, a manager would do relatively badly. So, a manager with strong convictions about the most optimistic scenario would tend to choose securities from this quadrant.

In quadrant IV are what might be considered *defensive* securities. They are defensive in that, if the worst case scenario prevailed, a manager would do relatively well. But if the most likely scenario were to occur, a manager would do relatively poorly. So a manager who wanted to posture the portfolio defensively would concentrate it in securities that fall within quadrant IV.

Quadrant III contains securities that might be considered *inferior*. They are inferior because, regardless of scenario outcome—either the most likely or worst case—these securities would perform relatively worse than the portfolio average. Securities falling into quadrant III are the potential sales from the existing portfolio since, by definition, they are no-win situations.

That leaves the securities falling in quadrant I. These might be considered *superior* securities because, regardless of scenario outcome, these securities would always outperform the portfolio, providing a no-loss situation. If a portfolio manager were to increase holdings of the securities that fall in this quadrant, he or she would tend to move the portfolio results to the upper right portion of the quadrant. That would enhance the overall results for the portfolio, regardless of the scenarios being evaluated.

Figure 5 is another characterization of this type of analysis, and what we call a *strategic frontier*. This frontier essentially maps out the upper right

FIGURE 5. *Strategic Frontier Analysis.*

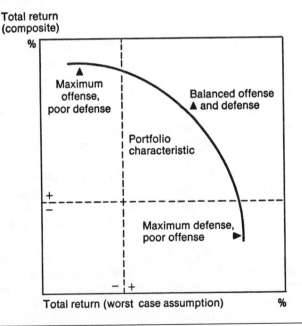

region, from which a manager can choose securities that would do the best job, given his or her convictions. For example, a manager who wanted maximum offense or maximum aggressiveness but was willing to give up the defensive nature of some of the other securities would choose securities along the strategic frontier mapped in or near the upper left quadrant. If the manager wanted a maximum defensive posture and was willing to live with the relatively poor returns should the most likely scenario prevail, then the securities chosen would be along the frontier in or near the lower right quadrant. The ultimate objective, especially in the face of high uncertainty and an unsteady conviction about either scenario, would be to drive the portfolio into the upper right quadrant as far as possible.

For our sample portfolio of 86 bonds, Figure 7 presents a plot of the trade-off based on the total return for the best and worst case. Table 6 lists the bonds and provides a summary of information for the securities in quad-

---

FIGURE 6. *Strategic Frontier Analysis for Sample Portfolio of 86 Bonds: Best Case versus Worst Case.*

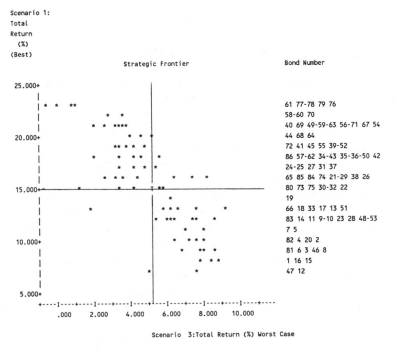

TABLE 6. *Scenario 1 Total Returns (%) for Quadrant I.*

64	CIT GROUP HOLDINGS INC	9.8500	08-15-04	20.0	11.0	5.2	12.1
42	AVCO FINL SVCS INC	9.1250	03-01-98	18.4	10.2	5.6	11.4
37	FORD MTR CO DEL	8.5000	04-01-96	16.9	9.4	5.4	10.6
26	IBM CR CORP	13.7500	03-15-94	16.3	11.0	8.2	11.8
29	HELLER FINANCIAL INC	13.0000	09-15-94	16.1	9.7	6.4	10.7
38	PHELPS DODGE CORP	8.1000	06-15-96	15.8	10.4	7.4	11.2
21	SECURITY PAC CORP	8.2500	07-01-93	15.7	9.5	6.3	10.5
	Quadrant Mean	10.2995	09-13-96	17.0	10.2	6.4	11.2

rant I. In Table 7, a plot of each bond in descending order of total return is displayed. The ranking may be based on the total return from any of the scenarios or the composite. The plot in Table 7 is based on the total return from scenario 1 (best case). The plot, which somewhat resembles a histogram, gives a visualization of the returns. For any one bond, both rank position and range of returns (generally analogous to variance) are seen at a glance. The return/risk characteristics of the portfolio composition are revealed by the overall wedge of the diagram.

V. Maturity Management Analysis

Table 8 displays a convenient asset mixing diagram that can assist a manager in maturity management. The bonds in the portfolio are first classified into the following three maturity classifications: short bonds (less than 3 years), intermediate bonds (3–12 years), and long bonds (greater than 12 years). Each cell in the table gives the upside (best case or scenario 1), downside (worst case or scenario 3), and composite total return for various allocations among the three maturity classifications. The columns indicate the percentage of the portfolio allocated to short bonds while the rows show the amount allocated to long bonds. For a given cell, the amount allocated to intermediate bonds is 100 percent minus the amount allocated to short and long bonds. For example, consider the cell representing 40 percent in short bonds and 10 percent in long bonds. Then 50 percent, of course, would be in intermediate bonds. For this allocation, the total return under the composite scenario is 9.6 percent. For the best case (Scenario 1) the total return would be 14.2 percent while for the worst case (Scenario 3) it would be 5.8 percent.

The maturity management table is useful because it is easy for a manager to see the effect of reweighting the maturity composition of a portfolio. For example, the composition of the portfolio under analysis (as shown in

TABLE 7. Scenario 1 Rank Order and Range Plot.

Bond No.	Total Return (%)			
	Scenario[a]			Com-posite
	1	2	3	
78	23.2	8.7	.0	10.6
77	23.1	8.7	.0	10.6
79	23.1	9.2	.7	11.0
76	22.9	9.2	.9	11.0
61	22.5	8.3	-.6	10.1
60	22.0	9.7	2.8	11.5
70	21.6	10.4	3.5	11.9
58	21.5	9.6	2.9	11.3
63	21.4	10.0	3.1	11.5
67	21.2	10.2	3.5	11.7
54	20.9	10.0	3.7	11.5
59	20.9	9.7	3.2	11.3
56	20.9	9.8	3.5	11.4
69	20.9	9.6	2.7	11.0
71	20.9	10.4	3.5	11.6
40	20.9	8.5	2.0	10.5
49	20.7	9.5	3.3	11.2
64	20.0	11.0	5.2	12.1
44	19.8	9.6	3.9	11.1
68	19.5	10.5	4.6	11.6

Total Return (%)

0.0	5.0	10.0	15.0	20.0

TABLE 7 *Continued*

Total Return (%)

Bond No.	Scenario[a]			Com-posite
	1	2	3	
41	19.4	9.0	3.4	10.6
45	19.4	9.5	3.9	10.9
52	18.9	10.0	4.8	11.3
55	18.9	9.5	4.1	10.8
72	18.6	10.2	3.2	10.6
39	18.5	9.6	4.7	10.9
43	18.5	9.4	4.2	10.7
86	18.4	7.4	1.9	9.2
62	18.4	10.0	3.5	10.6
50	18.4	9.8	4.6	10.9
42	18.4	10.2	5.6	11.4
35	18.1	9.3	4.6	10.6
36	18.1	9.3	4.6	10.6
57	18.0	8.8	3.4	10.1
34	17.9	8.9	4.2	10.4
24	17.4	8.1	3.4	9.6
25	17.4	8.1	3.4	9.6
31	17.4	9.1	4.7	10.4
27	17.1	8.4	4.1	9.9
Port.	15.5	9.0	5.1	9.9

Total Return (%): 0.0   5.0   10.0   15.0   20.0

TABLE 7 *Continued*

Bond No.	Scenario[a]			Com- posite	Total Return (%) 0.0 — 5.0 — 10.0 — 15.0 — 20.0
	1	2	3		
37	16.9	9.4	5.4	10.6	3 - - - - - 2 - C - - - - - - 1
85	16.4	7.5	3.1	9.0	3 - - - - - 2 - C - - - - - - - 1
26	16.3	11.0	8.2	11.8	3 - - - - - 2 - C - - - - - - 1
29	16.1	9.7	6.4	10.7	3 - - - - - 2 - C - - - - - - 1
38	15.8	10.4	7.4	11.2	3 - - - - - 2C - - - - - - - 1
21	15.7	9.5	6.3	10.5	3 - - - - - 2 - C - - - - - - 1
74	15.7	10.6	4.4	10.3	3 - - - - - - C - - - - - - - 1
84	15.6	7.5	3.6	8.9	3 - - - - - 2 - C - - - - - - 1
65	15.6	8.5	2.6	8.9	3 - - - - - - 2C - - - - - - 1
22	15.3	9.0	5.8	10.0	3 - - - - - 2 - C - - - - - - 1
75	15.1	10.5	4.2	10.0	3 - - - - - - C2 - - - - - - 1
73	15.1	10.7	3.3	9.7	3 - - - - - - C - 2 - - - - - 1
80	15.0	9.5	1.2	8.6	3 - - - - - - C - 2 - - - - - 1
30	14.8	9.6	5.5	10.0	3 - - - - - - 2C - - - - - - 1
32	14.6	9.2	5.5	9.8	3 - - - - - - 2 - C - - - - - 1
19	14.5	8.9	6.1	9.8	3 - - - - - - 2 - C - - - - - 1
66	13.4	8.8	1.8	8.0	3 - - - - - - C - 2 - - - - - 1
17	13.2	8.7	6.6	9.5	3 - - - 2 - C - - - - - - 1
33	12.9	8.4	6.3	9.2	3 - - - 2C - - - - - - 1
13	12.8	9.3	7.7	9.9	3 - - - - 2C - - - - - - 1

TABLE 7 *Continued*

Total Return (%)

Bond No.	Scenario[a] 1	2	3	Composite	Total Return (%) graph (scale: 0.0 5.0 10.0 15.0 20.0)
18	12.7	8.1	5.9	8.9	3 - - 2 - C - - - - - 1
51	12.6	10.2	9.2	10.7	3 - 2C - - - - 1
28	12.5	9.1	7.5	9.7	3 - - 2C - - - - - 1
23	12.5	9.1	7.4	9.7	3 - - 2C - - - - 1
48	12.4	10.3	8.6	10.4	3 - - C - - - - 1
53	12.4	9.7	8.5	10.2	3 - 2C - - - - 1
14	12.0	7.9	5.9	8.6	3 - - 2C - - - - - 1
83	11.9	7.5	5.5	8.3	3 - - 2 - C - - - - 1
9	11.8	8.1	6.5	8.8	3 - - 2 - C - - - - - 1
10	11.8	8.1	6.5	8.8	3 - - 2 - C - - - - - 1
11	11.8	7.9	6.2	8.6	3 - - 2C - - - - - 1
7	10.9	8.1	7.0	8.7	3 - 2C - - 1
5	10.5	8.6	7.9	9.0	3 2C - - 1
4	10.4	8.1	7.2	8.6	3 - 2C - - 1
2	9.6	8.4	8.0	8.7	3C - 1
20	9.5	8.2	7.7	8.4	3 2C - 1
82	9.5	7.3	6.4	7.7	3 - C - - 1
6	9.5	8.6	7.8	8.6	3C - 1
3	9.4	8.3	7.9	8.6	3C - 1
Port.	15.5	9.0	5.1	9.9	3 - - - - - 2 - C - - - - - - 1

TABLE 7 *Continued*

Total Return (%)

Bond No.	Scenario[a] 1	2	3	Composite	Total Return (%)
8	9.4	9.8	9.8	9.7	13 (≈10.0)
81	8.7	7.3	6.7	7.6	3 - C - 1 (≈5.0–7.5)
46	8.5	8.6	8.6	8.6	1 (≈7.5)
15	8.5	8.9	8.9	8.8	1C (≈8.5)
1	7.8	7.8	7.8	7.8	1 (≈7.8)
16	7.8	8.2	8.3	8.1	13 (≈8.0)
12	7.5	7.6	7.7	7.6	1 (≈7.5)
47	7.3	5.7	5.1	6.0	3 2C - - 1 (≈4.0–6.0)
Port.	15.5	9.0	5.1	9.9	3 - - - - - 2 - C - - - - - - - 1 (≈5.0–15.0)

Total Return (%) axis: 0.0   5.0   10.0   15.0   20.0

a. Probability for each scenario is 33⅓%.

TABLE 8. *Maturity Management Table of Total Return Expectations for Varying Maturity Concentrations.*

Percent Long Bonds		Percent Short Bonds										
		0%	10%	20%	30%	40%	50%	60%	70%	80%	90%	100%
100%	Scenario 1	19.4										
	Scenario 2	9.7										
	Scenario 3	2.9										
	Composite	10.7										
90%	Scenario 1	19.1	18.5									
	Scenario 2	9.7	9.6									
	Scenario 3	3.2	3.4									
	Composite	10.7	10.5									
80%	Scenario 1	18.8	18.2	17.6								
	Scenario 2	9.6	9.5	9.5								
	Scenario 3	3.4	3.6	3.8								
	Composite	10.6	10.4	10.3								
70%	Scenario 1	18.5	17.9	17.3	16.7							
	Scenario 2	9.5	9.4	9.4	9.3							
	Scenario 3	3.6	3.8	4.1	4.3							
	Composite	10.5	10.4	10.2	10.1							
60%	Scenario 1	18.2	17.6	17.0	16.4	15.7						
	Scenario 2	9.4	9.4	9.3	9.2	9.2						
	Scenario 3	3.8	4.0	4.3	4.5	4.8						
	Composite	10.5	10.3	10.2	10.0	9.9						
50%	Scenario 1	17.9	17.3	16.7	16.1	15.4	14.8					
	Scenario 2	9.4	9.3	9.2	9.2	9.1	9.0					
	Scenario 3	4.0	4.3	4.5	4.7	5.0	5.2					
	Composite	10.4	10.3	10.1	10.0	9.8	9.7					

TABLE 8 *Continued*

Percent Long Bonds		Percent Short Bonds										
		0%	10%	20%	30%	40%	50%	60%	70%	80%	90%	100%
40%	Scenario 1	17.6	17.0	16.4	15.7	15.1	14.5	13.9				
	Scenario 2	9.3	9.2	9.2	9.1	9.0	9.0	8.9				
	Scenario 3	4.2	4.5	4.7	4.9	5.2	5.4	5.7				
	Composite	10.4	10.2	10.1	9.9	9.8	9.6	9.5				
30%	Scenario 1	17.3	16.7	16.1	15.4	14.8	14.2	13.6	12.9			
	Scenario 2	9.2	9.2	9.1	9.0	9.0	8.9	8.8	8.7			
	Scenario 3	4.5	4.7	4.9	5.2	5.4	5.6	5.9	6.1			
	Composite	10.3	10.2	10.0	9.9	9.7	9.6	9.4	9.3			
20%	Scenario 1	17.0	16.4	15.8	15.1	14.5	13.9	13.3	12.6	12.0		
	Scenario 2	9.1	9.1	9.0	8.9	8.9	8.8	8.7	8.7	8.6		
	Scenario 3	4.7	4.9	5.1	5.4	5.6	5.9	6.1	6.3	6.6		
	Composite	10.3	10.1	10.0	9.8	9.7	9.5	9.4	9.2	9.1		
10%	Scenario 1	16.7	16.1	15.5	14.8	14.2	13.6	13.0	12.3	11.7	11.1	
	Scenario 2	9.1	9.0	8.9	8.9	8.8	8.7	8.7	8.6	8.5	8.5	
	Scenario 3	4.9	5.1	5.4	5.6	5.8	6.1	6.3	6.5	6.8	7.0	
	Composite	10.2	10.1	9.9	9.8	9.6	9.5	9.3	9.2	9.0	8.9	
0%	Scenario 1	16.4	15.8	15.2	14.5	13.9	13.3	12.7	12.0	11.4	10.8	10.2
	Scenario 2	9.0	8.9	8.9	8.8	8.7	8.7	8.6	8.5	8.5	8.4	8.3
	Scenario 3	5.1	5.3	5.6	5.8	6.0	6.3	6.5	6.8	7.0	7.2	7.5
	Composite	10.2	10.0	9.9	9.7	9.6	9.4	9.3	9.1	9.0	8.8	8.7

the last panel of Table 1; see p. 355) is 31.16 percent short bonds, 35.73 percent intermediate bonds and 33.11 percent long bonds. From Table 4, the portfolio summary, the composite total return is 9.88 percent and the best case (scenario 1) and worst case (scenario 3) total returns are 15.47 percent and 9.88 percent, respectively. If the portfolio is rebalanced to 20 percent short bonds, 40 percent intermediate bonds and 40 percent long bonds — which is essentially shifting the current portfolio holding from shorts to longs — then there will be an imperceptible change in the composite total return; however, the best case total return is improved by 93 basis points (from 15.47 percent to 16.40 percent) while the worst case declines by only 42 basis points (from 5.12 percent to 4.70 percent).

In addition to providing a useful tool to analyze the "risk/return" trade-off from portfolio rebalancing, the maturity management table allows a manager or sponsor to determine the alternative portfolio rebalancing necessary to achieve a minimum total return. For example, suppose a sponsor establishes a minimum portfolio return of 7.0 percent. By looking at the portfolio maturity composition that would produce a total return of at least 7.0 percent in the worst case, a manager could determine how the portfolio must be rebalanced. In this illustration, these are the four portfolios in the lower right-hand corner of the table.

Although the foregoing analysis was performed utilizing maturities, the same could be performed using duration.

VI. Timing

The timing of active strategies can be important. Over a given planning horizon, judgment is necessary to determine when a strategy is to be implemented. When a positively sloped yield curve exists, and if it is interpreted as a forecast of higher future interest rates, the strategy taken must be carefully timed. To benefit from an ensuing rate increase, a shortening of maturity (duration) is called for. However, by shortening maturity, a lower yield to maturity must be accepted. Premature rate anticipation under these circumstances would result in a lower realized return for the time frame before rates increase; if the increase never materializes, significant return give-up may be experienced.

Conversely, if a negatively sloped yield curve exists and rates are expected to decrease, again timing is important since a premature lengthening of maturity results in a lower yield to maturity with much riskier longer maturity (duration) portfolios. The conclusion is that effective timing of rate anticipation is a necessary and important consideration.

Moreover, rate anticipation should not be considered complete after the initial timing issue is resolved. When to reverse or modify the strategy must be continually considered. The return component interactions originally estimated will be constantly in flux, and the manager must continually balance anticipated capital changes against current yield and reinvestment return effects. This makes the "round-trip" character of successful rate anticipation apparent. That is, the rate anticipation efforts of the manager cannot be judged to be successful until the move taken in anticipation of any given rate increase (decrease) is reversed with a timely opposite move when rates are expected to decrease (increase). It should be pointed out, however, that the manager's performance is most appropriately judged over an entire interest rate cycle and in the context of the entire portfolio rather than on individual transactions.

In addition, other terms of a security should be analyzed, such as the effects of embedded options. For example, suppose that in a scenario of rising rates the prepayment experience of mortgage pass-through securities is expected to decline as homeowners tend to want to hold on to lower interest rate mortgages. Conversely, if rates decline, there is an incentive to refinance; hence, higher refunding and shorter lived Ginnie Maes can be expected. Forearmed with knowledge of the anticipated average life of a GNMA security under various interest rate scenarios, the manager can decide whether to embrace or avoid these securities with their potentially altered average maturity.

As another example, the call feature of bonds tends to be unused by issuers if rates rise because the issuer will not want to retire or refinance bonds issued at rates lower than current rates. As a result, callability is not of concern to the manager when scenarios call for rising rates. The opposite is true when rates are expected to fall. In such case, the issuer will have an incentive to retire callable bonds and refinance at lower rates.

Fortunately, all considerations can be integrated into the return simulation analysis described. This allows the manager to focus attention on the most important dimensions of direction, shape, and timing of interest rate change.

VII. Conclusion

Interest rate forecasting in the United States and Canada may be thought of as a good example of an activity associated with a highly efficient market. That is, wide distribution of information, low transaction costs, and many intelligent participants contribute to the difficulty of consistently and correctly forecasting the direction of rate changes. This does not say that some people cannot do it well, but it does suggest success will be extremely difficult to achieve on a consistent basis. However, the rewards of being right are great, not only in terms of realized returns, but in the amount of investment management business one can accrue. Unfortunately the converse is also true.

26

Use of an Immunized Bond Portfolio in Portfolio Protection*

H. Gifford Fong
President
Gifford Fong Associates

Eric M.P. Tang
Vice President
Gifford Fong Associates

I. Introduction

An investor often wants to ensure that his or her portfolio will produce at least a specified minimum return. To achieve this, the investor may consider purchasing protection for the investment. A protected portfolio would allow participation in a rising market while limiting the downside risk to a pre-specified level.

There are several methods to protect a portfolio. First, the portfolio manager can purchase protection directly. An example of a directly protected portfolio would be the purchase of a put option contract against the existing portfolio. Under a declining market scenario the investor can exercise the put option. The gain in the put option would offset part or all of the losses in the underlying securities. In this case the strike price of the put option effectively sets a floor to the portfolio's return.

In contrast, if the underlying assets performed well, the investor would let the put option expire without exercise and benefit from the appreciation of the underlying securities. The total return on the protected portfolio would be the profits on the actual portfolio minus the premium paid for the put option. Thus the options premium is equivalent to an insurance premium.

---

*This article is a significantly expanded version of one with the same title that appeared in the Winter 1988 issue of *The Journal of Portfolio Management*.

Another method to protect a portfolio is to pursue a synthetic option strategy. This technique uses only the cash and the futures markets without relying on any option contract. The synthetic option would structure and rebalance various asset classes in the portfolio over the investment horizon in such a fashion that the risk and return characteristics of the entire investment would replicate those of a portfolio protected by a put option. For instance, if an investor wants to protect a portfolio consisting of a risky or a volatile asset via the synthetic strategy, only part of the portfolio would be allocated to that asset. The rest of the portfolio would be invested in cash or a relatively risk-free security. When the risky asset performs poorly, the synthetic strategy would distribute more funds to the risk-free instrument. If the risky asset performs well, however, a larger portion of the portfolio would be invested in it. By properly rebalancing between the risky and the risk-free asset over the investment horizon, the return pattern on the overall investment would duplicate that of a portfolio protected by a put option.[1] This alternative protection method is valuable because direct portfolio protection is not always feasible. Direct protection is uncommon since publicly traded options are available only for a limited number of securities and asset types. Moreover, the expiration date and the strike price of traded option contracts are determined by the exchange. An investor may not always find a publicly traded option contract that is suitable for his or her portfolio.

The synthetic strategy, on the contrary, allows the investor to protect any one asset or combination at any strike price or expiration date desired. Most important, it is possible to extend synthetic option asset allocation to alter the risk characteristics of the portfolio in a fashion that is not achievable with publicly traded option contracts. For instance, the dynamic approach can be used to capture the best return among several risky securities instead of one.[2] It is even possible to apply the synthetic technique to asset and liability management in preserving the surplus of a portfolio. Thus synthetic option asset allocation is an extremely powerful approach that has a much wider appeal and more practical flexibility than direct portfolio protection.

II. Applications of Portfolio Protection

There are several major uses for portfolio protection. First, an investor such as a pension fund sponsor often wants to guarantee that the investment will generate a certain minimum rate of return that is required by the actuary.

---

1. M. Rubinstein and H. E. Leland, "Replicating Options with Positions in Stock and Cash," *Financial Analyst Journal* (July/August 1981).
2. See Oldrich A. Vasicek, "The Best Return Strategy," Gifford Fong Associates, Walnut Creek, California, 1987.

One way to satisfy the minimum rate is to immunize the portfolio.[3] An immunized portfolio would lock in the current spot rate of return on a fixed-income portfolio over the investment horizon regardless of movements in interest rates. Immunization is typically a passive strategy, however. Once a portfolio is immunized, the rate of return is fixed. The investor would not be able to earn a return significantly higher than the rate at which the portfolio was originally immunized.

Portfolio protection, on the contrary, allows an investor to participate in the movements of risky assets while setting a minimum return on the portfolio. If the risky assets perform well, the portfolio would achieve the return on these securities less the protection cost. And the investor is not limited to just a fixed rate of return. Moreover, by setting the floor return on the portfolio at the appropriate level, the investor can be assured that the actuarially set required rate of return will be satisfied. But there is one drawback to portfolio protection: the minimum floor return on the protected portfolio must be set at a level lower than the rate of the risk-free asset.

An alternative but similar strategy to portfolio protection is contingent immunization.[4] Under contingent immunization an investor would initially invest the portfolio entirely in risky assets. If the risky securities produce a high return, the investor would benefit from it. But in order to avoid catastrophic losses, the investor would monitor the portfolio closely. If at any time the market value of the portfolio drops to the same amount as the portfolio's desired minimum terminal wealth, the investor would restructure the risky securities and immunize the entire portfolio. Therefore, even under a bear market, the manager can still be confident that the desired minimum rate of return will be met.

However, there is one major difference between contingent immunization and portfolio protection. Contingent immunization is similar to a stop-loss order. For instance, suppose a portfolio is initially invested in risky assets. If the value of the risky securities drops to a point where the investor is forced to immunize, the portfolio can never be reactivated even if the risky assets recover. In contrast, a portfolio that is protected can participate in any rally of the risky assets — even after a major bear market. The protection strategy is similar to a protective put option where the investor can be continuously exposed to the upside potential of the risky securities. Thus the advantage of protecting a portfolio is that the investment is never totally detached from the potential of the risky asset.

3. H. Gifford Fong and Frank J. Fabozzi, "Immunization and Cash Flow Matching Strategies," in *Fixed Income Management* (Homewood, Ill.: Dow Jones-Irwin, 1985), chap. 6.
4. Martin L. Leibowitz and Alfred Weinberger, "The Uses of Contingent Immunization," *The Journal of Portfolio Management* (Fall 1981).

Besides ensuring a required rate of return, portfolio protection is also a powerful analytical tool for dynamic asset allocation decisions. It is possible to extend the protection program to the asset allocation process because the strategy of protecting a portfolio involves periodic redistribution of the assets in the portfolio. The assets are reallocated systematically over the investment horizon to pursue the initial investment objectives. For example, an investor may be very uncertain about future economic events. If the investor wants to protect the portfolio against major losses, an arbitrary amount of risky assets may be sold and the proceeds may be invested in cash or other risk-free instruments. This way, loses will be limited by the reduced proportion of the portfolio in the risky asset. Alternatively, the investor can employ a more systematic approach such as portfolio protection. By using the dynamic asset allocation strategy, the investor can be assured of a minimum return on the portfolio regardless of the outcome in the risky asset.

Thus portfolio protection is a disciplined way to achieve the investment objectives of an actively managed portfolio. In the preceding example, the investor can measure the risk/return trade-off of the portfolio by how high the floor return is. A portfolio that has a high floor return is considered defensive because it assures a high minimum rate of return by sacrificing some upside potential. Similarly, an offensive portfolio would have a low minimum floor rate. Such a portfolio would carry a lower protection cost and, hence, opportunity for greater appreciation. Of course, the downside risk on an offensive portfolio is greater.

III. Comparison with Traditional Asset Allocation

There are several differences between portfolio protection and other asset allocation methods. (A comparison of the major characteristics of the various asset allocation strategies is provided in the appendix to this article.) First, portfolio protection is a dynamic strategy. The investor sets the investment objectives and the investment horizon in the beginning. The portfolio protection program will determine the optimal allocation of assets over time. If one security is performing better than another, more funds will automatically be allocated to it. The investor simply follows the recommendations of the program in rebalancing his portfolio.

Most traditional methods of asset allocation utilize the static approach. The amount of investment in each security is decided initially. Reallocation among asset classes occurs only at the end of the investment horizon. A change in the investor's economic outlook may lead to redistribution of the assets prior to the horizon date. But any change in asset allocation would require new inputs in terms of the expected return and risk characteristics of the assets in the portfolio.

Another difference between portfolio protection and other asset allocation approaches is that the dynamic strategy does not require an investor to generate the expected return of the risky securities in the portfolio. Anticipated returns are not needed because portfolio protection relies on modern options pricing theory. The only inputs required to calculate the optimal asset allocation are the risk-free rate of return, the volatility, and the correlation of the return on the risky assets. This is a major advantage over the traditional static asset allocation procedure, which requires the investor to estimate the expected return on every asset in the portfolio in addition to their risk characteristics. Thus, substantially fewer user inputs are needed to run the dynamic asset allocation strategy.

IV. The Mechanics of Protecting a Portfolio with the Synthetic Option Allocation Strategy

The main objective of the synthetic option asset allocation strategy is to replicate the return pattern of a portfolio insured by a protective put option. To do so, the strategy relies on a property of options contracts that suggests that the return pattern of an asset protected by a put option is identical to a position that holds only a safety asset plus a call option on the same security. This property is called the put-call parity of options.

To illustrate how this property works, consider the simple case where a portfolio consists of only one 10-year zero coupon bond with a current market price of $50. Suppose the investor purchases a six-month over-the-counter (OTC) put option on that bond with a strike price of $50 and an options premium of $5. The return pattern on this portfolio can be represented by Figure 1. If on the expiration date the market price of the bond drops below $50, the put option would be exercised and the terminal value of the portfolio would be the strike price of the options contract less the premium or $45. This return pattern is shown as line AB in Figure 1.

If the price of the bond rises above $50, the put option would expire without being exercised. The ending value of the portfolio would be the value of the bond less the option premium. This is shown as line BC in Figure 1. Thus, the line ABC represents the final payoff pattern of a risky asset protected by a put option.

Suppose the investor, instead of purchasing a protective put option, decides to hold only the safety asset plus an OTC call option on the same bond. If the call option has the same strike price ($50) and the same premium ($5) as the put option, the return pattern of the cash plus call position would be exactly the same as in Figure 1.[5] To see why this is true, suppose the bond

---

5. This example assumes that the option can be exercised only on the expiration date and that the underlying bond does not pay coupons. Moreover, the interest rate on cash is assumed

FIGURE 1. *Exercise Value of an Option.*

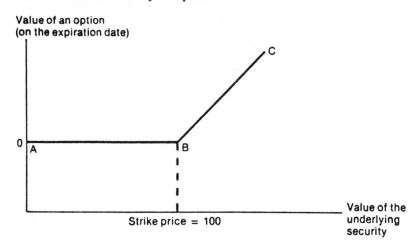

price rises above $50; the call option would be exercised. The terminal value of the portfolio would again be the value of the bond less the options premium as shown in line BC of Figure 1. If the price of the bond drops below $50, the call option would expire without being exercised. The ending value of the portfolio would be the amount of cash less the premium paid on the call option or $45. This can be represented by line AB. Therefore the payoff distribution of a combined position in a safety asset and a call option is identical to holding the underlying security protected by a put option.

Because of the put-call parity, an investor can protect a portfolio either by buying a protective put option against the existing assets or by holding only a safety asset plus a call option. Similarly, a dynamic asset allocation strategy can protect a portfolio if the strategy reproduces the payoff pattern of a call option plus a safety asset. It is possible to duplicate the payoff pattern of an option contract with only cash securities because there is a predictable relationship between the theoretical value of an option contract and the price of the underlying asset even prior to the expiration date. By varying the amount of the underlying cash securities that is held in the portfolio, one can reproduce the return distribution of an option.

The value of an option contract at any time is closely tied to the price of the underlying security. Consider the previous example where the strike

---

to be zero. The put-call parity, however, still holds even if these restrictive assumptions were dropped. See John Cox and Mark Rubinstein, *Options Markets* (Englewood Cliffs, N.J.: Prentice-Hall, 1985).

FIGURE 2. *Value of an Option Prior to the Expiration Date.*

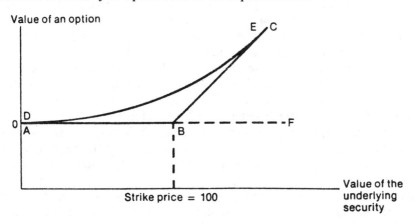

price of the call option is $50. If the price of the underlying bond rises far above the strike price, the option would be considered "deep in the money." The value of a deep-in-the-money option contract or the option premium is likely to move one-to-one with the price of the underlying bond.

If the price of the underlying bond drops substantially below the strike price, the option contract is considered "out of the money." The value or the premium of an out-of-the-money option is likely to change very little in response to movements in the price of the underlying security. In the extreme case where the price of the underlying bond falls close to zero, the value of the option approaches zero also.

This relationship between the price of the underlying asset and the value of the option is shown in Figure 2. Line ABC represents the value on the expiration date of a call option contract with a strike price of $50. The value of the option prior to expiration is represented by the curve DE. At one extreme when the price of the underlying stock drops far below $50, the option premium falls toward zero. The curve DE becomes flat and its slope becomes zero. When the bond price rises significantly above $50, however, the option premium moves one-to-one with the underlying security. In this case curve DE approaches the 45° line BC. The slope of curve DE becomes 1.

The slope of curve DE is also known as the hedge ratio. The hedge ratio is an important concept in portfolio protection or dynamic asset allocation because it suggests the proportion of the portfolio to be invested in the risky asset. Using the previous example, suppose the current price of the underlying bond is $50 and the slope of curve DE at that point is 0.5. If the price of the underlying asset changes, the value of the option would move by only half as much. Thus a portfolio that is composed of 50 percent in safety asset and 50 percent bonds would experience the same profit and loss as a position in a safety asset plus a call option contract whose underlying value is equal to the value of the portfolio. To replicate the return pattern of the call option, half the portfolio should be allocated to bonds and the rest in the safety asset. So the correct hedge ratio is 0.5. Similarly, when the price of the underlying bond rises to $55, the hedge ratio will be increased. If the slope of curve DE is 0.8 at that point, 80 percent of the portfolio should be invested in bonds. The ratio is 0.8 because any change in the options premium will only be 80 percent of the fluctuation of the bond price.

In summary, the value of an option contract will move with the price of the underlying security. The sensitivity of the option's price relative to the bond price will depend on the slope of curve DE or the hedge ratio. By setting the strike price at the appropriate level to reflect the desired minimum floor return and by adjusting the hedge ratio continuously throughout the investment horizon, it is possible to duplicate the return pattern of the option contract.

V. An Immunized Bond Portfolio as the Safety Asset

In a dynamic hedging strategy the portfolio is invested in two assets: the target asset and a safety asset. Since the safety asset is the instrument that provides the downside protection to a portfolio, the choice of this asset is very important.

A popular safety asset in dynamic hedging strategies is cash or Treasury bills. Cash is assumed to be risk-free because it has a short duration, and hence its price is less volatile. More important, an investor does not have to worry about losing the principal on a short-duration instrument.

However, cash is not the proper safety asset in dynamic asset allocation. Cash is inappropriate because the reinvestment return is unknown. For instance, suppose the current yield on a three-month Treasury bill is 10 percent and an investor wants to assure that his or her portfolio return will be at least 2 percent per annum for the next five years. The investor may compute the hedge ratio of the portfolio assuming that the 10 percent risk-free rate of return would remain unchanged over the investment horizon. When the portfolio is rebalanced or when the Treasury bill matures, however, the reinvestment rate could be substantially different from 10 percent. Therefore, using cash as the safety asset in dynamic hedging would subject the portfolio to significant reinvestment risk. Moreover, because of this uncertainty in the reinvestment rate, neither the desired minimum return nor the cost of protection can be determined with great confidence in the beginning of the plan.[6]

---

6. The reinvestment risk of cash can pose a serious problem under the following two scenarios. First, if the target asset is a bond portfolio, a steepening of the yield curve could cause bond

To minimize the reinvestment risk, an immunized bond portfolio with a duration equal to the investment horizon should be used as the safety asset. An immunized portfolio is the more appropriate choice because the terminal value of this instrument is predetermined. Knowing the terminal value of the safety asset, however, is not sufficient to control the reinvestment risk. Under dynamic asset allocation, an investor would rebalance his protected portfolio frequently. The investor may sell some risky securities and add the proceeds to the immunized portfolio. At other times the investor may liquidate part of the immunized portfolio and invest in the risky asset. Since the timing and the amount of these rebalancings are not known in advance, funds will be added or withdrawn from the immunized portfolio at some uncertain future rates. Thus even an immunized portfolio is not completely risk-free in a portfolio protection context.

However, two unusual features of immunized portfolios allow the investor to have strong control over the reinvestment risk in a dynamically hedged portfolio. First, the return on an immunized portfolio is negatively correlated over time. For example, suppose the initial yield on a five-year immunized portfolio is 10 percent. If the return on that portfolio is 12 percent in the first year, then the return in the remaining four years must be lower than the initial yield. In fact, the immunized return would have to be 9.51 percent per annum for the remaining investment horizon. Second, the volatility of return on a immunized portfolio would systematically decrease during the investment horizon. The volatility changes over time because the duration of this instrument shortens automatically.

Because of these two properties, the stochastic nature of an immunized portfolio can be modeled much more accurately than cash. Therefore a dynamic strategy that properly takes these factors into consideration would have much greater control over the reinvestment risk. That is why an immunized portfolio is the more appropriate choice of safety asset to assure a minimum rate of return on a protected portfolio.

VI. Determinants of the Hedge Ratio

In addition to the difference between the price on the underlying asset and the strike price, the hedge ratio is also determined by the shape and position of the curve DE. Curve DE is the option value curve because it represents the value of an option contract or the size of the option premium. Under modern options pricing theory, the value of an option contract also depends on the following four factors: the volatility of the target security, volatility

---

prices to drop and simultaneously lower the reinvestment rate on cash. Second, if the target asset is a stock portfolio, a severe recession may lead both stock prices and interest rates to drop at the same time.

of the term structure of interest rates, correlation between the target and the safety asset, and the time to expiration.[7]

The volatility of the target security and the time to expiration are included in most standard portfolio protection models. Hedging dynamically with an immunized portfolio, however, requires additional parameters. First, the return on an immunized portfolio prior to the horizon date is not constant. And its return may be correlated with the target asset. Second, the volatility of the immunized portfolio declines systematically over time. A single volatility parameter such as the standard deviation is not enough to capture this effect. It is necessary to specify the volatility of the whole term structure of interest rates to correctly quantify the stochastic nature of the immunized portfolio.

VII. Optimal Rule of Portfolio Rebalancing

The dynamic asset allocation strategy requires frequent rebalancing of the portfolio because the hedge ratio does not remain constant. To assure that the dynamically hedged portfolio closely replicates the return on an options contract, the portfolio should be rebalanced every time the hedge ratio changes. In practice, however, it is unfeasible and costly to make instantaneous adjustments.

The drawback of rebalancing infrequently, of course, is that the actual performance of the protected portfolio may be different from the theoretical prediction. For instance, if the risky securities performed well, the return on the portfolio may be lower than the risky asset less the protection cost. This can happen because as the value of the risky security appreciates, the hedge ratio should be raised. If the portfolio is not rebalanced fast enough, the portfolio's exposure to the risky security would be lower than the required level, and the return on the portfolio would fall behind the risky securities by more than the cost of protection.

If the portfolio is rebalanced very often, however, the transaction fees would be substantially greater. The transaction expenses can become an even bigger factor if the securities in the protected portfolio are not liquid. Thus frequent rebalancing can narrow the difference between the theoretical and the actual return (tracking error), but these gains must be evaluated against the higher transaction cost.

To achieve the optimal trade-off between tracking accuracy and transaction expenses — that is, to minimize transaction fees for a given standard deviation of tracking error — an investor should pursue the following rule:

---

7. Several other factors such as interest rates, cash dividends on the underlying stock, tax rate, margin requirement, transaction cost, and market structure also affect the value of an option contract.

Periodically compute the absolute difference in return between the target and the safety asset since the last time the portfolio was rebalanced. If this difference exceeds a certain trigger point prespecified by the investor, then the portfolio should be rebalanced to reflect the new hedge ratio. If the difference is smaller than the trigger point, no rebalancing is necessary. For example, if the investor decided on a trigger point of 3 percent, the portfolio should be rebalanced only if the absolute difference in return between the target and safety asset is greater than 3 percent.

To decide on a proper trigger point, the investor should look at trade-off diagrams such as Figures 3a–c. A large trigger point means that the portfolio would be rebalanced less frequently. This would result in smaller transaction costs but less tracking accuracy. A small trigger point, in contrast, implies greater transaction expenses and better tracking precision.[8]

It can be proved that the rebalancing criteria described above is, indeed, the optimal rule. Any other decision rules such as rebalancing by changes in the hedge ratio or by the passage of time would result in more portfolio turnover than necessary. In other words, if the investor's portfolio were rebalanced according to time or changes in the hedge ratio, the resulting trade-off curve between transaction expenses and tracking error would be suboptimal. In Figure 3c the suboptimal rebalancing rule is depicted by a curve farther away from the origin.

One way to improve this trade-off between transaction cost and tracking error is to use futures contracts. Futures contracts are valuable because they provide leverage in the portfolio. A small deposit (or margin requirement) on a futures contract would allow an investor to have a large exposure to the underlying asset; the hedge ratio of a protected portfolio can thus be adjusted easily and economically with the purchase or sale of a relatively small number of futures contracts. This tends to reduce the transaction cost of a dynamically hedged portfolio for any given level of tracking error.

VIII. The Cost of Portfolio Protection

One major consideration in dynamic asset allocation is the cost of this strategy. There is a cost to protect a portfolio because the program allows an investor to shun the downside risk of a risky asset while capturing its upside potential. The cost of protection can be expressed as a percentage of the portfolio's value. For instance, if the cost of protection is 2 percent per annum, the protected portfolio's return would be the return on the risky asset less 2 percent or the prespecified floor rate, whichever is higher.

---

8. The actual relationships among tracking error, trigger point, and transaction costs are as follows: Standard deviation of tracking error and trigger point—proportional; transactions cost and trigger point—inversely proportional; and standard deviation of tracking error and transaction cost—inversely proportional.

FIGURE 3. *Trigger between Transaction Cost and Tracking Error.*

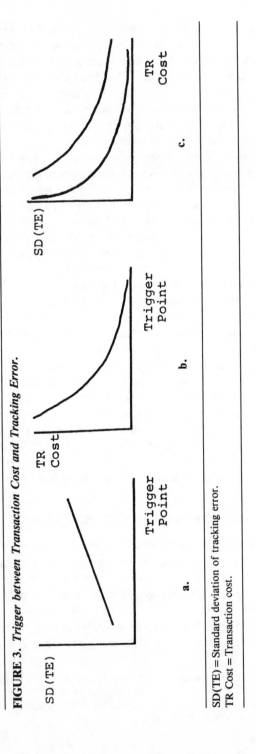

SD(TE) = Standard deviation of tracking error.
TR Cost = Transaction cost.

Intuitively, the cost of protecting a portfolio is the price that the investor pays for not investing 100 percent in the risky asset. Under a dynamic asset allocation strategy the hedge ratio or the portion of the portfolio invested in the risky security will vary between 0 and 1 depending on the performance of the risky asset. If the risky security earns a high return, the portfolio's return will be smaller because a certain portion of the portfolio has been invested in the lower earning risk-free securities. Therefore the implied cost of protecting a portfolio is the price the investor pays for not being fully invested in the risky security if the risky asset outperforms the risk-free security.

The net cost of portfolio protection, however, is lower than the implied cost. The implied cost is relevant only if the risky security is performing well. But if the return on the risky asset less the implied cost of protection is lower than the minimum rate of return, the portfolio return will be the prespecified floor rate. In this case the investor recovers part or all of the paid insurance premium. At the inception of a protection program, an investor would not know with certainty the future performance of the risky security. The expected price of this dynamic strategy (versus holding 100 percent of the risky asset) is the implied cost of protection less the probability-weighted amount of claims that the investor collects if the risky securities perform poorly.

IX. Extensions of the Strategy: Return Ceiling, Multiple Assets, and Surplus Protection

Besides assuring a minimum return, the dynamic asset allocation strategy can be extended to other important applications. First, the same strategy can be used to impose a ceiling or a maximum return on the portfolio. Placing a maximum return is equivalent to writing a call option against the risky asset. If the risky securities performed well, they would be called away and the portfolio return would be capped. If the return on the risky assets did not exceed the ceiling, however, the investor would keep the call premium. In this case the dynamically hedged portfolio would actually outperform the target asset by the amount of the call premium. This strategy would thus guarantee a superior portfolio return against the benchmark within a certain range. In addition, an investor may want to combine both minimum and maximum return constraints on a portfolio to achieve the desired insurance cost.

The dynamic asset allocation strategy can also be extended to protect a portfolio that contains more than one risky asset. For a multiple risky asset portfolio, the protection program would allow the portfolio to earn the highest return among all the risky assets less the cost of protection. For example, if the risky assets are U.S. stocks, U.S. bonds, international bonds, and gold then the return on the composite portfolio would be equal to the best return among the four assets less the corresponding protection premium.[9]

---

9. See Vasicek, forthcoming.

There are two major differences between the multiple risky asset protection strategy and buying a separate call option on each risky security. When an investor purchases call options on several risky assets and invests the remaining funds in a safety instrument, the return on that portfolio would be tied not only to the best performing asset but to every asset that has a high return. This difference is caused by the fact that the investor would exercise every call option that is in the money on the expiration date. Thus the total portfolio return would be a weighted average of the return on every risk asset that performed well minus the total call premium paid in the beginning of the plan.

Moreover, when an investor buys call options on every risky asset, the terminal value of the portfolio is guaranteed. If all the risky securities performed poorly, the call options would expire nonetheless. The ending value of the portfolio would be determined by the initial amount invested in the safety asset and the risk-free interest rate. Multiple risky asset protection, in contrast, does not automatically impose a minimum return on the portfolio. The minimum floor return is assured only if one of the risky securities is chosen to be an immunized portfolio with a duration equaled to the horizon date.

For example, if an investor is interested in capturing the best return between two risky assets, the return on the composite portfolio on the horizon date can be described in Figure 4. In that figure line DE represents the return on the composite portfolio if 100 percent of the portfolio were invested in asset 1. Under the multiple asset protection scheme, however, the final return on the portfolio would be described by line ABC. If the return on asset 1 less the protection cost is lower than the return on asset 2 less its insurance cost, the total return on the portfolio would be tied to asset 2. This is represented by the line AB. If the peformance on asset 1 is better, however, the portfolio return would be the return on that security less the protection cost. In this case portfolio return can be measured by line BC. The vertical distance between line DE and BC equals the cost of insurance on asset 1.

Under the multiple asset protection strategy, the investor is not always assured of a floor nominal return. If all the risky assets performed poorly, the composite portfolio would do the same. In Figure 4, if the return on both asset 1 and asset 2 were negative, line AB would fall below the 0 percent horizontal axis. And the portfolio return would be negative also. If asset 2 were an immunized portfolio, however, the return on asset 2 would be known in advance. More important, a floor return on the composite portfolio would be assured.

The multiple risky asset protection approach offers investors several advantages. First, the protection cost on this strategy is much lower than purchasing separate call options on every risky asset. Second, a diversified portfolio typically consists of numerous classes of assets. This strategy would

FIGURE 4. *Payoff Diagram on a Two-Risky-Asset Portfolio.*

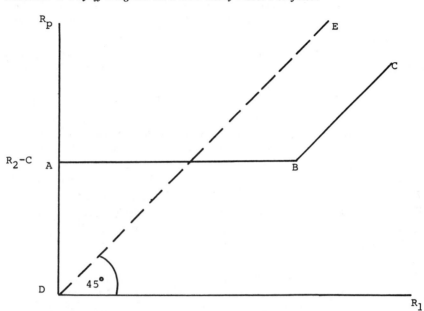

R_p = Return on composite portfolio.
R_1, R_2 = Return on assets 1 and 2.
C_1, C_2 = Protection cost on assets 1 and 2.

help the portfolio manager to allocate the assets within that portfolio over the investment horizon. The allocation would be made in a systematic fashion that is consistent with the investment objectives. Furthermore, the potential for a very large return may be higher under the multiple risky asset strategy than the single risky security case. This is true because the more classes of assets one includes in the portfolio, the more likely it is that at least one of them, and hence the portfolio, will earn a high return. An investor, however, would have to mitigate this extra opportunity against the additional cost — the protection premium on a multiple risky security portfolio would be higher.

One very important application of dynamic asset allocation is to perform asset and liability management. Very often, investors such as pension plan sponsors or insurance companies may want to protect or preserve a surplus in their net financial position. In other words, they may want assurance that the market value of assets will always exceed the present value of liabilities by a certain amount or percentage.

To preserve a surplus with the dynamic hedging strategy, the investor would pick an immunized bond portfolio as one of the two or several risky assets; the bond portfolio would be immunized against the liability stream. The remaining risky assets would be instruments such as stocks or an actively managed bond portfolio. Since the duration of the liabilities may be different from the investment horizon, the duration of the immunized portfolio does not have to be the same as the horizon.

Intuition suggests that the immunized portfolio would serve as a proxy to the liabilities. Because the bond portfolio is immunized against the liabilities, the market value of the fixed-income securities will change at the same percentage rate as the present value of the liabilities. For example, if interest rates decline, the present value of both the immunized portfolio and the liabilities will increase at the same percentage rate. Since a protected portfolio's total return would not fall behind the return on the immunized portfolio by more than the amount of the protection cost, an investor can assure that the market value of the portfolio will exceed the present value of the liabilities by a predetermined level. Thus it is possible to preserve the surplus by selecting the proper protection cost on the immunized portfolio.

An immunized bond portfolio is the crucial element in surplus protection because the future value of liabilities is unknown. For example, an investor may want to hedge against the liabilities with a dynamically managed portfolio consisting only of stocks and Treasury bills. Suppose the equities market rallies; then the value of the portfolio would appreciate with the price of the stocks. It is possible, however, that the present value of the liabilities can increase at an even faster pace. This can happen if the duration of the liabilities was very long and interest rates fell substantially. In this case the surplus can actually shrink or even turn negative despite the strong stock market. To protect the surplus of a portfolio, therefore, an immunized portfolio should be used as the hedging asset.

X. Simulation Results

To demonstrate how the dynamic hedging strategy would have worked, two simulations were performed on protecting a bond portfolio tied to the Shearson Lehman Government-Corporate Bond Index. In both cases the projected volatility and correlation on the assets were estimated with historical data available only in the beginning of the plan; no prior knowledge of the performance of the assets was assumed. The performance on the bond index and the immunized portfolio, however, was based on actual results.

The first simulation started on January 1, 1980 and ended on July 1, 1982. The investor was assumed to have chosen a minimum return of 7.5 percent without any limit on the upside. The projected protection cost at the plan's inception was 2.02 percent (compounded annually). Table 1 shows the

TABLE 1. *Portfolio Simulation.*

Plan # 6: Guarantee a Minimum Return on an Indexed Bond Portfolio

Target Asset: SLINDEX (Shearson Lehman Government-Corporate Bond Index)

Safety Asset: IMMU (Immunized Portfolio, Initial Duration = 2.5 Years)

Inception Date	01-01-80	*Investment Objectives:*		*Target Asset:*	
Horizon Date	07-01-82	Minimum Return	7.50%	Standard Deviation	12.00%
Transaction Cost	.25%	Maximum Return	NOMAX	*Safety Asset:*	
Horizon Length	2.50 years	Protection Cost:	.25%	Yield to Horizon	11.17%
Initial Investment ($000)	100,000	*Interest Rate:*		*Correlation:*	.15
Target Returns Filename	BND1	Volatility Factor	1.00		
Safety Returns Filename	IM1				

Date	Years to Horizon	Return in Last Period (%)				Return since Inception (%)					Hedge Ratio	Turn-over (%)	Invest-ment Total ($000)	New Cash-flow ($000)	Trans. Costs ($000)
		Target Asset	Safety Asset	Sched-uled	Actual	Target Asset	Safety Asset	Sched-uled	Actual before Trans. Cost	Actual after Trans. Cost					
01-01-80	2.50										.581		100,000	0.	
02-01-80	2.41	−2.87	−.44	−1.89	−1.85	−2.87	−.44	−1.89	−1.85	−1.85	.524	5.1	98,150	0.	13
03-01-80	2.33	−5.81	−5.90	−5.95	−5.85	−8.51	−6.31	−7.73	−7.59	−7.61	.531	.8	92,394	0.	2
04-01-80	2.25	.19	2.36	1.15	1.20	−8.34	−4.10	−6.67	−6.48	−6.50	.481	4.6	93,503	0.	11
05-01-80	2.17	10.76	9.70	10.09	10.21	1.52	5.20	2.75	3.07	3.04	.510	2.7	103,039	0.	7
06-01-80	2.08	4.68	3.22	3.84	3.97	6.27	8.59	6.70	7.15	7.12	.552	3.8	107,118	0.	10
07-01-80	2.00	1.83	1.25	1.45	1.57	8.22	9.95	8.24	8.84	8.79	.574	2.0	108,792	0.	6
08-01-80	1.92	−1.68	−1.24	−1.60	−1.49	6.40	8.58	6.50	7.21	7.16	.569	.4	107,161	0.	1
09-01-80	1.83	−3.49	−1.67	−2.73	−2.70	2.69	6.77	3.60	4.31	4.26	.523	4.2	104,261	0.	11
10-01-80	1.75	−1.15	−.59	−.99	−.89	1.50	6.13	2.58	3.39	3.33	.514	.7	103,326	0.	2

TABLE 1 Continued

Date	Years to Horizon	Return in Last Period (%) Target Asset	Safety Asset	Sched-uled	Actual	Return since Inception (%) Target Asset	Safety Asset	Sched-uled	Actual before Trans. Cost	Actual after Trans. Cost	Hedge Ratio	Turn-over (%)	Invest-ment Total ($000)	New Cash-flow ($000)	Trans. Costs ($000)
11-01-80	1.66	−1.01	−.51	−.87	−.77	.48	5.59	1.69	2.59	2.53	.507	.6	102,530	0.	1
12-01-80	1.58	−.23	.09	−.18	−.07	.25	5.69	1.50	2.52	2.46	.505	.1	102,456	0.	0
01-01-81	1.50	2.81	2.28	2.38	2.55	3.06	8.10	3.91	5.13	5.07	.529	2.3	105,067	0.	6
02-01-81	1.41	−.03	.60	.18	.26	3.03	8.75	4.10	5.41	5.34	.518	.9	105,339	0.	2
03-01-81	1.33	−1.63	.11	−.73	−.79	1.35	8.87	3.34	4.57	4.50	.467	4.7	104,501	0.	12
04-01-81	1.25	2.39	2.24	2.15	2.31	3.77	11.30	5.56	6.99	6.90	.482	1.4	106,902	0.	4
05-01-81	1.17	−3.22	−.90	−1.82	−2.02	.42	10.31	3.63	4.83	4.74	.404	7.2	104,742	0.	19
06-01-81	1.08	3.19	1.60	1.96	2.24	3.63	12.08	5.66	7.19	7.07	.466	5.8	107,074	0.	16
07-01-81	1.00	.15	1.20	.71	.71	3.78	13.42	6.41	7.95	7.82	.438	2.5	107,819	0.	7
08-01-81	.92	−1.79	−.07	−.68	−.82	1.93	13.34	5.69	7.06	6.92	.380	5.3	106,923	0.	14
09-01-81	.83	−1.68	.55	−.03	−.30	.21	13.96	5.66	6.73	6.59	.300	7.6	106,588	0.	20
10-01-81	.75	.02	1.78	1.44	1.25	.23	15.99	7.18	8.07	7.90	.243	5.3	107,904	0.	14
11-01-81	.66	5.45	2.49	2.77	3.21	5.69	18.88	10.14	11.54	11.35	.347	9.9	111,349	0.	28
12-01-81	.58	8.04	2.76	3.85	4.59	14.18	22.16	14.38	16.66	16.43	.551	19.3	116,433	0.	56
01-01-82	.50	−3.19	.13	−.93	−1.70	10.54	22.32	13.32	14.67	14.40	.373	17.0	114,396	0.	49
02-01-82	.41	.49	.78	.57	.67	11.07	23.28	13.96	15.45	15.12	.382	.9	115,116	0.	3
03-01-82	.33	1.77	1.15	1.08	1.38	13.04	24.69	15.20	17.04	16.71	.445	6.2	116,707	0.	18
04-01-82	.25	1.25	.94	.80	1.08	14.46	25.86	16.12	18.31	17.95	.510	6.5	117,947	0.	19
05-01-82	.17	2.73	1.36	1.33	2.06	17.58	27.57	17.66	20.74	20.36	.670	15.6	120,358	0.	47
06-01-82	.08	1.60	1.14	.94	1.44	19.46	29.02	18.77	22.49	22.05	.825	15.4	122,048	0.	47
07-01-82	.00	−1.53	.98	.87	−1.10	17.63	30.29	19.80	21.14	20.66			120,665	0.	

TABLE 2. *Simulation Summary.*

Plan # 6: Guarantee a Minimum Return on an Indexed Bond Portfolio

Target Asset: SLINDEX (Shearson Lehman Government-Corporate Bond Index)
Safety Asset: IMMU (Immunized Portfolio, Initial Duration = 2.5 Years)

Plan Inception Date	01-01-80	*Investment Objectives:*	
Plan Horizon Date	07-01-82	Minimum Return	7.50%
Horizon Length (years)	2.50	Maximum Return	NOMAX
Initial Investment ($000)	100,000	Protection Cost	2.02%
Target Returns Filename	BND1		
Safety Returns Filename	IM1		

	Target Asset	Safety Asset	Plan Scheduled	Plan Actual Before Trans. Cost	Plan Actual After Trans. Cost
Balances ($000)					
Horizon Date	99,127.656	21,537.248	119,801	121,145	120,665
Return since Inception (%)					
Total Return	17.63	30.29	19.80	21.14	20.66
Return/Year (Annl. Comp)	6.71	11.17	7.50	7.98	7.81
Return/Year (Cont. Comp)	6.50	10.59	7.23	7.68	7.52

Notes: Total turnover = 158.76%; total transaction costs ($000) = 443.619.

month-by-month results of the two assets and the composite portfolio. The hedge ratio, which represents the portion of the portfolio invested in the indexed bond fund, ranged from 0.243 to 0.825.

A summary of the simulation is presented in Table 2. The summary shows that the annual return on the bond index during the two and one-half year period was 6.50 percent. Since the return on the index minus the protection cost (2.02 percent) was 4.48 percent—lower than the desired minimum level—the scheduled return on the composite portfolio should be 7.23 percent (continuously compounded) or 7.50 percent (annually compounded). The actual return on the portfolio, however, was 7.68 percent—0.45 percent higher than expected.

The actual and scheduled returns can be different because of several reasons. First, the projected volatility of the assets may be wrong. Since the actual volatility is not observable beforehand and the hedge ratio is computed on the assumed volatility, an incorrect projection could cause tracking error. Second, the portfolio was not rebalanced continuously. As a result, the actual exposure of the portfolio would not be the same as the ideal hedge ratio. And tracking error may occur. In this example the tracking error was positive, which worked in favor of the investor. In other instances the tracking error can be negative, however.

The second simulation covered the period from June 1, 1984 to November 1, 1986. The target and safety assets were (again) the Shearson Lehman Government-Corporate Bond Index and an immunized portfolio. The minimum floor return on this portfolio also was set at 7.5 percent.

Results of the simulation are reported in Tables 3 and 4. During this period the bond market rallied. Since the return on the index (19.41 percent, less the protection cost of 1.91 percent) was higher than the minimum floor, the scheduled return on the composite portfolio should have been 17.5 percent. However, the actual performance was 18.54 percent, resulting in a +104 basis point tracking error. The large tracking error in this case was caused mainly by the fact that the portfolio was rebalanced on a monthly basis even though the intramonth changes in interest rates were very large. With a real portfolio, the manager would rebalance the portfolio when the return on the bond index exceeds the prespecified trigger point. Thus the tracking precision is likely to be much higher in practice.

XI. Summary

Portfolio protection is a powerful strategy for an investor to alter the risk and return characteristics of his or her assets. To protect a portfolio properly, however, an investor must consider several issues of implementation. First, the choice of the safety asset is crucial. If an investor wants to assure at least a minimum return, an immunized bond portfolio or a zero coupon bond are the only assets that allow control over the reinvestment risk. Second, in the actual operation of the strategy, an investor should follow the optimal rebalancing procedure described earlier. To do otherwise is to incur unnecessary transaction costs. Third, the cost of protection may be prohibitively high if the time horizon of investment is short. In this case an investor may consider imposing a return ceiling on the portfolio to lower the protection cost.

The basic form of portfolio protection can also be extended to other important investment applications. By choosing the proper instruments and protection cost, this strategy can be used to preserve a surplus and hence allows an investor to manage his assets relative to his funding needs. Moreover, portfolio protection can be enhanced to capture the best return among several risky securities. Multiple asset protection can even be considered as an alternative method of allocating assets in a diversified portfolio.

Appendix:
Comparing Alternative Asset Allocation Strategies

Many different asset allocation strategies are currently available to investors. These strategies range from the traditional static asset allocation technique

TABLE 3. *Portfolio Simulation.*

Plan # 6: Guarantee a Minimum Return on an Indexed Bond Portfolio

Target Asset: SLINDEX (Shearson Lehman Government-Corporate Bond Index)
Safety Asset: IMMU (Immunized Portfolio, Initial Duration = 2.4 Years)

Inception Date 06-01-84	Investment Objectives:	Target Asset:
Horizon Date 11-01-86	Minimum Return 7.50%	Standard Deviation 15.00%
Transaction Cost .25%	Maximum Return NOMAX	Safety Asset:
Horizon Length 2.42 years	Protection Cost: 1.91%	Yield to Horizon 13.28%
Initial Investment ($000) 100,000	Interest Rate:	Correlation: .15
Target Returns Filename BND2	Volatility Factor 1.00	
Safety Returns Filename IM2		

Date	Years to Horizon	Return in Last Period (%)				Return since Inception (%)					Hedge Ratio	Turn-over (%)	Invest-ment Total ($000)	New Cash-flow ($000)	Trans. Costs ($000)
		Target Asset	Safety Asset	Sched-uled	Actual	Target Asset	Safety Asset	Sched-uled	Actual before Trans. Cost	Actual after Trans. Cost					
06-01-84	2.42										.657		100,000	0.	
07-01-84	2.34	1.08	.72	.84	.96	1.08	.72	.84	.96	.96	.669	1.2	100,960	0.	3
08-01-84	2.25	4.24	2.23	3.47	3.57	5.37	2.97	4.34	4.57	4.57	.710	3.6	104,566	0.	10
09-01-84	2.17	1.68	1.13	1.40	1.52	7.14	4.14	5.80	6.16	6.15	.726	1.5	106,145	0.	4
10-01-84	2.08	2.27	1.93	2.05	2.17	9.56	6.14	7.97	8.46	8.45	.738	1.2	108,447	0.	3
11-01-84	2.00	4.15	3.04	3.73	3.86	14.11	9.38	12.00	12.65	12.63	.763	2.3	112,628	0.	6
12-01-84	1.92	1.73	1.90	1.65	1.77	16.08	11.45	13.85	14.64	14.61	.767	.5	114,612	0.	1
01-01-85	1.83	-.17	1.65	.18	.25	15.88	13.29	14.05	14.93	14.90	.742	2.2	114,901	0.	6
02-01-85	1.75	2.19	1.26	1.81	1.95	18.42	14.72	16.12	17.17	17.14	.766	2.3	117,136	0.	7
03-01-85	1.67	-1.91	-.17	-1.56	-1.50	16.16	14.52	14.30	15.41	15.37	.741	2.2	115,368	0.	6

TABLE 3 *Continued*

Date	Years to Horizon	Return in Last Period (%)				Return since Inception (%)					Hedge Ratio	Turnover (%)	Investment Total ($000)	New Cashflow ($000)	Trans. Costs ($000)
		Target Asset	Safety Asset	Scheduled	Actual	Target Asset	Safety Asset	Scheduled	Actual before Trans. Cost	Actual after Trans. Cost					
04-01-85	1.59	1.90	1.15	1.55	1.71	18.36	15.84	16.08	17.38	17.33	.763	2.1	117,329	0.	6
05-01-85	1.50	2.06	1.70	1.83	1.98	20.81	17.80	18.20	19.70	19.64	.779	1.5	119,642	0.	4
06-01-85	1.42	5.02	2.15	4.24	4.39	26.87	20.34	23.21	24.95	24.89	.834	5.1	124,886	0.	16
07-01-85	1.34	.98	1.29	.92	1.03	28.12	21.89	24.34	26.24	26.16	.838	.5	126,159	0.	1
08-01-85	1.25	-.32	.31	-.33	-.22	27.71	22.26	23.93	25.96	25.88	.838	.0	125,883	0.	0
09-01-85	1.17	1.80	.85	1.49	1.65	30.01	23.30	25.79	28.04	27.96	.863	2.4	127,957	0.	8
10-01-85	1.08	.51	.69	.42	.53	30.68	24.14	26.31	28.72	28.63	.870	.8	128,633	0.	2
11-01-85	1.00	2.01	.87	1.71	1.86	33.30	25.22	28.47	31.12	31.03	.898	2.6	131,028	0.	8
12-01-85	.92	2.29	.75	1.99	2.13	36.35	26.16	31.03	33.92	33.81	.926	2.7	133,809	0.	9
01-01-86	.83	3.09	.86	2.81	2.93	40.57	27.24	34.70	37.83	37.71	.955	2.8	137,714	0.	10
02-01-86	.75	.59	.59	.51	.59	41.40	27.99	35.40	38.65	38.52	.963	.8	138,517	0.	3
03-01-86	.67	4.19	.69	4.00	4.06	47.32	28.88	40.81	44.28	44.14	.986	2.2	144,141	0.	8
04-01-86	.59	3.54	1.03	3.47	3.51	52.54	30.21	45.70	49.34	49.19	.995	.9	149,186	0.	3
05-01-86	.50	.45	.62	.44	.45	53.22	31.01	46.33	50.01	49.85	.997	.2	149,855	0.	1
06-01-86	.42	-1.98	.45	-1.98	-1.97	50.19	31.60	43.44	47.05	46.90	.997	.0	146,897	0.	0
07-01-86	.34	2.90	.66	2.88	2.89	54.54	32.47	47.57	51.30	51.15	1.000	.3	151,147	0.	1
08-01-86	.25	.65	.57	.65	.65	55.55	33.22	48.53	52.29	52.13	1.000	.0	152,128	0.	0
09-01-86	.17	2.64	.61	2.64	2.64	59.65	34.04	52.45	56.31	56.14	1.000	.0	156,144	0.	0
10-01-86	.08	-1.25	.43	-1.25	-1.25	57.66	34.61	50.54	54.35	54.19	1.000	.0	154,193	0.	0
11-01-86	.00	1.45	.45	1.45	1.45	59.94	35.21	52.72	56.59	56.43	1.000	.0	156,428	0.	0

TABLE 4. *Simulation Summary.*

Plan # 6: Guarantee a Minimum Return on an Indexed Bond Portfolio

Target Asset: SLINDEX (Shearson Lehman Government-Corporate Bond Index)
Safety Asset: IMMU (Immunized Portfolio, Initial Duration = 2.4 Years)

Plan Inception Date	06-01-84	*Investment Objectives:*	
Plan Horizon Date	11-01-86	Minimum Return	7.50%
Horizon Length (years)	2.42	Maximum Return	NOMAX
Initial Investment ($000)	100,000	Protection Cost	1.91%
Target Returns Filename	BND2		
Safety Returns Filename	IM2		

| | | | | Plan Actual | |
	Target Asset	Safety Asset	Plan Scheduled	Before Trans. Cost	After Trans. Cost
Balances ($000)					
Horizon Date	156,420	7.773	152,725	156,591	156,428
Return since Inception (%)					
Total Return	59.94	35.21	52.72	56.59	56.43
Return/Year (Annl. Comp)	21.43	13.28	19.13	20.37	20.32
Return/Year (Cont. Comp)	19.41	12.47	17.50	18.54	18.50

Notes: Total turnover = 41.60%; total transaction costs ($000) = 127.605.

(mean-variance analysis) to the more sophisticated portfolio insurance models. The diversity of strategies, however, often causes confusion among investors. The purpose of this section is to summarize the strength and weakness of each strategy. Table 5 provides a list of the available strategies and their major characteristics.

In comparing the various strategies, it is obvious that no one method dominates all the others. Strategies that are relatively easy to understand and implement, such as contingent immunization and process-free insurance, have severe limitations. However, more advanced models such as Assured Return Technique (ART) require more inputs and greater user sophistication to appreciate. Thus an investor must consider an investment objective carefully before choosing a particular strategy.

Specifically, the various asset allocation strategies can be distinguished by several characteristics:

1. *Required inputs.* Investor may be required to generate expected return and volatility for each asset under consideration. The resulting portfolio mix is often sensitive to these inputs.
2. *Minimum return guarantee.* Can the strategy provide assurance that the portfolio return would be above a certain minimum level?

TABLE 5. *Asset Allocation Strategies.*

Strategies	Required Inputs		Minimum Return Guarantee	Path Independence	Max Upside Capture	Fixed Horizon	Surplus Protection	Hedge Ratio
	$E(R)$	Variance						
Mean-variance	Yes	Yes	No	Yes	NA	Yes	No	Constant
Contingent immunization	No	No	Yes	No	?	Yes	Yes	0 or 1
Process-free insurance	No	No	Yes	No	?	No	Yes(?)	0 to ∞
Portfolio insurance (cash)	No	Yes	?	Yes	Yes	Yes	No	0 to 1
ART (immunized portfolio)	No	Yes	Yes	Yes	Yes	Yes	Yes	0 to 1
Ideal	No	No	Yes	Yes	Yes	No	Yes	0 to 1

3. *Path independence.* The realized return on the portfolio depends only on the cumulative return of the individual assets. It is independent of the particular paths by which the return is achieved. Path independence is a desirable property of any options-related strategy.
4. *Maximum upside capture.* Can the strategy capture the upside potential of the target asset less some insurance cost?
5. *Fixed horizon.* Can the strategy guarantee a minimum return, capture the appreciation of the target asset, or preserve a surplus for only a predetermined horizon, or can it perform these functions indefinitely?
6. *Surplus protection.* This very important feature in asset and liability management allows the investor to preserve the surplus of assets over the present value of liabilities by a predetermined amount.
7. *Hedge ratio.* Proportion of portfolio allocated to the target asset, the ideal range of this ratio should be greater than zero and less than or equal to one.

A detailed description of each asset allocation strategy is provided next.

Mean-variance Analysis   Mean-variance analysis is a strategy that maximizes the expected return on a portfolio for any given level of risk. Once an allocation is determined, it is held constant throughout the investment horizon. The allocation of the portfolio, however, is highly sensitive to the expectational inputs generated by the investor. Moreover, the strategy can neither guarantee a minimum return nor protect a surplus.

Contingent Immunization   Contingent immunization requires the investor to initially invest the entire portfolio in the target asset. If the target asset performs poorly, the investor would sell all the risky securities and immunize the proceeds. This way, a certain predetermined terminal value of the portfolio can be guaranteed. The major advantage of this strategy is that it is simple to understand and implement. The major drawback, however, is that once the portfolio is immunized, it will be locked into the safety securities even if the target asset recovers. Furthermore, it is impossible to predetermine the upside potential of this strategy since the outcome depends on the particular path of return of the target asset.

Process-free Portfolio Insurance   This is a strategy that achieves a certain degree of downside protection on a risky security while retaining its upside potential. The basic form of this strategy can be characterized by the following equation:

$$E = M * C,$$

where

E = exposure in target asset,
M = a multiple selected by the investor at the inception of the plan, and

C = cushion, or the market value of portfolio minus a predetermined floor.

If the risky asset performs well, the cushion of the portfolio would expand and the portfolio's exposure to the risky asset increases. Similarly, if the risky asset performs poorly, the exposure would be reduced. In the extreme case where the cushion shrinks to zero, the portfolio would be invested entirely in the safety asset. More important, the floor value of the portfolio is assured. The strength of this strategy is that it is easy to understand. It does not require the user to project volatility of the target asset. In addition, this strategy can be used to preserve the surplus of a portfolio indefinitely.

However, there are several drawbacks to this strategy. First, the investor has to decide on the value of the multiple. A higher multiple means that the hedge ratio of the portfolio will be more volatile and the return on the portfolio will be closely tied to the target asset. A high multiple, however, can cause the exposure to the target asset to be greater than 100 percent of the portfolio. For instance, suppose the initial investment is $100 with a desired floor of $80. If the multiple is set at 3, then the initial exposure to the target asset is $60, or 60 percent of the portfolio. If on some future date the value of the target asset increased by 50 percent, the new required exposure will be $3*(130-80) = 150$, which is greater than the actual portfolio value of $130. To achieve this kind of exposure, the investor would have to leverage in the risky security and take a short position in the safety asset.

Since leveraging or shorting is considered undesirable by many investors, one remedy to this problem is to arbitrarily set a ceiling on the exposure at say, 100 percent of portfolio value. Setting a ceiling, however, would result in path dependence; that is, the total cumulative return on the portfolio at any point in time is sensitive to the return path of the target asset. Consequently, there is significant uncertainty regarding the kind of insurance policy the investor is actually purchasing.

Basic Portfolio Insurance (Using Cash as the Safety Asset)   The basic portfolio insurance strategy uses dynamic asset allocation to replicate the return pattern of a portfolio protected by a put option. The solution of the model is path independent and provides a weak form of return guarantee; the minimum return guarantee is not certain because this technique uses cash as the safety asset, and future return on cash is not known. This type of model would thus subject the investor to a lot of reinvestment risk. Another drawback of this strategy is that it cannot be applied to surplus protection.

Assured Return Technique (ART): Portfolio Insurance with an Immunized Portfolio   This represents the most complicated and advanced strategy in asset allocation. It is similar to the basic portfolio insurance strategy with the exception that an immunized portfolio is used as the safety asset. By using an immunized portfolio, the reinvestment risk is minimized and the minimum return can be assured. In addition, the strategy can be applied to surplus preservation.

Although ART requires the user to project the volatility of the target asset, the resulting tracking error seems to be insensitive to this estimate. Performance both of simulations (random and historical) and live portfolios using ART has demonstrated that unless projected volatility is unreasonably wrong, the tracking error of the portfolio is likely to be small.

Compared to the process-free insurance strategy, ART can also protect a minimum surplus for a given horizon. Moreover, if the surplus is defined to be the ratio of assets to liabilities, the surplus will not fall below this minimum level at any time during the investment horizon. However, ART does require the investor to project the volatility of different assets, which is not necessary under the process-free strategy.

27

Customized Benchmarks in Structured Management*

Sharmin Mossavar-Rahmani
Senior Vice President
Fidelity Management Trust Company

I. Introduction

From the "buy and hold long-term bonds" investment style of the 1960s through the "Nips for Blips"[1] swaps of the early 1970s, the "interest rate anticipation" of the late 1970s, and the "dedication, immunization, and horizon matching" of the early 1980s, bond managers have turned now to a new investment technique—"structured management." Structured management plays down interest rate anticipation on the part of portfolio managers who match the duration of a portfolio with that of a benchmark. Rather, this approach encompasses an array of investment styles including indexation, enhanced indexation, and duration-controlled sector rotation. In indexation, the duration of a portfolio closely tracks that of a benchmark. In enhanced indexation and duration-controlled sector rotation, the duration of a portfolio deviates from that of a benchmark within a wider predetermined range; the range is widest in the latter style.

Traditionally, managers have selected these benchmarks from among the generic market indexes introduced since the late 1970s, notably the Shear-

---

*This article is a revised and expanded version of the article with the same title appearing in the Summer 1987 issue of *The Journal of Portfolio Management*.
1. Nips stands for Northern Indiana Public Service, and Blips for Bell Telephone of Pennsylvania.

son Lehman Government/Corporate Index, the Salomon Brothers Broad Investment-Grade Bond Index, and the Merrill Lynch Domestic Master Index. More recently, however, the investment community has moved away from generic indexes toward "customized benchmarks."

This article aims to answer the following questions: What is a customized benchmark? What factors account for the interest in customized benchmarks? What are some of the considerations in designing such benchmarks? Finally, how can the performance of such benchmarks be monitored?

II. What Is a Customized Benchmark—And Why?

A customized benchmark is a benchmark designed to meet the specific requirements and long-term objectives of a fund, given the fund's risk tolerance over short and long horizons. The growing interest in customized benchmarks can be attributed to at least six developments:

- Financial Accounting Standards Board Statements 87 and 88 have prompted pension plan sponsors to link the expected return on assets more closely to particular liabilities. Risk-averse pension plan sponsors could, for example, use a customized benchmark to maintain stable or favorable asset–liability ratios.
- Increasingly, the investment community has recognized that funds have different long-term objectives and risk preferences, and that fund performance should not be compared to just one market index. The requirements and objectives of an endowment fund, for example, are not the same as those of an overfunded large pension plan. Structured management requires customized benchmarks designed to meet different objectives and constraints.
- Investment advisors adopting structured management have sought to establish market niches by promoting their specific capabilities and services in designing and using customized benchmarks.
- Investment advisors can command higher fees for managing structured portfolios based on customized benchmarks than for those based on generic benchmarks.
- Members of the broker/dealer community design and market customized indexes in an effort to capture market share in index and index-related products. Salomon Brothers introduced its Large Pension Fund Baseline Bond Index in December 1986 as a standardized customized benchmark designed specifically for large long-term oriented pensions funds.[2] This index was adopted by the California State Teachers Retirement System in August 1987 as the benchmark for indexing some $7.0 billion.

---

2. See "Introducing the Salomon Brothers Large Pension Fund Baseline Bond Index," Salomon Brothers Inc, December 1986.

- The ban on incentive fees (which tie the compensation of investment advisors to their performance relative to a benchmark) was removed by the Securities and Exchange Commission in November 1985 and by the Department of Labor in August 1986. Often, a customized benchmark is designed to accurately incorporate all constraints imposed on the investment advisor by a plan sponsor.

III. Designing the Benchmark

The first step in designing a customized benchmark is to specify the fund's objectives. Maximizing long-term expected return, producing a minimum annual real rate of return, matching liabilities, maximizing liquidity, preserving capital, and maintaining favorable asset–liability ratios are popular objectives among plan sponsors. Some of these objectives are short-term, while others are long-term. In addition, plan sponsors also may specify different levels of risk tolerance.

The most important and certainly the most difficult task in designing a customized benchmark is translating these broad and sweeping objectives into concrete goals and risk parameters. Often, nonfinancial considerations have to be incorporated into the design as well. Some public pension funds, for example, have demanded benchmarks that exclude securities of corporations involved in South Africa.

The second step in the design process is to determine a duration (and maturity distribution) and a sector distribution for the benchmark that can best meet the fund's objectives. The duration of the customized benchmark can be tied either to that of a broad-based market index, or to that of a particular liability schedule. Alternatively, the duration can simply be set at an absolute level. For example, some plan sponsors specify long-duration benchmarks, given the greater expected return of long-term securities over extended periods.

A critical decision is whether to design a fixed-duration benchmark or an interest rate–sensitive one. A fixed-duration benchmark holds the duration at a fixed level irrespective of the level of interest rates. For example, a 5-year duration benchmark is held at five years whether interest rates rise or fall. In an interest rate–sensitive benchmark, on the other hand, the duration increases (decreases) as interest rates fall (rise). The Shearson Lehman Aggregate Index is such a benchmark. It is important to note that the two approaches result in different total returns.

The sector distribution determines the weightings assigned to government securities, corporate securities, and mortgage-backed securities. Plan sponsors seeking the higher yields from corporate bonds and mortgage-backed securities (see Figure 1) may choose to overweight these two sectors relative to their actual distribution in the market. Other sponsors may be averse to

FIGURE 1. *Current-Coupon GNMAs and A Industrials vs. Ten-Year U.S. Treasuries (spreads in basis points).*

Source: Salomon Brothers, Inc.

the risk of exposure to adverse spread movements between corporate and mortgage-based securities on the one hand and government securities on the other. The significant deterioration in credit quality (see Table 1) over the last few years may also discourage some sponsors from seeking the higher yields of corporate bonds. Finally, sponsors with large liquidity requirements may choose to overweight Treasuries.

TABLE 1. *Changes in Credit Quality: Upgrades versus Downgrades.*

	1982	1983	1984	1985	1986	1987*
No. of upgrades	49	91	161	124	143	59
No of downgrades	169	149	148	153	246	101
Downgrades as percent of total	77.5	62.1	47.9	55.2	63.2	63.1

*First six months.
Source: Moody's Investors Service, Inc.

Customized benchmarks also may be designed to include specialized market sectors such as the high-yield ("junk") or convertible bond markets. Plan sponsors, for example, may choose to include high-yield bonds in a customized benchmark if their investment advisors are allowed to invest in this sector.

IV. Expected Performance

Once the key parameters of a customized benchmark are set, the next step is to advise the plan sponsor of the expected performance of the benchmark under alternative market scenarios. If a short-duration benchmark is selected, the plan sponsor should be informed of the expected underperformance of this benchmark relative to the broad-based market indexes in a period of falling interest rates. Similarly, if corporate bonds are overweighted, the benchmark will underperform as spreads between corporate and government securities widen. Such a risk may be acceptable to some plan sponsors and consistent with their funds' long-term objectives; nonetheless, these types of risks must be clearly spelled out.

Such a scenario analysis can be complemented by a review of the historical return and risk levels of the customized benchmark. A historical review advances the plan sponsor's understanding of the benchmark and provides some useful insights into the impact of various duration/maturity and sector biases.

As Tables 2 through 5 illustrate, the insights gained from a historical review depend largely on the market trends during the specific period examined. Table 2 highlights the impact of the maturity distribution on portfolio returns. For example, over the course of the complete market cycle from December 1976 to September 1986, the intermediate sector of the Treasury market outperformed both the short and the long sectors of the market despite two of the strongest annual rallies in bond market history. Table 3

TABLE 2. *Return Analysis of Maturity Distribution (in percent).*

Maturity	Complete Market Cycle 12/31/76–9/30/86	Bear Market 12/31/76–9/30/81	Bull Market 9/30/81–9/30/86
T-Bills	142.06	53.87	57.32
Intermediate Treasuries	169.47	23.26	118.63
Long Treasuries	149.74	−16.05	197.49

Source: Shearson Lehman Indexes, Ibbotson Associates series, Payden & Rygel T-Bill Indexes.

TABLE 3. *Risk Analysis of Maturity Distribution.*

Maturity	Complete Market Cycle Duration Date 12/31/76	Bear Market Duration Date 9/30/81	Bull Market Duration Date 9/30/86
T-Bills			
Volatility (in percent)	0.24	0.29	0.18
Duration (in years)	0.25	0.25	0.25
Intermediate Treasuries			
Volatility (in percent)	1.74	1.76	1.58
Duration (in years)	3.08	2.54	3.09
Long Treasuries			
Volatility (in percent)	3.89	3.40	4.03
Duration (in years)	10.88	6.95	9.90

Source: Shearson Lehman Indexes, Ibbotson Associates series, Payden & Rygel T-Bill Indexes.

TABLE 4. *Return Analysis of Sector Distribution.*

Maturity	Complete Market Cycle 12/31/76–9/30/86	Bear Market 12/31/76–9/30/81	Bull Market 9/30/81–9/30/86
Governments	169.46	15.78	132.73
Corporates	156.38	−6.83	175.17
MBS	162.72	−7.16	182.99
Aggregate index	162.10	5.09	149.42

Source: Shearson Lehman Indexes, Ibbotson Associates series, Payden & Rygel T-Bill Indexes.

shows the risk levels associated with the three maturity sectors, where risk levels are measured by duration and volatility of monthly returns.

Table 4 highlights the impact of varying the sector distribution on portfolio returns. Over the bull market cycle from September 1981 to September 1986, mortgage-backed securities and corporate bonds outperformed government securities. In fact, mortgage-backed securities outperformed corporate bonds despite a shorter begining and ending duration. Over the complete market cycle, however, government securities outperformed mortgage-backed securities and corporate bonds. Such outperformance was due partly to the intermediate maturity bias of the government market and partly to widening spreads between corporate bonds and mortgage-backed securities, and government securities.

TABLE 5. *Risk Analysis of Sector Distribution.*

Maturity	Complete Market Cycle Duration Date 12/31/76	Bear Market Duration Date 9/30/81	Bull Market Duration Date 9/30/86
Governments			
Volatility (in percent)	2.07	2.02	1.96
Duration (in years)	3.98	3.20	4.62
Corporates			
Volatility (in percent)	3.02	2.99	2.78
Duration (in years)	9.18	5.68	6.96
MBS			
Volatility (in percent)	3.31	3.22	3.14
Duration (in years)	6.67	5.32	3.51
Aggregate index			
Volatility (in percent)	2.48	2.46	2.28
Duration (in years)	6.46	4.16	4.89

Source: Shearson Lehman Indexes, Ibbotson Associates series, Payden & Rygel T-Bill Indexes.

V. Common Pitfalls

Two common pitfalls must be avoided when designing a customized benchmark. A benchmark must not be unduly complex. A complex benchmark may lead to unreliable pricing of securities, unrealistic constraints, and impractical assumptions. Moreover, a benchmark must avoid high turnover of its universe. For example, a barbell Treasury benchmark with a one-to-two-year maturity range at the short end will lead to an annual 100 percent turnover for that portion of assets; as securities age, those with less than one year to maturity drop out of the benchmark and are replaced with new ones.

VI. Monitoring the Benchmark

The last step in design is to set up an information system for monitoring the customized benchmark. We can measure performance and profile characteristics of customized benchmarks in several ways. The most simple and direct approach is to use various subsectors of publicly available indexes to obtain the desired duration and sector distribution. The client should monitor the subsector indexes regularly to ensure that the profile characteristics of the customized benchmark are consistent, practical, and replicable. For example, one cannot use the Treasury subsector of the Shearson Lehman Aggregate Index to obtain a long-term duration benchmark.

An alternative and more precise approach is to maintain a complete data base of the fixed-income market. The data base then can be used to generate the necessary performance and profile characteristics of the customized benchmarks. The costs of maintaining data bases and the problems associated with pricing fixed-income securities will prohibit most investment advisors from using such an approach. Of course, smaller investment advisors can turn to major broker/dealers for research and support services to monitor the former's customized benchmarks.

Looking ahead, we can surmise that structured management using customized benchmarks, like past techniques, will give way to new investment styles over time. While they last, however, customized benchmarks will affect plan sponsors and investment advisors alike.

In developing and designing customized benchmarks, plan sponsors face the task of better describing their objectives and risk tolerance levels. At the same time, investment advisors will set up portfolios that are more responsive to the plan sponsors' priorities. In the process, the advisors either will devote greater resources to separately managing customized portfolios, or they will specialize in structured management based on standardized customized benchmarks that can be used for plan sponsors with similar requirements and objectives.

28

Realized Return Optimization:
A Strategy for Targeted Total Return Investing in Fixed Income Markets

Llewellyn Miller
Vice President
Drexel Burnham Lambert

Uday Rajan
Associate
Drexel Burnham Lambert

Prakash A. Shimpi
Associate
Drexel Burnham Lambert

I. Introduction

The fixed income markets have been characterized by innovation over the past several years. The mortgage sector in particular has seen the rapid growth of new and more complex products such as CMOs and MBS Strips. The techniques used to value such securities have also evolved in complexity, with the use of sophisticated models based on option pricing theory to value option features embedded within securities. Callable bonds, for example, are analyzed as combinations of non-callable bonds and call options, with option pricing techniques used to value the latter.

The substantial increase in interest rate volatility in the early to mid '80s is primarily responsible for the increasing emphasis on options, both embedded and explicit. One consequence of this emphasis is that recent innovations in portfolio strategy focus on hedging techniques, especially those incorporating the use of options. The basic elements involved in choosing fixed income portfolios remain unquestioned. For example, the virtues of modified duration and convexity in controlling interest rate risk are taken for granted.

From the viewpoint of a total return investor, conventional portfolio selection strategies do not seem to provide an answer to the problem of efficiently managing the trade-off between risk and return. The measures typically used to quantify risk (duration mismatch) and expected return (yield

---

TABLE 1. *Advantages of RRO in Liability Funding.*

- Ensures ability to meet cash outflows
- Matches present values of assets and liabilities
- Handles cash flow uncertainty caused by option features on either the asset or liability side
- Flexible with respect to objectives and targets
  - Allows for multiple investment horizons
  - Accounts for diverse shifts in interest rates
- Identifies untenable positions well in advance
- Determines a risk-return frontier based on investor's targets
- Can incorporate margins for profit and error

---

or spread over the yield curve) have no direct bearing on the one used to evaluate historical performance (total return). This article introduces a scenario-based strategy, *realized return optimization* (RRO), that directly targets total return and is therefore an improvement over existing methods.

One of the most important applications of RRO is in the process of liability funding, that is, choosing asset portfolios to offset future cash outflows. Pension funds and insurance companies, for example, have streams of promised future cash outflows that need to be currently funded. Table 1 outlines some of the features that make RRO attractive for liability funding.

The Investor's Goal

The goal of a total return investor is to identify an appropriate balance between risk and return. In the context of liability funding, an additional requirement is that the portfolio chosen must be able to meet the liability outflows as they come due.

When measuring the performance of a portfolio, return refers to the total return earned by the portfolio over some specified period. This is measured from the cost of the original portfolio and the total market value of the portfolio at the end of the period. When purchasing assets, yield or spread over some Treasury benchmark is often used as a proxy for return. This may be misleading in some cases because the relative total returns on securities over a specific time period and under a particular interest rate scenario need not correspond to their relative yields or spreads.

Risk in the fixed income markets refers either to credit risk or interest rate related risk. Credit risk is controlled through allocation among sectors distinguished by industry and quality. In this article, the focus is on interest rate related risk, that is, the risk of the return on an asset or portfolio deviating from what was expected due to unanticipated changes in interest rates.

Currently, the most common strategies used within the context of liability funding are immunization and portfolio insurance. Immunization typically involves matching the modified duration of the assets to that of the liabilities, sometimes ensuring that the assets have greater convexity.

Modified duration measures the sensitivity of the present value or price of a stream of cash flows to interest rates and convexity the interest sensitivity of modified duration. Another version of duration that is sometimes used is Macaulay duration, which is computed for default-free and option-free bonds. It measures the horizon over which the total return on the security is "guaranteed." For example, the Macaulay duration of a Treasury strip would be equal to its term to maturity.

Portfolio insurance involves the continuous rebalancing of a risky asset and a riskless asset, depending on market moves. The riskless asset is often assumed to be an immunized portfolio. Hence, for risk management, this strategy also depends on the same parameters—modified duration and convexity—as immunization.

When duration and convexity are used as targets, interest rate risk is measured by the difference between the durations and convexities of the assets and liabilities. Active positions on interest rates are taken by increasing or reducing the duration of the portfolio. Portfolios with lower durations do well when rates rise, since reinvestment rates are higher, while those with higher durations do well when rates fall and the price appreciation on the portfolio is high.

Is Duration a Valid Target?

The problem with using modified duration as a target is that it does not provide any information about the return that may be expected from an asset over any particular time period or change in interest rates. In other words, it does not relate to the performance measure, total return. Macaulay duration does provide information about the return on the asset over one specified time horizon. However, the measure itself loses any economic interpretation when the stream of cash flows from the asset can vary across interest rate scenarios, as is the case with all securities with option features, such as callable bonds and mortgage-backed securities.

Since the real concern is total return, why not use that as the target? The problem is that returns on fixed income securities are generally *path dependent*. The return depends not just on interest rates at the terminal date when the security may have to be sold, but also on how they got there; that is, on the interest rate environment at each previous point in time. This is particularly true of securities with option features, where the prior exercise of an option may affect all future cash flows.

The strategy proposed here, *realized return optimization* (RRO), recognizes the path dependency of returns and uses it to define explicitly targets and risk measures in terms of total returns.

II. Realized Return Optimization

The key concepts in RRO are realized return, which refers to the return earned on an asset, and required return, which defines an investor's targets.

Realized Return

The realized return (RR) on an asset refers to the total return earned on it over any specified time period. An examination of the components of realized return helps to illustrate the sources of path dependency.

1. *Initial cost:* The cost of buying the asset at the beginning of the period.
2. *Cash flows:* The cash flows received from the asset during the period, including coupons and principal, both scheduled (as on maturity) and unscheduled (e.g., prepayments). These may be path dependent.
3. *Reinvestment income:* The amount earned on reinvesting the cash flows until the end of the period. This depends on interest rates when the cash flows are realized.
4. *Terminal value:* The resale value of the asset at the end of the period. This depends on rates at the horizon date and on previous rate environments. For example, if a bond is called before the horizon, there is nothing left to sell.

The realized return over the period in question is now defined as:

$$RR = \left(\frac{\text{Cash Flows} + \text{Reinvestment Income} + \text{Terminal Value}}{\text{Initial Cost}} \right) - 1.$$

Over any past time period, the realized return on a security or portfolio can be computed easily. All the required data are available. For example, to compute the one-year realized return on a bond purchased a year ago, the amount paid for it, the cash flows received, the amount earned on reinvestment and what the bond could be sold for today are all known.

In projecting a return over some future time period, however, the only known information is the cost of the security today. The other three values must be forecast.

Cash flows: For a non-callable bond, these are easily predicted. However, for a callable bond, a model is required to predict when the bond will be called in any given scenario. For a mortgage-backed security, a prepayment model to help predict the monthly cash flows is needed.

Reinvestment income: Given the cash flows, reinvestment income to the horizon date is computed at some expected reinvestment rate. For example, one could assume that all cash flows will be reinvested daily at the overnight funds rate. This rate would depend on the assumed scenario.

Terminal value: Particularly for securities with option features, this could be the most difficult component to project. An accurate pricing model is essential.

Sophisticated option pricing models to value the option components of callable corporate bonds and mortgage-backed securities have been developed.[1] These models permit the accurate evaluation of such securities and facilitate forecasting the price at any point in the future under any given interest rate scenario. Furthermore, a prepayment model can be used to forecast prepayment rates for the universe of actively traded and liquid mortgage-backed securities.

The explicit computation of each component of realized return allows an investor to assume a realistic or achievable reinvestment rate for cash inflows from the asset portfolio. This is an improvement over implicitly assuming that these inflows all can be reinvested at the same yield or spread of the original portfolio. Incoming cash is often reinvested at short term rates before being used to meet cash outflows or to purchase new assets. Should the latter be necessary, the original portfolio itself may need to be rebalanced. Therefore, it may be incorrect to assume that all cash inflows are reinvested back in the original portfolio.

The computation of a one-year realized return for a 10% 10-year bond priced at par, in a situation of rising interest rates, is illustrated in Table 2. If

---

1. See the article by Andrew D. Langerman and William J. Gartland, "Callable Corporate Bonds: Pricing and Portfolio Considerations," in this book and David J. Askin, Woodward C. Hoffman, and Steven D. Meyer, "The Complete Evaluation of the Option Component of Mortgage Securities," in *The Handbook of Mortgage-Backed Securities,* edited by Frank J. Fabozzi (Chicago: Probus Publishing, 1988).

TABLE 2. *Realized Return Calculation.*[a]

Initial cost (price of bond at beginning of year) = 100.00

Cash flow (coupon income over the year)	= 10.00[b]
Reinvestment income (5×0.04)	= 0.20[b]
Terminal value (price of bond at end of year)	= 95.00[b]
Total accumulated value over the year	= 105.20

Realized return $= (105.20/100.00) - 1 = 5.20\%$.

---

a. All figures are quoted as a percentage of par.
b. Projected value.

FIGURE 1. *One-Year Realized Returns.*

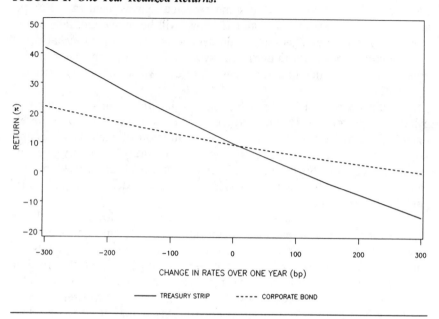

the first coupon can be reinvested at 8% until the end of the year, the reinvestment income is $0.20 on an initial investment of $100. To project the price of the bond at the end of the horizon, a pricing model is needed.

The way in which the one-year realized returns on a security depend on changes in interest rates over the year is illustrated in Figure 1. For simplicity, it is assumed throughout this article that interest rate shifts are represented by parallel movements of the yield curve. The realized returns are computed for the Treasury strip maturing on 08/15/1997 and the Associates Corp. 7⅝s maturing on 04/15/1998. Over one year, the dominant component of the realized return is the terminal value, so that the return on both bonds is high when rates fall and low when they rise.

The ten-year realized returns on the same two bonds under various interest rate shifts are shown in Figure 2. The strip matures in ten years and so has a constant return over that period. The return on the corporate bond is higher under rising rates than falling ones, because cash flow and reinvestment income now dominate the realized return.

For any particular time period, an expected (probability-weighted average) return may be computed for each security by assigning probabilities to the scenarios considered. This measure indicates the average return that one may expect to earn on that asset across all interest rate scenarios.

FIGURE 2. *Ten-Year Realized Returns.*

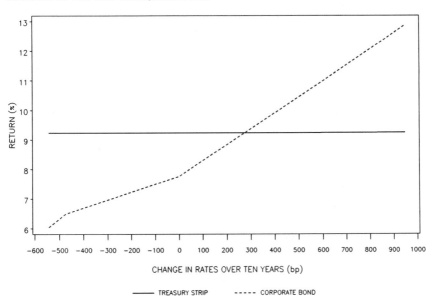

Required Return

Required return (RQ) refers to the investor's target return. Like realized return, a required return also depends on a particular scenario of interest rates and is computed for a particular period of time. An expected required return for any time period is computed in similar fashion to an expected realized return.

Required returns vary among investors, depending on needs and preferences. For pension funds and other investors funding liabilities, they are derived from the structure of the liability schedule. For active managers seeking to maximize return, they may be computed from the expected return on a benchmark portfolio such as an index. Alternatively, an investor can choose in each scenario an acceptable level of return and use that as the target.

In the context of liability funding, the required return can be computed in an analogous manner to realized return. The parallel components are listed below.

1. *Funds available:* The amount available to purchase the funding portfolio.
2. *Cash outflow:* The total cash flow to be paid out over the period.
3. *Borrowing cost:* This is the converse of reinvestment income. For convenience, any cash flows occurring during the period can be assumed

to be offset by short-term borrowing until the end of the period. This component represents the interest paid on the borrowing.

4. *Terminal amount:* This is the amount that must be available at the end of the period to fund the remaining liabilities. It may be computed as either the present value of future cash flows or the actuarially equivalent lump-sum amount.

The required return is computed as:

$$RQ = \left(\frac{\text{Cash outflow} + \text{Borrowing cost} + \text{Terminal Amount}}{\text{Funds Available}} \right) - 1.$$

Table 3 provides an example of this computation for the purpose of liability funding.

The one-year required returns for two kinds of liabilities under different interest rate scenarios are shown in Figure 3. The first liability considered is a retired lives benefits schedule for a pension fund. In this case, the cash outflows are generally independent of interest rate movements, since the only uncertain element is the mortality rate. For this schedule, required returns vary across scenarios because of differences in the present value of the future liabilities and the borrowing rates.

The second liability shown is a Single Premium Deferred Annuity (SPDA) issued by an insurance company. In this case, the cash outflows themselves are path dependent because of the presence of several option features. The policyholder has the option to withdraw the investment at any time and the insurance company has the option to set the rate at which accounts will be credited. Such liabilities are termed interest sensitive.[2]

---

2. For a description of SPDA features, see the Drexel Burnham research report "Single Premium Deferred Annuity: Product and Risk Considerations," by Prakash A. Shimpi, March 1987.

TABLE 3. *Required Return Calculation.*

Funds available	= $100 million
Cash outflow (at end of year)	= $ 5 million[a]
Borrowing cost	= 0[a]
Terminal amount (present value of liability at end of year)	= $110 million[a]
Total estimated liability at end of year	= $115 million

Required return = ($115 million/$100 million) − 1 = 15%.

---

a. Projected value.

FIGURE 3. *One-Year Required Returns.*

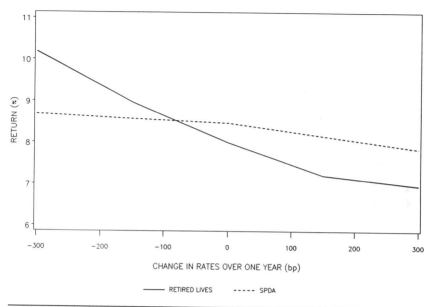

The one-year required returns for the SPDA are high in all interest rate scenarios because the crediting rate is normally guaranteed for an initial period of up to five years. For the retired lives pension schedule, the required returns are high in falling rate scenarios and lower in rising ones. This is because the terminal value, measured as the present value of future benefits, is higher when rates fall and is the dominant component of the one-year return.

The ten-year required returns for both sets of liabilities are shown in Figure 4. As with the asset returns, these returns are higher when rates rise. This is because the cash outflows are paramount in the return computation.

Specification of the Targets

The path dependency of returns requires that a scenario-based approach be used to project realized and required returns over future time periods. Since the goal is to control interest rate risk, these scenarios are characterized in terms of future interest rate environments. Each interest rate environment is defined by the sequence of forward rates underlying the Treasury yield curve. Probabilities are assigned to each scenario to facilitate computation of averages for return and risk across all scenarios.

FIGURE 4. *Ten-Year Required Returns.*

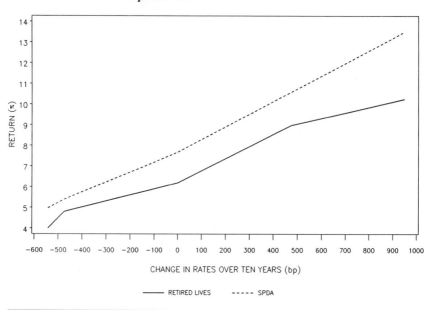

The investor's targets are defined by the required returns over specified scenarios and specified periods of time. Theoretically, all possible interest rate scenarios and all possible periods of time may be of interest. As a practical matter, the number of scenarios and time periods of concern must be reduced. Some of the considerations involved in choosing scenarios and time periods are mentioned below.

Choice of Time Periods   The strategy can cater to different investment horizons on the part of the investor. For example, a pension fund with long liabilities may have a long horizon, such as over ten years. However, the fund also may be concerned with returns over a shorter time period such as one year, possibly due to liquidity requirements.

In general, the investor should attempt to identify time periods which are risky and others which are of concern. For example, for the SPDA liabilities mentioned earlier, the high one-year required returns imply that the first year is a risky period in rising rate environments. For most investors, a combination of a short term, an intermediate term and a long term (for example, 1, 3 and 10 years) may be adequate.

Definition of Scenarios   The scenarios considered do not necessarily have to be specified in terms of interest rates. For example, a pension fund may wish to examine the impact on its liabilities of changes in mortality rates or rates of inflation, while a taxable investor may be concerned with after-tax returns under varying tax rates.

Moreover, interest rate scenarios may be defined by the investor in any manner. For example, an interest rate scenario may be defined in terms of parallel shifts of the yield curve or in terms of a particular shape of the yield curve at the horizon date(s).

Choice of Scenarios   An investor either can use a stochastic process such as a binomial model to choose and assign probabilities to interest rate scenarios or consider particular scenarios of concern. The probability of occurrence for each scenario can be tailored to suit a particular investor's preferences. For example, an investor concerned just with rising interest rates may wish to assign a very low probability to falling rate scenarios.

As an example, scenarios over a three-stage period are indicated in Figure 5. They are generated from a binomial process which assumes that, at each stage, rates can go up or down by 100 basis points with equal probability. In this example, each stage is assumed to be one year long and the shift in rates is considered to be a parallel shift in the term structure. Figure 5 also provides an example of the implications of path dependence of returns. The interest rate environments at nodes (5) and (6) are the same but the two points are on different paths and therefore are shown separately.

FIGURE 5. *Interest Rate Scenarios Generated Using a Binomial Process.*

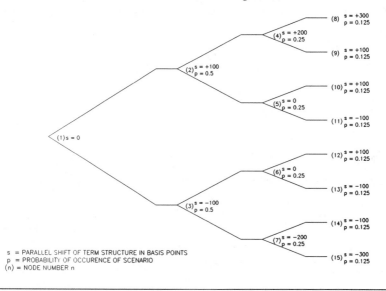

s = PARALLEL SHIFT OF TERM STRUCTURE IN BASIS POINTS
p = PROBABILITY OF OCCURENCE OF SCENARIO
(n) = NODE NUMBER n

Once the targets are defined in terms of required returns, the strategy involves choosing a portfolio that will earn realized returns as close as possible to the profile of required returns. In the most riskless case, this would involve selecting a portfolio that achieves at least the required return in every scenario and for every time period under consideration. It may not be possible to meet these strong conditions. This brings us to one of the most elegant features about RRO—the ability to quantify the risk–return trade-off.

III. Risk Management Using RRO

Choosing the Best Measure of Risk

In trying to achieve a target, risk should refer only to the possibility of not achieving that target. Referring to Figure 6, which again shows the one-year required returns from Figure 3, the risky situations are those in which the realized returns fall short of the required returns. Risk is incurred whenever the realized returns are projected to fall in the shaded region of the diagram, below the required return line.

For such situations, a measure of risk is needed which recognizes that no risk is incurred in situations where the realized returns exceed the required returns. The risk measure proposed is the average downside deviation of the realized returns from the required returns. For comparison purposes, alternative measures of risk are first examined.

FIGURE 6. *Identifying Risk over One Year Using Projected Required Return.*

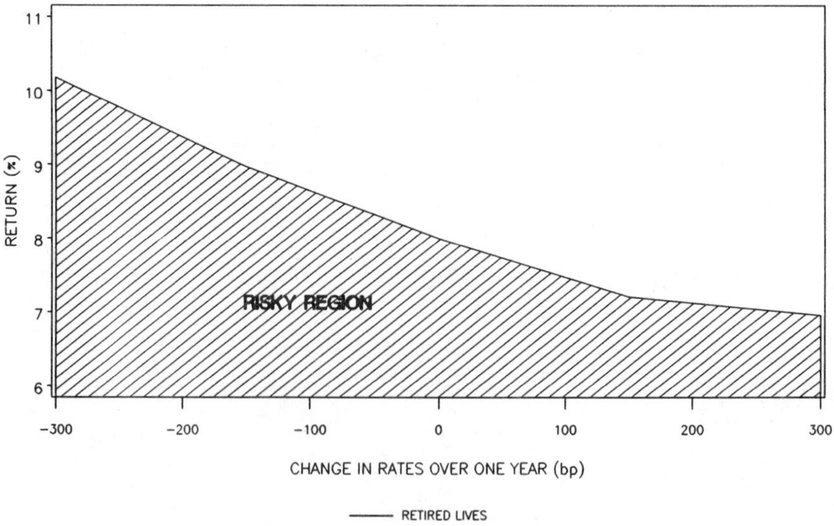

CHANGE IN RATES OVER ONE YEAR (bp)

——— RETIRED LIVES

Standard Deviation about Average Return

Typically, the measure of risk used in portfolio management is the standard deviation of the returns on the portfolio about the expected or average return. This was the measure proposed by Markowitz in the context of efficient portfolio selection and the generation of risk–return frontiers.[3] Such a risk measure implies that the goal of the investor is to earn a constant return regardless of interest rate scenario. The implied required return function is the horizontal line shown in Figure 7. Using the two assets referred to earlier, along with several others, a portfolio X is chosen to minimize this risk measure for an expected return of 8.25%. Figure 8 illustrates the one-year realized returns on this portfolio.

Total Deviation about Required Returns

Figure 7 also shows the required return function considered earlier. In this example, the required returns are also scenario dependent. To facilitate comparison, the expected required return is 8.25% in this case as well. From the figure, it is seen that a portfolio which would earn a constant 8.25% in all scenarios would have no risk in a Markowitz sense, since the average return is always earned. However, it would result in the investor missing the target in falling interest rate scenarios. This is indicated by region 1 in Figure 7.

---

3. See Harry M. Markowitz, "Portfolio Selection," *Journal of Finance* (March 1952): 77–91.

FIGURE 7. *Identifying Risk over One Year Using Implied Required Return.*

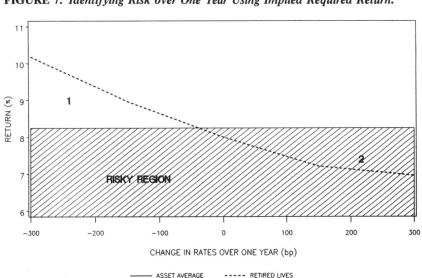

FIGURE 8. *Portfolio X Chosen to Minimize Variance of Returns.*

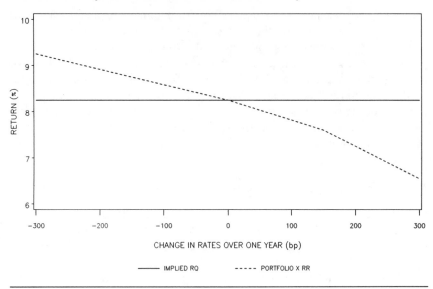

This suggests that a more appropriate measure of risk would be deviation from the required return in each scenario rather than the overall average return. Referring back to Figure 7, a portfolio manager would be willing to surrender some of the gains in the rising rate scenarios (region 2) to cover losses under falling rates (region 1). Minimizing this measure would result in a portfolio with a realized return profile closer to the required returns. Figure 9 shows the one-year realized returns on a portfolio Y which minimizes this measure without regard to the expected return.

Downside Deviation about Required Returns

A measure which minimizes total deviation of realized returns about required returns would consider upside deviations from required returns to be as risky as downside ones. In other words, if in one scenario the required return was 8%, a portfolio which earned 10% would be considered as risky as one which earned 6%. This is inappropriate because all risk has been removed once the target is met. A portfolio which earns a return in excess of the required return should be desired, not shunned. Therefore, the most appropriate measure of risk would be downside deviation from the required returns.

Intuitively, minimizing the total deviation about the required returns results in a portfolio that matches the required return profile as closely as possible, while using downside deviation results in a portfolio that matches or exceeds the required returns. The latter situation is preferred.

FIGURE 9. *Portfolio Y Chosen to Minimize Total Deviation of RR about RQ.*

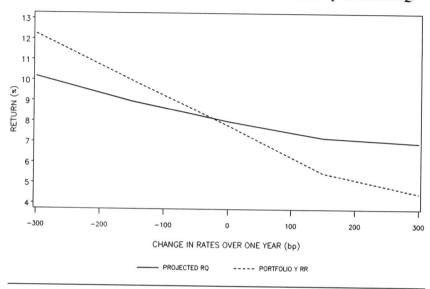

FIGURE 10. *Portfolio Z Chosen to Minimize Downside Deviation of RR about RQ.*

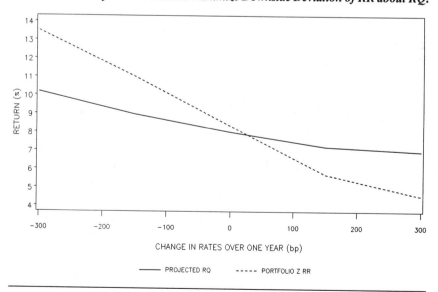

The performance over one year of a portfolio Z is shown in Figure 10. This portfolio minimizes the downside deviation from the required returns for all levels of expected return.

FIGURE 11. *Comparison of Portfolios X, Y and Z.*

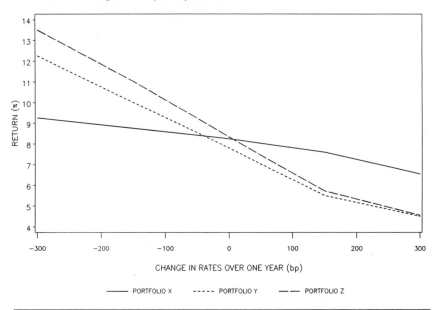

Comparison of the Three Measures

For purposes of comparison, the realized returns of the three portfolios X, Y and Z are illustrated in Figure 11. Portfolio X earns the most stable returns across all scenarios, but does not match the required returns very well. Portfolio Z, which minimizes downside deviation from the required returns, dominates (that is, in each scenario earns higher returns than) portfolio Y, which minimizes total deviation from required returns. This need not always happen. It occurs here because minimizing total deviation penalizes both the upside and the downside equally, whereas minimizing downside deviation penalizes just the downside and allows the upside to be unrestricted. The reverse situation can never happen; that is, the portfolio minimizing total deviation will never dominate in all scenarios the portfolio which minimizes downside deviation.

The Risk–Return Frontier

Now that downside deviation from the required returns is defined as the appropriate measure of risk, the least risky portfolio for any level of expected return can be determined. This generates a risk–return frontier which defines the set of efficient portfolios. A portfolio is said to be efficient if it earns the

FIGURE 12. *Risk–Return Frontier.*

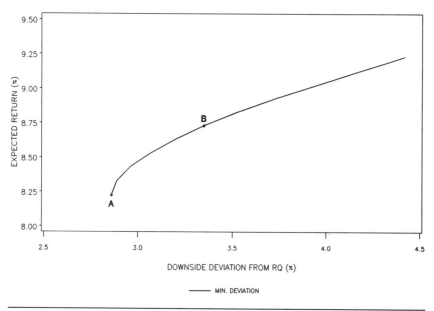

maximum return for any given level of risk. An investor wishing to avoid risk would prefer portfolios on the risk–return frontier to those within it.

A risk–return frontier is shown in Figure 12. All efficient portfolios are on the line representing the frontier. The area below the line indicates portfolios which result in unnecessary risk being incurred. No portfolio would lie in the area above the line because risk cannot be further reduced for any level of expected return. Along the frontier, the risk of not achieving the required returns increases with higher levels of expected return, as the investor trades off higher projected gains in some scenarios with higher projected losses in others.

Given a risk–return frontier for any set of required returns, the investor must choose a preferred level of expected return and find the least risky portfolio for that return from the frontier. By moving along the risk–return frontier, the investor can trade off risk for return in an efficient manner. For example, from Figure 12, portfolio A represents the least risky portfolio for all levels of expected return. An investor wishing to earn a higher return could instead choose portfolio B, which has both a higher return and a higher risk than A. This position is achieved by trading off higher returns in situations where the realized return exceeds the required return against lower returns in situations where the realized return falls short of the target.

Alternative Objectives

One of the biggest advantages of RRO is its flexibility. This adaptivity has already been mentioned in the context of choosing scenarios and time horizons. The strategy is also flexible with regard to the following goals that can be used to choose a portfolio.

1. Minimize risk across some particular scenarios (for example, just the upward sloping scenarios) rather than the entire set of scenarios.
2. Maximize expected return across either the entire set of scenarios or a chosen subset.
3. Maximize the spread earned over the required returns in some or all scenarios. This is particularly appropriate in situations where there is no risk, that is, the required returns are met in all scenarios.

IV. Applications of RRO

Any situation where an investor wishes to maximize total return with control over risk presents a potential application of RRO. The differences in the various situations where it can be applied stem purely from the methods used to determine the required returns. Once the targets are fixed, the strategy adopted is the same.

Below, one application of RRO is presented in detail within the context of liability funding. It is compared to the previously mentioned strategies that are currently used in that context.

Liability Funding

This presents one of the most useful areas for the application of RRO. The strategies currently used — portfolio insurance and immunization — were mentioned previously.

Apart from the problems involved with using modified duration as a tool for risk control when it does not relate to the performance measure, there are other difficulties.

1. Modified duration and convexity are local measures, that is, they are valid only for small changes in interest rates. Furthermore, they are static, since they are computed at a particular point in time. Their values change daily. Continual rebalancing is required to maintain the immunized position. As a result two difficulties arise:
   (a) frequent transactions costs are incurred and
   (b) the portfolio may not be protected against interest rate changes between rebalancings.
2. Modified duration and convexity work effectively only for parallel shifts in the yield curve. Historically, however, the term structure has often experienced changes in slope, with short-term rates being more volatile than long-term ones.

FIGURE 13. *Surplus under Immunization.*

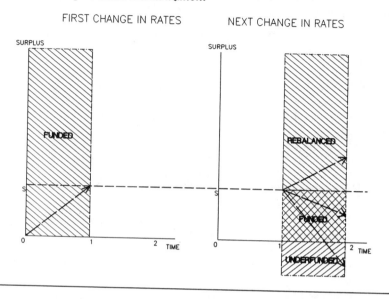

Possible changes in surplus (defined as the market value of the assets less the present value of the liabilities) when interest rates change are shown in Figure 13. Starting from an immunized position at time zero, the first change in rates results in the surplus being in the shaded region, that is, zero or positive. However, this also results in a duration mismatch between the assets and the liabilities and, if the position is not rebalanced, the next change in rates may result in a deficit. In contrast, Figure 14 shows the surplus under RRO as rates change. If both times 1 and 2 are chosen as investment horizons, the realized return will exceed the required return regardless of changes in rates and there will not be a deficit at time 2. In the worst case, if there is some interest rate scenario under which the required return cannot be earned, that situation will be recognized in advance.

The other common funding strategy, portfolio insurance, attempts to protect the return on the portfolio over the short term. As mentioned before, it often relies on using an immunized portfolio as the riskless asset. This exposes the strategy to all the dangers inherent in immunization. Furthermore, frequent market movements can result in high transactions costs.

Interest Sensitive Liabilities

There is a large class of liabilities where immunization breaks down completely because the parameters on which it relies, modified duration and convexity, cannot be computed with sufficient precision. These liabilities are

FIGURE 14. *Surplus under RRO.*

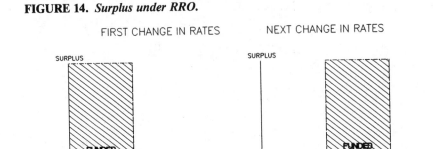

termed interest sensitive because the cash outflows depend on interest rates. They include several insurance company liabilities such as single premium deferred annuities and universal life policies.

Briefly, the estimation of parameters for these liabilities is complicated by the interplay of various option features. The insurance company has the option of choosing a crediting rate to give the policyholder each year and the policyholder has the option to withdraw the entire accumulated investment at any time for a small penalty. Furthermore, there is no market in these liabilities, so that accurate pricing is much more difficult. For such liabilities, RRO provides a very effective solution.

Evaluation of RRO

The key features of RRO that make it appealing for liability funding were introduced in Table 1 and are briefly described below.

1. It ensures that the chosen asset portfolio will be able to meet the liability cash outflows, either through cash flows received from the assets or by liquidating some of the assets. This is because the definitions of realized and required returns include both the cash flows and the present values of the assets or liabilities.

2. For the same reason, RRO ensures that, provided sufficient funds are available initially, the market value of the asset portfolio will at least equal the present value of the liabilities at the specified horizon dates, regardless of interest rate movements.

3. Since RRO is a scenario-based approach, option features on either the asset or liability side are accounted for explicitly. Under each scenario, one can determine when it is optimal to exercise any option. Moreover, when past history is available, as in the case of prepayment rates, one can also account for options being exercised when this seems suboptimal financially.
4. RRO is extremely flexible with respect to the goals and targets of the investor.
   (a) The investor can choose multiple horizons that are of concern in funding the liabilities.
   (b) The strategy allows for diverse shifts in interest rates.
5. RRO explicitly identifies the situations where risk has to be incurred, that is, the interest rate shifts and time horizons where the realized return falls short of the required return. This facilitates the design of optimal hedging strategies.
6. By using an explicit measure of risk, RRO facilitates risk–return trade-offs, along a frontier consisting of a set of efficient portfolios. The measure of risk is based on the investor's targets, which relate directly to the measure of performance.
7. A margin for profit or error can easily be incorporated into the strategy by boosting the required returns. In situations where there is no risk, the strategy can be modified to minimize the risk related to earning a defined profit margin in each scenario.

RRO does have some potential weaknesses.

1. The set of scenarios used may not be sufficiently representative. The goal in choosing scenarios should not be to consider every possible scenario of interest rates but rather to choose a subset that accounts for the likely volatility of future rates. The scenarios should represent extreme shifts.
2. Accurate asset and liability pricing models are necessary for successful implementation, since computing the returns requires the ability to value assets and liabilities under specified interest rate scenarios at future points of time. For the assets, this is not as drastic as it may seem; the same capability is required by any scenario-based option pricing model such as the binomial model. Valuing the liabilities may be more difficult because of the absence of a liquid secondary market.

Another Application: Active Management

By explicitly quantifying the risk–return trade-off, RRO enables the active manager to take properly evaluated positions on interest rates. An investor expecting rates to rise could, for example, choose to maximize return in rising rate scenarios, while ensuring that some floor level would be earned even if the prediction were wrong and rates were to fall instead. Using RRO, the investor could analyze the trade-off between increasing return in rising rate scenarios and risk incurred in falling rate scenarios by constructing a customized risk–return frontier.

For active management, the required returns may be determined either solely on the basis of the investor's preferences or from the expected returns on some benchmark such as a market index.

V. Conclusion

Realized return optimization is a strategy designed to protect total return over any given horizon and under many interest rate scenarios. The key to the strategy is the ability to define the targets in the same terms as the performance measure. The flexibility afforded by the strategy makes it particularly suitable for funding liabilities, especially interest sensitive ones, and for active management.

Strategies presently used for total return maximization tend to rely on modified duration and convexity as tools for risk control. These parameters do not relate directly to the total return on an asset over any particular period of time. In addition to the theoretical difficulties mentioned earlier, it may not be possible to estimate accurately duration and convexity. Interest sensitive liabilities provide an example of such a situation.[4]

A scenario-based approach can be an improvement over conventional portfolio selection techniques because interest sensitivity can be captured explicitly, rather than summarized by two parameters. RRO goes one step further by defining the investor's targets in terms of total returns and using these targets to compute a measure of risk. This enables it to determine the most efficient manner in which to achieve the targets. It is therefore a very powerful and practical tool for risk management in total return maximization.

---

4. Detailed examples of the application of RRO are provided in "Funding SPDA Liabilities: An Application of Realized Return Optimization," by Llewellyn Miller, Prakash A. Shimpi, and Uday Rajan, and "Optimal Funding of Guaranteed Investment Contracts," by Llewellyn Miller and Nancy Roth in Frank J. Fabozzi (ed.), *Fixed Income Portfolio Strategies* (Chicago: Probus Publishing, 1989).

29

Treasury Bond Behavior at the Long End:
Implications for Hedging and Spread Trading

Laurie S. Goodman*
Vice President
Financial Strategies Group
Fixed Income Division
Goldman Sachs & Co.

Joseph Snailer*
Vice President
Capital Markets Assurance Corp.

Raj Daryanani
Associate
Fixed Income Research
Citicorp North American
    Investment Bank

I. Introduction

The behavior of long Treasury bonds is perplexing: when the bond market rallies, pre-1985 30-year bonds, which are callable, appear to become more valuable relative to newer non-callable 30-year bonds, just the opposite of how the call feature should affect their value. After careful consideration, it appears that this occurs because long bonds (except for the most recent issues) have relative price movements that reflect their CBT factors rather than the value of the embedded call.

This behavior has dramatic implications for trading and hedging long Treasury bonds. In particular, CBT factor weighting is appropriate for both spread trading and hedging one long bond with another.

II. The Paradox

One can think of a callable bond as a combination of a non-callable bond and a call option. That is:

$$\text{callable bond} = \text{non-callable bond} - \text{call option}.$$

*Laurie Goodman and Joe Snailer were vice presidents of the Capital Markets Analysis Unit of Citicorp North American Investment Bank when this article was written.

FIGURE 1. *Treasury 14 of 11/15/2011 (06) versus 10-5/8 of 8/15/2015 (Weekly, 23 August 1985 to 20 March 1987).*

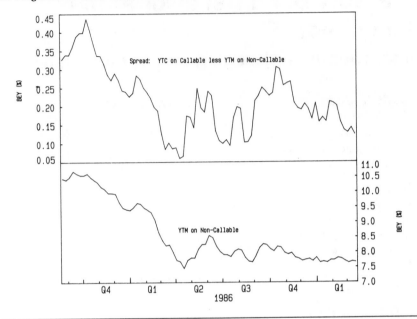

When interest rates fall, the value of the non-callable bond and the value of the call option both rise.[1] Consequently, the price of the callable bond should rise less than the non-callable bond due to the rise in the value of the option the bond holder has written. This suggests that yields to maturity on callable bonds should decline less than yields to maturity on comparable coupon non-callable bonds. That is, yield spreads (callable less non-callable) on a yield to maturity basis should widen as yields fall. It should be noted that if the option is very deep in-the-money, the callable bond essentially behaves as if its maturity date is the call date. In this case, the yield to call on the callable bond should move equally with the yield to maturity on the comparable coupon non-callable bond. But, in fact, yield spreads narrow significantly as rates fall (see Figure 1).

Suppose, however, that the market behaves as if all old 30-year issues have relative price movements that reflect their relative CBT factors (that is,

---

1. The mechanics are described in more detail in Laurie S. Goodman, "Callable Treasury Bonds: Profitable Arbitrage at the Long End," Capital Markets Analysis Unit, Citicorp Investment Bank, September 26, 1986.

TABLE 1.

Initial Interest Rate Scenario

Price of non-callable 10⅝ of 2015 at 7.70 yield	133.54
Price of hypothetical non-callable 14 of 2011 at 7.70 yield	169.09
Price of call option, exercisable in 2006 at par (volatility = 6.5%)	6.70
Price of callable 14 of 2011	162.39
Yield to call of 14 of 2011	7.76
Price spread between 14 of 2011 and 10⅝ of 2015	28.85
Yield spread: YTC on 14 of 2011 less YTM on 10⅝ of 2015	0.06

Interest Rates on 10⅝ Fall by 20 Basis Points

Price of 10⅝ at 7.50 yield	136.51
Price of callable 14 of 2011 assuming prices move by relative factors[a]	166.05
Yield to call of callable 14 of 2011	7.52
Price spread between 14 of 2011 and 10⅝ of 2015	29.54
Yield spread: YTC on 14 of 2011 less YTM on 10⅝ of 2015	0.02

Interest Rates on 10⅝ Rise by 20 Basis Points

Price of 10⅝ of 12 at 7.90 yield	130.66
Price of callable 14 of 2011 assuming prices move by relative factors[a]	158.86
Yield on callable 14 of 2011	8.00
Price spread between 14 of 2011 and 10⅝ of 2015	28.20
Yield spread: YTC on 14 of 2011 less YTM on 10⅝ of 2015	0.10

a. The factor on the 14 of 2011 is 1.5875, while the factor on the 10⅝ of 2015 is 1.2921.

the delivery factors on the bond futures contract).[2] In this case, when the market rallies, prices on the high coupon callable bonds rise more than their lower coupon, non-callable counterparts because their factors are higher. Under this assumption, yield spreads narrow when rates fall.

Table 1 shows an example that will highlight this point. Looking at the prices of the 14 of 2011, callable in 2006, and the non-callable 10⅝ of 2015 and assuming the yield curve is flat at 7.70 between 2006 and 2015, the yield spread is 6 basis points between the two bonds. As the market rallies (rates fall by 20 basis points) and the bond prices move by their relative factors, the yield spread will narrow to 2 basis points. As the market tanks (rates rise by 20 basis points) and the bond prices move by their relative factors, the yield spread will widen to 10 basis points.

2. CBT factors are described in detail in Arak et al., "The Cheapest to Deliver Bond on the Treasury Bond Futures Contract," Capital Markets Analysis Unit, Citicorp Investment Bank, May 15, 1985.

Thus, *if* the market behaves as if relative price movements are determined by relative CBT factors, the perplexing behavior of long bonds would be explained. We now show empirically that the long bond market does, in fact, trade according to CBT factors.

III. Market Behavior and Hedge Ratios

To compare the actual price movement of one bond with another, we ran a regression of the price changes of the bond to be hedged against the price changes of the bond to be used as the hedging instrument. The regression equation takes the following form:

$$\Delta P_i = a + b\Delta P_j + \tilde{e}$$

where:

ΔP_i = change in price of security i, the bond to be hedged;
ΔP_j = change in price of security j, the bond being used as the hedging instrument;
a, b = regression coefficients;
$\tilde{e}$ = error term.

The estimated value of the regression coefficient b is the hedge ratio.

Table 2 contains hedge ratios for twelve long bonds, both callable and non-callable. For example, suppose we want to hedge the 14 of 2011 with the 10⅝ of 2015. Thus, we use the "14 of 2011" row and the "10⅝ of 2015" column in Table 2. The hedge ratio based on the regression results is the first number in the square −1.27. Alternately, if one simply weighted by the relative CBT factors, the hedge ratio would have been 1.23 (the second entry in the square). This is simply the factor on the 14 of 2011 (1.5875) divided by the factor on the 10⅝ of 2015 (1.2921).

As you can see, with the possible exception of the 7¼ of 2016, the 7½ of 2016, and the 9¼ of 2016 − the active issues over the past year − the regression hedge ratios are very close to the factor hedge ratios. For example, the regression hedge ratio between the 10⅜ of 2012 and the 10⅝ of 2015 was .95, exactly the same as the factor hedge ratio, while the regression hedge ratio between the 12 of 2013 and the 9⅞ of 2015 was 1.20 versus a factor hedge ratio of 1.16.

An alternative way of constructing hedge ratios is to ask what would happen to relative price movements if interest rates on the two bonds experienced the same yield change. This corresponds to a view of the world in which yield spreads should be unresponsive to changes in the level of interest rates. That is, since most of the callable bonds are so deep in-the-money that they behave as non-callable (but shorter maturity) bonds, the yield spread of a callable bond's yield to call vis-à-vis the yield to maturity on a non-callable bond should remain constant.

The constant yield spread hedge ratio can be formed by recognizing:

$$\Delta P_i = 1/(YV_i\ 32)$$
$$\Delta P_j = 1/(YV_j\ 32)$$
$$\Delta P_i/\Delta P_j = (YV_j\ 32)/(YV_i\ 32)$$

where $YV_i\ 32$ is the yield value of a 32nd for bond i. Thus, if you want to use the 10⅝ of 2015 to hedge the 14 of 2011, the constant yield spread hedge ratio would be (.2131)/(.2151) or .99.

The constant yield spread hedge ratios are reported in Table 2 as the third entry in each square. As you can see, the constant yield spread hedge ratio in our example, .99, is quite different from the regression hedge ratio of 1.27. Results for other hedges reported in Table 2 are similar—CBT factor hedge ratios more closely match the regression hedge ratios than the hedge ratios based on YV 32s.

The implication of this for hedging is clear—for the purposes of hedging one long bond with another, one should use factor weights rather than YV 32 weights.

IV. Implications for Spread Trading

The relative CBT factor weights used for hedging one long bond with another should also be used when spread trading long bonds. If you believe that spreads are misaligned in some relative sense but you don't have a view about the general direction of rates, then you would want to put on a spread trade that would profit from a realignment of rates but would not be dependent upon market direction. Weighting by relative factors—which we have just shown more accurately reflect actual relative price movements than YV 32 weights—would achieve this.

For example, suppose you thought the 12.4 basis point (b.p.) spread prevailing on March 20, 1987 between the 14 of 2011 and the 10⅝ of 2015 was too narrow. Then, since the weight based on relative factors is 1.23, you should buy five 10⅝ of 2015 bonds for each four 14 of 2011 bonds that you sell. (Note that the weight based on historical movements is 1.27 while the YV 32 weight is .99.) With this factor weighted trade, a widening (narrowing) of 1 b.p. per 5 b.p. rise (fall) in rates is treated as "normal". The trade works if, when rates rise, the spread widens by more than 1 b.p. for each 5 b.p. rise in rates or, when rates decline, the spread narrows less than 1 b.p. for each 5 b.p. change in rates.

It is somewhat difficult to identify a relative spread misalignment when looking at a factor weighted trade. One identification method which we have

TABLE 2. *Hedge Ratios on Long Bonds, 3/14/86–3/16/87 (explanatory series).*

Response Series	Factor YV 1/32	14.000% Nov–2011 1.5875 0.2151	10.375% Nov–2012 1.2216 0.2541	12.000% Aug–2013 1.4053 0.2275	13.250% May–2014 1.5394 0.2083	13.875% May–2011 1.5689 0.2201
14.000%	Nov–2011		1.31	1.10	1.03	1.03
	1.5875		1.30	1.13	1.03	1.01
	0.2151		1.18	1.06	0.97	1.02
10.375%	Nov–2012	0.73		0.82	0.77	0.75
	1.2216	0.77		0.87	0.79	0.78
	0.2541	0.85		0.90	0.82	0.87
12.000%	Aug–2013	0.88	1.18		0.92	0.90
	1.4053	0.89	1.15		0.91	0.90
	0.2275	0.95	1.12		0.92	0.97
13.250%	May–2014	0.94	1.26	1.05		0.97
	1.5394	0.97	1.26	1.10		0.98
	0.2083	1.03	1.22	1.09		1.06
13.875%	May–2011	0.97	1.27	1.07	1.00	
	1.5689	0.99	1.28	1.12	1.02	
	0.2201	0.98	1.15	1.03	0.95	
12.500%	Aug–2014	0.90	1.20	1.00	0.95	0.92
	1.4640	0.92	1.20	1.04	0.95	0.93
	0.2156	1.00	1.18	1.06	0.97	1.02
11.250%	Feb–2015	0.79	1.07	0.89	0.83	0.82
	1.3599	0.86	1.11	0.97	0.88	0.87
	0.2056	1.05	1.24	1.11	1.01	1.07
10.625%	Aug–2015	0.74	1.00	0.84	0.78	0.77
	1.2921	0.81	1.06	0.92	0.84	0.82
	0.2131	1.01	1.19	1.07	0.98	1.03
9.875%	Nov–2015	0.71	0.96	0.80	0.74	0.73
	1.2093	0.76	0.99	0.86	0.79	0.77
	0.2245	0.96	1.13	1.01	0.93	0.98
9.250%	Feb–2016	0.60	0.82	0.68	0.64	0.62
	1.1396	0.72	0.93	0.81	0.74	0.73
	0.2335	0.92	1.09	0.97	0.89	0.94
7.250%	May–2016	0.51	0.69	0.57	0.53	0.52
	0.9159	0.58	0.75	0.65	0.59	0.58
	0.2743	0.78	0.93	0.83	0.76	0.80
7.500%	Nov–2016	0.48	0.70	0.58	0.51	0.49
	0.9437	0.59	0.77	0.67	0.61	0.60
	0.2649	0.81	0.96	0.86	0.79	0.83

a. Calculations are based on daily 3 P.M. price quotes.

12.500% Aug−2014 1.4640 0.2156	11.250% Feb−2015 1.3599 0.2056	10.625% Aug−2015 1.2921 0.2131	9.875% Nov−2015 1.2093 0.2245	9.250% Feb−2016 1.1396 0.2335	7.250% May−2016 0.9159 0.2743	7.500% Nov−2016 0.9437 0.2649
1.07	1.20	1.27	1.34	1.45	1.78	1.90
1.08	1.17	1.23	1.31	1.39	1.73	1.68
1.00	0.96	0.99	1.04	1.09	1.28	1.23
0.80	0.90	0.95	1.01	1.10	1.32	1.34
0.83	0.90	0.95	1.01	1.07	1.33	1.29
0.85	0.81	0.84	0.88	0.92	1.08	1.04
0.96	1.07	1.14	1.20	1.31	1.58	1.62
0.96	1.03	1.09	1.16	1.23	1.53	1.49
0.95	0.90	0.94	0.99	1.03	1.21	1.16
1.03	1.15	1.21	1.28	1.40	1.70	1.80
1.05	1.13	1.19	1.27	1.35	1.68	1.63
1.04	0.99	1.02	1.08	1.12	1.32	1.27
1.04	1.16	1.23	1.30	1.41	1.72	1.86
1.07	1.15	1.21	1.30	1.38	1.71	1.66
0.98	0.93	0.97	1.02	1.06	1.25	1.20
	1.10	1.16	1.22	1.34	1.61	1.64
	1.08	1.13	1.21	1.28	1.60	1.55
	0.95	0.99	1.04	1.08	1.27	1.23
0.87		1.04	1.10	1.20	1.45	1.36
0.93		1.05	1.12	1.19	1.48	1.44
1.05		1.04	1.09	1.14	1.33	1.29
0.81	0.92		1.03	1.13	1.37	1.32
0.88	0.95		1.07	1.13	1.41	1.37
1.01	0.96		1.05	1.10	1.29	1.24
0.77	0.88	0.93		1.08	1.30	1.28
0.83	0.89	0.94		1.06	1.32	1.28
0.96	0.92	0.95		1.04	1.22	1.18
0.66	0.75	0.80	0.85		1.16	1.13
0.78	0.84	0.88	0.94		1.24	1.21
0.92	0.88	0.91	0.96		1.17	1.13
0.55	0.63	0.66	0.71	0.79		0.95
0.63	0.67	0.71	0.76	0.80		0.97
0.79	0.75	0.78	0.82	0.85		0.97
0.56	0.69	0.71	0.74	0.83	1.00	
0.64	0.69	0.73	0.78	0.83	1.03	
0.81	0.78	0.80	0.85	0.88	1.04	

found useful is to look at the average yield and average spread over, say, the past 3 or 6 months. Essentially, this methodology assumes that yield spreads have been "correctly" priced on average over the past 3 or 6 months. Today's correct (or predicted) yield spread should not be simply the average yield spread over the past 3 or 6 months, but this average spread adjusted for the level of yields. That is, if prices move by their factors, we know a fall in yields will cause yield spreads to narrow. If actual yield spreads are lower than would be expected by this occurrence alone, a realignment in the future may be suggested. Thus, if you put on a factor weighted trade, it would allow you to take advantage of a relative realignment without taking a bet on market direction.

This method can be illustrated more clearly by means of an example. Say we have the following 3- and 6-month history:

	Average Yield (past 3 months)	Average Yield (past 6 months)
14 of 2011	7.868	7.984
10⅝ of 2015	7.711	7.805
Yield Spread	15.7 b.p.	17.9 b.p.

On March 20, 1987 the yield on the 14 of 2011 was 7.80, which was 6.8 basis points below the mean for the past 3 months of 7.868. Since factor weighting relates to relative prices we must translate this yield differential into a price differential:

$$\frac{\text{price differential}}{\text{on 14 of 2011}} = \frac{\text{yield differential}}{\text{on 14 of 2011}} \times \frac{1}{\text{YV 32 on 14 of 2011}}. \quad (1)$$

The price differential on the 10⅝ of 2015 consistent with the relative factor pricing scenario is calculated by:

$$\frac{\text{price differential}}{\text{on 10⅝ of 2015}} = \frac{\dfrac{\text{price differential}}{\text{on 14 of 2011}}}{\text{hedge ratio}}$$

$$= \frac{\text{price differential}}{\text{on 14 of 2011}} \times \frac{\text{factor on 10⅝ of 2015}}{\text{factor on 14 of 2011}}. \quad (2)$$

The yield differential on the 10⅝ of 2015 can be calculated as follows:

$$\frac{\text{yield differential}}{\text{on 10⅝ of 2015}} = \frac{\text{price differential}}{\text{on 10⅝ of 2015}} \times \frac{\text{YV 32 on}}{\text{10⅝ of 2015}}. \quad (3)$$

The differential in the yield spread from its average would be given by:

$$\frac{\text{yield spread}}{\text{differential}} = \frac{\text{yield differential}}{\text{on 14 of 2011}} - \frac{\text{yield differential}}{\text{on 10⅝ of 2015}}. \quad (4)$$

Substituting (1), (2) and (3) into (4) we get:

$$\text{yield spread differential} = \text{yield differential on 14 of 2011} \times \left[1 - \frac{\text{factor on } 10\tfrac{5}{8} \text{ of 2015}}{\text{factor on 14 of 2011}} \times \frac{\text{YV 32 on } 10\tfrac{5}{8} \text{ of 2015}}{\text{YV 32 on 14 of 2011}}\right]. \quad \text{(4a)}$$

Plugging actual values (from Table 2) into equation (4a):

$$\text{yield spread differential} = -6.8 \times \left(1 - \frac{1.2921}{1.5875} \times \frac{.2131}{.2151}\right) = -1.3.$$

Finally, the yield spread between the 14 of 2011 and the 10⅝ of 2015 consistent with the relative pricing scenario can be obtained by adding the average yield spread to the yield spread differential:

$$\begin{aligned} \text{predicted yield spread} &= \text{average yield spread} + \text{yield spread differential} \\ &= 15.7 - 1.3 \\ &= 14.4 \text{ b.p.} \end{aligned}$$

Remember that the actual spread was 12.4 basis points. Thus, it would have been reasonable to bet that the spread would widen.

Table 3 was constructed using this methodology to identify misalignments. The example given above can be found in the top part of the table: the predicted spread for the 14 of 2011 versus the 10⅝ of 2015 using a three month average is 14.3 b.p., while the actual spread is 12.4 b.p.; the predicted spread based on the six month average is 14.4. Another example shows the spread between the 10⅜ of 2012 and the 10⅝ of 2015 was 6.5 b.p. on March 20, very close to the 6.9 b.p. predicted spread based on the three month average.

Table 3, like any analysis based on historical trading relationships, must be carefully interpreted to allow for structural changes. For example, when the 7¼ of 2016 was reopened, the spread between the 9¼ of 2016 and the 9⅞ of 2015 collapsed. Thus, average spreads over the past 3 months between high coupon callable bonds and the 9¼ of 2016 (which are shown in the bottom half of Table 3) are higher than they should be based on this structural change. The predicted spreads are biased upwards, indicating opportunities when, in all likelihood, none exist.

Nonetheless, a table such as Table 3 can be valuable in indicating good spread trading opportunities. For example, on February 6, 1987, the yield to call on the 10⅜ of 2012 was 7.79 and the yield to maturity on the 10⅝ of 2015 was 7.69, resulting in a spread of 10 basis points. On that same date, the 3-month and 6-month predicted spreads were 7.0 and 6.0 basis points, respectively. Hence, expecting a narrowing of the spread, you could have sold short $10,000,000 par of the 10⅝ at 133:20 and bought $10,000,000 par

TABLE 3. *Callable and Non-Callable Long Bond Spread Analysis, 3/20/87.*

Callable Issue	Relative Factor	Average Yield	Average Spread	Today's Yield	Predicted Spread	Actual Spread
Callable Issues Vis à Vis 10.625 – 8/15/15 (3-Month Averages)						
12.750 – 11/15/10	0.8898	7.855	14.3	7.796	13.1	12.0
13.875 – 5/15/11	0.8251	7.867	15.5	7.797	14.1	12.0
14.000 – 11/15/11	0.8154	7.868	15.7	7.800	14.3	12.4
10.375 – 11/15/12	1.0577	7.787	7.5	7.741	6.9	6.5
12.000 – 8/15/13	0.9201	7.842	13.1	7.792	12.4	11.5
13.250 – 5/15/14	0.8404	7.872	16.0	7.811	15.2	13.5
12.500 – 8/15/14	0.8833	7.859	14.8	7.796	14.0	12.0
11.750 – 11/15/14	0.9315	7.787	7.6	7.756	7.2	8.0
Callable Issues Vis à Vis 10.625 – 8/15/15 (6-Month Averages)						
12.750 – 11/15/10	0.8898	7.964	15.9	7.796	12.6	12.0
13.875 – 5/15/11	0.8251	7.982	17.7	7.797	14.0	12.0
14.000 – 11/15/11	0.8154	7.984	17.9	7.800	14.4	12.4
10.375 – 11/15/12	1.0577	7.889	8.4	7.741	6.6	6.5
12.000 – 8/15/13	0.9201	7.954	14.9	7.792	12.6	11.5
13.250 – 5/15/14	0.8404	7.987	18.2	7.811	15.7	13.5
12.500 – 8/15/14	0.8833	7.974	16.9	7.796	14.6	12.0
11.750 – 11/15/14	0.9315	7.889	8.4	7.756	7.0	8.0
Callable Issues Vis à Vis 9.250 – 2/15/16 (3-Month Averages)						
12.750 – 11/15/10	0.7850	7.855	21.7	7.796	20.3	15.9
13.875 – 5/15/11	0.7280	7.867	22.9	7.797	21.3	16.0
14.000 – 11/15/11	0.7194	7.868	23.0	7.800	21.5	16.3
10.375 – 11/15/12	0.9329	7.787	14.9	7.741	14.2	10.5
12.000 – 8/15/13	0.8118	7.842	20.4	7.792	19.6	15.5
13.250 – 5/15/14	0.7415	7.872	23.4	7.811	22.4	17.4
12.500 – 8/15/14	0.7793	7.859	22.1	7.796	21.2	15.9
11.750 – 11/15/14	0.8218	7.787	14.9	7.756	14.5	11.9
Callable Issues Vis à Vis 9.250 – 2/15/16 (6-Month Averages)						
12.750 – 11/15/10	0.7850	7.964	27.2	7.796	23.5	15.9
13.875 – 5/15/11	0.7280	7.982	29.1	7.797	24.9	16.0
14.000 – 11/15/11	0.7194	7.984	29.2	7.800	25.2	16.3
10.375 – 11/15/12	0.9329	7.889	19.7	7.741	17.5	10.5
12.000 – 8/15/13	0.8118	7.954	26.2	7.792	23.5	15.5
13.250 – 5/15/14	0.7415	7.987	29.5	7.811	26.6	17.4
12.500 – 8/15/14	0.7793	7.974	28.2	7.796	25.5	15.9
11.750 – 11/15/14	0.8218	7.889	19.7	7.756	17.9	11.9

of the 10⅜ at 126:12.[3] On March 12, the yield to call on the 10⅜ had narrowed to 7.74 while the yield to maturity on the 10⅝ was unchanged at 7.69, result-

---

3. Note the relative factor weight was 1.0577, close enough to 1 to justify an equal par weighted trade.

ing in a spread of 5 basis points. In addition, the relative factor model had 3-month and 6-month predicted spreads of 6.9 and 6.5 basis points, respectively, indicating that the trade should be unwound. This would have been accomplished by buying the 10⅝ at 133:25 and selling the 10⅜ at 126:27. The profit on this trade, net of financing costs, would have been about $26,000.

V. A Caveat: Hedging Long Bonds with Bond Futures

It is interesting to note that while the cash bonds move relative to each other by their CBT factors, they generally move less relative to futures prices than their factors would indicate. Table 4 shows the movement on long bond prices relative to futures prices over the recent past as well as their factors.[4] Note that for all bonds over most periods the relative price movement is less than would be dictated by the factor. Some of these overstatements are minor—the 14 of 2011 has a factor of 1.5875 as compared to the 1.53 result during the 2/16/87 to 3/16/87 time period. However, a number of the mismatches are quite large. For example, the 1.2921 factor for the 10⅝ of 2015 significantly overstates the 1.02 result over the 9/16/86 to 3/16/87 time period.

Thus, if you are to use bond futures to hedge bonds for short time periods, you should buy or sell fewer bond futures than the factor dictates. You

---

4. These calculations are based on daily closing future prices and 3:00 P.M. cash prices.

TABLE 4. *Movements of Long Bond Prices Relative to Bond Futures.*

	14 Mar 86 to 16 Mar 87	16 Sep 86 to 16 Mar 87	16 Dec 86 to 16 Mar 87	16 Feb 87 to 16 Mar 87	Factor
14.000 – 2011	1.32	1.43	1.58	1.53	1.5875
10.375 – 2012	1.01	1.02	1.13	1.13	1.2216
12.000 – 2013	1.19	1.22	1.33	1.36	1.4053
13.250 – 2014	1.27	1.31	1.55	1.64	1.5394
13.875 – 2011	1.29	1.37	1.55	1.49	1.5689
12.500 – 2014	1.21	1.23	1.41	1.60	1.4640
11.250 – 2015	1.08	1.07	1.18	1.24	1.3599
10.625 – 2015	1.02	1.02	1.11	1.13	1.2921
9.875 – 2015	0.96	0.98	1.07	1.05	1.2093
9.250 – 2016	0.83	0.86	0.94	0.95	1.1396
7.250 – 2016		0.73	0.77	0.77	0.9159
7.500 – 2016			0.80	0.76	0.9437

Calculations are based on daily closing futures prices and 3 P.M. cash prices.

would probably want to use a hedge ratio based on the past 3 or 6 months of experience.

VI. Conclusion

This article has established that long Treasury bond cash prices move roughly in proportion to their relative CBT factors. This has important implications for both hedging and spread trading. One should hedge one cash bond with another by the factor based weights. For hedging a cash bond with futures, however, the factor weight will result in an over-hedged position. For spread or basis trading between long bonds one should decide at the outset whether or not the trade is to be made independent of market direction. If so, factor weighting is appropriate.

30

The Relative Value of Floating Rate Notes

Laurie S. Goodman
Vice President
Financial Strategies Group
Fixed Income Division
Goldman Sachs & Co.

Jess B. Yawitz
Vice President
Fixed Income Division
Goldman Sachs & Co.

I. Development of the Floater Market

The floating-rate note (FRN) is one of many financial products spawned in the 1970s in response to the dramatic increase in interest rate volatility. In this environment the attributes of FRNs are of interest to both investors and issuers. For *investors* the prices of these securities are relatively insensitive to changes in general market conditions, since the coupon is set for short periods. At reset the coupon will reflect the new level of market yields. The floating-rate note allows *issuers,* mainly financial institutions, to match the repricing dates and maturities of their assets (longer term floating-rate loans) with similar liabilities. In contrast, fixed-rate financing does not allow for repricing the liabilities, and the short-term debt markets do not guarantee the availability of funds.

These features have spurred rapid growth in the popularity of FRNs. Outstanding issues in the domestic market total approximately $23 billion. Outstanding issues in the Euromarket exceed $150 billion.

Despite the large volume of FRNs outstanding, valuation of these securities is generally not well understood. Traditional methods of floating-rate analysis do not allow comparisons of relative value between floating-rate instruments of different maturities or between floating-rate and fixed-rate instruments. In this article we develop a way to value the price of an FRN relative to another instrument. In essence, we combine the note with other financial products (swaps, zeros, and annuities) to design a synthetic security with cash flows similar to those of the comparison instrument.

Our method, explained in Section IV, involves decomposing an FRN into two components: a par floating-rate instrument and a *credit annuity*. Section V explains how to compute the value of these securities relative to other floaters and to fixed-rate instruments. We show that the credit annuity plays a crucial role in the calculation of relative value.

Before presenting our approach to valuation, however, we describe the characteristics and variations of floating-rate instruments and then examine traditional methods of valuing these securities.[1]

II. The Nature of Floating-Rate Instruments

An FRN is a debt instrument with a coupon that is reset periodically at a margin over a benchmark interest rate, such as the Treasury-bill rate or the London Interbank Offered Rate (LIBOR).

Investors and Issuers

Market participants often view the use of floating-rate debt as nearly equivalent to the employment of a rollover strategy using short-term debt. From the standpoint of both investors and borrowers, however, floaters are preferable to the rollover strategy because they entail lower transaction costs. FRNs also have advantages over the traditional fixed-rate bond for some investors and borrowers, as listed below.

Advantages to Investors of FRNs

1. Buying an FRN versus rolling over short-term debt:
   a. With an FRN the investor need purchase only one security rather than a series of securities at regular intervals.
   b. Floating-rate instruments allow an investor to lock in what appears to be good value in credit spreads over long periods. In a rollover strategy the investor locks in the credit spread only for the life of the short-term security.
2. Buying an FRN versus buying a fixed-rate instrument:
   a. Floating-rate instruments have relatively low price sensitivity to fluctuations in the general level of interest rates.
   b. For financial institutions, which tend to be the largest investors, FRNs have the same economic characteristics as floating-rate loans. This makes FRNs convenient securities to incorporate into their asset portfolios.

---

1. Readers familiar with these securities may wish to skip directly to Section III.

Advantages to Borrowers of FRNs

1. Issuing an FRN versus rolling over short-term debt:
   a. The borrower benefits by not incurring the transaction costs from continually rolling over short-term debt.
   b. The borrower is guaranteed a term source of funding. An institution (such as a commercial bank or thrift) that desires the permanence of long-term borrowing but has outflows highly correlated with inflation and interest rates will find floaters particularly attractive.
   c. FRNs allow a borrower to lock in a financial spread relative to the benchmark rate, even if the borrower's actual or perceived credit quality worsens after issuance.
2. Issuing an FRN versus issuing a fixed-rate instrument:
   a. Floating-rate debt allows many institutions to better match fund their existing floating-rate assets.
   b. If the yield curve incorporates a liquidity premium, expected borrowing costs using floating-rate debt will be lower, on average, than those associated with fixed-rate debt of the same maturity.

U.S. financial institutions, especially commercial banks, have been the major issuers in the U.S. domestic FRN market. However, U.S. industrial firms have had a small but noticeable presence (10–15 percent of the market). In the Euromarket U.S. and foreign banks tend to be the major issuers, followed by sovereign borrowers. For sovereign borrowers the FRN market is an alternative to the syndicated loan market. They can sometimes borrow in the FRN market at narrower margins—with more attractive option features—than those they could obtain directly from banks.

Characteristics

An important feature of an FRN is its coupon payment rule. This rule specifies:

1. *The "reference" or base rate to which the FRN is tied.* For U.S. floating-rate instruments, the FRN is generally tied to either the Treasury-bill rate or LIBOR. For Eurodollar floaters, the FRN is generally tied to LIBOR, the London Interbank Bid Rate (LIBID), or the arithmetic mean of LIBID and LIBOR (LIMEAN).
2. *The term of the reference interest rate* (for example, one month, three months, or six months).
3. *The frequency of the coupon payment* (for example, quarterly or semiannually). This is typically, but not always, the same as the term of the reference interest rate.
4. *The frequency of the coupon reset* (for example, weekly, monthly, quarterly, or semiannually). This is typically the same as, or shorter than, the term of the reference interest rate.

5. *The margin over the reference rate.* When LIBOR is the base rate, A or AA issuers can obtain funds at margins of ⅛–¼ in the domestic market or Euromarket. Bill-based floaters in the domestic market are typically priced at approximately 50 basis points over the 3-month bill rate for AAA issuers or 100 basis points over the 3-month bill rate for single-A issuers.

For a normal floating-rate note, items 2–4 will be identical. A U.S. domestic instrument may be based on the 6-month U.S. Treasury bill rate (or 6-month LIBOR), pay semiannually, and have a coupon reset twice a year, shortly before the beginning of the semiannual period. For example, if a domestic FRN pays interest on May 1 and November 1, the coupon to be paid in November might be determined by the six-month T-bill rate at the auction held the last week of the previous April. In the Eurodollar market, the coupon is generally based on LIBOR at 11:00 A.M. London time, two business days prior to the start of the interest period.

For a "mismatched" floating-rate note, the coupon is paid less frequently than it is reset. For example, many U.S. domestic FRNs are based on the 3-month T-bill rate and pay quarterly but have a coupon reset weekly. Thus the coupon received at the end of the quarter is the average bill rate prevailing over the quarter. In the Euromarket, a number of issues tied to 6-month LIBOR pay semiannually but have a coupon reset monthly. These mismatched FRNs appeal to two groups of investors:

- Investors who expect rates to rise in the next three to six months but also expect the yield curve to remain upward sloping. This group prefers the combination of a more frequent coupon reset and a longer term base rate.
- Investors who borrow money on a one-week or one-month rollover basis to buy FRNs and who expect the yield curve to remain upward sloping. For this group, mismatched floaters allow the coupon on the FRN to be reset when their funding rolls over, eliminating the risk of harm from large swings in rates. Moreover, when the yield curve slopes upward, these investors will receive a higher coupon than a short base rate would allow.

The range of coupon payment rules is wider in the U.S. domestic market than in the Euromarket. Table 1 classifies domestic floating rate notes by their coupon payment rules. Note that mismatched FRNs are quite common. Mismatched floaters are less common in the Euromarket. The overwhelming majority of these issues are reset monthly off 3-month or 6-month LIBOR, LIBID, and LIMEAN. The remaining three issues are reset weekly.

The needs of the issuers, especially with regard to regulatory constraints, have heavily influenced the maturities of FRNs in both the domestic market and the Euromarket. As indicated earlier, most of the issuers and investors have been financial institutions; approximately half the issuers are banks.

TABLE 1. *Types of Domestic Floating Rate Notes.*[a]

Category of Instrument	Amount Outstanding ($ millions)	Frequency of Coupon Reset	Frequency of Coupon Payment	Base Rate	Characteristic Feature
Weekly floaters	950	Weekly	Quarterly	3-month T-bills	
Weekly extendable floaters	2,579	Weekly	Quarterly	3-month T-bills	Extension (put/call/reset)
Weekly extendable floaters over 6-month bills	5	Weekly	Quarterly	6-month T-bills	Extension (put/call/reset)
Monthly extendable floaters	367	Monthly	Quarterly	3-month T-bills	Extension (put/call/reset)
Quarterly floaters	500	Quarterly	Quarterly	3-month T-bills	
Quarterly extendable floaters	152	Quarterly	Quarterly	3-month T-bills	Extension (put/call/reset)
Treasury bill-CD spread floaters	250	Monthly	Semiannually	T-bill + % (CD − T-bill) spread	
Extendable floaters	149	Semiannually	Semiannually	6-month T-bill	Extension
Intermediates	1,140	Semiannually	Semiannually	6-month T-bill	
Long-term	1,283	Semiannually	Semiannually	6-month T-bill	Maturity 1998 or after
LIBOR floaters	50	Quarterly	Semiannually	3-month LIBOR	
"	100	Monthly	Monthly	1-Month LIBOR	
"	7,022	Quarterly	Quarterly	3-month LIBOR	
"	200	Semiannually	Semiannually	6-month LIBOR	
"	850	Weekly	Quarterly	3-month LIBOR	
"	100	Monthly	Quarterly	3-month LIBOR	
Prime CD floater	1,750	Weekly	Quarterly	Lesser of: Prime−x, CD+y	

TABLE 1 *Continued*

Category of Instrument	Amount Outstanding ($ millions)	Frequency of Coupon Reset	Frequency of Coupon Payment	Base Rate	Characteristic Feature
CD floaters	250	Quarterly	Quarterly	90-day CD	
LIBOR floaters	470	Annually	Annually	1-year LIBOR	
Long-period floaters	50	Annually	Semiannually	2-year Treasury	
ECU floater	150	Weekly	Quarterly	3-month T-bill	
"	150	Quarterly	Quarterly	3-month T-bill	
Australian floater	625	Quarterly	Quarterly	3-month A$ bank bills	
New Zealand $ floaters	430	Quarterly	Quarterly	3-month NZ$ bank bills	
Inverse floaters[b]	1,300	Semiannually	Semiannually	6-month LIBOR	Base rate 6-month LIBOR
VCRs[c]	2,125	Weekly	Quarterly	3-month T-bills	Putable at par on any quarterly payment date on 9 months prior notice

a. A listing of domestic floating rate notes issues is available periodically from Goldman Sachs. See, for example, John Steinhardt and Christopher L. Stanwich, "Domestic Floating Rate Note Issues," Goldman, Sachs & Co., April 1987.

b. Characteristics of inverse floaters are discussed in detail in Jess B. Yawitz, "Pricing and Duration of Inverse Floating Rate Notes," Goldman, Sachs & Co., March 1986.

c. Characteristics of variable coupon renewable notes (VCRs) are discussed in detail in Laurie S. Goodman and Jess B. Yawitz, "The Structure and Pricing of VCRs," Goldman, Sachs & Co., August 1987.

Under U.S. bank regulations, for example, floaters qualify as equity capital on bank holding company balance sheets, provided that (1) the debt is subordinated, (2) the maximum maturity is 12 years, and (3) arrangements exist to finance the debt retirement from equity proceeds. British banks may include perpetual floaters in their calculation of primary capital. French banks make good use of the Euro-FRN market to fund medium-term lending because French regulations exclude from current credit controls any lending funded by bond issues.

In addition to specifying the maturity and the coupon payment rule, many floating rate instruments contain one or more option features. The most common of these are as follows.

Common FRN Option Features

Minimum and Maximum Coupon   Most floating-rate notes have a minimum coupon. If the coupon payment rule would produce a lower coupon, the minimum coupon will apply. This protects investors against rates going too low. Some FRNs have maximum coupons or caps. For example, a First Interstate Bank Corporation LIBOR-based FRN maturing June 10, 1997 has a maximum coupon of 12¾ percent. A LIBOR-based Bankers Trust issue maturing November 7, 1992 has a 13⅛ percent cap.

Put Options   Some FRNs contain options that entitle the investor to "put" the note back to the issuer, generally at par, at a set date or date prior to maturity. This feature is included because some investors have maturity limits on their holdings (for example, they cannot hold assets with a maturity longer than five years). Put options also protect the investor against a deterioration of the issuer's credit. FRNs with put options are often referred to as extendable notes.

Call Options   Some FRNs contain options that entitle the issuer to "call" the note back from the investor (redeem the note), generally at par. The issuer will exercise this call when the margin is lower in the secondary market or through alternative borrowing sources than the initial offering margin. Most perpetual floaters contain issuer calls.

Reset Options   Some FRNs contain options that entitle the issuer to reset the spread on the note at some prespecified date. The reset date is generally also a call date. For example, a $150 million Mellon Bank issue has a final maturity of April 30, 2000, with a put, call, and reset of April 30, 1988. Thus, on April 30, 1988, investors can put the issue while the borrower can call the issue or reset the spread. The spread reset is determined before the investor has to decide whether to exercise the put.

Conversion Options   Some FRNs contain options allowing the investor or borrower to convert the bond to a fixed-rate issue during certain periods. For example, the holder can convert a Mellon Bankcorp issue in the U.S. domestic market, maturing June 15, 1989, into the 8½s of June 15, 2009. The issuer can convert it into the higher of 8½ percent or 65 basis points over 30-year Treasuries. The holder of a small Norwest issue maturing May 1, 1989 can convert it into the 8⅜ of May 1, 2009.

Drop-Lock Features   Some FRNs automatically become fixed-rate instruments when the base rate "drops" to a prespecified minimum value. The coupon on the fixed-rate bond is prespecified (the lock).

Options on the Index   A few FRNs specify that the index used is to be the greater of two possibilities (an option to the investor) or the lesser of two possibilities (an option to the issuer). For example, a large ($1.5 billion) Kingdom of Sweden issue in the U.S. domestic market, maturing May 15, 1991, specifies that the issuer will pay the lesser of either prime minus 40 basis points or 90-day CD plus 55 basis points.

III. Relative Value Comparisons

Some investors are not able to exercise much discretion in selecting maturity or in choosing between floating and fixed assets. Most investors, however, have considerable flexibility in structuring their portfolios. If one sector currently represents a good value they would like to take advantage of it, making adjustments elsewhere in the portfolio to maintain the desired duration. Consequently, there is a great deal of interest in making relative value comparison across dissimilar instruments. Unfortunately, conventional methods of doing so have not proved satisfactory.

Traditional Valuation Methods

Since an FRN pays many coupons over its life, most of them unknown in advance, it is impossible to calculate a yield to maturity as in the fixed-rate market. However, because yield has become the standard yardstick for relative value, market participants have need for a yield-based measure for FRNs. Two such measures have come into general use.[2] The so-called *yield to maturity* (YTM) method evolved in the U.S. domestic market so that FRNs could be compared with fixed-rate bonds. The *discounted cash flow*

---

2. Many market participants use simple approximations to value floating-rate securities—for example, simple margin, total margin, and adjusted total margin. These approximations give answers extremely close to internal rate of return calculations for floaters selling close to par. For floaters selling at a deep discount, the simple approximations will be highly inaccurate.

margin (DCFM) method emerged in the Euromarket. The difference between the two methods, generally less than 1 basis point (bp), arises because of minor differences in day counts. The YTM spread assumes that all complete semiannual periods have 182.5 days, whereas the DCFM takes into account the actual number of days in each semiannual period.

Both methods essentially involve computing an internal rate of return, using a stream of expected cash flows. In order to calculate the internal rate of return for a floating-rate note, we must assume an annual coupon rate (LIBOR or T-bill plus margin). That is, we forecast an average index rate over the remaining life of the FRN, and add the quoted margin to this rate to get the coupon rate. The YTM is the discount rate that equates the present value of the assumed cash flow stream to the price of the bond. We can compute the spread over the index (the YTM spread) simply by subtracting the assumed coupon rate from the YTM.

Limitations of Conventional Methods

The problem with these calculations is that the YTM spread and the DCF margin do not lend themselves to comparing anything except two floating-rate notes that have similar maturities and are tied to the same index. Consider the following situations:

- A 5-year FRN is priced to a DCFM of 11 bp over 3-month LIBOR. A 10-year FRN of similar credit quality is priced to a DCFM of 14 bp over 3-month LIBOR. Which instrument is preferable? Traditional approaches cannot help us here, although we could conceivably address this question by calculating the breakeven forward credit spread.
- A 5-year LIBOR-based FRN is currently priced so that the DCF margin is 11 bp. A 5-year T-bill-based floater is currently priced such that the DCF margin is 78 bp. For investors, does the T-bill-based floater represent relatively greater value for their money? We cannot make this evaluation with traditional methods.
- A 5-year LIBOR-based FRN is currently priced such that the DCF margin is 11 bp. How does this compare with a 5-year fixed-rate instrument of similar credit quality priced to yield 8.67 percent (5-year Treasury notes + 90 bp)? We again cannot evaluate this alternative.

Clearly, yield-based methods are of limited help to investors who wish to make relative value comparisons involving FRNs. The next section describes an alternative approach to the pricing of floaters, which is applied in Section V to the relative valuation of these securities.

IV. A New Look at FRN Valuations

Consider an FRN issued at par that pays semiannual coupons at a spread of 100 bp over the prevailing 6-month bill rate. The coupon payments are scheduled to occur May 1 and November 1 of each year, and the face value is to be repaid on May 1, 1997. A typical structure would specify that the coupon of November 1, 1987, be set on May 1, 1987, based on the results of the last Treasury-bill auction in April 1987. The coupon rate for May 1988 would be set in November 1987 in a similar fashion.

Assume for the moment that the appropriate credit risk spread for the borrower remains constant at 100 bp. On the repricing dates this security would be priced at par. That is, on the next repricing date, the same borrower could issue a May 1997 floater at 100 bp over the T-bill rate. Thus, the outstanding issue must be priced at par.

The pricing of FRNs becomes more complicated when we allow for credit risk to change after issuance. When this happens, an original issue par floater will no longer be priced at par on coupon reset dates. Instead, it will be priced at a discount if credit risk has deteriorated and at a premium if credit risk has improved.

This leads us to a critical insight: When credit risk changes after issuance, we can calculate the size of the discount or premium relative to par by viewing the price of the floater (P) as the sum of two positions:

- the value of a par floater (V), offering the new spread over the benchmark rate necessary for pricing at par; and
- an implicit interest subsidy to the borrower or bonus to the lender that is equivalent to a short or long position in a credit annuity (A). We can think of this as the present value of the difference between the old credit spread and the new credit spread for the remaining life of the FRN.

In symbols:

$$P = V + A.$$

A will be negative (short annuity position) — reducing the value of the bond — if the borrower's credit quality has deteriorated since the bond was issued. Thus the FRN will sell at a discount. A will be positive (long annuity position) — increasing the floater's value — if credit quality has improved. Thus the FRN will sell at a premium.

Credit Quality Deterioration

To demonstrate this point, we will continue to examine the 10-year floater described above, adding the assumption that the credit quality of the issuer has deteriorated since the note was issued. To be precise, we will specify that if the borrower were to issue new debt, the new current rate would be 200 bp above the prevailing T-bill yield. Obviously the holder of the original FRN continues to receive the original 100 bp spread specified at issuance.

Since credit quality has deteriorated, the bond will be priced below par on coupon reset dates. To calculate the size of the discount to par, we can regard the price P of this floater as the sum of the following two positions: the value V of a par floater priced to offer the necessary 200 bp over T-bills, and a rebate A of interest from the lender to the borrower of 100 bp per year. The second component, A, is negative in this case, since it represents an annuity that has the effect of reducing the value of the bond when the borrower's credit risk has deteriorated. The discount floater is thus equivalent to a portfolio consisting of a par floater and a *short position in an annuity.*

As an example, if the 6-month Treasury yield is 9 percent, the *new* par floater would command a coupon of 11 percent. The coupon paid is only 10 percent. The value of this annuity for a 10-year FRN is the present value of (11 percent − 10 percent) × \$100 face value = \$1 per year (or \$0.50 per 6-month period) for ten years, discounted semiannually at a rate of 11 percent. This "credit annuity" has a value of \$5.98, implying that the floater should sell for \$100 − \$5.98 = \$94.02 as of May 1, 1987.[3]

For purposes of this discussion, we are using such terms as "credit risk" and "credit quality" quite broadly. This obviously includes firm-specific credit changes. But we also define credit risk to encompass basis risk, which involves the possibility of a change in the relationship between the benchmark rate used for resetting the coupon and the benchmark rate used for valuing the issue. For example, consider an FRN that has a coupon reset at a spread over the Treasury-bill rate but is actually valued in the market at a spread over LIBOR. Holding credit risk constant, a change in the LIBOR/T-bill spread will affect the pricing of the FRN. This type of spread risk, which we fold into the "credit risk" category, is a marketwide phenomenon not limited to a specific security. Finally, our definition of credit risk incorporates the risk that the spreads for a class of securities may widen for technical reasons, even when no change occurs in the credit quality of the firms involved. In the FRN market, supply and demand "technicals" have been far more important than firm-specific risk.

Table 2 shows the effects of different levels of deterioration in credit risk on the price of a 10-year FRN and on the price of an identical floater with five years to maturity. The magnitude of the credit annuity obviously depends on the size of any change in credit risk that has taken place. It also depends on the bond's maturity, since the subsidy to the borrower (if risk has increased) or the bonus to the lender (if risk has diminished) lasts until the bond matures or is retired.[4] Specifically, note that for a given deterioration in the borrower's credit standing, the (negative) value of the credit annuity

---

3. For illustrative purposes, we have discounted the credit annuity at the yield for a par floater. In general, if the maturity of the floater is significantly longer than the reset period, we would discount the credit annuity at a rate appropriate for the term.

4. This logic also points out the importance for valuation of the call and put provisions of these notes. We do not consider these complications in this basic analysis.

TABLE 2. *Price Effect of Various Levels of Credit Risk Deterioration.*

Deterioration in Credit Quality (basis points)	10-Year Maturity FRN ($)			5-Year Maturity FRN ($)		
	V	A	P	V	A	P
0	100	0	100	100	0	100
60	100	−3.65	96.35	100	−2.29	97.71
100	100	−5.98	94.02	100	−3.77	96.23
160	100	−9.33	90.67	100	−5.94	94.06
200	100	−11.47	88.53	100	−7.36	92.64

Note: V = Value of par floater. A = Value of annuity position. P = Price of floater $(P = V + A)$.

is larger for the longer term bond. That is, for a given credit deterioration, longer dated bonds will have a lower price.

We have established that the longer the term to maturity, the greater the price impact of a given deterioration in credit quality. For example, as Table 2 shows, a 160 bp credit quality deterioration for a 5-year floater and a 100 bp deterioration for a 10-year floater have a similar price impact ($5.47 versus $5.98). It follows that for a perpetual floater, which in effect has an infinite term, even a relatively small credit spread deterioration could have an extremely large price effect. In Appendix A we consider the theoretical impact of changes in credit spread on perpetuals and relate it to recent developments in the London market for these instruments.

Comparing the Annuity and Yield Approaches

Conceptually, we have used a "synthetic securities" approach to decompose any floater into two more easily understood parts: a floater that we expect to reset to par, and the added margin needed to adjust for changes in credit risk. The synthetic securities approach is easy to implement. The investor need ask only two questions:

- At what margin could the issuer borrow new money on a floating-rate basis?
- At what rate could the issuer borrow new money on a fixed-rate basis for a security of the same term as the floater?

The difference between the old spread and the current market spread determines the cash flow on the credit annuity. The discount rate on the credit annuity should equal the fixed borrowing rate that the issuer would pay.

This approach does not differ in principle from the more conventional DCFM technique. However, as we discussed in Section III, the DCFM approach requires an estimate of the average level of the benchmark rate and hence of the future coupons. No such forecast is necessary with the synthetic securities approach. The credit annuity that may arise from changes in credit risk should be discounted at a rate consistent with the term of the annuity. If we choose the assumed average level of the benchmark appropriately (that is, equal to the implied forward rates), then the annualized value of the credit annuity plus the stated spread will equal the DCFM.

Besides eliminating the need for a rate forecast, the synthetic securities method has a critical advantage over the yield approaches: By decomposing an FRN, we can compare its value with that of other instruments. The next section demonstrates this technique.

V. Assessing Relative Value

To evaluate an FRN relative to a dissimilar instrument, we equate both the initial costs of the two securities and their coupon payments until the end of the life of the shorter one. We do this by first making a series of conceptual adjustments and then calculating the breakeven value of the longer instrument at the end of the life of the shorter one.[5] We can make four types of adjustments, although not all are necessary for every comparison.

1. Price Adjustment   If two floaters pay on different dates or have different option features, they are not directly comparable. If, for example, one FRN has an option and the other does not, or one FRN pays a submarket coupon for five months and the other for two months, we must take account of these differences. To do so, we assign the same repricing dates and option characteristics to each security and adjust the price of one security accordingly.

2. Swap Adjustment   Where necessary, we place a swap on the longer instrument. (If both securities are LIBOR-based, this is unnecessary.) The swap should have the same maturity as the shorter instrument. This allows us to price both securities off the same reference index.

3. Annuity Adjustment   We buy or sell an annuity on the longer instrument to achieve the same coupon on both securities.

4. Zero Adjustment   We purchase or sell zeroes on the longer instrument to equate the initial investment costs.

After making the appropriate adjustments, we calculate the breakeven value of the longer instrument at the end of the life of the shorter security.

---

5. When comparing the prices of two perpetuals, we must choose an arbitrary horizon and compute the breakeven value of one instrument assuming the liquidation value of the other.

This value is simply $100 minus the dollar amount of zeroes purchased and sold. But this breakeven value is exactly the same as par plus the value of the credit annuity on that future date. That is, the A term in the decomposition of the previous section is simply the negative of the amount of zeroes purchased. Thus, in comparing one FRN with another, we end up with a breakeven A term that may be positive or negative. If you expect the actual credit annuity to be worth more than the breakeven value, you should consider purchasing the longer security; otherwise, the shorter security is preferable. We can translate this A term back into a breakeven credit deterioration.

A Generic Example

We illustrate this procedure here with an example comparing two hypothetical FRNs with different maturities and reference rates but identical payment dates.

> Security 1: A twenty-year FRN with coupon at 3-month LIBOR + 12.5 bp. The current price is $98 and the payment dates are February 15, May 15, August 15, and November 15.

versus

> Security 2: A 5-year FRN with coupon at 3-month T-bill + 95 bp. The current price is $100 and the payment dates are February 15, May 15, August 15, and November 15.

Because the securities pay on the same date, no price adjustment is required. The swap market allows us to swap LIBOR for T-bill + 90 bp for five years.[6] Thus, in a 5-year swap, the coupon on the 20-year FRN would be T-bill + 102.5 bp (90 + 12.5 = 102.5). Since the spread on the 5-year FRN is T-bill + 95 bp, we must sell an annuity to reduce the cash flows on the 20-year FRN. The annuity to be sold is worth $0.075 per year ($0.0375 per semiannual period) for five years, or $0.30 (at an 8.7 percent discount rate, which is the approximate rate on a 5-year bond of the same credit quality). We must subtract this annuity from the price of the 20-year FRN, since it represents the cost of a 20-year FRN paying 3-month T-bill + 95 bp for five years and LIBOR + 12.5 bp thereafter. The 20-year FRN price, taking into account the annuity adjustment, is $97.70.

The final step is to purchase a sufficient amount of zeroes to equate the original purchase prices of the two instruments. In this case we will have to spend $2.30 on zeroes maturing in five years. Assuming a yield of 8 percent, we must purchase a par amount of $3.52. Thus, if the breakeven on the current 20-year floater after five years is greater than $96.48 ($100 − 3.52), the

---

6. The introduction of swaps raises a question as to which side of the swap market we should use for the adjustment, the bid side or the offered side. If we are selling one floater and buying another, we should use the more conservative side, to fully account for transaction costs. If we are trying to decide which floater to buy, the midmarket price is appropriate.

20-year FRN is the more attractive instrument. This corresponds to a credit annuity of 41 bp per year over the remaining fifteen years. To sell at a price of $98, the current credit annuity is 20 bp. Thus, as long as the credit deterioration during the next five years is no more than 21 bp, the 20-year FRN is the more attractive possibility.

Table 3 summarizes the cash flows. The four adjustments are examined in detail in the following paragraphs.

The Price Adjustment

A three-part price adjustment is necessary to compare two securities.

1. Adjustment for Option Futures Many FRNs have option features. Since we wish to duplicate the cash flows on the shorter instrument, the simplest way to do this is to create optionless FRNs synthetically. We can do this by valuing the options explicitly and making a price adjustment in the underlying security. If the security contains an investor *put* option, we can *subtract* the option price from the security price. If the security contains an issuer *call* option, we can *add* the option price to the security price. This is not as easy as it sounds. It is extremely difficult to value the options explicitly, since they are credit options rather than interest rate options. To complicate matters further, many FRNs contain both investor options and issuer options. Nonetheless, an ad hoc adjustment to the price may be in order.

2. Adjustment for Different Coupon Payment Rates The coupon payment dates on any two bonds or FRNs will generally be different. The coupon for each period is set at the beginning of the period. To understand what might be involved in a date adjustment, assume that it is now September 15 and that we are comparing the two FRNs depicted in Figure 1, where each full horizontal line segment represents a coupon period. The shorter-maturity FRN, represented by line A, pays May 15 and November 15, and the longer one (line B) pays February 15 and August 15. The rate on the longer FRN (LIBOR + margin) was last set at 7 percent, but LIBOR plus the appropriate margin is now 8 percent. We must therefore imagine that the coupon on the longer FRN has been raised to 8 percent for November 15 through February 15 (dotted portion of line C). This requires us to adjust the purchase price upward on the longer FRN to reflect the shorter period of negative carry.[7] That is, the 1 percent negative carry is in effect for only two months

---

7. "Carry" is defined as the difference between the coupon interest earned and the cost of financing (or alternative investment rate) for the period from the FRN purchase date to the first rollover date. A LIBOR flat note carrying an 8 percent coupon when LIBOR is 6.5 percent will generate a positive carry of 150 basis points until the next rollover date, when the coupon is refixed at market level. Conversely, a FRN carrying a below-market coupon would produce a negative carry.

TABLE 3. *Cash Flows Summarized.*

Cash Flows	20-Year FRN + Swap + Zero + Annuity	Five-Year FRN
1. Total purchase price	$100	$100
Original purchase price of bond	$98	$100
Purchase price of annuity	−$0.30	0
Purchase price of zero	$2.30	0
2. Net coupon for five years	3-month T-bill + 95 bp	3-month T-bill + 95 bp
Coupon for five years	3-month LIBOR + 12.5 bp	3-month T-bill + 95 bp
Swap for five years	−3-month LIBOR	0
	+3-month T-bill + 90 bp	
Annuity for five years	−7.5 bp	0
3. Payment at end of five years (zeroes or principal)	$3.52	$100
4. Cash flows after year 5	3-month LIBOR + 12.5 bp	0

FIGURE 1. *Coupon and Date Adjustments.*

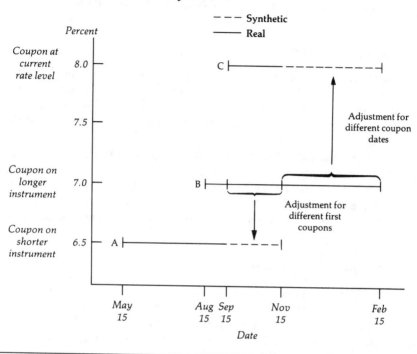

(to November 15) rather than five months (to February 15). The required price adjustment is roughly $0.25.[8]

3. Adjustment for Different First Coupons The first coupons due (which have already been set) will generally be different. Continuing the example of Figure 1, if the coupon on the longer FRN is 7 percent and the coupon on the shorter FRN is 6.5 percent, the owner of the longer FRN will receive a larger amount on November 15. We therefore imagine that on September 15, we reduce the coupon on the longer instrument to 6.5 percent (dotted portion of line A). This requires us to reduce the price of the longer issue by (.50 × 2/12), discounted back by two months — a downward price adjustment of approximately $0.08.

---

8. Many traders believe the market overreacts to the carry effect. That is, if the coupon is higher than the value to which it will reset, the market overvalues carry and bids up the price of the issue. If the coupon is lower than the value to which it will reset, the market discounts the issue more than it should.

Thus our overall price correction, including adjustments for disparities in both the payment dates and the first coupons, nets out to ($0.25 − 0.08) = $0.17.

The Swap Adjustment

The swap adjustment is necessary in two cases: when comparing two FRNs based on different indexes, and when comparing a floater with a fixed-rate bond. In the first case, if one floater is priced off T-bills and the other off LIBOR, a swap will be necessary. The generic example at the start of this section illustrates this point.

In the second case, if one bond is floating and the other fixed, we must execute a swap to place the two instruments on the same basis. Appendix B shows how to compare a fixed-rate bond with an FRN. It gives a detailed example of a case in which the floater is the longer instrument, and briefly discusses the differences in interpretation and procedure when the fixed-rate bond is longer.

The Annuity Adjustment

The annuity adjustment serves several purposes. We may use the annuity adjustment to equate the margins of two issues of the same credit quality that were issued at different times. If we raise the margin on the longer issue by a certain number of basis points per year, we must add the present value of this annuity to the initial cost of the FRN.

We may use the annuity adjustment to equate different Eurodollar-based issues. Some Eurodollar issues are priced over LIBOR, others over LIMEAN, and still others over LIBID.

We may use the annuity adjustment to take account of credit differentials. For example, suppose we wish to compare values of a Lloyd's perpetual FRN and a 7.5-year Phillips Petroleum FRN. The Lloyd's floater pays 3-month LIBOR + 18.75 bp. The Phillips FRN pays 3-month LIBOR + 150 bp. To correct for the credit differential, we ask how much lower a spread over LIBOR Lloyd's would command than Phillips for a 7.5-year issue. At the time of comparison, a Lloyd's 7.5-year bond would carry a yield of 9.60 percent while a Phillips 7.5-year bond would command a yield of 0.63 percent—103 bp higher. We may therefore conclude that 103 bp of the total 131.25 bp yield difference between the two floaters is due to the difference in credit quality.[9] We would want to achieve a net coupon on the Lloyd's issue of LIBOR + 47 bp (150 − 103). Since no actual coupon is 18.75 bp, we must

9. The Lloyd's perpetual counts as primary capital and hence has a lower standing in bankruptcy than senior subordinated debt. Consequently, 103 basis points may slightly overstate the actual credit difference. We cannot make a more exact comparison, however, because there is no primary capital that matures in 7.5 years.

purchase an annuity of 28.25 bp per year (47 – 18.75). We would add this annuity to the purchase price of the Lloyd's issue, since we are pretending that the perpetual pays LIBOR + 47 bp.

The Zero Adjustment

We must make the zero adjustment in virtually all cases to equate initial purchase prices. This is the crucial ingredient in the analysis, because it gives us the breakeven value of the credit annuity.

Some Shortcuts

For certain types of comparisons, it is not necessary to go through all four adjustments outlined above. In fact, several shortcuts to this approach have come into limited use by sophisticated investors. These shortcuts can be considered as special cases of the generalized four-step method we have presented.

One common shortcut is simply making only the zero adjustment. This adjustment is not a bad approximation in certain instances. If, for example, you are comparing a long-dated FRN with a perpetual, the margins will be quite similar. No swap is necessary, since both instruments are based on LIBOR. By purchasing zeroes to mature at or near the maturity of the long-dated floater (to equate the initial purchase prices), you will get an approximation of the breakeven value of the credit annuity at the maturity of the shorter instrument. This approximation is not exact, as it ignores the different first coupons, the different payment dates, the different option features, and the different margins. If the breakeven value of the credit annuity is high enough, however, these differences will not markedly change the basic result.

A second shortcut for comparing two FRNs is using the swap market to synthetically create two fixed-rate instruments maturing at the end of the life of the shorter instrument. For example, assume we are trying to compare a 3-year LIBOR-based floater with a 7-year LIBOR-based floater. If we swap both securities from floating into fixed for three years, calculate the internal rate of return on the shorter security, and impute this internal rate of return to the longer security, we could compute the breakeven horizon value at the end of the three years. This breakeven horizon value is simply par plus accrued interest minus the value of the credit annuity.

Since the longest swap is ten years, this shortcut is difficult to apply when the shorter FRN has a maturity greater than ten years. This precludes an easy comparison of perpetuals with long-dated floaters, a comparison that lately has been of keen interest. Some market participants have related long-dated FRNs to perpetuals by swapping to ten years, assuming liquidation values for both the perpetual and the long-dated FRN, and comparing the internal rates of return. This comparison, however, will be highly sensitive to the assumed liquidation values, both of which must be estimated. In contrast, the generalized approach we propose in this article requires a qualitative evaluation of only one FRN. All we need ask is whether its price will be greater or less than the breakeven value.

For comparisons in which at least one of the securities has a maturity under ten years, the "swap" shortcut allows the user to avoid several traps. In effect it substitutes a swap adjustment for a price adjustment, an annuity adjustment, and a zero adjustment. If the two FRNs have dissimilar option characteristics, however, we would have to take account of this with an explicit price adjustment.

As special cases of our generalized method, these shortcuts can be handy timesavers. In many instances, however, they either will not be applicable or will introduce conceptual problems (for example, assigning the same internal rate of return to two very different cash flow streams). For reasons of both precision and broad applicability, the full four-step approach will generally be the preferred procedure.

VI. Summing Up

The four adjustments discussed in the previous section—the price adjustment, the swap adjustment, the annuity adjustment, and the zero adjustment—constitute what we call the synthetic securities approach to relative value. We have taken the longer security and, by packaging it with other instruments, we have exactly duplicated the cash flows on the shorter security.

Specifically, in relative value comparisons involving FRNs, we have calculated the breakeven price of the longer instrument at the end of the life of the shorter one and used this value to create a synthetic shorter security. The difference between this breakeven value and our expected value is the key to regarding a security as over- or under-valued. If the breakeven value is lower than the expected value, the longer security is the preferable alternative. Stated differently, if the breakeven credit annuity is less positive or more negative than we expected, we would prefer the longer security.

In sum, the synthetic securities approach offers market participants a consistent way to compare relative value across securities when a floater is involved. It ensures that they have selected the less expensive way to achieve a given set of cash flows. We can use this approach to compare the value of an FRN with any other FRN or with a fixed-rate bond.

Appendix A:
The Perpetual Floater Market—An Analysis

Decomposition

The decomposition of a perpetual floater into a par bond and a credit annuity takes a particularly simple form.

$$\text{Price of a perpetuity} = 100\,\frac{c+r}{c'+r}, \tag{A-1}$$

where (in decimal notation)

$c =$ credit spread at issuance = quoted margin
$r =$ risk-free base rate
$c' =$ new credit spread after a change in credit quality

Thus, if $r = 9$ percent, $c = 1$ percent, and $c' = 2$ percent, the price of the annuity is $100(.10/.11)$ or \$90.91. We can easily decompose the perpetuity into a par floater and credit annuity, as follows:

$$\text{Price of a perpetuity} = 100\,\frac{c+r}{c'+r} = 100\,\frac{c'+r}{c'+r} + \frac{c-c'}{c'+r}. \tag{A-2}$$

Let $c' = c + x$, where x is the change in credit spread:

$x > 0$ indicates a credit deterioration;
$x < 0$ indicates a credit improvement.

Rewriting (A-2), we obtain:

$$\text{Price of the perpetuity} = 100\left(1 + \frac{c-c-x}{c+x+r}\right) = 100\left(1 - \frac{x}{c+x+r}\right). \tag{A-3}$$

Therefore, the value of the credit annuity $= -100[x/(c+x+r)]$.

Table 4 shows the value of a perpetuity under different interest rate and credit risk scenarios. As you can see, the lower the level of interest rates, the greater the price effect of a given credit risk deterioration. For example,

TABLE 4. *Pricing Perpetual FRNs under Different Interest Rate and Credit Risk Scenarios.*

Credit Spread Change[a]	Original Interest Rate $(r+c)$[b]			
	6%	8%	10%	12%
+200 bp	\$75.00	\$80.00	\$83.33	\$85.71
+150	80.00	84.21	86.96	88.89
+100	85.71	88.89	90.91	92.31
+50	92.31	94.12	95.23	96.00
+25	96.00	96.97	97.56	97.96
+10	98.36	98.76	99.01	99.17
0	100.00	100.00	100.00	100.00
−10	101.70	101.27	101.01	100.84
−25	104.35	103.23	102.56	102.13
−50	109.09	106.67	105.26	104.35

a. A positive change in credit spread indicates credit deterioration. A negative credit spread change indicates credit improvement.
b. Risk-free base rate + credit spread at issuance.

a 25 bp worsening of credit quality will cause a $3.03 price drop from par at an original interest rate of 8 percent but only a $2.04 price decline at an original interest rate of 12 percent.

The London Market

The foregoing analysis will be helpful in interpreting recent events in London's perpetual FRN market. The perpetual floating-rate note market originated with the U.K. clearing banks (NatWest, Barclays, Midland, Lloyd's, Standard Chartered, Royal Bank of Scotland, and Bank of Scotland), which could structure their FRN issues as primary capital. The market began to grow rapidly in early 1986. As the market grew, the number of participants expanded to include Canadian, French, and Hong Kong banks. Outstanding perpetuals totaled about $18 billion by the summer of 1986. Spreads were exceptionally tight, with the Banque National de Paris issuing a perpetual with a coupon of LIBOR plus only 7.5 bp. Clearly, the market was not requiring a credit risk premium for longer maturity issues.

Two events occurred in the autumn of 1986 that sapped the liquidity from the perpetuals market. First, fears arose that the Bank of England, the Bank of Japan, and the Federal Reserve would impose uniform regulatory capital rules. U.K. banks currently have strict capital requirements (1:1) on the holding of primary capital of other banks. Market participants felt that if uniform regulatory capital rules were adopted, it was likely that this rule would be extended to Japanese and U.S. banks. These fears deepened when the Bank of Japan informally voiced concerns about the level of perpetual holdings of Japanese banks.

The second event that sapped liquidity was the creation of collateralized mortage obligation (CMO) floaters. These new floaters represented a dated alternative to the perpetual FRN—at significantly wider spreads, even factoring in the value of the cap—prompting holders of perpetuals to reassess their investment.

Japanese banks constitute the largest investor group in the perpetual FRN market, accounting for at least 70–80 percent of the holdings. In response to the events we have described, Japanese banks attempted to reduce the size of their positions without taking a large loss. Market makers, however, were unwilling to take on significant long positions. Bid-asked spreads widened from $0.10 to 1 point on perpetuals issued by top-tier U.K. clearing banks. The issues of second-tier U.K. clearing banks and foreign banks had even wider bid-asked spreads. Little trading in perpetuals took place in the last two months of 1986, but the relatively few transactions that did occur were at prices very close to previous levels.

In January 1987, with the approach of the end of Japanese banks' fiscal year in March, prices declined as Japanese banks began a concerted effort to sell some of their holdings of perpetuals. In terms of our analysis, the "credit risk" of this market deteriorated on the order of 90 bp between January and March 1987 for the prime issuers (NatWest, Barclays, Lloyd's) and by substantially more for second-tier issuers (such as Standard Chartered). Using equation (A-3), we calculate that a 90 bp deterioration in credit quality — assuming an original interest rate $(r + c)$ of 7.5 percent — would cause a price decline of $10.71. A typical case was that of NatWest Perpetual Series A, which was trading at $100.50 in late December 1986. By mid-March, the mid-market price was $89.73, a $10.75 drop. This had little to do with the specific risk of the issuers. Rather, it resulted from supply and demand forces stemming from regulatory concerns and competing investments, which drove up the required margin on the issues. Between April and August 1987, the market bounced around in roughly a two-point range. In September 1987 bid-asked spreads were $0.50 for the top-tier U.K. clearing banks.

Meanwhile, long-dated FRN prices in the Euromarket, particularly for U.S. banks, also fell in early 1987. This resulted primarily from fears of the impact of Latin American debt on the balance sheets of U.S. financial institutions, in the wake of Brazil's nonpayment of interest for the first quarter. Some market participants also expressed fears that the uniform regulatory capital rules might be extended to include the capital notes and perhaps the long-dated subordinated debt of U.S. banks. The market took another blow in May and June when major U.S. institutions greatly increased their loan loss reserves. Nonetheless, during the first half of 1987, the long-dated FRN market declined considerably less than did the perpetual market. From January through March 1987, a Chase Manhattan floater (see example below) maturing December 5, 2009, declined from par to $98. The issue fell another two points between April and June before rebounding to roughly $97.

We can readily explain these price responses with the credit annuity analysis presented in this article. You will recall that our broad definition of credit risk encompasses supply/demand developments in the FRN market as well as firm-specific events. Even though little change has occurred in the firm-specific credit risk of the perpetual issuers, credit spreads on perpetuals have widened considerably in response to supply and demand forces. In contrast, the long-dated FRNs have suffered less of a decline, even though they are primarily the subordinated debt of U.S. banks. The credit deterioration of these securities has been both firm-specific and industry-specific, reflecting market concerns about the long-term financial health of the largest U.S. banks. Nevertheless, the credit quality deterioration of long-dated floaters has been outweighed by the worsening of credit risk in the perpetual FRN market that resulted from weakened demand.

A concrete example will further clarify these ideas and illustrate the uses of our analytical approach. We will compare the values of a U.K. bank's perpetuity and a U.S. bank's long-date floater at two very different moments: (1) during August 1986, before the market declines described above, and (2) exactly one year later.

Perpetuity: NatWest Series A, perpetual FRN with coupon at 6-month LIMEAN + 25 bp. The bid price as $100.65 on August 18, 1986, and $89.50 on August 18, 1987. Coupon payment dates are January 9 and July 9.

versus

Long-dated FRN: Chase Manhattan FRN of December 5, 2009, with coupon at 3-month LIBOR + 12.5 bp. The bid price was $100.125 on August 18, 1986, and $96.90 on August 18, 1987. Coupon payment dates are March 5, June 5, September 5, and December 5.

The price adjustments — which ensure (1) that the NatWest issue pays on the same dates as the Chase floater and (2) that the first coupons are identical — are sufficiently small (currently $0.06 per $100 par) that they can be ignored. Both the NatWest Series A perpetual and the Chase FRN contain issuer call options. In both cases the options are sufficiently out of the money that we can ignore them. We do not need a swap adjustment in this case since both issues are based on similar London reference rates. (The Chase issue is based on 3-month LIBOR while the NatWest issue is based on 6-month LIBOR. A 22-year floater based on 3-month LIBOR would command the same margin in the market as a 22-year floater based on 6-month LIBOR).

Under the conservative assumption that the securities are of equal credit quality, we have to make an annuity adjustment to equate the margins.[10] The NatWest floater pays LIMEAN + 25 bp. This is equivalent to LIBOR + 18.75 bp. Since the Chase floater pays LIBOR + 12.5 bp, we must sell an annuity equal to $0.0625 per year for 22 years in order to equate cash flows. At a 9 percent discount rate, the value of this annuity is $0.60. We therefore imagine that the NatWest issue has a coupon of LIBOR + 12.5 bp, and we reduce the value of the perpetual to reflect the lower coupon.

We must now make the zero adjustment. Let us consider the situation as of August 18, 1987, with the long-dated floater priced at $96.90 and the price of the perpetuity minus the annuity at ($89.50 − 0.60) = $88.90.

To equate the initial purchase prices, we must purchase $8.00 ($96.90 − 88.90) market value of zeroes maturing December 5, 2009. Using a yield of 9.39 percent (the actual yield on a Treasury zero maturing November 15, 2009), we would be able to purchase $61.77 par amount (reflecting a price of $12.95 per $100 par).

The cash flows are summarized in Table 5.

We have now simulated identical purchase prices and identical cash flows until the maturity of the zero and long-dated floater in 2009. On December 9,

---

10. NatWest is actually of considerably higher credit quality than Chase, but this NatWest issue has primary capital status in bankruptcy and hence a lower standing than senior subordinated debt.

TABLE 5. *Cash Flows Summarized.*

Cash Flows	NatWest Perp. + Annuity + Zero	Chase FRN
1. Total purchase price	$96.90	$96.90
Original purchase price of bond	$89.50	$96.90
Purchase price of annuity	–$0.60	0
Purchase price of zero	$8.00	0
2. Net coupon until December 5, 2009	LIBOR + 12.5 bp	LIBOR + 12.5 bp
Coupon until December 5, 2009	LIMEAN + 25 bp (= LIBOR + 18.75 bp)	LIBOR + 12.5 bp
Annuity until December 5, 2009	–6.25 bp	0
3. Payment at end of five years (zeroes or principal)	$61.77	$100
4. Cash flows after December 5, 2009	3-month LIMEAN + 25 bp	0

2009, we will receive either $61.77 plus a NatWest perpetuity (under our first alternative), or $100 plus a final coupon payment (if we buy the Chase floater). Note that since the adjusted perpetuity will reset on December 5, 2009, we can decompose its resale price on that date into a par floater and the credit annuity. Thus the negative of the amount of zeroes purchased ($61.77) can be interpreted as the breakeven value of the credit annuity.

If the perpetuity were to sell for more than $38.23 ($100 − 61.77) on December 5, 2009, it would be the more attractive possibility. In fact, this is quite likely to be the case, since it requires only that the credit spread be less than 1,454 bp over LIMEAN.

Now, let us consider the situation one year earlier, on August 18, 1986. The NatWest perpetual was priced at $100.65, the Chase FRN at $100.125, and annuity (assuming an 8 percent discount rate) at $0.66. Thus the base price minus the annuity was $99.99. The amount of zeros that could be purchased was therefore ($100.125 − 99.99) = $0.135. The par amount of these zeroes is roughly $1. Consequently, the NatWest perpetual must sell for $99 on December 5, 2009, in order for it to be the better value. This corresponds to LIMEAN + 34 bp, a very slim margin.

Thus, in August 1986 the Chase floater was more attractive; the breakeven was represented by a 9 bp credit deterioration over 22 years. In August 1987, however, the NatWest perpetual represented far better value. Current efforts to package perpetuals with other products represent an attempt to capitalize on the currently underpriced market.

Appendix B:
Comparing an FRN with a Fixed-Rate Bond

In the following comparison, the floater is the longer instrument.

Floating-rate note: Chase Manhattan FRN of December 5, 2009, with coupon at 3-month LIBOR + 12.5 bp. The current price is $96.90 and the payment dates are March 5, June 5, September 5, and December 5.

versus

Fixed-rate bond: Chase Manhattan note maturing December 1, 1989, with coupon at 6¾ percent. At the current price of $96.62, the yield to maturity is 8.40 percent.

To create identical cash flows until December 1, 1989, we must first make a price adjustment to put the two securities in the same coupon cycle. Second, we must change the FRN into a fixed-rate instrument until December 1, 1989, via a swap. We must then correct for the differential coupon by buying or selling an annuity on the FRN. Finally, we must calculate how many zeroes we can purchase to equate the initial purchase price. We can then compute the breakeven credit annuity on the FRN.

The price adjustment necessary to place the two securities on the same coupon cycle is trivial, on the order of $0.01. Consequently, we will ignore it.

To equate the cash flows, the investor must pay floating and receive fixed until December 1, 1989. If we assume that the swap rate is 70 bp over the 3-year rate, or 8.72 percent, the investor would on net receive the swap rate plus the quoted margin of .125, or 8.845 percent.

We now have a large differential coupon, with the 3-year fixed note paying 6.75 percent and the FRN + swap paying 8.845 percent. We must therefore reduce the proceeds on the FRN + swap to match the coupon on the fixed rate, reducing the price on the FRN + swap to reflect this adjustment. We wish to sell an annuity of $2.095 per year ($1.0475 per semiannual period) from June 1, 1987, to December 1, 1989. The price of this annuity, if we assume an 8.5 percent discount rate, is $4.82. Reducing the price on the Chase 2009 FRN + swap by $4.82 to equalize the coupon, we obtain a price of $92.08.

The $4.54 difference between this synthetic price ($92.08) and the price of the fixed-rate bond ($96.62) must be invested in zeroes to mature on June 1, 1989. The $4.54 can purchase $5.40 of zeroes (at a yield of 7.778 percent). Thus the breakeven price of the Chase FRN on December 1, 2009, must be greater than ($100 − 5.40) = $94.60. Since the current price is $96.90, the choice between the two instruments becomes a close call, with the ultimate decision resting on whether the credit annuity on December 1, 1989, will be worth less than $5.40. Stated differently, if the value of the credit annuity on December 1, 1989, is less than 59 bp per annum, the FRN is the superior choice.

We may summarize the cash flows as shown in Table 6 (see following page).

In a case in which the fixed-rate bond is the longer instrument, the breakeven value takes on a slightly different meaning because we are selling a fixed-rate bond at the horizon. But the methodology is the same. We do a swap in which we pay fixed and receive floating. The coupon on the fixed-rate issue plus the swap plus the annuity can be equated to the coupon on the FRN. We buy or sell zeroes to equate the initial purchase prices. We assume that at the end of the life of the FRN, we sell the fixed-rate bond. We can compute the breakeven sale price for the fixed-rate bond and compare it with the forward price currently prevailing in the market. The difference between the breakeven price and the forward price is the annuity value of the credit deterioration.

TABLE 6. *Cash Flows Summarized.*

Cash Flows	Chase FRN + Swap + Annuity + Zero	Chase 6.75 Note
1. Total purchase price	$96.62	$96.62
Original purchase price of bond	$96.90	$96.62
Purchase price of annuity	−$4.82	0
Purchase price of zero	$4.54	0
2. Net coupon until December 1, 1989	6.75 percent	6.75 percent
Coupon until December 1, 1989	3-month LIBOR + 12.5 bp	6.75 percent
Swap until December 1, 1989	3-month LIBOR + 8.72 percent	0
Annuity until December 1, 1989	−209.5 bp	0
3. Payment on December 1, 1989 (zeroes or principal)	$5.40	$100
4. Cash flows after December 1, 1989	3-month LIBOR + 12.5 bp	0

31

Striking the Right Performance Fee Arrangement for Fixed Income Managers

Edgar A. Robie, Jr.
Managing Director
 and Senior Portfolio Manager
Western Asset Management Company

I. Introduction

Some of the more recent research performed by the investment management, plan sponsor and consultant communities has centered around the issue of performance fees and the motivations for managers and plan sponsors to employ them. Serious questions have arisen as a result of this research, including Will performance fees have an impact on manager performance? Who wins? Who loses?[1] What form should performance fee arrangements take? How should a performance fee structure be administered? Are there any unwanted side effects? These and other questions have thrown a number of plan sponsors, consultants and money managers into a debate on striking the right performance fee arrangements. This article will present some important background information with regard to performance fees, provide a framework for administering performance fees and discuss some of the unresolved issues facing sponsors and managers on this important topic.

The author wishes to thank Peter Lambert for his assistance in preparing the article.
1. A discussion of these issues is presented in Richard Grinold and Andrew Rudd, "Incentive Fees: Who Wins? Who Loses," *Financial Analyst Journal* (January/February 1987).

II. Characteristics of Performance Fees

The potential merits of performance fees notwithstanding, a considerable number of positive side effects have resulted from the introduction of these fees. Just as U.S. efforts to put a man on the moon have produced such beneficial side effects as miniaturized electronic components, lightweight durable materials and enhanced communications systems, the growing interest and research in performance fees are beginning to produce favorable side effects for the management of plan assets. Sponsors are now examining and evaluating manager objectives, performance standards and the communications link with the manager. Further, documenting the proper characteristics of a performance fee arrangement focuses the sponsor on whether the manager's investment goals are coincident with his own.

Several desirable elements should be considered when developing a performance fee arrangement. We discuss six that we believe are most important.

Promote Coincidence of Goals

The goals of the manager's investment process should coincide with those of the sponsor whose assets are being managed. The responsibility of the plan sponsor is to construct a portfolio of managers with differing styles in a range of asset classes such that the aggregate performance of all managers meets the stated goals of the plan and conforms to the desired level of risk dictated by the plan's objectives. Given that managers are chosen for their individual investment processes, it is crucial that each manager adhere to his particular process. Excess risk should be undertaken only in pursuit of investment opportunities that correspond with the objectives of a particular manager's portfolio and its contribution to the total fund. A good performance fee structure rewards the manager for taking successful controlled risks that are in the best interest of the plan sponsor.

Reward Manager Performance, Not Market Performance

The right performance fee arranagement rewards the manager for superior performance resulting from the application of his investment skills. In contrast, the common fee structure, which is based solely on the market value of the managed assets, rewards managers for upward moves in the market and penalizes them in negatively performing markets; the manager's fee is largely dependent on events beyond his control. A performance fee structure should reward a manager for his value added relative to his appropriate benchmark.

Provide a Logical Reward Structure to the Manager

Managers should be both rewarded and held accountable for portfolio returns that exceed or fall below their given benchmark. Returns far in excess of the manager's target bogey suggest that the bogey has been set too low. Likewise, if a manager consistently underperforms his given bogey, the target may be too high. The fee arrangement should be designed so that the manager is motivated and rewarded for providing returns that approach the target bogey, yet not motivated to "build-in" excess return by setting an unappropriately low target bogey. There is some debate on whether target returns can be attained by employing a passive or structured approach that replicates the manager's long-run strategy or "normal portfolio." Furthermore, a passive management fee may or may not be appropriate for a structured approach based on a particular manager's strategic investment style that provides superior performance. Clearly, the beginning point in designing a logical performance fee structure must be some mutually agreed upon active return or target bogey relative to the manager's benchmark that will serve as the base from which the performance fee is determined.

Enhance Communication between the Manager and the Sponsor

Both the manager and the sponsor can benefit from a properly designed performance fee arrangement. The manager is rewarded with greater fees for providing superior performance relative to his bogey. The sponsor gains a systematic framework for monitoring the types and levels of risk the manager is taking, and thus can easily determine if the portfolio is being managed according to the stated objectives.

Consider the Additional Business Risk Being Accepted by the Manager

Inherent in any performance fee arrangement is the increased volatility of the manager's revenue stream. Determining the appropriate performance measurement time horizon and termination guidelines are important tasks that must be factored into the design of any performance fee arrangement. By choosing to implement a performance fee structure, the sponsor does not want to inadvertently preselect only those larger management organizations that are unusually well capitalized. The sponsor hopes to attract managers confident of providing superior returns, not just managers whose business can accept the additional volatility in their revenue streams.

Discourage "Gaming" the Fee Structure

The right performance fee arrangement does not provide the manager with incentives to abandon the investment style for which he was hired in order to protect fees already earned or increase the probability of earning a fee above the base amount. Such problems are usually associated with fee "caps" and "floors" that have been set at inappropriate levels. While caps and floors provide protection to both the sponsor and manager by avoiding an adversarial relationship due to extreme under or overperformance, they must be set such that the probability of the manager's returns hitting the cap or floor in any measurement period is very low.

These six elements provide a backdrop against which sponsors may think about the overall investment objectives of their funds. Managers will be hired with a better understanding of how their investment styles fit into the overall goals of the sponsor's portfolio. The sponsor will be more inclined to establish a well-defined and measurable set of guidelines for each manager, and the managers will see that their compensation is dependent upon their performance relative to the prescribed guidelines. As sponsors begin to address the role of each manager in the context of the fund's overall objectives, the task of identifying a particular manager's investment style will be of the greatest importance. In order to choose an appropriate benchmark for assessing the success of a particular manager's investment process, it may be necessary to develop concrete, quantifiable benchmarks where none exist. The concept of a "normal portfolio" is useful for this task.

III. Normal Portfolios

In considering the desirable characteristics described above and in grappling with the various difficulties they pose for structuring a performance fee arrangement, we found that a well-constructed, customized benchmark or "normal" portfolio was key to the design of a performance fee arrangement. Given that the performance fee concept focuses on the manager's actual contribution to returns relative to some predetermined benchmark, the definition of the benchmark portfolio is crucial to satisfactory implementation of a performance fee. The most logical choice for a benchmark in this situation is a portfolio that represents the desired risk level and the expected level of return for which the manager was hired.

For equity portfolios the construction of such a normal portfolio is relatively simple. For a large-cap manager the appropriate benchmark portfolio may be as simple as the S&P 500 index; for a small-cap manager perhaps the Wilshire 5000 less the S&P 500. For fixed income managers the exercise is more complex.

The normal portfolio represents the set of "passive" or "neutral" investment positions that best depicts the manager's long-run strategy and average exposures to market characteristics. Through its exposure to market characteristics such as duration, sector, coupon and quality, the normal portfolio serves as the best predictor of the manager's portfolios' expected risk and return profile. The normal portfolio captures the essence of a manager's long-run investment style and so serves as a point of reference for evaluating the success of his active investment decisions.

Given that the normal portfolio represents a manager's long-run passive investment strategy, departures from the normal portfolio represent the strategic (active) investment decisions. These departures are made in response to changes in current market conditions with the expectation of capturing excess return or of protecting the value of the portfolio during adverse market conditions. It is from these departures that active returns are generated and active fees are paid by the plan sponsor. Consequently, the use of a normal portfolio allows the success of a manager's active investment strategies to be evaluated and performance fees to be administered based on the value added by the manager's active process. The use of normal portfolios addresses several of the important problems encountered in designing a performance fee arrangement.

Perhaps most importantly, a manager's normal portfolio provides the plan sponsor with valuable information for choosing a "portfolio" of managers who, individually or collectively, will meet the desired risk and return objectives of the sponsor's plan. A well-constructed normal portfolio serves as an objective representation of the manager's investment process, which is the basis on which a particular manager is hired. Because the sponsor now has a benchmark that is tailored to a manager's individual investment style, the returns on the managed portfolio can be evaluated against a benchmark that truly indicates what the portfolio returns should be given that manager's style. Even though the managed portfolio may underperform the broad market, the manager may have added value relative to what he was hired to do, as represented by his normal portfolio. Clearly, the use of manager normal portfolios will enhance the communication between the sponsor and manager. The focus of discussions can be on the portfolio tactics that have increased or decreased the risks and returns of the managed portfolio relative to the manager's long-run strategy. Such discussion helps both sponsor and manager avoid the harmful "horse-race" syndrome, where the returns from diverse investment styles are directly compared to one another without regard for the appropriate risk levels inherent in the various styles. This provides a motivation for managers to focus solely on near-term performance rather than on the long-term goals of the fund. Whether or not normal portfolios are used in conjunction with a performance fee structure, the information they provide gives the sponsor and manager common ground to discuss the investment tactics employed in pursuit of the goals set forth for that manager.

Having first established the correct benchmark for a given manager, normal portfolios can be used to design a logical performance fee structure that rewards the manager for pursuing the goals of the sponsor. Merely having a performance benchmark is not enough; the manager's expected performance relative to that benchmark must be considered. In our research we considered seven years of quarterly returns for an actively managed portfolio and its normal portfolio. The active portfolio outperformed the normal in eighteen of the twenty-eight quarters by an average of 26 basis points per quarter or 105 basis points per year. We refer to the value added by the active management process relative to the normal as "excess return." Clearly, if the normal portfolio return itself is the bogey in a performance fee arrangement, the sponsor will be rewarding the manager for superior performance most of the time. Assuming that the historical expected excess return is the best predictor of future excess returns, we believe that the true bogey should be based on what the manager's active process can be expected to add to his passive normal portfolio return.

Rather than starting with a minimal base fee and then deciding at what rate the manager should be rewarded for his performance, it is more logical to approach the problem from the perspective of the manager's expected excess return. If the active portfolio has historically returned 105 basis points per year above the normal, then at this level of excess return the manager's fee should be comparable to the fee paid under the current fee structure. Excess returns greater than the expected excess returns should reward the manager with a greater fee, and positive excess returns that are less than the expected level should provide a fee somewhat less than the usual active fee. Such a fee structure is sound because it is based on the manager's actual past performance relative to his normal portfolio and ensures continuity when changing from a fixed fee schedule to a performance fee arrangement. This may also mitigate some of the manager's anxiety over the increased volatility of his revenue stream because his expected fee under the new arrangement will be comparable to his usual fee.

IV. The Problem of "Gaming"

Inherent in establishing a performance fee arrangement for fixed income managers is the problem of "gaming," that is, actions taken by the manager to subvert the performance fee arrangement to gain a higher fee. The most obvious gaming tactic is to set the return bogey too low, so that the manager is practically assured of outperforming it. More complex and difficult to detect gaming tactics arise when caps and floors are part of the fee structure.

Under the circumstances where a "floor" level is attained, the manager might take substantial risk in areas where no expertise has historically existed with the expectation that there is nothing to lose yet everything to gain in the future (betting-the-ranch). Floors are similar to the manager owning a long call option—when the active return is less than the floor trigger point, the manager has nothing to lose and increased fees to gain by increasing the portfolio's exposure to risk. At a "cap" level of return the manager has nothing to gain by taking risk, and he may wish to index the portfolio to the normal in order to ensure capturing the maximum performance fee. Caps are similar to the manager selling a call option—when the active return is greater than the level that triggers the fee cap, the manager has an incentive to reduce the portfolio's risk in order to protect the maximum fee. Performance fee structures should offer sufficient latitude for the manager to take risk on the sponsor's behalf in search of opportunities of increased return, yet have a minimal probability of achieving either a floor or cap return level.

V. Proposed Structure for Performance Fees

A performance fee structure should provide the manager with adequate incentives that are in the sponsor's best interest at all times. Such a structure would guard against the manager either taking excessive risk or "closet indexing" by introducing the notion of a manager's forecasted alpha (relative to his normal). This approach has the advantage of being sufficiently flexible to be used in any sponsor/manager relationship; however, it does require the rigorous specification of the manager's normal portfolio in order to be implemented properly.

The following notation can be used to describe this fee concept. Let:

R_n = Normal portfolio return
R_p = Active portfolio return
$R_e = R_p - R_n$ (excess return)
a = Base fee
b = Participation or incentive rate
r = Risk aversion factor
c = Penalty adjustment $(b \times r)$
A_f = Forecasted alpha

Thus:

$$\text{Fee (basis points)} = a + b(R_e) - c(A_f - R_e)^2.$$

Thus the base fee plus the incentive minus the penalty would provide the basic equation for the performance fee. Floors and caps are outside of the equation and should be agreed upon by the sponsor and manager. The significant input to this decision is the variability of the excess return. In order to ensure against hitting either the floor or the cap too frequently, and so to provide sufficient latitude to capture the appropriate fee for the level of active performance, the floor and cap must be set wide enough around the expected excess return, yet not at too high or low a level to nullify the purpose of including them in the fee structure. We believe that the setting of these levels should be based on the statistical probability of hitting either one, given the manager's expected excess return and the historical volatility of the excess return. If, for example, the cap and floor are each triggered at a level of excess return that is two standard deviations away from the expected excess return, then the probability of hitting the cap or the floor is only 4.56 percent. For purposes of illustration we have used a 3 basis point floor and a 50 basis point cap. A graphic representation of the performance fee concept is presented in Figure 1.

Figure 1 shows a floor of 3 basis points and a cap of 50 basis points with an average excess return fee of 30 basis points. The active fee is positioned at the point where the average historical excess return (105 basis points) represents the manager's active fee. This positioning of the base fee equals the average seven-year historical excess return for the active portfolio. The proposed fee structure is somewhat symmetrical with sufficient incentives for the manager to add value over a predetermined time horizon. Additionally,

---

FIGURE 1. *Performance Fee Framework.*

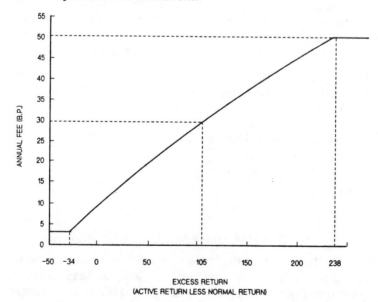

there is a sufficient disincentive for the manager should performance be less than the forecasted alphas over the same time horizon.

Because the squared penalty term is included in the fee equation, the graph of the function between the cap and floor levels is concave rather than a straight line. Essentially, we are seeing the center section of the left leg of a parabola, above zero on the Y-axis and below the inflection point of the parabola.

A particularly appealing feature of the proposed structure is the fact that the slope of the line tangent to the incentive fee curve is equal to 1.0 where $R_e = A_f$. Below the manager's forecasted alpha (A_f), fees are rising at an increasing rate. Above the manager's forecasted alpha, fees are rising at a decreasing rate. Consequently, any variance from the manager's forecasted alphas has the effect of decreasing the marginal fee. *In order to maximize his marginal fee, the manager should deliver the excess returns provided by historical experience and fairly represent his managerial skills.* It is far more difficult to obtain a higher fee under this structure given a manager's historical experience, but encouragement to be creative in adding value is provided by the sponsor as long as the manager adheres to his style of management.

VI. Revenue Volatility and Performance Measurement Horizon

One of the primary issues surrounding the current controversy over performance fees is the potential increase in the volatility of the manager's revenue stream. As can be seen from Figure 2, the volatility of the quarterly management fee is significantly increased under the performance structure fee presented here. Performance fees transfer the risk-bearing associated with the volatility of excess returns from the sponsor to the manager. Unfortunately, this situation may prevent many managers from accepting an incentive fee arrangement.

The problem of fee volatility stems from the fact that the performance measurement period has remained unchanged from that under the usual fixed-fee schedules. If, instead of looking at performance on a quarter-by-quarter basis, we were to measure the cumulative excess return relative to the cumulative forecasted alpha, we could calculate a range into which the cumulative excess return could be expected to fall for any given measurement period. Figure 3 illustrates this notion. The horizontal line at +105 basis points represents the expected annual excess return at the beginning of the contract and performance measurement period based on historical data supplied by the manager. The cone of points that converge around the +105 basis point line represents the range of values plus or minus one standard deviation from the expected excess return for the annualized cumulative return

FIGURE 2. *Impact of Performance Fees on Manager Revenue, $100 Million Portfolio as of 12/31/79.*

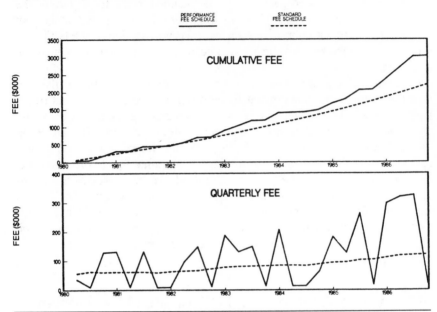

for the number of periods of management return indicated on the X-axis. Clearly, the more quarters of actual return data that are used in the calculation, the greater the probability of achieving an annualized cumulative excess return that is near the long-run historical average.

Given that a sponsor implicitly accepts the return volatility inherent in a particular manager's investment style by actually hiring the manager, the sponsor should be willing to pay a performance fee based on excess returns that fall within an acceptable range around the long-run expected excess return. We have used the range of plus or minus one standard deviation here solely for the purpose of illustrating the concept.

The actual range will depend on the degree of probability of matching the forecasted alpha that the sponsor is willing to accept. Such an arrangement need not necessarily be symmetrical. That is, the manager might be willing to accept more deviation from the forecasted alphas on the up side than on the down side. Employing this probability range methodology will require some adjustment to the penalty function in the fee equation in order to maintain consistency in the calculation of the peformance fee.

Obviously, neither the manager nor the sponsor will want to rely solely on past performance as the determinant of the forecasted alpha. We suggest that the returns achieved in each subsequent quarter be added to the

FIGURE 3. *Standard Deviation of Return Spreads, January 1980 – December 1986.*

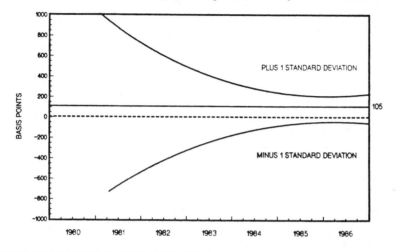

calculation of the expected excess return and standard deviation, and that the oldest return figure be dropped from the calculation. This results in a rolling twelve-quarter figure that will eventually incorporate only those returns earned while under contract to the sponsor. The probability of falling within the acceptable range will not change, but the range itself (in basis points) may narrow or widen depending upon the return volatility actually experienced.

Finally, a relatively long (compared to current practice) performance measurement horizon and contract length must be employed to implement this structure effectively. A three-year (twelve-quarter) period is probably a reasonable period over which to calculate expected excess returns. The effect here is to smooth the volatility of the manager's revenue stream by incorporating the performance of prior periods in the calculation of the fee for the current period. While some managers may object to the burden of poor past performance, this type of rolling cumulative fee calculation enforces the importance of hiring managers to provide the fund with long-term performance as the goal. This will help bring the goals of the manager into coincidence with those of the sponsor and, indeed, will encourage the sponsor as well as his managers to focus on the longer-term objectives of the total fund.

VII. Further Issues

Because the normal portfolio concept is essential to striking the right performance fee arrangement, the resources devoted to construction, maintenance and ongoing monitoring of the manager's normal is a key issue to be faced by both the sponsor and the manager. Fixed-income normals are difficult to construct and in many cases may require the assistance of the consultant community. Probably the most desirable methodology for constructing a fixed income normal is first to determine the representative long-term characteristics of the manager's active process, then to construct an index with weightings that provide the best representation of the risk factors anticipated by the manager's style. This approach has the distinct advantage of being the easiest to calculate and understand by the sponsor. Further, maintenance of the normal index is less complicated, and performance evaluation more accurately portrays the manager's style by eliminating return that is directly related to the manager's ability to select securities. It is important to note that the index should be priced and returns calculated by an independent source so that performance is objectively determined.

Some thought should be given to the appropriate floor level for performance fee calculations. It seems reasonable that the floor fee should be that fee with which the sponsor could purchase a passive portfolio that captures the essence of a desired style of management. Particular styles of management are provided by the money management community and vary in their complexity. Consequently, it is reasonable to assume that replicating a portfolio strategy of greater complexity will require a higher cost. Thus, the floor compensation may need to be adjusted to reflect the actual cost of replicating the manager's style. Furthermore, the manager provides the sponsor with several services that are not generally taken into account, but are thrown into the basket of services that a sponsor pays for under fixed fee arrangements. These ancillary services include transaction services, liquidity services, diligence and prudence, assistance (either implicit or explicit) in the sponsor's asset allocation decision, and, most importantly, a proprietary investment style. It is this last service, which includes not only the objective representation of investment strategy represented by the normal portfolio but also intangibles such as the synergy of the investment team and the trader's relationships with the brokers, that causes us to hold that the return on the normal portfolio is a result of more than a mere passive strategy and, thus, should earn more than a passive fee.

A manager is taking a part of the excess return as his fee (at the given participation rate b) and so is acting as a financial intermediary. To the extent that the manager may be required to rely on his own capitalization in order to guarantee the normal return when the excess return is negative, an extremely undesirable situation is created, which will benefit neither sponsor nor manager. The sponsor should realize that most managers are not in a position to act as financial intermediaries; they simply do not have the capital to borrow substantial sums of money during periods when returns are under pressure. Further, people within the investment community are extremely mobile and can be easily lured away from an adverse circumstance under a performance fee arrangement that has negative fees or a payback scheme to the sponsors. Finally, larger firms would benefit from a negative performance scheme and may be willing to enter into agreements that include such schemes simply as a marketing ploy to gain some advantage over smaller firms. Consequently, the sponsor should carefully assess any performance fee arrangement that includes a negative or payback scheme.

Most investment advisory contracts contain a clause specifying a thirty- to ninety-day notice before a manager may be terminated. Under a performance fee arrangment, consideration should be given to this notification period so that the performance measurement period more closely corresponds to the effective termination dates.

VIII. Summary

Implicit in this article is the view that performance fees should not have a meaningful impact on the actual performance of an investment manager. However, there is a great deal of value associated with the manager/sponsor establishing a normal portfolio and measuring performance in a meaningful way. Further, performance fees can enhance the communications between the sponsor and the manager as both parties understand the peaks and valleys a particular style may encounter during a full market cycle. The sponsor focuses on the manager's performance, not market performance, which is key to the communications issue. Finally, under a performance fee arrangement, the manager may be motivated to be innovative in improving his investment process so that performance is enhanced by taking controlled risks relative to his normal portfolio in pursuit of opportunities that correspond to the sponsor's goals.

Essential to any performance fee is the degree to which it can be easily understood and administered by all parties. However, a performance fee arrangement should be based on the manager's ability to provide an active return relative to his style of management, not upon some expectation of added value above a market index; this demands a clear understanding (and representation) of the manager's investment process.

Finally, sponsors should be aware of the problems associated with performance fees and ensure that thoughtful consideration is given to the added business risks of the manager. Performance fees can be structured to achieve fairness to both parties and to promote an atmosphere conducive to the highest quality of portfolio management.

32

High Yield Mortgage Securities

Andrew S. Carron
Vice President
First Boston Corporation

Eric I. Hemel
Vice President
First Boston Corporation

Bennett W. Golub

I. Introduction

Over the last few years, a new market has developed for a variety of high yield mortgage-related securities that offers both rewards and risks far greater than those offered by previously available mortgage-related instruments. Only a thorough examination of these different securities will enable an investor to take full advantage of the new opportunities that their development affords, as well as to avoid the associated hazards.

Mortgages and mortgage securities have traditionally provided yields substantially above other products of comparable credit quality. This yield differential may be attributed primarily to the recognition that mortgage cash flows are inherently uncertain.

High yield mortgage securities are created when mortgage cash flows are divided into two or more pieces, creating at least one instrument that has a set of performance characteristics substantially different from the underlying mortgages. The defining features of these derivative securities are high yield, high credit quality, and returns that are extremely sensitive to interest rates and/or prepayment rates. At present, high yield mortgage securities encompass residuals from CMOs and REMICs, certain stripped mortgage backed securities, and leveraged floating rate mortgage securities.

High yield mortgage securities have developed out of the increasing ability of mortgage securities issuers to create derivative cash flow streams which, when viewed individually, bear little resemblance to the primary cash flows of the underlying mortgages themselves. As a result, it is now possible to construct securities based on mortgage cash flows that possess extraordinarily different risk and reward characteristics from those of the underlying mortgages. While the interest rate risk and prepayment risk inherent in residual mortgages transfer in full to the derivative securities as a whole, different portions of those securities can be configured to meet the desires of investors with a wide array of risk/reward preferences. High yield mortgage securities can concentrate both the risks and rewards of the underlying mortgages into instruments that require a considerably lower cash investment than that required to invest in the underlying mortgages themselves.

High yield mortgage securities have negative attributes other than their performance risk. Due to their relatively recent introduction to the market, these securities lack the liquidity associated with the traditional mortgage pass-through market. More important, they are quite complex in comparison to traditional mortgage investments and therefore require greater effort and consideration by investors. As with other complex investments, the range in value among different high yield mortgage securities is wide. Apparently similar instruments may have radically different performance profiles and intrinsic values. Investor success will depend upon the ability to make relevant distinctions among high yield mortgage products.

High Yield Mortgage Securities

Traditional fixed income securities, including mortgage-related securities, have clearly defined principal (face value) and interest components. With a non-callable bond, the future cash flows (principal and interest) are known with certainty. Even with a traditional mortgage security, where prepayments are not fully predictable, several things are certain: ultimately, the face value of the instrument will be repaid at par; the coupon interest payable at any time is a function of the then-remaining principal; and prepayment variations will tend to reduce the gains in a falling rate environment and accentuate the losses in a rising rate environment.

High yield mortgage securities are different. Several of these instruments —CMO residuals and interest only (IO) strips—have little or no principal, as that term is usually understood. Leveraged floaters have a face amount of principal and a coupon, but the coupon is determined by a formula quite unlike that for traditional floating rate securities. Principal only (PO) strips have a face amount of principal but no coupon. It is therefore useful to characterize high yield mortgage securities as streams of cash flows rather than as packages of principal and interest. Assignment of these flows to interest income and return of principal can be made for accounting purposes, but investors should consider the economic returns—the cash flows—rather than the accounting treatment, when making investment decisions. Calculations of yield and total return depend not on the characterization of the cash, but only on the amount and the timing of the cash flow.

The lack of principal amounts for some high yield security types requires that price quotations be based on notional principal. That is, the price is expressed as a percentage of the principal amount of the underlying collateral, even though the security itself does not include the principal. Once this pricing convention is understood, it can be used in the same manner as more traditional investments.

Reasons to Invest in High Yield Mortgage Securities

The first reason to own these instruments is, of course, yield. Quoted yields can be substantially higher than on any other investment of comparable quality, and from 100 to 800 basis points or more over the highest yielding Treasury securities. But there are other considerations as well.

High yield mortgage securities are more sensitive to economic conditions than other fixed income investments. That is, the price, or present value of future cash flows, can change more in response to a given move in market interest rates and/or prepayment rates than virtually any other security in the market except options and futures. This can make some high yield mortgage securities valuable as hedging tools.

The extent to which this risk is viewed negatively will depend on whether prospective investors evaluate the risk factors in isolation or with respect to an entire portfolio. A number of high yield securities are high-risk investments when viewed in isolation in that they have substantial positive or negative durations and/or are highly sensitive to prepayment shifts. Nevertheless, when these instruments are added to a general mortgage portfolio in appropriate quantities, they may serve to reduce overall interest rate risk or prepayment risk. Although many of the same risk reduction objectives can, in theory, be accomplished through the use of futures, options, and interest rate swaps, high yield mortgage securities offer many advantages: they are available for longer terms than futures and options; they offer higher yields during the holding periods than traditional hedging instruments, which tend to reduce portfolio yield; there is no maintenance margin requirement or overcollateralization required; and they may be considered qualifying real estate investments for savings institution tax purposes. High yield mortgage securities also provide an alternative for those investors prevented by regulation from using futures and options to hedge their portfolios.

Analysts and investors specializing in equities have long recognized that assessing the risk of an investment depends on its "portfolio effect" — that is, its effect on total portfolio risk. The potential for raising aggregate portfolio yield while reducing overall portfolio risk presents intriguing opportunities for financial institutions with significant investments in mortgages and other fixed rate debt instruments.

II. Characteristics of High Yield Mortgage Securities

High yield mortgage securities offer high yield, high credit quality, and a pattern of returns unlike those of other securities in the market. The presence of high yield mortgage securities in a portfolio can enhance returns, reduce maturity gaps, hedge mortgages and bonds, and create synthetic instruments with desirable performance profiles. These advantages can be seen most clearly when the performance of these products is compared over a range of possible economic scenarios.

Yield and Duration

As their name suggests, high yield mortgage securities offer investors higher yields than any other security of comparable quality. Some CMO residuals, interest only strips, and leveraged floaters have been offered at yields of 3% or more above comparable Treasury securities, based on reasonable pricing and prepayment assumptions. Yields on some CMO residuals have been as high as 25%. Moreover, payback periods can be relatively short, often 3 to 5 years (see Table 1).

To quantify price sensitivity for securities with variable cash flows, the concept of "effective duration" is more appropriate than modified duration. Effective duration is an empirically determined relationship between changes in market interest rates and the price of a security. For securities without embedded options, effective and modified duration are equal, and can be expressed as unmodified duration divided by one plus the periodic yield. For securities with embedded options, such as callable bonds or mortgages that

TABLE 1. *Characteristics of High Yield Mortgage Securities.*

Security	Average Life Range (years)	Cash Flow Duration Range (years)	Effective Duration Range (years)	Yield Spread over Treasuries (%)
CMO residuals	2–5	1–4	−15–+1	2–16
IO strips	N/M	3–7	−20–+1	0–3
PO strips	3–9	3–7	+8–+18	0–3
Leveraged floaters	3–9	3–7	−2–+14	0–3

can be prepaid, effective duration is no longer equal to modified duration. In the case of CMO residuals, the disparity is particularly great: while the modified duration of bearish residuals is 2 to 4 years, the effective duration may be in the range of -10 to -15 years.

Credit Quality

Unlike many high yield corporate securities, the attractive returns on residuals, strips, and leveraged floaters are not a reflection of actual or perceived credit risk. Some high yield mortgage securities such as FNMA strips carry agency guarantees. Others, such as reverse floaters and privately issued strips, are rated AAA or AA. CMO residuals are backed by collateral rated AAA or AA. The trustee structure and segregated collateral employed in structured financings provides further protection to investors. These are securities of high quality that are unlikely ever to experience downgradings, because they are fully collateralized by assets that tend to appreciate even as the debt is paying down.

Patterns of Returns

The patterns of returns depend primarily on the movement of market interest rates. Interest rate levels affect not only the discount rate but also the cash flows themselves because of the sensitivity of mortgage prepayments to interest rate changes. In CMOs with floating rate tranches, they can also affect the coupons being paid on the bonds. Typically, much of the effect of prepayment variability on the underlying mortgages is passed through to the holder of the high yield mortgage security.

Although variability of returns is a characteristic of all high yield mortgage securities, the direction and pattern of movement varies. Because of the partitioning of the principal and interest components, these securities can offer investors a wide range of investment alternatives. Some perform better when interest rates rise, others when rates fall. Returns may be symmetric or asymmetric, in either up or down markets.

Each pattern of returns suggests appropriate applications for high yield mortgage securities. For investors with a clear point of view on market direction, these instruments provide the greatest potential for value appreciation. Institutions with large portfolios of long-term fixed rate assets may find it more advantageous to accomplish restructuring objectives through the purchase of IO strips or CMO residuals than through the sale of existing assets or the acquisition of longer-term liabilities. High yield mortgage securities may be used to hedge other instruments or to create synthetic instruments with returns superior to traditional products.

How to Analyze High Yield Mortgage Securities

Because the performance of high yield mortgage securities is so sensitive to economic conditions, it is not sufficient to evaluate their purchase strictly on the basis of a single quoted yield to maturity. Investors should evaluate the sensitivity of returns to changes in the financial environment. This technique is generally termed *scenario analysis*.

The amount, timing, and value of the cash flows of high yield mortgage securities are dependent on the course of economic events. Investors must understand how the value of these instruments will vary under the most likely scenarios. Scenarios are typically characterized by a projected path of future interest rates and mortgage prepayment rates. Each of these can vary independently, although there is a strong relationship between the level of market interest rates and the prepayment rates on fixed rate mortgages. Interest rate changes influence investor discount rates, cash flow reinvestment rates, and coupon levels on floating rate bonds. Prepayment rate changes affect the amount of cash flow from principal paid to bondholders and the size of the remaining balance on which interest continues to accrue.

Traditional yield calculations are insufficient to describe the complex interactions among these factors and the resulting impact on the value of the investments. Scenario analysis is a technique for modeling the performance of an investment under a variety of circumstances, aggregating these forecasts, and comparing alternative strategies.

For high yield mortgage securities, scenario analysis begins with a set of possible market interest rate movements. This may range from a small number of highly simplified events (stable rates, rates up 100 basis points, rates down 100 basis points) to a random simulation of interest rate paths that can involve thousands of trials. It is also necessary to account for the fact that interest rate changes are not uniform across maturities and sectors: a model of yield curves and yield spreads is helpful. Finally, it is necessary to forecast mortgage prepayment rates for each interest rate scenario based on the level and pattern of mortgage rates, the age of the mortgages, and other factors. A typical prepayment model is shown in Figure 1.

Models like this can provide a realistic view of the cash flows anticipated from high yield mortgage securities. Often, probabilities are assigned to each scenario, allowing calculation of an average expected return weighted by the probabilities. This reliable method of comparing alternative investments takes into account the fact that the realized performance of most securities in the market — and high yield mortgage securities in particular — is dependent on future market conditions.

While scenario analysis is a powerful tool that may be used to evaluate a wide variety of fixed income investments, it is not a perfect predictor. Actual prepayment rates may diverge from the model's estimate for reasons

FIGURE 1. *Prepayment Model.*

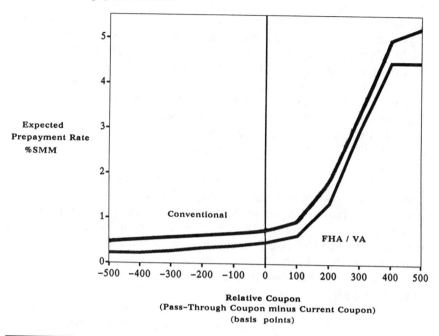

Relative Coupon
(Pass-Through Coupon minus Current Coupon)
(basis points)

unrelated to interest rates, mortgage age, and other factors accounted for. This variance is as likely to work to the benefit as to the detriment of the investor. Similarly, unanticipated events may cause yield spreads to narrow or widen, or yield volatility to increase or decrease. Scenario analysis nevertheless provides the best means of assembling all of the currently available market information into a structure that permits meaningful comparison among very different instruments.

III. CMO Residuals

Collateralized mortgage obligation (CMO) residuals present a relatively new investment opportunity for sophisticated investors. Previously, investments in residuals were available only to those institutions willing to issue CMOs. This required the expense and effort of creating issuing subsidiaries, filing shelf registrations with the Securities and Exchange Commission (SEC), developing or arranging for bond administration capabilities, and establishing investment banking and mortgage finance relationships. Because of several recent legal and accounting developments, investors can now purchase interests in residual cash flows directly from CMO issuers. This can involve purchasing existing residuals "off the shelf" from CMO issuers such as mortgage bankers, home builders, mortgage conduit operations, or investment banks. Or it can entail the purchase of "custom tailored" residuals created by a special issuer according to the investor's specifications.

CMO residuals are the equity of the corporation or trust that issued the CMO. Generally, this equity is sold to investors on a private-placement basis, where the investor purchases common stock or Certificates of Beneficial Interest in the Owner Trust. A few CMO issuing corporations have issued common stock to the public. Residuals may be issued as REMIC residual interests.

Residuals arise from the creation of a structured financing in which the cash flows of a pool of assets are used to fund the cash flow requirements of one or more classes of collateralized debt. For the most part, residual cash flows result from the positive spread between the cash flow generated by a pool of assets and the cash flow required to serve one or more classes of bonds collateralized by those assets. This is shown schematically in Figure 2. Indeed, the spread between the mortgage and CMO cash flows is the primary reason for issuing a CMO.

All investments in residuals assign to the investor an expected (but uncertain) stream of future cash flows. Figure 3 shows a typical pattern for residual cash flows in relation to the CMO bond cash flows. Initially, the level of cash flow is high. It begins to drop rapidly with the amortization of the assets collateralizing the bonds. As the shape of the expected cash flow in-

---

FIGURE 2. *CMO Cash Flows.*

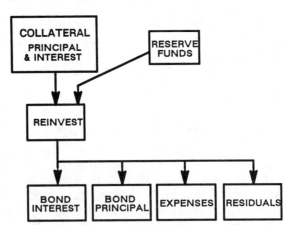

FIGURE 3. *CMO Cash Flows.*

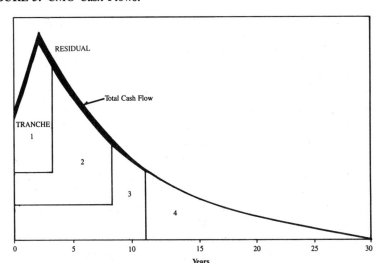

dicates, residuals typically have a final cash flow corresponding to the final maturity of the collateral, but the expected cash flow duration of the investment is very short.

Unlike most fixed income investments, these cash flows are not explicitly divisible into principal and interest components. As CMO equity, residuals represent the ownership of the stream of excess cash flows generated by the trust — that is, the net income or "profits."

Residuals essentially represent a leveraged investment in a closed-end, match-funded bond portfolio. Economically, ownership of residuals amounts to ownership of a pool of collateral that is partially funded through a series of liabilities, generally CMOs. The economic characteristics of residuals depend on the characteristics of the assets, the characteristics of the liabilities, and how they are combined. The structural integrity required of the CMO bonds by the rating agencies ensures that the assets will always prove sufficient to support the bonds with the same degree of creditworthiness as the assets. Therefore, unlike investments in some mismatched asset/liability strategies, an investment in residuals will not produce cash shortfalls after the investment has occurred.

Components of Residual Cash Flows

Residuals are cash flows resulting from the difference between the cash generated by a pool of collateral and that required to fund bonds that are entirely supported by that collateral. Behind the seemingly complicated nature of residual cash flows are a number of basic building blocks, each of which behaves in a straightforward manner. By understanding each component individually, it becomes possible to understand how and why residuals behave the way they do. The components of residual cash flow are:

- Collateral principal payments
- Collateral interest payments
- Reinvestment interest on collateral cash flow
- Bond principal retirements
- Bond interest payments
- Bond administration expenses

The behavior of each of these components will vary depending upon the type of collateral, the types of bonds, and other details specific to the structured financing. Each of the six components of residual cash flow will respond differently to the general state of the economy and general conditions in the financial markets.

Collateral principal payments have two parts: scheduled payments and unscheduled prepayments. In fact, the majority of the principal paid from a pool of mortgages in a given period consists of unscheduled principal. Because of this, the amount of cash flow available to the residuals will vary substantially with the rate of prepayments. Generally, the slower the prepayment rate, the greater the longevity of the cash stream payable to residual holders. The exact impact of prepayment changes on residual cash flows, and thus on total performance, can vary significantly from one residual to the next.

Collateral interest payments are another major source of cash inflow in a CMO. Unlike collateral principal payments, in which only the timing of cash flows is affected by prepayments, both the timing *and* the total amount of collateral interest payments will vary with prepayments. As prepayment rates increase, the total amount of collateral interest payments that will be received decreases, and vice versa.

Reinvestment interest on collateral cash flow is the third source of residuals. All CMO structures require some delay between the receipt of collateral cash flows and the scheduled payments to bondholders. While collateral pays monthly, most CMOs pay quarterly. Therefore, there is usually some period during which collateral cash flows must be reinvested. Most, if not all, of the reinvestment interest earned on the cash flows awaiting payment to bondholders is paid to residual holders. While this is not typically a main source of residual cash flow, its effect will be greater in CMOs where the size of the residual is small in percentage terms, or where the reinvestment period is longer.

An important determinant of the amount of reinvestment interest payable to the residual holder is the actual interest rate available on the funds to be reinvested. For residual holders, this component of their cash flow will generally increase as interest rates increase, since these temporary cash balances are invested in money market instruments earning current market rates.

Bond principal retirements absorb collateral cash flow and its reinvestment interest. Most CMOs have been issued with the provision that the rate of prepayment on the collateral will determine the rate of principal retirement on the bonds. This means that rapid amortization of the bonds almost always occurs when the collateral prepays rapidly. Similarly, if the collateral prepayment slows down, so will that of the bonds. Because the size of the residual cash flows is a function of the amount of bonds outstanding, rapid retirements of CMO bond principal tend to hurt residual holders, while slow retirements tend to help them.

Bond interest payments, like bond principal retirements, absorb collateral cash flow and reinvestment interest. Increases in these interest payments always reduce the amount of cash flow available to residual holders. The amount of interest to be paid varies directly with the remaining amount of bond principal and, in the case of floating rate tranches, with the level of the bond's index rate.

Most CMO floaters have had their coupons indexed to three-month LIBOR. The cash flow to residual holders in these transactions will tend to increase as the index rate decreases and decrease as the index rate increases. The position of the floating rate CMO residual holder is analogous to that of a financial institution that finances fixed rate assets with floating rate liabilities. Unlike such a financial institution, however, the residual investor is ensured that there will never be a negative spread between the collateral and the liabilities it supports.

Bond administration expenses are the last and least significant end to which collateral cash flows must be applied. To the extent that these bond expenses increase, the returns to the residual holders decrease. These fees include expenses for the Indenture Trustee, accountants, rating agencies, and legal counsel. Some of these expenses will increase over time because of inflation. Thus, bond administration expenses, as a percentage of residual cash flow, will have a tendency to rise, since the compounding effects of expense inflation occur simultaneously with the amortization of both the collateral and the bonds.

The timing of cash flows under a characteristic scenario for residuals produced by a typical CMO, FBC Mortgage Securities Trust V, is illustrated in Table 2.

Different Types of Residual Investments

Residuals represent the differential between mortgage collateral and CMO bond cash flows; as such, they are highly sensitive to minor alterations in the

TABLE 2. *FBC Mortgage Securities Trust V, Summary of Residual Cash Flows (FHLMC 9.4% WAC Collateral, Priced at 185% PSA).*[a]

For the Year Ending January 20	Principal & Interest on FHLMC Certificates	Reinvestment Income at 6.00%	Principal & Interest on Bonds	Bond & Trust Expenses	Draws from Reserve Funds[b]	Bond Administrator Fee[c]	Distributable Cash Flow
1988	$75,964	$431	$72,049	$87	$ 0	$39	$4,220
1989	94,515	539	90,520	100	0	50	4,383
1990	83,718	477	80,257	94	0	50	3,794
1991	74,083	422	71,099	89	0	50	3,267
1992	65,523	374	62,970	84	0	50	2,793
1993	57,919	330	55,753	80	0	50	2,366
1994	51,165	292	49,350	77	0	50	1,980
1995	45,166	258	43,670	73	0	50	1,630
1996	39,838	227	38,636	70	0	50	1,309
1997	35,107	200	34,175	68	0	50	1,015
1998	30,906	176	30,219	65	0	50	748
1999	27,177	155	26,719	63	0	50	500
2000	23,867	136	23,590	62	0	50	302
2001	20,929	119	20,700	60	0	50	238
2002	18,322	105	18,126	59	0	50	191
2003	16,009	91	15,843	57	0	50	150
2004	13,958	80	13,819	56	0	50	113
2005	12,139	69	12,023	55	0	50	80

TABLE 2 *Continued*

For the Year Ending January 20	Principal & Interest on FHLMC Certificates	Reinvestment Income at 6.00%	Principal & Interest on Bonds	Bond & Trust Expenses	Draws from Reserve Funds[b]	Bond Administrator Fee[c]	Distributable Cash Flow
2006	$10,527	$60	$10,431	$54	$ 0	$50	$51
2007	9,097	52	9,020	54	0	50	25
2008	7,831	45	7,771	53	0	49	4
2009	6,710	38	6,664	52	0	32	0
2010	5,718	33	5,684	52	0	15	0
2011	4,840	28	4,817	51	2	1	0
2012	4,063	23	4,050	51	15	0	0
2013	3,377	19	3,373	51	27	0	0
2014	2,333	14	2,337	50	40	0	0
2015	1,574	9	1,582	50	48	0	0
2016	420	3	422	38	603	340	227
Total	842,799	4,804	815,668	1,858	736	1,427	29,387

a. Dollars in thousands rounded to the nearest thousand.
b. Draws from the Reserve Funds are sufficient to cover shortfalls as well as to release funds from the Bond Reserve Fund upon the retirement of the Bonds.
c. Fees due to the Bond Administrator that are not payable from funds released from the lien of the Indenture are deferred until sufficient cash flow from the Reserve Funds becomes available.

collateral or bond structures. Thus, the economic characteristics of residuals do not lend themselves to a single stereotype.

In order to demonstrate how residuals can perform differently, this section will discuss the three basic kinds of CMO residuals produced to date, which we will label as "bearish," "humped," and "stable." As new CMO structures continue to evolve, it is likely that hybrids of these residual types will emerge.

Bearish residuals increase in yield as interest rates increase, and decrease in yield as interest rates fall. The overwhelming majority of CMO residuals produced prior to the Fall of 1986 were bearish residuals. This kind of residual was created by using mortgage securities as collateral for CMOs with only fixed-coupon tranches. The large negative duration of bearish residuals, comparable to shorting an ordinary bond, makes them attractive for hedging purposes. This feature can be seen in Figure 4, where a typical investment in bearish residuals is shown to yield in excess of 20% for interest rate increases in excess of 100 basis points, with a steep decline in yield for interest rate drops of more than 50 basis points. Bearish residuals are offered at wide spreads over long U.S. Treasury bonds, and are especially attractive in light of their counter-cyclical performance characteristics.

FIGURE 4. *Scenario Yields on Bearish Residuals.*

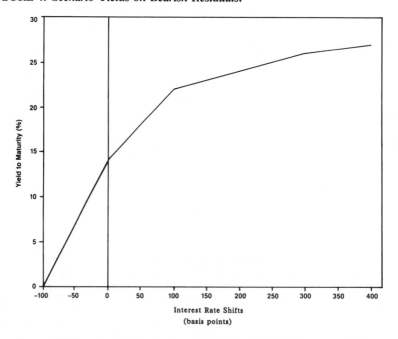

The shorter maturity tranches of a multi-class, fixed rate CMO will have lower coupons than the longer tranches when the yield curve is positively sloped. Thus, as the underlying mortgages prepay and amortize and the shorter, lower-coupon tranches pay down, the average coupon rate on the remaining bonds will rise. For example, FBC Mortgage Securities Trust III Series A at issue had three tranches of unequal size bearing coupon rates of 8.825%, 9.70%, and 9.50%, respectively, resulting in a weighted average coupon of 9.073%. The underlying collateral has a coupon rate of 10%. Initially, therefore, the residual cash flows are approximately equal to 0.927% of the amount of the bonds outstanding: 10% received from the collateral, less 9.073% on average paid on the bonds. After the first tranche is retired, however, the weighted-average coupon of the CMO would be 9.638%. At that point, the residual cash flows would be smaller, because there are fewer bonds outstanding and because the weighted-average coupon on the remaining bonds increases. These residuals have a relatively short payback period, or "stated" duration. (Stated duration is calculated by projecting the cash flows and then determining the average amount of time until receipt of present value.) The amount of residual cash flow declines sharply over time. Stated duration on most residuals of this type ranges from 2 to 4 years. Events in the more distant future have little impact on the return to residual holders.

As a consequence, if interest rates fall and prepayments rise, rapid prepayments of the shorter classes will both reduce the coupon spread between the CMO and the mortgage collateral and shorten the longevity of the residual cash flows. Conversely, in a rising rate environment, residual holders will enjoy both a wider spread and longer-lasting residual cash flows. Due to these relationships, the performance of bearish residuals will tend to be inversely related to that of most fixed income securities. Whereas most fixed income investments perform best in a falling rate environment, bearish residuals will perform better in a rising rate environment.

Humped residuals tend to command a higher yield than bearish residuals because their yield at pricing generally represents their best possible performance. They do not have the substantial upside of bearish residuals, nor are they "natural" hedges. Their most attractive characteristic is their current yield. These residuals exhibit extremely high returns if interest rates remain relatively stable after the CMO is issued; their performance declines if interest rates either increase or decrease dramatically. Scenario yields on humped residuals are shown in Figure 5.

Stable residuals offer lower yields than humped residuals because they have much less downside risk. Within a wide range of market rates — generally 200 basis points above and below the market level at issuance — these residuals behave like short-term money market instruments. Their yield rises and falls with market rates, but at a spread substantially above competing investments. As shown in Figure 6, under a falling interest rate environment,

FIGURE 5. *Scenario Yields on Humped Residuals.*

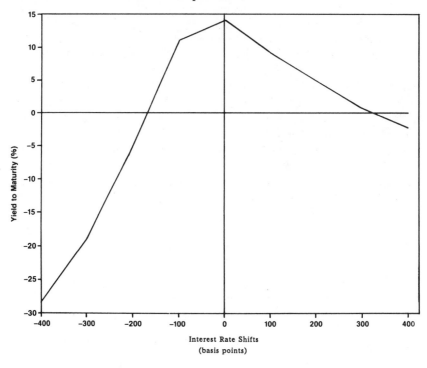

the yield drops as rates decline up to 200 basis points, and then begins to rise. Under a rising rate environment, the yield increases as interest rates increase up to 200 basis points, and then begins to decline.

Stable residuals were first created with FBC Mortgage Securities Trust VI, the first CMO consisting primarily or exclusively of floating rate tranches. The residual cash flows in cases like this arise from the difference between the coupon payment on fixed rate mortgage collateral and the floating rate payments to CMO holders.

Stable residuals, like floating rate securities, have an expected effective duration close to zero. As interest rates change, two opposing forces affect the residual cash flows. First, changes in interest rates cause the spread between the fixed rate assets and floating rate liabilities to change. Lower levels of LIBOR, for example, create a greater spread between the fixed rate collateral and the floating rate liabilities. That is, as LIBOR declines, the size of residuals increases. Conversely as LIBOR increases, the size of residuals decreases.

FIGURE 6. *Scenario Yields on Stable Residuals.*

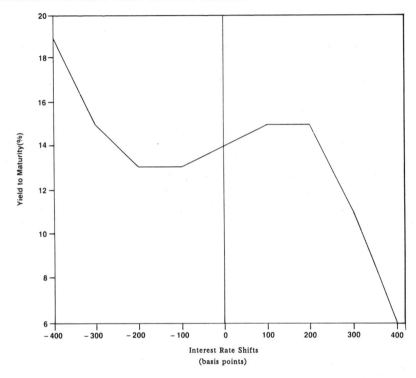

Second, changes in interest rates cause changes in prepayment speeds. Declining rates accelerate prepayments, and vice versa. Higher prepayment rates, in turn, reduce the level of residual cash flows. Conversely, lower rates of prepayment increase residual cash flows.

Figure 7 demonstrates the effect of simultaneous changes in LIBOR and prepayment rates on residual cash flows. For stable residuals, if mortgage and short-term rates go down, residual cash flows per period go up, but they are received for a shorter period of time than they otherwise would have been. Conversely, if mortgage and short-term rates go up, residual cash flows go down, but their expected longevity increases since the underlying mortgages prepay at slower rates.

As long as mortgage rates and short rates move roughly in tandem, these two effects will offset each other to a large extent, producing fairly constant present values. The value of stable residuals can be affected, however, by divergences from the historical inverse relationship between LIBOR and prepayment rates. When spreads between mortgage rates and short-term rates

FIGURE 7. *FBC Mortgage Securities Trust X Residual Cash Flow under Alternative LIBOR and Prepayment Rates.*

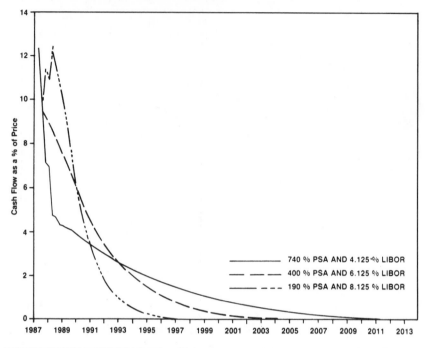

shift, investors will receive the greatest return when mortgage rates rise and short-term rates fall, that is, when the yield curve steepens. Conversely, investors will receive their poorest return when mortgage rates fall while short-term rates rise.

Bonds Taxable as REMIC Residual Interests

An alternative CMO structure eliminates non-securitized residual cash flows. Instead, the cash flow that would have gone into residuals is structured into high coupon CMO bonds, which are publicly offered. The first appearances of this structure were the Collateralized Mortgage Securities Corporation, CMO Series J and K. In each of these transactions the traditional first tranche was stripped of some of its coupon interest, which was subsequently placed in a new second tranche with a small amount of principal. The J-2 and K-2 bonds are rated securities with face principal amounts and coupon rates. They carry high coupon rates (e.g., 100% or more) and prices (e.g., 300 or higher). Their yields tend to be lower than those for residuals sold as private placement owner trusts or limited partnerships, reflecting the fact that they constitute AAA-rated debt rather than unrated equity.

This new structure was facilitated by the 1986 tax law that created Real Estate Mortgage Investment Conduits (REMICs). While these instruments are corporate bonds, they are, for income tax purposes, REMIC residual interests. This is in contrast to the other CMO bonds, which are, for income tax purposes, REMIC regular interests. The analysis of the after-tax returns of REMIC residual interests is complicated and beyond the scope of this article.

Analyzing Residuals

Unlike most fixed income investments, residuals are not explicitly separated into principal and interest components. They do not carry a stipulated rate of return on an identifiable notional amount. Rather, their cash flows are "contingent," depending for their ultimate size on the performance of a given pool of collateral. Market rates of interest, collateral yields, and mortgage prepayment rates all affect cash flows.

When a price is quoted, it is quoted at a certain pricing speed and discount rate, and the investor typically examines a range of internal rates of return over different shifts in interest rates and prepayment speeds. This range shows the investor how the residuals will perform in different cases and makes clear the shape of the residuals. In analyzing residuals, investors focus on yield or payback period; because the secondary market for residuals is limited, projected total rate of return is less meaningful than for other high yield mortgage securities.

Investors can purchase residual cash flows without the expenses and encumbrances of issuing CMOs directly. With high yields and a variety of performance characteristics — characteristics that can be tailored to fit an investor's needs — CMO residuals present new opportunities for financial management.

IV. Strips

Mortgage strips are created by altering the distribution of interest and principal on a pass-through from pro rata to an unequal allocation. In the extreme case, interest only (IO) is paid to one class of investor while principal only (PO) is paid to the other class of investor. More moderate allocation can be made as well. FNMA 8s, for example, can be broken down into equal principal amounts of 5% and 11% strips.

A variant of stripped mortgage-backed securities was the forerunner of today's high yield mortgage securities. Even before mortgage-backed securities were created, trading of whole loans took place, and often the coupon rate associated with these loans was less than that paid by the borrower. The originator, who typically continued to service the loan, would retain a portion of the coupon interest. Over time, these servicing portfolios were seen to generate cash flows in excess of the costs of servicing; hence the term "excess servicing." An active market in the trading of servicing portfolios developed. Mortgage bankers and thrifts could originate new loans at or near par, strip a portion of the coupon, and resell the loans at a discount. The stream of excess servicing, although somewhat uncertain, was expected to have a present discounted value in excess of the discount on the loans sold.

Stripped mortgage-backed securities are a refined descendant of excess servicing. A stripped mortgage-backed security is either a pass-through or a pay-through instrument with two or more different tranches. Unlike traditional serial pay CMOs, where payments of principal are made sequentially, in the strip structure payments are usually made concurrently to all classes. Unlike traditional pass-throughs, which have a single class and where all certificate holders receive pro rata shares of principal and interest, the allocation of principal differs from the allocation of interest in a strip. For example, a security may be created with two tranches, each representing a half share in the underlying principal amount. The interest payments may be allocated differently: one third may be allocated to one class, for example, and two thirds to the other class. Thus, the tranches would have a coupon rate below and above that of the underlying collateral, respectively.

This process is valuable because it separates the linkage between the dollar price of the security and its prepayment rate. In the pass-through market, prices above par are associated with higher prepayment rates, and prices below par are associated with lower prepayment rates. The stripping process allows the creation of premium securities with slow prepayment rates when discount collateral is used, or discount securities with fast prepayment rates when premium collateral is used. This innovation expands the range of performance for mortgage securities, creating instruments that fit a wider variety of investor needs. Mortgage strips are typically created as agency pass-through or private-label rated pass-through securities, or as tranches of CMOs/REMICs. They therefore enjoy the same credit quality and financing ability as more traditional instruments. Like traditional pass-throughs, strips are generally considered qualifying mortgage assets for savings institutions.

The first publicly offered stripped mortgage-backed securities were issued in the second half of 1986. Premiums and discounts were created from seasoned collateral, as shown in Figures 8 and 9. The coupon on the collateral was such that the collateral itself would have been priced near par. In one transaction, the coupon of the premium tranche was raised to a super premium 600%, with most of the principal of course allocated to the discount tranche. In early 1987, the "ultimate" stripped mortgage-backed securities were issued: the interest-only/principal-only (IO/PO) structure. All of the interest and none of the principal go to one tranche, while the other

FIGURE 8. *Graphical Analysis of SMBS: Parent Is a FNMA 8%.*

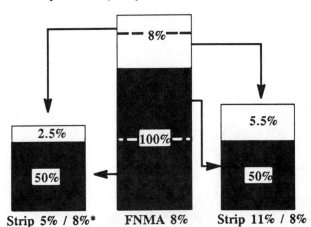

Strip 5% / 8%*   FNMA 8%   Strip 11% / 8%

■ Principal   □ Interest

*Strip 5% / 8% means that a Synthetic 5% Coupon Security has been derived from an underlying 8% Security.

FIGURE 9. *Graphical Analysis of SMBS: Parent Is a FNMA 9%.*

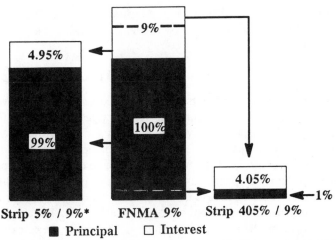

Strip 5% / 9%*   FNMA 9%   Strip 405% / 9%

■ Principal   □ Interest

*Strip 5% / 9% means that a Synthetic 5% Coupon Security has been derived from an underlying 9% Security.

tranche is a zero coupon instrument. Most strip offerings have been of the IO/PO variety. Generally speaking, it is the IO stripped security that will most often fit into the "high yield" category, because its value is more likely

---

FIGURE 10. *Cash Flow on a FNMA 7-1/2% MBS (8% WAC, 240 Month WAM, 0.55% SMM).*

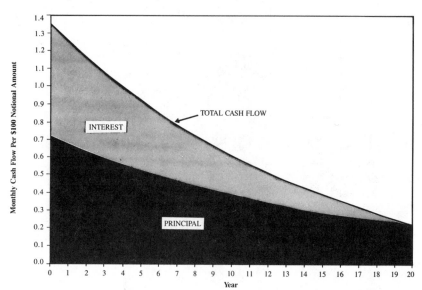

---

to demonstrate acute sensitivity to fluctuations in interest rates and prepayment rates. PO securities backed by higher collateral will also offer higher yields.

Determinants of Cash Flow and Yield in IO/PO Strips

The cash flows from a typical mortgage-backed security are shown in Figure 10. If the underlying pass-through were stripped to produce IO and PO classes, the holders would receive the amounts shown by the areas marked "Interest" and "Principal," respectively. PO holders receive both amortization and prepayments while IO investors receive all of the coupon payments.

Investors in IO strips face uncertainty with respect to the timing and ultimate amount of cash that will be realized. Prepayments are the major factor that affect the timing and amount of IO cash flows. The slower the rate of prepayments on the underlying collateral, the higher the rate of return to the IO holder. Figure 11 shows the cash flows to IO investors at different prepayment rates. Because of the concentration of prepayment risk in IO securities, and the concomitant uncertainty of cash flow, investors in IO strips are compensated with higher yields than they would receive on other types of mortgage securities. The highest yields occur with collateral just above the current coupon, because those securities have the greatest potential for

FIGURE 11. *Prepayment Sensitivity: Interest Only Strip.*

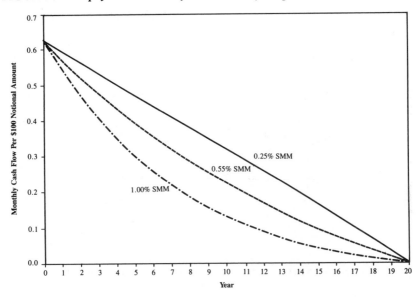

substantially faster prepayments and a consequent loss of value with modest declines in interest rates. Conversely, lower yields occur when the collateral prepayment rate remains level or slows down for small changes in market interest rates, that is, for discount or higher premium collateral.

Investors in PO strips can be certain of the amount of cash that will be realized, but not the timing of the cash flows. The faster the rates of prepayments on the underlying collateral, the higher the rate of return to the PO holder. Figure 12 shows the cash flows to PO investors at different prepayment rates. Because of the defined face amount and the stabilizing effect of scheduled principal amortization, PO strips are slightly less sensitive to prepayment rates than are IO strips. Nevertheless, PO strips can still demonstrate substantial price volatility, particularly when backed by higher coupon mortgages. In such circumstances, PO strips would be offered at higher yields to compensate for the prepayment uncertainty. Higher coupon mortgages have more potential for a deceleration in cash flow than do current coupon or discount mortgages already demonstrating a low prepayment rate.

Different Types of Strips

Investors can purchase strips in a wide variety of forms. Strips are available either as direct agency securities or as securities issued by private issuers

FIGURE 12. *Prepayment Sensitivity: Principal Only Strip.*

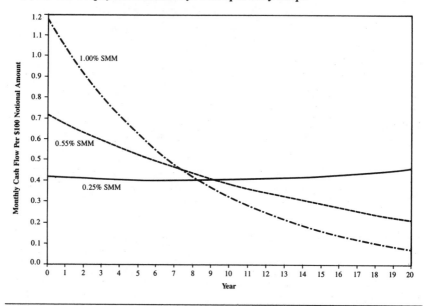

backed by agency collateral. For instance, FNMA issued its Trust 1 IO/ PO Strip backed by its own mortgage pools. Similarly, First Boston Mortgage Securities Corporation issued its SPLITS™, Series B IO/PO backed by FNMA 9s.

SPLITS backed by FNMAs and FHLMCs have exactly the same collateral as synthetics issued by those agencies directly. Payments from the underlying collateral are passed to investors when received.

Privately issued strips can also be purchased in the form of CMO bonds. Some CMO tranches have been issued that do not entail sequential payment of principal. For instance, one tranche of First Boston Mortgage Securities Corporation CMO Trust XI was issued with a coupon of 100%. This gave the tranche almost exactly the same financial properties as an IO backed by GNMA 11s, which was the collateral backing the CMO. Regardless of whether a strip is a direct agency issue, a private pass-through, or a tranche of a CMO, investors should focus almost exclusively on the collateral to determine investment performance.

IO Strips and Portfolio Hedging

Strips can prove effective in hedging both bond and mortgage-based portfolios. Bearish investors can use strips and certain CMO residuals to reduce the volatility and increase the yield of a range of fixed income debt and mortgage-based portfolios.

The performance of the IO tranche will depend disporportionately on prepayments. The amount of cash received in each period is determined by the principal amount of mortgages outstanding at the beginning of the period. As the mortgages amortize and prepay, the notional principal upon which the coupon is computed will decrease. Higher rates of prepayment therefore reduce the return to the investor in IO strips. Since higher prepayments are associated with declining interest rates, the value of an IO strip will generally move inversely with those of other fixed income debt instruments. Specifically, because IO strips perform better with lower prepayment rates, they should prove especially effective in raising the yield while reducing the prepayment sensitivity of portfolios consisting largely of current coupon and discount mortgages. IO strips may be thought of as a long put option (or short call option) on prepayments. The same is true for bearish CMO residuals.

As an example, consider a thrift institution holding $100 million in recently originated 8.5% and 9.0% mortgage securities, with an approximate market value of $102 million, yielding 7.95%. That firm could purchase $40 million notional principal amount of an IO strip backed by GNMA 11s, at an approximate cost of $12 million. The aggregate portfolio would then have a yield spread of approximately 140 basis points over short-term funding costs that is protected over a range of −100 to +200 basis point shifts in interest rates. In a rising rate environment, the strip position would appreciate at approximately the same rate as the mortgage portfolio declined in value. Conversely, in a 100 basis point declining rate environment, the GNMA portfolio would appreciate and the IO strip would decrease in value, but the combined market value would be stable. These results are shown schematically in Figure 13. This strategy has an advantage over other hedging techniques in that the cash flows on the IO strip decline over time, roughly matching those on the mortgage portfolio. The average life of the IO strip will lengthen and shorten approximately in lock step with the mortgage security portfolio.

PO Strips and Synthetic Securities

Principal only strips generally have very long effective durations. When backed by premium mortgages, they may be offered at relatively high yields. Taking advantage of these two properties, investors can combine PO strips with money market, floating rate, or other short duration securities to form intermediate duration synthetics. These synthetics may have higher yields than comparable maturity securities found in the market.

For example, $10 million face amount in PO strips backed by FNMA 9s may be combined with $30 million of 2-year Treasuries. The combination has performance characteristics similar to a 7-year Treasury over a ±200 basis point range of yield curve shifts, but consistently provides higher total returns. Over a one-year holding period with no change in rates, the synthetic

FIGURE 13. *GNMA plus IO Strip Portfolio.*

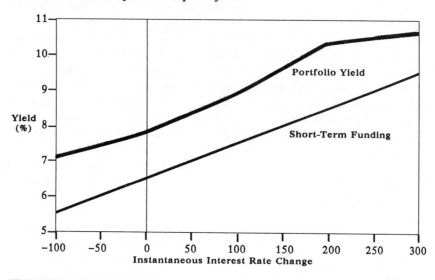

security returns 9.1% to the 7-year's 7.1% In rising rate environments, the short maturity of the 2-year Treasury prevents the return of the synthetic from declining as sharply as the 7-year Treasury. With falling interest rates, rising prepayments on the PO strip more than offset the small appreciation of the 2-year to maintain a return advantage over the 7-year.

V. Leveraged Floaters

A third type of high yield mortgage-backed security is the leveraged floater. A leveraged floater is a security whose interest rate varies by a multiple of a specified index, and/or inversely with that index. Thus, unlike traditional floaters, whose hallmark is a coupon that remains close to market and a price that remains close to par, the leveraged floater will react sharply to changes in market yields.

Leveraged floating rate mortgage-backed securities have been created as tranches of CMOs and share many of the attributes of other mortgage securities, including prepayment uncertainty. There are two basic types of leveraged floaters.

One subcategory of leveraged floaters is the "super floater": when the index rises, the coupon is reset upwards by more than the move in market rates, and when the index declines the coupon shifts downward by a multiple of the drop. The coupon rate is quoted according to a multiple of the index and a constant, such as "2 × LIBOR − 7%." The super floater is a bearish instrument, increasing in value when rates are rising and declining in value when rates are falling.

The other subcategory is the "reverse floater": when the index declines, the coupon is reset upwards, and vice versa. A simple reverse floater might have a coupon of "14% − LIBOR." Reverse floaters are bullish instruments, increasing in value when rates are falling and declining in value when rates are rising. Reverse super floaters have also been created, so that a one-point rise in the index generates more than a one-point drop in the coupon (and vice versa). Reverse floaters were introduced to the market before super floaters.

Reverse floaters were first developed in early 1986 for the corporate bond sector. These securities had relatively short maturities, but had coupons that varied inversely with market rates, thus providing investors with a means of participating in the market rally with instruments of short final maturity.

The value of a reverse floater varies inversely with interest rates as a result of two factors: the coupon and the rate of discounting. When market yields decline, the reverse floater coupon rises while the discount rate declines. Both factors increase the value of the security.

A reverse floater has an effective duration longer than its cash flow duration − longer even than its final maturity − which is to say it will be more volatile than even a zero-coupon bond of the same maturity. Figure 14 shows

FIGURE 14. *Reverse Floater Expected Yield Analysis.*

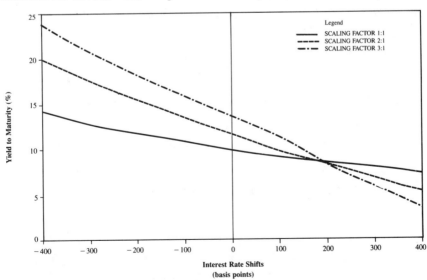

how reverse floaters with different leverage factors can be expected to perform across a range of interest rate shifts.

A mortgage-backed reverse floater has an additional characteristic not found in traditional reverse floating rate notes. As interest rates decline, the coupon on a reverse floater will increase and the discount rate will drop, which by themselves would give a sharp boost to the value of a reverse floater. But at the same time, the rate of prepayments on the underlying collateral will increase, more quickly reducing the outstanding balance on which the coupon is earned, thereby attenuating some of the increase in value.

Conversely, in a rising rate environment, the coupon will decrease, the discount rate will rise, and prepayments will slow, all of which combined will sharply depress the value of the instrument. In the terms of fixed income analytics, these securities have substantial negative convexity. Unlike CMO residuals and IO strips, however, leveraged floaters do have "principal" assigned to them, and a rapid acceleration of prepayments will not result in the evaporation of the security's value.

Super floaters offer investors a highly bearish security with attractive immunization properties in a rapidly rising rate environment. Because its coupon resets at a multiple of the underlying index, super floater investments provide yields higher than the cost of short-term liabilities when interest rates

FIGURE 15. *Performance of Leveraged Floaters.*

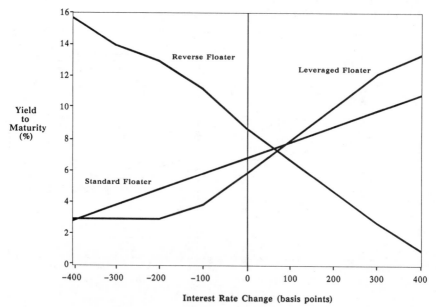

increase. Because of this property, super floaters are offered at relatively low initial yields, usually somewhat below that obtainable on a traditional floater.

Reverse floaters are offered at high initial yields. These yields will improve with any decline in rates. Because of their initially high yields, reverse floaters will generally outperform a traditional floater or a super floater until rates rise by more than 100 basis points. Figure 15 presents typical performance profiles for standard, super, and reverse floaters. The exact performance of these instruments will be specific to the issue, depending on the leverage factor, initial rate, and price.

Reverse floaters are suited either for the investor with a definite belief that market rates are stable or heading downwards, or for the sophisticated investor in the context of a portfolio of other securities. For example, they may be used to offset high cost floating rate liabilities, such as interest rate swaps. They may also be used with other high yield mortgage securities to create stabilized yields in excess of what is obtainable from traditional mortgage securities. Figure 16 shows the performance of a reverse floater combined in a ratio of two to one with an IO strip. The reverse floater exhibits bullish performance, while the IO strip exhibits bearish performance. The synthetic, however, exhibits a surprising degree of stability at attractive yields.

FIGURE 16. *Performance of a Reverse Floater Combined with IOs.*

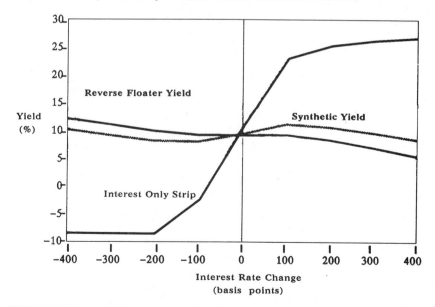

VI. Conclusions

While the evolution of high yield, high risk mortgage securities presents new opportunities to investors, it is not an unmixed blessing. Many forms of high yield mortgage securities are extremely complex, and the value range is wide; investor success will require the ability to analyze and discriminate among various high yield products. Investors who do not take the time and effort to understand the performance characteristics and qualitative differences between individual high yield mortgage securities are not likely to enjoy maximum economic performance. For those who do, however, the rewards could prove substantial.

High yield mortgage securities are not for all investors; they are powerful vehicles that tend to have large degrees of interest rate risk, prepayment risk, or both. Like most new markets, the market for high yield mortgage securities often exhibits considerable inefficiencies and can therefore offer abnormally high yield spreads, both before and after adjustment for risk. It is inevitable that these spreads will narrow over time as the high yield mortgage market matures. In the interim, investors who are already familiar with mortgages and the associated risks may find that the effort to understand the evolving forms of high yield mortgage securities will result in considerable benefits.

33

An Investor's Guide to CMOs*

Janet Spratlin**   **Paul Vianna****

Steven Guterman
Vice President
Mortgage Research
Salomon Brothers Inc

I. Introduction

The first collateralized mortgage obligation (CMO) was issued by the Federal Home Loan Mortgage Corporation (FHLMC) in June 1983. Since that time CMOs have become a major segment of the fixed-income market. By year-end 1987, securities dealers, home builders, mortgage bankers, thrift institutions, commercial banks, and insurance companies had also issued CMOs, and total issuance exceeded $130 billion.

This new form of mortgage-backed security provides several benefits to traditional purchasers of corporate bonds. CMOs retain the credit quality and yield advantages of mortgage pass-throughs, while offering investors semiannual or quarterly payment schedules, a range of maturities and a limited form of call protection that enables investors to avoid some of the reinvestment risk associated with the early paydown of the underlying mortgages.

---

*The authors wish to thank the many people who contributed to this article; in particular, Bernard Carl, John Cavanagh, Thomas Delehanty, Andrew Furer, Robert Geitz, Jerry Hartzog, Keith Maillard, Phil Matthews, Bill Oliva, John Thompson, Michael Waldman, Paul Ullman, and Thomas Zimmerman. Special thanks go to Matt Kunka for his assistance in preparing the charts and to Andrea Learer for her meticulous attention to the details of the production process.
**Dr. Spratlin and Dr. Vianna worked in Mortgage Research at Salomon Brothers Inc when they coauthored this article.

The development of CMOs has opened the mortgage market to investors who are not equipped to deal with monthly payment schedules and irregular mortgage cash flows and to those who need securities with more targeted maturities than are available with mortgage pass-throughs.

II. Structural Characteristics

How CMOs Differ from Traditional Mortgage Pass-Through Securities

The main innovation of the CMO structure is the segmentation of mortgage cash flows, which converts long-term mortgage securities with irregular and widely dispersed cash flows into high-quality, short-, medium- and long-term mortgage-collateralized bonds. In contrast, traditional mortgage-backed securities simply pass through to investors their respective pro rata shares of the monthly payments on the underlying mortgages.

The mortgage cash flows distributed to holders of a traditional pass-through security include any principal prepayments that occur when a mortgage is paid off (for example, when the home is sold or the mortgage is refinanced). Since residential mortgages usually allow the borrower the option to prepay whenever he chooses, mortgage pass-throughs are investments that can be called at any time at par. Although it is unlikely that all mortgages in a pool will be paid off at the same time (since home owners make their decisions independently), investors can expect to experience unpredictable, partial calls of their principal.

The home owner's call option, combined with the pro rata distribution of mortgage cash flows, imparts some unique investment characteristics to mortgage pass-through securities: uncertain, irregular and widely dispersed cash flows, and average lives and durations that are significantly shorter than the final maturity of the security. (See Exhibit 1 for definitions of average life and duration.)

Whereas investors in mortgage pass-throughs own undivided interests in a pool of mortgages, CMO investors own bonds that are collateralized by a pool of mortgages or by a portfolio of mortgage-backed securities. These bonds are serviced with the cash flows from the mortgage collateral. The variability and unpredictability of the underlying mortgage cash flows remain, but since the CMO substitutes a sequential distribution process for the pass-through's pro rata distribution of these cash flows, the stream of payments received by CMO bondholders differs dramatically from that received by the holder of a (hypothetical) pass-through security backed by the same collateral.

The CMO structure creates a series of bonds with varying maturities that appeal to a wider range of investors than do mortgage pass-throughs.

Exhibit 1. *Maturity Measures Used in the CMO Market.*

Although a major feature of the CMO is the variation in the maturities of the various classes of bonds, the unpredictability of the cash flows inherent in mortgage-backed securities makes the concept of maturity less well-defined in this market than in other fixed-income markets.

At issuance, each CMO bond class carries a stated maturity, and one can compute a projected final maturity as the issue pays down. The final maturity is not the key to analyzing the characteristics of a CMO bond. Market participants recognize that given the structure of mortgage cash flows, CMOs are effectively much shorter-term instruments than their stated or projected maturities indicate. As a result, these bonds never trade on the basis of either their stated or projected maturities. Instead, a CMO, like other mortgage-backed securities, typically trades on the basis of its projected weighted average life (WAL), a measure that more accurately summarizes the security's maturity characteristics.

A short glossary of various maturity measures used to describe CMOs follows.

Stated Final Maturity A stated final maturity is assigned to each class of bonds when a CMO is issued. The stated maturity is the time needed to retire all of the bonds in that class under the conservative prepayment and reinvestment assumptions employed by the rating agencies. In most cases[a] this conservative approach assumes that principal payments from the mortgage collateral include standard amortization, but no prepayments. With any reasonable prepayment assumption, the actual maturity of any class will be much shorter than its stated maturity. Consequently, analyzing these bonds in terms of stated final maturity can be misleading and should be avoided — except in cases in which the investor must know the maximum maturity of a class of bonds.

Projected Final Maturity The projected final maturity is calculated using some reasonable prepayment assumption. This is a more realistic measure of final maturity than stated maturity. Within the CMO structure, the fixed cash flow, interest-only period of each class of bonds is determined by the final maturity of the previous class of bonds. Consequently, investors in CMO bonds (other than in the the shortest-maturity class) will normally want to know the projected final maturity of the previous class of bonds.

Weighted-Average Life The weighted-average life of an amortizing security is the average time to receipt of principal, weighted by the size of each principal payment. Like projected final maturities, WALs for CMOs (and mortgage pass-throughs) are calculated under some specific prepayment assumption. The weighted-average life is the most commonly used maturity measure in the mortgage market. Since the weighted-average lives of Treasuries (and corporates without sinking funds) are equal to their maturities, the par yield curve for Treasuries provides a natural benchmark for pricing mortgage-backed securities of various projected average lives. The total principal value used in computing the WAL of a CMO Z bond is not the original balance of the Z bond; rather, it is the (projected) largest balance reached before principal payments commence.

Exhibit 1 *Continued*

Duration The duration is the average time to receipt of cash flows weighted by the present value of the cash flows. This is a widely used measure of the sensitivity of a security's market value to shifts in the discount rate used to value it. For a bond with known cash flows, the percentage change in the security's price in response to a small change in the discount rate is approximately equal to the product of the security's modified duration and the rate shift.[b] For mortgage-backed securities such as CMOs, whose cash flows can only be estimated and are known to change systematically with movements in interest rates, the calculated duration is only an initial indication of market risk, since it does not adjust for the impact of changing interest rates on prepayment rates.

a. For CMOs that are issued with a guaranteed repayment schedule, the stated maturity is equal to the maximum maturity that is guaranteed by the schedule. See Guaranteed Minimum Repayment Schedules.
b. See Robert W. Kopprasch, "Understanding Duration and Volatility," in *The Handbook of Fixed-Income Securities,* edited by Frank J. Fabozzi and Irving Pollack (Homewood, Ill.: Dow Jones-Irwin, 1987), chap. 5.

Investors in the shorter-maturity classes of CMOs can avoid the market risk of the long "tail" on mortgage pass-throughs. In addition, because CMOs involve a sequential distribution of cash flows, there is a period of time during which the investors in the longer-maturity classes receive no principal paydowns. This provides investors in these longer-maturity bonds with a modified form of call protection.

The Prioritization of Mortgage Cash Flows

All CMOs follow the same basic structure:

1. Several classes of bonds are issued against a pool of mortgage collateral. The most common CMO structure contains four classes of bonds: The first three pay interest at their stated rates beginning with the issue date; the final one is typically an accrual class (or Z bond).[1]
2. The cash flows from the underlying mortgages are applied first to pay interest and then to retire bonds.
3. The classes of bonds are retired sequentially. All principal payments are directed first to the shortest-maturity class A bonds. When those bonds are completely retired, all principal retirement is then directed to the next-shortest-maturity bonds — the B class. This process continues until all of the classes have been paid off.

---

1. A wide range of different structures has been employed. There have been as many as 17 classes; some CMOs have a Z bond, some have more than one Z bond, others have none.

FIGURE 1. *Allocation of the Cash Flows from a Pool of Mortgages Among CMO Classes (Salomon Brothers Mortgage Securities II Inc CMO, Series 1984-2, $ millions).*[a]

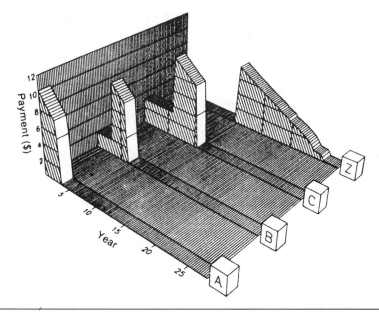

a. Assumes prepayment at 100% PSA. See Appendix I for a review of the PSA benchmark.

Figure 1 illustrates the allocation of cash flows from a mortgage collateral pool among the classes of a CMO.

Although the various classes of bonds are identified differently from issue to issue, market participants often refer to them generically by letter: A bonds have the shortest maturity, B bonds have the next-shortest maturity, and so on. An accrual bond class is often called the Z class, or Z bond. The prioritization of mortgage cash flows creates a series of CMO bonds with different maturities that, because of their varying investment characteristics, appeal to different types of investors.

■ *Class A.* The cash flows from the shortest-maturity class of any CMO will resemble those from a short-term mortgage security (that pays quarterly or semiannually). Since prepayments from the entire pool of mortgage collateral are initially directed to retire A bonds (and only A bonds as long as they are outstanding), holders of these bonds will begin to receive significant principal payments from the first payment date.

- *Classes B and C.* The cash flows from later-maturity coupon-bearing CMO bonds more closely resemble those from a medium-term corporate or Treasury bond. Since the B and C classes will not begin to be called until all shorter-maturity bonds have been retired, investors in these classes can expect a period during which they will receive only interest. Investors will know the amount of their quarterly or semiannual interest payments in advance, but they will not know the length of time that this fixed, known payment will be received, because that will depend on how quickly the mortgage collateral pays down.
- *Class Z.* Z bonds combine characteristics of zero-coupon bonds and mortgage pass-throughs. They receive no coupon payments until all earlier classes have been retired, at which time the cash flow from the remaining collateral is directed to the Z bond holders.

While the earlier classes are being paid down, the interest earned by the Z bonds accrues (is added to the principal balance); thus, the balance of the Z bond grows at the coupon rate, compounded quarterly or semiannually, depending on the payment frequency. After all of the earlier classes are retired, the accrual period ends, and interest and principal payments to Z bondholders commence. During the accrual perod, the cash that would otherwise

---

FIGURE 2. *Outstanding Balances of CMO Classes (Salomon Brothers Mortgage Securities II Inc CMO, Series 1984-2, $ millions).*[a]

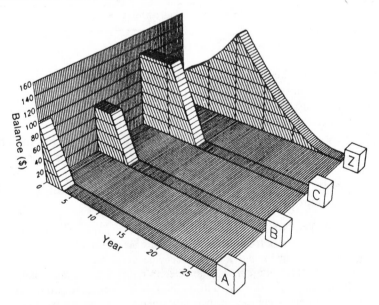

---

a. Assumes prepayment at 100% PSA. See Appendix I for a review of the PSA benchmark.

be used to pay interest on the Z bonds is used to accelerate the retirement of the shorter-maturity classes.

Figure 2 illustrates that with the sequential retirement of CMO bonds, the outstanding balances of coupon-paying classes remain constant during their interest-only periods and then decline when principal payments begin to retire bonds in that class. In contrast, the principal balance of the Z bond grows until all previous bond classes are completely retired. At that point, the Z bond's balance declines as the remaining mortgages continue to pay down and the cash flow is used to retire bonds.

III. What Benefits Do CMOs Offer Investors?

Credit Quality is Superior to Corporate Bond Alternatives

High credit quality is a major advantage of CMO bonds. Most are rated AAA based not on the creditworthiness of the issuer, but rather on their collateralized structure and the quality of the underlying collateral.

In order to obtain a AAA rating, CMOs must be structured to ensure that the underlying mortgages will always generate enough cash to support the number of bonds issued — even at the most conservative prepayment and reinvestment rates. In fact, the conservative structuring of CMOs means that virtually all are overcollateralized.[2]

The credit risk of the collateral that backs CMO bonds is minimal. Some CMOs are backed by so-called agency collateral — mortgages or mortgage pass-throughs whose creditworthiness has been further enhanced by the guarantees of one of the housing finance agencies (GNMA, FHLMC or FNMA). Most CMO issues that are not backed by agency collateral are FHLMC-issued CMOs, which carry FHLMC's guarantee and, therefore, trade with agency credit standing regardless of the credit quality of the collateral. For those remaining CMO issues that are backed by nonagency collateral, the collateral normally carries private insurance (typically at two levels: pool insurance guaranteeing timely payment of principal and interest, and private mortgage insurance (PMI) on any loans with loan-to-value ratios above some specified limit).

Finally, most CMOs are issued by single-purpose, finance subsidiaries that have been incorporated solely for the purpose of issuing these securities; the mortgage collateral is held in trust by a third-party custodial bank; and in most cases, all bond administration expenses are covered by a special reserve fund set up specifically for this purpose.

One can argue that because of their collateralized structures, AAA-rated CMOs are higher-quality credits than AAA-rated corporate bonds. With a

---

2. See Appendix IV: Structuring CMOs.

corporate bond, the AAA rating represents the low likelihood of the issuer defaulting. With a CMO, the AAA rating reflects a collateralized structure that normally makes the creditworthiness of the issuer irrelevant. Even if the parent of the issuer goes into bankruptcy, the investors can expect to be paid as the mortgage collateral pays down. Most people would agree that AAA-rated corporate bonds are more subject to downgrading than are AAA-rated CMOs, because it is far easier to construct a collateralization scheme that protects investors than to forecast the future viability of any corporation.

Because of their solid collateralized structures, the credit ratings on CMOs are typically higher than those of their issuer-sponsors. In fact, issuing a CMO is a way for an unrated borrower to lower its borrowing costs. Normally the creditworthiness of the CMO issuer-sponsor is a factor only in the case of a CMO with a guaranteed principal retirement that might require contributions from the issuer. Aside from CMOs issued by FHLMC, such guaranteed repayment schedules are the exception in the CMO market.[3]

Yields Are Higher than Those on High-Grade Corporates

The CMO market is remarkable in that corporate bond investors can move up in credit quality and pick up yield. Figure 3 compares CMO yield spreads (to Treasuries) with those of similar-maturity AA and AAA corporate bond alternatives.

Payment Frequencies and Range of Maturities Are Attractive to Investors

Many investors—particularly international ones—shy away from mortgage pass-throughs because of their monthly payment schedules. CMOs offer such investors high-quality, high-yielding mortgage investments with quarterly or semiannual payment schedules.

CMOs also offer investors a more defined maturity than that available with mortgage pass-throughs. Most fixed-income investors seek securities within a specified maturity range. They may be funding known future liabilities; they may be constrained by regulations to maintain a particular maturity structure; or they may be working within some asset allocation objective reflecting either the overall objectives of the institution or its current position on interest rates. In any case, such investors will find that CMOs, with their range of maturities, often fit their needs better than mortgage pass-through securities.

It has become standard practice for institutional investors to try to minimize the market risk of their portfolios by managing the maturity gap between their assets and liabilities. Many financial institutions are functioning

---

3. See the subsection Guaranteed Repayment Schedules Reduce Maturity Uncertainty.

FIGURE 3. *Yield Spreads to Treasuries of New Issues — CMOs and High-Grade Corporates.*[a]

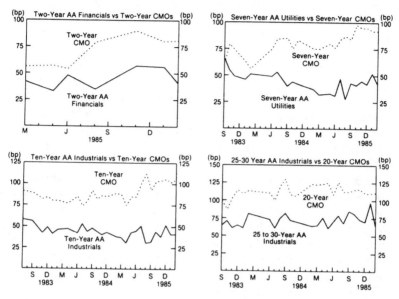

a. CMO spreads are cash flow yield spreads to Treasury benchmarks at initial pricing. See Appendix I for a review of mortgage securities pricing conventions.

like "spread bankers" in that when possible, they raise funds at one rate and invest at a higher rate, and try to lock in that spread by matching off liabilities and assets.

The irregular and unpredictable cash flows from mortgage investments can make it more difficult to apply such strategies to mortgage portfolios. CMOs are potentially well suited to these types of strategies, because they are available in a range of more specified maturities, and many CMO bonds have periods during which the cash flows are more predictable, since the investor receives only interest.

Most of the strategies that have been devised to help investors manage their market risk — and at the same time enjoy the high quality and high yields of mortgage investments — are based on the general concept of duration matching. Since duration is an indicator of the price volatility of a security, by matching the assets in a balance sheet with liabilities of similar durations, movements in interest rates should affect both sides of the balance sheet similarly; thus, the initial spread is preserved over time.

Maintaining a duration-matched portfolio containing mortgage-backed securities requires active management. Over time, the duration of the liabilities used to fund the mortgage pass-throughs tends to shorten faster than that of the asset portfolio. This "duration drift" is a direct result of the differences in the time profiles of the cash flows of the mortgage pass-throughs and the payments due on the liabilities.[4] Thus, some periodic rebalancing is needed in order for institutions investing in mortgage securities to remain duration matched. An even greater need for rebalancing results from the changes in prepayment rates that occur when interest rates move.

Many investors would prefer to minimize this ongoing management and periodic rebalancing of their portfolios. In particular, many institutions have liabilities over which they have relatively little control, because they are closely tied to other activities of the organization. For example, banks take in a variety of deposits as a part of their banking activities, and insurance companies tend to concentrate on relatively few types of policies (each with its own maturity profile).

Other sources of funding can always be tapped, but often the institution is more comfortable investing in assets with a maturity profile that matches that of their typical liabilities. By investing in CMO bonds rather than in mortgage pass-throughs, the institution can pick high-quality mortgage assets whose durations more closely approximate those of its liability stream. Since the durations of the CMO bonds initially decrease over time in a manner similar to liabilities with bullet maturities, the need for rebalancing *resulting from duration drift* is lessened.

IV. Who Buys CMOs?

The preference of specific types of investors for particular maturities is reflected in the profile of investors in the different classes of CMO bonds (see Table 1).

CMO A Bonds Go to Liquidity Investors

The short average lives, high yields and high-credit quality of A bonds make them attractive alternatives to short-term Treasuries and agencies for liquidity investors—even though portfolio managers must be prepared to accept less certainty in the timing of the repayment of principal. The yield advantage has been significant enough in many cases to motivate managers of comercial bank portfolios and corporate treasurers to reevaluate their cash requirements and identify a core short-term portfolio that, because it is so rarely needed, can be targeted for somewhat less liquid investments, such as CMO A bonds.

---

4. For example, in one year, the duration of a 5-year 10% bullet liability shortens by 0.7 year, from 4.1 to 3.4 years. In contrast, because of the dispersion in its cash flows, the duration of a pool of mortgages will shorten much less with the passage of time.

TABLE 1. *Characteristics of Different Bond Classes.*

	A Class Bonds	B Class Bonds	C Class Bonds	Z Bonds
Stated Maturity	5–10 years	7–15 years	10–20 years	25–30 years
Projected final maturity	2–5 years	4–7 years	7–12 years	20–30 years
Projected average life/duration	1–3 years	3–10 years	5–10 years	15–25 years
Projected interest-only/accrual period	None	2–5 years	4–7 years	8–12 years
Major investors	Thrifts Commercial bank portfolios Money market funds Corporate treasurers	Insurance companies Pension funds Bank trust departments Investment advisors International investors	Insurance companies Pension funds Bank trust departments Investment advisors International investors	Insurance companies Pension funds Bank trust departments Investment advisors Bond funds
Alternative investments	Short treasuries Money market instruments	Corporate bonds	Corporate bonds Eurobonds	CATS, STRIPS Corp. discounts, zero-coupon bonds
Benefits versus Treasuries	Yield	Yield	Yield	Yield
Benefits versus money market instruments	Credit quality Yield	NA NA	NA NA	NA NA
Benefits versus corporates	Credit quality Yield	Credit quality Yield	Credit quality Yield	Credit quality Yield No reinvestment uncertainty for number of years
Benefits versus mortgages	Short maturity Some bonds qualify as liquidity investments	Period of interest only Quarterly or semiannual pay Maturity profile	Period of interest only Quarterly or semiannual pay Maturity profile	Period of interest only Long duration No reinvestment uncertainty for a number of years
Potential investor concerns	Maturity/yield uncertainty No access to repo market (except for FHLMC CMOs) Liquidity less than Treasuries	Maturity/yield uncertainty No access to repo market (except for FHLMC CMOs) Liquidity less than Treasuries, GNMAs	Maturity/yield uncertainty No access to repo market (except for FHLMC CMOs) Liquidity less than Treasuries, GNMAs	Maturity/yield uncertainty No access to repo market (except for FHLMC CMOs) Liquidity less than Treasuries, GNMAs

Certain investors are more attracted to A bonds that carry maximum maturities that fit the maturity limits on their liquidity portfolios. The most obvious examples are the thrift institutions, which are required by Federal Home Loan Bank (FHLB) regulations to keep a specified fraction of their total portfolios in liquid assets,[5] and money market funds, whose legal investments are generally constrained to maturities under one year. Such maturity limits (or guidelines) may effectively prevent many institutions from investing in new A bonds with longer stated maturities.

However, not all CMO A bonds will be off-limits to such investors. For example, the guaranteed repayment schedules on the Citicorp issues shortened the initial maximum maturities of these A bonds to meet the liquidity constraints of thrifts. In addition, several seasoned A bonds have a stated maturity that is now less than three years. A few CMOs have paydowns to date that have been rapid enough that their A bonds will be retired within the one-year limit for money market mutual funds — even if the underlying collateral experiences no further prepayment of principal. The supply of these "maximum maturity bonds" should increase as CMOs pay down over time. When they are available, the yields can be extremely attractive.

CMO B and C Bonds Attract Buyers of Intermediate-Term Corporates

The general structures of B and C bonds are similar — both have periods during which investors receive interest payments, but no principal. Typically, the B and C classes of the same CMO differ only with respect to the expected maturity and the expected length of the interest-only period.

B and C classes have been attractive to institutional investors who traditionally meet their intermediate-maturity needs with corporate bonds: insurance companies, commercial bank trust departments, pension funds, and investment advisors. Many are international investors, who are looking for high-quality securities but who cannot tolerate the monthly payment frequency and widely dispersed cash flows inherent in mortgage pass-throughs.

Investors in B bonds differ from investors in C bonds primarily with respect to their maturity needs. For example, insurance companies looking to match liabilities in the five-year range — Guaranteed Investment Contracts (GICs) and Single-Payment Deferred Annuities (SPDAs) — find B pieces to be attractive alternatives to high-grade corporates or private placements. The same institutions find C bonds more attractive when they seek to match longer-term liabilities.

---

5. The specific maturity requirement for thrift investments to qualify as liquid assets varies, depending on the type of security. Corporate bonds such as CMOs must have maturities of three years or less to qualify as liquid assets.

Z Bonds Lock Up High Yields for Long-Term Investors

Z bonds offer long-term investors high yield and quality, a long (but uncertain) duration and automatic reinvestment of cash flows for a number of years. They provide yields that are often higher than those available from typical rate-of-return investments — lower-quality bonds, private placements and traditional mortgage products. In contrast to lower-quality issues that require vigilance with regard to potential adverse credit changes, Z bonds are generally AAA-rated and backed by agency-guaranteed mortgage securities.

Unlike other mortgage products, Z bonds eliminate the problems related to reinvestment of cash flows over a number of years — a benefit similar to that provided by zero-coupon Treasuries. Since they offer a significant yield spread over CATS[RM] or STRIPs with little sacrifice in credit quality, Z bonds are attractive to investors who want to lock in yields for long periods.

Pension funds and insurance companies have been the biggest investors in Z bonds to date. They have found the yield advantage attractive enough to outweigh the uncertainty of cash flows after the end of the Z bond's accrual period.

V. Analyzing the Investment Characteristics of CMOs

CMO Investors Must Accept Some Uncertainty of Cash Flows

CMOs provide corporate bond buyers with an opportunity to significantly increase the credit quality of their portfolios while gaining yield. In return for the step-up in yield and quality, however, CMO investors must be prepared to accept some maturity uncertainty. By changing the nature of mortgage cash flows going to investors, the CMO structure has created bonds with distinctly different maturities and varying amounts of call protection; but because the prepayments on the underlying mortgages cannot be known in advance, the maturity uncertainty inherent in mortgage investments has not been eliminated.

Figure 4 illustrates how the cash flows to investors in the various classes of CMOs will change as the prepayments of the mortgage collateral change.

Guaranteed Repayment Schedules Reduce Maturity Uncertainty

Recognizing that the remaining maturity uncertainty may be unattractive to potential CMO investors, some issuers have chosen to guarantee minimum repayment schedules for their CMO bonds that are faster than those that could be guaranteed based on the minimum possible prepayment of the

FIGURE 4. *CMO Cash Flows for Various Prepayment Rates (Salomon Brothers Mortgage Securities II Inc CMO, Series 1984-2, $ millions).*

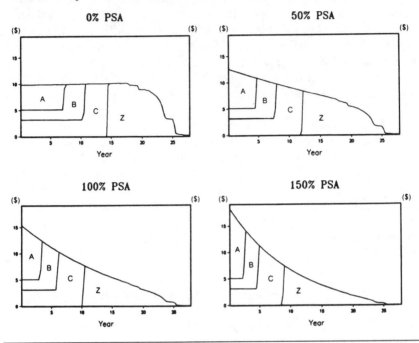

underlying collateral.[6] Whenever the cash flows from the underlying mortgages fall short of what is needed to retire the specified minimum amount of these bonds, the issuer makes up the difference. Such advances by the issuer are most likely to be necessary during periods of rising interest rates when prepayments tend to decline.

The effect of such a minimum repayment schedule (also called a guaranteed sinking fund schedule) is to guarantee, for each class of CMO bonds, a maximum (stated) maturity that is significantly shorter than the zero prepayment maturity. This feature is particularly attractive to certain investor groups. For example, CMOs with guaranteed repayment schedules can be structured to ensure that the guaranteed maximum maturity of the A class bonds is three years or less, which qualifies these bonds as liquidity investments for thrift institutions.

All CMOs that have been issued to date with minimum repayment schedules also provide the issuer with the opportunity to recover advances in subsequent periods, whenever prepayments rise enough that the cash flow from

---

6. To date FHLMC and Citicorp are the only issuers to do this.

the underlying mortgage collateral exceeds that necessary to meet the guaranteed minimum repayment schedule. The issuer may then retain any excess cash flow up to an amount equal to previous (unrecovered) advances. The net effect of an issuer advancing and subsequently recovering any shortfalls from the guaranteed minimum repayment schedule will be to reduce the variability in the rate at which CMO bonds pay down.

Since CMOs with guaranteed minimum repayment schedules are not "fully collateralized,"[7] the issuer is, in effect, assuming part of the prepayment risk. Consequently, the ultimate credit quality of these CMOs will be determined by the credit standing of the issuer — not by the structure of the issue and the underlying collateral.

Projecting Yield and Evaluating Prepayment Risk Dominate CMO Valuation Analysis

Any evaluation of the investment characteristics of a CMO will focus primarily on prepayment risk, because the credit risk is minimized by the collateralized structure. The key question is: "Given an investor's objectives and his position on interest rates, how does this security compare to his available alternatives?"

With a mortgage-backed security, the answer to this question is much less straightforward than with a Treasury or corporate bond whose income stream is known in advance. With Treasury or corporate securities, there are a variety of analytical tools that can be applied directly to that known cash flow to calculate indicators of value such as yield or duration, to create portfolios with cash flows that match future liabilities or to develop other investment strategies.

With a mortgage-backed security whose income stream is not known in advance, there is an entire level of analysis that must take place before the standard fixed-income analytical tool box can be brought to bear. Specifically, some projection must be made of the cash flows from the security. In addition, since these cash flows are expected to vary with interest rates, that expected variation must be factored into any analysis of performance or yield under different interest rate environments.

Yield Tables Capture Structural Differences Among CMOs

With a traditional mortgage pass-through security, projecting the payment stream to an investor is equivalent to projecting prepayments on the underlying mortgages, because the cash from the underlying mortgages is simply

---

7. "Fully collateralized" in the sense that they are structured specifically to guarantee that the collateral itself will always be sufficient to meet the sinking-fund requirement, even in the "worst-case scenario."

passed through on a pro rata basis to investors. In contrast, with CMOs it is necessary to translate the projected cash flow from the mortgage collateral into a projected stream of payments to the CMO bondholders before one can begin to value the investment.

The process that transforms mortgage cash flows into bond cash flows is determined by the particular structure of the CMO, which is set when the CMO is issued and does not change over the life of the bonds.[8] Because this structure is known precisely, it is possible, given any series of mortgage cash flows, to determine the cash flows to the CMO bondholders. Beginning with a stream of mortgage cash flows that are consistent with a specified prepayment rate, one can generate the resulting cash flows to CMO bondholders. These CMO cash flows can in turn be subjected to the usual fixed-income analysis to determine, for example, CMO yields or durations that are consistent with that prepayment rate. By repeating this process, one can generate projected yields for CMO bonds over a wide range of prepayment rates and prices.

CMO issuers or their investment bankers perform this analysis, and they summarize it in the form of yield tables that are circulated among the dealer community (usually monthly). The most recent set of yield tables is normally available to investors. CMO structures vary, and the structure of a particular issue will affect the returns to investors. Since the structural impact is effectively captured in the yield table, investors with ready access to current yield tables can focus attention there when evaluating expected CMO returns, rather than on the structural details of each individual CMO issue.

Projecting Prepayments on the Mortgage Collateral

It is impossible to meaningfully evaluate a CMO bond without first developing some projections of prepayment rates for the mortgage collateral. Two CMOs with exactly the same structure, but different underlying collateral, will prepay at different rates, with the result that the average lives, final maturities and yields of similar classes of the two CMOs may diverge dramatically. Only after developing a probable range of prepayment rates for the mortgage collateral can an investor refer to the CMO yield table to obtain yield projections.

Market participants look to a variety of sources for indications of future prepayment rates. Normally the first step is to examine historical prepayments — for the CMO itself and for mortgage pass-through securities similar to the CMO's collateral.

---

8. This includes the number of bond classes, the size of each, the different coupons, the bond value method used, whether spread is passed through to the bondholder or retained by the issuer, the assumed reinvestment rate between coupon dates, and the existence of a sinking fund schedule. See Appendix IV on CMO Structure.

For example, during the payment period ended February 28, 1986, the mortgages collateralizing the Salomon Brothers Mortgage Securities II Inc CMO, Series 1984-2 (SBMSI II-2) paid down at an annual rate of 11.8%. The prepayment rate from date of issuance (November 27, 1984) had been 8.1%. The yield table for the C class of the SBMSI II-2 CMO indicates that at a price of 105, the projected yield would be 8.94% under a prepayment assumption of 200% PSA (equivalent to 12% constant prepayment rate (CPR)) and would rise to 9.15% if prepayments slowed to 125% PSA (equivalent to 7.5% CPR) (see Table 2).[9]

It is also useful to "cross-check" the prepayment experience of the CMO with the prepayment history of the sector of the mortgage-backed securities market that compares most closely with the particular collateral that is backing the CMO to see if the two are similar. For example, the SBMSI II-2 CMO is backed by FHLMC participation certificates (PCs) and FNMA mortgage-backed securities (MBs) with coupons of 9.75%, 10.00% and 10.25%. Consider the average prepayment rates for securities with these coupons.

Since the average prepayment rates of the types of securities backing this CMO have been somewhat slower than those experienced by the specific CMO collateral, a prospective investor might be inclined to view the most recent CMO prepayment history as an upper bound and evaluate the CMO accordingly. That would probably be a reasonable conclusion during periods when interest rates have been (and are expected to remain) stable. During such periods, recent prepayment experience is a good indicator of the future. However, during periods of rapidly changing rates (or when rates are expected to move significantly over the not-too-distant future), it is necessary to judge the likely impact of the new (or changing) rate environment on prepayments.

Until recently, it has been standard practice to make a variety of ad hoc adjustments to the published prepayment data to try to account for changes (or expected changes) in rates. One of the more commonly used rules of thumb is based on relationships between mortgage securities of different coupons and the current mortgage interest rate. For example, consider a period during which mortgage rates have fallen rapidly to 10% after having been 12% for an extended period of time. Assume further that during the 12% rate environment, 12% coupons prepaid at 9%, while 10% coupons prepaid at only 8%. One might argue that in the new 10% interest rate environment, 10% coupons would prepay the same way that the 12% coupons prepaid in the 12% interest rate environment, which would imply that prepayments on 10% coupons will rise from 8% to 9%.

---

9. Yields quoted here are bond-equivalent, cash flow yields based on an assumed constant prepayment rate (CPR) or percentage of PSA. See Appendix I for a discussion of the pricing and yield conventions that are used in the mortgage securities market.

TABLE 2. SBMSI II-2 Class Yield Table.[a]

Price	0% PSA		50% PSA		75% PSA		100% PSA		125% PSA		150% PSA		200% PSA	
	Yield	Dur.	Yield	Dur.	Yield	Dur.	Yield	Dur.	Yield	Dur.	Yield	Dur.	Yield	Dur.
104-16	9.49%	7.24	9.40%	6.35	9.35%	5.93	9.30%	5.53	9.24%	5.17	9.18%	4.85	9.06%	4.27
104-20	9.47		9.38		9.33		9.28		9.22		9.16		9.03	
104-24	9.46		9.36		9.31		9.25		9.19		9.13		9.00	
104-28	9.44		9.34		9.29		9.23		9.17		9.11		8.97	
105-00	9.42		9.33		9.27		9.21		9.15		9.08		8.94	
105-04	9.41		9.31		9.25		9.19		9.12		9.05		8.91	
105-08	9.39		9.29		9.23		9.16		9.10		9.03		8.88	
105-12	9.37		9.27		9.21		9.14		9.07		9.00		8.86	
105-16	9.36	7.27	9.25	6.37	9.19	5.94	9.12	5.55	9.05	5.19	8.98	4.86	8.83	4.28
105-20	9.34		9.23		9.17		9.10		9.03		8.95		8.80	
105-24	9.32		9.21		9.15		9.08		9.00		8.93		8.77	
105-28	9.31		9.19		9.12		9.05		8.98		8.90		8.74	
106-00	9.29		9.17		9.10		9.03		8.96		8.88		8.71	
106-04	9.27		9.15		9.08		9.01		8.93		8.85		8.69	
106-08	9.26		9.13		9.06		8.99		8.91		8.83		8.66	
106-12	9.24		9.11		9.04		8.97		8.89		8.80		8.63	
106-16	9.22	7.29	9.10	6.38	9.02	5.96	8.95	5.56	8.86	5.20	8.78	4.87	8.60	4.29
106-20	9.21		9.08		9.00		8.92		8.84		8.75		8.57	
106-24	9.19		9.06		8.98		8.90		8.82		8.73		8.54	
106-28	9.17		9.04		8.96		8.88		8.79		8.71		8.52	
107-00	9.16		9.02		8.94		8.86		8.77		8.68		8.49	
107-04	9.14		9.00		8.92		8.84		8.75		8.66		8.46	
107-08	9.12		8.98		8.90		8.82		8.73		8.63		8.43	
107-12	9.11		8.96		8.88		8.79		8.70		8.61		8.40	

TABLE 2 *Continued*

Price	0% PSA Yield	0% PSA Dur.	50% PSA Yield	50% PSA Dur.	75% PSA Yield	75% PSA Dur.	100% PSA Yield	100% PSA Dur.	125% PSA Yield	125% PSA Dur.	150% PSA Yield	150% PSA Dur.	200% PSA Yield	200% PSA Dur.
107–16	9.09%	7.32	8.95%	6.40	8.86%	5.97	8.77%	5.58	8.68%	5.21	8.58%	4.88	8.38%	4.30
107–20	9.07		8.93		8.84		8.75		8.66		8.56		8.35	
107–24	9.06		8.91		8.82		8.73		8.63		8.53		8.32	
107–28	9.04		8.89		8.80		8.71		8.61		8.51		8.29	
108–00	9.02		8.87		8.78		8.69		8.59		8.48		8.27	
108–04	9.01		8.85		8.76		8.67		8.57		8.46		8.24	
108–08	8.99		8.83		8.74		8.65		8.54		8.44		8.21	
108–12	8.98		8.82		8.72		8.62		8.52		8.41		8.18	
108–16	8.96	7.34	8.80	6.42	8.70	5.99	8.60	5.59	8.50	5.22	8.39	4.89	8.16	4.31
108–20	8.94		8.78		8.68		8.58		8.47		8.36		8.13	
108–24	8.93		8.76		8.66		8.56		8.45		8.34		8.10	
108–28	8.91		8.74		8.64		8.54		8.43		8.32		8.07	
109–00	8.90		8.72		8.62		8.52		8.41		8.29		8.05	
109–04	8.88		8.70		8.60		8.50		8.38		8.27		8.02	
109–08	8.86		8.69		8.58		8.48		8.36		8.24		7.99	
109–12	8.85		8.67		8.56		8.46		8.34		8.22		7.97	
Average life	12.4 yrs.		9.9 yrs.		8.9 yrs.		8.0 yrs.		7.2 yrs.		6.6 yrs.		5.6 yrs.	
Paydown start	10.3		7.6		6.6		5.8		5.1		4.6		3.8	
Paydown end	14.3		11.8		10.8		10.1		9.3		8.6		7.6	

a. Salomon Brothers Mortgage Securities II Inc CMO, Series 1984-2. Payment period is quarterly; amount outstanding is $126 million; interest accrues from 1 Mar. 86; final maturity is 1 Sep. 02; settlement date is 29 Apr. 86.

Using the Salomon Brothers Prepayment Model to Evaluate CMOs

Although such rule-of-thumb adjustments are sometimes helpful, they do not account for several important factors (see Exhibit 2). The Salomon Brothers prepayment model uses more sophisticated statistical methods to obtain estimates of the impact on prepayments of factors such as interest rates, type of mortgage, coupon, aging, and seasonality.

The prepayment model can be used to project prepayment rates for a wide range of different types of mortgage collateral over any specified interest rate environment. The model takes into account the impact of recent moves in interest rates on current and projected prepayment rates.

The prepayment rates projected by the Salomon Brothers prepayment model provide useful benchmarks for evaluating CMO yields. For example, projected prepayment rates for the types of collateral backing the Salomon II-2 CMO (see Table 3) indicate that the prepayment experience for this CMO over the first quarter of 1986 (11.8% CPR or 198% PSA) was not high relative to what was expected from this type of collateral in the second quarter and probably should not have been viewed as a potential upper limit.

The Salomon Brothers prepayment model projections, used in conjunction with CMO yield tables, also help investors to develop a sense of how much variability in prepayments is possible or likely over some realistic range of economic scenarios. This is particularly important when comparing different CMO investments. For example, even if at current prices two CMOs have the same projected yields under what is considered to be the most likely

TABLE 3. *Historical and Projected Prepayments for SBMSI II-2 Collateral.*

		Historical		
	March	Past Three Months	Past Six Months	Projected[a]
FHLMC 9.75%	7.6%	7.3%	8.3%	13.5%
FHLMC 10.0%	7.5	8.1	8.8	14.0
FHLMC 10.25%	7.3	7.8	8.8	14.4
FNMA 9.75%	8.8	9.4	9.4	13.5
FNMA 10.0%	5.9	6.7	8.4	14.1
FNMA 10.25%	11.4	8.3	9.2	14.5
SBMSI II-2 CMO		11.8	(1 Dec 85–1 Mar 86)	

a. Projected long-term average prepayment rate as of March 31, 1986, from the Salomon Brothers prepayment model.

EXHIBIT 2. *Many Factors Influence Mortgage Prepayment Rates.*

Economic Factors Affect the Decisions of all Home Owners' Interest Rate Variability Prepayment rates on the underlying collateral will tend to vary inversely with interest rates; hence, the average lives and durations of CMO bonds normally shorten when rates fall, and they tend to lengthen when rates rise.

The inverse relationship between interest rates and prepayments reflects the incentive for home owners to refinance their mortgages when mortgage rates fall to levels that are 200–300 basis points below those on their outstanding loans. It also reflects the fact that when mortgage rates are low, home owners are more likely to adjust to changing housing needs by moving (which typically results in the existing loan being paid off). Conversely, when rates rise, home owners may find themselves "locked in" to their current housing situation by the increase in mortgage costs that they would face if they moved.

Economic Activity Economic activity, as measured by indicators such as inflation and unemployment, will affect prepayments through their impact on turnover in housing, independent of the effect of interest rates.

Seasonality Monthly prepayment rates show a definite seasonal pattern because families are more likely to move in the spring and summer months.

The Variation in Prepayment Rates Among Pools Are Related to the Particular Characteristics of the Mortgages Backing Them

Age of the Mortgages In a stable interest rate environment, prepayment rates on pools of newly issued mortgages tend to increase steadily over the first few years and level out in later years. This observed seasoning effect underlies the construction of the PSA Prepayment Benchmark (see Appendix I).

Coupon The higher the coupon on a mortgage-backed security relative to current mortgage rates, the faster (and more responsive to changes in interest rates) prepayments tend to be. This is because the home owner's incentive to refinance is greater (and his disincentive to sell the home and move is smaller), the greater the difference between the rate on the household's outstanding mortgage and the currently available mortgage rate.

Due-on-Sale FNMA and FHLMC securities tend to prepay faster than similar GNMA securities. This difference primarily reflects differences in the underlying mortgages. Most FNMA pass-throughs and FHLMC PCs are backed by conventional mortgages, which typically contain enforceable due-on-sale clauses, meaning that the lender can require that the mortgage be paid off when the home is sold. In contrast, GNMA securities are all backed by FHA/VA loans, which are assumable by law.

Payment Schedules of Different Types of Mortgages The standard mortgage contract provides for a level payment schedule, and the overwhelming majority of outstanding mortgages are level-pay mortgages. In recent years, however, new types of mortgages with nonlevel payment schedules have been developed, such as

---

EXHIBIT 2 *Continued*

graduated payment mortgages (GPMs), adjustable-rate mortgages (ARMs) and early-ownership mortgages (EOMs). These different structures not only change the payment schedules, they also affect the incentives for the home owner to prepay. (To date, only level-pay and GPM mortgages — or mortgage pass-throughs — have been used as collateral for CMOs.)

Geographic Distribution   At any point in time, mortgages on homes located in particular areas of the country tend to experience faster (or slower) prepayment rates than average, reflecting the impact of regional and local economies on housing turnover.

---

interest rate scenario, their yields might respond differently to any deviation from this most likely scenario. Investors may find it useful to consider the model's projected prepayment rates for the particular type of collateral backing the CMO over a possible range of interest rates and then apply these rates to the appropriate CMO yield table. In this way, investors can develop some boundaries on the potential impact of the variability in prepayments on their expected yields, weighted average lives and durations.

Conceptually, one can view the impact of changing interest rates on CMO yields as a two-stage process. First, a change in interest rates affects prepayments and, therefore, the cash flows from the mortgage collateral. The specific CMO structure then transforms these cash flows into CMO bond payments. These two relationships are complex. Fortunately, one can turn to the Salomon Brothers prepayment model to obtain assistance in analyzing the first — and to the CMO yield table for assistance in analyzing the second.

It is important, however, to understand that the final impact of any change in interest rates on CMO yields will depend on the collateral and the structure. For example, it is well-known that all else being equal, prepayments on discount mortgages tend to be less responsive to changes in interest rates than prepayments on current-coupon or premium mortgages. Does this mean that a CMO backed by discount mortgages is less risky and should therefore command premium prices over a similar CMO backed by current or premium mortgages?

In most cases, the answer is probably yes, but it ultimately depends on how the two issues are structured. For example, during market rallies, the price of a CMO backed by discount mortgages, but carrying a current coupon, will reach par and "stall out" sooner than will the price of a discount-coupon CMO backed by discount collateral. Moreover, since discount-coupon CMOs are issued below par, investors receive a yield premium if prepayments pick up as interest rates fall.

Similarly, a guaranteed repayment schedule normally reduces yield responsiveness to interest rate changes, while sensitivity to interest rate moves can be increased by other structural features (for example, passing through to bondholders any mortgage cash flows that exceed those required for debt service).

Optional Redemption Provisions Can Affect Yields

In addition to the sequential retirement of bonds that accompanies the paydown of the underlying mortgages, many CMOs also specify certain conditions under which the issuer is allowed to call *all* of the outstanding CMO bonds. These optional redemption provisions in some cases can dramatically reduce the expected average life (and, hence, affect the expected return) of longer-maturity CMO bonds. Prospective investors will want to examine the call provisions of each issue separately, since unlike most other structural aspects of a CMO, optional redemption provisions frequently are not taken into account by CMO yield tables.

Of most concern to investors are so-called "refunding call provisions," which are designed to benefit the issuer in the event of a bond market rally — at the expense of the investor. Such provisions allow the issuer to direct the trustee to sell the collateral, use the proceeds to retire the bonds and return the excess cash to the issuer. The exercise of this type of call can significantly reduce an investor's return from a CMO and will affect secondary market trading whenever prices approach or rise above par. In some CMOs, the outstanding bonds are callable in as few as ten years after issuance with no restrictions.

Of much less immediate concern to investors are "cleanup calls" that enable issuers to avoid the cost of servicing large numbers of almost-retired bonds.[10] For example, an indenture may provide that all outstanding bonds can be retired at 100% of their remaining principal balance, plus accrued interest, after the balance on the final class of bonds has declined to some specified fraction of that class's original balance. To illustrate, the Z bonds might be callable on any payment date fifteen or more years from origination, if the total balance of the Zs has declined to 10% of its original value.

In most cases, cleanup calls will not significantly affect the return to investors in long-term CMO Z bonds; by the time that the call is permitted, little principal will remain outstanding.[11] Nevertheless, as the outstanding

---

10. The last bond class of a CMO could linger on until the last mortgage is retired. The main exceptions are those CMOs that pass the spread through to investors (see Appendix IV on CMO Structure). For these issues, the final class of bonds is likely to be retired well before the final maturity of the underlying mortgages. Any remaining collateral would revert to the issuer.

11. Following the example above, a quarterly pay Z bond with a coupon of 10.250% might start to pay down after ten years, at which point its total principal would have grown to 275% of its original balance. By the time that this bond can be called (in this example, after the outstanding balance falls below 10.0% of the original balance), only 3.6% of the maximum balance would be outstanding.

balance approaches the specified fraction at which the remaining bonds can be called, prices in the secondary market are likely to be affected.

In addition to these more standard types of call provisions, it is now standard practice for CMO indentures to include provisions that require the trustee to make "mandatory redemptions of principal" whenever a combination of rapid mortgage prepayments and low reinvestment rates may prevent the trustee from making scheduled payments at the next coupon date, unless some principal is retired between the scheduled payment dates.[12]

Appendix I:
Pricing and Yield Conventions

The variety and complexity of the pricing and yield conventions of mortgage securities often perplex investors. As the CMO market has adopted many of these conventions, we review them briefly.

Cash Flow Yield: The Mortgage Market's Yield to Maturity

As yield to maturity is for bonds, the cash flow yield is the basic yield measure for the mortgage market. The cash flow yield is the discount rate that equates the present value of a mortgage security's future cash flows, based on a projected principal payment schedule, to its current market price. Cash flow yields on mortgage pass-throughs and CMOs are commonly quoted on a semiannually compounded or bond-equivalent basis. The bond-equivalent yield accounts for the value of receiving monthly or quarterly — rather than semiannual payments; it implicitly assumes that these cash flows are reinvested at the yield rate.

CMOs, like other fixed-income securities, are benchmarked against the Treasury yield curve, and the standard procedure is to compare the CMO's cash flow yield with the yield to maturity of the Treasury security. If, for example, a CMO bond is quoted as "50 basis points over the 10-year Treasury at a 6% constant prepay rate (CPR)," the assumed cash flows are those that would occur if the underlying mortgages were to prepay at the specified prepayment rate over the remaining term of the bond. The above quote indicates that at current prices, if the collateral prepays at 6% per year, then the cash flow yield of the CMO will be 50 basis points higher than the yield to maturity of the 10-year Treasury.

In general, the benchmark security chosen for comparison is a Treasury whose maturity is close to the projected average life of the CMO. This may be the active issue with the maturity closest to the projected average life, on

---

12. See Appendix IV.

the presumption that that particular Treasury issue is the appropriate benchmark. At other times, the spread is quoted over an interpolated point on the yield curve that exactly matches the projected average life of the CMO on the assumption that this is a better representation of the true yield spread being offered to investors.

For instance, the CMO yield quoted in the example above used the 10-year Treasury as a benchmark, even though the average life implied by the assumed 6% prepayment rate was 8.9 years. If the same bond were quoted at a spread over the interpolated yield for a Treasury security with a maturity of 8.9 years, the wording would more likely be: "50 basis points over the curve at a 6% prepay rate and an 8.9-year average life."

Cash Flow Assumptions Used in Calculating Mortgage Yields

Since the projected cash flows underlying any mortgage yield calculation are arbitrary, it is possible for two different dealers to sell the same security at the same price and represent it as having different yields reflecting their differing cash flow assumptions. In light of this, the industry has adopted some standard ways of quoting mortgage securities that have been designed to minimize confusion and promote the development of a consistent secondary market. These standards have changed over the years to meet the changing needs of the market and to reflect an increasing understanding of mortgage prepayment patterns.

Cash Flow Yields to a Constant Prepayment Rate

In the secondary market, cash flow yields on mortgage securities are normally quoted on the basis of an assumed constant prepayment rate (CPR). The prepayment rate is the percentage of the outstanding mortgage balance that is prepaid per year. For example, when a particular pool is said to have a 10% CPR, it indicates that if the current monthly rate were to continue for an entire year, the pool's outstanding balance at year-end would be 90% of what it would have been without prepayments. A cash flow yield calculated on the basis of a 10% CPR would take the monthly mortgage cash flows that result under a 10% constant prepayment rate and calculate the discount rate that would equate the present discounted value of this payment stream to the price of the security.

When yields are quoted on a CPR basis, the quote makes explicit the particular prepayment rate that has been assumed (for example, "11.45% to a 6% prepay"). The prepayment rate chosen could, in principle, be any rate, but in practice, CPR yields are frequently based on the recent historical prepayment experience of that type of security (for example, the rate for the past month or the past 12 months). This provides historical justification for the prepayment rate chosen, but it implicitly assumes that past prepayment rates will prevail for the remaining life of the security.

The mortgage-backed securities market has recently begun to focus more on CPR yields that are based on projected prepayment rates such as those generated by the Salomon Brothers prepayment model. The model's projections of prepayment rates for the major types of mortgage-backed pass-throughs can be helpful in evaluating CMOs, since in most cases, CMO collateral comprises mortgage-backed securities or whole loans with mortgage rates and other characteristics similar to those that have been pooled into pass-throughs. For example, in a case where the collateral backing a CMO is all or mostly 11% GNMAs, it makes sense to examine CMO bond yields calculated on the basis of the model's projected CPR for GNMA 11s.

Cash Flow Yields to a Percentage of PSA

Calculations of yields to a constant prepayment rate assume that the specified prepayment rate will prevail for the remaining term of the security. This assumption of a constant CPR reflects observed prepayment behavior of seasoned mortgages during periods of stable interest rates. It is much less representative of the prepayment rates of newly issued mortgages. These have tended to increase for the first few years after the mortgages are issued and then level off. Given the historical prepayment pattern for new mortgages, it can be misleading to quote a CMO backed by newly issued mortgages on the basis of a constant prepayment rate. This is particularly true for the short-maturity pieces that pay down during the first few years of the CMO, which for current-coupon CMOs, is likely to correspond to the first few years after the mortgages were issued.

To promote CMO pricing that reflects reasonable expectations regarding prepayments, the major dealers in CMOs adopted a new prepayment benchmark for pricing CMOs. This benchmark is called the Public Securities Association (PSA) Standard Prepayment Model. In essence, the industry has endorsed a specific prepayment curve (or series of prepayment rates over the life of a mortgage) as a benchmark, and it has agreed to relate the prepayment experience of all CMOs to this specific pattern. The PSA prepayment rate curve starts at 0.2% per year in the first month that a pool of mortgages is outstanding, increases by 0.2% each month until month 30, after which it remains at 6% per year for all succeeding months. Any security whose underlying mortgages prepay according to this pattern is said to be prepaying at 100% PSA. Figure 5 presents the PSA Prepayment Curve at 50%, 100% and 150% PSA.

The securities industry has agreed that published yield tables for newly issued CMOs will be constructed on the basis of the PSA benchmark and that the issues themselves will be priced on this basis. Assume, for example,

FIGURE 5. *PSA Prepayment Curve.*

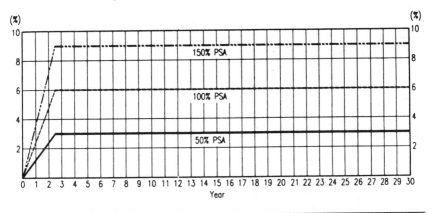

that CMOs backed by current-coupon GNMAs are priced "at 100% PSA," based on expectations that prepayments on the underlying collateral will approximate the PSA prepayment curve. In the same economic environment, a CMO backed by current-coupon conventional collateral (that normally prepays faster than GNMA collateral) might be priced "at 150% PSA." The projected cash flows from the underlying mortgages would be generated assuming that the prepayment rates will increase from 0.3% per year in the first month after the underlying mortgages were issued to 9% per year in the thirtieth month and then remain at 9% for the remaining term of the mortgages.[13]

Appendix II:
Accrued Interest on Z Bonds

During their accrual perod, accrued interest on Z bonds is treated differently than on coupon-bearing fixed income securities. Since these differences have been a source of confusion, we review them below.

Between coupon dates, bond prices normally are quoted as "a percentage of par value plus accrued interest." The principal value of the bond that

---

13. The Public Securities Association Standard Prepayment Model has generally replaced FHA experience as a prepayment benchmark, because it more accurately represents the pattern of prepayments on a pool of mortgages over time, and because the periodic revisions of the FHA "standard" created confusion among market participants. See Thomas Delehanty, *A New Prepayment Benchmark for CMOs—the PSA Model* (New York: Salomon Brothers Inc, June 14, 1985).

will be returned to the bondholder at maturity is being quoted at the market price, but the accrued interest that will be paid back to the bondholder at the next coupon date is, in effect, being priced at par.

Mortgage-backed pass-through securities and coupon-bearing CMO bonds follow the same convention, although the par value of a mortgage-backed security, unlike that of a Treasury bond, does not remain constant over the life of the security: it changes over time. The market accounts for this paydown of principal by defining the par value on any date as the principal balance as of the previous payment date.

For example, consider the B-piece of the Salomon Brothers Mortgage Securities Inc II CMO, Series 1984-2 (SBMSI II-2). This quarterly pay bond carries a 10% coupon. On November 4, 1985, the quoted bid price of the bond was 99. Since the previous coupon date was September 1, 1985, there were 63 days of accrued interest to be paid. At a quoted price of 99, the total cost on November 4, 1985 of a bond that on September 1, 1985, had a balance of $1,000 would be:

Total Cost = Principal Value + Accrued Interest

= (Price/100) * Balance

+ (Days Since Last Payment/360) * (Coupon/100) * Balance

= (99/100) * 1000 + (63/360) * (10/100) * 1000

= 1,007.50.

In contrast, Z bonds are "traded flat" (without accrued interest). This does not mean that an investor who purchases a Z bond part of the way through a coupon period does not have to pay for whatever interest has accrued since the previous period. It just means that the accrued interest is accounted for differently.

Instead of multiplying the balance (as of the previous payment date) by the quoted price and adding the accrued interest, the dollar cost of a Z bond is obtained by multiplying the "current balance" by the quoted price. This current balance is an intraperiod trading balance that is updated daily by adding to the previous day's current balance another day's accrued interest.

In practice, the computation of the current balance is accomplished via "principal balance factors" or "Z-factors." The Z-factor for a given day is the ratio of the current balance on the bond, as of that day, to its original balance. Therefore, given the original balance on a Z, the current quoted price, and a table of Z-factors for the bond, the total price to be paid on the bond is obtained by simple multiplication, without making any reference to accrued interest.

For example, the Z bond of the SBMSI II-2 was quoted on November 27, 1985 at 84⅛. Since the dated date for this 10% coupon CMO was November 27, 1984 and the first coupon date was March 1, 1985, the long first coupon had 94 days in it. Subsequent to the long first coupon, there were two full coupon periods from the dated date to November 4, 1985: March 1, 1985–June 1, 1985, and June 1, 1985–September 1, 1985, as well as a final period of 63 days.

The Z-factor on November 4, 1985, is therefore:

$$[1 + .10 * (94/360)] * [1 + .10 * (90/360)]^2 * [1 + .10 * (63/360)] = 1.096924.$$

For a Z bond of $1,000 original face value, bought at 84⅛:

$$\text{Total Cost} = (\text{Z-Factor}) * (\text{Original Balance}) * (\text{Price}/100)$$
$$= (1.096924) * (1000) * (84.125/100) = 922.79.$$

Trade confirmations may break down the remittance amount for the purchase of a Z bond into two cost figures: one for the principal value as of the last coupon date and one for the accrued interest. In the above example, these items are as follows:

$$\text{Principal Value} = \text{Principal Amount as of the Last Coupon Date} * \text{Price}/100$$
$$= (\text{Z-Factor as of the Last Coupon Date})$$
$$* (\text{Original Balance}) * (\text{Price}/100)$$
$$= [1 + .10 * (94/360)] * [1 + .10 * (90/360)]^2$$
$$* (1,000) * (84.125/100)$$
$$= (1.07806) * (1,000) * (.84125) = 906.92; \quad \text{and}$$

$$\text{Accrued Interest Value} = \text{Accrued Interest Since the Last Coupon Date}$$
$$* \text{Price}/100$$
$$= (\text{Days Since Last Payment}/360) * (\text{Coupon}/100)$$
$$* (\text{Balance as of Last Coupon Date}) * (\text{Price}/100)$$
$$= (63/360) * (.10) * (1078.06) * (.84125) = 15.87.$$

For a coupon-bearing bond, say Class B, with the same balance (as of the last coupon date), coupon, settlement date, and price, the settlement amount would differ only in that the accrued interest term would not be multiplied by the price. For such a hypothetical issue, the total cost would break down as:

$$\text{Total Cost} = \text{Principal Value} + \text{Accrued Interest}$$
$$= (\text{Price}/100) * (\text{Banance as of Last Coupon Date})$$
$$+ (\text{Days Since Last Payment}/360) * (\text{Coupon}/100) * (\text{Balance})$$
$$= (.84125) * (1,078.06) + (63/360 * .10 * 1,078.06)$$
$$= 906.92 + 18.87 = 925.79.$$

The market convention for Z bonds is, in effect, "pricing" the accrued interest at the price at which the principal balance of the bond is being quoted (rather than at par), since the Z bond's accrued interest will not be paid out to the investor on the next coupon date (as it would on a coupon-bearing bond), but will instead be added to the principal balance of the bond and paid out in the future.

Note that once principal payments commence on the Z bonds, their prices will be quoted like the price on any other coupon bond.

Appendix III: Payment Delays

1985 saw the addition of payment delays to the standard CMO structure. Payment delays have always been a standard feature of the mortgage pass-through market. For example, an investor who purchases a GNMA pass-through on the first of a month will not receive the first payment on the certificate until the fifteenth of the following month. This can be considered a delay of 15 days in the payment of the interest that accrued in the first month. Accrued interest on a trade in midmonth is always computed from the first day of a month, rather than from the prior date on which a payment was actually made to certificate holders.

CMO payment delays are analogous to delays on pass-throughs. As an illustration, consider two hypothetical quarterly pay CMOs, both dated January 1, 1986. The first has no payment delay, which means that principal and interest payments will be made on April 1, July 1, October 1, and January 1 of each year. Any interest accrued on a purchase will be computed using the number of days from the previous payment date to the settlement date.

The second issue has a 30-day payment delay. This means that while April 1, July 1, October 1, and January 1 (which one might call "pseudo payment dates") continue to have the same significance as before for computing accrued interest (and Z-factors), the quarterly principal and interest payments will not actually be made until 30 days later, on May 1, August 1, November 1, and February 1 (the actual payment dates).

So, for example, the investor who purchased a nonaccrual bond from this second issue on April 10, 1986, would have to pay accrued interest from April 1, 1986 (the previous pseudo-coupon date), and would receive his first payment from the bonds only on August 1, 1986. This payment would include interest accrued from April 1, 1986, to July 1, 1986, in addition to any principal.

One simple way to remember what a payment delay does and does not affect is by the "check in the mail" analogy. From the investor's viewpoint, the cash flow received from the issue with a 30-day delay is the same as he would receive from the issue with no delay if, in the latter case, his checks were sent to him by such slow means that he only received them after one month. The computation of accrued interest and the determination of record date are identical in the two bonds, but the computation of the investor's projected cash flow yield and projected total return must take into account the delay in his receipt of the cash flows.

For Par-Priced Bonds with Payment Delays, the Rules of Thumb Do Not Apply

Yield computations on CMO bonds with payment delays sometimes produce apparently paradoxical results. For example, it is well known that the semiannual yield of a par bond with no payment delay will equal its coupon. With a par-priced CMO bond with a payment delay, however, the cash flow yield will be less than the coupon because the payment delay reduces the present value of the projected cash flows by pushing them farther out in time.

For example, consider the Class A-1 bonds of the Great Western 85-A CMO. This quarterly pay issue is dated September 1, 1985, the A-1 coupon is 10.20%, and the issue was priced at 100% PSA. The Great Western A-1 bonds have a 30-day payment delay and were originally offered for September 27, 1985, delivery at a price of 100. At 100% PSA, the projected cash flow yield is 9.89%, which is 31 basis points less than the coupon, despite the price being at 100.[14]

In addition to being less than the coupon, the projected cash flow yield of a par-priced CMO with a payment delay will also decline as the prepayment rates on the mortgage collateral rise. This is in contrast to the more familiar situation for the par bond with no payment delay, in which the cash flow yield is insensitive to the timing of cash flows. For example, consider the cash flow yields for the Great Western A-1 bonds over a range of prepayment rates.

Projected Cash Flow Yields, Great Western 85 A-1 CMO

Pct. PSA	Yield (%)
100	9.89
125	9.84
150	9.78
175	9.73
200	9.68

To understand why bonds that are apparently priced at par would trade like bonds priced at a premium, consider that the same Great Western 85-A1

---

14. In addition, it is fully 44 basis points less than the semiannual-equivalent coupon rate of 10.33%.

10.20% bonds with identical cash flows but with no delay would be priced on October 1, 1985, at 100.84 to provide the same 9.89% yield. It is no surprise that the yield on this hypothetical CMO bond, with its premium price, decreases as prepayments speed up.

Appendix IV:
Structuring CMOs

The need to satisfy the rating agencies that even under the most adverse conditions, sufficient cash will be generated to service the outstanding bonds places certain constraints on the structure of any CMO. The CMO issuer's objective is to maximize the value of the bonds that can be issued from the available collateral, while obtaining the highest credit rating possible based on the quality of the underlying collateral and the CMO structure (without reference to the creditworthiness of the issuer-sponsor). The objective of the rating agencies is to protect investors from default. Their requirements are based on insuring against the worst-case scenario and effectively place conservative upper limits on the amount of bonds that can be issued against a given amount of collateral.

In setting structural requirements for CMOs, the rating agencies have three major concerns:

1. The credit risk must be minimal. Typically, to obtain a AAA rating the collateral must be either insured against default by a AAA-rated insurance company or guaranteed by one of the Federal housing agencies.
2. The CMO must be fully collateralized. This means that it must be structured so that even under the worst-case prepayment scenario — immediate prepayment of all premium mortgages and zero prepayments on all discounts — the value of the bonds outstanding would not exceed the maximum amount that can be serviced by the underlying collateral.

   In practice this limits the principal value of bonds issued to an amount less than the outstanding principal balance of the underlying collateral. In cases in which the coupons on the bonds exceed the coupons on the underlying mortgages (for example, current coupon bonds backed by discount mortgage collateral), the maximum value of the bonds that can be issued may be significantly less than the mortgage principal.
3. The reinvestment risk must be minimized. Since CMOs pay quarterly or semiannually, they must include provisions that ensure the soundness of the issue in low interest rate environments when rates at which monthly cash flows can be reinvested between coupon dates will be less

than the coupon on the outstanding bonds.[15] A variety of approaches have been adopted to minimize reinvestment risk during periods of low interest rates:

- The principal value of bonds issued is calculated assuming conservative reinvestment rates on the monthly cash from the mortgage collateral — currently 4½% the first year, 4% the second year and 3% thereafter. Only if the issuer obtains a guaranteed investment contract (GIC) from a AAA-rated issuer guaranteeing a higher reinvestment rate can the principal value of the bonds issued be calculated assuming that higher rate.
- The issuer may also overcollateralize the issue sufficiently so that there is, in effect, a reserve to make up any shortfall between the reinvestment income on monthly cash flows from the collateral and what is needed to service the outstanding bonds.
- Most CMOs also include "mandatory redemption provisions" that require issuers to revert to monthly principal payments whenever necessary to prevent a shortfall from developing. This would occur only under conditions of extremely rapid prepayments or extremely low reinvestment rates.

In virtually all cases, the worst-case prepayment and reinvestment rate assumptions that are implicit in the structural requirements for a AAA rating will prove to be too conservative; the cash thrown off from the pool of mortgages between coupon dates will exceed that needed to ensure that the outstanding bonds can be serviced, and the CMO will turn out to be, in effect, overcollateralized. And even in the highly unlikely event of the worst-case scenario, the mandatory redemption provisions would guarantee that bondholders be paid in full.

Bond Value

The actual amount of bonds issued against a given collateral pool depends in practice on the way the "bond value" of the collateral is calculated for that particular CMO. Conceptually, the bond value is the total outstanding face amount of CMO bonds that can be safely collateralized by that pool alone, given the particular structure of the CMO in question.

The bond value calculation provides the formula for deciding the maximum-sized CMO that can be issued with all available pools: Add up the

---

15. At the end of each quarter (or semiannual period), bondholders are entitled to the interest on the principal balance that was outstanding at the beginning of that period. Since the cash flow from the underlying mortgages will be received over the period in monthly payments (part of which will reduce the outstanding principal balance), however, the issuer's ability to meet the quarterly (or semiannual) interest payments will depend on the rate at which these intervening principal payments can be reinvested.

bond values of the individual collateral pools to get an aggregate bond value, which is the upper limit on the size of the CMO. In practice, the bond value of a pool of mortgages rarely exceeds the principal balance of mortgage collateral, because an instantaneous prepayment of all the mortgages will pay only the mortgage balance plus one month's interest.

Since the cash flows on the underlying collateral are uncertain, any bond value calculation must be based on some assumption about prepayments and the reinvestment rates at which monthly cash flows can be invested until the quarterly or semiannual coupon dates. As noted above, to meet the requirements of the rating agencies, bond values for CMOs are computed using only scheduled distributions from the mortgages (assuming no prepayments), and assuming rather low reinvestment rates (currently 4½% the first year, 4% the second and 3% thereafter).

Two common schemes for calculating bond value follow.

1. The coupon-to-coupon ratio method under which the bond value of all mortgages with coupons less than the maximum CMO coupon is equal to the present balance of the mortgages multiplied by the ratio of the annual coupon on the underlying mortgages to the maximum annual coupon on the CMO bonds. For all mortgages with coupons greater than the maximum CMO coupon, the bond value is equal to the present balance of the mortgages.
2. The present-value method, which projects the future scheduled cash flow from the mortgage collateral (reinvesting to the appropriate points in time) and then discounts this cash flow back to the present using the highest coupon on the CMO bonds as a discount rate.[16] In most cases, the highest coupon is carried by only the longest-maturity class bonds. Its use as the discount rate when calculating the bond value of a CMO is a conservative practice that limits the size of the issue more than is strictly necessary. Such bond issues are, in effect, overcollateralized, because as the mortgage pays down, more cash will be thrown off than is needed to service the outstanding bonds.

The bond value calculation must also hold over time as the mortgages and bonds pay down: The total outstanding bond balance at any time must not exceed the total bond value of the collateral at that point. So the bond value calculation not only determines how many bonds can be issued initially, it also determines how much of the existing cash needs to be used to retire bonds and how much is "spread" that can either be passed back to the issuer or used to speed the retirement of bonds.

In those issues that are structured to return the spread to the issuer, by definition the principal value of the outstanding bonds over time will always

---

16. See Patricia A. Jehle, *Collateralized Mortgage Obligations* (New York: Salomon Brothers Inc, February 1985).

equal the bond value (as long as the original total balance on the bonds equals the aggregate bond value of the collateral). Since issuers of such CMOs are allowed, typically on each coupon date, to withdraw any funds over and above those necessary to ensure that the issue will remain fully collateralized, bonds in these issues will be retired at approximately the same rate as the underlying collateral, even though the CMO bonds may become over-collateralized between coupon dates.

In contrast, if the spread is passed through to the bondholder, the bonds will be retired at a faster rate than the prepayment rate on the mortgage collateral, and over time, the issue will become increasingly overcollateralized. With the faster retirement of bonds, average lives will be reduced, as will the expected length of the interest-only periods of the longer-maturity classes of the CMO. This does not present any problem to investors as long as their expectations regarding average lives, yields and total returns reflect the shorter expected maturities on such bonds. Because the monthly CMO yield tables circulated among the dealer community reflect the impact of these structural characteristics on paydowns, they provide investors with a framework in which to evaluate different CMO bonds without becoming immersed in the details of each CMO issue.

Relative Size of the Different CMO Classes

When structuring a CMO from a pool of mortgage collateral, issuers can exercise some discretion in deciding how large to make the different classes of bonds. This means that within limits, CMOs can be structured to take advantage of the market conditions prevailing at the time of issuance. For example, if there appeared to be a strong demand for short-maturity bonds, the A class of a CMO could be increased by increasing the size of the Z class and compressing the sizes of the B and C classes. Since interest on the Z bonds is accrued but not paid out until all previous classes are retired, an increase in the relative size of the Z class will reduce the amount of cash flow from the underlying mortgages that is needed to pay coupon interest and, hence, will increase the amount available in early years to retire A bonds.

In general, the larger the earlier classes, the longer the expected interest-only period of the later classes will be. At the same time, increasing the size of the A class will lengthen its expected maturity and average life. Since there appears to be some maximum acceptable expected average life for A bonds among short-maturity investors, this places an effective upper limit on the size of the earlier CMO classes.

34

Hedging Prepayment Risk with Derivative Mortgage Securities

Steven J. Carlson
Vice President and Manager
Shearson Lehman Mortgage Securities

I. Introduction

Investors in mortgage-backed securities have long desired a tool to hedge prepayment risk. This desire is particularly prevalent among investors in premium- and discount-coupon securities, as unexpected changes in prepayments will substantially affect these coupons' values. A greater than expected increase in prepayments in the underlying collateral will reduce the value of premium coupons while raising the value of discount securities. This risk can be effectively hedged since the advent of derivative mortgage securities (derivative mortgage securities' prepayment risk can also be hedged). For the purposes of this article, derivative mortgage securities include stripped principal only (PO) securities and the tranches of collateralized mortgage obligations (CMOs) whose coupon rates are substantially below those of the underlying collateral, both called synthetic discounts. Derivative securities also include synthetic premiums such as stripped interest only securities (IOs), fixed-rate CMO residuals, and excess servicing. This article introduces a prepayment hedging technique that allows investors to construct portfolios whose price value is insulated from unexpected changes in prepayments. This portfolio may be called a synthetic par portfolio. Once a synthetic par portfolio is constructed, then its overall interest rate risk can be addressed.

Prior to the issuance of large quantities of derivative securities, the only way to immunize mortgage portfolios against prepayment risk was to short like securities — that is, to take a short position in a security with attributes similar or identical to the security being hedged. This method could be costly and in some cases was not a plausible option. Other hedging techniques — such as hedging mortgage securities with interest rate swaps, financial futures, or shorts on Treasury securities — covered market direction risk but left investors exposed if prepayments diverged from expectations. What investors needed was a hedging vehicle that specifically addressed prepayment risk.

For derivative mortgage securities, the impact on value due to changes in the prepayment behavior of the underlying collateral is substantially different from the impact on the underlying pass-through collateral itself. Assuming identical collateral, an increase in prepayments would substantially enhance the value of synthetic discounts but reduce the value of synthetic premiums. The prepayment sensitivities of selected derivative mortgage securities are shown in Table 1. For example, many CMO offerings have included several

TABLE 1. *Price Prepayment Sensitivity for Derivative Mortgage Securities.*

	E^a	Collateral Prepayment Rate (PSA%)	Current Price (32nds)[b]	Yield (CBE%)	Standard Modified Duration
Stripped MBS					
9% IOs	−0.175	180	36-21	9.00	3.1
9% POs	0.082	180	68-22	7.24	4.4
Discount CMO Bonds[c]					
Santa Barbara A-4	0.095	165	75-24	8.50	7.9
Santa Barbara A-3	0.054	165	85-05	7.81	4.9
Fixed-Rate CMO Residual[c]					
SICMO Series C	−0.268	165	6.420	14.00	3.7
Excess Servicing					
100 bp Current Production	−0.261	150	5-04	10.00	4.7
Pass-throughs					
GNMA 30-year 13s	−0.015	500	109-19	7.39	1.8
GNMA 30-year 9s	−0.001	150	103-12	8.49	7.0
GNMA 30-year 7.5s	0.006	150	97-21	8.06	6.9
FNMA 15-year 9s	−0.007	180	103-10	8.22	4.0

a. E is equal to the percentage change in price (P) given a one percentage point change in PSA or $(\Delta p/\Delta PSA)/P$ where $\Delta p/\Delta PSA$ is the first derivative of price given a change in PSA. (For more details, see the Shearson Lehman Brothers special report, *Assessing the Duration of Mortgage Securities: A New Approach* by Steven J. Carlson [New York, 1987]).
b. Price is expressed as a percentage of face value. In the case of the fixed-rate CMO residual, price is expressed in millions of dollars.
c. See Table 2 for summary of bond terms.

TABLE 2. *Pricing Analysis of CMO Bond and Residual Interest.*

a. CMO Discount Bond: Santa Barbara Funding II, Inc. – Series A

Sequence	Current Principal Balance ($ million)	Bond Coupon (%)	Stated Maturity	Average Life[a]	Projected Maturity
A-1	337.450	Floater	03/20/18	8.97	09/20/16
A-2	82.375	5.00	03/20/09	2.46	06/20/91
A-3	51.100	5.00	12/20/12	5.71	06/20/94
A-4	86.475	5.00	12/20/16	11.01	03/20/03
A-5	42.600	5.00	03/20/18	21.35	09/20/16

b. Residual Interest: Shearson Lehman CMO – Series C

Bond Class	Current Principal Balance ($ million)	Bond Coupon (%)	Stated Maturity	Average Life[a]	Projected Maturity
C-1	51,883,386.	7.45000	10/20/01	2.09	07/20/90
C-2	68,000,000.	8.25000	04/20/08	5.59	01/20/95
C-3	67,500,000.	9.12500	01/20/12	10.92	04/20/01
C-4	11,259,875.	9.45000	10/20/17	19.95	10/20/16

a. Weighted average life based on a 165 percent PSA assumption.

deep discount tranches. Because of the deep discount in price, these tranches are favorably affected by increases in the prepayments of the underlying collateral. Investors in CMO residuals can reduce their exposure to the effects of rising prepayments by purchasing discount CMO bonds from another offering with similar collateral. As a result, the CMO bond is favorably affected even though the CMO residual's value is adversely affected by unexpected increases in prepayments. With the availability of these securities, the investor can construct a synthetic par portfolio whose current value is largely immunized from the effects of prepayments.

In essence, a synthetic par security can be created by combining various synthetic or generic premium pass-throughs with synthetic or generic discount pass-throughs. To be assured of an effective prepayment hedge, both securities must have similar collateral characteristics, underlying mortgage types, coupons, and age. After identifying two securities with similar collateral characteristics whose values would move in opposing directions if unexpected changes occurred in prepayment behavior, a prepayment hedge can be constructed. The following discussion describes how to construct a synthetic par security.

FIGURE 1. *Asset Value and Prepayments for a $100 Purchase at the Projected Prepayment Rate for Residual and CMO Discount Bond.*

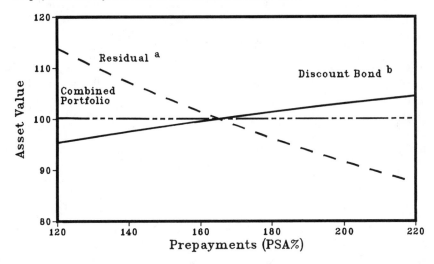

* Residual refers to ownership of a residual interest in SLCMO Series C (see Table 2 for details).
** CMO Discount Bond refers to Santa Barbata A-4s (see Table 2 for details).

FIGURE 2. *Asset Value and Prepayments for a $100 Purchase at Projected Prepayment Rate for FNMA 15-Year 9% Pass-Throughs and POs.*

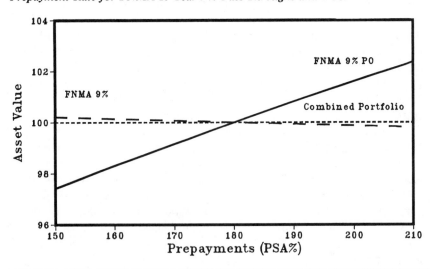

II. Synthetic Par Portfolios

Figure 1 depicts the relationship between asset value and prepayments for a $100 investment in a fixed-rate CMO residual and a deep-discount CMO bond. Both are backed by similar collateral: Federal Home Loan Mortgage Corporation (FHLMC) 9½s. Figure 2 shows asset value and prepayments for two stripped mortgage-backed securities, Federal National Mortgage Association (FNMA) 15-year, 9% PO strips and FNMA 15-year, 9% pass-through securities. The analysis is based on a pricing prepayment rate of 165% PSA (Public Securities Association model) for the CMO residual and discount bond (Figure 1), and 180% PSA for the stripped mortgage-backed securities (Figure 2).

As is shown, the fixed-rate CMO residual and the 9% pass-through decrease in value as the prepayment rate increases. Conversely, the discount CMO bond and the PO strip increase in value as the prepayment rate rises. A synthetic par security can be constructed by forming a portfolio that balances the price-weighted prepayment sensitivity of a security whose price moves directly with prepayments with a security whose price moves indirectly with prepayments. Such a portfolio would be insulated against prepayment fluctuations that may occur even when interest rates remain stable.

Figures 1 and 2 also display the value/prepayment relationship of two such synthetic par portfolios (see line labeled "combined portfolio"). As is evident, the combined portfolios are relatively immunized against changes in prepayment expectations. In the first example (see Figure 1), the investor can create an synthetic par portfolio by purchasing $2.823 million worth of discount CMO bonds ($2.145 million face value) and $1 million worth of CMO fixed-rate residuals. In the second case (Figure 2), a purchase of $8.82 million of POs and $103.313 million worth of pass-throughs or a $12.84 million face value purchase of POs is made for every $100 million of pass-throughs in the portfolio. Similar synthetic par portfolios can be created using a variety of securities — servicing portfolios hedged with POs, for example. The following discussion describes the concept more fully.

III. The Prepayment Hedge Concept

Immunizing one mortgage-backed asset (asset 1) from the price risk imposed by unexpected changes in prepayments requires purchasing a second asset (asset 2) whose price change is equal in magnitude yet opposite in direction. If the changes in the prices of the two assets in the hedge interval are ΔP_1 and ΔP_2, the value of asset 2 that must be purchased to hedge an equal value is

$$\text{PHR} = -\frac{\Delta P_1}{\Delta P_2},$$

where PHR = prepayment hedge ratio.

Prepayments on the underlying collateral can respond differently depending on the attributes of the collateral. As a result, the relative prepayment behavior effect must be incorporated. This is accomplished by multiplying and dividing the numerator by PSA_1 and the denominator by ΔPSA_2, with the new result:

$$PHR = -\frac{\Delta P_1/\Delta PSA_1}{\Delta P_2/\Delta PSA_2} \times \frac{\Delta PSA_1}{\Delta PSA_2},$$

where

$\Delta P/\Delta PSA = $ the price sensitivities of assets 1 and 2 to respective prepayment changes (or similarly, the partial derivative of price with respect to prepayments); and

$\Delta PSA_1/\Delta PSA_2 = $ the change in the prepayment expectations of asset 1 relative to the change in the prepayment expectations of asset 2.

If assets 1 and 2 come from similar or identical mortgage collateral, then $\Delta PSA_1/\Delta PSA_2 = 1$. If the collateral is dissimilar, then the hedge is less likely to prove effective. However, $\Delta PSA_1/\Delta PSA_2$ can be determined empirically using statistical techniques.[1]

E can be employed to simplify the equation:

$$PHR = -\frac{E_1 P_1}{E_2 P_2} \times \frac{\Delta PSA_1}{\Delta PSA_2},$$

where E is equal to the percentage change in price given a one percentage point change in PSA.

In the case where similar or identical collateral underlies both assets 1 and 2, $\Delta PSA_1/\Delta PSA_2 = 1$. In this case a further simplified result is:

$$PHR = -\frac{E_1 P_1}{E_2 P_2}.$$

IV. Numerical Example of Hedge Ratio

Assume that an investor owns $100 million face amount of 15-year FNMA 9s priced at 103.313% of par and wishes to immunize any exposure to prepayment variations. Upon identifying a security with similar collateral characteristics, such as 15-year 9% PO strips, the investor can now construct a prepayment hedge ratio.

---

1. One technique for empirically estimating the relative prepayment relationship is to regress PSA_1 with PSA_2; the best statistical results are likely to occur when the collateral from both assets is similar.

Substituting values from Table 1 and using the prepayment hedge ratio formula, the result can be calculated as follows:

$$PHR = -\frac{-.007 \times 103.313}{0.082 \times 68.688} = .1284.$$

Investors can immunize the price value sensitivity to changes in prepayments of a $100 million portfolio purchase of 15-year FNMA 9s by purchasing $12.84 million face value of 15-year 9% PO strips.

Modifications in this hedge ratio will be necessary as yield and expected prepayment levels change. As is the case with all hedging techniques, the portfolio may require adjustment should market conditions and/or prepayment expectations change significantly. Interest rate risk of the prepayment-hedged portfolio can be addressed separately using more traditional hedging approaches.

35

An Introduction to
Interest Rate Futures*

Francis H. Trainer, Jr.
Manager, Fixed-Income Investments
Sanford C. Bernstein & Co., Inc.

I. Introduction

A financial future on a Treasury note or bond represents a commitment to buy or sell a Treasury security at a specified time in the future.[1] When a futures contract is purchased, the portfolio is exposed to the risks of owning the underlying security. Conversely, when a future is sold against an existing position, the interest rate risk is neutralized. The position is, in a sense, eliminated from the portfolio.

One would expect a future to trade at a price that is very close to its intrinsic value; that is, there should be very little incentive to use the futures contract as a substitute for an actual bond transaction. Yet this does not seem to be the case for financial futures on Treasury securities. There have been many times in the past when these contracts have been mispriced, either over- or underpriced, and could have been used to enhance returns.

1. The specifications of the note and bond contracts are identical (except for maturity). The remainder of this article refers exclusively to the relationship of the futures contract and Treasury notes, but all comments apply to Treasury bonds as well.

One of the characteristics of a future that is difficult to understand is that it does not cost anything.[2] When we "buy" a future, what we are really doing is making a *commitment* to purchase a note. The execution price is determined when the futures contract is initiated. Thus a futures trade is similar to a trade for forward delivery or delayed settlement — but not exactly the same. In a forward contract the delivery price is established at the time of the trade, but generally no money passes hands until the actual settlement. At that time the market price can be higher or lower than the initial execution without affecting the settlement price. In a futures trade the execution price is also locked in, but the process is somewhat different.

When a note future is purchased at $100, it is equivalent to purchasing $100,000 par value of notes. If, at the end of the first day, the price rises to $101, the purchaser of the contract (who is said to be "long" the contract) receives $1,000 per contract. If the contract falls the next day to $99, the long holder is required to pay $2,000. The futures contract "marks to the market" daily, and all changes in the market value of the contract must be offset by cash transfers. (In addition, a margin deposit must be maintained with the broker who executes the trade.)

If, on the last day of trading, the contract settles at a price of $99, that becomes the delivery price — that is, the price that the purchaser of the futures contract must pay for the Treasury note that is delivered to him. Although the purchaser of the note is buying it one point below the original price, this point had already been paid when the price fell to $99. In other words the delivery price plus the net cash transfers (other than the initial margin deposit) equals the price at which the trade first took place.

II. The Factor System — A Method to Equilibrate Prices

The commitment to buy or sell the underlying security may be extinguished at any time prior to expiration by simply reversing the original trade.[3] But, as noted above, if the contract is held through the delivery month, it will expire and the seller of the contract (the short) will be called upon to deliver to the long holder of the contract a security. The delivery price will be the price of the future at the close of trading adjusted for the specific security that is delivered. This adjustment is effected through the use of the factor system.

---

2. A future does not cost anything in terms of principal value; that is, there are no payments made to the seller. To be sure, there are transaction charges and bid/asked spreads, but they are very small relative to the value of the underlying security.
3. The Chicago Board of Trade imposes a three-point limit on the daily movement of the futures price (as of August 3, 1987). This limit may temporarily prevent the reversal of the original trade. However, this limit is not applied to the spot future in the delivery month.

When a futures contract is purchased, the exact security that will be received through the delivery process is not known. For example, as of December 31, 1985, there were 13 notes and 33 bonds that were deliverable against the U.S. Treasury note and bond futures contracts respectively. The prices on these securities ranged from $85.06 to $150.25. Since there is only one closing futures price (one each for notes and bonds), it is clear that there must be a way to adjust the price of the future to allow for an equitable delivery system. One way to establish an indifference price between two bonds with similar maturities is to value them at the same yield to maturity. This is the solution developed by the Chicago Board of Trade. Since interest rates were near 8 percent when the Treasury bond contract was created, an 8 percent yield has been used to derive the equivalence price for each deliverable bond. When the Treasury note contracts were introduced in 1982, the same convention was used.

In Table 1, the factors for each of the deliverable notes against the March 1986 note contract are presented.

TABLE 1. *Computation of the Factor Treasury Note Futures (December 31, 1985).*

1	2	3	4	5
			Price at an	(4/100)
Coupon		Adjusted	8% Yield[a]	
(%)	Maturity	Maturity	($)	Factor
9.750	10/15/92	09/01/92	108.737	1.08737
10.500	11/15/92	09/01/92	112.482	1.12482
10.875	02/15/93	12/01/92	114.751	1.14751
10.125	05/15/93	03/01/93	111.223	1.11223
11.875	08/15/93	06/01/93	120.986	1.20986
11.750	11/15/93	09/01/93	120.847	1.20847
13.125	05/15/94	03/01/94	129.859	1.29859
12.625	08/15/94	06/01/94	127.521	1.27521
11.625	11/15/94	09/01/94	122.050	1.22050
11.250	02/15/95	12/01/94	120.151	1.20151
11.250	05/15/95	03/01/95	120.571	1.20571
10.500	08/15/95	06/01/95	116.101	1.16101
9.500	11/15/95	09/01/95	109.850	1.09850
8.989[b]	02/15/96	12/01/95	106.586	1.06586

a. Assumes a settlement date of March 1, 1986.
b. Hypothetical security.
Source: Sanford C. Bernstein & Co., Inc.

There are two additional conventions that are used in the calculation of a factor. First, the maturity of the note is assumed to be the first day of the delivery month immediately preceding the actual maturity date or call date (if callable). Second, the settlement date used in the price calculation is the first day of the delivery month. Column 4 of Table 1 lists the price of each note at an 8 percent yield. Since the standard for delivery is an 8 percent note priced at $100, the equivalence ratio (column 5) for other notes is derived by dividing their price at an 8 percent yield by $100. Thus, if the March future settled at $92.91, the delivery price on the 9.75 percent notes that are due on October 15, 1992 would be equal to 1.08737 times $92.91, or $101.02. Not only is the factor important in the delivery process, but it plays a critical role in evaluating the futures contract at any point in time.

III. Evaluating the Price of a Futures Contract

There are a wide variety of securities that can be delivered against the note and bond contracts. For example, any U.S. Treasury note with a maturity between 6.5 years and 10 years is deliverable. However, depending upon the slope of the yield curve and the absolute level of interest rates, there will usually be only one note that is the cheapest to deliver. This is the note that maximizes the profit (or minimizes the loss) to the deliverer. The process for identifying this note is detailed in Table 2.

Table 2 contains all of the notes that can be delivered against the March 1986 contract and our analysis of their relationship to the futures contract.[4] For example, on December 31, 1985 the 9.75 percent notes due October 15, 1992 were priced at $104.50 when the March future finished trading for the day at $92.91. The March factor for these notes was 1.08737. Therefore, the delivery price was $101.02—the product of the futures price and the factor.

The difference between the delivery value of a security and its actual price is called the basis. Since the delivery value was lower than the current market price of the bond, the basis was negative, in this case, $-3.48. Before reaching a conclusion about the relationship of the futures price to the actual market, there are several additional factors to consider.

Let us assume that we are interested in buying an intermediate maturity note. We can purchase this note in the cash market or in the futures market. Furthermore, let us say that the basis on this note is zero; that is, its cash

---

4. Since the U.S. Treasury issues a 10-year note on a quarterly cycle, there is likely to be a new 10-year note outstanding when the March contract expires. Therefore we need to include this note in our universe of deliverable securities. Since we cannot know the coupon in advance, we assume a coupon equal to the yield on the current 10-year note. On December 31, 1985, the yield on 10-year notes was 8.989 percent. Therefore we have used this figure as the coupon on the hypothetical note.

TABLE 2. Identification of the Cheapest to Deliver Treasury Note Futures (December 31, 1985).

1	2	3	4	5	6	7	8	9
Coupon (%)	Maturity	Market Price ($)	Factor	Delivery Price ($)[a]	(5−3) Basis ($)	Cost of Carry ($)[b]	(6+7) Adjusted Basis ($)	(8/3) Percent Basis
9.750	10/15/92	104.50	1.08737	101.02	−3.48	0.30	−3.18	−3.04
10.500	11/15/92	108.47	1.12482	104.50	−3.97	0.42	−3.55	−3.27
10.875	02/15/93	110.19	1.14751	106.61	−3.58	0.44	−3.14	−2.85
10.125	05/15/93	106.69	1.11223	103.33	−3.35	0.37	−2.98	−2.79
11.875	08/15/93	115.69	1.20986	112.40	−3.28	0.55	−2.73	−2.36
11.750	11/15/93	115.25	1.20847	112.47	−2.98	0.57	−2.41	−2.09
13.125	05/15/94	123.28	1.29859	120.65	−2.63	0.73	−1.90	−1.54
12.625	08/15/94	120.78	1.27521	118.47	−2.31	0.63	−1.68	−1.39
11.625	11/15/94	115.37	1.22050	113.39	−1.98	0.54	−1.44	−1.25
11.250	02/15/95	113.28	1.20151	111.63	−1.65	0.46	−1.19	−1.05
11.250	05/15/95	113.34	1.20571	112.02	−1.33	0.50	−0.83	−0.73
10.500	08/15/95	109.13	1.16101	107.87	−1.26	0.37	−0.89	−0.82
9.500	11/15/95	103.28	1.09850	102.06	−1.22	0.29	−0.93	−0.90
8.989[c]	02/15/96	100.00	1.06586	99.02	−0.98	0.21	−0.77	−0.77

a. Assumes a futures price of $92-29/32 (that is, $92.90625).
b. Incorporates a 7.75 percent certificate of deposit rate.
c. Hypothetical security.
Source: Sanford C. Bernstein & Co., Inc.

price is its delivery value. If the purchase is made in the futures market, we don't have to pay anything and so we can temporarily invest our funds in short-term securities. If the yield on these short-term investments is lower than the current return on the bond (which we would expect when the yield curve is upward sloping), then the futures alternative is less attractive by the amount of this income differential.

However, this income differential can be offset if the future trades at a lower price than the note. The difference in price that will exactly offset the income differential is called the cost of carry (column 7). Because of the potential for arbitrage, we expect that the future price *should* reflect this differential, and therefore we adjust the basis for the cost of carry (column 8).

The adjusted basis is the potential gain *per note*. We are more concerned with the value *per dollar* invested. Therefore we normalize the adjusted basis by dividing the adjusted basis on each note by the market price. The result, the percentage basis in column 9, is an unbiased measure of the relationship of the future to the market prices of the deliverable securities.

In Table 2, the basis is negative for all of the deliverable notes. This means that the deliverer will incur a loss on every security. We can assume that the deliverer will attempt to minimize this loss; that is, he will deliver the bond with the least negative basis. On December 31, 1985 this was the 11¼ percent due May 15, 1995 with a basis of −0.73 percent. This note was the cheapest to deliver and, consequently, it is the note that will determine the price and the day-to-day price changes of the futures contract (as long as it remains the cheapest-to-deliver note).

IV. How Futures Are Used in Management of a Portfolio

The purchase of a future represents a commitment to purchase a security at a specified price on a given date or within a certain range of dates. If this commitment is selling for less than its fair value (that is, if the adjusted basis is negative), it may be attractive to buy the future as a substitute for the cheapest-to-deliver note. On the other hand selling a future is equivalent to selling a note. If the cheapest-to-deliver note is held in a portfolio and an equivalent amount of futures is sold, the interest rate risk of this position is eliminated (that is, a short-term security is created). If the return on this synthetic security is higher than that on certificates of deposit, it is attractive to sell futures against the long-term maturity as a substitute for conventional short-term securities.

Creating a Synthetic Short-Term Security

A synthetic short-term security is, in an economic sense, the equivalent of a repurchase agreement. In a repo, the purchase and sale price are agreed to and they define a contractual return over a specific period. Even though the security that is used as collateral may have a long-term maturity, it is immaterial; a fixed sales price transforms its interest rate risk into that of a short-term security. Similarly, when a futures contract is sold against an existing long-term security, the sales price of that security is locked in and its interest rate risk is virtually eliminated.

To illustrate, we shall use the prices as of December 31, 1985 and make a few simplifying assumptions: First, the prices of all of the deliverable notes are constant. Second, at the close of the March futures contract, the price of the cheapest-to-deliver note is equal to the invoice price of the future (that is, there is no gain or loss upon delivery). Third, we shall use the delivery price of the futures contract (the futures price times the factor) as a proxy for the futures price. The relationship of the future price and the cheapest-to-deliver note from December 31, 1985 to the close of trading on March 19, 1986 is as shown in Figure 1.

On December 31, 1986, the price of the cheapest-do-deliver note—the 11.25 percent due May 15, 1992—was $113.344 and the price of the future was $112.018. We have assumed that prices are constant and that the future converges to the cheapest-to-deliver note. Under these assumptions the futures price rises from $112.018 on December 31, 1985 to $113.344 by March 19, 1986. Since the futures contract is held on the short side (it was sold), the rise in price results in a loss of $1.326. The net price realized is $112.018 — the actual sales price of $113.344 less the loss on the future of $1.326. When the futures contract was sold for $112.018 on December 31, 1985, the sales price of the 11.25 percent note, 2.5 months later on March 19, was effectively locked in.

It might seem that this result is in some way related to the assumption that prices do not change. To demonstrate that this is not the case, let us assume that prices rise and fall over the interim and that the price of the 11.25 percent note ends up at $117.878 (a net increase of 4 percent). We shall continue to assume that the future price converges to the cheapest-do-deliver note at the close of trading. The relationship of the future to the cheapest-to-deliver note is shown in Figure 2.

As the price of the cheapest-to-deliver note changes, the price of the futures contract should also change. Prior to the close of trading, these two prices do not have to change synchronously. In fact they will often diverge slightly on a day-to-day basis. However, because we have assumed convergence by the close of trading, the potential divergence decreases as the expiration date approaches.

The actual sales price of the 11.25 percent notes is $117.878. However, the price of the short futures position rose from $112.018 to $117.878, resulting in a loss of $5.860. The net sales price is $112.018 — $117.878 minus $5.860.

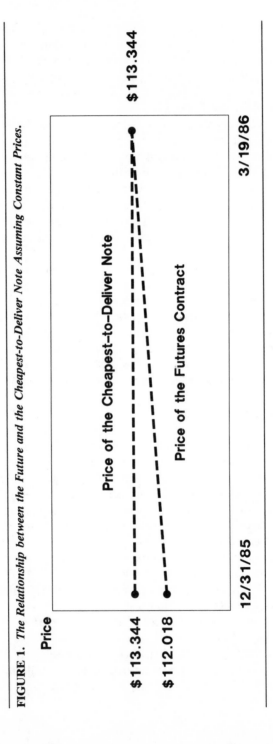

FIGURE 1. *The Relationship between the Future and the Cheapest-to-Deliver Note Assuming Constant Prices.*

FIGURE 2. *Relationship of the Future and the Cheapest-to-Deliver Note When Prices Change.*

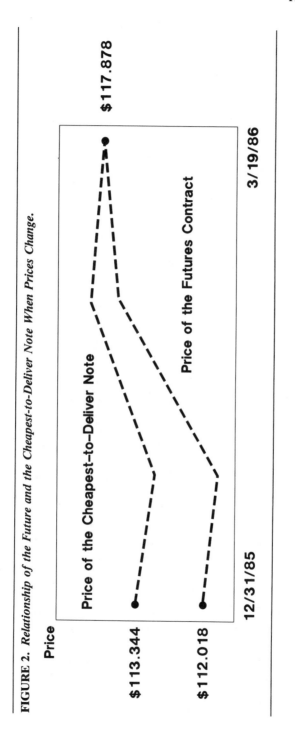

TABLE 3. *Calculation of the Total Return on the Synthetic Short-Term Security.*

a. The formula is:

$$\frac{\begin{array}{c}\text{Change in price} \\ \text{of note position}\end{array} - \begin{array}{c}\text{Change in price} \\ \text{of future position}\end{array} + \begin{array}{c}\text{Change in ac-} \\ \text{crued interest}\end{array}}{\text{Beginning price} + \text{accrued interest}} \times \frac{360}{n}.$$

b. Substituting:

$$\frac{0 - \$1.326 + \$2.424}{\$113.344 + \$1.430} \times \frac{360}{78} = 4.42\%.$$

As long as we assume convergence, the price at which the futures contract is sold represents the effective sales price of that security. Therefore, a note position that is hedged with a future is a synthetic security that matures on the date the futures contract stops trading, generates income equal to the income on the note and has a price at maturity equal to the sales price of the futures contract. The rate of return on the synthetic security (Table 3) is equal to the net change in the prices of the note and futures positions plus the accrued interest divided by the cost of the note (principal plus accrued interest).

The return on the synthetic security over the 78-day period is 4.42 percent (see Table 3), substantially less than the 7.75 percent return available from a certificate of deposit.

It is important to note that the 4.42 percent return is the *minimum* return that may be earned on the synthetic security. Because we have assumed a basis of zero at the close of trading, we have postulated the maximum loss on the futures contract relative to the note position. It is unlikely that the future would close at a higher price than the note (that is, a positive basis) because an arbitrageur could buy the cheapest to deliver note, sell the future, and deliver the note for an immediate (on the same day) and *certain* profit. However, it is highly likely that the future will expire at a lower price (in adjusted terms) than the cheapest to deliver note. To understand why a negative closing basis is likely, we need to explore the delivery process.

The Delivery Process

It might seem strange to postulate a negative basis at the close of trading. One of the primary tenets of the commodity markets is the convergence of the future and spot prices upon delivery. The reason that the basis rarely rises to zero in the bond and note futures contracts is that the short position has the option to deliver a wide variety of securities with different market values.

If $100,000 par value of the 11.25 percent notes due May 15, 1995 are held, 1.20571 contracts need to be sold to hedge this position. (The figure 1.20571 is the factor for the March 1986 contract. We have used fractional contracts to facilitate this presentation. In practice, the hedge ratio will be 12 futures contracts for every $995,000 par value of this particular note.) Let us assume that the note component of the synthetic security is held until the futures contract expires. The futures contract calls for delivery of $100,000 par value per contract. Since 1.20571 contracts have been sold, $120,571 par value of notes must be delivered. But there are only $100,000 of the 11.25 percent notes in position. What can be done?

Trading on the future stops on the eighth business day before the end of the month. The short holder of the note contract has until the next to last business day of the month to announce which security he intends to deliver. If he chooses to deliver the 11.25 percent notes, he needs to purchase an additional $20,571 par value notes.

If interest rates do not change, the additional notes can be purchased at $113.344 for a cost of $23,316. The market value of the original position at the close of trading is $113,344. Thus, the total value of the notes delivered is $136,660 (see Table 4).

The delivery price on the futures contract is $113.344 (assuming a zero basis). Thus the delivery value of $120,571 par value of notes is $136,660. Since the delivery value is equal to the market value of notes delivered, there is no gain or loss and the additional purchase is immaterial.

However, if interest rates fall and prices rise, the purchase of additional 11.25 percent notes results in a loss. This occurs because the market price on the additional $20,571 par value of notes is higher than the invoice price that was established when the future stopped trading. To illustrate, we shall assume that the market price of each note increases by 4 percent (see Table 5).

When the future stops trading, the delivery price is fixed at $113.344. However, the price of the additional $20,571 of notes has risen to a price of

TABLE 4. *Profit (Loss) from Delivery of 11.25 Percent Notes When Prices Do Not Change.*

	Initial Position ($)	Additional Purchase ($)	Total ($)
Par value	100,000	20,571	120,571
Market price	113.344	113.344	—
Market value (par × market price)	113,344	23,316	136,660
Delivery price	113.344	113.344	—
Delivery value (par × delivery price)	113,344	23,316	136,660
Gain (delivery value − market value)	0	0	0

TABLE 5. *Loss from Delivery of 11.25 Percent Notes When Prices Rise 4 Percent.*

	Initial Position ($)	Additional Purchase ($)	Total ($)
Par value	100,000	20,571	120,571
Market price	113.344	117.878	—
Market value (par × market price)	113,344	24,249	137,593
Delivery price	113.344	113.344	—
Delivery value (par × delivery price)	113,344	23,316	136,660
Gain (delivery value − market value)	0	−933	−933

$117.878 and a loss of $933 is incurred on the purchase. However, it may be possible to avoid this loss.

If we assume that there is a second note—Treasury 8 percents due November 15, 1995 (a hypothetical note)—which is equally cheap to deliver, the 11.25 percent notes can be swapped for 8 percent notes and the loss eliminated. Since we assumed that prices rise by 4 percent, the sale of the 11.25 percent notes raises proceeds of $117,878 and results in a gain of $4,534 (see Table 6).

If the $117,878 in proceeds are invested in 8 percent notes, how many notes can be purchased? To answer this, we need to determine the price of the 8 percent notes (see Table 7).

TABLE 6. *Gain on Sale of 11.25 Percent Notes When Prices Rise 4 Percent.*

Par value	$100,000
Initial market price	113.344
Initial market value	113,344
Adjusted market price	117.878
Adjusted market value	117,878
Gain on sale	4,534

TABLE 7. *Derivation of the Price of 8 Percent Notes.*

Delivery price of 11.25 percent notes	$113.344
Factor on 11.25 percent notes	1.20571
Closing price of future (delivery price/factor)	$ 94.006
Factor on 8 percent notes	1.00000
Delivery price of 8 percent notes	$ 94.006
Price of 8 percent notes after 4 percent increase	$ 97.766

TABLE 8. *Loss from Delivery of 8 Percent
Notes When Prices Rise 4 Percent.*

Par value	$120,571
Market price	97.766
Market value (par × market price)	117,878
Delivery price	94.006
Delivery value (par × delivery price)	113,344
Loss (market value − delivery value)	4,534

The delivery price of the 11.25 percent notes at the close of trading is $113.344. The factor for these notes is 1.20571, which implies a closing future price of $94.006 − $113.344/1.20571. Given our assumption that the 8 percent notes have a zero closing basis, and incorporating a factor of 1.0000, the price of the 8 percent notes at the close of trading is $94.006. If prices subsequently rise 4 percent, the price of this 8 percent note increases to $97.766.

At a price of $97.766, $117,878 will purchase $120,571 par value of 8 percent notes — the exact amount required for delivery. The delivery value of these notes is $113,344 (see Table 8). Therefore, when these notes are delivered in satisfaction of the contract, a loss of $4,534 results. Since the loss on the delivery of the 8 percent notes is exactly equal to the gain on the sale of the 11.25 percent notes, the loss from delivery when prices rise can be avoided.

When prices rise, the best strategy — that is, the one that minimizes losses — is to shift into the security that obviates the additional purchase of securities at a higher price. In our example the assumption of an 8 percent alternative that was equally cheap to deliver provided a way to avoid a loss.

Since the additional purchase requirement is unattractive when prices rise, it is reasonable to assume that it is beneficial when prices fall, and this is exactly the case. To illustrate, we shall assume a 4 percent decline in prices, as shown in Table 9.

TABLE 9. *Profit from Delivery of 11.25 Percent Notes When Prices Fall 4 Percent.*

	Initial Position ($)	Additional Purchase ($)	Total ($)
Par value	100,000	20,571	120,571
Market price	113.344	108.810	—
Market value (par × market price)	113,344	22,383	135,727
Delivery price	113.344	113.344	—
Delivery value (par × delivery price)	113,344	23,316	136,660
Gain (delivery value − market value)	—	933	933

As in the two previous cases, there is no loss upon delivery of the initial position of the 11.25 percent notes. But with the delivery price frozen at $113.344, the additional $20,571 notes can be purchased at $108.810 and delivered at $113.344, for a gain of $933. Thus the total profit from the delivery of $120,571 notes is $933. (Although not demonstrated here, a swap into the 8 percent notes would result in a zero gain.)

The variety of securities that can be delivered by the seller, in effect, creates an option. If the closing basis is zero, the delivery process can be viewed as a *free option* on a Treasury note. If interest rates are unchanged or decline, there is no gain or loss. However, if interest rates rise and prices fall, additional notes can be purchased at a lower price and "put" to the holder of the long contract at the closing delivery price. Since this option clearly has value, the basis is unlikely to close at zero. The value of this option should be equal to the closing basis and, of course, will be negative. Based upon the volatility of interest rates over the past several years, a negative basis of $-0.10 was a reasonable approximation of the value of this option at the close of the March 1986 contract.

Recomputing the Synthetic Return Assuming a Negative Basis

In our computation of the return on the synthetic security, we assumed a zero closing basis and derived a 4.42 percent return (Table 3). What happens when we assume a $-0.10 basis at expiration?

If we assume constant prices, the closing price of the 11.25 percent notes will be $113.344 and the price of the future will be $113.244−$0.100 lower (see Figure 3). Because the closing basis is negative, the price of the future does not converge to the note and the loss on a short future position is reduced to $1,226 ($113,244−$112,018).

As shown below, the return on the synthetic short-term security is now 4.82 percent−40 basis points higher than our first example but still substantially less than the 7.75 percent return on a certificate of deposit:

$$\frac{\$2.424 - \$1.226}{\$114.774} \times \frac{360}{78} = 4.82 \text{ percent.}$$

Even the assumption of a negative basis of $-0.100 does not translate into a competitive return on the synthetic security. If the return of the synthetic security is lower than money market yields, it is an indication that the future is underpriced and that it is unattractive to sell. This begs the question: If the future was too cheap to sell, was it cheap enough to buy?

Buying Futures—An Alternative to Buying an Actual Security

As of December 31, 1985, the basis on all of the Treasury notes eligible for delivery against the T-note futures contract was negative—so much so that the

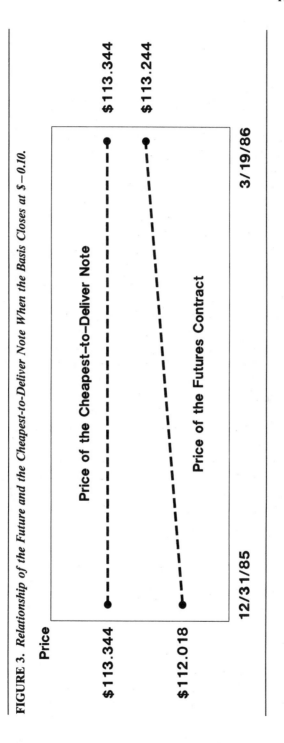

FIGURE 3. *Relationship of the Future and the Cheapest-to-Deliver Note When the Basis Closes at $ − 0.10.*

highest return on a synthetic security was well below money market yields. When the adjusted basis on the Treasury note or bond contract is negative, it is possible that futures can be used as a substitute for actual securities to enhance returns. To illustrate, we shall compare the returns on a position in the 11¼ percent notes to an alternative investment in futures and short-term securities over the period December 31, 1985 through the close of trading on March 19, 1986. The following simplifying assumptions are made:

1. The initial margin requirements on a financial futures contract can be met with the deposit of an interest-bearing Treasury bill.
2. No subsequent margin deposits are required.
3. The basis is assumed to be $-0.100 at the close of trading.
4. Prices are constant.

On December 31, 1985, a position of $100,000 par value of the 11.25 percent represented an investment of $114,774 − $113,344 in principal and $1,430 in accrued interest. Since we have assumed constant prices, the only change in the value of this investment through March 19, 1986 is the accrual of $2,424 of interest.

Because a future does not cost anything, there is no investment when a future is purchased − just the deposit of margin to serve as a "good faith" balance. Since this margin can be met with a Treasury bill and because there are no margin calls (assumptions 2 and 4), the entire amount available for investment − $114,774 − can be placed into a Treasury bill. The gain in value from the combined futures/Treasury bill position is equal to $3,153 (Table 10). This is the sum of a $1,226 gain on the futures contract over the December 31, 1985 to March 19, 1986 period plus $1,927 income on the Treasury bill. (Since the futures contract was assumed to be purchased in this example, the rise in the price of the future results in a gain.)

Thus, if we invest $114,774 in each strategy, the change in the market value of the futures/Treasury bill strategy at the end of the 2.5 month period is $729 higher than the change in the value of the cheapest-to-deliver note (Table 11).

TABLE 10. *Change in the Market Value of a Futures/Treasury Bill Position.*

	12/31/85	3/19/86	Change
Delivery value	$112,018	$113,244	$1,226
Treasury bill	114,774	116,701	1,927
Change in delivery value plus income on Treasury bill			$3,153

TABLE 11. *Summary of the Changes in Market Value.*	
Change in future/Treasury bill	$3,153
Change in cheapest to deliver	2,424
Incremental value of future/Treasury bill	729

If the basis does not go to $-0.100 versus the 11.25 percent notes, the profit will be less. While $-0.100 is our best estimate of the closing basis versus the cheapest-to-deliver note, there is no guarantee that the 11.25 percent notes example will be the cheapest to deliver at the close of trading. The yield relationship between the deliverable notes changes over time as a result of changes in the level of interest rates, changes in the shape of the yield curve, as well as random variation. Since the future is priced off the cheapest-to-deliver note, it may underperform the security that is was used as a substitute for—even though the original basis was negative.

Conversely, the potential change in the cheapest-to-deliver note enhances the return of a synthetic short-term security. If another note becomes cheaper to deliver, the future will underperform the note originally purchased, resulting in a smaller than expected loss on the future and a higher than expected return on the synthetic security.

While this effect cannot be calculated precisely, we have been able to estimate its likely magnitude and incorporate this into our analysis. If, after taking into account the substitution effect, the future is underpriced, it is attractive to purchase it as a substitute for an actual holding. If the future is overpriced, returns can be enhanced by creating a synthetic short-term security. In either case, since the future is used as a substitute for an actual security, *the use of futures does not alter the risk characteristics of the portfolio.*

36

Short-Term Liability Hedging*

Frank J. Jones
Managing Director
Kidder, Peabody & Co., Inc.

Beth A. Krumholz
Vice President
Kidder, Peabody & Co., Inc.

I. Introduction

Short-term interest rates have become much more volatile in recent years, as indicated in Figure 1. As a result, financial and nonfinancial institutions that have short-term debt, as most institutions do, have found that their interest costs and overall profits are very sensitive to changes in short-term interest rates.

For this reason, many institutions have attempted to immunize themselves from the effects of variable short-term interest rates by issuing long-term debt. But some institutions have found that they cannot issue long-term debt, and others have found that they can issue long-term debt only at a prohibitive cost.

This article discusses methods for hedging short-term liabilities with short-term futures contracts as a method for locking in borrowing costs over a longer time period even though short-term liabilities are issued. Among the types of borrowing to which these techniques apply are

1. one issue or a series of issues of commercial paper by corporations;
2. borrowings on a variable rate loan tied to the Eurodollar rate, the Treasury bill rate, or the prime rate;
3. one issue or a series of issues of certificates of deposit by commercial banks or savings and loan associations;

*The authors wish to thank Frank Fabozzi for his assistance in the preparation of this article.

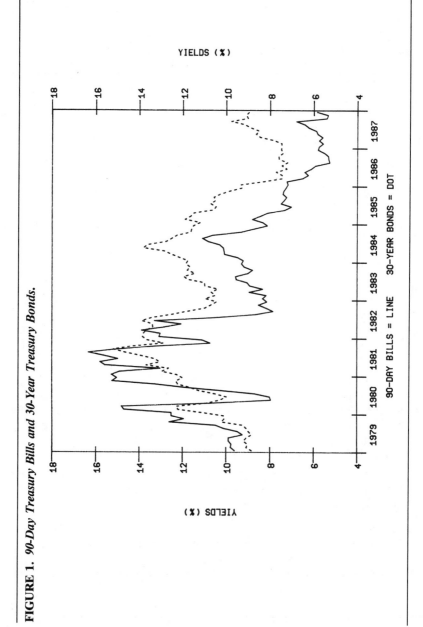

FIGURE 1. *90-Day Treasury Bills and 30-Year Treasury Bonds.*

4. issuances of money market certificates (MMCs) by savings and loan associations or savings banks;
5. issuances of money market deposit accounts (MMDAs) by commercial banks, savings and loan associations, or savings banks; and
6. issuances of one or a series of Eurodollar deposits by commercial banks.

Section II provides the specifications of the various short-term futures contracts available for hedging short-term liabilities and shows the interest rate relationships among them. Sections III, IV, V, and VI discuss techniques for hedging with these futures contracts. Specifically, after a general introduction to hedging in Section III, Section IV discusses methods for the selection of the correct futures contract and how the number of futures contracts used for a hedge (the hedge ratio) is determined. Section V discusses the choice of contract month(s) used for a hedge and when the contract(s) should be initiated and liquidated. Section VI provides an overview of how a hedge may be managed.

Section VII discusses the accounting practices for hedging short-term liabilities with futures contracts as specified by Financial Accounting Standards Board Statement No. 80. Section VIII provides a summary of this article.

II. Futures Contracts

There are currently two short-term futures contracts available for hedging short-term debt. They are the

- 90-day Eurodollar futures contract; and
- 90-day Treasury bill futures contract.

Indications of the level of activity of these contracts are shown in Table 1. Table 2 shows an example of the daily quotations for these contracts, as they appear in *The Wall Street Journal*.

TABLE 1. *Money Market Futures Contracts.*

Contract	Exchange[a]	Date Listed	Average Daily Volume[b]	Open Interest (12/31/87)
90-day Eurodollar	IMM	December 1982	81,017	292,326
90-day Treasury bill	IMM	January 1976	7,647	18,752

a. IMM denotes the International Monetary Market of the Chicago Mercantile Exchange.
b. 1987.

TABLE 2. *Money Market Futures Contract Quotations.*

Eurodollar (IMM) − $1 million; pts. of 100%

	Open	High	Low	Settle	Chg	Yield Settle	Chg	Interest
Mar	92.50	92.54	92.43	92.44−	.14	7.56+	.14	128,466
June	92.23	92.26	92.19	92.20−	.11	7.80+	.11	55,474
Sept	91.91	91.92	91.86	91.86−	.10	8.14+	.10	27,728
Dec	91.57	91.57	91.52	91.52−	.10	8.48+	.10	18,992
Mr89	91.29	91.29	91.23	91.23−	.10	8.77+	.10	14,398
June	91.05	91.05	91.00	90.98−	.10	9.02+	.10	8,882
Sept	90.84	90.84	90.82	90.78−	.10	9.22+	.10	7,792
Dec	90.65	90.65	90.65	90.61−	.10	9.39+	.10	5,688
Mr90	90.51	90.52	90.50	90.47−	.10	9.53+	.10	8,659
June	90.40	90.40	90.37	90.35−	.10	9.65+	.10	9,907
Sept	90.31	90.31	90.26	90.24−	.10	9.76+	.10	3,832
Dec	90.21	90.21	90.16	90.14−	.10	9.86+	.10	1,367

Est vol 22,181; vol Wed 43,980; open int 291,185, −2,686

Treasury Bills (IMM) − $1 million; pts. of 100%

	Open	High	Low	Settle	Chg	Discount Settle	Chg	Interest
Mar	94.01	94.10	93.97	93.99−	.11	6.01+	.11	16,834
June	93.72	93.79	93.69	93.70−	.08	6.30+	.08	1,649
Sept	93.40	93.42	93.34	93.34−	.08	6.66+	.08	598
Dec	....	....	....	92.99−	.07	7.01+	.07	107
Mr89	....	....	....	92.71−	.07	7.29+	.07	71

Est vol 2,401; vol Wed 4,695; open int 19,260, −632

Source: *The Wall Street Journal,* prices for December 31, 1987.

A. Contract Specifications

Table 3 provides a summary of the specifications of these two futures contracts. Both are based on 90-day instruments, have denominations of $1 million, and have March, June, September, and December contract months. The major differences between them are in their deliverable instrument and delivery mechanisms, which are summarized as follows:

1. The Eurodollar futures contract is based on cash settlement, that is, normal settlement variation margin on the last day of trading settles the contract, based on an index of 90-day LIBOR;
2. The Treasury bill futures contract requires the delivery of a 91-day Treasury bill on, in effect, one delivery day (in some instances 90- or 92-day Treasury bills can be delivered when no 91-day Treasury bills are available).

TABLE 3. *Short-Term Futures Contract Specifications: A Summary.*

	Treasury Bill (IMM)	Eurodollar (IMM)
Denomination	$1,000,000	$1,000,000
Method of quotation	Index equal to 100 minus Treasury bill discount rate	Index equal to 100 minus Eurodollar yield (add-on basis)
Minimum price fluctuation ($ value)	.01 (1 basis point) ($25)	.01 (1 basis point) ($25)
Price limits ($ value)	None	None
Last day of trading	Last business day before the first delivery day	Two business days prior to the 3rd Wednesday in the delivery month
Delivery period	First Thursday of spot month on which 13-week Treasury bill is issued and a one-year Treasury bill has 13 weeks to maturity	Same as last day of trading
Trading months	March, June, September, December	March, June, September, December
Trading hours	8:30 A.M.–3:00 P.M. EST	8:30 A.M.–3:00 P.M. EST
Deliverable grade	U.S. Treasury bills with maturity of 91 days on first delivery day (or 90 or 92 days, if there are no 91-day Treasury bills due to a holiday)	No delivery; cash settlement based on an IMM LIBOR rate[a]
Invoice price mechanism	$IP = 1,000,000[1 - (SY \times 91/360)]$ where IP = Invoice Price, SY = Settlement Yield = $100 -$ Settlement Price, N = Days to Maturity of Instrument Delivered on Delivery Date	No delivery; cash settlement on LDT.

a. The London Interbank Offer Rate (LIBOR) is determined by the IMM on a daily basis. Twice a day, once at a random time within 90 minutes before the close of trading (3:30 P.M. London time, 9:30 A.M. Chicago time) and again at the time trading terminates, the following steps are taken to determine this rate:

(1) 12 major banks in the London Eurodollar market are randomly selected from a list of 20.
(2) The rate at which the 3-month Eurodollar time deposits of these banks are offered to prime banks is obtained.
(3) The two highest and the two lowest rates are eliminated, and the remaining rates are averaged.
(4) The two mean rates (from the two times of day) are averaged and rounded to the nearest 1/100th of a percentage point. This final average is the IMM LIBOR rate used for settlement.

A detailed set of contract specifications for these two contracts is available from the exchanges.

B. Interest Rate Relationships

While these two futures contracts are based on 90-day interest rates, they, nevertheless, exhibit different interest rate behavior over the interest rate cycle because they are based on different 90-day instruments.

The Treasury bill futures contract is based on a 90-day Treasury bill, which has a risk-free interest rate. Since the Eurodollar futures contract is based on a commercial bank liability and, thus, has credit risk, the interest rate on the Eurodollar futures contract is higher than on Treasury bills (the futures prices are lower).

Eurodollar deposits, because they are based on the liabilities of foreign banks or foreign subsidiaries of U.S. banks, are perceived to have, in addition to normal business credit risk, sovereign risk, that is, the risk that actions by foreign governments could impair the timely withdrawal of these deposits by U.S. citizens. As a result, Eurodollar interest rates are higher than CD interest rates. (Eurodollar futures prices are lower.) And the Eurodollar/CD yield spread will vary as perceptions of changes in risks of these two banking sectors change.

The spread between both CD and Eurodollar interest rates on the one hand and Treasury bill rates on the other hand tends to widen when interest rates are high and narrow when interest rates are low. This behavior is a reflection of a "flight to quality," a preference for low-credit-risk instruments (specifically Treasury debt) when interest rates are high and the economy is perceived to be vulnerable. These spreads also widen when there are concerns about the major U.S. or London banking sectors, as there were during October 1982 and June 1984, respectively.

Figures 2, 3, and 4 show the interest rate relationships among Treasury bills, CDs, and Eurodollars.

III. Hedging Methodology

The objective of a perfect hedge with futures contracts is to maintain a futures position that will experience a change in dollar value equal in magnitude and opposite in sign to a change in the dollar value of the cash position being hedged, which results from a change in the yield on the cash instrument. For example, if $10 million of 180-day CDs are being hedged with Eurodollar futures contracts, the number of Eurodollar futures contracts transacted and the contract month(s) used should cause a dollar gain in the futures position equal to the dollar loss on the CDs if the yield on the CDs increases. Thus, there are three choices in constructing a futures hedge: (1)

FIGURE 2. *90-Day Treasury Bills versus 90-Day LIBOR.*

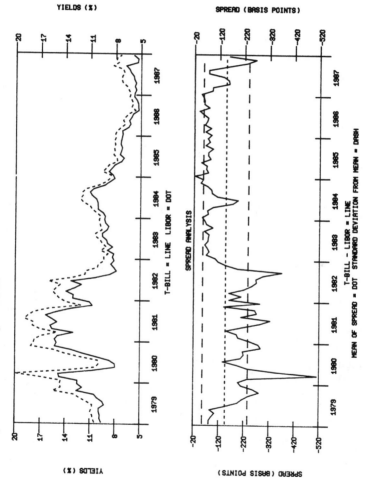

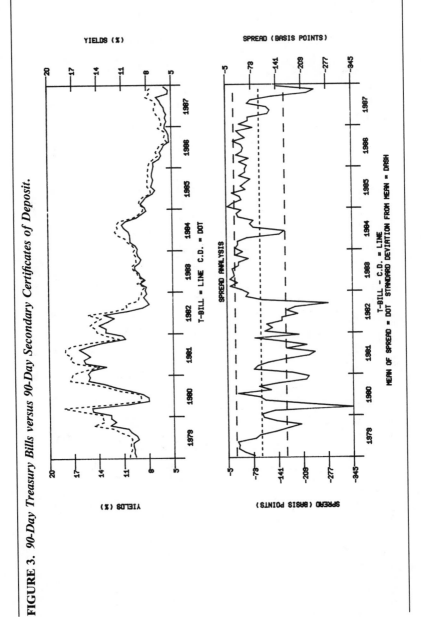

FIGURE 3. *90-Day Treasury Bills versus 90-Day Secondary Certificates of Deposit.*

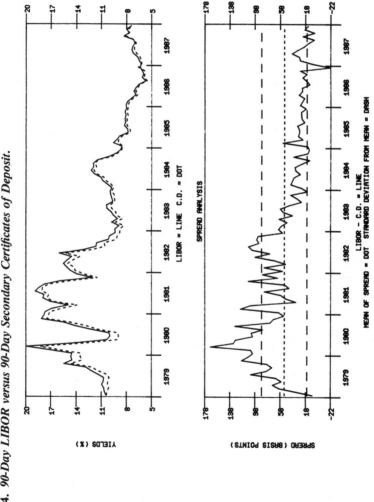

FIGURE 4. *90-Day LIBOR versus 90-Day Secondary Certificates of Deposit.*

which futures contract to use; (2) how many futures contracts to transact (called the hedge ratio); and (3) which contract month(s) of the futures contract to use. This report discusses these three choices in designing a hedge.

On the day a hedge is initiated, the initial cash and futures prices are known. To completely quantify the results of a hedge, the cash and futures prices at the end of a hedge, or at least the relationship between them, must also be known. In a perfect hedge, the change in the cash price during the hedge will be exactly equal in magnitude and opposite in sign to the change in the futures price during the hedge multiplied by the number of futures contracts transacted.

There are two aspects to specifying the relationship between the cash price and the futures price at the end of the hedge: (1) the relationship between the price of the cash instrument being hedged and the price of the instrument underlying the futures contract and (2) the relationship between the price of the instrument underlying the futures contract and the futures price, which depends on the time at which the hedge is terminated relative to the delivery period on the futures contract used. For example, if 180-day CDs are being hedged with Eurodollar futures contracts, the relationship between the price of the 180-day CDs and the price of the 90-day Eurodollars and the relationship between the 90-day Eurodollar price and the Eurodollar futures price at the end of the hedge both determine the outcome of the hedge. The risk that results from changes in the first price relationship is called cross hedge basis risk; the risk that results from changes in the second price relationship is called time basis risk. Thus, there are two types of risk in a hedge.

Consider first cross hedge basis risk. If 90-day Treasury bills are hedged with Treasury bill futures contracts, the instrument underlying the futures contract and the cash instrument being hedged are the same, so the price and yield of the futures contract should behave similarly to the price (and yield) of the cash instrument being hedged. In this case there is no cross hedge basis risk—this type of hedge is called a pure hedge.

If, however, 180-day CDs are hedged with Eurodollar futures contracts, the instrument underlying the futures contract and the cash instrument being hedged are not the same and so their prices (yields) may change by different amounts; and a hedge must, therefore, consider this difference. Cross hedge basis risk is introduced into this hedge when the hedger cross hedges one instrument with a futures contract based on another instrument. Obviously, the basis risk in this example, as with any type of risk, can work either to the advantage or disadvantage of the hedger. For example, if a short Eurodollar futures position is used to hedge a 180-day CD issue, the hedger will be disadvantaged if CD prices decrease (yields increase) relative to 90-day Eurodollar prices (yields). If CD prices increase (yields decrease) relative to 90-day Eurodollar prices (yields), the hedger will benefit.

When the cash instrument being hedged and the instrument underlying the futures contract are not the same, there are two aspects to minimizing the resulting cross hedge basis risk: (1) selecting the correct futures contract and (2) determining the correct hedge ratio, that is, the correct number of futures contracts to transact. These two aspects of the hedge are discussed in Section IV.

Next consider the time basis risk. The degree of time basis risk depends on the time at which the hedge is terminated relative to the futures delivery day. Consider first a hedge terminated on a futures delivery day. In this case, the price of the instrument underlying the futures contract and the futures price will be equal at the termination of the hedge because of convergence, and there is no time basis risk. In a pure hedge of this type, since the instrument being hedged and the instrument underlying the futures position are the same and the price (yield) on the instrument underlying the futures contract and the futures price (yield) are equal on the futures delivery day, the price (yield) on the instrument being hedged and the futures contract price (yield) will be equal at the termination of the hedge. Thus, at the beginning of a pure hedge that will be terminated on a futures delivery day, the price relationship between the hedged instrument and the futures price at the end of the hedge is known — they will be equal. For a cross hedge that will be terminated on a futures delivery day, the price of the futures contract will equal the cash price of the instrument underlying the futures contract on the futures delivery day, and so the relationship between the futures price and the price of the instrument being hedged will equal the cash market price spread between these two instruments.

But if the hedge is terminated on other than a futures contract delivery day, the futures price will not equal the cash price of the instrument underlying the futures contract — the futures price may be either greater or less than the cash price of the instrument underlying the futures contract, depending on the slope of the yield curve at this time, as discussed in Section V. If a short futures position is used in the hedge, obviously (since the futures contract will be bought back to liquidate it), the lower the futures price relative to the cash price of the instrument underlying the futures contract at the termination of the hedge, the more beneficial for the hedger, and vice versa. The risk associated with the termination of a hedge before the futures delivery day and the resulting risk due to variations in the difference between the prices of the futures contract and the instrument underlying the futures contract, that is, time basis risk, can be eliminated or minimized by the proper selection of the contract months. Section V discusses methods for treating time basis risk.

Sections IV and V discuss methods to minimize cross hedge and time basis risk, respectively, that is, methods to develop a hedge with minimum risk. Section VI discusses techniques for managing, rather than minimizing, these two types of basis risk. The objective of a managed hedge is to attempt to achieve a lower hedge rate (for the borrower) than can be achieved from simply minimizing the basis risk. Of course, a greater risk is borne by managing, rather than minimizing, basis risk and a higher hedge rate may, thus, result.

IV. Cross Hedge Basis Risk

This section discusses two issues involved in minimizing cross hedge basis risk: (1) selecting the correct futures contract and (2) determining the correct number of this futures contract to sell (the hedge ratio).

A. Selecting the Correct Futures Contract

The first decision in constructing a short-term liability hedge is choosing which of the futures contracts discussed in Section II to use.

There are two major elements of this choice, cross hedge basis risk and liquidity. The way to minimize cross hedge basis risk, since it stems from a different instrument being hedged than the instrument underlying the futures contract, is to select the futures contract whose underlying instrument has the yield that is most highly statistically related to the yield of the instrument being hedged.[1] In terms of the figures in Section II, the futures contract whose yield plot is most similar to the yield of the instrument being hedged would be selected.

Using the yield relationship as the basis for choosing the correct contract, the hedge ratio can then be used to correct for different price responses to a yield change and, if appropriate, for systematic differences in yield changes, as discussed below.

But no matter how small the basis risk (cross hedge or time basis risk), a hedge cannot be effectively implemented if the futures contracts cannot be transacted (sold and then bought) with reasonable transaction costs. For this reason, the liquidity of the futures contract chosen is critical. Published data on trading volume and open interest are useful in assessing the liquidity of futures contracts. But bid/ask spreads with size are the ultimate indicator of liquidity. These can be obtained from the exchange floor. Particularly when trying to transact large volumes of deferred month futures contracts, the liquidity of the contract month chosen should be assessed. And illiquidity may prevent a hedger from using the futures contract and month desired on the basis of minimizing basis risk.

---

1. The data in Table 5 provide statistics relevant to this discussion.

B. Hedge Ratios

The choice of which futures contract to use in a hedge is based on yield relationships. But different instruments experience different price changes in response to equal yield changes. In addition, the yields are usually not perfectly correlated. And, in some cases, there may be systematic differences in the way their yields change. For these reasons, once the futures contract is chosen, the number of futures contracts to be transacted (the hedge ratio) must be determined.

The objective of a perfect hedge is a futures position whose change in dollar value is equal in magnitude and opposite in sign to the change in the dollar value of the cash position being hedged. In many hedges, however, simply having futures positions of equal dollar value to the dollar value of the cash instrument being hedged will not achieve this objective. For example, $10 million of 90-day Treasury bill futures contracts (10 futures contracts) will not provide a perfect hedge for $10 million of 180-day Treasury bills or $10 million of 90-day commercial paper. To achieve a perfect hedge may require an adjustment in the number of futures contracts transacted.

The hedge ratio has two components. The first component considers the change in the price of the instrument being hedged relative to the change in the futures price, given equal yield changes in the instrument being hedged and the instrument underlying the futures contract. Assume, in this regard, that the cash price (PC) changes by DPC and the futures price (PF) changes by DPF upon equal yield changes in the two instruments. Then the hedge ratio (h) is the ratio of the change in the cash price to the change in the futures price:

$$h = \frac{DPC}{DPF}.$$

The hedge ratio indicates the number of futures contracts sold (or bought) against the cash instrument having the same dollar value as the futures contract. That is, if $10 million of a cash instrument is being hedged with Treasury bill futures contracts and the cash market instrument has a hedge ratio of h, the hedge would consist of selling $10 \times h$ Treasury bill futures contracts, since each futures position represents $1 million. If equal yield changes, either up or down, in the cash instrument and futures contract then occur, the gain or loss on the cash instrument would be offset by an equal loss or gain on the futures contracts. For example, with a hedge ratio of 1.5, 15 Treasury bill futures contracts would be sold against $10 million of the cash instrument being hedged.

The second component of the hedge ratio considers the effects of different yield changes in the instrument being hedged and the instrument underlying the futures contract.

These two components of the hedge ratio, different price responses to equal yield changes (price volatility) and different yield changes (yield volatility) are considered in the next two sections.

1. Price Volatility — Maturity The major determinant of the first component of the hedge ratio is the maturity of the instrument being hedged. Instruments of different maturities incur different price changes when their interest rates change by equal amounts. For example, a one-basis-point change in the discount rate of $1 million of 90-day Treasury bills causes a $25 change in the price, but $1 million of 180-day Treasury bills changes in price by $50 in response to the same interest rate change. Thus, to hedge a $1 million 180-day Treasury bill with 90-day Treasury bill futures contracts, assuming equal rate changes, requires two, not one, Treasury bill futures contracts. The hedge ratio on this basis would therefore be 2.

Table 4 shows the hedge ratios for discount instruments by maturity vis-à-vis the 90-day Treasury bill futures contract.[2] The appendix to this section illustrates how these hedge ratios are determined.

2. Yield Volatility The first component of a hedge ratio, discussed in the previous section, is based on the assumption that the interest rate changes on the cash instruments being hedged and the instrument underlying the futures contracts are equal. In fact, rates on different instruments do not typically

---

2. For hedging long-term debt instruments, additional factors, including the coupon and the callability of the instrument, affect the price volatility of the instrument and, thus, the hedge ratio, given equal yield changes.

TABLE 4. *Hedge Ratios by Maturity.*

Maturity (days)	BPV(.01)[a] ($)	Hedge Ratio (h)
15	4.17	0.167
30	8.33	0.330
60	16.67	0.670
90	25.00	1.000
180	50.00	2.000
360	100.00	4.000

a. BPV(.01) (referred to as the basis point value of an "01") is the dollar value of the change in the price of an instrument due to a one basis point change in discount rate (or, often, in yield).

change by equal amounts. Rates on different short-term cash instruments change by different amounts for two reasons: credit risk and maturity.

Interest rate spreads between private and government credit instruments typically change over the interest rate cycle because of their different credit risks. As indicated in Figures 2 and 3, these yield spreads typically widen at high rates and narrow at low rates because of a flight to quality. In addition, vulnerabilities in the banking or corporate sectors cause private/government debt instrument yield spreads to widen. Systematic changes in the yield spread, such as those due to changes in the level of interest rates, can, however, be adjusted for, as indicated below. Adjustments for nonsystematic, or random, changes in the spreads, however, cannot be made.

Interest rate spreads between instruments of different maturities also vary. Typically, longer-term rates vary by less than shorter-term rates over the interest rate cycle. As indicated in Figure 5, short-term rates are less than long-term rates when interest rates are low and the yield curve is upward sloping, and vice versa. If this were the case, and it typically is, the rate on a 180-day instrument would usually vary by less than the rate on a 90-day instrument and the rate on a 30-day instrument by more than the rate on a 90-day instrument. For this reason, hedge ratios calculated on the basis

FIGURE 5. *Yield Spreads Due to Maturity.*

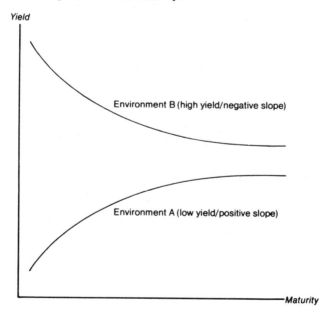

of an assumption of equal rate changes in the hedged instrument and futures contract may not be appropriate if these two instruments have different maturities.

The relationship between interest rate changes on different instruments (the hedged instrument and the instrument underlying the futures contract) of different credit risk and/or maturities is called the "yield beta." Yield betas are calculated using standard statistical methods (regression analysis) with the equation below:

$$YC = (a+b)YF,$$

where

YC = yield of cash market instrument being hedged;
YF = yield of instrument underlying futures contract; and
a, b = statistical coefficients.[3]

Given the data on YC and YF, statistical techniques are used to estimate the coefficients a and b in the context of this equation. The coefficient b, the yield beta, measures the change in the yield of the cash instrument for a one basis point change in the yield of the instrument underlying the futures contract.

If $b = 1$, the yields of the two instruments change by the same amounts and, thus, the assumption of equal yield changes is appropriate. If $b > 1$, however, the yield of the instrument being hedged changes by more than the yield of the instrument underlying the futures contract, and the futures contracts must be sold in greater dollar value than the dollar value of the cash instrument being hedged. If $b < 1$, the opposite is true.

Table 5 provides yield betas between various cash market instruments of different maturities and credit risks, and the instruments underlying the three short-term futures contracts.

3. Synthesis Section IV-B-1 shows how hedge ratios (h) can be calculated when there are different price responses to equal yield changes by the instrument being hedged and the instrument underlying the futures contracts. The yield beta (b), discussed in Section IV-B-2, shows how to adjust for unequal yield changes.

The overall hedge ratio for a cash instrument that has a different price response to a given yield change and also a different yield change than the instrument underlying the futures contract is the product of these two terms. Thus, the overall hedge ratio, denoted by H, is

$$H = h \times b.$$

---

3. More sophisticated variations of this equation can also be used.

TABLE 5. Short-Term Yield Betas: Regression Coefficients (Yield Betas) and Correlation Coefficients (R2) (in Parentheses).[a]

	30-Day T-Bill	60-Day T-Bill	90-Day T-Bill	180-Day T-Bill	One-Year T-Bill	90-Day Eurodollar	90-Day CD	90-Day C.P.	90-Day B.A.	180-Day CD	180-Day Eurodollar
90-Day T-Bill											
Last 3 months	.391694 (.5792)	.65268 (.7606)	NC	1.05276 (.9168)	1.05780 (.9027)	.743203 (.5307)	.744045 (.4866)	1.10216 (.5258)	.765763 (.5549)	.72185 (.5461)	.698636 (.5698)
Last 1 year	.30067 (.3047)	.693198 (.7020)	NC	.681445 (.7321)	.500423 (.6315)	.350277 (.3738)	.335736 (.3498)	.438162 (.3920)	.351868 (.3886)	.327257 (.4134)	.349825 (.4373)
Last 3 years	.840819 (.8260)	.974906 (.9644)	NC	.91819 (.9662)	.839318 (.9114)	.938049 (.8108)	.945118 (.7951)	1.02822 (.8246)	.926022 (.8082)	.844127 (.7894)	.841921 (.8081)

TABLE 5 *Continued*

	30-Day T-Bill	60-Day T-Bill	90-Day T-Bill	180-Day T-Bill	One-Year T-Bill	90-Day Eurodollar	90-Day CD	90-Day C.P.	90-Day B.A.	180-Day CD	180-Day Eurodollar
90-Day Eurodollar											
Last 3 months	.315381	.588247	.724401	.917816	.923802	NC	1.02064	1.33782	.984409	.938695	.300670
	(.3797)	(.6311)	(.5307)	(.7112)	(.7027)		(.9548)	(.8034)	(.9525)	(.9597)	(.3047)
Last 1 year	−.0336546	.440996	1.07438	1.2474	1.00638	NC	.976294	1.1712	.978903	.862324	.910147
	(−.0028)	(.0891)	(.3738)	(.8002)	(.8339)		(.9706)	(.9184)	(.9877)	(.9402)	(.9701)
Last 3 years	.645648	.808113	.864579	.850607	.811584	NC	1.01214	1.06126	.986569	.90038	.892478
	(.5279)	(.7186)	(.8108)	(.8996)	(.9246)		(.9902)	(.9563)	(.9953)	(.9758)	(.9855)

a. Terminal Date: 12/31/87.

b. NC = no change.

Note: Figure 5 indicates that 180-day rates vary by less than and 30-day rates vary by more than 90-day rates. The data in Table 5 indicate the opposite. The data provided below show these relationships for Eurodollar rates annually over 1980–87.

Yield Betas

1-Month and 6-Month LIBOR versus 3-Month LIBOR

	1 Month	6 Months
1980	1.05778	0.8891
1981	1.09971	0.8227
1982	1.01673	0.9520
1983	0.84159	1.13901
1984	0.94652	1.04857
1985	0.71621	1.2658
1986	0.961309	1.01108
1987	0.79443	1.06874

Note that during 1980, 1981, and 1982, when the level of rates changed substantially, the relationships are consistent with Figure 5. However, during 1983 and 1984, when rates were less variable, the relationships reversed. These data indicate the need for measuring and analyzing these interest rate relationships.

Two observations about the hedge ratio can be made. First, maturity has opposite effects on h and b. For example, a 180-day maturity instrument has double the price response to a yield change that a 90-day maturity instrument has $(h = 2)$. But, the yield change over the interest rate cycle is often smaller for a 180-day instrument than for a 90-day instrument. Thus, b would be less than 1 for a 180-day cash market instrument being hedged. Consequently, H, the product of h and b, will be less than 2 but most likely greater than 1. The data in Table 5, however, show that recently the yield beta for 180-day instruments has been greater than 1 and so, on this basis, H would be greater than 2.

Second, there is an important difference between the ways in which h and b are determined. The h term is determined analytically by the equations relating price and rate of return for the appropriate instruments. It will, thus, be constant over time.

But b is determined statistically from data over a given period of time. Its value, thus, depends on the particular time period considered. It may be that this coefficient is very reliable (has a high correlation coefficient) or is unreliable. Calculations of the b term should, thus, be done over various periods of time, as shown in Table 5, to test for stability. These calculations should also be updated frequently.

Based on these observations there are three ways to use the yield beta. Some hedgers use the yield beta mechanically, simply measuring it over a single specific time period and using this number. Others do not use it at all because it is too subjective and often not stable over time. Finally, other hedgers use a yield beta that is consistent with the time period they *expect* over the hedge period — that is, they use a forecasted rather than a historical yield beta. Thus, while h is a product of science, b is a product of a combination of art and science.

Appendix to Section IV:
Interest Costs by Maturity

Consider the change in interest costs due to changes in the interest rate from 10% to 15% for various maturities of an instrument.

1. *10% Rate*

$$\begin{array}{r} \$1,000,000 \\ \underline{.10} \\ \$ \ \ 100,000 \end{array}$$

Interest Costs (in Dollars) Over Various Periods

Period	1 yr.	3 mos.	4 mos.	1 mo.
Interest Cost	100,000	50,000	25,000	8,333

2. *15% Rate*

$1,000,000

.15
_____

$ 150,000

Interest Costs (in Dollars) Over Various Periods

Period	1 yr.	3 mos.	4 mos.	1 mo.
Interest Cost	150,000	75,000	37,500	12,500

3. *Change From 10% to 15%*

	1 yr.	6 mos.	3 mos.	1 mo.
10%	$100,000	$50,000	$25,000	$ 8,333
15%	150,000	75,000	37,500	12,500
5%	$ 50,000	$25,000	$12,500	$ 4,167
(500 basis points)				
Dollar Value of 1 basis point	100	50	25	8.33
No. of 90-day T-bill futures contracts needed to hedge	4	2	1	1/3

V. Time Basis Risk

Section IV discusses the methods for selecting the futures contract to use and determining the number of futures contracts to transact in order to effectively hedge short-term cash market instruments. These elements of a hedge affect the cross hedge basis risk.

But, as indicated above, there is another type of basis risk, time basis risk, which results from uncertainty about the relationship between the cash price of the instrument underlying the futures contract and the futures price at the termination of the hedge. The element of a hedge that affects the degree of time basis risk is the choice of the contract month (or months) of the futures contract selected. For example, should the March or June contract month of the futures contract selected be sold?

If the hedge (or series of hedges) terminates on a futures delivery day (or days), there is no intrinsic time basis risk in the hedge because the cash price of the underlying instrument and the futures price will be equal, or approximately equal, on the last day of trading of the futures contract as the result of convergence. Subsection A below discusses how time basis risk can be eliminated in this case. However, even when there is not intrinsic time basis risk in a hedge, the hedger may decide to design a hedge with basis risk in an attempt to reduce the cost of the hedge, as discussed in Sections C and D.

If the hedge (or series of hedges) does not terminate on a futures delivery day (or days), however, there is intrinsic time basis risk in the hedge because the relationship between the cash price of the instrument underlying the futures contract and the futures price prior to the termination of the hedge is not known. As discussed below, the relationship between these two prices depends on the slope of the yield curve at the termination of the hedge. The uncertainty and variability in this price relationship cause time basis risk in a hedge. Time basis risk cannot be eliminated in this case. However, an understanding of the relevant relationships, how they affect the outcome of a hedge, and an estimate of the likely future relationships among the relevant variables may permit the hedger to minimize the time basis risk. Typically, the futures contract that expires nearest and subsequent to the transaction being hedged is used. Subsection B below discusses an alternate method for minimizing the time basis risk in this case.

In the former case, a hedger can make a precise calculation at the beginning of the hedge of the effective hedge rate; in the latter case, the hedger can only estimate the effective hedge rate. In either case, the hedger may decide, instead of eliminating or minimizing time basis risk, to manager time basis risk in an attempt to reduce the effective hedge rate. Subsection C discusses a method for managing time basis risk that can be applied to the assumptions and methods in either Subsection A (where the hedge terminates on a futures delivery day) or Subsection B (where the hedge does not terminate on a futures delivery day).

A. The Basic Hedge—No Time Basis Risk

This section considers one or a series of hedges terminating on one or a series of futures delivery dates and how time basis risk may be eliminated in this case. In this context, consider an institution that is issuing one or a series of Eurodollar deposits of varying maturities and is initiating a hedge of these prospective liability issues on January 1. Assume that the Eurodollar issues will occur on a futures delivery day (or days) and the hedge (or hedges) are, thus, terminated on this day (or these days). The implementation and liquidation of the hedge (or hedges) in the five examples are summarized in Table 6.

Example 1: Single 90-Day Eurodollar Issue   Assume that the institution will issue $12 million of 90-day Eurodollar deposits during mid-March. To hedge this issue requires 12 March Eurodollar futures contracts. These contracts are liquidated in mid-March at the same time the Eurodollar deposits are issued. Since the futures contracts mature at the same time the deposits are issued, there is little or no time basis risk in this example.

Example 2: Single 30-Day Eurodollar Issue   Assume everything is the same as in Example 1 except that 30-day rather than 90-day Eurodollar deposits

TABLE 6. *Summary of Examples 1–5.*[a]

Example		J	F	M	A	M	J	J	A	S	O	N	D	Total
1				−12										−12
				+12										+12
2				−4										−4
				+4										+4
3				−24										−24
				+24										+24
4				−12			−12			−12			−12	−48
				+12			+12			+12			+12	+48
5				−12			−12			−12			−12	−48
		+4	+4	+4	+4	+4	+4	+4	+4	+4	+4	+4	+4	+48

a. The minus numbers (−) indicate the number of futures contracts, of the futures contract month under which the number occurs, sold on January 1. The plus numbers (+) indicate the number of contracts bought back, or liquidated. These purchases are, in all cases, the nearby futures contract at the time of purchase and are listed under the month in which the purchase occurs.

will be issued during mid-March. In this case 4, rather than 12, March Euro-dollar futures contracts are sold on January 1 and liquidated in mid-March.[4]

Example 3: Single 180-Day Eurodollar Issue   In this case, $12 million of 180-day Eurodollar deposits will be issued during mid-March. To hedge this issue, 24 March Eurodollar futures contracts are sold on January 1 and liquidated during mid-March.[5]

In Example 1, hedging a 90-day Eurodollar instrument with a 90-day Eurodollar futures contract has no cross hedge basis. In Examples 2 and 3, however, where 30- and 180-day instruments, respectively, are hedged with 90-day futures contracts, there is a cross hedge basis due to potential changes in the spreads between 90-day Eurodollar deposits on one hand and 30- or 180-day Eurodollar deposits on the other hand. The hedges in Examples 2 and 3 become less effective if the 30-day or 180-day Eurodollar rates, respec-tively, increase relative to the 90-day Eurodollar rates.

A yield beta, if utilized, attempts to correct for these spread changes, but, as discussed, does not always precisely accomplish this objective. For example, if in Example 3 a yield beta of 1.33 were used for 180-day Eurodol-lars against 90-day Eurodollars, 32 (1.33×24) rather than 24 March Euro-dollar futures contracts would be sold on January 1 to attempt to reduce cross hedge risk.

Example 4: Series of 90-Day Eurodollar Issues   Consider next, instead of a single Eurodollar deposit, a series of 90-day Eurodollar issues of $12 mil-lion each during mid-March, -June, -September, and -December. The obvi-ous extension of Example 1 to this example indicates that on January 1, 12 March, 12 June, 12 September, and 12 December Eurodollar futures con-tracts should be sold. Then, as the Eurodollar deposits are issued, the fu-tures contracts are liquidated. Specifically, the 12 March contracts are liq-uidated during mid-March; the 12 June contracts during mid-June; the 12 September contracts during mid-September; and the 12 December contracts during mid-December.

Selling a series of futures contracts of different months is called a *strip of futures*. In this example, there is no basis risk due to either cross hedge basis (90-day Eurodollars are hedged with 90-day Eurodollar futures con-tracts) or time basis (Eurodollars are issued at the same time the futures con-tracts mature).

---

4. In Examples 2 and 3, the hedge ratios are based only on the BPV(.01) due to maturity and not on the yield beta due to maturity. If the yield betas shown in Table 5 had been used, the number of contracts sold in Examples 2 and 3 may have been 0.67 and 1.33, respectively, based on the previous three months.

5. See note 4.

Example 5: Series of 30-Day Eurodollar Issues Assume $12 million of 30-day Eurodollars are issued every 30 days beginning in mid-January. As indicated above, four futures contracts are required to hedge each Eurodollar issue. The existing money market futures contracts mature only during March, June, September, and December; therefore, the January, February, and March Eurodollar issues can be hedged with the March contract; the April, May, and June issues hedged with the June contract, etc.

In this case, the futures contracts sold in January 1 would be 12 March, 12 June, 12 September, and 12 December contracts. Subsequently, four of the nearby futures contracts would be liquidated during the middle of each month when Eurodollar deposits were issued. For example, during mid-January four March contracts would be liquidated, during mid-February four more March futures contracts would be liquidated, and during mid-March the last four March futures contracts would be liquidated. Beginning in mid-April, the hedger would begin to close out the June positions.

There are both cross hedge and time basis risks in this example. The cross hedge basis risk results, as in Example 2, from hedging a 30-day instrument with a 90-day futures contract. In addition, this is the first example with time basis risk. The time basis risk results from the fact that Eurodollars are being issued and futures contracts liquidated at times that are not futures contract maturity days. This occurs during the eight months other than March, June, September, and December. During these eight months, the futures price will not converge to the 90-day Eurodollar cash price. The relation between the cash price and the futures price at these times will depend on the slope of the yield curve, as discussed below. Ways to minimize this time basis risk are discussed in the following section.

Note that the number of futures contracts, total and in each month, is the same in Examples 4 and 5; this is due to the fact that each example has the same amount of issues outstanding over the same period of time. Only the pattern of liquidating these contracts is different.

B. The Basic Hedge with Time Basis Risk — Minimizing Time Basis Risk

The previous discussion was concerned with hedges that terminate on futures delivery dates, for which time basis risk can be eliminated. This section discusses hedges that terminate on dates that are not futures delivery dates. For such hedges there is time basis risk and this time basis risk cannot be eliminated.

As indicated above, time basis risk depends on the relationship between the spot price and the futures price at the time the hedge is terminated. If the hedge is to be terminated on the last day of trading of a futures contract, at the beginning of the hedge it is known that the futures price and the price of the instrument underlying the futures contract will be equal at the end of the hedge (at least for a pure hedge) because of convergence. If the hedge is terminated on other than a futures delivery day, however, the final relationship is not known at the beginning of the hedge. This uncertainty is the source of time basis risk. Time basis risk, as with any type of risk, can serve either to the advantage or disadvantage of the hedger. For example, as demonstrated below, if the futures price is higher (lower) than the spot price at the termination of the hedge, the hedge will be less (more) effective than if the futures price was equal to the spot price.

Typically, for hedges that do not terminate on a futures delivery date, hedgers use the contract month that matures just after the termination of the hedge, as in Example 5 above. However, under some circumstances, other methods may provide better hedge results. This section considers an alternate method for analyzing and managing time basis risk for hedges whose termination dates do not coincide with futures delivery dates.

Time basis risk depends on two factors: (1) the date of the termination of the hedge relative to the maturity of the futures contract used in the hedge and (2) the change in the slope of the short-term yield curve between the time the hedge is initiated and when the hedge is terminated (if the hedge is not terminated at the maturity of a futures contract).

Consider three examples to illustrate the effect on a hedge of a change in the slope of the yield curve during a hedge. As indicated, if the hedge is terminated at the maturity of a futures contract, the spot price of the instrument underlying the futures contract and the futures rate will be equal because of convergence. In this case, the effective rate on the hedge will equal the initial futures rate, as shown by the example in Table 7 for a hedge initiated on December 15 by selling a June futures contract, which matures on June 15, at 9.00%. If the hedge is terminated on June 15, the delivery day of the futures contract, the futures rate will equal the spot rate on this day. As shown in Part b of Table 7, the effective rate on the hedge is 9%, whether the spot rate on June 15 is 10% (Case 1), 9% (Case 2), or 6% (Case 3). This result occurs because the futures rate at the termination of the hedge equals the spot rate and there is no time basis risk.

This result does not apply when the hedge is terminated on *other than a futures delivery day,* that is, when there is time basis risk. To demonstrate this result, consider the same hedge terminated on May 1 instead of June 15, as in Table 8.[6] In this case, on May 1 it cannot be assumed that the spot and futures rates will be equal. The example in Table 8 considers three assumptions (cases X, Y, and Z) that can be made about the futures rate on May 1 and the effect of the assumptions on the outcome of the hedge. If the spot

---

6. The discussion in this section is based on the assumption of an initially positive yield curve. Many of the conclusions are reversed when the yield curve is initially inverted.

TABLE 7. *Perfect Convergence — Zero Time Basis Risk.*

a. Data

	December 15	June 15		
		Case 1	Case 2	Case 3
Spot	8.00%	10.00%	9.00%	6.00%
March 15 futures	8.50	—	—	—
June 15 futures	9.00	10.00	9.00	6.00
September 15 futures	9.50	10.50	9.50	6.50

b. Effective Rate on Hedge

Case 1
Issue at 10.00%
Profit/loss on hedge:

		June Futures Contract	
	12/15	9.00%	
	6/15	10.00%	
		1.00%	Profit
Effective rate:		10.00%	
		−1.00%	
		9.00%	

Case 2
Issue at 9.00%
Profit/loss on hedge:

		June Futures Contract	
	12/15	9.00%	
	6/15	9.00%	
		0.00%	Profit
Effective rate:		9.00%	
		0.00%	
		9.00%	

Case 3
Issue at 6.00%
Profit/loss on hedge:

		June Futures Contract	
	12/15	9.00%	
	6/15	6.00%	
		3.00%	Loss
Effective rate:		6.00%	
		+3.00%	
		9.00%	

TABLE 8. *Non-Convergence – Time Basis Risk.*

a. Data

	December 15	May 1 Case X	May 1 Case Y	May 1 Case Z
Spot (three-month):	8.00%	10.00%	10.00%	10.00%
March 15 futures	8.50	—	—	—
June 15 futures	9.00	10.25	10.00	10.50
September 15 futures	9.50	(same slope)	(flatter)	(steeper)

b. Effective Rate on Hedge (issue rate: 10.00%)

	Profit/Loss on Hedge Case X	Profit/Loss on Hedge Case Y	Profit/Loss on Hedge Case Z
	Same Slope Yield Curve	Less Positive Yield Curve	More Positive Yield Curve
Sale price of June contract	9.00%	9.00%	9.00%
Purchase price of June contract	10.25	10.00	10.50
Difference (profit/loss)	+1.25	+1.00	+1.50
Issue rate	10.00	10.00	10.00
Effective hedge rate	8.75	9.00	8.50

c. Analysis

Case X: Yield curve retains same slope:
- Original time basis was 1.00% (9.00% − 8.00%).
- Futures contract is held ¾ of its initial time to maturity (12/15–6/15 is 6 months; 12/15–5/01 is 4½ months; 4½ ÷ 6 = 0.75 of total time).
- Expect to experience 75% of total convergence, a total amount equal to (0.75) × (1.00%) = 0.75%.
- Expect to lock in spot rate plus 75% of difference between spot rate and futures rate, that is, 8.00% + (0.75)(9.00% − 8.00%) = 8.75%.

Case Y: Yield curve becomes less steep:
- Take off short position (buy back) at lower yield (higher price) than in Case X, so experience a higher effective rate of 9.00%.
- Due to flatter yield curve there is a more than proportional convergence: proportional convergence would have provided a 25 b.p. basis between spot and futures at the termination of the hedge, and in this case there is a 0 b.p. basis (10.00% − 10.00%).
- Since convergence works against short hedge position, faster convergence hurts the short hedger and the hedger experiences a higher than expected hedge rate, 9.00% rather than the 8.75% effective rate with yield curve of same slope.

Case Z: Yield curve becomes steeper:
- Take off short position (buy back) at higher yield (lower price) than in Case X, so experience a lower effective rate of 8.50%.
- Due to a steeper yield curve there is a less than proportional convergence: proportional convergence would have provided a 25 b.p. spread between spot and futures at the termination of the hedge (original basis was 100 b.p.) and there actually is convergence of only 50 b.p. (10.50% − 10.00%).
- Since convergence works against a short futures contract (with positive yield curve), the less than full convergence benefits the hedger, and the hedger experiences a lower than expected hedge rate, 8.50% rather than 8.75%.

rate is 10.00% on May 1, what can be assumed about the futures rate? The answer depends on the slope of the yield curve on May 1. Initially, on December 15, the yield curve is such that the futures rate increases by 0.50% every three months into the future.[7]

For example, as shown in Part a of Table 8, the March rate of 8.50% is 50 basis points greater than the 8.00% spot rate, the June futures rate is 50 basis points greater than the March rate, etc. If the yield curve retains the same slope on May 1 despite the increase in the level of rates (the three-month spot rate increases from 8% to 10%), then, since the time between May 1 and June 15 is 1½ months, the June futures rate will be 25 basis points over the spot rate on May 1, that is, the June futures rate will be 10.25%. As shown in Case X in Table 8, the effective rate on the hedge will be 8.75%.

The reason that with no change in the slope of the yield curve the effective hedge rate is 8.75%, rather than 9.0% as in the example in Table 7, relates to the nature of convergence. On December 15 there was a 1% difference between the spot rate of 8.00% and the futures rate of 9.00%. This difference is called the basis. At the maturity of the futures contract, these two rates will be equal. Thus, over the life of the futures contract there will be a convergence of 1% between cash and futures. How does this convergence affect the effective rate on a hedge?

A positive yield curve is assumed, so futures rates are higher than spot rates. Futures contracts are, however, actually transacted in price rather than interest rate. On the short-term futures contracts, the futures price equals 100 minus the discount rate. Thus, a spot rate of 8% and a futures rate of 9% are, in effect, equivalent to prices of 92 and 91, respectively. Thus, complete convergence, in this case, will cause the futures price to increase by 1.0 relative to the spot price, that is, from 91 to a spot price of 92 at the end of the hedge. Since a liability hedge requires a short futures position, the relative increase in the futures price will serve to the disadvantage of the hedger.[8]

---

7. While asserting that the futures rate increases by 0.50% every three months permits one to calculate the change in the spot yield curve, the change in the spot yields for instruments with maturity differences of three months (for example, if futures contracts with six- and nine-month maturities were being considered, the appropriate spot yields would be on six- and nine-month instruments) will not necessarily be 0.50%. The relationship between a futures (or a forward) rate and the corresponding spot rates for Eurodollars and CDs is given by:

$$\text{Implied Forward Rate} = \frac{R_1 T_1 - R_2 T_2}{(1 + [R_2 * T_2 / 360])(T_1 - T_2)},$$

where: R_1 = Rate on Longer Maturity Instrument
R_2 = Rate on Shorter Maturity Instrument
T_1 = Number of days to Maturity of Longer Instrument
T_2 = Number of days to Maturity of Shorter Instrument.

For Treasury bills, the denominator is $(1 - [R_2 * T_2 / 360])(T_1 - T_2)$. See Marcia Stigum, *Money Market Calculations*, pp. 83, 163.

8. Convergence is a relative rather than absolute phenomenon. In case X in Part b of Table 8, the effect of a convergence of 0.75 on the hedge rate will not be altered by the level of the spot

Between the initiation of the hedge on December 15 and the termination of the hedge on May 1, 75% of the initial time to maturity of the futures contract has decayed. If there is no change in the slope of the yield curve over this period, 75% of the initial basis of 1% will decay, or 25% of the initial basis will remain. Because of this, the effective hedge rate, as shown in Case X in Table 8, will be 8.75% rather than 9% as in Case 1 in Table 7, for which complete convergence occurred.

Consider next the effects of flattening or steepening yield curves between December 15 and May 1 on the hedge. In Case Y in Table 8, the June futures rate on May 1 is 10%, the same as the spot rate. Thus, since the two rates are equal, the yield curve has flattened from December 15 to May 1. As shown in Part b of Table 8, the effective rate on the hedge is 9% for Case Y. This rate is 25 basis points higher than for Case X (an unchanged yield curve) and the same as for the examples in Table 7 (complete convergence). In fact, in Case Y both the spot and futures rates are 10%, so complete convergence has occurred. Therefore, if the yield curve flattens during the hedge, convergence occurs more quickly, and this serves to the disadvantage of the hedge, as discussed in Part c of Table 8.

Case Z in Table 8 considers an example of a yield curve that steepens during the hedge. The spot/futures basis remains 50 basis points even though there is only 1½ months until the maturity of the futures contract at the termination of the hedge. In this case, there is less than proportional convergence during the hedge—only 50% of the initial basis decays even though 75% of the initial time to maturity of the futures contract elapses—due to the steepening yield curve. As a result, the effective hedge rate of 8.50% is lower than the case for which the yield curve maintained the same slope.

The examples in Table 8 illustrate how changes in the slope of the yield curve during a hedge affect the spot/futures basis and, thus, affect the degree of convergence and the effective rate on a hedge. This time basis risk is present in all hedges that do not end on a delivery day of a futures contract.

Next consider how time basis risk can be minimized. Figure 6 shows the initial basis for the March and June futures contracts for the example in Table 7 and the convergence based on the assumption that the slope of

---

rate at the end of the hedge. For example, at the end of the hedge the spot rate (price) could remain at 8% (92) and the futures rate (price) would be 8.25% (91.75)—in this case the futures rate moves toward the spot rate. Or the spot rate (price) could be 8.75% (91.25) and the futures rate (price) would be 9.00% (91)—in this case the spot rate moves to the futures rate (which would indicate that the futures rate had been a good predictor of future spot rates). Or the spot rate could be any other level, such as 6%, 8.5%, or 12%, with the futures rates 0.25% higher (futures price 0.25 lower). In any of these cases the degree of convergence would be 0.75 (the futures price was initially 1.0 less than the spot price and was only 0.25 less at the end of the hedge) and the effective hedge rate would be the same. Thus, in a hedge, it is the degree to which the futures and spot price converge, independent of the final level of the spot price, that affects the hedge rate.

FIGURE 6. *Basis and Convergence.*

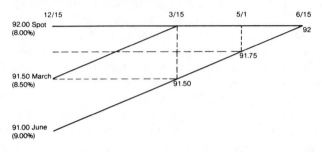

the yield curve remains constant. With the yield curve maintaining the same slope, the convergence, or the decrease in the basis, is assumed to be linear. Figure 6 assumes that the spot rate remains constant over time. But as indicated in note 8, changes in this assumption would not affect the conclusions. That is, while changes in the slope of the yield curve affect the degree of convergence, changes in the level of the yield curve (the level of interest rates) do not.

Consider the paths of convergence when the yield curve steepens or flattens during the hedge. Based on the considerations of Table 8, when the yield curve steepens, convergence occurs more gradually; and when the yield curve flattens, convergence occurs more quickly, as shown in Figure 7. These different convergence paths do not affect the effective rate on a hedge that ends at the maturity of the futures contract. However, as discussed in the context of Table 8, the path of convergence does affect a hedge that is terminated prior to the maturity of the futures contract. A steepening yield

FIGURE 7. *Convergence Paths.*

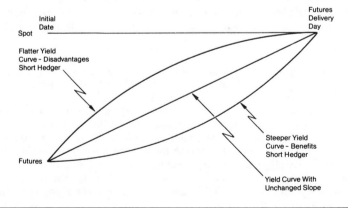

curve retards convergence and benefits a short hedger; a flattening yield curve accelerates convergence and serves to the disadvantage of the short hedger.

Given these relationships between the slope of the yield curve, basis, and the path of convergence and their effect on a short hedge, the minimization of time basis risk can be considered. The choice in minimizing time basis risk by the selection of the contract month(s) of the hedge, in this context, is whether to

- short a futures contract that matures prior to the termination of the hedge and, when it matures, roll into the next deferred contract (and, of course, liquidate the deferred contract at the termination of the hedge); or
- short a futures contract that matures after the termination of the hedge and liquidate it (buy it back) prior to its maturity (as indicated above, this is a common approach); or
- short a combination of these two contracts.

Consider, as summarized in Figure 8, some potential convergence paths for futures contracts that mature nearest prior to (called "the nearby future") and nearest after (called "the deferred future") the date of termination of a hedge. Each convergence path begins with a positively sloped yield curve, which is the reason that point C, the initial price of the deferred futures contract, is less than point A, the initial price of the nearby futures contract. The four cases consider convergence when: (1) the yield curve maintains its initial (positive) slope; (2) the yield curve becomes more positively sloped ("steeper"); (3) the yield curve becomes less positively sloped ("flatter"), but not inverted; and (4) the yield curve becomes negatively sloped ("inverted").

Figure 8-A shows the convergence path for the nearby and deferred futures contracts when the slope of the yield curve remains constant. Note that the effective rate on the hedge will be the same whether the hedger uses the nearby contract and then rolls into the deferred contract at the expiration of the nearby or uses the deferred contract (or uses any combination of the two contracts). If the former method is used, the hedger experiences convergence along path AB, of amount OA, on the nearby contract and then along path DE, of amount XD, after the roll into the deferred contract. If the latter approach is used, the hedger experiences a convergence along path CE of amount YC. As a result of the linearity of these convergence paths, $OA + XD = YC$, and, thus, the effective hedge rates according to the two approaches are identical.

Figure 8-B shows, via the solid lines, the effect of convergence when the yield curve steepens. The linear convergence paths are shown as dotted lines as a frame of reference. When the nearby contract is used until its maturity and then rolled into the deferred contract until the termination of the hedge, the convergence on the nearby contract along the curve AB is OA. Note that

FIGURE 8. *Convergence Paths and Time Basis Risk Management.*

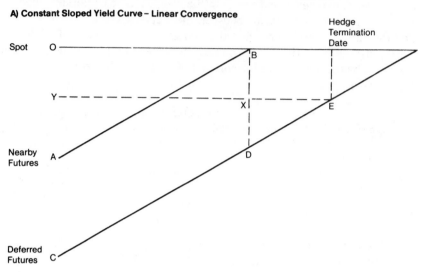

A) Constant Sloped Yield Curve – Linear Convergence

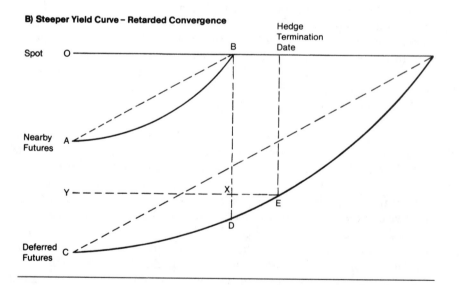

B) Steeper Yield Curve – Retarded Convergence

the nearby contract, if used, is always held until maturity and has a total convergence of *OA*, whether convergence is linear as in Figure 8-A, slower than linear as in Figure 8-B, or faster than linear as in Figure 8-C. So changes in the slope of the yield curve do not affect the convergence experienced by the nearby contract. At the maturity of the nearby contract, however, the short futures position is rolled into the deferred contract until the termination

FIGURE 8 *Continued*

C) Flatter Yield Curve – Accelerated Convergence

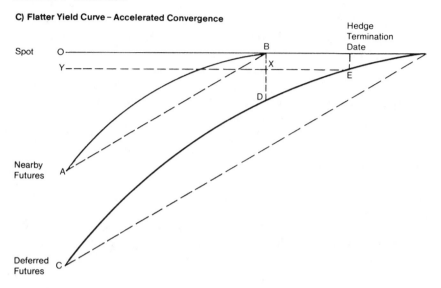

D) Inverted Yield Curve – More Than Complete Convergence

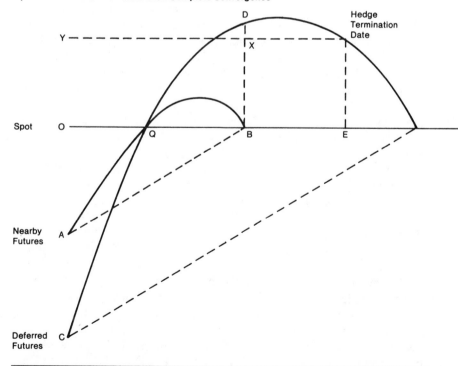

of the hedge, and the deferred contract experiences convergence along path *DE* of amount *XD*. Thus, according to this strategy, the total convergence experienced is *OA + XD*. This result concerning the convergence of the nearby contract applies to Figures 8-A, B, C, and D for any change in the slope of the yield curve.

If only the deferred contract is used, convergence occurs along path *CE* of total amount *YC*. With a steeper yield curve and the resultant retarded convergence, the use of the deferred contract, rather than the use of the nearby contract, to initiate the hedge experiences less convergence (*OA + XD* is greater than *YC*) and, consequently, provides a lower effective hedge rate. Thus, if a hedger thought the yield curve would steepen during a hedge, it is optimal to initiate the hedge with the deferred rather than the nearby futures contract. The use of the deferred contract permits the hedger to take advantage of the retarded convergence of the deferred contract.

The comparison of the results of the two methods of hedging when the yield curve flattens is shown in Figure 8-C. When the hedge is initiated with the nearby futures contract, the total convergence experienced by this contract, as in the two previous cases, is *OA*. After rolling into the deferred contract upon the maturity of the nearby, the convergence experienced by the deferred contract along the convergence path *DE* is *XD*. Thus, the total convergence experienced using this method is *OA + XD*.

If the hedge is initiated with the deferred contract, convergence will occur along path *CDE* and the total convergence will equal *YC*. Obviously, because of accelerated convergence *OA + XD* is less than *YC*. Therefore, there is less convergence (and a lower effective hedge rate) if the hedge is initiated with the nearby contract and then rolled to the deferred contract — this permits the hedger to avoid the accelerated convergence of the deferred contract. Since the accelerated convergence is due to a flattening yield curve, if the yield curve is expected to flatten during the hedge, it is optimal to initiate the hedge with the nearby rather than with the deferred futures contract. These results are summarized in Table 9.

The examples considered seem to indicate that the effective hedge rate can be no higher than the rate on the futures contract sold. This is, however, not the case. Returning to the example in Table 8, if the yield curve inverted between December 15 and May 1, the June futures rate could be 9.50%, with the spot rate equal to 10.00% on May 1. In this case the issue rate would be 10.00%, but there would be a 0.50% gain (from 9.00% to 9.50%) on the short futures position for a 9.50% effective hedge rate. This is higher than the 9.00% rate at which the futures position was originally sold. The inversion of the yield curve (from an initially positive curve) causes more than complete convergence and, thus, is more disadvantageous to the short hedger than full convergence or just the flattening of the yield curve, as shown in Figure 8-C. The hedge should, in this case, be initiated with the nearby contract, as shown in Figure 8-D and summarized in Table 9. Note that in Figure

TABLE 9. *Summary of Optimal Strategies.*

Change in Yield Curve During Hedge	Amount of Convergence					Effect of Yield Curve Change on Convergence	Optimal Strategy (Initial Contract Sold)
	Hedge with Nearby Contract and Rolled into Deferred Contract			Hedge with Deferred Contract	Relationship		
	Nearby Contract	Deferred Contract	Total				
Constant slope yield curve	OA	XD	$OA+XD$	YC	$XD+OA=YC$	Linear convergence	Either contract
Steeper yield curve	OA	XD	$OA+XD$	YC	$XD+OA=YC$	Retarded convergence	Deferred contract
Flatter yield curve	OA	XD	$OA+XD$	YC	$XD+OA=YC$	Accelerated convergence	Nearby contract

8-D the prices of the nearby and deferred futures contracts are equal (and equal to the spot rate) when the yield curve is flat, as shown at point Q.

If a futures contract matures on the same day as the termination of the hedge, the time basis risk of the hedge can be eliminated, that is, the hedge can be insulated against changes in the slope of the yield curve by selling the futures contract that matures at the termination of the hedge. In this case, the effective hedge rate will equal the initial futures rate. However, if the hedge is terminated between futures contracts, the effective hedge rate depends on the futures contract chosen and whether the yield curve steepens, flattens, or maintains the same slope before the contract is liquidated. As summarized in Table 9, if the yield curve is expected to become steeper between the initiation and the termination of the hedge, it is better to initiate the hedge with the deferred contract and liquidate it at the termination of the hedge. If the yield curve is expected to become flatter during the hedge, it is better to initiate the hedge with the nearby contract and roll to the deferred contract at the maturity of the nearby contract and then liquidate the deferred contract at the termination of the hedge.

Obviously, if the hedger knows how the slope of the yield curve will change during the hedge, time basis risk can be minimized in this manner. The hedger, however, does not usually know how the slope of the yield curve will change.

In the absence of knowledge about changes in the slope of the yield curve, however, time basis risk can be minimized by using a weighted combination of the nearby and deferred futures contracts. To determine the number of each contract to use, that is, the weights of the two contracts in the hedge, assume there are T days between the maturities of the nearby and deferred futures contracts. Assume also that there are X days between the maturity of the nearby contract and the termination of the hedge and Y days between the termination of the hedge and the maturity of the deferred contract; as shown in Figure 9, $X + Y = T$. Given that H is the hedge ratio (that is, the number of futures contracts to be sold), to minimize time basis risk

FIGURE 9. *Composite Hedge.*

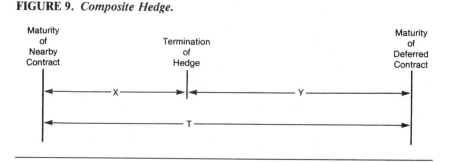

$(Y/T) \times H$ nearby contracts and $(X/T) \times H$ deferred contracts should be sold. This type of hedge composed of a combination of contract months is called a composite hedge, or a mixed hedge. According to this method, the effective or weighted delivery date of the hedge is the same as the termination date of the hedge.

C. Managing Time Basis Risk —
Strip Hedging Versus Stack Hedging

This section discusses two alternative methods for initiating and terminating the hedge of a series of liability issues and discusses the relative advantages of each. These two methods are called strip hedges and stack hedges. These methods can apply to hedges whether or not the hedge terminates on a futures delivery date, that is, the methods apply in conjunction with the methods discussed in either Section V-A or Section V-B.

Consider again a series of examples. Assume that on January 1 an institution develops a plan to issue during mid-March, mid-June, and mid-September $10 million of 90-day liabilities at a rate equal to the 90-day Eurodollar rate. As shown in Table 10, the current 90-day Eurodollar rate is 10.00% and the current rates on the March, June, and September Eurodollar futures contracts are 10.50%, 11.00%, and 11.50%, respectively (that is, the Eurodollar futures prices are 89.50, 89.00, and 88.50, respectively). The sequential cash/futures and futures/futures spreads are, thus, 50 basis points.

TABLE 10.

	January	March	June	September
a. Constant Spreads (constant slope yield curve).				
Cash	10.00%	12.00%	14.00%	16.00%
March future	10.50	12.00	–	–
June future	11.00	12.50	14.00	–
Sept. future	11.50	13.00	14.50	16.00
b. Widening Spreads (more positive yield curve).				
Cash		12.00%	14.00%	16.00%
March future		12.00	–	–
June future		13.00	14.00	–
Sept. future		14.00	15.50	16.00
c. Narrowing Spreads (less positive yield curve).				
Cash		12.00%	14.00%	16.00%
March future		12.00	–	–
June future		12.30	14.00	–
Sept. future		12.60	14.10	16.00

These spread relationships describe an environment of an upward sloping yield curve and a corresponding expectation of higher interest rates. Consider two different ways the institution could initiate and manage a hedge of this series of liability issues.

Strip Hedge A strip hedge involves selling futures contracts that mature on the day the liability will be issued or as close to the issue date as possible. In the context of this example, as discussed in Section V-A, a strip hedge would involve selling 10 March, 10 June, and 10 September contracts on January 1, that is, selling a "strip of futures." During March, at the time $10 million of liabilities are issued, the 10 March contracts would be bought back or liquidated. During June the 10 June contracts would be bought back as the June liabilities are issued, and during September the 10 September contracts would be bought back as the September liabilities are issued.

In this example, there is neither any cross hedge nor time basis risk. Thus, the rate at which the futures contracts are initially sold is the rate "locked-in" on the ultimate liability issues. The outcome of this example is illustrated below. This example is similar to Examples 4 and 5 in Section V-A. The results of this section apply not only to this example but also if the institution issued the Eurodollars during February, May, August, and November and hedged them with the March, June, September, and December contracts, respectively.

Stack Hedge While in a stack hedge the same number of futures contracts are initially sold as in a strip hedge, in a stack hedge all the contracts are sold in the nearby contract month rather than spread across two or more contract months. But, of course, the hedge must continue after the maturity of the nearby contract month. Thus, just prior to the maturity of the nearby futures contract, all the contracts in the nearby month are bought back and the correct number of futures contracts in the next month are sold. This is called "rolling" the hedge.

A roll is essentially a spread transaction, buying the nearby contract to liquidate the previous short position and selling the deferred contract to reestablish a new short position. This rolling procedure is used until the end of the hedge. At the time each liability is issued, some or all of the nearby futures contracts are liquidated and rolled into the next deferred position. Because liabilities are issued at the time of the roll, fewer deferred contracts are sold than nearby contracts bought back (liquidated) in the roll.

In the example above, for a stack hedge during January, 30 March Eurodollar futures contracts are sold. During mid-March, these 30 contracts are bought back (liquidated) and 20 June contracts are sold. Ten fewer June contracts are sold because $10 million of liabilities are issued at the time of the roll. Then during mid-June, the 20 June contracts are bought back and 10 September contracts sold. During mid-September, of course, the 10 September contracts are bought back as the last of the series of liabilities are issued.

Strip Hedge Versus Stack Hedge: A Comparison   In a strip hedge the futures contract months can be identified with the transactions hedged at the time the futures contracts are sold. These same futures contract positions are maintained until the liability they are hedging is issued, whereupon they are liquidated. For example, September futures contracts are initially sold to hedge a September issue of deposits and are liquidated at the time of the issue.

This is not the case, however, with a stack hedge. In a stack hedge only nearby futures contracts are sold. Thus, at most only the first debt issue is directly identified with the futures contracts initially sold. In this example, the deposits issued in March are identified with March contracts initially sold. But no June contracts are initially sold to hedge the June liability issues. Instead, March contracts are initially sold and then rolled into June contracts to hedge the June issue. So the effect of the hedge on the June liability issue depends on, in addition to the initial price of the March futures contract, the prices of the March and June futures contracts at the time of the roll from the March to the June contract. This roll would typically be done during late February or early March.

Similarly, the September liability issue is initially hedged with a March contract that is rolled into a June contract and then rolled into a September contract. Thus, the effect of the hedge of the September liability issue depends on the relative prices of the March, June, and September futures contracts, specifically the spreads between consecutive pairs of these contracts, at the time of the rolls between them. Therefore, the analysis of more relationships is necessary to determine the outcome of a stack hedge than for a strip hedge.

Which is more effective, the strip hedge or the stack hedge? Consider the answer to this question via another series of examples, the data for which are provided in Table 10. Various cash/futures and futures/futures spreads for the outstanding futures contracts during the time of the hedge are provided. At the maturity of the futures contract, its rate equals the cash rate because of convergence. But prior to the maturity of the futures contract, the cash/futures and futures/futures spreads are determined by the slope of the short-term yield curve.

Initially during January, as shown in Table 10, the cash/futures and futures/futures spreads are 50 b.p. (basis points). What are the relevant spreads during March, June, and September when the Eurodollar issues are made and the futures contracts rolled? Table 10 shows three different possibilities. Part a shows the rates under the assumption that the 90-day Eurodollar rate increases by 200 b.p. every three months (from the initial 10.00% to 12.00% during March, to 14.00% during June, and to 16.00% during September); but the cash/futures and futures/futures spreads remain at 50 b.p., that is, the slope of the yield curve remains constant.

Part b of Table 10 shows the rates for the 200 b.p. per period increase in the cash rate but with a widening of the spreads; that is, a more positive yield curve. For example, instead of a 50 b.p. spread between the cash rate and the June futures rate during March (12.50%–12.00%), as in Part a, there is a 100 b.p. spread (13.00–12.00%). Assume also a 100 b.p. spread in the June/September futures rate spread (14.00%–13.00%) during March. A further widening of the spread exists during June, at which time the cash rate/September futures rate spread is 150 b.p. (15.50%–14.00%).

Part c of Table 10 shows rates for the 200 b.p. per period increase in the cash rate but with a narrowing of the cash/futures and futures/futures spreads from their initial 50 b.p. to 30 b.p. during March and to 10 b.p. during June. This narrowing of the spreads is consistent with a change to a less positive yield curve.

What effects do these changes in the cash and futures spreads have on the hedges of a series of Eurodollar liability issues via strip and stack hedges? Consider the strip hedge first.

Strip Hedge   The outcome of a strip hedge based on this example is shown in Table 11. The effective issue rate, including hedge profits/losses, is 10.50% for the March issue, 11.00% for the June issue, and 11.50% for the September issue. These hedge rates result for any of the three yield shifts shown in Table 10. Note that these effective hedge rates are the same rates at which the March, June, and September futures contracts were sold during January. The initial futures rates are, therefore, the final effective hedge rates because, in this example, there is no cross hedge basis risk or time basis risk. Cross hedge basis risk would, however, have affected these outcomes. And, as shown in Section V-B, if the hedges had not terminated on a futures delivery day (there is time basis risk) changes in the slope of the yield curve would have affected the hedge rate.[9]

Changes in the level or slope of the yield curve, thus, do not affect the outcome of a strip hedge that terminates on futures delivery days. The initial futures rates alone determine the outcome of the hedge.[10] These conclusions result from the fact that for a strip hedge, the initial futures contracts

---

9. Changes in the slope of the yield curve will affect the time pattern of variation margin the hedger pays or collects during the hedge even in this example.

10. Again, changes in the slope of the yield curve will affect the outcome of the hedge. And changes in the cash/futures spreads during the hedge affect the pattern of variation margin payments or collections.

TABLE 11. *Strip Hedge versus Stack Hedge.*

Transaction Hedged	Cash Rate (at time of transaction)	Strip Hedge		Stack Hedge		
				Widening Spread	Constant Spread	Narrowing Spread
1. March issue	12.00%	*March contract*		*March contract*		
		Sell rate	10.50%	Sell rate	10.50%	
		Buy rate	12.00	Buy rate	12.00	
		Profit (loss)	1.50	Profit (loss)	1.50	
		Issue rate	12.00	Issue rate	12.00	
		Effective issue rate	10.50	Effective issue rate	10.50	
2. June issue	14.00%	*June contract*		*March contract*		
		Sell rate	11.00%	Sell rate	10.50%	10.50%	10.50%
		Buy rate	14.00	Buy rate	12.00	12.00	12.00
		Profit (loss)	3.00	Profit (loss) on first roll	1.50	1.50	1.50
		Issue rate	14.00				
		Effective issue rate	11.00	*June contract*			
				Sell rate	13.00%	12.50%	12.30%
				Buy rate	14.00	14.00	14.00
				Profit (loss)	1.00	1.50	1.70
				Total			
				Net profit (loss)	2.50%	3.00%	3.20%
				Issue rate	14.00	14.00	14.00
				Effective issue rate	11.50	11.00	10.80

TABLE 11 *Continued*

Transaction Hedged	Cash Rate (at time of transaction)	Strip Hedge		Stack Hedge		
				Widening Spread	Constant Spread	Narrowing Spread
3. September issue	16.00%	*September contract*		*March contract*		
		Sell rate	11.50%	Sell rate	10.50%	10.50%	10.50%
		Buy rate	16.00	Buy rate	12.00	12.00	12.00
		Profit (loss)	4.50	Profit (loss) on first roll	1.50	1.50	1.50
		Issue rate	16.00				
		Effective issue rate	11.50	*June contract*		
				Sell rate	13.00%	12.50%	12.30%
				Buy rate	14.00	14.00	14.00
				Profit (loss) on second roll	1.00	1.50	1.70
				September contract		
				Sell rate	15.50%	14.50%	14.10%
				Buy rate	16.00	16.00	16.00
				Profit (loss)	0.50	1.50	1.90
				Total		
				Net profit (loss)	3.00%	4.50%	5.10%
				Issue rate	16.00	16.00	16.00
				Effective issue rate	13.00	11.50	9.90

mature at exactly or approximately the same time as the corresponding cash market transaction, and there is no need to roll from one futures contract to another.

Stack Hedge   In a stack hedge, however, it is necessary to roll from one futures contract to another. So changes in futures/futures spreads affect the outcome of the hedge.

Table 11 shows the results of a stck hedge for the three changes in the yield curve environment described in Table 10. Consider the effects of the various subsequent yield curve environments on the hedges of the March, June, and September liability issues separately.

March Liability Issue   For the March transaction, only the March futures contract is used as a hedge. So this hedge is, in effect, a strip hedge and the 10.50% effective rate (the same as for the strip hedge) is equal to the initial March futures contract rate.

June Liability Issue   However, the June liability issue is hedged first with the March futures contract and then with the June futures contract after the March contract is rolled into the June contract during March. The effective rate on the transaction will, therefore, depend on the relationship between the March and June contract rates at the time of the roll. As shown in Table 11, for constant spreads (50 b.p.) the effective rate is 11.00%, the same as for the strip hedge. Thus, this stack hedge provides the same result as the strip hedge if the slope of the yield curve remains constant.

For spreads that widen (a yield curve that becomes more positively sloped) the effective hedge rate is 11.50%, as shown in Table 11, which is higher than the strip hedge rate. The reason for this outcome is that at the time of the roll from the March to the June contract, the rate of the June contract has increased relative to the rate on the March contract (that is, the price of the June contract has decreased relative to the price of the March contract). Since at the time of the roll the March contract is bought and the June contract is sold, the relatively higher price of the March contract and the relatively lower price of the June contract work to the disadvantage of the roll and consequently the hedge. Thus, a yield curve becoming more positive works to the disadvantage of a stack hedge, with a result inferior to that of a strip hedge.

The effective issue rate for the June transaction for narrowing spreads (a less positive yield curve) is 10.80%, which is lower than the strip hedge rate. With the less positive yield curve, the June rate has decreased relative to the March rate (the June price has increased relative to the March price), and at the time of the roll the March contract can be bought and the June contract sold at a more favorable spread. Thus, a change toward a less positive yield curve provides a better outcome for this stack hedge than for the strip hedge.

September Liability Issue   Table 11 also shows the effects of changes in the slope of the yield curve on the September transaction for a stack hedge. A stack hedge of the September issue requires the initial sale of March futures contracts, a roll into the June contract, and subsequently a roll into the September contract. Thus, the effect of the hedge depends on the relative prices of these futures contracts at the times of the two rolls.

The conclusions for the stack hedge of the September deposit are the same as for the stack hedge of the June transaction. If the yield curve maintains its initial slope, the results of the stack hedge are the same as for the strip hedge. But if the yield curve becomes more positive, the stack hedge is less effective than the strip hedge, and vice versa.

Thus, in deciding between the use of a strip hedge and a stack hedge, a forecast of changes in the slope of the yield curve is critical. As summarized in the table below, a forecast of a more positive yield curve warrants the use of a strip hedge; a forecast of a less positive yield curve warrants the use of a stack hedge. For a forecast of no change in the slope of the yield curve, the hedger would be indifferent between using strip and stack hedges on this basis.

Expected Change in Slope of Yield Curve	Strategy
More positive	Strip
No change (only change in level of yield curve)	Strip or stack −indifferent
Less positive	Stack

There is, however, a difference in the risk of the two strategies. A strip hedge is unaffected by changes in the slope of the yield curve because the deferred rates are already locked in, while stack hedges are affected by changes in the slope because the hedger has to roll out of the deferred contract. Thus, the strip hedge is the less risky strategy. An appropriate strategy reconciling the effects of the changes in the slope of the yield curve on a hedge and risk may be to generally use a strip hedge to minimize time basis risk, and to use a stack hedge only when the yield curve is judged to have an abnormally positive slope.

There may be an apparent contradiction between the conclusions in this section and those in Subsection B. To summarize the results of the effects of a change in the slope of the yield curve on a hedge, a steeper yield curve is to the advantage of a short hedge position already put on (as was the case in Subsection B) but to the disadvantage of a short hedge that will be put on in the future (in the context of rolling from a nearby to a more deferred

TABLE 12. *Summary of Effects of Changes in the Slope of the Yield Curve on Hedges.*

	Existing Hedge	Prospective Hedge in Deferred Contract (or Strip Out a Stack Hedge)
Steeper (more positive) yield curve	Advantage (retards convergence)	Disadvantage
Constant slope yield curve	No effect	No effect
Flatter (less positive) yield curve	Disadvantage (accelerates convergence)	Advantage

contract — for example, to strip out a stack hedge, as discussed in this subsection). A flatter yield curve is to the disadvantage of an existing hedge but to the advantage of a hedge to be put on in the future in a more deferred contract. These conclusions are summarized in Table 12.

D. Overview

Section V-A discusses methods for minimizing time basis risk when the hedges terminate on futures delivery days, that is, when there is no intrinsic time basis risk; Section V-B discusses methods for minimizing time basis risk when the hedges do not terminate on futures delivery days, that is, when there is intrinsic time basis risk. When the hedges terminate on a sequence of futures delivery dys, selling a strip of futures contracts eliminates time basis risk. When the hedges terminate on days that are not futures delivery days, weighted combinations of futures contracts maturing immediately before and immediately after each hedge termination data minimize, but do not eliminate, time basis risk.

Section V-C adds a new dimension to Sections V-A and V-B — it discusses managing time basis risk, rather than eliminating it as discussed in Section V-A or minimizing it as discussed in Section V-B, in an attempt to reduce the cost of the hedge. If it was thought that the yield curve was going to flatten during the hedge, there would be an advantage to stacking the hedge in the nearby contract, whether the hedge terminated on a futures delivery date or not, and to strip out the hedge after the yield curve flattened. When the hedge was stripped out, it could be stripped out according to the methods in either section V-A or V-B, depending on whether the hedges terminated on futures delivery days or not. That is, it could be stripped out to the appropriate futures contract in the former case or to the combination of

TABLE 13. *Summary of Optimal Hedges Considering Time Basis Risk.*

	Hedges Terminating on Futures Delivery Dates		Hedges Not Terminating on Futures Delivery Dates	
	Minimize Time Basis Risk	Manage Time Basis Risk	Minimize Time Basis Risk	Manage Time Basis Risk
Steeper (more positive) yield curve (Figure 8-A)	Strip of futures	Strip of futures[a]	Strip of mixed futures[b]	Strip of mixed futures (there would be a tendency to use more of the deferred contract in each pair in the mixed hedge)
Constant slope yield curve (Figure 8-B)	Strip of futures	Either strip or stack of futues	Strip of mixed futures[b]	Either strip of mixed futures, simple strip of futures (in nearby or deferred contract) or a stack of futures
Flatter (less positive) yield curve (Figure 8-C, D)	Strip of futures	Stack of nearby futures	Strip of mixed futures[b]	Stack of nearby futures (if a strip hedge were used, there would be a tendency to use more of the nearby contract in each pair in the mixed hedge)

a. In this case, a stack of futures in the deferred contract could be used.
b. Mixed futures are a combination of nearby and deferred futures contracts with the relative number of each contract calculated as shown in Section V-B.

futures contracts indicated in Section V-B in the latter case. And even if a strip hedge were used, when the yield curve was expected to flatten there would be a tendency to use the futures contract that matured before rather than after the hedge termination date for hedging each transaction.

If the yield curve were expected to steepen, a strip hedge would be used rather than a stack hedge.[11] And for hedges that terminate between futures maturity dates, there would be more of a tendency to use the futures contract maturing immediately after rather than immediately prior to the futures maturity date.

Thus, there is an interaction between the issues discussed in Section V-C and those discussed in Sections V-A and V-B. A summary of the appropriate strategies for various assumptions about changes in the yield curve and various goals regarding risk is provided in Table 13.

VI. Managing the Hedge

Hedging is frequently thought of by the novice as being completely mechanical and nonjudgmental. Indeed, some of the techniques discussed in this report could be applied in mechanical and nonjudgmental ways. Hedges conducted according to this philosophy are called "static hedges." Such hedges, designed to minimize basis risk, are put on according to risk minimization methods discussed in this report and are not taken off until the initially specified date, the termination of the hedge. But anyone familiar with risk management, of which hedging is one type, knows that risk management is typically very judgmental. And many of the techniques discussed in this report are the basis for the use of judgment in hedging. Some times to decrease and increase risk are better than others, and some methods of managing risk are better than others. The concept "risk/reward ratio" is often used in considering how to manage risk.

One element of judgment in hedging is introduced in the section on strip versus stack hedging. Another very important element of judgment concerns when a hedge should be "left on" and when the hedge should be "taken off." Two aspects of hedging make this "timing" decision very important. One aspect concerns the effect of a hedge on the return of the relevant hedged transaction or position. A hedge removes the potential loss due to interest rates "going against" a cash transaction or position. But a hedge also eliminates the benefit of decreasing rates for a liability issuer. Thus, it is desirable to hedge a liability issue when rates are increasing but not when rates are decreasing, if this goal can be achieved.

---

11. A more aggressive strategy under these assumptions, not discussed in this article, would be to stack all the futures contracts in the most deferred contract and then to strip into the more nearby contracts as the yield curve steepened.

The second aspect of the desirability of being hedged only when rates are going against the cash transaction or position exacerbates the first. Futures gains and losses are marked to the market on a daily basis, that is, they are settled in cash on a daily basis. Thus, independent of how the gains and losses on the futures position and the cash position are accounted for or when they are realized on the cash position, the gains or losses on the futures positions are realized in cash on a daily basis. So even if the hedge is effective in the sense that futures losses are offset by cash market gains, the cash market gains may be deferred (or in a worse case be only unrealized, or paper, gains), while the futures losses are settled in cash on a daily basis.

These two aspects of hedging make the timing of when hedges are put on, kept on, and taken off even more important. How is such timing determined? Hedge timing methods are identical to methods of forecasting interest rates, and are mainly fundamental and technical.

Fundamental forecasts are based on the economic and financial determinants of interest rates. Such fundamental determinants may be combined in either mathematical (often econometric) models or by judgment. Economic forecasts are usually fairly long term (typically on a quarterly basis), and judgmental forecasts are, by their nature, subjective. While either is often difficult to use in a short-term, disciplined way, fundamental methods are nevertheless frequently used for the timing of hedge management. Some types of fundamental models, particularly those that depend on analyzing government policy, including "Fed watching," are, however, much more short-term oriented.

Technical methods are based mainly on a consideration of the prices of the underlying instrument considered (including the high, low, and closing prices) and may include the trading volume and open interest. Types of technical methods include oscillators, relative strength indicators, bar charts, chart formations, and others. Technical methods are often formulated in quantitative models with explicit entry and exit levels for the market, although some methods, particularly the use of chart patterns, are subjective.

Stop orders may also be used to determine the timing of a hedge. Stop orders are orders to liquidate a position if the futures price moves to a specific price against the existing futures position. While stop orders may be useful in limiting futures losses, the danger is that futures prices may move temporarily against the futures position, "taking out the stop," and then reverse and move against the cash position with no futures position remaining as a hedge. For example, with the short-term rate at 10% (a futures price of 90), a short prospective liability hedge may be initiated with a stop at 9.50% (90.50). A potential disadvantage is that the market may strengthen to 9.50% (90.50), taking out the stop, then reverse and weaken to 12.00% (88.00). This move from 9.50% to 12.00%, then, is unhedged. The stop order, on the other hand, given the initial short-term rate of 10%, would protect against a decline in rates from 9.50% to 6%.

There are also other aspects of hedge management. These include deciding the timing of rolling the hedge from one contract month to another and adjusting the hedge ratio due to changes in the level of the futures price, changes in the yield beta, or other changes in the hedge. In cross hedges, the spread between the rates on the instrument being hedged and the instrument underlying the futures contract should also be continuously monitored. If this spread worsens, the hedge ratio may be changed or the hedge terminated due to the ineffectiveness of the hedge.

There is a spectrum of activeness with which hedges may be managed. At one extreme is the static (or completely passive) hedge. At the other extreme is a very active, continuously managed hedge. In practice, most hedge applications are between these extreme approaches.

Overview The basic, or static, method or hedging a series of short-term liability issues is to transact a strip of short futures contracts whose maturity dates are the nearest after the corresponding liability issues (or a weighted combination of nearby and deferred contract months around the hedge termination date). The futures contracts corresponding to each liability issue are subsequently liquidated at the time the liability is issued. This type of hedge also uses the futures contract whose underlying instrument is most closely related to the instrument being hedged (for example, uses the Treasury bill futures contracts to hedge MMCs); uses the strip rather than stack method to minimize time basis risk; and after initiating the short futures contract liquidates them at the time the liabilities are issued.

There are three ways to deviate from this standard, static hedge, that is, there are three ways to manage the hedge. These three methods can be used separately or in any combination. Managing the hedge in any of these ways is more aggressive than the standard, static hedge. It is an attempt to manage rather than minimize risk, an acceptance of more risk in an attempt to reduce the cost of the hedge.

The first method of managing the hedge involves market timing and attempts to maintain short futures positions when interest rates are rising and liquidate the short futures positions and be unhedged when the interest rates are declining. It is, therefore, based on projections of the level of short-term interest rates. Methods used for market timing are indicated above.

The second method of hedge management involves the use of the stack hedge rather than the strip hedge. The basis for the use of the stack or strip hedge is a projection of the *slope,* not the *level,* of the short-term yield curve. In this type of hedge management, a stack hedge is used when the short-term yield curve is judged to be relatively steep and is expected to become less positive (less steep). When the short-term yield curve flattens the initial stack hedge can be "stripped out," that is, the stack hedge replaced by a strip hedge, to minimize basis risk. If the yield curve is initially relatively flat and is expected to steepen, a strip hedge is initiated.

TABLE 14. *Managing the Hedge.*

Type of Management	Basis for Management
Market timing	Level of short-term interest rates
Strip versus stack	Slope of short-term yield curve
Cross hedge	Intermarket yield spreads

The third type of hedge management is the cross hedge. Typically, the appropriate futures contract for a hedge is chosen on the basis of the highest yield correlation with the instrument being hedged. For example, the Eurodollar futures contract is used to hedge future LIBOR-based liabilities, and the Treasury bill futures contract is used to hedge MMCs based on Treasury bill rates. This selection minimizes cross hedge basis risk.

But the hedger could, instead of minimizing this basis risk, manage it and attempt to profit from expected changes in the basis. For example, if the yield spread between Eurodollars and Treasury bills was judged to be abnormally low, hedgers would benefit from a widening of this spread if Eurodollar futures contracts were used to hedge MMCs. On the other hand, this change in the yield spread would work to the disadvantage of a hedge of LIBOR-based liabilities with Treasury bill futures contracts. If the Eurodollar/Treasury bill yield spread was initially abnormally wide and then narrowed, however, the outcomes would be the opposite.

An historical evaluation of these spread relationships based on graphs, such as shown in Figures 2, 3, and 4, and the corresponding statistics can be used to make decisions on the selection of the hedge instrument in view of expected yield spread changes.

Table 14 summarizes the three types of hedge management and the basis for the decisions regarding them. All three of these types of hedge management are used in practice.

VII. Accounting Issues

During August 1984, the financial Accounting Standards Board (FASB) issued Statement of Financial Accounting Standards (SFAS) No. 80, Accounting for Futures Contracts. This section describes how SFAS No. 80 applies to hedging short-term liabilities with futures contracts.

SFAS No. 80 requires that interest rate futures contracts be accounted for on a market value basis (that is, gains and losses be recognized as income when they occur) unless they meet all the criteria for hedge accounting. Thus, if all the hedge criteria are not met, futures gains and losses must be included in income on a current basis. With this accounting treatment, the use of futures contracts would, in many cases, tend to destabilize income rather than stabilize income.

This leaves two questions: (1) If the hedge criteria are met, how are futures gains and losses accounted for? (2) What are the hedge criteria?

A. Hedge Accounting Treatment

If the hedge criteria are met, SFAS No. 80 requires symmetry between the transaction being hedged and the futures contract (whether on a market value basis or a lower-of-cost-or-market basis or an historical cost basis). For example, an institution that sells futures contracts to hedge against the interest rates of subsequent short-term borrowings can treat, for accounting purposes, the gain or loss on the futures contracts as a component of the cost of the debt. Thus, the gain or loss on the futures contract can be treated as a premium or discount (that is, an adjustment) on the interest expense of the debt over its expected life. The gains or losses on the futures contracts can, in these circumstances, be deferred — this is called "deferral accounting."

SFAS No. 80 permits deferral accounting for futures contracts if all the criteria for hedge accounting are met. What are the criteria for deferral accounting?

B. Criteria for Hedge Accounting Treatment

There are two criteria for all hedges and two additional criteria for anticipatory hedges, which include the hedges of future issues of liabilities. The two criteria for all hedges are the following:

1. the transaction hedged must expose the institution to the risk of increasing interest rates; and
2. the futures contract must reduce the interest rate risk of that transaction.

There are several aspects of each criterion that should be discussed. An issue with respect to the first criterion relates to the measurement of the interest rate risk of an institution. If an institution has a negative gap (subject to the risk of rising interest rates) over the short term, say from zero to 270 days, but a positive gap (subject to risk of declining interest rates) thereafter, can it enact both short and long hedges? This issue becomes more difficult when both strip and stack hedges are considered.

The FASB also made the following exception to the statement: "An enterprise that cannot assess risk by considering other relevant positions and transactions for the enterprise as a whole because it conducts its risk management activities on a decentralized basis can meet this condition if the item intended to be hedged exposes the particular business unit that enters into the contract." While there will be some questions about what is a "business unit" when conducting risk management activities on a "decentralized basis," this exception seems to reinforce the micro-view as opposed to the macro-view of hedge accounting.

The second criterion requires that the futures contract be a hedge of a specific position or transaction or an essentially similar collection of positions or transactions. Thus, according to this criterion also, hedges must be micro-hedges rather than macro-hedges, and hedging gaps does not qualify for hedge accounting. Simultaneously, analysts of gaps have come to believe that it is not gaps but the specific liabilities or assets comprising the gap that should be hedged. Thus, these standards should not limit gap hedging as it has come to be practiced.

To satisfy the second criterion also requires that there will be a "high degree of correlation" between the position or transaction being hedged and the hedge instrument. This is initially a statistical issue leading to questions about the length of time over which a high degree of correlation should be demonstrated and how high the correlation should be to satisfy this criterion. Obviously, given statistics such as shown in Table 5, accounting judgment and managerial discretion must resolve this issue.

C. Anticipatory Hedges

There are two additional criteria for anticipatory hedges:

1. the significant characteristics and expected terms of the anticipated transaction must be identified; and
2. the anticipated transaction that is being hedged must be probable.

These criteria mean that the hedger must be able to identify the expected date of the transaction, the dollar amount, and the expected maturity of the transaction and also that the expected transaction is likely to occur. To qualify for hedge (deferral) accounting, subsequent issuers of short-term liabilities must satisfy these four criteria.

D. Overview

The deferral of the gains or losses on futures contracts is permitted as long as all of these criteria are met. Once any of these criteria are not met, hedge accounting is not appropriate and the gains or losses on futures contracts must be reported on a market value (current) basis.

SFAS No. 80 makes it appropriate to continue to defer gains and losses on futures contracts, whether greater or less than losses or gains on corresponding hedged instruments, as long as there is a high degree of positive correlation. However, once there is no longer high correlation, the cumulative futures gains or losses in excess of the cumulative unrecognized losses or gains on the positions being hedged must be recorded in income immediately. Past futures gains or losses of an amount equal to the unrecognized losses or gains on positions being hedged can, however, continue to be treated on a deferred basis. Either a profit or loss may be recorded in income when high correlation ceases. (If the cumulative futures gains or losses are less than the cumulative unrecognized losses or gains on positions being hedged, no entry in current income is made immediately after high correlation ceases.) For this reason, the hedge criteria must be monitored throughout the hedge.

More detailed discussions on accounting for futures transactions are available from several public accounting firms.

VIII. Summary

This article discusses how short-term liabilities can be hedged with Eurodollar, Treasury bill, and CD futures contracts. Hedging prospective liability issues permits institutions to lock in the interest rates on their future short-term liability issues and insulate themselves against increases in short-term interest rates.

While the basic principles of hedging short-term liabilities are quite simple, there are several aspects of the hedge that must be considered to improve the effectiveness of the hedge. This report discusses the various issues that must be considered to provide an effective hedge. Among them are:

- choosing the futures contract to use based on the correlation of the yields of the hedged instrument and the instrument underlying the futures contract and the management of the resulting cross hedge basis risk;
- calculating the correct hedge ratio;
- choosing the appropriate contract month or months of the futures contract to use based on the current and expected changes in the slope of the yield curve, and managing the resulting time basis risk. This issue involves determining both:
  - whether to use a strip or stack hedge and
  - whether to use the futures contract that matures prior to or after the date of the termination of the hedge or a combination of these two contracts when the hedge does not terminate on a futures maturity day;
- methods for timing the hedge, that is, removing the hedge when interest rates are changing in favor of the prospective liability issue.

A brief summary of how these futures transactions are accounted for is also provided.

The Eurodollar, Treasury bill, and CD futures contracts provide flexibility, liquidity, and low transactions costs in managing the interest rate risks associated with short-term liability issues.

The option on the Eurodollar futures contract can also be used to put an upper limit, or "cap," on borrowing costs rather than locking in the rate.

Appendix: Measures of Rates of Return

Rates of return on different instruments are often cited as if they are comparable, even though, as is well known, the rates of return on Treasury bills and Treasury bonds are not. Neither are the rates of return on various money market instruments. The differences in the methods of determining rates of return on various short-term and long-term instruments are summarized in Table A-1. This appendix summarizes some of the relationships among these rates of return.

1. Discount Rate (d)

$$d = \frac{F-P}{F} \times \frac{360}{M},$$

where:

d = discount rate
F = maturity (or face) value (usually expressed in base of 100)
P = market price
M = time to maturity

Or $P = F - D$, where D is the dollar amount of discount from the face value and

TABLE A-1. *Rates of Return on Various Fixed-Income Securities.*

	Maturity	
	360 Days	365 Days
Discount basis (on basis of maturity value)	Treasury bills Commercial paper BAs	—
Yield basis (on basis of current market value)	CDs (add-on yield) Euro CDs and TDs (add-on yield) Repos (add-on yield)	Treasury bonds and notes (semiannual coupon/365 days)

	Municipal bonds (semi-
	  annual coupon/360 days)
	Corporate bonds (semi-
	  annual coupon/360 days)
	GNMAs (monthly pay-
	  ment, including amor-
	  tization/360 days)	

$$D = F\left(\frac{d \times M}{360}\right).$$

2. Yield (on 360-day basis)

$$Y = \frac{F-P}{P} \times \frac{360}{M} = d \times \frac{F}{P}$$

$$= d \frac{1}{(1-(d \times M/360))}.$$

3. Bond Equivalent Yield of Discount Rate (y)[12]

(a) For M between 0 and 182 days:[13]

$$y = \frac{F-P}{P} \times \frac{365}{M} = \frac{365}{360} \times \frac{F}{P} \times d.$$

This can also be expressed as

$$y = \frac{365 \times d}{360 - (d \times M)}.$$

(b) For M between 183 and 365 days:

$$F = P\left(1+\left(\frac{y}{CP}\right)\right)^{CP \times (M/365)},$$

where:

y = annual compound rate,
M = time to maturity of the money market instrument (in days),
P = present value (or current market price) of the security,
F = maturity value of the security, and
CP = compounding periods per year.

For semiannual compounding periods,

$$P = F/(1+y/2)^{2(M/365)}.$$

4. CD Yield   Add-on yield; also applies to Euro CDs and TDs and repos:

$$P = \frac{\text{Principal} + \text{Interest at Maturity}}{1+(Y \times Lt/360)} = \frac{V(1+LoC/360)}{1+(YCD \times Lt/360)},$$

---

12. The Security Industry Association, which provides the "street" convention, specifies method (a) for Treasury bills with maturities between 0 and 182 days and an alternative method (specified in Marcia Stigum, *Money Market Calculations*, p. 35) for Treasury bills with maturities between 183 and 365 days. Many analysts use method (b) for Treasury bills of all maturities.

13. The equation $y = (F-P)/P \times 365/M$ can be rewritten as $F = P(1+y \times M/365)$, which is linear in yield, y. The equation in (b) is obviously nonlinear in yield.

where:

P = current price of CD,
YCD = yield on CD (add-on yield),
V = amount of initial deposit,
O = CD yield,
Lo = initial maturity,
Lt = current maturity, and
C = coupon.

Note that $V(1+LoC/360)$, the numerator in the price equation, is equal to the maturity value of the CD, which equals the "principal plus interest at maturity."

Expressing YCD in terms of P gives

$$YCD = \left(\frac{360}{Lt} \times \frac{V(1+LoC/360)-P}{P} \right),$$

where $V(1+(LoC/360))$ is the maturity value of the CD. Thus, this is a yield on a 360-day basis. It can be converted to a yield on a 365-day basis by multiplying by 365/360.

5. Relation between Discount (d) and CD Yield (YCD) Since

$$d = \frac{F-P}{F} \times \frac{360}{M}$$

and a yield on a 360-day basis is

$$Y = \frac{F-P}{P} \times \frac{360}{M},$$

as indicated in (1) and (2) above, to convert from discount to short-term yield (CD add-on yield) use

$$d = \frac{P}{F}Y \quad \text{and} \quad Y = \frac{F}{P}d,$$

where:

P = the current price; and
F = maturity value, which equals $V(1+LoC/360)$ for a CD.

PART III

Real Estate

37

Real Estate in the Portfolio*

David J. Hartzell
Vice President
Salomon Brothers Inc.

I. Introduction

The relative size of the equity real estate market is frequently cited as one reason for allocating increasing proportions of portfolios to real estate. For example, we estimate that the total value of commercial real estate equity is approximately $1.8 trillion, while the total value of domestic corporate equity outstanding is about $2.6 trillion. Given these figures, an index portfolio should hold approximately 60% of the amount committed to domestic corporate equity as real estate. Using this type of analysis, the allocation to real estate should be at least 25% in a value-weighted index portfolio.

This type of analysis is only appropriate for the large institutional investor whose strategy involves combining assets in weights proportional to the market value of those assets in the domestic wealth portfolio. This is also the case in the stock market, where investors are primarily institutional, because the structure of the investment vehicle lends itself well to institutional investors. In real estate, however, the market is mainly dominated by individual investors, not the institutional investors of the stock and bond markets. This phenomenon is changing, however, as institutions increasingly enter the domain of equity real estate investment and as the number of real estate investment vehicles broadens.

For the past five years, portfolio analysts have been arguing the merits of increasing the allocation in equity holdings of real estate in large investment portfolios for reasons not entirely related to index portfolios.[1] Most of these recommendations arise and are generated from investment models, which use past information to provide the optimal allocations. Unfortunately, the bulk of these works utilizes information as of the early 1980s, after which time major real estate markets ceased outperforming financial assets. Furthermore, these models generally use information from the mid-1970s; thus, recommendations are based on an interval characterized by increasing rates of inflation and a general improvement in the real estate markets. Within this framework, it is not surprising that asset selection models prescribe large allocations to equity real estate, because on a return/risk basis, the asset has dominated stocks and bonds.

These analyses are flawed, however, because they are period-specific studies. Vacancies in the office market — the blue chip institutional real estate investment — have increased to an average 20% in nearly all markets from 5% in 1982. While reported values have not yet decreased in all markets, returns have as effective rents have fallen. Given this economic background, the previous recommendations of high real estate allocations may be upwardly biased. For those institutions currently investing in real estate, allocations should be at the low end of the policy range. However, for those not holding real estate, diversification benefits are achieved by adding the asset to portfolios of financial assets.

---

1. See Russell Fogler, "20% in Real Estate: Can Theory Justify It?" *Journal of Portfolio Management* (Winter 1984) and J.R. Webb and J. Rubens, "Portfolio Considerations and the Valuation of Real Estate," *The AREUEA Journal,* Fall 1986.

TABLE 1. *The Changing Role of Real Estate in the Pension Portfolio, 1981–85 (top 200 pension funds).*

	1981	1982	1983	1984	1985
Real estate equity	3.7%	3.5%	3.3%	3.3%	4.2%
Stocks	40.6	37.0	44.2	41.2	41.6
Bonds	37.5	39.0	34.9	33.4	33.3
Cash	12.1	10.5	8.2	10.4	8.5
Mortgages[a]	NA	4.0	3.5	2.2	2.2
Mortgage-backed securities	NA	NA	NA	2.9	3.1
Guaranteed investment certificates	NA	3.0	2.4	3.0	3.7
Other	6.1	3.0	3.5	3.6	3.4

a. In 1981, mortgages are included in real estate totals.
NA = Not available.
Source: *Pensions and Investment Age,* various issues.

The overall holdings of pension funds in real estate have remained near-ly constant, despite increased recommended allocations to the asset class. While pension funds have marginally increased their real estate holdings since 1980, their holdings still account for only 4% of the total portfolio (see Table 1). Thus, there remains a wedge between actual holdings of pension funds and recommended holdings. In the context of the declining real estate markets, it currently appears that the wedge is appropriate. In real estate, as with other assets, however, efficient investment is a matter of timing; thus, normal weights should serve as benchmarks only, with policy weights deter-mined with respect to current market conditions. Despite the stable asset al-location to real estate, however, the rapid growth of pension funds has led to absolute real estate commitments that have risen each year. For example, the 0.9% increase in the 1984–85 period represented a gain of $13 billion.

II. The Recent Performance of Real Estate

Average returns for the three major asset holdings of pension funds over three periods are shown in Table 2. In the fourth-quarter 1977 to first-quar-ter 1986 period, real property returns averaged 13.95%, compared with the 16.73% and 10.70% earned by stocks and bonds, respectively, The variabil-ity of the real estate returns was only one quarter of the variability associ-ated with the two financial assets. Low standard deviations result from the

TABLE 2. *Annualized Returns, Selected Asset Classes, Fourth Quarter 1977–First Quarter 1986.*

	Real Estate[a]	Bonds[b]	Stocks[c]
4Q77–1Q86			
Mean	13.95%	10.70%	16.73%
Standard deviation	2.52	10.8	13.98
4Q77–4Q81			
Mean	17.34%	1.45%	12.39%
Standard deviation	2.32	13.44	12.26
4Q81–1Q86			
Mean	10.84%	19.06%	20.46%
Standard deviation	1.76	7.94	14.64

a. Returns calculated from the Frank Russell Company Prop-erty Index.
b. Returns calculated from the *Salomon Brothers Broad In-vestment-Grade Bond Index.*™
c. Total returns earned by the S&P 500.

FIGURE 1. *Quarterly Returns, Selected Asset Classes, 1978–85.*

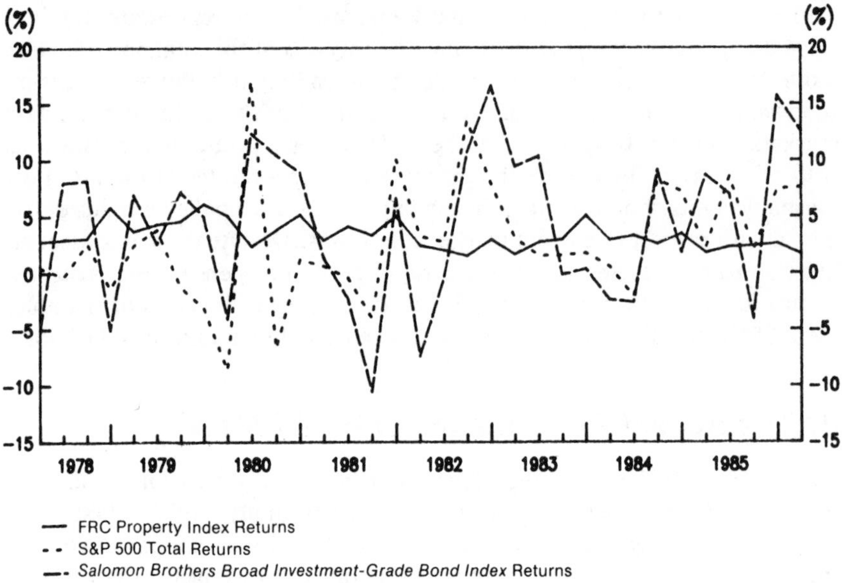

— FRC Property Index Returns
- - S&P 500 Total Returns
—- *Salomon Brothers Broad Investment-Grade Bond Index* Returns

appraisal process employed by the commingled real estate funds that report to the Frank Russell Company. The use of appraisals smooths returns, creating a less variable return series.[2] The extent of the low variability is shown in Figure 1, in which quarterly returns are plotted for real estate, stocks and bonds.

The evidence from the fourth-quarter 1977 to fourth-quarter 1981 period shows the superiority of real property investment. The nominal annual return earned by the real estate portfolio over the period was 17.34%, compared with smaller returns for stocks and bonds. The performance of real estate over this period led many to argue for increased allocations to the asset class for institutional investors.

Since 1981, however, the relative performance of the assets has changed drastically. The FRC Index return fell to 60% of its average in the fourth-quarter 1977 to fourth-quarter 1981 period, to an average annualized return of 10.84%. Stock and bond returns rose substantially to annualized average rates of 20.46% and 19.06%, respectively, for the fourth-quarter 1981 to first-quarter 1986 period. Thus, the effect of the real estate market slowdown

---

2. See David Shulman, "The Relative Risk of Real Estate and Common Stock: A New View," the following article in this book.

and the recent booms in the stock and bond markets are clear. In fact, the total effect may be even greater, because the FRC Index calculates the appreciation component of return from often-outdated appraisals. Because the reporting funds appraise properties at different intervals, the market values reported may be one to four quarters old. Thus, reported values may not be current with respect to a more widely declining market, and overall returns may be overstated. Even with this potential overestimation, the FRC Index shows a lower average return for the fourth-quarter 1981 to first-quarter 1986 period, compared with the first-quarter 1977 to fourth-quarter 1981 period.

The market performance of real estate in the past year is also interesting, compared with the overall performance of the stock and bond markets. The recent bond and stock market booms have generated significantly higher returns in these markets relative to real estate. For example, total rates of return on all property types were lower than the five financial assets surveyed in 1985 (see Table 3). Stocks and bonds earned 31.1% and 30.3%, respectively, while the overall FRC Index registered only a 9.8% annual return. Office properties returned only 8.6%, but because of the appraisal methodology and the problems that arise from using appraisals to calculate returns, even that figure may be overstated. Therefore, from a recent return perspective, real estate is in a slump compared with other typically held institutional assets.

The degree to which real estate correlates with other assets is described in Table 4, which shows that real estate serves as an excellent diversifier when the asset class is combined with financial assets. When assets are combined into a portfolio, the portfolio return is simply a weighted average of the

---

TABLE 3. *Comparative Total Rates of Return, 1985.*

	Total
Comparable Assets Return	
S&P 500	31.1%
Long-term *Salomon Brothers Broad Investment-Grade Index*	30.3
Long-term Treasury index	31.5
Medium-term *Salomon Brothers Broad Investment-Grade Index*	20.0
Medium-term Treasury index	18.2
Real Estate Equity	
Frank Russell Company (FRC) property index	9.8%
Office	8.6
Industrial	11.8
Retail	11.5
Hotel	4.5
Apartment	8.0

TABLE 4. *Correlation of Asset Returns, Fourth Quarter 1977–First Quarter 1986.*

	Real Estate	Bonds	Stocks	Inflation
Real estate	1.00	(0.46)	(0.25)	0.58
Bonds		1.00	0.52	(0.30)
Stocks			1.00	(0.16)
Inflation				1.00

returns earned by the separate assets. The overall risk of the portfolio, however, is dependent not only on the separate asset risks, but also on the manner in which the separate asset returns move together. If there is perfect correlation among returns, there is no risk-reduction benefit from combining the assets. If correlations are less than perfect (correlation coefficients are less than one), the portfolio risk is lower than that of the individual assets. Maximum benefits are obtained the closer the correlation coefficient is to minus one. Real estate correlations with common stocks over the 33-quarter period ended in the first quarter of 1986 are less than zero, indicating that total portfolio risk could be substantially reduced if both asset classes are combined. Furthermore, real estate and bond returns are even more negatively correlated, indicating even greater diversification potential. In contrast, stock and bond return correlations are strongly positive. Therefore, mixed-asset portfolios of stocks, bonds and real estate offer more superior risk/return profiles than portfolios held solely in stocks and bonds.

Despite the strongly negative correlations, there is currently some question concerning the appropriate correlation levels for real estate returns and returns on other financial assets. In particular, the usual caveat pertains in that the appraisal process biases correlations downward, although the extent of this occurrence is unknown. Although data are not available for longer intervals, the conventional wisdom is that correlations should be near zero, indicating the potential for diversification benefits.

As expected, real estate returns are highly correlated with inflation, consistent with the conventional wisdom that real estate provides an inflation hedge. In the recent period of disinflation, however, high correlations with inflation indicate declining nominal returns. Given the long-term risk of a return to higher inflation levels, real estate will continue to be an important component of institutional portfolios.

III. Portfolio Allocation Estimation

While past performance serves as a useful guide in terms of analyzing investment strategies, future portfolio performance is a more important concern.

In the face of continued declining returns and slowing inflation, it is instructive to reconsider the appropriate portfolio allocation to real estate, stocks and bonds utilizing information from the past, but adjusting real estate returns and risks to more accurately represent the current state of the market. Various allocation algorithms are available that utilize information concerning expected returns, expected standard deviation and expected correlation coefficients. The algorithm used in this study uses the concept of mean-variance efficiency, which was pioneered by Dr. Harry Markowitz. The algorithm is simple to employ and depends strongly on the estimates used as inputs. The output consists of several portfolios that lie along the efficient frontier, which is the set of portfolios that provides the maximum rate of return for a given level of risk, or equivalently, the minimum risk for a given level of return. In terms of portfolio performance, the Sharpe reward-to-variability ratio, a measure of relative portfolio performance, is used to analyze that portfolio of the efficient set that achieves the best performance (in terms of risk and return). Three scenarios are analyzed to determine the sensitivity of results to the potential underestimation of risk created by the appraisal process.

Simulation Inputs

Three different assumptions concerning real estate risk are assumed for the portfolio allocation model. Because there is no doubt that the volatility reported in Table 2 is underrepresented, more realistic assumptions are required for meaningful allocation results. These assumptions are as follows: (1) Real estate risk is equal to historical stock volatility as reported in Table 2; (2) real estate risk is equal to three quarters of historical stock volatility; and (3) real estate risk is equal to one half of historical stock volatility. Furthermore, because the extent to which the correlations are affected by the appraisal process is unknown, conservative estimates of zero correlation of bond and real estate returns and low but positive correlation (0.2) of stock and real estate returns are used. Finally, historical returns for the full period reported in Table 2 are used for stock and bond return expectations, but real estate returns are assumed to be lower than those reported in Table 2. Because of the current state of most real estate markets, the expected real estate return employed in the allocation algorithm is 7.5%.

Simulation Results

The extent to which the differing risk assumptions affect the portfolio allocations are shown in Table 5. Intuitively, as the expected risk for real estate decreases, holding all else constant, a larger portfolio allocation to the asset class is indicated. In the worst-case scenario, where real estate risk is equal to full stock return volatility, the allocation to real estate is 3.01%, below

TABLE 5. *Asset Allocation Results.*

	Simulation A[a] (%)	Simulation B[b] (%)	Simulation C[c] (%)
Expected portfolio return	15.375	14.725	12.745
Portfolio standard deviation	12.260	11.436	8.889
Allocations			
Real estate	3.01	10.81	33.08
Bonds	17.85	16.72	15.48
Stocks	79.14	72.46	51.45

a. Real estate volatility equal to 100% of stock volatility.
b. Real estate volatility equal to 75% of stock volatility.
c. Real estate volatility equal to 50% of stock volatility.

the current portfolio holdings of the pension funds surveyed in Table 1. For comparison purposes, when expectations of real estate risk are reduced to three quarters of stock volatility, the allocation increases to 10.81% of the portfolio. When real estate risk is reduced to one half of stock volatility, the portfolio share increases to 33.08%. Given our view that real estate volatility is higher than currently reported,[3] the appropriate range of a current allocation to real estate is 3%–11%. Thus, despite the expectation of lower returns to real estate in the future, the asset class retains a significant allocation in efficiently constructed portfolios.

IV. Summary and Conclusions

In the late 1970s and early 1980s, real estate significantly outperformed alternative asset classes. In that period, many institutional investors increased their commitment to real estate to capture the benefits of equity real estate investment, although industry average allocations have remained unchanged. Since 1982, the investment situation has changed significantly. Reported real estate returns have fallen, while returns earned on stocks and bonds have skyrocketed. In this new environment, an efficient investment strategy calls for a new look at allocation to real estate as an asset class.

Ultimately, the efficient allocation to real estate depends on the investor's expectations of risk and return. Under various assumptions concerning the performance of real estate, the efficient allocation falls in the 3%–11%

---

3. For a discussion of stock and bond volatility, see Martin L. Leibowitz, *Total Portfolio Duration: A New Perspective on Asset Allocation* (New York: Salomon Brothers Inc, February 1986).

range. The low end of this range corresponds to current actual portfolio holdings of large pension funds, while the high end is somewhat lower than those recommended in academic studies. In the current market, these new allocations are more sensible and suggest that institutional investors should still consider real estate as a viable asset class for a diversified portfolio. Of course, the results are dependent on the expectations used in the simulation algorithm, but the real estate return and the correlation coefficients employed are deemed conservative. If an investor believes that correlations are lower or that real estate returns will not dip as low as 7.5%, the efficient allocation increases to higher levels for real estate than those reported in Table 5.

Furthermore, as institutional investors increase their attention to real estate and the market becomes more institutionally dominated — as has the stock market — the trend toward even greater investment in real estate will continue. Over time, as passive index portfolios are constructed, real estate allocations should increase to more than 25% of institutional portfolios. In this way, the short-term strategic weightings represent a drastic underweighting for real estate, given the total value of equity investment in the asset class. This increase will require the creation of properly constructed real estate investment vehicles, which more closely meet the needs of institutional investors. In this way, the 3%-11% recommendations supported above are appropriate in the short term, while over the longer term, the allocations should be higher.

38

The Relative Risk of Equity Real Estate and Common Stock:
A New View

David Shulman
Director
Salomon Brothers Inc

I. The Traditional View

In recent years, institutional investors have considered direct investment in real estate equities as a low-risk alternative to corporate equities. This view is grounded in the fact that real estate returns measured by Frank Russell Co. Property Index (FRC Index) have exhibited significantly less volatility than common stock returns measured by the S&P 500.[1] Several widely publicized articles in the investment literature have supported this view.[2] Perhaps even more importantly, real estate returns have exhibited low or negative correlations with stocks and bonds, which has made it a valuable asset class in constructing well-diversified institutional portfolios.

The FRC Index is based on the investment results of 31 real estate money managers. The Index was initialized on December 31, 1977, composed of 236 properties with a total market value of $594 million. As of December 31, 1985, the Index represented 960 properties with a market value of $10.3 bil-

---

1. See FRC, *Property Index,* Fourth Quarter 1985, Frank Russell Company and National Council of Real Estate Investment Fiduciaries.
2. See H. Russell Fogler, "20% in Real Estate: Can Theory Justify It?" *Journal of Portfolio Management* (Winter 1984); Robert H. Zerbst and Barbara R. Cambon, "Real Estate: Historical Returns and Risks," *Journal of Portfolio Management* (Spring 1984); and Mike Miles and Tom McCue, "Commercial Real Estate Returns," *AREUEA Journal* (1984).

TABLE 1. *Annual Total Return—FRC Index and the S&P 500, 1978-85.*

Year	FRC Index	S&P 500	REITs
1978	15.9%	6.4%	−0.1%
1979	20.6	18.1	28.6
1980	17.9	31.6	20.1
1981	16.6	−4.8	9.3
1982	9.3	20.3	27.1
1983	13.3	22.3	24.5
1984	12.9	6.0	13.1
1985	9.8	31.1	5.2
Mean	14.5	16.4	16.0
Std Dev	3.7	12.0	10.0

Sources: Standard & Poor's, Frank Russell Co., and NAREIT.

lion. The underlying portfolio is diversified by product type and geographic region.

Over the 1978–85 time period, the FRC Index recorded an average annual return of 14.5%, with a standard deviation of 3.7%. (We use standard deviation as a measure of the absolute risk of an asset class.) Comparatively, the S&P 500 recorded a 16.4% average annual return, with a standard deviation of 12.4%. Because real estate returns as measured by appraisals exhibit less volatility, real estate appears to be less risky than common stock. In response to this observation and the high returns reported over 1978–81, institutional investors have increased their asset allocation to real estate over the past several years. This view is held despite the fact that real estate investment trusts (REITs), a form of securitized real estate that includes equity and debt assets, performed remarkably similarly to common stocks over 1978–85, with a 16% average annual return and a 10% standard deviation (see Table 1). This result resembles previous studies that compared equity real estate investment trusts with common stock.[3]

II. The Market Model versus the Appraisal Model

The data in Table 1 are not strictly comparable. The S&P 500 and REIT returns are based on actual market prices, while the FRC Index is overwhelmingly based on property appraisals that occur periodically. Properties are

---

3. See Keith V. Smith and David Shulman, "The Performance of Equity Real Estate Investment Trust," *Financial Analysts Journal* (September-October 1976).

typically appraised annually on their purchase anniversary date; thus, the valuation of a real estate portfolio on a given date could be based on inputs that are as much as one year old. This appraisal convention works to average returns.

More importantly, the appraisal process itself is long-term oriented; thus, as such, short-term changes in the level and structure of interest rates are less significant than in the trading orientation of the stock market. The long-run orientation is embedded in the three basic approaches to real estate appraisal:

1. income capitalization;
2. replacement cost; and
3. comparable sales.

All three approaches work to artificially smooth returns. The income capitalization approach involves forecasting long-run inflation rates to project the future income from a given property. This clearly requires some form of averaging. Conceptually, the discount rate applied to future income streams can vary with market interest rates; however, the realized income component of returns has remained remarkably stable (see Table 2). One cannot detect the extreme volatility in the market interest rates that occurred over 1978–85 in the income returns from real estate.

Although the income portion of return is not a discount rate per se, it is analogous to what those in real estate term the capitalization rate. That rate is defined as next year's income divided by value. It is the shorthand way of pricing real estate.

TABLE 2. *FRC Index*
Realized Return from
Income, 1978–85.

Year	Return from Income
1978	8.7%
1979	8.8
1980	8.4
1981	8.0
1982	7.8
1983	7.8
1984	7.2
1985	7.6

Source: Frank Russell Co. and NACREIF.

The second appraisal approach involves estimating the replacement cost of a property. This is largely a function of estimating current land and construction costs. The recent history of replacement cost appraisals has reflected overall changes in the price level. Finally, although the comparable sales approach is market-based, its utility is limited. This is because there are few sales relative to the stock of buildings, which causes significant comparability problems, because no building is exactly like another. Further, in soft markets, sales volumes tend to dry up; thus, the comparable sales data that do exist more reflect a previous boom than a current bust.

III. The S&P 500 Appraised

Stocks can be valued similarly to real estate appraisal. Assume that the market for corporations were a private one with only an occasional transaction for an entire corporation. In this scenario, appraisers would value whole corporations much as they currently appraise privately held corporations. The methodology for valuation would be similar to that for real estate, although here we emphasize the income capitalization approach.

The well-known dividend discount model is the most widely used income capitalization model.[4] The DDM follows in its simplest form:

$$P = D1/(k - g)$$

where:

P = price;
$D1$ = dividend in the next period;
k = required return; and
g = expected growth rate of future dividends.

Although there are many variations to the basic model, we make the following underlying assumptions:[5]

1. Inflation expectations equal the three-year moving-average percentage change in the consumption deflator.
2. The *required return* (k) equals the historical 6.1% premium over inflation.[6]
3. The *growth rate of future dividends* (g) equals the recent trend of growth in real gross national product (GNP) of 2.8% annually plus 85% of expected inflation.
4. The *dividend in the next period* ($D1$) equals the actual current-period dividend multiplied by $(1 + g)$.

---

4. See *Financial Analysts Journal* (November-December 1985).
5. See Tony Estep, Nick Hanson, Michelle Clayman, Cal Johnson, and Jonathan Singer, *Values and Factors* (New York: Salomon Brothers Inc, March 1981).
6. See Roger G. Ibsotson and Rex A. Sinquefield, *Stocks, Bonds, Bills and Inflation: The Past and the Future* (Charlottesville: Financial Analysts Research Foundation, 1982).

FIGURE 1. *Actual Value of the S&P 500 versus Dividend Discount Model Estimates, 1974–85 (year-end data).*

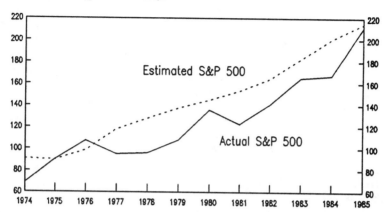

In this form, the DDM explicitly ignores current-market interest rates in defining the required return. This smooths returns, but it is actually no different from what is done in real estate appraisal. Real estate capitalization rates have been remarkably stable over the past eight years. Further, the model seems to track the year-end values of the S&P 500 reasonably well (see Figure 1).

The DDM used here is not a corporate cash flow model. Dividends represent the portion of corporate cash flow distributed to investors — not the cash flow itself. Thus, the flow of dividends is inherently more stable than the actual cash flow to the corporation over time. This distinction is important, because real estate income distributions are generally equal to cash flow. The real estate capitalization rate is applied to cash flow, which is usually fully distributed to investors. An added attribute of real estate is that the ultimate investor generally has more control over the cash flow, while the investor's agents (management) have control in the case of common stocks, which makes it difficult to estimate the actual discretionary cash flow of a corporation.

The dividend discount model results for the S&P 500 presented in Table 3 should be read with the cash flow distinction in mind. The estimated returns are remarkably stable with an average annual return of 12.1% and a standard deviation of 1.8% for the 1978–85 time period. The return is lower than the actual S&P 500, because the model valuation indicates that the stock market was undervalued in the late 1970s.

By 1985, however, the gap closed measurably (see Table 4). This result would not trouble an appraiser, because replacement cost estimates for the S&P 500 well exceeded the actual values, and the sales prices in buyouts of

TABLE 3. *Dividend Discount Model Estimate of S&P 500 Returns, 1977–86.*

Year	k	g	Actual Div.	Est. Div.	Est. S&P	Est. Return
1977					117.91	
1978	12.7%	8.4%	$5.07	$5.07	127.91	12.8%
1979	13.8	9.3	5.65	5.50	137.33	11.8
1980	15.2	10.5	6.16	6.18	144.89	10.0
1981	15.8	11.0	6.63	6.81	153.33	10.4
1982	14.6	10.0	6.87	7.36	164.35	11.7
1983	12.4	8.2	7.09	7.56	182.62	15.4
1984	10.7	6.7	7.53	7.67	200.75	14.1
1985	9.8	5.9	7.90	8.03	214.62	10.8
1986				8.37		
Mean return	12.1%					
Standard deviation	1.8					

TABLE 4. *Actual versus Dividend Discount Model Estimated Values of the S&P 500, 1978–85.*

Year	Actual S&P 500 Closing Value	Est. S&P 500 Value	Actual as a Percentage of Estimated
1978	96.11	127.91	75%
1979	107.90	137.33	79
1980	135.80	144.89	94
1981	122.60	153.33	80
1982	140.60	164.35	86
1983	164.90	182.62	90
1984	167.24	200.75	83
1985	211.28	214.62	98

entire corporations were well above the actual prices that prevailed when the transaction announcement was made.

IV. A New View

The results indicate that when measured on a common-appraisal basis, equity real estate compared with common stocks appears to be more risky than previously believed. The smoothed returns reported by real estate investment managers compared with stocks appear to largely reflect the appraisal process. If stocks were valued on the same basis as real estate, the returns would be far more stable than those reported.

Investors may be systematically underestimating real estate risk; consequently, investment allocation decisions could be biased in favor of real estate. This last point is more theoretical than practical, because most large pension funds hold less than 5% of their assets in real estate.

Investment allocation decisions involve the concept of covariance as well as variance. Even when measured by the DDM, the FRC Index exhibits extremely low correlations (essentially zero) with common stock returns. Thus, real estate remains an important asset in a diversified portfolio. Real estate's main attribute is its ability to lower the risk of a portfolio of financial assets, consistent with the traditional view of real estate's role in a portfolio.

Finally, the real need is to develop an index of real estate returns based on actual transaction prices and the pricing that would prevail in distressed markets when transactions volume is low. Only when such an index is available will the "true" returns and risks of equity real estate be known.

PART IV
Asset Allocation

39

Time Diversification
Surest Route to Lower Risk?*

Richard W. McEnally
Meade H. Willis Sr. Professor
  of Investment Banking
University of North Carolina
  — Chapel Hill

I. Another Look at Time Diversification

Will saying something often enough make it so? If the answer is yes, then time diversification is indeed the surest route to lower risk — for this has certainly been the message of a number of articles in recent years.[1]

Unfortunately, it is probably not so. Now we are all free to frame our own definitions of risk; the state mandates nothing in this respect. Nevertheless, under most reasonable definitions, risk increases rather than decreases with the time horizon.

Most people who have thought carefully about the matter seem to agree that risk relates to the chance of unpleasant surprise. Since deviations from what is expected are approximately symmetric on the upside and downside — at least in the security investments arena — some measure that considers both

*This article was published in the Summer 1985 issue of *The Journal of Portfolio Management* and has been updated by the author.

1. Peter L. Bernstein, "The Time of Your Life," *The Journal of Portfolio Management* (Summer 1976): 4; Robert A. Levy, "Stocks, Bonds, Bills, and Inflation over 52 Years," *The Journal of Portfolio Management* (Summer 1978): 18–19; William P. Lloyd and Richard L. Haney, Jr., "Time Diversification: Surest Route to Lower Risk," *The Journal of Portfolio Management* (Spring 1980): 5–9; and William P. Lloyd and Naval K. Modani, "Stocks, Bonds, Bills and Time Diversification," *The Journal of Portfolio Management* (Spring 1983): 7–11.

favorable and unfavorable deviations is often used to quantify risk. The standard deviation around the mean is popular for this purpose, the implication being that on average what occurred was expected.

Where the battle is joined is in identifying what it is to which the surprises relate.

A number of observers have looked at something like the average annualized rates of return over single-year and multiple-year horizons reported by Ibbotson and Sinquefield. The first column of Table 1 shows some summary statistics for 1-year through 5-year and 10-year horizons.[2] We can see that the standard deviation of average annualized returns does decline as the horizon lengthens. For example, the average annualized percentage returns over 5-year horizons have a standard deviation of 6.59 percent versus 21.04 percent for returns over 1-year periods. Can we then conclude that the risk of a single period tends to be averaged out as the horizon increases, much as the risk is reduced when it is averaged over more securities in a portfolio? In short, have these observers discovered the perfect risk-reducing machine?

It all sounds plausible, even if it does run counter to intuition and experience. If, however, most of us were to think deeply about the matter for a moment, without benefit of clues provided by the Ibbotson–Sinquefield or equivalent data, we would be likely to come to a different conclusion. We would recognize that the whole purpose of investing is to enhance wealth—to see the total worth of holdings increase in value—and that the relevant risk is the chance that the value of assets at the end of the horizon may diverge from our expectation. In other words what matters is unpleasant surprises in *total* returns or terminal wealth—the values to which the annual rates of return would compound—not surprises in the average *annualized* rates of return themselves.[3]

---

2. The annual returns for one-year periods and average annualized returns for the multiple-year horizons are developed directly from the Ibbotson–Sinquefield data as described in Roger G. Ibbotson and Rex A. Sinquefield, *Stocks, Bonds, Bills, and Inflation: The Past and the Future* (Charlottesville, Va.: The Financial Analysts' Research Foundation, 1982). These average annualized returns are simply geometric means of the annual returns over the appropriate holding periods. The decision to show multiple-year returns beginning with 1926 for all horizons is essentially arbitrary, but the starting year has little effect on the dispersion numbers. The data for the various horizons do not contain a uniform number of years' returns, but once again the effect is not consequential.

Notice, however, that I resist the temptation to look at all possible holding periods of a given length, in the manner of Robert Levy, who, for example, finds 28 holding periods of 25 years each in the 1926–1977 period! Such overlapping holding periods are not independent, and can give misleading impressions where investment risk analysis is concerned.

3. As stated, this argument ignores the possibility of withdrawal for consumption purposes, but it makes no difference. With consumption we would compute a series of periodic or time-weighted returns, determine their geometric mean, and compound at this average rate over the horizon.

TABLE 1. *Summary Measures of Common Stock Return Distributions.*

	Average Annualized Returns	Total Returns
Annual Horizons, 1926–1986		
Number of holding periods	61	61
Standard deviation	21.04	21.04
Variance	442.5	442.5
Mean absolute deviation	17.22	17.22
Range	95.9	95.9
Semi-standard deviation	15.47	15.47
Two-Year Horizons, 1926–1985		
Number of holding periods	30	30
Standard deviation	14.21	30.21
Variance	202.0	909.0
Mean absolute deviation	10.62	22.92
Range	76.4	158.2
Semi-standard deviation	10.91	21.70
Three-Year Horizons, 1926–1985		
Number of holding periods	20	20
Standard deviation	11.23	37.27
Variance	126.1	1389.2
Mean absolute deviation	7.08	25.88
Range	52.6	159.8
Semi-standard deviation	8.87	25.68
Four-Year Horizons, 1926–1985		
Number of holding periods	15	15
Standard deviation	9.50	48.51
Variance	90.2	2451.2
Mean absolute deviation	8.01	43.28
Range	37.3	187.3
Semi-standard deviation	7.05	34.17
Five-Year Horizons, 1926–1985		
Number of holding periods	12	12
Standard deviation	6.59	51.93
Variance	43.4	2696.2
Mean absolute deviation	5.43	41.91
Range	20.8	189.4
Semi-standard deviation	4.41	31.89
Ten-Year Horizons, 1926–1985		
Number of holding periods	6	6
Standard deviation	4.65	115.20
Variance	21.6	13269.9
Mean absolute deviation	4.09	99.44
Range	10.8	330.1
Semi-standard deviation	3.26	74.62

But lo and behold, when one looks at total holding period returns, as in the second column of Table 1, a very different picture emerges.[4] The variability in these numbers, which show the percentage change in the value of the initial investment over the horizon, now *increases* with the length of the holding period. For example, while the standard deviation of total returns over annual horizons is 21.04 percent, as noted previously, for five-year periods the standard deviation of total returns is 51.93 percent. This means that the confidence interval, the range within which an investor might anticipate ending portfolio value to fall with a given probability, has more than doubled!

II. Why It Is This Way

What appears to have misled many previous observers is excessive concentration on *average annualized* rates of return, and variations in these averages. Such periodic rates of return clearly have their place. They are, for example, indispensible in comparing rewards per unit of time over different horizon lengths, or for expressing rates of growth per unit of time. Moreover, variations in periodic returns over a specific time holding period provide an appropriate and useful way of evaluating risk, such as the risk of different investment strategies or portfolio managers. On the other hand, a comparison of variation in annualized returns over horizons of different length is a classic example of comparing things that are not comparable and is an inappropriate application of a single-period risk measure in a multiple-period investment context.

It is no accident that the standard deviation of annualized rates of return decreases with the length of the investment horizon while the standard deviation of total returns increases with the horizon. Common stock returns, and returns of other primary securities, are comparatively well behaved in a statistical sense. That is, they are approximately "independently and identically distributed" over time, so investing in them is somewhat akin to the experiment of drawing colored balls from an urn, with replacement. In such an experiment the color of one ball that is drawn does not influence the color of another, so that the probability of drawing a ball of a given color remains constant over time. As one reaches in and draws a handful of balls, the larger the handful the more likely the proportionate composition of the balls drawn

---

4. These total holding period returns are simply the average annualized returns for the respective holding periods compounded for the appropriate number of years. Formally, the annual returns must be converted to decimal returns, augmented by 1, and then raised to the nth power. The values in Table 1 are based on the resulting numbers, sometimes called wealth relatives, or wealth indexes, less 1 times 100 percent.

will approximate the composition of those in the urn. This convergence is what happens to average annualized rates of return when averaged over more and more periods.

Nevertheless, the larger the handful the larger the variation in the *number* of a given color of balls that are apt to be drawn. (This is so obvious it doesn't get much play in standard statistics discussions!) Now associate, say, a 10 percent gain in value with the red balls and a 10 percent loss with the blue balls. From a portfolio perspective what matters is the *number* of red versus blue balls, not the relative proportions of the two.[5]

Substantially the same thing can be said more simply in another way. As the investment horizon lengthens, the deviation of average periodic returns from the expected periodic return gets smaller and smaller. But this effect is more than offset by the fact that the smaller and smaller deviations are multiplied by more and more occurrences.[6]

What of risk measures other than standard deviations of returns? Table 1 also shows what happens when risk is measured by some other popular measures of dispersion of outcomes, including the variance, mean absolute deviation, range, and semi-standard deviation considering only outcomes below the mean. As long as the focus is on total returns over the investment horizon, risk uniformly increases with the length of the horizon.

---

5. A detailed exploration of the statistics of such series is beyond the scope of this article. However, it is worth noting that for an independently and identically distributed series that reproduces additively, such as continuously compounded security returns, the variance of the cumulative result (that is, the total return in log form) increases proportionately with the length of the time horizon, while the standard deviation increases with the square root of the horizon. On the other hand, the variance of the average outcome (that is, the average annual return in log form) decreases at a rate equal to the reciprocal of the proportionate increase in the horizon. For example, a doubling in the horizon cuts the variance in half. The relationships become considerably more complex for series that reproduce multiplicatively, such as periodic security returns. These properties have been used in investigations of whether stock market returns are independent; see William E. Young, "Random Walk of Stock Prices: A Test of the Variance-Time Function," *Econometrica 39,* no. 5 (September 1971): 797–812.

An excellent review of the statistics of multiperiod wealth distributions is provided by William E. Avera in a dissertation completed at the University of North Carolina in 1972, "The Geometric Mean Strategy as a Theory of Multiperiod Portfolio Selection." Unfortunately, this dissertation remains unpublished.

6. Or with discrete returns, raised to higher and higher powers. But as the preceding footnote implies, this is so only if the behavior of the return series is approximately independent. If, for example, stock market returns showed sufficient negative correlation (for example, a large loss in one period increases the chance of gain in the next period), then it would be possible for the variation in the total returns actually to decline as the horizon lengthens. Indeed, when appropriate techniques for estimating the changes in variances and standard deviations as the horizon changes are applied to the stock market series in Table 1, they consistently overestimate the variations. This result suggests that, at least over long horizons, stock market returns do display some mean-reverting behavior.

Several authors have taken a somewhat different tack on risk, arguing in effect that what matters in investment is the likelihood of doing worse than some lower limit.[7] They then show that, historically, the chance of common stocks having negative nominal or real returns decreases as the investment horizon is extended.[8] If these are the kinds of risks they worry about, no one can say they are wrong. Personally, when I look at, say, the annual returns over five-year horizons in the numbers underlying Table 1, I draw rather cold comfort from the fact that they are all positive since in 4 of the 12 cases these returns averaged 3.3 percent or less per annum. But risk is in the eye of the beholder.

III. When Time Diversification Makes Sense

Is there any sense in which some sort of "time diversification" is valid? I believe that there is, and that it is the sort of thing which is implied by the title of one of Peter Bernstein's editorial comments in *The Journal of Portfolio Management* several years ago, "The Time of Your Life."[9] It is very different from the erroneous notion that risk decreases with the length of the holding period. It is based on the simple premise that predicting "good" and "bad" markets is difficult if not impossible. Under these conditions, if we investors hope to achieve even average returns, then we must "be there" year after year in order to do so.

To see what I mean, consider the data in Table 2. The first line shows the geometric mean annual return over the 61 years 1926–1986 for the same Ibbotson–Sinquefield data used to construct Table 1. The figure is about 10 percent, a figure many investors have engraved on their minds as *the* long-run return from holding common stocks. Successive lines of the table show the geometric mean return when the best single year's return (54 percent in 1933) is removed and the geometric mean is recomputed over the remaining 60 observations, the second best (52.5 percent in 1954) is removed, and so on. What is so striking about this simple experiment is that the 10 percent is extremely dependent on the returns of just a few years. For example, simply

---

7. For example, Bernstein comments on the fact that common stock returns over 20-year horizons in some unspecified span of years always exceeded the inflation rate, while Levy counts the number of loss periods (total returns less than zero) or periods with returns of less than the rate of return on stocks, corporate bonds, and Treasury bills over horizons of 1, 5, 10, and 25 years as shown by the Ibbotson–Sinquefield data.

8. This means that the relationship between the mean and the standard deviation of both nominal and real total returns is such that the distributions shift to the right (higher average returns) more quickly that the left tail (adverse outcomes) extends itself; thus, the probability of returns below zero decreases. This result is in no way inconsistent with the observation that the dispersion in the probability distribution of total returns increases with time.

9. (Summer 1976): 4.

TABLE 2. *Effects of Large Annual Returns on Geometric Mean Return, 1926–1986.*

Return Deleted (%)	Year	Returns Remaining	Geometric Mean (%)
00.0	0000	61	9.98
54.0	1933	60	9.37
52.5	1954	59	8.75
47.7	1935	58	8.18
43.6	1928	57	7.64
43.4	1958	56	7.09
37.5	1927	55	6.61
37.2	1975	54	6.11
36.4	1945	53	5.61
33.9	1936	52	5.13
32.4	1980	51	4.65
32.2	1985	50	4.16
31.7	1950	49	3.67
31.6	1955	48	3.15
31.1	1938	47	2.63
26.9	1961	46	2.16
25.9	1943	45	1.68
24.0	1951	44	1.22
24.0	1967	43	0.75
23.8	1976	42	0.25

eliminating the five best years cuts the mean return to only 7.09 percent. The last entry shows that if the best 19, or 31 percent, of the total observations are eliminated, then the average return is only marginally above zero. (Eliminating the twentieth would reduce it to *below* zero.)

When I showed these numbers to a group of institutional investment managers recently, one of them exclaimed, "There have only been four of these great years in my life!" I think he might have been underestimating his age a bit, but his observation makes the point nonetheless. There will only be a very few "great years" during our professional lifetimes; if we are not in the market when they come, we are probably doomed to a lifetime average of below-average returns. As Bernstein observed, "What assurance can we have that any particular moment is the *best* time to hold any particular asset or asset group? Or, indeed, that any particular moment is so fraught with horrendous prospects that we should flee from any sector of the capital markets entirely?"

40

Volatility of Pension Expense under FASB Statement 87*

Lawrence N. Bader
Vice President
Bond Portfolio Analysis
Salomon Brothers Inc

Martin L. Leibowitz
Managing Director
Bond Portfolio Analysis
Salomon Brothers Inc

I. Introduction

Financial Accounting Standards Board (FASB) Statement 87 is having a far-reaching influence on the reporting of pension liabilities and expenses by companies that sponsor defined pension plans. Many companies have already adopted FASB 87 and found it very beneficial, lowering pension expense by several hundred million dollars in some instances. Results may not be as gratifying for those companies that delay adopting FASB 87 until compliance becomes mandatory in 1987. For the great majority of companies, however, the initial effect of adopting the new rules is to lower pension expense.

The lowering of expense results from essentially transitory phenomena. Most important are the one-time revaluation of pension plan assets to market value and the use of current market interest rates for valuing pension liabilities. In calculating these values, plan sponsors have generally used five-year moving averages, which are well below current market value, and interest rate assumptions that, until this year, were well below market rates. An enduring result of FASB 87, however, is the potential volatility of pension expense. This volatility results primarily from the sensitivity of pension obligations to changes in market interest rates, and can be managed only with

---

*Copyright © 1986 by Salomon Brothers Inc.

an understanding of how those changes affect pension assets, liabilities and expenses. This article aims to promote such an understanding by illustrating the sometimes surprising impact that different economic scenarios would have on two typical pension plans.

II. Determining Pension Expense Under FASB 87

Pension expense under FASB 87 is the sum of several items: service cost, net interest cost and amortization cost.[1]

- The *service cost* is the actuarial present value of pension benefits credited for service during the current year.
- The *net interest cost* is equal to interest on the "projected benefit obligation" (the actuarial present value of pension benefits credited for service before the current year), *less* the expected return on plan assets.

  If the interest rate used to determine the projected benefit obligation equals the expected earnings rate on plan assets, the net interest cost is simply the interest on the plan deficit, if any. An overfunded plan produces an interest *credit* equal to the interest on the plan surplus.
- The *amortization cost* is the charge or credit that results from amortizing the plan deficit or surplus. Deficit or surplus accumulated at the date of transition to FASB 87 is aggregated into the "transition amount." Additional deficit or surplus can develop after transition as a result of plan amendments ("prior service cost") or deviations of plan experience from that anticipated by the actuarial assumptions ("actuarial gains and losses"). These three types of deficit or surplus are generally amortized over the future service of the active plan participants. Actuarial gains and losses, however, need not be amortized until their cumulative amount exceeds 10% of either the assets or the projected benefit obligation, whichever is greater.

III. Sources of Volatility

FASB 87 does not introduce significant new volatility on the asset side of pension accounting. After the initial revaluation of plan assets to market value, plan sponsors will be permitted to average subsequent market value changes over five years, as is now common practice.

---

1. For a more comprehensive discussion, see Lawrence N. Bader and Martin L. Leibowitz, *An Overview of FASB Statement 87 on Pension Accounting* (New York: Salomon Brothers Inc, November 1986).

On the liability side, however, FASB 87 introduces substantial potential volatility. The interest rate used to determine the service cost and projected benefit obligation is the "settlement rate" — the interest rate at which pension benefits can be settled through an annuity purchase.

This rate is redetermined each year based on current market conditions — in contrast to the pre-FASB 87 practice of using a stable, below-market interest rate assumption. Since pension obligations extend over many decades, their discounted values are very sensitive to changes in interest rates. This interest-rate sensitivity can cause severe fluctuations in pension liabilities and expenses.[2] For example, a drop in interest rates can increase the following expense components:

- Service cost, representing the discounted value of pension benefits earned during the year, will rise when the discount rate falls — generally, service cost will increase by 10%–20% for each 1% drop in rates. The sensitivity would be somewhat less for a pay-related plan if the assumed salary growth rates, and therefore projected pension benefits, decline in tandem with interest rates.
- The projected benefit obligation will also increase with a decline in interest rates, again with a potential offset for a declining salary growth assumption. This increase may generate an actuarial loss requiring amortization.
- The expected return on assets, a credit against expense, may decrease if the interest rate decline necessitates a lower assumption for the expected long-term rate of return on assets.

Of course, the decline in interest rates would increase the value of interest-sensitive assets, thereby offsetting some or all of these effects.

IV. Description of Sample Pension Plans

We will use the two sample pension plans described below to illustrate the range of responses of FASB 87 pension expenses to a variety of economic conditions. Table 1 compares their main features. The major differences between the two plans are as follows:

Benefit Formula Plan A provides a pension related to final pay, such as 2% of the employee's final five-year average pay for each year of service. Final-pay plans, which are commonly used for salaried workforces, have

---

2. See Terence C. Langetieg, Lawrence N. Bader, Martin L. Leibowitz, and Alfred Weinberger, "Measuring the Effective Duration of Pension Liabilities," in *Advances in Bond Analysis and Portfolio Strategies,* edited by Frank J. Fabozzi and T. Dessa Garlicki (Chicago: Probus Publishing, 1987).

TABLE 1. *Sample Plan Statistics at January 1, 1987 ($ thousands).*

	Plan A: Overfunded Plan	Plan B: Underfunded Plan
Benefit Formula	Final Average Pay	Flat Dollar
Assets		
Market value	$125,000	$50,000
Equity percentage	65%	50%
Equity dividend rate	3%	3%
Fixed income percentage	35%	50%
Fixed income duration	5	5
Liabilities		
Projected Benefit Obligation (PBO)	$100,000	$100,000
PBO duration		
Salary growth rate constant	15	11
Salary growth rate changes	8	11
Service cost	$5,000	$2,000
Service cost duration		
Salary growth rate constant	20	18
Salary growth rate changes	10	18
Cash Flow		
Annual contributions	0	$9,000
Annual benefit payments	$3,500	$7,000
Average Future Service	15 years	15 years

generally become well funded in recent years, as contributions were based on below-market actuarial interest assumptions while market values appreciated substantially.

Plan B, like most poorly funded plans in the United States, uses a flat-dollar pension formula, such as $20 monthly for each year of service. Flat-dollar plans are commonly used for unions, with the dollar level being periodically negotiated upward. The periodic increases cannot be prefunded on a tax-deductible basis, and most have been funded over the 30-year periods following their adoption. Many of these plans have, therefore, been chronically underfunded, with asset bases insufficient to benefit significantly from the strong markets of the past few years.

Assets The overfunded plan is invested somewhat more aggressively than average, with 65% in equities, while the underfunded plan has a 50/50 allocation. The equity portfolios have dividend rates averaging 3%. The fixed-income portfolios have durations of 5, approximating that of the Salomon Brothers Broad Investment-Grade Bond Index™ and implying that a 1%

decrease in interest rates would result in approximately a 5% appreciation in fixed-income market values. (This approximate relationship between the duration of an asset or liability and its response to interest rate movements is used throughout this article.) Appreciation in equities is smoothed over a five-year period, so interest sensitivity of the equity portfolio, which would be modest at best,[3] will be ignored.

Liabilities Both plans have projected benefit obligations of $100 million. Plan B, with a large proportion of retirees, has a PBO duration of 11.[4] Two figures are shown for Plan A. The first, 15, indicates that a 1% decrease in the discount rate applied to the PBO cash flow would increase the PBO by 15%. The second, 8, is based on the assumption that a 1% decrease in the discount rate would be accompanied by a 1% drop in salary growth rates, thereby reducing the PBO cash flow and partially offsetting the effect of the lower discount rates; the result would be an increase of only 8%. (Plan B, with its fixed-dollar benefits, does not have this dual sensitivity.)

Plan A has a larger proportion of active employees than Plan B and therefore a larger service cost. It also has two service cost durations: 20 if salary growth rates do not change with changes in discount rates, and 10 if they do.

Cash Flow Plan A, being overfunded, has no contributions being made; contributions to Plan B are $9 million annually. Contributions and benefit payments are assumed to be made at the end of the year.

Actuarial Basis Both plans are using the same actuarial basis on the date of adoption of FASB 87, as shown in Table 2.

The asset valuation method is designed to minimize expense volatility. It recognizes changes in fixed-income security values immediately, since they should correlate with and therefore help to offset changes in liability values caused by interest rate changes. The asset valuation method smooths changes in equity values over a five-year period; while equity prices tend to move somewhat in response to market interest rate changes, their noninterest-related movements are far more dramatic and could cause severe fluctuations in pension expense if reflected immediately.

Projections Apart from changes due to the accrual of interest or fund earnings and changes due to the interest sensitivity of assets and liabilities,

---

3. See Martin L. Leibowitz, *Total Portfolio Duration: A New Perspective on Asset Allocation* (New York: Salomon Brothers Inc, February 1986).
4. See Langetieg, Bader, Leibowitz, and Weinberger, "Measuring the Effective Duration of Pension Liabilities."

TABLE 2. *Sample Plan Actuarial Basis.*

Actuarial discount rate (settlement rate)	8.5%
Expected long-term rate of return on plan assets	8.5%
Amortization of actuarial gains and losses	Minimum rate required by FASB 87[a]
Asset valuation	
Fixed-income securities	Market value
Equities	Five-year average market value

a. Amortization applies only to gains and losses of more than 10%. Such gains and losses are amortized over the average future service of active participants.

we assume that all data in Table 1 remain constant. The actuarial discount rate changes in a specified way for each economic scenario. Because accounting policies regarding adjustment of the expected long-term rate of return on plan assets have not yet become clear, two possibilities are considered:

1. The expected rate of return is held constant because of its long-term nature; and alternatively,
2. The expected rate of return is kept equal to the settlement rate, since at any given time the settlement rate is the market estimate of the long-term expected rate of return. (This reasoning applies to bonds, at least. For simplicity, this article ignores the argument that the expected rate of return on a diversified portfolio should be set and maintained somewhat above the settlement rate, to reflect the expected superiority of returns on common stock and other equity investments.)

For a comparison among the three economic scenarios presented here, Table 3 shows baseline forecasts, which give the three-year expense figures that would obtain if the actuarial assumptions were precisely realized throughout the period.

TABLE 3. *Baseline Expense Forecasts.*

	1987	1988	1989
Plan A	$1,208	$1,453	$1,718
Plan B	9,583	9,350	9,096

The increase of Plan A costs is due to the unfavorable trend in the net interest cost: Liabilities and interest thereon continue to grow, while assets and their expected return do not keep pace because no contributions are being made. Contributions *are* being made to Plan B, so the deficit is shrinking and net interest costs are falling.

V. Economic Scenario 1: "Good Times"

Table 4 shows the favorable conditions of Economic Scenario 1, together with three-year summaries for Plans A and B.

The cost increases for the overfunded Plan A, under what appear to be favorable economic conditions, are quite striking, with costs rising by over 250% if a continued 8.5% asset return is justified and by nearly 500% if the expected asset return falls to 6.5%.

The escalation of expense results from several factors:

- Equity returns are, in effect, only 5% during 1987, because the 3% dividend rate is recognized in full but the 10% appreciation is spread over five years.
- Fixed-income returns during 1987 are equal to the initial yield of 8.5% plus 10% appreciation, which results from the 2% interest rate decline and the duration of 5.

TABLE 4. *Economic Scenario 1.*

Settlement rate	Drops from 8.5% to 6.5% at the end of 1987.		
Equities	Appreciate by 10% in 1987 and 1988 (in addition to 3% dividend rate).		
Salary growth rate	No change.		

	Three-Year Expense Summaries		
	1987	1988	1989
Plan A			
Baseline (all assumptions realized)	$1,208	$1,453	$1,718
Expected rate of return 8.5%	1,208	4,393	4,686
Expected rate of return 6.5%	1,208	7,068	7,302
Plan B			
Baseline (all assumptions realized)	$9,583	$9,350	$9,096
Expected rate of return 8.5%	9,583	9,865	9,600
Expected rate of return 6.5%	9,583	11,028	10,807

- The "liability return,"[5] however, is 30% — the 2% interest rate change multiplied by the duration of 15. The result is that the $25-million surplus disappears, turning into a deficit of $2.6 million. Amortization of the resulting actuarial loss, after five-year spreading of the equity gain and application of the 10% corridor, amounts to $1.1 million. The net interest cost also changes, by an amount that depends on which asset return assumption is used.
- Apart from the disappearance of the surplus, the service cost rises by 40% (2% interest rate change multiplied by 20 duration), from $5 million to $7 million.

Both in percentage and absolute dollar terms, the consequence of the change in rates is far less dramatic for the underfunded Plan B than for Plan A. This is due primarily to the fact that the service cost, which is highly vulnerable to interest rate movements, is a relatively small part of the cost for an underfunded plan.

VI. Economic Scenario 2: "Stagflation" (Inflation without Growth)

Table 5 shows the unfavorable conditions of Economic Scenario 2, together with the three-year expense summaries.

In contrast to the "favorable" Economic Scenario 1, the "unfavorable" Scenario 2 is remarkably benign in its effect on Plan A's pension expense. The increase in the interest rate used to discount liabilities is very helpful, although somewhat muted by the increase in salary growth rates. The five-year averaging of equity values defers the effect of the equity losses, although the bond losses are recognized in full; the resulting asset loss is outweighed by the liability decrease caused by the increase in the discount rate. Overall, if the expected return on assets is raised to 10.5%, there is actually "pension income" rather than expense in 1988. Even if the expected return is held at 8.5%, the near-term increase over the baseline figure is far less dramatic than under the other scenarios considered here.

This scenario is uniformly favorable for Plan B because of its fixed benefits; the favorable effect of the increase in the discount rate is not offset by an increase in expected benefits caused by inflation. Of course, such benefit increases may ultimately become necessary. Under FASB 87, however, plan

---

5. See Martin L. Leibowitz, "Liability Returns: A New Perspective on Asset Allocation," in *Advances in Bond Analysis and Portfolio Strategies,* edited by Frank J. Fabozzi and T. Dessa Garlicki (Chicago: Probus Publishing, 1987).

TABLE 5. *Economic Scenario 2.*

Settlement rate	Increases from 8.5% to 10.5% at the end of 1987.
Equities	Depreciate by 10% in 1987 and 1988.
Salary growth rate	Increases by 2%.

	Three-Year Expense Summaries		
	1987	1988	1989
Plan A			
Baseline (all assumptions realized)	$1,208	$1,453	$1,718
Expected rate of return 8.5%	1,208	1,705	2,796
Expected rate of return 10.5%	1,208	(725)	370
Plan B			
Baseline (all assumptions realized)	$9,583	$9,350	$9,096
Expected rate of return 8.5%	9,583	8,037	8,172
Expected rate of return 10.5%	9,583	7,005	7,125

amendments are reflected in pension expense only when they are made,[6] so the cost effect of such amendments would be deferred, while the saving from the higher interest rate is immediate.

VII. Economic Scenario 3: Disinflation

Table 6 shows the unfavorable conditions of Economic Scenario 3, together with the three-year expense summaries.

These results are unfavorable for Plan A, but it is interesting to compare them with the even more unfavorable results of Scenario 1, "Good Times." Scenario 3 differs from "Good Times" in that the salary growth rate declines by 2% instead of remaining stable, and equities depreciate by 10% rather than appreciating by 10%. Because of the five-year spreading of changes in equity values, the market performance is slow to help in Scenario 1 and slow to hurt in Scenario 3. The Scenario 3 drop in the salary growth rate, however, reduces the liability immediately, or moderates the rise caused by the discount rate decrease; FASB 87 does not provide smoothing of liabilities comparable to that available for assets.[7]

---

6. FASB 87, paragraph 41 provides that future plan amendments pursuant to a "substantive commitment" by the company may be anticipated, but application of this provision will be rare.
7. In practice, the benefit of the lower salary growth assumption may be difficult to realize. Although interest rates and salary growth rates are likely to show a reasonable correlation over time, the salary growth assumption may have considerable short-term "stickiness," particularly on the downside, and may be slow to respond to interest rate changes.

TABLE 6. *Economic Scenario 3.*

Settlement rate	Decreases from 8.5% to 6.5% at the end of 1987.
Equities	Depreciate by 10% in 1987 and 1988.
Salary growth rate	Decreases by 2%.

	Three-Year Expense Summaries		
	1987	1988	1989
Plan A			
Baseline (all assumptions realized)	$1,208	$1,453	$1,718
Expected rate of return 8.5%	1,208	1,952	3,316
Expected rate of return 6.5%	1,208	4,561	5,720
Plan B			
Baseline (all assumptions realized)	$9,583	$9,350	$9,096
Expected rate of return 8.5%	9,583	10,031	10,151
Expected rate of return 6.5%	9,583	11,173	11,285

The results for Plan B are unfavorable, slightly worse than those of Scenario 1. Since the benefits of Plan B are independent of the salary growth rate, the only difference between Scenarios 1 and 3 is the poor equity performance in Scenario 3. As explained, the effect of good and bad equity performance is spread so that the impact on the three-year expense is negligible.

VIII. Conclusion

As the examples show, FASB 87's requirement to measure pension liabilities at market interest rates can lead to surprising and adverse movements in pension expense. What can be done to minimize these movements, without compromising the long-term objective of securing benefits at minimum cost? There is no single solution to the problems of all companies, or even to all the problems of any single company, but there are ways to control volatility.

Actuarial Policy

Selection of the Settlement Rate   The wording of FASB 87 has fostered a widespread belief that the settlement rate is not a unique interest rate for a particular plan at a particular date, but any rate between the Pension Benefit Guaranty Corporation rate and the rates available on high-quality fixed-income securities, which is typically a 2%–3% range. The FASB has indicated that this view is not correct, and it may issue guidance to tighten the range. Plan sponsors may, however, retain some flexibility to move the assumed settlement rate by less than the market movement would suggest.

Selection of the Salary Growth Rate   As indicated in the discussion of Plan A under Scenario 3, moving the assumed salary growth rate in tandem with the settlement rate can help significantly in reducing volatility, by shortening the effective durations of the projected benefit obligation and service cost. Any change in the assumed salary growth rate would have to be disclosed in the corporate annual report, which might have undesirable labor relations consequences.

Selection of the Expected Long-Term Rate of Return on Plan Assets   FASB 87 gives only vague guidance on this assumption, so companies are apparently free to set this rate in accordance with subjective long-term views rather than being tied to current market rates. The illustrations in this article indicate that keeping the rate stable, or at least keeping a floor under it, will generally promote expense stability, since the main threat to expense stability is a decline in interest rates.

Pension Fund Investment Strategy

Investment strategies should be set primarily for the long term, with plan sponsors focusing on benefit security and cost control over time. Some companies may feel that volatility can be controlled through actuarial adjustments. Others may feel that as long as rates bounce back eventually, they can ignore short-term fluctuations. (Prolonged rate shifts, however, can mean real economic loss.) Companies whose potential pension expense fluctuations are material relative to their earnings may, however, need to constrain their long-term strategies with concern for short-term fluctuations. This concern may be particularly strong when a significant decline in interest rates appears possible. Because liability durations are generally much longer than total portfolio durations, lengthening the portfolio duration—by holding more bonds, longer bonds or derivative instruments—will generally be helpful in moderating fluctuations. Complete protection against interest-related expense volatility may, however, require durations that are unachievably long, or undesirable for other reasons.

Hedging Outside the Plan

A company may be concerned about the risk of pension expense fluctuations but unwilling or unable to achieve the desired protection within the plan. Such a company may consider hedging its interest rate risk outside the plan —with bond futures, for example. This approach involves evaluating pension expense in terms of its interest rate risk, like any other corporate revenue or expense item; if the total interest rate risk faced by the company is a problem, it can then be hedged. Note that a natural hedge may exist in that declining interest rates may benefit other aspects of the company's operations at the same time that they increase pension expense.

The problem of stabilizing expense is not a simple one, especially because there are other destabilizing factors not considered here. Further, an expense stabilization policy will not be fully consistent with other pension objectives, such as stabilizing contributions or avoiding FASB 87's balance sheet liability and, of course, the fundamental objective of maximizing long-term benefit security at minimum cost. Plan sponsors must, however, understand the risks to which their earnings statements are exposed and, if appropriate, take steps to moderate those risks while they pursue their longer-term objectives.

41

Risk Management in a FASB 87 Environment

Edward A. Brill
Head, Quantitative Investment Products
Bankers Trust Investment Management Ltd.

Is FASB (Financial Accounting Standards Board) 87 a relatively harmless accounting convention or could it adversely affect your pension fund's balance sheet and earnings statement? Does FASB 87 reflect the economic realities and funding status risk of your fund? If so, how should you be redefining your risk? Indeed, what should you be doing differently to manage this risk?

I. Introduction

FASB 87 forces fund managers to deal with the volatility of fund surplus, rather than just the volatility of fund assets, by insisting the fund recognize certain changes in funding status on both the balance sheet and earnings statement. These include changes in asset value and changes in liabilities as accompanies a change in the discount factor.[1]

As concerns the balance sheet, FASB 87 demands the following of a fund:

- That any "deficit" be placed on its balance sheet at year's end
- That a deficit (surplus) be calculated by valuing fund assets at year end, and liabilities as the present value of vested and accrued benefits comprising the Accumulated Benefit Obligation

---

1. Lawrence Bader and Martin Leibowitz, "An Overview of FASB Statement 87 on Pension Accounting," Salomon Brothers, New York, 1986.

- That "significant" changes in surplus (deficit) be recognized on the earnings statement

As concerns the earnings statement, FASB 87 permits a fund to smooth the effects of annual surplus fluctuations on annual pension expense in the following ways:

- Cumulative surplus changes less than 10 percent of assets (or 10 percent of liabilities, if larger) are ignored.
- Changes in excess of 10 percent can be amortized over 10–15 years.
- Asset value can be based on a five-year moving average.

What are the likely effects of FASB 87? In looking back over 1980–1986, Leibowitz and Bader[2] found that *disclosed* funding ratios of the *Fortune* 500 increased from 1980 to 1986, while the FASB 87 equivalent for the same companies and time period were decreased!

In other words some pension funds' euphoria over stock market gains would surely have been dampened by red ink on both the balance sheet and earnings statement. And all due to a drop in interest rates!

Can a case be made for ignoring current interest rates and arguing that sooner or later rates will come full circle? If the fund's short-term risk tolerance and position on interest rates permit, yes! If the sponsor is contemplating plan termination, or if there is concern over short-term balance sheet impact, no!

Will a dedicated bond portfolio solve the problem of a potential drop in rates (rising liabilities) while assuring funding status? Certainly! But at what opportunity cost? If interest rates rise, we lose value. If rates drop, we potentially lose participation in a bull stock market that may outperform a dedicated bond portfolio.

Finally, how should one define risk? Do we address the risk of becoming underfunded, or the risk of the fund's surplus declining below a certain value, or the overall risk of the parent company?

II. Asset Risk or Asset-Liability Risk?

Asset Risk Management

A popular method of asset risk management is that of protecting the fund's assets over a fixed time horizon, through a system a dynamic hedging designed to replicate the effect of a protective put. We term this Standard Portfolio Protection (SPP).

SPP provides a fund with the opportunity to share in the upside of a risky asset, such as stock, while maintaining a prespecified minimum level

---

2. Martin Leibowitz and Lawrence Bader, "FASB 87—Equivalent Funding Ratios: Pension Surplus Trends, 1980–86," Salomon Brothers, New York, March 1987.

of return over the given time horizon. It is accomplished by dynamically allocating assets between the risky asset (stocks) and a reserve asset such as T-bills.[3] A dynamic strategy allows for limited downside risk and greater upside potential than a static mix. See Figure 1.

What about the other side of the asset liability equation? What of the possibility that interest rates might drop? For those funds unable or unwilling to tolerate large fluctuations in surplus, and for those not otherwise hedged against a drop in interest rates, SPP would appear inappropriate on both economic and accounting grounds.

Protecting against a Drop in Interest Rates?

A drop in interest rates reflects the economic reality that a dedicated bond portfolio, necessary to fund liabilities, costs more. FASB 87 forces the fund to recognize a portion of the added cost on a stand-alone basis. For a sponsor contemplating termination, the complete effect of the rate will be felt.

The recent period beginning in December 1985, is a prime example. Figure 2, taken from Salomon Brothers' FASB 87-Equivalent Funding Ratios,[4] compares asset and liability growth over the past several years for a hypothetical plan with assets taken to be the Standard and Poor's 500 and liabilities assumed to follow the 10-year new "A" industrial rates.

Dedication

Why not simply neutralize the risk of an interest rate drop with a fully dedicated bond portfolio? Dedication is designed to act as a "liability-matching" portfolio in the sense that matching durations matches the interest rate sensitivities of the liabilities and bond portfolio. To the extent that the two move in concert, there is assurance that liabilities will be funded. The surplus can be left unhedged or be protected to a desired floor.

Full dedication and immunization is plausible but may be too conservative for a fund whose risk tolerance allows it to seek potential added return from a "risky" asset, such as the stock market.

There is an alternative.

III. Asset Liability Protection

What may be appropriate to a fund is a relative protection strategy, where one protects the financial condition of the fund as measured by its asset/liability ratio. The goal is to capture the better performing of two assets — stocks and a dedicated bond portfolio — protecting this ratio to a specified

3. Mark Rubinstein, "Alternative Paths to Portfolio Insurance," *Financial Analysts' Journal* (July-August 1985).
4. Leibowitz and Bader, "FASB 87 – Equivalent Funding Ratios."

FIGURE 1. ***Profit Pattern of Standard Portfolio Protection.***

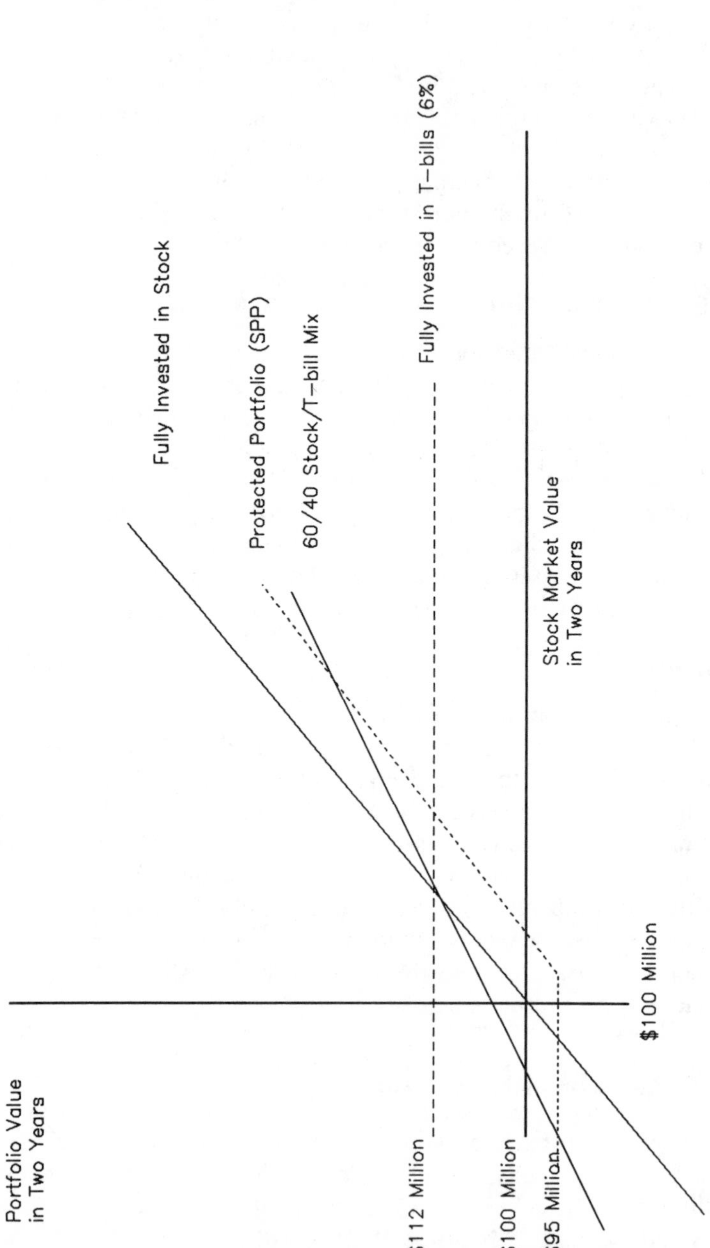

FIGURE 2. *Asset/Liability Ratio for Hypothetical Plan, 1980–1986.*

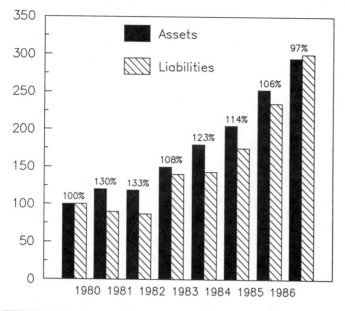

Source: Leibowitz and Bader, "FASB 87—Equivalent Funding Ratios," Salomon Brothers, New York, March 1987.

floor while capturing the bulk of an upward move in the stock market relative to liabilities (and relative to a fully dedicated bond portfolio).

This strategy, termed asset liability protection, may take the form of option replication over a specified time horizon or a perpetual-style policy. Either way, the strategy takes the form of conditional asset allocation, dynamically managed between a risky asset (stocks) and a reserve asset (dedicated/immunized bond portfolio). With option replication, one seeks to replicate the payoff pattern of an option, over a fixed time horizon, to exchange one risky asset (stock) for another (dedicated bond portfolio).

The strategy directly addresses funding status and FASB 87, by protecting assets to a floor relative to liabilities. Moreover, any positive correlation between the reserve and risk assets would lower the cost of protection.

IV. Illustrations

Standard Portfolio Protection

SPI seeks to protect a fund's assets from dropping below some absolute floor while allowing it to share in the upside of a risky asset. The strategy may be accomplished by shifting the asset mix between the risky asset (stocks or bonds) and the hedge asset (say, T-bills) in a way that replicates the payoff pattern of a protective put. It also may take the form of a perpetual-style strategy that will be discussed later. The floor that is chosen is absolute.[5]

Note how SPP compares with being fully invested in stocks, with being fully invested in a "riskless" asset (T-bills) and with a 60/40 static mix. For example, in Figure 2 we have assets of $100 million, and set a floor of $95 million over two years. SPP generates a conditional asset allocation strategy dynamically managed to give the desired payoff pattern at the end of two years. The upside cost of SPP is the percentage of underperformance by the strategy relative to an unhedged (fully invested) program. If our upside cost were 3 percent, then a stock market increase of 30 percent over two years to the $130 million level would net us $126.1 million—or 97 percent of what we could have had were we fully invested. Our "upside capture" is 97 percent.

A higher floor, say $100 million, would result in a lower upside capture, say 95 percent. Note how the profit pattern of the SPP strategy compares to being fully invested in either the risky or reserve asset. One can see that the strategy is an attempt to capture the better of two assets, stocks or T-bills.

The upside cost can be estimated in advance from options pricing theory by estimating market volatility and interest rates. However, due to replication error (discrete tracking of a continuous process), misestimation of volatility, changing interest rates, and other factors, the upside cost can be estimated to be within some confidence band.

Again SPP seeks to protect assets from falling below a dollar floor.

Asset Liability Protection

Protecting the fund's asset/liability ratio (or surplus) is a strategy that protects the assets to a floor relative to liabilities, so that the ratio (or surplus) is protected while allowing the fund to share in the upside of the risky asset relative to liabilities. The protection is accomplished by shifting between a risky asset (stocks) and the reserve asset (a liability-matching dedicated bond portfolio). The policy may be perpetual or fixed life.[6]

For example, suppose we begin with assets of $100 million, the present value of liabilities at $80 million, and therefore an initial ratio of 1.25. If we set the floor ratio at 1.15 over two years, the replication of a protective put (to exchange the risky asset for the "safe" bond portfolio) will generate a conditional asset allocation strategy to give the desired payoff pattern after two years. (See Figure 3.)

5. Rubinstein, "Alternative Paths to Portfolio Insurance."
6. William Margrabe, "The Value of an Option to Exchange One Asset for Another," *Journal of Finance* (March 1978).

FIGURE 3. *Profit Pattern of Asset-Liability Protection.*

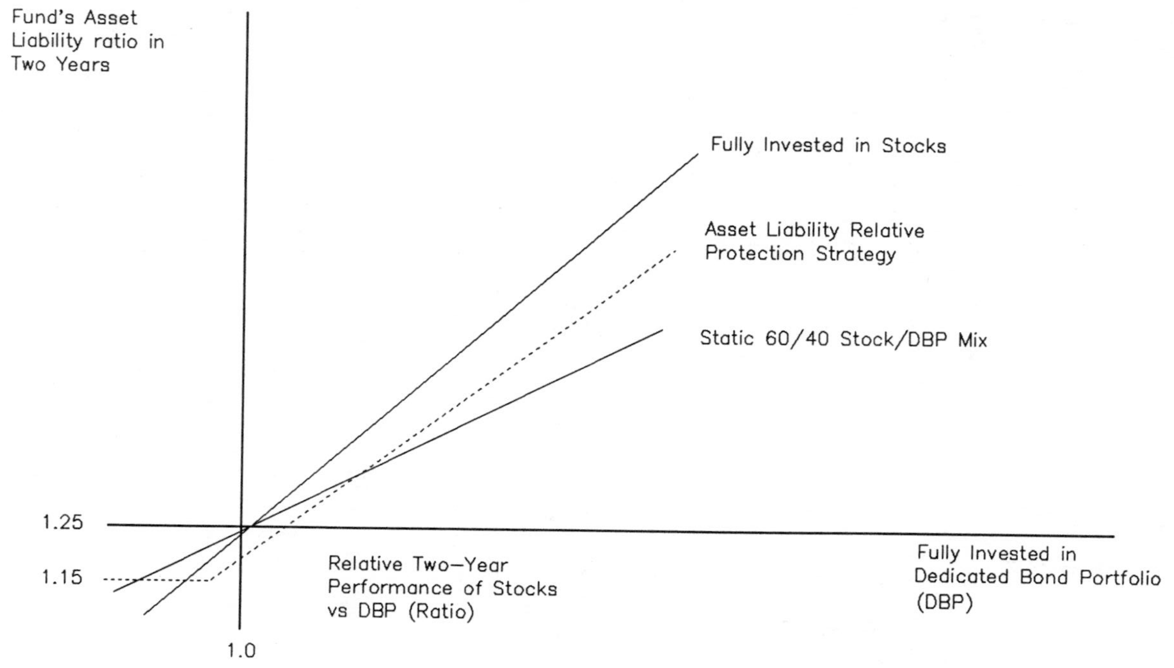

Fund's Asset
Liability ratio in
Two Years

Fully Invested in Stocks

Asset Liability Relative
Protection Strategy

Static 60/40 Stock/DBP Mix

Fully Invested in
Dedicated Bond Portfolio
(DBP)

Relative Two-Year
Performance of Stocks
vs DBP (Ratio)

1.25

1.15

1.0

Note that the horizontal axis represents the relative performance of the risky asset to the dedicated bond portfolio over two years, while the vertical axis represents the financial condition of the fund as measured by the asset/liability ratio. The upside cost of protection in this case is the percentage of underperformance by the strategy relative to an unhedge program (fully invested in the risky asset).

Suppose our upside cost is 2 percent, and suppose a stock market increase of 30 percent in two years is accompanied by an increase in liabilities of 10 percent. The resultant increase in the asset/liability ratio would have been to $130/88 = 1.477$, had we remained fully invested in stocks. Had we adopted a 60/40 static mix of stocks and dedicated bonds, our ratio would have been 1.39 $[(60 \times 1.3 + 40 \times 1.1)/88]$. With asset liability protection we would have "captured" 98 percent of 1.477 or 1.447.

On the downside, suppose the market stayed flat at the $100 million level, while liabilities increased by 25 percent to $100 million. The would-be ratio of $100/100 = 1$ would have been realized had we been fully invested in the risky asset. However, because our strategy limits the ratio (or relative performance) to 1.15 on the downside, we would have gradually shifted assets into the better performing bond portfolio and kept the asset/liability ratio to the 1.15 floor.

Similarly, had we kept a static 60/40 mix of stocks and (dedicated) bond portfolio, the portfolio would have had a value of 110 (60 for stocks and 50 for bonds) with a realized ratio of 1.1.

Exactly what does protecting the asset/liability ratio accomplish? It protects funding status and protects against the potential negative impact of FASB 87 on the corporate balance sheet and earnings statement. Standard portfolio insurance addresses only assets.

Protecting the Surplus with Complete Dedication

Full dedication may be appropriate for a fund unable to tolerate *any* deterioration in funding status. Consider the example where assets are $100 million and liabilities are $80 million, giving us a surplus of $20 million. The strategy is to dedicate an $80 million bond portfolio that will match the duration of liabilities, assuring that future benefit obligations will be paid.

Whether we protect the surplus or not, it is clear that, in terms of upside capture, this strategy is inferior to asset liability protection. This is due to the severe risk aversion of the fund. To wit, its risk aversion will not allow funding status to go below the 1.25 ratio, and the price paid for this protection is low upside capture.

If the equity index goes up to $120 million with liabilities staying the same, our asset liability protection program would have netted $117.6 million (assuming 98 percent capture). A surplus protected to a 0 percent floor could yield no more than a 20 percent gain to $24 million, giving us a net portfolio value of no more than $104 million ($80 plus $24).

It may be overly conservative to completely dedicate an $80 million bond portfolio at the outset. A strategy that gradually allocates funds to the dedicated bond portfolio as the risky asset declines will be superior in terms of upside capture, to a fund able to tolerate a bit of funding status loss.

V. Perpetual Asset Liability Protection

Unlike fixed life policies, perpetual strategies do not replicate options, and therefore do not have the same hockey-stick profit patterns of options. Although perpetual policies target minimum returns over a given time horizon, their asset allocations, unlike options, are time invariant. That is, they do not depend on a time horizon.

The time dependence often seems irrelevant to the long-term concerns of a pension fund, and for this reason as well as others, perpetual policies have been gaining in popularity and should continue to do so as they are better understood.

One perpetual policy that is pertinent to asset liability management is known as Constant Proportion Portfolio Protection (CPPP), which was introduced simultaneously by Black–Jones and by Perold.[7,8] CPPP can actually be applied to either asset protection or to asset liability protection. It has a firm basis in utility theory and is simple to implement.

The fundamental idea behind CPPP is that one's exposure (e) to the risky asset be directly proportional to one's cushion (c), which is defined as the difference between assets and a floor level. The proportionality constant, m, is called the multiple and the entire strategy is summarized by the equation

$$e = mc.$$

The spirit of the strategy is its recognition of a risk tolerance which increases with an increasing cushion. Moreover, within a mathematical framework, a linear risk tolerance function leads to a CPPP strategy with appropriate multiple. (See the appendix for a brief review and Merton[9] for an in-depth treatment. The reader is referred to Perold[10] for an in-depth treatment of CPPP.)

---

7. Fisher Black and Robert Jones, "Simplifying Portfolio Insurance," *Journal of Portfolio Management* (Fall 1987).

8. André Perold, "Constant Proportion Portfolio Insurance." Harvard Business School, August 1986.

9. Robert Merton, "Optimum Consumption and Portfolio Rules in a Continuous Time Model," *Journal of Economic Theory 3* (1971): 373–413.

10. Perold, "Constant Proportion Portfolio Insurance."

Assume, for example, that we have assets of $160 million, liabilities of $100 million, and that we are protecting our asset/liability ratio to a floor of 1.20. Our cushion in ratio terms is 0.40, which translates to $40 million. If we choose an initial exposure of $120 million in stocks and $40 million in a dedicated bond portfolio, our multiple is 3 (120/40).

The multiple represents the speed of adjustment of exposure relative to the cushion. Should liabilities rise to $120 million while assets remain flat, our floor, or protection level, becomes $144 million (1.2 times $120 million) and the cushion shrinks to $16 million. Our exposure to equity is reduced to 3 times $16 million or $48 million.

As stocks rise relative to liabilities, exposure increases and vice versa. In Figure 4 the profit pattern of a CPPP strategy over one year is overlaid onto that of a one-year protective put with the same floor. Multiples of $m = 3$ and $m = 5$ are used.

As long as the risk asset increases at the same rate as the reserve asset, the cushion remains the same, as will dollar exposure. When the risky asset overperforms (underperforms) the reserve asset, exposure is increased (decreased).

The strategy in Figure 4 calculates the cushion (in dollars) as the difference between the existing surplus and the floor surplus, as inferred from the floor ratio of 1.10. The CPPP strategy would work analogously if our goal were a surplus dollar floor instead of a ratio floor. CPPP can be applied either way depending on the plan's objectives.

A couple of observations are obvious from Figure 4:

- The expected upside capture is not constant for CPPP as it is for protective put replication.
- The higher m, the better we do in a strong market, but the worse we perform in a mediocre market.

VI. Risk Tolerance and Asset Allocation

Long-Term Asset Allocation

Any strategy has associated with it a certain payoff pattern that may or may not be consistent with one's risk tolerance. In discussing *long-term asset allocation (LTAA) decision rules,* we assume that the risky asset has an expected return that is constant and higher than the reserve asset. LTAA is to be contrasted with Tactical Asset Allocation (TAA), in which "changes" in expected returns are used to alter the asset mix. TAA, of course, is synonymous with market timing.

We have found, for example, that for some plan sponsors, risk tolerance increases with wealth (decreasing risk aversion) prompting more aggressive investment allocation as wealth increases. This is entirely consistent with

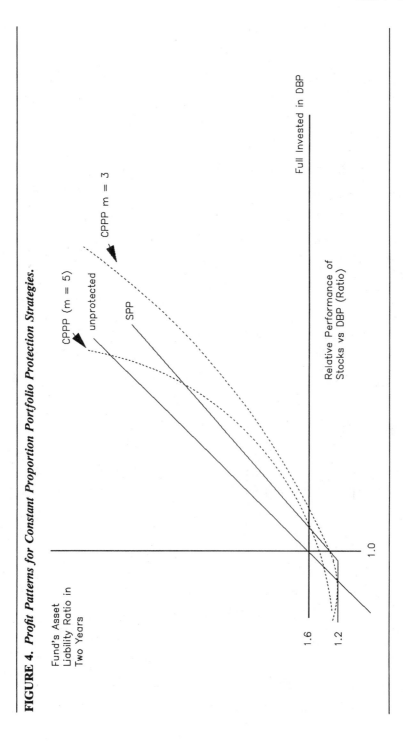

FIGURE 4. *Profit Patterns for Constant Proportion Portfolio Protection Strategies.*

CPPP having multiples greater than 1, SPP, and a static buy/hold strategy. (See appendix.)

Some sponsors, however, display decreasing risk tolerance with increasing wealth (increasing risk aversion). In this case a manager may exhibit less aggressive investment allocation as wealth increases. This is consistent with CPPP having multiples less than 1, with covered call writing and a constant asset mix strategy. (See appendix.)

Ratcheting

Some plan sponsors express a desire to protect not only original wealth but also accumulated wealth. For either an SPP or perpetual program, this could mean raising the floor in some prescribed manner (ratcheting) as wealth increases. Ratcheting may be done in the name of changing risk tolerance, but is often a form of closet market timing and therefore is usually considered a tactical rather than long-term strategy.

Ratcheting strategies are path dependent, while CPPP with multiples less than 1 are not (assuming we can trade continuously). Consider, for example, an SPP strategy on $100 million of assets. Suppose the portfolio value increases to $120 million and that we ratchet by raising the floor to $120 million. Any subsequent drop to previous levels is averted by ratcheting. However, had the equity index first gone down and then up, we would not have had an opportunity to ratchet.

VII. Summary

In conclusion, it is clear that one's risk aversion directly impacts, implicitly or explicitly, one's risk management strategy. It is also clear that the aversion to risk may not remain constant over time. Therefore, a risk management strategy that is set in motion today may not be appropriate next year.

A plan sponsor must choose a strategy (dynamic or static) consistent with the fund's aversion to risk; this risk aversion should include plan funding status, FASB 87, and company-specific risk tolerance. Finally, changes in risk tolerance must be addressed periodically.

Appendix: Choosing the Multiple

A simple method for matching the multiple of a CPPP strategy with the more familiar protective put replication is to equate their expected payoffs. The procedure is to equate the closed-form expression for the expected payoff of a CPPP strategy with that of a protective put, and solve for m. Table 1

TABLE 1. *Matching the Multiple of CPPP with Put Replication.*

Put Replication		Multiple with Equal Expected Return
Number of Years	Floor	
1	0	7.4
1	−5	5.9
2	0	6.1
2	−5	4.5
5	0	5.3
5	−5	3.1

Note: Expected returns are equated with risk-free rate at 5.5 percent, volatility at 16 percent, mean stock return at 12 percent.

produces some typical results. Those interested in the mathematics are referred to Perold.[11]

Table 1 indicates the method of matching m using expected value as a criterion. More to the point, we should be viewing the entire probability distribution of the payoff pattern in light of our risk tolerance, and in light of our market viewpoint, in determining m. Expected value is appropriate only for someone who is risk neutral. The discussion in the appendix relates m to risk tolerance.

Risk Tolerance

The utility function of the plan, and its risk tolerance, are actually at the heart of choosing the appropriate long-term asset allocation decision rule. For the two asset problem, Sharpe[12] has shown that one's dollar exposure to the risky asset is proportional to one's absolute risk tolerance (ART), defined as

$$ART = -U''/U',$$

where U' and U'' are the first and second derivatives, respectively, of utility, U, with respect to wealth, W.

Symbolically, $e = k \times ART$, where k is a constant. As one's wealth increases, so does one's ART and exposure. It is clear that if risk tolerance is

---

11. Ibid.
12. William Sharpe, "Integrated Asset Allocation," Sharpe-Russell Research, February 1987.

directly proportional to the cushion then exposure also is directly proportional to the cushion, rendering a CPPP strategy optimal.

Following Merton,[13] consider the family of utility functions given by

$$U(W) = (W - F)^{1-a},$$

where W is end-of-period wealth, F is end-of-period floor, and a is a positive constant.

This family has linear risk tolerance (ART is directly proportional to cushion). A CPPP strategy, for this investor, is optimal with the multiple m given by

$$m = (m_s - r)/av^2,$$

where m_s = expected annual mean logarithmic stock return, r = risk-free rate, and v = annualized logarithmic volatility of the risky asset.

Viewed within the context of risk tolerance, the asset allocation decision rule is reduced to $e = m(c) \times c$, where $m(c)$ is a *changing multiple* that will depend on how ART relates to c. CPPP, therefore, is associated with one type of increasing risk tolerance (linear).

Option replication has a murkier association with risk tolerance. A protective put, for example, is associated with a utility curve whose ART is, *initially,* an increasing concave function of the cushion with a maximum exposure equal to the total asset value. As time elapses toward the expiration of the option, the ART curve degenerates to a step function that equals zero when the cushion is at or below zero, and equals its maximum when the cushion is above zero. In other words the utility curve is quite dependent on the time horizon. On these grounds option replication is difficult to justify, particularly since the choice of horizon is usually quite arbitrary and unrelated to any utility changes.

---

13. Merton, "Optimum Consumption."

42

Constant Proportion Portfolio Insurance and the Synthetic Put Option:
A Comparison

Fischer Black
Partner
Goldman, Sachs & Co.

Ramine Rouhani*
Vice President
Goldman, Sachs & Co.

I. A Preview

In an earlier article, we introduced Constant Proportion Portfolio Insurance (CPPI for short).[1] In this paper we compare CPPI with the Synthetic Put Option (SPO).[2] Both strategies set a floor on your portfolio's value to protect it in falling markets; both allow the portfolio to appreciate in rising markets.

In comparing CPPI and the SPO, three main points emerge:

- Neither strategy outperforms the other all the time. As Figure 1 shows, the SPO's payoff is greater in a moderate market rise. In a market drop, small market rise or large market rise, CPPI performs better.
- Because CPPI is perpetual, it doesn't have many of the drawbacks of the fixed-life SPO.
- While both strategies call for dynamic adjustment, CPPI is much simpler to carry out.

To draw the comparison, we first describe the synthetic put option – how it grew out of market-traded puts, how trading takes place and its sensitivity to volatility. Then we review constant proportion portfolio insurance – how

*Ramine Rouhani has since joined Franklin Savings Association where he is Vice President, Financial Engineering Department.
1. Fischer Black and Robert Jones, "Simplifying Portfolio Insurance," *The Journal of Portfolio Management* (Fall 1987). The original version was published in August 1986.
2. The original version of this paper was published in May 1987.

FIGURE 1.

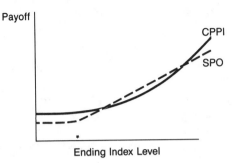

Payoff

CPPI

SPO

Ending Index Level

* Initial Index

trading takes place, the effect of changing the multiple, and the strategy's sensitivity to volatility. We end the article by comparing the SPO and CPPI payoffs in different markets.

II. Synthetic Put Option (SPO)

Before we tackle a synthetic put, let's back up and look at how a "real" put works. Real puts are those bought and sold on an exchange or over the counter.

Real Puts

First some facts. Suppose you have $100 to invest in the stock market (for instance, the S&P 500). Your investment horizon is two years, and the annual interest rate is 7%. The S&P 500 index price is $100, its expected annual return over the next two years is 13%, and its expected annual volatility is 20%. Assume transaction costs are zero.

You want to be sure that your portfolio's value isn't below $95 in two years. How can you put this $95 floor on your portfolio? One way is to buy a European put option to cover your investment in the S&P 500 index. It should have a two-year maturity and a strike price that will effectively fix a floor of $95 on the final value of your portfolio.

We use a formula to find the put's strike price and value. That formula works with several variables, including our floor, the prevailing interest rate, our estimate of market volatility and our investment horizon. (The Appendix covers option mathematics.) In our example, the correct strike price for the put is $100.2 and its value is $5.5. This means you will use $94.8 of your $100 portfolio to buy the S&P index and $5.2 to buy put options. Your portfolio will have .948 shares of the S&P index at $100 per share and .948 shares of the put option at $5.5 a share.

At the end of two years, if the index is above the $100.2 strike price, your puts will be worthless. But the .948 shares of the index in your portfolio will be worth more than the $95 floor. (.948 × $100.2). If the index drops below the strike price, your index shares will be worth less than your floor. Your final portfolio value, however, will be the $95 floor since you can exercise your put.

Since you don't know the index level in two years, your portfolio's return is uncertain. However, you can estimate its *expected return:* it is 24.4%, which corresponds to an expected portfolio value of $124.4. This return is less than the index expected return of 27.7% (13% coupounded for two years), but more than the two-year riskless return, 14.5% (7% compounded for 2 years).

Curve (1) of Figure 2 shows how the portfolio's value will depend on the value of the index in two years and its relation to the $100.2 strike price:

If the index is less than $100.2, the portfolio's value will be at its floor, $95 (horizontal line AB). If the index is above $100.2, the payoff is traced by BC, a line whose slope is .948. When the index goes above $120.8, the breakeven point, your portfolio's return exceeds the 7% riskless return, which corresponds to a 9.9% market rate of return per year.

If everything else remains the same, any floor you choose through a put option will define a unique payoff pattern, similar to curve (1) of Figure 2. The value of the index in two years determines the payoff—no matter which path the index takes to that value, or how interest rates and volatility change. The put is an insurance policy for your portfolio.

Even though it is perfectly reliable, a put is not always practical to use. Here's why:

- Long-maturity European options are not available. All listed options have maturities of less than 11 months.
- Even if your investment horizon is under 11 months, you may not find options with the strike prices and maturities you need — particularly if your basket of stocks does not follow the S&P index (or some other index with traded options). Listed options for individual stocks have standard strike prices and expiration dates.

To get around these roadblocks, you can create synthetic options of any maturity and exercise price on a basket of stocks.

Creating the SPO

Synthetic put options can be put together in different ways. The one we describe below has two parts: a reserve asset which you create by lending cash (for instance, buying T-bills) and an active asset (for instance, the S&P index or any other basket of stocks) which you sell and buy according to an option pricing model. Other versions call for selling futures instead of the

FIGURE 2.

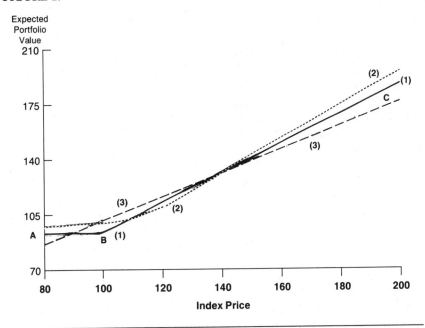

Note: (1) SPO; (2) CPPI with a multiple of 5.30. Final floor = 95, interest rate = 7%, volatility = 20%, time = 2 years, initial portfolio value = 100, initial index level = 100; (3) Buy-and-hold strategy with 75% invested in risky asset.

Expected Payoff Tables

Index Level	SPO	CPPI	Buy & Hold
90	95.00	97.66	96.12
100	95.00	99.89	103.62
110	104.29	103.63	111.12
120	113.77	109.96	118.62
130	123.25	119.66	126.12
140	132.73	130.90	133.62
150	142.21	142.05	141.12
160	151.69	152.92	148.62
170	161.17	163.57	156.12
180	170.65	174.08	163.62
190	180.13	184.47	171.12
200	189.61	194.79	178.62

active asset or rolling over short-term index options to make longer-term options. These also require option models.

To create a synthetic put on one share of the active asset, you lend cash equal to the present value of the strike price, and sell less than one share of the active asset. As the market climbs, you buy shares of the active asset and decrease your lending – buy stocks and sell T-bills. As the market falls, you sell shares of the active asset and lend the proceeds – sell stocks and buy T-bills.

You cover each share of the active asset that you hold with a synthetic put. To do this, you let the option pricing model determine your initial portfolio exposure to the active asset. As the market changes, the model gives you your target exposure: the number of active asset shares to hold. By continuously rebalancing your portfolio to maintain your exposure at its target value, your expected payoff at maturity will be the same as that of the real put [curve (1) of Figure 2] – if transaction costs are zero.

But of course transaction costs are not zero. That's why continuous rebalancing is costly. It's also impractical. So unlike a market-traded put, a synthetic put's expected payoff differs from the theoretical one, and its actual payoff will differ from its expected payoff.

Take a closer look at rebalancing with the synthetic put. In practice, you adjust your portfolio only when your exposure strays from your target exposure by a certain tolerance, say 3%. Such discrete rebalancing introduces a discrepancy between the strategy's expected payoff and that of a real put. And if the price of the active asset can jump suddenly, the discrepancy will be larger. Assuming the price of your active asset moves in small steps, decreasing your tolerance (for instance, from 3% to 2%) will make the actual discrepancy smaller; this will mean trading more frequently and incurring higher transaction costs.

The synthetic put's finite life presents another drawback. When you reach the maturity of the synthetic put, you reallocate your portfolio's assets to continue the strategy – no matter what has happened in the market. Here's what we mean:

At expiration, the synthetic put is either worthless or in the money, and your portfolio is either fully invested in the reserve asset or fully invested in the active asset. To roll your position into another synthetic put, you will have to radically reallocate your portfolio between the two asset classes. Your outlook and the market's movements have nothing to do with this shift; the strategy's fixed life makes it necessary.

If you approach expiration and the synthetic put is at the money, then your exposure's sensitivity to the active asset's price increases. Your exposure will fluctuate significantly and you will trade more often. Again, these changes reflect only the fact that the option is nearing expiration.

Let's look at how market volatility affects the SPO.

Volatility and the SPO

The SPO strategy is sensitive to both expected and actual market volatility. Recall that your estimate of the market's volatility is one of the variables that determine the strike price of your synthetic put. An increase in expected volatility raises the market level that will keep you above your floor. In our example, if the expected volatility is 15%, you create a two-year put with a strike price of $97.4. At 20% expected volatility, the strike price rises to $100.2; at 25%, it goes up to $103.7.

As volatility increases, the SPO strategy captures less and less of a market rise. The slopes of the SPO payoff lines fall from .976 to .948 to .916 as expected volatility rises from 15% to 20% to 25%.

The break-even index values where the portfolio yields the 7% interest rate are $117.3 for 15% expected volatility, $120.8 for 20% volatility and $125 for 25% volatility. These prices correspond to 8.3%, 9.9%, and 11.8% market returns for the year.

At each rebalancing point in the SPO strategy, you must put your expected market volatility in an option pricing model to calculate the hedge ratio. This ratio gives your portfolio's exposure to the market. Actual market volatility, however, is usually different from expected volatility. While your expected volatility affects your portfolio adjustment, actual market volatility determines the final payoff. If actual volatility is higher than expected volatility, your payoff declines; if it is below expected volatility, your payoff increases.

Let's move on to Constant Proportion Portfolio Insurance.

III. Constant Proportion Portfolio Insurance (CPPI)

The key concepts in Constant Proportion Portfolio Insurance are summarized below:

$$e = mc$$

e = exposure
m = multiple
c = cushion

Floor = Lowest value for the portfolio
Cushion = Portfolio value minus floor
Exposure = Amount in the active asset
Multiple = Exposure divided by cushion
Tolerance = Deviation from target exposure that triggers a trade

Again you start with a portfolio of $100 and a $95 floor. To be sure the portfolio is worth at least $95 in two years, you could invest $82.98 in your reserve asset today. This becomes the present value of your floor. It will grow at an annual rate of 7% over the next two years to $95.

The difference between your portfolio and your floor is your cushion. In this example you start with a cushion of $17.02. You invest in the S&P

index an amount equal to the smaller of these two numbers: (i) your multiple times your cushion or (ii) your portfolio value. This amount is your exposure.

Suppose you choose a multiple of 4. Since your multiple times your cushion (4 times $17.02), $68.08, is less than your portfolio value ($100), your exposure is $68.08. This is the amount you invest in the index. To keep the multiple constant, you buy stocks after the index rises, and sell stocks after it falls.

If you choose a multiple of 8 and multiply it by your $17.02 cushion, the result ($136.16) is larger than your portfolio value ($100). Again, you choose the smaller number for your exposure. This means you invest your entire portfolio, $100, in the index. If the index declines, your cushion will also decline. When your exposure becomes smaller than your portfolio, you sell stocks until you bring the ratio of your exposure to your cushion back to 8.

Before we move on, note that CPPI is a perpetual strategy. Approaching the end of your investment horizon does not affect your trading decisions. As we saw, this is not true for the SPO. Expiration of the synthetic put can dictate how you allocate assets.

On the other hand, like the SPO, CPPI calls for rebalancing your portfolio. In a world with no transaction costs, you would continuously rebalance your portfolio throughout the trading day as the market moved. But in real life this is impractical and costly. For this reason CPPI calls for discrete rebalancing. Here's how a discrete rebalancing policy works.

Discrete Rebalancing with CPPI

With CPPI in place, you follow the market to monitor your exposure and the ratio of your exposure to your cushion. If the exposure is your entire portfolio, you don't trade. If your exposure is less than your portfolio, but its ratio to your cushion is within a certain tolerance of your multiple, you still don't trade.

Suppose that tolerance is 2% and your multiple is 4. You won't trade so long as your exposure-to-cushion ratio falls between 3.92 and 4.08. If the ratio is larger than the multiple and outside this range, you decrease your exposure until its ratio to your cushion falls back to the upper edge of the range—4.08 in our example. If the ratio is less than the multiple and below the range, you increase your exposure until the ratio equals the lower edge of the range—or 3.92. You only need your multiple and your cushion to rebalance. You don't need a model.

You can increase the frequency of rebalancing by decreasing the tolerance, say from 2% to 1%. This will narrow the difference between the actual and expected payoffs, if the price of your active asset moves in small steps.

FIGURE 3.

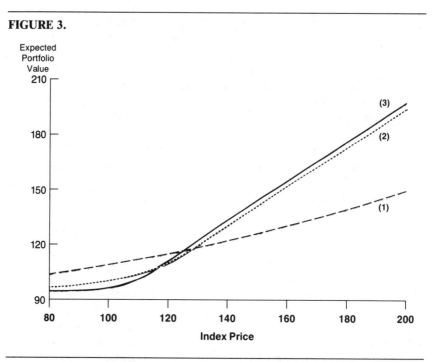

Note: (1) CPPI (multiple = 2); (2) CPPI (multiple = 5.3); (3) CPPI (multiple = 8). Final floor = 95, interest rate = 7%, volatility = 20%, time = 2 years, initial portfolio value = 100, initial index level = 100.

| | *Expected Payoff Tables* | | |
Index Level	CPPI (multiple = 2)	CPPI (multiple = 5.3)	CPPI (multiple = 8)
90	106.17	97.66	95.83
100	108.79	99.89	97.41
110	111.68	103.63	101.73
120	114.85	109.96	110.57
130	118.30	119.66	121.90
140	122.02	130.90	133.62
150	126.02	142.05	144.93
160	130.30	152.92	155.87
170	134.85	163.57	166.57
180	139.69	174.08	177.09
190	144.79	184.47	187.49
200	150.18	194.79	197.81

But decreasing your tolerance increases your transaction costs. And if the price of the active asset jumps suddenly, the actual payoff may be far from the expected one, even with a small tolerance.

Effect of the Multiple

Figure 3 shows the payoffs expected at the end of two years for CPPI strategies with multiples of 2, 5.3, and 8. To estimate these payoffs we have assumed continuous rebalancing. We have also adjusted the ratio of exposure to cushion to match the multiple exactly. Even though all the strategies have the same floor, the different multiples produce different payoffs.

Here is a summary of the findings in Figure 3:

With multiples of 2, 5.30 and 8, the initial exposures will be $34.04, $90.21 and $100.00.

With a multiple of 2:

- the expected payoff increases slowly with the index, but is larger than that of a strategy using a multiple of 5.30 if the index remains below $128.2;
- the expected payoff remains above that of a multiple 8 strategy for index levels below $125.5.

Compared to multiples of 2 and 5.30, the expected payoff of a multiple 8 strategy starts low; but it moves up faster as the index rises.

When the index value is $90, the expected payoff is $95.8 with a multiple of 8, $97.7 with a multiple of 5.30, and $106.2 with a multiple of 2.

Plots of Figure 3, as well as the table accompanying it, show that as the multiple increases the strategy becomes more aggressive: it captures more of a rising market, and drops to the floor faster in a falling market.

In general, as you raise the multiple your expected payoff becomes larger for high market levels, and stays closer to the floor for low market levels. Although your floor limits your risk, the expected payoffs vary significantly, as curves (1) and (3) of Figure 3 show. Two investors with the same floor and the same estimates of expected market return and volatility may very well select two different multiples: the more conservative investor, a lower multiple; the more aggressive investor, a higher multiple.

Your estimate of the stock market's expected return may also influence your choice of multiple. The higher the multiple, the smaller the expected payoff for small-to-moderate increases in the index. But as the index rises sharply, the payoff curve steepens. So other things equal, if you expect a sharp rise in the market, you want to choose a higher multiple. If you expect a small-to-moderate market rise, you want a lower multiple.

In short, the multiple lets you shape your portfolio's expected return to reflect your view of the market. As that view changes, you can adjust your multiple without affecting your floor.

Volatility and CPPI

A rise in actual volatility reduces the CPPI payoff. Tables 1 and 2 show this. Table 1 lists CPPI payoffs using a multiple of 2; Table 2 lists CPPI payoffs

---

TABLE 1. *Expected Payoffs, Multiple of 2.*

Index Level	CPPI (vol. = 15%)	CPPI (vol. = 20%)	CPPI (vol. = 25%)
90	106.53	106.17	105.72
100	109.24	108.79	108.24
110	112.23	111.68	111.02
120	115.51	114.85	114.06
130	119.07	118.30	117.37
140	122.91	122.02	120.95
150	127.05	126.02	124.79
160	131.46	130.30	128.90
170	136.17	134.85	133.27
180	141.15	139.69	137.91
190	146.43	144.79	142.82
200	151.99	150.18	148.00

CPPI payoffs: final floor = 95; interest rate = 7%; multiple = 2; time horizon = 2 years; initial portfolio value = 100; initial index level = 100. Volatilities: 15%, 20%, 25%.

---

with a multiple of 5. In both tables, the floor is $95 and the investment horizon two years.

With a multiple of 2, the break-even index values (where the portfolio yields 7%) are $116.8, $119 and $121.3 for volatilities of 15%, 20% and 25% (8.1%, 9.1% and 10.1% yearly returns).

With a multiple of 5, the break-even index values are $120.9, $124.1 and $130 for volatilities of 15%, 20% and 25% (9.9%, 11.4% and 14% yearly returns).

As volatility increases, these break-even index values and their corresponding rates of return rise. Payoffs decline also. And the higher the multiple, the more they decline.

Suppose your multiple is 5. As market volatility rises you should expect a larger fall in your payoff than you would with a multiple of 2. For instance, if volatility rises from 15% to 20% (a 33% increase), your expected payoff with an index value of $130 drops from $124.2 to $119.9 (a 3.5% decrease). With the same increase in volatility and a multiple of 2, the expected payoff for an index value of $130 falls from $119.1 to $118.3 — a 0.7% drop.

So if you think the market will be very volatile, you should choose a low multiple. You can change it as your expectation of volatility changes.

Keep in mind the roles expected and actual volatility play: expected volatility affects your choice of multiple, and actual volatility affects the strategy's payoff. If actual market volatility is higher than expected, your payoff will be lower since you will trade more frequently than you expected. If actual volatility stays below expected volatility, your payoff will be higher.

TABLE 2. *Expected Payoffs, Multiple of 5.*

Index Level	CPPI (vol. = 15%)	CPPI (vol. = 20%)	CPPI (vol. = 25%)
90	98.98	98.14	97.25
100	101.88	100.54	99.05
110	106.43	104.37	102.01
120	113.62	110.50	106.86
130	124.17	119.85	114.49
140	135.19	130.88	124.50
150	145.85	141.90	135.55
160	156.30	152.67	146.67
170	166.62	163.25	157.59
180	176.85	173.69	168.33
190	187.01	184.04	178.93
200	197.13	194.31	189.42

CPPI payoffs: final floor = 95; interest rate = 7%; multiple = 5; time horizon = 2 years; initial portfolio value = 100; initial index level = 100. Volatilities: 15%, 20%, 25%.

IV. SPO versus CPPI — Payoff Comparison

Plots (1) and (2) of Figure 2 show the expected payoffs of the SPO and CPPI strategies after two years. The CPPI strategy has a multiple of 5.30. *Both* strategies have a floor of $95, and *both* have an expected return of 24.4% at maturity. Their payoffs, however, are quite different.

With the SPO, the portfolio value drops to the floor when the index stays at or below the exercise price. With CPPI, you stay above the floor so long as the index stays above zero. Since this is almost certain, we can assume that the CPPI payoff always stays above the floor. However, no matter which strategy you use, a sudden, sharp market drop may put you at or under your floor if you cannot trade and adjust your exposure in time.

The payoff table in Figure 2 shows which strategy has the greater payoff depending on the index at maturity. That is:

- for index values below $108.5, the CPPI payoff is greater;
- for index values of $108.5 to $152.2, the SPO payoff is greater;
- for index values greater than $152.2, the CPPI payoff is greater.

As the index increases beyond $152.2, the difference between the payoffs of the two strategies increases. To help explain this, let's examine the upside capture of the strategies.

Upside Capture

Upside capture is the slope of the strategy's payoff curve. It tells how much of the market's appreciation the strategy lets you capture. Put another way, it is the rate of increase of the expected payoff in relation to an increase in the index.

The slope of the SPO payoff curve shows that the upside capture is constant and therefore independent of the index level. The slope is always less than 1. In Figure 2, the SPO's upside capture is equal to .948. For instance, as the index moves from $150 to $160, the corresponding SPO payoff increases by $9.5, moving from $142.2 to $151.7.

For CPPI, the upside capture is not constant and depends on the index level. The slopes of the CPPI payoff curves in Figures 2 and 3 reflect this. Typically, the strategy's upside capture stays below 1 for low index levels; increases to 1 or more for medium to high levels of the index; and decreases to 1 as the index level goes still higher. For instance, with a multiple of 5.30, the upside capture is .34 for an index level of $100. It increases to 1.12 for an index level of $130, and decreases to 1.03 for an index level of $190.

As Figure 3 shows, the CPPI upside capture (slope of the curve) hinges on the multiple. When the multiple is small, the upside capture is small, even for high index values [curve (1)]. And when the multiple is larger, the upside capture becomes greater than 1 for moderate levels of the index.

While the slope of the payoff curve for CPPI in Figure 2 is smooth, that of the SPO payoff curve is not. When the index is lower than the strike price at maturity, the SPO curve is flat; it steepens abruptly when the index goes above the strike price. This implies that SPO investors are extremely risk averse when the index is less than the exercise price (point B), but willing to accept risk as soon as the index goes past that point. The smooth CPPI payoff curve suggests nothing of this sort.

For comparison, curve (3) of Figure 2 corresponds to a buy-and-hold strategy that assigns 25% of the portfolio to the reserve asset and the rest to the active asset. The investment horizon is two years. Like the SPO and CPPI, the expected return of this strategy is 24.4%. Its floor, however, is much lower — $28.6. The upside capture is .75.

V. Summary

- Both the SPO and CPPI strategies protect your portfolio from market declines by setting a floor on its value. The SPO is a fixed-life strategy while CPPI is perpetual.
- Both strategies are dynamic. Rebalancing your portfolio with the SPO requires an option model. Rebalancing with CPPI requires two numbers: your multiple and your cushion.
- The SPO payoff depends on estimated market volatility, actual market volatility, the interest rate, the investment horizon and the floor. The CPPI payoff depends on the multiple, actual market volatility, the interest rate, the investment horizon and the floor.

- If you use CPPI, you will choose your multiple to reflect your attitude toward risk, and your estimates of stock market volatility and expected return. The multiple shapes your expected payoff. You can change it as your attitude toward risk or your expectations change.
- In general, the SPO performs better if the market increases moderately. CPPI does better if the market drops or increases by a small or large amount.

Appendix: Put Option Mathematics

Definitions

T = time to maturity
K = exercise price
σ = volatility
S = index price at time T
$S(O)$ = index price at time O
r = one plus the riskless interest rate
$P(K)$ = price of one share of European put with exercise price K and maturity T
W = total portfolio value at time T
$W(O)$ = total portfolio value at time O
f = floor ratio at maturity

Determining the Exercise Price

Suppose we start with a portfolio of $W(O)$. At maturity we want our portfolio value to be at least equal to:

$$f \cdot W(O)$$

We use $W(O)$ to purchase n shares of stock index and n shares of European put options on the index maturing in T years, with an exercise price of K (to be determined). Clearly:

$$W(O) = n \cdot (P(K) + S(O)) \tag{1}$$

The payoff of this portfolio at maturity is:

$$\begin{aligned} W &= n \cdot S & \text{for } S > K \\ &= n \cdot K & \text{for } S < K \end{aligned}$$

To guarantee the floor we require that:

$$n \cdot K = f \cdot W(O) \tag{2}$$

Substituting the value of n in (1) we get the following equation:

$$K = f \cdot (S(O) + P(K)) \tag{3}$$

Note that K is the only unknown in the above equation. P is the Black–Scholes expression for a European put that depends on $S(O)$, T, σ, r and K. Equation (3) is nonlinear in K. We can solve it by using a simple Newton algorithm. The number of shares n, which is also the slope of the payoff line for $S > K$, is then calculated from (2).

43

Simplifying Portfolio Insurance for the Seller

Fischer Black
Partner
Goldman, Sachs & Co.

Erol Hakanoglu
Vice President
Goldman, Sachs & Co.

I. A Preview

In an earlier article, Black and Jones described a simple kind of portfolio insurance from a buyer's point of view.[1] Here we look at the seller's side.[2]

Throughout our strategy, the seller always trades with the same buyer. He decides when, what and how much the seller trades. These trades reflect why the buyer and seller use portfolio insurance. That is: The buyer wants a floor on his portfolio's value to protect it in falling markets; he also wants to capture some appreciation in rising markets. In trading, he buys after the market rises and sells after the market falls.

In total contrast, the seller wants to buy after a market fall and sell after a market rise. Countering the buyer's trades permits this, and allows him to realize capital gains.

In describing portfolio insurance for the seller, we begin by showing how he trades in rising and falling markets. We then discuss how the buyer's trading strategy affects the seller. Finally, we use market data from 1974 through 1986 in simulations. They show how the buyer's trading strategy

---

1. Fischer Black and Robert Jones, "Simplifying Portfolio Insurance," *The Journal of Portfolio Management* (Fall 1987). The original version was published in August 1986.
2. The original version of this paper was published in May 1987.

affects the performance of both the buyer and seller of portfolio insurance; how our strategy's payoffs compare with those of a buy-and-hold strategy; and the role of realized capital gains for the portfolio insurance seller.

II. Key Concepts

The key concepts needed to understand our simplified approach to portfolio insurance are summarized below.

$$e = mc$$

$$e = \text{exposure}$$
$$m = \text{buyer's multiple}$$
$$c = \text{buyer's cushion}$$

Reserve asset	Asset that has an acceptable minimum rate of return
Active asset	Asset whose expected return exceeds that of the reserve asset
Floor	Lowest value for buyer's portfolio
Cushion	Buyer's portfolio value minus floor
Buyer's (seller's) exposure	Amount buyer (seller) has in active asset
Multiple	Buyer's initial exposure divided by initial cushion
Tolerance	Percentage difference between actual and target cushions that triggers a trade
Limit	Maximum percentage of the buyer's portfolio in the active asset
Ceiling	Maximum number of shares seller might ever hold
Provision in active assets	Number of shares seller must hold to satisfy buyer's limit
Provision in reserve assets	Reserve assets the seller must have to purchase his ceiling

III. The Seller's Point of View

The market in buying portfolio insurance has rapidly grown beyond $40 billion. Portfolio insurance buyers, many of them pension funds, use the strategy for two reasons: to set a floor on the value of their stocks (or any risky assets) in case the market drops; and to capture some appreciation in rising markets. To do this, they buy stocks after a market rise, and sell after a market fall.

But to many investors such trading seems backward. They think buying after a market fall and selling after a market rise makes more sense. They do not need a floor on their portfolios. Such investors are potential sellers of portfolio insurance — particularly if they favor stocks with low P/E ratios; use dividend discount models; or expect volatile, non-trending markets.

We begin our discussion by looking at how you set up and adjust your position as a portfolio insurance seller. We describe the strategy as though you were matched with an appropriate buyer through a clearing organization. No such entity exists now, but later we touch on the practical side of establishing one.

IV. The Link between Buyer and Seller

As a portfolio insurance seller, you are paired with a portfolio insurance buyer. Both of you need portfolios with the same active and reserve assets — for instance, the S&P 500 and Treasury bills. You must also agree on the buyer's multiple and tolerance. More on these later.

Because you always take the other side of his trades, the buyer determines how you trade. The buyer participates in the upside, you participate in the downside. That is, as he buys after a market rise, you sell to him; as he sells after a market decline, you buy from him.

You profit from the losses the buyer incurs as he buys high and sells low. In addition to the capital gains you realize, you share the buyer's transaction costs with the entity that sets up the trade. The fraction that you collect is determined by the market. These costs are an incentive for you to sell portfolio insurance, particularly when market conditions favor the buyer.

V. The Buyer Leads

Recall that the buyer starts by choosing a *floor* for his portfolio. The difference between his current portfolio value and his floor is his *cushion*. He invests part of his portfolio in a reserve asset that has an acceptable minimum rate of return. The remainder he invests in an active asset, one whose expected return exceeds that of the reserve asset; this is his *exposure*. (In our examples, the active asset is the S&P 500 index and the reserve asset is T-bills.)

The buyer's strategy is to maintain his exposure at a constant *multiple* of the cushion. No matter what multiple he picks, as the cushion approaches zero, his exposure will approach zero too. Normally, this strategy will keep his portfolio value above the floor. His portfolio can drop below the floor, however, if the market drops sharply before he has a chance to trade.

VI. The Seller Follows

As the portfolio insurance seller, you sell stocks to the buyer when he wants to buy them, and buy his stocks when he wants to sell them.

Your portfolio also contains the S&P 500 index and T-bills. Your exposure equals the amount you have invested in stocks. But unless you are willing to buy stocks in the market to meet your buyer's demands, the number of shares in your initial portfolio should be at least equal to the maximum number of shares the buyer could ever want to buy. We call this amount your *provision in active assets*. You can calculate it if you know the buyer's multiple (his exposure divided by his cushion), his floor, his initial portfolio value and his *limit*—the maximum percentage of his portfolio the buyer is willing to invest in stocks. You use the same variables to calculate the maximum number of shares you might ever hold. This amount is your *ceiling*.

You may also want to hold a *provision in reserve assets* to pay for the shares in your ceiling, excluding those in your initial portfolio. Assuming the buyer's limit is 100% and you only trade with each other, the ceiling equals the total stocks you both hold when the strategy starts.

Suppose you and the buyer begin with portfolios of equal value. You trade when he wants to. He trades when the market moves his cushion beyond its *tolerance*. His tolerance is the percentage change he allows in his cushion before he trades with you to bring the relation between his cushion and exposure back in line. After a market rise, such trading lowers your exposure because you sell stocks to the buyer; after a market drop, such trading increases your exposure because you buy stocks from the buyer. Given his tolerance, you know what market moves will spark trading and how much stock will change hands.

Let's look now at how our portfolio insurance strategy works in a rising market and a falling market.

VII. A Rising Market

Suppose the buyer has a portfolio of $100. He chooses a floor of $80 and a multiple of 2. Keeping in mind "exposure = multiple × cushion," the buyer's cushion is $20, and his initial stock exposure is $40. He invests the remaining $60 in T-bills. You, a portfolio insurance seller, take the other side of his trades. Your initial exposure is $60, and you have $40 invested in T-bills.

If stock prices rise 10%, the buyer's exposure rises to $44 ($40 plus 10% of $40). This brings his cushion to $24 (the $104 new portfolio value minus his $80 floor). The buyer must now increase his exposure to $48 ($24 cushion times multiple of 2) to restore the ratio between his cushion and exposure. To do this he buys $4 of stock from you, using $4 he collects from selling some of his T-bills.

Before you trade with the buyer, the 10% stock price increase raises your exposure from $60 to $66. After trading, your exposure drops to $62. Your T-bill holdings go from $40 to $44 because you buy T-bills with the $4 you collect from the buyer.

In the extreme — that is, with stock prices rising unchecked — you continue selling stock to the buyer. Your exposure keeps falling until you own only T-bills. At this point, the buyer is at his limit, with the maximum allowable percentage of stocks in his portfolio. Trading stops until the market retreats.

VIII. A Falling Market

Suppose stock prices drop 10%. The buyer's exposure falls to $36 ($40 minus 10% of $40), and his cushion falls to $16 ($96 new portfolio value minus $80 floor). To restore the ratio between his cushion and exposure to a multiple of 2, the buyer wants to reduce his exposure to $32 ($16 cushion times the multiple of 2). He sells $4 of stock to you, and replaces it with $4 of T-bills.

Before trading with the buyer, your exposure drops to $54. After you trade, it goes up to $58, but your T-bill holdings fall to $36. If stock prices keep tumbling, you will continue to buy stock from the buyer, and your T-bill holdings will continue to decline. You go right on buying stock so long as prices fall and the buyer doesn't run out of stock to sell.

The more the market drops, the closer you come to depleting your T-bill holdings and reaching your ceiling in stocks. But unlike a rising market which can easily bring the buyer to his limit, a falling market probably won't drop far enough to leave him with only reserve assets and you with only active assets. On the other hand, you will probably lose more than the buyer in such a market. Even though you collect part of his trading costs, your gains won't cover your losses from steadily buying when prices are low and still dropping.

No matter what direction it takes, a large number of portfolio insurance buyers can force the market to move more than it would otherwise. A market rise will trigger buying by all portfolio insurance buyers and a fall will trigger selling. And if the two extremes occur close together, the seller will benefit from even more opportunities to buy low and sell high.

On top of market movements, the buyer's tolerance and multiple also influence trading patterns and profits in a portfolio insurance strategy.

IX. The Effects of Tolerance and Multiple

How frequently you trade with the buyer depends on the tolerance he chooses. The lower it is, the more closely his exposure will be related to his cushion and the more frequently he will trade with you.

The buyer's multiple also affects trading. The higher it is, the faster he approaches his limit as the market rises or loses his cushion as the market falls. This is why a higher multiple will favor you, the seller, when stocks move up and down, or down and up. Since you profit from buying low and selling high, the higher multiple increases the value of these trades. By contrast, the buyer with a high multiple loses from buying higher and selling lower.

Next we examine simulation results for portfolio insurance buyers and sellers using multiples of 2 and 4.

X. Simulations

In our simulations, the buyer's trading costs are 0.5% of the value of the trade. These costs are equally split between the seller and the entity that matches buyer and seller.

With a Multiple of 2

Suppose that in 1974 you began selling portfolio insurance. Your buyer had a portfolio value of $100 million; an $80 million floor; an initial stock exposure of $40 million; a $20 million cushion ($100 million minus $80 million); and a multiple of 2. He set his tolerance to trade with you each time his cushion rose or fell 5%.

Your portfolio's value was also $100 million, but you had $60 million invested in stock and $40 million in T-bills. You rebalanced your portfolio according to the buyer's moves. Each time you traded with him, you received as payment half of the associated trading costs.

In 1974, the market was down 26%. By year-end, you had traded 65 times with the buyer. Your portfolio declined to $86.4 million. The buyer's portfolio declined to $95.7 million, and his floor increased to $86.5 million because of interest earned on the reserve asset. His cushion dropped to $9.2 million.

On the other hand, if you and the buyer had maintained your initial portfolios with no rebalancing (a buy-and-hold strategy), you would have ended up with $87.7 million and the buyer with $94.5 million. Following the portfolio insurance strategy, the buyer fared better by $1.2 million, while you did worse by $1.3 million. The buyer's trading costs produce the $.1 million imbalance.

In 1975, the market was up 37%. Using our strategy you and the buyer made 84 trades from the beginning of 1974 to the end of 1975. Your portfolio value rose to $107 million. The buyer ended the year with a $107.3 million portfolio — a $91.6 million floor and a $15.7 million cushion. But, if you had followed the buy-and-hold strategy, you would have ended up with a $106.1 million portfolio and the buyer with a $108.9 million portfolio. You fared better by $1.3 million using the portfolio insurance strategy, while the buyer did worse by $1.6 million. Again, trading costs produce the imbalance.

Table 1 summarizes simulation results for each year from 1974 to 1986 for buyers and sellers following portfolio insurance and buy-and-hold strategies. A tolerance of 5% was used. The table compares the performance of the portfolio insurance strategy with three different buy-and-hold strategies:

TABLE 1. *Simulation Results with the Strategy Restarted Each Year (Results Are Not Cumulative).*

Active asset	S&P 500 index
Reserve asset	One-year Treasury bill

Buyer		*Seller*	
Initial portfolio	100	Initial portfolio	100
Initial floor	80	Initial exposure	60
Initial cushion	20		
Initial exposure	40		
Multiple	2		

Tolerance: Rebalance after 5% move in the cushion
Trading cost for buyer: 0.5% of amount traded
(the seller receives half of this amount)

		Buyer			Seller's	Buy-and-Hold Strategies		
		Portfolio			Portfolio	100%	60%	40%
Year	Cost	Value	Cushion	Floor	Value	in S&P	in S&P	in S&P
1974	0.2	95.7	9.2	86.5	86.4	74.2	87.7	94.5
1975	0.4	118.7	34.0	84.7	124.1	137.1	124.6	118.4
1976	0.1	112.8	28.7	84.1	116.0	123.7	116.3	112.6
1977	0.1	100.5	16.1	84.3	98.0	93.1	98.0	100.5
1978	0.1	106.4	20.5	85.9	107.4	106.5	106.9	107.0
1979	0.1	113.0	24.6	88.4	115.0	117.6	114.7	113.3
1980	0.2	119.6	30.1	89.6	123.9	131.7	123.8	119.8
1981	0.1	106.9	15.1	91.8	102.8	95.0	102.9	106.8
1982	0.2	114.1	25.2	88.8	117.3	120.4	116.6	114.8
1983	0.1	114.8	27.7	87.1	118.0	123.9	117.9	114.9
1984	0.1	108.1	20.2	87.9	108.0	106.3	107.7	108.4
1985	0.1	118.0	31.9	86.2	121.0	131.4	121.9	117.2
1986	0.2	110.6	25.7	84.9	114.1	118.7	113.7	111.1

investing the entire portfolio in the S&P 500; investing 60% of the portfolio in the S&P 500 and the rest in T-bills; and investing 40% of the portfolio in the S&P 500 and the rest in T-bills.

Table 2 lists cumulative year-end portfolio values from the beginning of 1974 to the end of 1985. The first two charts in the table track the performance of the buyer in a portfolio insurance strategy and in a buy-and-hold strategy. The third and fourth charts track the performance of the seller in the two strategies.

The simulations reveal that portfolio insurance helps the buyer most when the market goes straight up or straight down relative to his floor. By contrast, a buy-and-hold strategy is more profitable to the buyer when markets are volatile but not trending—that is, when the market fluctuates but finishes very close to where it began.

TABLE 2.

Insured Portfolio Performance of Buyer—Multiple of 2

Active asset	S&P 500
Reserve asset	One-year Treasury bill
Initial portfolio	100
Initial floor	80
Initial cushion	20
Initial exposure	40
Multiple	2

Tolerance: Rebalance after a 5% change in the cushion
Trading cost: 0.5% of amount traded (the seller receives half of this amount)

From the Beginning of

Final Portfolio Values

To the End of	1974	1975	1976	1977	1978	1979	1980	1981	1982	1983	1984	1985	1986
1974	95.7												
1975	107.3	118.7											
1976	118.8	137.8	112.8										
1977	119.6	133.0	111.7	100.5									
1978	127.5	141.0	118.8	107.1	106.4								
1979	143.5	161.4	134.6	120.7	120.5	113.0							
1980	169.6	200.0	162.1	143.1	144.8	136.0	119.6						
1981	181.3	200.5	168.9	152.3	151.3	141.8	125.8	106.9					
1982	205.5	231.6	192.8	172.8	172.7	161.9	143.3	121.1	114.1				
1983	232.4	271.4	221.3	195.9	197.6	185.7	163.5	136.8	130.7	114.8			
1984	251.4	289.6	238.1	211.8	212.8	199.8	176.2	148.0	140.6	123.7	108.1		
1985	294.2	362.9	286.5	249.0	255.0	240.3	210.0	172.7	168.9	147.6	126.9	118.0	
1986	328.4	422.9	324.2	278.7	288.5	271.9	238.8	192.5	191.3	166.3	141.6	132.2	110.6

TABLE 2 *Continued*

Buy-and-Hold Portfolio Performance of Buyer

40% in the S&P 500 and 60% in one-year Treasury bill

Initial portfolio value: 100

From the Beginning of

Final Portfolio Values

To the End of	1974	1975	1976	1977	1978	1979	1980	1981	1982	1983	1984	1985	1986
1974	94.5												
1975	108.9	118.4											
1976	121.3	134.2	112.6										
1977	122.3	133.5	112.6	100.5									
1978	131.0	142.9	120.5	107.6	107.0								
1979	147.8	162.3	136.5	121.7	121.4	113.3							
1980	174.2	194.1	162.3	144.2	144.9	135.7	119.8						
1981	189.1	207.4	174.6	155.6	155.2	144.8	127.7	106.8					
1982	214.8	237.1	199.0	177.2	177.3	165.6	146.2	122.0	114.8				
1983	241.8	269.4	225.3	200.1	201.1	188.3	166.3	138.5	131.2	114.9			
1984	263.3	292.7	245.0	217.8	218.6	204.5	180.6	150.5	142.3	124.6	108.5		
1985	299.9	338.4	281.4	249.4	252.1	236.7	209.2	173.7	166.2	145.6	126.4	117.2	
1986	329.2	374.6	310.4	274.6	278.7	262.1	231.9	192.2	185.0	162.1	140.6	130.7	111.1

TABLE 2 Continued

Insured Portfolio Performance of Seller

Active asset	S&P 500
Reserve asset	One-year Treasury bill
Initial portfolio	100
Initial exposure	60

Tolerance: Rebalance after a 5% change in the cushion

Trading cost for buyer: 0.5% of amount traded (the seller receives half of this amount)

From the Beginning of

Final Portfolio Values

To the End of	1974	1975	1976	1977	1978	1979	1980	1981	1982	1983	1984	1985	1986
1974	86.4												
1975	107.4	124.1											
1976	124.1	141.8	116.0										
1977	122.5	141.7	114.3	98.0									
1978	131.5	152.7	122.9	105.2	107.4								
1979	150.3	174.0	140.7	120.9	123.7	115.0							
1980	181.1	206.3	169.6	147.1	150.8	141.1	123.9						
1981	194.1	227.1	182.4	156.1	160.1	148.9	129.2	102.8					
1982	223.1	259.9	210.1	180.4	185.3	172.9	150.6	120.2	117.3				
1983	253.9	291.7	238.6	206.6	212.2	198.6	174.2	140.0	136.8	118.0			
1984	276.9	320.5	260.7	225.0	231.4	216.3	189.4	151.8	148.4	127.8	108.0		
1985	315.4	351.6	294.5	258.4	264.9	248.7	220.4	179.2	174.6	151.7	129.9	121.0	
1986	345.4	373.7	321.3	284.2	290.7	274.1	244.2	200.3	194.6	170.2	146.8	137.2	114.1

TABLE 2 *Continued*

Buy-and-Hold Portfolio Performance of Seller

60% in the S&P 500 and 40% in one-year Treasury bill

Initial portfolio value: 100

From the Beginning of

Final Portfolio Values

To the End of	1974	1975	1976	1977	1978	1979	1980	1981	1982	1983	1984	1985	1986
1974	87.7												
1975	106.1	124.6											
1976	121.8	145.7	116.3										
1977	120.0	141.6	113.5	98.0									
1978	128.4	151.3	121.3	104.8	106.9								
1979	146.5	173.8	139.1	120.0	122.8	114.7							
1980	177.1	213.2	169.9	146.3	151.0	141.7	123.8						
1981	187.0	221.7	177.4	153.1	156.6	146.2	127.4	102.9					
1982	214.9	256.4	204.8	176.6	181.3	169.7	148.0	119.4	116.6				
1983	245.8	296.1	235.8	203.1	209.6	196.7	171.9	138.5	136.4	117.9			
1984	266.5	320.2	255.2	219.9	226.6	212.5	185.6	149.6	147.0	127.0	107.7		
1985	311.5	379.5	301.3	259.1	269.1	253.4	221.9	178.5	177.7	153.9	130.4	121.9	
1986	346.9	426.0	337.4	289.8	302.3	285.4	250.2	201.1	201.6	174.8	148.1	138.9	113.7

TABLE 3. *Simulation Results with the Strategy Restarted Each Year (Results Are Not Cumulative).*

Active asset	S&P 500 index
Reserve asset	One-year Treasury bill

Buyer		*Seller*	
Initial portfolio	100	Initial portfolio	100
Initial floor	80	Initial exposure	20
Initial cushion	20		
Initial exposure	80		
Multiple	4		

Tolerance: Rebalance after 5% move in the cushion
Trading cost for buyer: 0.5% of amount traded
(the seller receives half of this amount)

	Buyer				Seller's	Buy-and-Hold Strategies		
		Portfolio			Portfolio	100%	80%	20%
Year	Cost	Value	Cushion	Floor	Value	in S&P	in S&P	in S&P
1974	1.1	89.5	3.0	86.5	92.3	74.2	81.0	101.3
1975	0.2	134.5	31.2	84.7	108.4	137.1	130.8	112.1
1976	0.1	122.2	28.7	84.1	106.6	123.7	120.0	108.8
1977	0.5	95.9	11.6	84.3	102.3	93.1	95.6	102.9
1978	1.1	103.6	17.7	85.9	109.7	106.5	106.7	107.2
1979	0.9	114.0	25.7	88.4	113.6	117.6	116.2	111.9
1980	0.9	126.2	29.5	89.6	116.9	131.7	127.7	115.9
1981	0.7	100.8	9.0	91.8	108.6	95.0	98.9	110.7
1982	1.5	112.7	23.8	88.8	118.0	120.4	118.5	112.9
1983	0.3	121.6	28.2	87.1	111.1	123.9	120.9	111.9
1984	0.9	104.3	16.4	87.9	111.4	106.3	107.0	109.2
1985	0.3	129.6	31.5	86.2	109.4	131.4	126.6	112.4
1986	0.2	117.0	27.4	84.9	107.7	118.7	116.2	108.6

With a Multiple of 4

To see the effects of using a multiple of 4, we repeated the simulations that produced Tables 1 and 2. Tables 3 and 4 give the results.

Now we assume that in the beginning of 1974 you started to trade with a buyer who had an initial stock portfolio of $80 million, $20 million in T-bills, an initial cushion of $20 million and a 5% tolerance. You started with the same initial portfolio value as the buyer, but with $20 million in stocks and $80 million in T-bills.

By the end of 1974, your total portfolio decreased to $92.3 million, while the buyer's decreased to $89.5 million. If you and the buyer had maintained

TABLE 4.

Insured Portfolio Performance of Buyer—Multiple of 4

Active asset	S&P 500
Reserve asset	One-year Treasury bill
Initial portfolio	100
Initial floor	80
Initial cushion	20
Initial exposure	80
Multiple	4

Tolerance: Rebalance after a 5% change in the cushion
Trading cost: 0.5% of amount traded (the seller receives half of this amount)

Final Portfolio Values

To the End of	From the Beginning of												
	1974	1975	1976	1977	1978	1979	1980	1981	1982	1983	1984	1985	1986
1974	89.5												
1975	98.6	134.5											
1976	108.7	164.6	122.2										
1977	108.6	154.6	113.1	98.9									
1978	115.2	164.9	117.3	100.7	103.6								
1979	128.5	192.7	134.4	113.2	117.8	114.1							
1980	148.5	245.1	171.3	134.2	147.2	145.5	126.2						
1981	160.9	245.0	162.9	138.6	141.4	138.6	121.2	112.7					
1982	179.2	288.2	183.2	154.8	158.7	156.2	136.3	112.7	112.7				
1983	198.2	340.4	218.2	173.6	182.5	187.0	158.6	127.2	136.0	121.6			
1984	214.7	365.9	224.9	185.8	190.9	192.8	164.8	135.3	143.8	128.3	104.4		
1985	241.2	448.9	291.3	216.4	237.1	251.7	208.1	160.2	186.2	166.8	130.3	129.6	
1986	261.8	513.0	343.3	239.1	281.0	297.3	246.6	181.7	218.7	196.3	154.6	153.3	117.0

TABLE 4 *Continued*

Buy-and-Hold Portfolio Performance of Buyer

80% in the S&P 500 and 20% in one-year Treasury bill
Initial portfolio value: 100

To the End of	From the Beginning of												
	1974	1975	1976	1977	1978	1979	1980	1981	1982	1983	1984	1985	1986
	Final Portfolio Values												
1974	81.0												
1975	103.3	130.8											
1976	122.3	157.1	120.0										
1977	117.7	149.7	114.4	95.6									
1978	125.8	159.8	122.1	102.0	106.7								
1979	145.1	185.4	141.6	118.3	124.2	116.2							
1980	180.0	232.4	177.5	148.4	157.0	147.7	127.7						
1981	184.9	236.0	180.3	150.7	158.1	147.7	127.1	98.9					
1982	215.0	275.8	210.6	176.1	185.4	173.7	149.8	116.7	118.5				
1983	249.9	322.7	246.4	206.1	218.0	205.1	177.4	138.4	141.6	120.9			
1984	269.8	347.7	265.6	222.1	234.6	220.5	190.6	148.6	151.7	129.5	107.0		
1985	323.0	420.7	321.1	268.0	286.8	270.2	234.6	183.3	189.2	162.2	134.5	126.6	
1986	364.6	477.5	364.4	305.1	325.9	308.7	268.6	210.1	218.1	187.4	155.6	147.1	116.2

TABLE 4 *Continued*

Insured Portfolio Performance of Seller

Active asset	S&P 500
Reserve asset	One-year Treasury bill
Initial portfolio	100
Initial exposure	20

Tolerance: Rebalance after a 5% change in the cushion
Trading cost for buyer: 0.5% of amount traded (the seller receives half of this amount)

Final Portfolio Values

To the End of	From the Beginning of												
	1974	1975	1976	1977	1978	1979	1980	1981	1982	1983	1984	1985	1986
1974	92.3												
1975	115.5	108.4											
1976	133.4	115.2	106.6										
1977	132.4	120.4	112.8	102.3									
1978	142.5	129.2	123.7	111.0	109.7								
1979	163.8	143.4	139.7	127.6	125.4	113.6							
1980	200.2	162.1	158.7	154.6	146.7	130.8	116.9						
1981	212.0	184.0	186.1	167.7	167.6	150.8	133.1	108.6					
1982	246.6	205.2	216.2	195.9	195.9	176.5	156.3	128.0	118.0				
1983	284.9	205.2	216.2	225.7	222.9	194.9	177.1	148.6	130.7	111.1			
1984	309.9	246.8	268.4	247.2	242.7	219.7	197.9	163.1	144.3	122.9	111.4		
1985	364.2	268.9	283.9	286.6	276.1	233.5	218.5	189.8	156.3	132.2	125.6	109.4	
1986	407.0	287.4	296.4	318.0	291.6	245.0	230.8	208.5	166.5	140.2	133.1	116.1	107.7

TABLE 4 *Continued*

Buy-and-Hold Portfolio Performance of Seller
20% in the S&P 500 and 80% in one-year Treasury bill
Initial portfolio value: 100

To the End of	From the Beginning of												
	1974	1975	1976	1977	1978	1979	1980	1981	1982	1983	1984	1985	1986
	Final Portfolio Values												
1974	101.3												
1975	111.7	108.4											
1976	120.8	122.8	108.8										
1977	124.6	125.4	111.7	102.9									
1978	133.6	134.4	119.7	110.4	107.2								
1979	149.2	150.7	134.0	123.3	120.0	111.9							
1980	171.3	175.0	154.7	142.1	138.8	129.6	115.9						
1981	191.2	193.1	171.7	158.1	153.8	143.3	128.1	110.7					
1982	214.7	217.8	193.2	177.7	173.2	161.6	144.4	124.7	112.9				
1983	237.8	242.8	214.7	197.2	192.7	179.9	160.8	138.6	126.0	111.9			
1984	260.1	265.1	234.6	215.6	210.5	196.5	175.6	151.5	137.6	122.1	109.2		
1985	288.3	297.2	261.6	239.7	235.1	219.9	196.5	169.0	154.7	137.2	122.4	112.4	
1986	311.5	323.1	283.5	259.3	255.1	238.9	213.5	183.2	168.5	149.5	133.1	122.5	108.6

your initial portfolios without rebalancing, you would have ended up with $101.3 million and the buyer with $81 million.

On the other hand, as portfolio insurance trading partners from the beginning of 1974 to the end of 1975, your portfolio increased to $115.5 million, and the buyer's dropped to $98.6 million. Using the buy-and-hold strategy your portfolio would have increased to $111.7 million and the buyer's to $103.3 million.

Compared to a multiple 2 strategy, a multiple of 4 gives you even higher returns in a rising market, and lower returns in a falling market. And in a volatile, non-trending market, the higher multiple gives you more chances to make money buy buying lower and selling higher.

Here is a summary of portfolio values from the simulations above:

1/74–12/74 (market down 26% in 1974)

Multiple of 2	Portfolio insurance	buyer	95.7	seller	86.4
	Buy and hold	buyer	94.5	seller	87.7
Multiple of 4	Portfolio insurance	buyer	89.5	seller	92.3
	Buy and hold	buyer	81.0	seller	101.3

1/74–12/75 (market up 37% in 1975)

Multiple of 2	Portfolio insurance	buyer	107.3	seller	107.4
	Buy and hold	buyer	108.9	seller	106.1
Multiple of 4	Portfolio insurance	buyer	98.6	seller	115.5
	Buy and hold	buyer	103.3	seller	111.7

XI. Realized Capital Gains for the Seller

As a portfolio insurance seller, you can realize capital gains by buying after a market fall and selling after a market rise. Table 5 shows the capital gains you could have realized every year from 1974 to 1986. It also lists your realized income from dividends and interest for each year. You started with a $100 million portfolio, an initial exposure of $50 million and a $10 million cushion. Your buyer's multiple was 5.

We assume you traded to maximize your realized capital gains. That is, when a market rise caused you to sell stocks to the buyer, you sold him the shares you bought for the lowest price first. Table 5 shows that you realized substantial capital gains in years when the market was highly volatile but non-trending (1976, 1980, 1982, 1983, and 1986).

XII. Is It Practical?

In this article we had no trouble bringing you and your buyer together as portfolio insurance trading partners. Anything is possible on paper. Finding and matching buyers and sellers may be much harder in the real world. Both

TABLE 5. *Realized Income for Portfolio Insurance Seller.*

Active asset	S&P 500 index
Reserve asset	One-year Treasury bill
Initial portfolio	100
Initial exposure	50
Initial cushion	10
Multiple	5

Tolerance: Rebalance after 5% move in the cushion
Trading cost: 0.5% of amount traded

	Realized Income					Buy-and-Hold Strategies		
Year	Divi-dend	Interest	Capital Gains	Total	Portfolio Value	50% in S&P	100% in S&P	100% in T-Bill
1974	2.9	2.3	1.9	7.1	83.8	91.1	74.2	108.1
1975	0.8	5.2	6.2	12.2	114.7	121.5	137.1	105.9
1976	1.2	3.9	8.3	13.4	114.2	114.4	123.7	105.1
1977	2.7	1.9	0.5	5.1	98.6	99.2	93.1	105.4
1978	2.8	3.6	5.1	11.5	109.0	106.9	106.5	107.4
1979	2.6	6.0	5.6	14.2	115.9	114.0	117.6	110.4
1980	2.5	7.1	13.2	22.8	125.1	121.8	131.7	111.9
1981	3.3	4.9	1.1	9.3	102.9	104.8	95.0	114.7
1982	3.7	4.1	9.6	17.4	120.3	115.7	120.4	111.0
1983	1.5	6.7	9.7	17.9	118.4	116.4	123.9	108.9
1984	2.9	3.9	2.2	9.0	109.7	108.1	106.3	109.9
1985	1.5	5.4	7.9	14.8	116.5	119.5	131.4	107.7
1986	1.4	4.1	9.8	15.3	115.2	112.4	118.7	106.1

parties must have the same types of active and reserve assets. Both must agree on the multiple and when to begin the strategy. And even if we clear these hurdles, what happens if one party wants to stop trading before the other? Who, if anyone, will take the other side of the position? And what happens if the buyer wants to change his multiple?

A portfolio insurance clearing house could help solve these problems if the market has enough groups of potential buyers and sellers with the same multiple and the same types of assets in their portfolios. The clearing house could regulate the traffic, match buyers and sellers, and come up with ways to roll positions from one party to the next.

44

Portfolio Insurance:
Volatility Risk and Futures Mispricing*

Joanne M. Hill
Vice President
Kidder, Peabody & Co.

Anshuman Jain
Assistant Vice President
Kidder, Peabody & Co.

Richard A. Wood, Jr.
Research Associate
Kidder, Peabody & Co.

I. Introduction

The concept of portfolio insurance has been the center of considerable attention in both the academic literature and the investment profession. Portfolio insurance generally refers to an investment strategy that attempts to alter the payoff pattern of a portfolio of risky assets in a manner that significantly reduces the risk of returns below a minimum or protected level over a horizon chosen for implementation of the insurance program. Portfolio insurance strategies have the capacity to modify returns by adding positive skewness to the return payoff pattern. This positive skewness is the primary attraction and innovation of portfolio insurance that warrants much of the attention it has been accorded among the investment management community. The most defensible rationale for buying or selling portfolio insurance is based on three-dimensional utility preferences in which investors prefer higher returns to lower, lower risk in terms of standard deviation to higher, and positively skewed payoff patterns to symmetric or negatively skewed payoffs.[1] Adding the third dimension introduces a new solution to

---

*This article is a significantly expanded version of one with the same title that appeared in the Winter 1988 issue of *The Journal of Portfolio Management*.

1. Hayne E. Leland, "Who Should Buy Portfolio Insurance?" *Journal of Finance* 35 (May 1980): 581–94.

the portfolio allocation problem. In this solution, one becomes either a buyer or seller of portfolio insurance, depending on the market price of positive skewness relative to the investors' willingness to trade-off higher returns and a lower standard deviation for positive skewness. In this framework, the market price of positive skewness, i.e., cost of portfolio insurance, depends primarily on the aggregate investor preference for skewness.

Rubinstein has reviewed the range of investment strategies that fit the broad definition of portfolio insurance, including simple stop-loss disciplines, the purchase of exchange-traded put options, and the creation of synthetic put options using cash or futures instruments.[2] Perold has recently offered a portfolio insurance decision rule known as Constant Proportion Portfolio Insurance in which the payoffs are not dependent on the path of prices over the insured interval and the allocation in the risky asset does not depend on the time to the end of the program.[3] This approach is not dependent on "option-type" variables such as time and a volatility forecast that play a role in other portfolio insurance programs. The latest version of the Dynamic Asset Allocation (DAA)[T] product of Leland, O'Brien and Rubinstein, Inc., "perpetual" portfolio insurance, and the "Process-free" approach of John Cox have much in common with Constant Proportion Portfolio Insurance. These recent advances seek to reduce the dependence of the allocation decision on the time remaining to the end of the protection horizon and provide for a more definable and controllable relationship between insurance cost and volatility.[4]

All of these portfolio insurance techniques may be implemented by dynamically allocating funds between a set of risky assets and a lower risk "reserve" asset based on the relative prices of the reserve and risky asset and the distance from the insured portfolio value. This need for dynamic adjustment forces the trading costs associated with implementation of the dynamic strategy to be explicitly recognized in assessing the merits of portfolio insurance strategies. Futures markets have been the key to the success of portfolio insurance programs primarily because of their low trading costs. This and other reasons why futures have played a large role in portfolio insurance programs are listed below.

- The frequent adjustments required in dynamic programs can be done in futures markets at low trading costs (ignoring mispricing) and in the markets with the greatest continuous liquidity.

---

2. Mark Rubinstein, "Alternative Paths to Portfolio Insurance," *Financial Analysts Journal* (July/August 1985): 42–52.

3. André F. Perold, "Constant Proportion Portfolio Insurance," Working Paper, Harvard Business School, 1986. See also Fischer Black and Robert Jones, "Simplifying Portfolio Insurance," *The Journal of Portfolio Management* (Fall 1987).

4. These approaches were discussed by Hayne Leland and John Cox at the conference entitled "Innovative Techniques in Portfolio Insurance," New York, 10–11 June 1986.

- The liquidity of the futures market allows protection programs to be undertaken on a larger scale than is feasible in option or cash markets.
- The use of futures (or options) permits the portfolio insurance program to be implemented independent of the management of the risky assets. External managers or internal stock or bond management procedures are not disrupted by the portfolio insurance strategy.
- The longer-term, European-type options that meet the parameters of the types of insurance programs that appeal to institutional investors are not available or have limited liquidity.

Weighed against these significant advantages of futures in asset allocation, two important issues have surfaced as the use of these portfolio insurance products has grown. These issues are the impact on insurance costs of futures mispricing and uncertainty regarding realized volatility. Both issues are relevant to option-based insurance strategies as well as to Constant Proportion Insurance strategies that are implemented using futures. The initial parameters of a portfolio insurance program — such as term, target floor return, expected volatility, and expected return on the reserve asset — prescribe a series of allocation decisions over the program life that typically will be implemented with futures transactions. Increases in volatility can interact with the path of prices on the risky assets to raise the cost of the insurance program to the buyer or increase the returns to the seller. (In Constant Proportion Insurance, volatility is not an input, but high volatility increases the frequency of trading and, therefore, the transaction costs.) Adverse futures mispricing when allocation adjustments are made can increase the realized cost of the insurance programs. An additional concern is that these volatility and mispricing changes may be correlated with each other. A large price move can reflect an increase in volatility, thereby adding cost, and can also be accompanied by adverse futures mispricing, adding further cost to the insurance program.

Despite the fact that volatility uncertainty and futures mispricing have been the source of objections to the strategy of portfolio insurance, their actual effects on insurance costs have not been examined thoroughly. The objective of this study is to derive a distribution of portfolio insurance costs that encompasses both normal and extreme conditions of volatility changes, transactions costs, and stock index futures mispricing. A put-option replication version of portfolio insurance is assumed for purposes of the analysis. This is probably the most basic version of portfolio insurance as well as the version likely to be most sensitive to volatility uncertainty and futures mispricing. Using a method of option replication inclusive of transaction costs suggested by Leland, a probability distribution of insurance costs for one- and three-year programs can be derived from a distribution of volatility levels.[5]

---

5. Hayne E. Leland, "Option Pricing and Replication with Transaction Costs," *Journal of Finance* (December 1985): 1283–1301.

This distribution incorporates mispricing volatility as well as the trading costs associated with futures transactons. With these results, one can more realistically assess the value of portfolio insurance as a strategy, in general, and also evaluate trade-offs between alternative methods of implementing protection programs.

This article is divided into six sections. Section II details the impact of changing S&P 500 volatility and futures mispricing on portfolio insurance costs and presents some empirical evidence on the statistical properties of mispricing. In Section III, the methodology for revising volatility to incorporate higher transaction costs associated with mispricing is reviewed along with the basis for deriving the volatility distribution and related portfolio insurance cost distribution. The results of measuring the range of protection costs with this methodology are presented in Section IV. Section V summarizes the results and discusses their implications for the further growth and refinement of portfolio insurance as a strategy.

II. The Impact of Changing Volatility and Futures Mispricing

Volatility Impact

When a portfolio insurance program is implemented using futures, the size of the futures position is adjusted at specific intervals to replicate the delta of a call or put option.[6] For the purpose of this discussion, we assume that the purchase of portfolio insurance is comparable to buying a risky asset and a put option on that risky asset.[7] The option has a life equal to the horizon of the program and a strike price set at the current value of that asset minus the net of the floor value of the asset and any income earned by the risky asset over the insurance period. An equivalent strategy would be the purchase of a call option on the risky asset along with a riskless asset, sometimes referred to as a reserve asset, that has a duration equal to the horizon of the

---

6. Some portfolio insurance strategies are not completely tied to option models or have modified the option model in certain ways. However, all approaches involve adjustments of the exposure to the risky asset as a function of price moves in that asset. This adjustment occurs automatically when an option is held but must be done via futures transactions or trades in the risky asset itself in other circumstances.

7. Funds for the purchase of the option may come from outside the portfolio or from the sale of some of the risky assets. The costs of insurance differ in these two cases depending on the relative opportunity costs of the funds involved, but the dynamics are the same. Put cost estimates presented here are based on a put with a strike price equal to 100% of the portfolio (0% floor) or 95% of the portfolio (−5% floor) excluding the put cost. The actual minimum return would be the floor return (0% or −5%) plus the dividend yield minus the put cost as a percent of the initial portfolio value.

insurance program. In the latter case, the strike price of the call would be set in accordance with the income yield of the reserve asset and the floor return for the insurance program. For the purposes of this study, the S&P 500 stock index is used as a proxy for the risky asset, and the nearby S&P 500 futures contract for the future on that risky asset. The index put replication strategy is the subject of this analysis.

In a put replication strategy, the proportion of the portfolio allocated to stocks is 1.0 plus the (negative) delta of the put option. The remaining allocation can be held in the reserve asset or in an equity portfolio hedged with stock index futures. Typically, because of advantages previously mentioned, dynamic adjustments are made with futures rather than by changing the stock/reserve asset mix. The interval or trigger point for adjusting the actual equity allocation to the target level varies. The factors that are relevant in establishing the interval usually include: the expected magnitude of index changes over a typical trading interval, the difference between the current allocation and the target allocation, the transaction costs (commission and market impact) involved in the adjustment, the sensitivity of the allocation level to subsequent index changes (the gamma), and price and liquidity conditions in the futures market. Different portfolio insurance managers place different weights on these factors depending on their particular style and expertise. The major trade-off is between the reduction in option replication error and the higher trading costs that accompany more frequent adjustments.[8]

Volatility plays an important role in a portfolio insurance program. If a put option was purchased outright, the volatility implicit in the put premium or insurance cost would be, in effect, "locked-in." The outright put option holder is not subject to futures mispricing risk or changes in volatility.[9] If realized volatility is actually less than the volatility implicit in the put option, however, it is probable that the insurance could have been created at a lower cost by engaging in option replication. In such replication, the volatility estimate determines the expected put cost and the dynamic path of allocations for the risky and reserve asset. These allocations are based on a combination of the deltas of a long stock index (delta of 1) and a long put (delta < 1). The insurance is paid for over the life of the program through the accrual of costs associated with the lag in allocation adjustment to that based on the

---

8. See the following articles for a more detailed treatment of the selection of an adjustment interval: Michael Asay and Charles Edelburg, "Can a Dynamic Strategy Replicate the Returns on an Option?" *Journal of Futures Markets* 8 (1986): 63–70; E.S. Etzioni, "Rebalance Disciplines for Portfolio Insurance," *Journal of Portfolio Management* (Fall 1986): 59–62; Leland, "Option Pricing and Replication with Transaction Costs."
9. The futures mispricing at the time the option is purchased is typically a factor in the implied volatility of the put option, but changes in mispricing beyond this point would not directly affect the option holder assuming the option is held to expiration.

delta of the put being replicated. As an example, assume a $100 million S&P 500 index fund is protected by a short stock index futures position of $30 million in accordance with a put option delta of −.3 or −30%.

At revision interval t, the index has fallen 5% and the portfolio has decreased in value to $95 million. The loss of $5 million is partially offset by a gain on the synthetic option of $1.5 million. At the new index level, assume that the appropriate cash allocation (option delta) is −.35. If this 35% level had been established prior to the market decline, the futures position would have moved from $35 to $33.25 million for a gain of $1.75. This amount is $.3 million greater than the gain associated with the 30% hedge position. Similarly, on the upside, the 30% hedged position loses $.3 million more in value than if the 25% hedge position (based on an option delta of −.25 at a $105 portfolio value) had been established on day t.[10] The revised allocation would have been established automatically with a long put option as its delta adjusted to the new value of the portfolio. The differential performance for a 5% up or down move in the portfolio can be thought of as a payment toward the cost of insurance.

An initial volatility estimate in a portfolio insurance program provides an estimate of the expected put cost that will be paid over the life of the program. If volatility in terms of the size of index moves is consistent over the life of the program with the volatility estimate (reflecting transaction costs) used to establish the allocation criteria, the actual insurance costs will be very close to the expected costs. That is, the dollar amount of underperformance of option replication relative to the actual put option's performance should accumulate to a sum equal to the price that would have been paid for such a put with the equivalent implied volatility.

Consider the results if volatility is greater than expected or if stock index futures are mispriced to the disadvantage of the buyer or seller. If the move over the same time interval is 10% rather than 5%, the hedge position gains less than if the larger hedge position had been established at the outset or if a put option had been purchased. This is an extreme example, but it does illustrate how high volatility in terms of larger than expected market moves per time interval can cause one to pay more for insurance than expected.

The impact of futures mispricing can be explained in a similar fashion. In the examples in Tables 1 and 2, the percentage change in the hedge position is assumed to be identical to that in the portfolio. Now, consider a scenario in which futures are mispriced to the disadvantage of the portfolio insurer, i.e., futures are cheap when the hedge position needs to be increased

---

10. The deltas of −.35 and −.25 are the mid-points of the delta ranges of −.30 to −.40 and −.30 to −.20 which are typical deltas for a 5% index move for a −3% floor program with approximately one year left to run (volatility of 15%, interest rate 7%, dividend yield 3.5%).

TABLE 1. *Example of Dynamic Hedge.*

	Case 1: 5% Decline				Case 2: 5% Rise		
	Long Portfolio	Delta – Short Hedge Position		Long Put[a]	Long Portfolio	Delta – Short Hedge Position		Long Put[a]
		−.30	−.35			−.30	−.25	
Day$_0$	$100	30	35	3.2	$100	30	25	3.2
Day$_{0+t}$	95	28.5	33.2	5.0	105	31.5	26.3	1.9
Gain (loss)	(5)	1.5	1.8	1.8	5	(1.5)	(1.3)	(1.3)

a. One-year put option with a strike price of 97, volatility of 15%, interest rate of 7%.

TABLE 2. *Example of One Period in the Life of a Dynamic Hedge.*

	Case 3: 10% Decline				Case 4: 10% Rise		
	Long Portfolio	Delta – Short Hedge Position		Long Put[a]	Long Portfolio	Delta – Short Hedge Position		Long Put[a]
		−.30	−.45			−.30	−.15	
Day$_0$	$100	30	45	3.2	$100	30	15	3.2
Day$_{0+t}$	90	27	40.5	8.1	110	33	19.5	1.6
Gain (loss)	(10)	3	4.5	4.9	10	(3)	(4.5)	(1.6)

a. One-year put option with a strike price of 97, volatility of 17%, interest rate of 7%.

(for declines in the index), and rich in the circumstances when the hedged position needs to be decreased by buying futures. In the first case of a declining market, the short position already established (30% in the example) has actually fallen more in value than expected, assuming futures have cheapened relative to the index. This is to the advantage of the insurer, and in Table 1 would make the gain greater than $1.5 million. However, the insurer must now sell more futures to increase the size of the hedged position. If these new futures are sold at "cheap" price levels, the gain (loss) in the next period on the hedged position can be expected to be less (greater) than the percentage change in the index (unless the futures cheapen further). By reducing gains in a declining market or by increasing losses in a rising market, adverse futures mispricing increases the accumulated portfolio insurance charges incurred over the protection horizon.

Stock Index Futures "Mispricing": Definition and Analysis

In order to assess the importance of stock index futures mispricing in portfolio insurance cost determination, it is useful to review the incidence and extent of this mispricing and its relationship to moves in the S&P 500 stock index. For purposes of this study, futures mispricing refers to the difference between the 4:00 P.M. S&P 500 index futures price and the fair value of the futures contract at that time. The futures data series is based on the 4:00 P.M. price levels of the nearby S&P 500 futures contract for the three months prior to the delivery month. Fair value is a very simple calculation:[11]

Fair value of future = Index level

+ Interest earned by investing index level of $ in a risk-free asset

− Dividends expected to be earned on the index

The interest and dividends are those accrued between the current date and contract expiration.

A better term for the relationship between S&P 500 index levels and S&P 500 futures prices would be "misaligned" prices. The S&P 500 index level is based on 500 individual stocks, some of which trade less frequently than others. The index level at any specific point may not reflect the actual price at which trades of a varying number of shares in these stocks could be simultaneously executed. The last sale indicates the price at which a specific quantity of stock traded. This price may not hold for larger or smaller blocks. Also, bid and ask prices from specialists are based on an assessment of a given level of supply and demand for an issue. The spread may change if significantly more stock is offered for purchase or sale. Information flows often influence index futures prices prior to being reflected in the individual stocks of the index. The futures market is a highly liquid, single instrument market; the S&P 500 is a composite market with a wide range of liquidity levels among its issues. Therefore, it is not unreasonable to expect some departure from the fair value relationships because of the rapid movement of both markets and disparities in trading costs. Extreme deviations from fair value can be viewed as signals that prices are misaligned to the point that a

---

11. Trades motivated by mispricing are often given the term "computer-generated." A computer is certainly not needed for this simple calculation except for the speed of calculation and for handling the information flow of prices from the floor. The origin of the term "computer-generated trading" is possibly the fact that these trades are determined from objective trading rules that do not involve an opinion on the prospective direction of the index. Also, many aspects of the execution of the index portion of the trade are handled by sophisticated telecommunications techniques.

TABLE 3. *Daily Data, June 1983–August 1986.*[a]

a. S&P 500 Futures Mispricing
(Futures Price − Fair Value)

Mean		Standard	Mispricing Observations		
Level	%	Deviation	% > 0	% > 1.00	% < −1.00
.536	.316	.905	72.3%	27.2%	3.6%

b. Correlation between Changes in Mispricing
and Daily Index Percentage Changes

Day in Relation	Entire	Index Changes		
to Index Change	Data Set	> .5%	>1.0%	>1.5%
Previous day	.135	.180	.192	.266
Same day	.061	.121	.214	.286
Next day	−.279	−.330	−.354	−.334
Std. deviation of mispricing changes	.532	.569	.664	.771
Number of observations	799	368 (46.0%)	132 (16.5%)	54 (6.75%)

c. Relative Volatility of S&P 500 and S&P 500 Futures

	S&P 500	Futures	Difference
Annualized std. deviation	12.17%	13.44%	1.27%
Autocorrelation			
1-day lag	.092	−.007	
2-day lag	.002	.037	
3-day lag	−.024	−.035	

a. Index closing level and futures price as of 4:00 P.M. or nearby contract. Fair values based on bond-equivalent yield of Treasury bill maturing closest to expiration date and dividends expected to be paid through the expiration date.

trading opportunity exists even after considering the trading costs of capitalizing on that opportunity and the risk of attempting to implement trades simultaneously in both markets.

Section a of Table 3 contains evidence on the levels of mispricing experienced over the three-year period extending from June 1983 through mid-August 1986. On average, S&P 500 futures were overvalued by .536 S&P points or .32% of the index value. This average level of mispricing is within the range of differential trading costs between the cash and futures market. (In the next section, some typical trading costs are presented.) The standard deviation of .905 is just under one index point. Figure 1 charts chronologically by contract the average level of mispricing for the three months prior

FIGURE 1. *Average of S&P 500 Futures Mispricing (by contract).*[a]

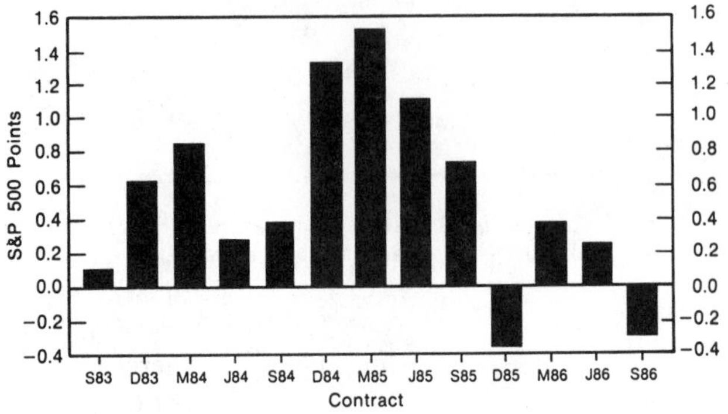

a. Data for three months prior to delivery month on S&P 500 future.

to the delivery month over the period. This figure shows that within the 1985–86 period the S&P 500 futures have moved from a position of average overvaluation to one averaging much closer to fair value. The December '85 and September '86 contract (through August 15) were the first contracts and the only 2 of the 13 contracts in the sample to record negative average mispricing behavior. This historical bias toward overvaluation is also reflected in the fact that on 72.3% of the sample days, mispricing was positive.

The relative volatility of the S&P 500 index and the nearby futures is shown in Section c of Table 3. The average annualized standard deviation is 12.2% for the index and 13.4% for the futures. The futures volatility was higher than the index volatility in 12 of the 13 three-month contract periods examined. One important source of the greater futures volatility is the volatility of the mispricing. This higher observed futures volatility supports the idea of incorporating the cost associated with adverse mispricing in analysis of insurance costs by incrementing the volatility estimate. (Another source of volatility in futures relative to the index is the variation in net carry costs as measured by the net of interest charges and dividends.)

Probably the most interesting results in Table 3 are those in Section b regarding the relationship between daily percentage changes in index levels and changes in mispricing. By screening the index return data for large index moves, one can explore the link between futures mispricing and index changes at the time when option replication trades are likely to occur. In a volatile market, where volatility is defined as an index move significantly larger than average, futures mispricing may be higher because stock index futures are able to digest the new information or a change of sentiment more quickly than is a broad stock index. The arbitrage mechanism helps to transmit new information or changes in sentiment to the stocks in the index. Therefore, one would expect to see a positive, contemporaneous relationship between mispricing changes and index returns when mispricing reaches a level that induces arbitrage.

The contemporaneous and one-day lead and one-day lag relationship are shown for the entire data set and for index changes of amounts greater than .5%, 1.0%, and 1.5% in absolute value. The contemporaneous relationship is positive but insignificant (.06) for the entire data set; however, the correlation increases as one moves to sample subsets which represent larger absolute index returns. A change of .64% represents one unit of standard deviation of daily percentage index changes. Therefore, a 1.5% index change represents a move of 2.4 standard deviations or over 98% of the distribution (assuming normality). In our sample 6.75% of the index returns were outside of this range, over 4% more than expected given a normal distribution. The mispricing results from this 1.5% index change subsample serve as the basis for developing worst case scenario insurance costs under varying volatilities. In this subsample, the contemporaneous correlation between the index and mispricing changes is .28, and the standard deviation of the changes in mispricing is .77 index points versus .53 points for the entire sample.

The significant and consistently negative correlation between index returns and mispricing changes the following day is also noteworthy. This can be interpreted as evidence that a positive (negative) index return tends to be followed by a decrease (increase) in mispricing on the next day, suggesting that from a mispricing standpoint it may be beneficial to delay adjustments to portfolio protection programs until the following day. If futures overvaluation increases on the day of a sharp index rise, there may be an opportunity for portfolio insurance managers to avoid buying overvalued futures by waiting until the next day for the mispricing change to reverse and decrease. The benefit of delaying the allocation adjustment also depends significantly on the direction of the index move on the next day. The index may move further in the direction of the initial change, negating any beneficial effects of reduced mispricing.[12] The day to day autocorrelation of index returns is slightly higher for the subsample representing index changes of greater than 1.5%, a correlation of .16 versus .09 overall. A higher autocorrelation at

---

12. A study of futures prices subsequent to days of greater than 1.5% index changes did show that on average the future closed (4:00 P.M.) slightly lower the following day for index declines and slightly higher the following day for index rises. This result was not uniform throughout the sample. Probably the most interesting result of this further study is that the significant negative correlation of mispricing changes do not necessarily imply an advantage to waiting until the following day of trade.

the 1-day lag was noted in index returns than in futures returns. This can arise because of the staggered response of the less actively traded stocks in a broad-based index to new information. It is interesting but not unexpected that the higher the volatility as defined by size of index move, the greater is the delayed response factor and hence the higher is the autocorrelation. The high volatility can be interpreted as a response to significant new information or to a change in sentiment.

III. Methodology

Volatility Adjustment

An approach suggested by Leland in a recent article is used to derive a distribution of put (insurance) costs that encompasses both normal and extreme conditions of volatility changes, transactions costs, and stock index futures mispricing.[13] Leland proposes a procedure that adjusts upward the volatility input to the option pricing and replication procedure. The increment to volatility is based on the fact that each time a transaction occurs the associated trading costs cause the purchase cost to be higher and the selling proceeds to be lower than in the absence of these costs. The key variables in the volatility revision are, therefore, the frequency of trading and the transaction cost level.

The adjustment to volatility takes the following form:

$$\sigma_A^2 = \sigma^2[1 + (\sqrt{(2/\pi)}\, k/\sigma\sqrt{t})] \tag{1}$$

where:

σ_A^2 = the transaction-cost adjusted volatility measure;
σ = the annualized standard deviation of the natural logarithm of price relative to holding period returns;
k = the round-trip transaction cost as a proportion of the volume of transactions; and
t = the revision interval as a proportion of a year.

Note that the difference $(\sigma_A^2 - \sigma^2)$ is an increasing function of the transaction cost, k. Also, as transactions become more frequent (t approaches 0), the adjustment becomes larger.

The innovative feature of the Leland approach is that the hedging strategy itself, i.e., the delta of the option, takes into account the trading costs. The total expected trading costs can be derived as the difference between the put cost based on the revised volatility compared to the put cost using unrevised volatility.

---

13. Leland, "Option Pricing and Replication with Transaction Costs."

Total expected trading and mispricing cost $= P(\sigma_A) - P(\sigma)$ \hfill (2)

where $P =$ the put option premium.

By estimating put option values using revised volatility estimates, insurance costs can be determined for a range of volatilities that reflect both typical trading costs and futures mispricing on days of significant index moves. When futures are mispriced to the disadvantage of the trader, a higher price is paid for purchases and lower proceeds realized for sales. Buying rich and selling cheap stock index futures is comparable, therefore, to incurring a higher round-trip transaction cost than would be incurred if futures were selling at fair value. Stock index futures mispricing can be thought of as a markup that one must pay as a penalty for "shopping" in busy periods or a discount one must take for selling when there is already a large supply.

Trading Cost and Mispricing Measurement

In the empirical analysis conducted here, 1% and 1.75% are used as round-trip trading cost estimates inclusive of moderate and extreme stock index futures mispricing. A third trading case, .5%, is an estimate of "pure" trading costs with only a small amount (.25%) of mispricing.[14] Trading costs k consist of three elements: (1) commissions, c; (2) the market impact of the trade itself, i; and (3) mispricing, m.

$$k = c + i + m \hspace{2cm} (3)$$

Commissions are typically fixed per contract. An amount of $15 one-way is a mid-range value for an institutional client. For a $100,000 contract value (S&P 500 at 200), $15 represents .015% or approximately $.006/share for an average $40 stock price. An index fund can expect to pay roughly

---

14. Some mispricing as defined here is expected at all times because of differential trading costs between futures and cash markets.

TABLE 4. *Stock Index and S&P 500 Futures Transactions Costs.*

	Stocks		Futures	
Commission per $100,000	$125[a]	(.125%)	$15	(.015%)
Market impact per $100 million		(.7%)		(.1%)
Total (one-way)		.825%		.115%
Total (two-way)		1.65%		.23%

a. Assumes commission of $.05 per share at average price of $40.
Source: Kidder, Peabody & Co., Inc. as published in "Corporate Pension Plans," *Intermarket,* August, 1986.

$.05 per share or .125% in one-way commissions. From a commission standpoint, therefore, futures are 1/8 to 1/10 the cost of trading stocks.

Market impact is harder to pinpoint because it depends not only on the size of the trade but also on the liquidity of the market at the time the trade occurs and the side of the market on which the trade will be executed. To capture trading costs on days when large index moves are occurring, assuming a portfolio insurer would be trading with that market move, it is critical to be as conservative as possible. Under normal market conditions, liquidity in S&P 500 futures is such that most trades can be done within one or at most two ticks of the price quoted on the same side of the market just before the trade appears. (One tick equals .05 S&P point or $25.) During more volatile market conditions, the impact would be larger. In this analysis, S&P 500 futures trades are assumed to be executed on average within four ticks of the last trade, on average .20 S&P points, or $100.[15] Individual trades may have a greater than four-tick market impact in a very fast moving market, but the four-tick assumption for the average insurance trade should be a conservative one. This would represent .1% (one-way) of a S&P 500 futures contract with $100,000 of underlying share value (S&P 500 at 200). Adding the commissions of .015% to .1% and multiplying by 2 results in round-trip commission and market impact charge of .23%. The comparable charge for an index fund trade in stocks under similar market conditions would be approximately .825%, of which .7% is an estimate of market impact. This .7% translates into roughly 1/4 points on a typical ($40) stock.

The final component of trading costs is the estimate of the futures mispricing expected to be present when a portfolio insurance trade occurs. Table 5 shows one and two standard deviation levels of mispricing changes (in S&P points) for percentage changes in the index greater than .5%, 1%, and 1.5% in absolute value. A 1.5% move in the index represents two standard deviations of daily index volatility (.77%) over the sample period.

The highest round-trip cost is 1.77% which assumes an index move of 1.5% in magnitude and mispricing of 1.54 S&P points, or two standard deviations from the average level of mispricing on days of index moves greater than 1.5% in magnitude. Note that this value is just above the round-trip trading cost that was assumed for stocks above.

The range of total trading costs shown in Table 5 indicates that a trading cost of 1% would be moderately high, but not an unreasonable assumption to use in evaluating the impact of mispricing. A 1.75% trading cost is an

---

15. The difficulty of conducting an index or program trade in a volatile stock market has not been taken into account in the market impact estimate for the stock market. The market estimate of .7% for stocks is based on a typical trading day and might be significantly higher on a day when a portfolio insurance trade would be called for because of the impact of higher volatility.

TABLE 5. *Transaction Cost Adjustment for Mispricing.*

Size of Index Move	Units of Std. Dev.	Standard Deviation of Mispricing Change			
		S&P Points	% of Index[a]	Round Trip	Total Cost[b]
.5%	1	.57%	.28%	.57%	.80%
	2	1.14	.57	1.14	1.37
1.0%	1	.66	.33	.66	.89
	2	1.32	.66	1.32	1.55
1.5%	1	.77	.38	.77	1.00
	2	1.54	.77	1.54	1.77

a. Index value of 200 assumed.
b. Round-trip mispricing plus commission and market impact.

example of an unusually high level mispricing. Incorporation of these trading cost levels in the volatility estimate implies that all trades executed over the entire life of the insurance program experience these high levels of transaction costs. This is a very conservative assumption and should, therefore, provide a very conservative estimate of portfolio insurance costs.

Estimating the Volatility Distribution

The put or insurance cost distribution can be directly derived from the probability distribution of volatility levels adjusted for transaction costs. The binomial option pricing model is used to effect the transformation of each adjusted volatility estimate to a put value.[16] Two different approaches are employed to arrive at a (unadjusted) probability distribution of annualized volatility levels. Both approaches use the Ibbotson Associates data base of monthly S&P 500 returns over the periods, 1926–85 and 1946–85. These returns serve as inputs for calculating a series of non-overlapping one-year and three-year volatilities from which a mean and standard deviation of volatility can be determined. By imposing a normal distribution assumption on the distribution of 1-year and 3-year volatility levels, this empirical mean and standard deviation can serve as a basis for deriving a distribution of volatilities.[17] Probabilities are assigned at 20 points evenly spaced along the distribu-

---

16. John C. Cox, Stephen A. Ross, and Mark Rubinstein, "Option Pricing: A Simplified Approach," *Journal of Financial Economics* 7 (1979): 229–63.
17. A normal distribution assumption is used here out of convenience. The standard assumption for variances is a Chi-squared distribution. Rather than work with other distributions, results are shown using a normal distribution and the actual frequency distribution encountered in the volatility data.

TABLE 6. *Statistics for Annualized Volatility (standard deviation of monthly S&P 500 returns).*

Period	One Year		Three Year[a]	
	Mean	Std. Dev.	Mean	Std. Dev.
1926–85	16.4%	10.7%	17.9%	10.0%
1946–85	12.5	3.9	13.3	2.6
1966–85	13.8	4.0	14.9	2.5

a. First observation is based on 1926–28, 1946–48, 1966–68.

tion, where the range of points is from −3 to +3 units of standard deviation. The means and standard deviations of 1-year and 3-year volatility measures (non-overlapping periods) are illustrated above for the last 60-, 40-, and 20-year samples.

Table 6 shows that the S&P 500 exhibited different volatility characteristics in the period 1926–85 than in the most recent 20- or 40-year period. In particular, inclusion of the dramatic decline and recovery of stock prices in the 1930s and early 1940s results in an average volatility statistic of 16.4% (1-year) and 17.9% (3-year) as compared to levels of 12.5% and 13.3% for the 1946–85 period. The 10% standard deviation of volatility levels is measured over the sixty-year period versus the 2.6–3.9% standard deviation in the last forty years. This result has important implications for the question at hand. If the volatility distribution is based on the period including the Depression years, the distribution of volatilities will be much wider and the expected and worst case portfolio insurance costs much higher. However, to simply exclude the portion of the sample that includes the Depression years is inappropriate because it captures the specific type of financial disaster against which portfolio insurance is designed to insulate investors. Put costs are, therefore, derived for two volatility scenarios: (1) an expected volatility of 13% with a standard deviation of 3% for three-year insurance (4% for one-year insurance), and (2) a mean volatility of 17% with a standard deviation of 10%. The former case should provide a distribution reflecting the volatility environment of the last 40 years; the latter case reflects a much wider range of outcomes including volatilities as high as 50% in the 1930s.[18]

The normality assumption is not appropriate to the extent that volatility is nonstationary or is otherwise distributed. The assumption of normality in the distribution of volatility levels seems appropriate for the last 40 years

---

18. The 10% standard deviation assigns a moderate probability to negative volatility levels. We have imposed a minimum standard deviation constraint of 5% throughout the distribution analysis.

but is violated in the subsets of the volatility data that include the Depression years.[19] To examine the sensitivity of the results to the normality assumption, a frequency distribution of insurance costs is determined from the actual, observed volatility levels over the two sample time periods. The median and 95% cumulative probability put cost level for this approach will indicate the impact of changing volatility and mispricing without imposing any distributional assumptions on the volatility series. In the next section, the results are reviewed for both the empirical and normal distribution approach as applied to the volatility scenarios prevailing in the 1926–85 period which includes the Depression years (Scenario I) and the 1946–85 period (Scenario II).

IV. Presentation and Discussion of Results

Some generic criteria, typical of those selected by portfolio insurers, were analyzed. The terms of the insurance programs (options) examined are one and three years, with return floors of 0 and −5%.[20] Put costs are expressed as a percentage of portfolio value; the cost of the insurance and dividend income is not included in the floor return. (The effective floor return inclusive of put cost is the target floor minus the percentage put cost plus the percentage dividend yield.) In calculating the revised volatility estimate, an average trading frequency of 1 week is assumed for the 1-year program and 3 weeks for the 3-year program. Both term programs then have the same expected number of trades. The characteristics of the distribution of volatilities, revised for the trading costs and mispricing, and the derived distribution of put values are linked by the Cos–Ross–Rubinstein put option pricing model.

A 4.5% dividend yield is assumed for the S&P 500, a level higher than the current dividend yield on the S&P 500 of approximately 3.5%, but in line with the long-term average dividend yield as estimated from the Ibbotson

---

19. To test the normality assumption, we considered the autocorrelation, skewness, and kurtosis of the relevant volatility series: 1-year volatility estimates (non-overlapping periods) from 1926 to 1985 and from 1946 to 1985 and 3-year estimates from 1926 to 1985 and from 1946 to 1985. The results showed that both 1- and 3-year volatility estimates for the 1926 to 1985 period had significant autocorrelation (at the 5% error level), but the same series over the 1946 to 1985 period did not. (Note, however, that the later series only contains 19 and 13 observations, respectively.) The results also showed that the 1926 to 1985 series exhibit skewness and kurtosis that are significantly different from normality at the 5% error level. These same effects were not found in the 1946 to 1985 series. Our conclusion, then, is that normality is probably a reasonable assumption under Scenario I (no-Depression), but is violated under Scenario II.

20. Based on a recent informal survey of portfolio insurers, programs of 1-year term or less represent about 20% of portfolio insurance funds currently under management. Another 20% of funds are in 1- to under 3-year programs and 60% are in 3-year or greater term programs.

data base.[21] A risk-free rate assumption of 7%, the average Treasury bill rate over the last 20 years, was used for the 1-year and 3-year interest rate. Put option values are sensitive to changes in this rate, but the focus here is confined to volatility changes over the life of the option.

Three-Year Programs

Sections a and b of Table 7 contain the results of the analysis for a 3-year protection program with a 0% floor return based on a normal distribution of volatility levels. The results for Volatility Scenario I are representative of the average level and range of S&P 500 volatilities over the last forty years. Volatility Scenario II is representative of the most recent sixty-year period reflecting a scenario that includes a "Depression"-type market. Characteristics of the volatility and put cost distribution are shown at three transaction cost levels for the 0% floor and −5% floor case. The .5% transaction cost reflects a conservative estimate of the "pure" trading cost plus a small mispricing component of .27% assumed for the stock index futures. The 1% and 1.75% transaction cost levels depict moderate and extreme scenarios for adverse stock index futures mispricing. By comparing the 1.75% results to those based on the assumed "pure" trading costs or .5% transaction cost level, we can assess the marginal effect of futures mispricing on the expected put cost.

For the 0% floor, 3-year, 13% volatility program as shown in Section a of Table 7, the volatility revision incorporating trading costs of .5% increases the expected volatility to 13.9% from 13%. Extreme futures mispricing (transaction costs of 1.75%) brings this figure up by another 1.7% to 15.6%. Volatility at the 95% cumulative probability level should be at the very high end of the range of volatilities (only 5% of the distribution of volatilities lies above this value). This volatility is 18.4% for transaction costs of .5%, and 20.2% for transaction costs of 1.75%, roughly 5% above the expected volatility value.

The impact on the insurance cost distribution in Volatility Scenario I can be measured in several ways. The range of expected put costs for different levels of transaction costs indicates the expected impact of mispricing. In this case, extreme mispricing results in an increase in the annualized option premium of .34% from 2.19% to 2.53%. The standard deviation of this

---

21. The average annualized monthly dividend yield and Treasury bill rate are:

	Div. Yld.	T-Bill Rate
1926–85	4.83%	3.41%
1946–85	4.50	4.62
1966–85	4.27	7.31

Source: Ibbotson Associates.

TABLE 7. *Analysis of Insurance Costs Based on Derived Normal Distribution.*

a. 0% Floor, 3-Year Term

Transaction Costs	Volatility Scenario I (Based on 1946-85)			Volatility Scenario II (Based on 1926-85)		
	.5%	1%	1.75%	.5%	1%	1.75%
Insurance cost						
Expected	2.194%	2.331%	2.530%	3.057%	3.184%	3.382%
Std. deviation	(1.04)	(1.05)	(1.07)	(3.08)	(3.09)	(3.12)
Extreme cost[a]	3.075	3.206	3.418	5.694	5.814	6.012
Volatility						
Revised expected[b]	13.9%	14.6%	15.6%	17.9%	18.6%	19.7%
Revised extreme	18.4	19.1	20.2	32.9	33.6	34.8

b. −5% Floor, 3-Year Term

Transaction Costs	Volatility Scenario I (Based on 1946-85)			Volatility Scenario II (Based on 1926-85)		
	.5%	1%	1.75%	.5%	1%	1.75%
Insurance cost						
Expected	1.543%	1.678%	1.867%	2.367%	2.497%	2.682%
Std. deviation	(0.94)	(0.96)	(0.98)	(2.85)	(2.88)	(2.92)
Extreme cost[a]	2.35	2.490	2.685	4.887	5.023	5.229
Volatility						
Revised expected[b]	13.8%	14.6%	15.6%	17.8%	18.6%	19.7%
Revised extreme	18.3	19.1	20.2	32.8	33.6	34.8

a. Extreme cost is defined as the cost for which there is only a 5% chance of higher costs or a 95% chance of the extreme cost or lower.

b. The unrevised expected volatility is 13% for Scenario I and 17% for Scenario II. The unrevised extreme value is 17.5% for Scenario I and 32% for Scenario II.

put cost is shown to be 1.04% for the lowest trading cost case and 1.07% for the 1.75% (including mispricing) trading cost case. The statistics for the put cost under an extreme volatility increase assumption (the 95% probability put cost level) show that insurance costs are much more sensitive to significant increases in volatility than they are to stock index futures mispricing. A volatility of 18.4% (.5% trading cost), which is not quite two standard deviations from the expected volatility level of 13.9%, raises the insurance cost from 2.19% to 3.07% by .88%. This is more than twice the impact of experiencing an unusually high level of futures mispricing throughout the program. The increase in insurance cost is identical for the higher trading cost (1.75%) case. The 95% probability put cost is .89% higher, 3.42% versus 2.53%.

For the Volatility Scenario II, a different picture emerges. Recall that the standard deviation of volatilities is 10% for this scenario versus only 3% for the 1946–85 period. Extreme futures mispricing is carried through as a .325% increase in the expected insurance cost. Note that the expected insurance cost is higher, by 3.38% versus 2.53% because of the higher average volatility. More important, the wider range of volatilities in this Scenario raises the extreme volatility insurance cost to an annualized value of 6.01%, almost twice the expected level of 3.38%. The revised volatility at the 95% probability level is 34.8%.

These results indicate that the biggest concern of the portfolio insurer should be adverse volatility changes in the form of an increase in volatility if an insurance program is implemented via option replication. The sharp cost increases in the Scenario including the Depression years should be considered in light of the actual returns during that period. In the event of a stock market decline such as the −27% annualized return over the 1929–31 period, anyone with a 0% floor program would not be particularly disturbed by a 6% insurance cost when a 3% cost was expected. On the other hand, in a period such as 1933–35 where the annualized total return of the S&P 500 was +30.9%, the 6% annualized cost in terms of underperformance in a high volatility environment may be a bit more uncomfortable. The bottom panel results are shown for a −5% floor. The expected put costs (annualized) are approximately .5% lower in all cases and .8% lower at the 95% probability level than the costs at the 0% floor.

A similar analysis is conducted for the 0% floor case using the frequency distribution volatilities occurring over the sample periods. These results are indicated in Figure 2. The sample distributions of 3-year volatilities over the 1926–85 and 1946–85 perios are shown in Section b, and the positive skewness in observed volatilities is noted. The 95% probability level for the 1946–85 volatilities is 19.7%, 2.2% greater than the 17.5% level given by the derived normal distribution. For the 1926–85 sample, the comparable empirical level is 33.5% versus the 32% derived from the normal distribution. In this time period, however, the maximum volatility of over 50% is the strongest evidence of the presence of skewness. These differences between the empirical and derived normal distributions suggest that the more conservative approach would be to base extreme cost estimates on an empirical distribution or a positively skewed derived distribution, such as the lognormal or Chi-squared distribution.

The insurance costs shown in Figure 2 can be compared to those in Section a of Table 7. The median unrevised volatility of 13.6% is close to the 13% estimate used in the normal distribution analyses for the 1946–85 period. This is not the case for the 1926–85 period, in which the median volatility of 14.1% is well below the average of 17% used in the normal distribution analysis. This lower value results in lower expected (median) put costs for the empirically-based analysis (1926–85).

FIGURE 2. *Analysis of Insurance Costs Based on Empirical Volatility Distribution.*

a. 0% Floor, 3-Year Term

Transaction Costs	Volatility Scenario I (Based on 1946–85)			Volatility Scenario II (Based on 1926–85)		
	.5%	1%	1.75%	.5%	1%	1.75%
Insurance cost						
Median	2.315%	2.446%	2.657%	2.412%	2.545%	2.755%
Extreme[a]	3.494	3.622	3.831	5.949	6.067	6.262
Volatility						
Median revised[b]	14.5%	15.2%	16.3%	15.0%	15.7%	16.8%
Minimum revised	8.6	10.1	11.1	10.3	11.8	12.9
Maximum revised	19.7	21.3	22.4	50.7	52.3	53.5

a. Extreme cost is defined as the cost for which there is only a 5% chance of higher costs or a 95% chance of the extreme cost or lower.
b. The unrevised median volatility is 13.6% for Scenario I and 14.1% for Scenario II. The unrevised extreme volatility is 19.7% for Scenario I and 33.5% for Scenario II.

b. 3-Year Volatility of Monthly S&P 500 Returns (frequency distribution)

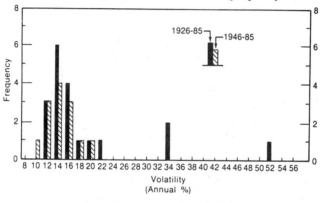

c. Distribution of Insurance Costs
(3-Year, 0% Floor, Annualized, 1.75% transaction cost)

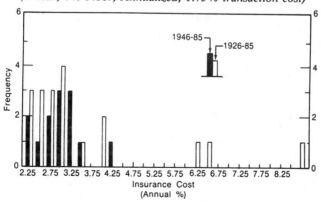

The median insurance cost based on the 1946–85 volatility distribution is slightly higher (2.66% vs. 2.53%) than that from the normal distribution results as shown in Section a of Figure 2, assuming high levels of futures mispricing. The extreme volatility cost is 3.83% compared to 3.42% from the derived normal distribution, using 1.75% as the full trading cost. The cost distribution calculated from Volatility Scenario II has a lower median, 2.76%, than the expected cost of 3.38% from the normal distribution. However, the 95% probability insurance costs are very similar to 6.26% (empirical) and 6.01% (normal).

One-Year Programs

Table 8 contains an insurance cost analysis for a one-year program with a −5% (Section a) and a 0% (Section b) floor. Note that a sequence of three 1-year insurance programs is more expensive than one 3-year program. The expected annualized put cost for a 0% floor is 2.33% assuming a 13% volatlity and moderate futures mispricing. For a one-year program, this cost would be more than double at a level of 5.86%. A −5% floor for a one-year program is more typical than a 0% floor (approximately one fourth of the distribution of annual S&P 500 returns is at a level of −5% or below).

The evidence that insurance costs are more sensitive to extreme volatility levels than to extreme futures mispricing is even more pronounced in the one-year program results. With a −5% floor, a one-year program would have an expected cost of 2.87% in Scenario I and 4.49% for the Scenario II case, assuming minor futures mispricing. Recall that the incremental cost associated with extreme futures mispricing for a 3-year program was .34%. These expected costs are incremented by approximately 1% to 3.80% (Scenario I) and 5.45% (Scenario II) with high levels of futures mispricing in a one-year program. The extreme volatility insurance costs are 5.98% and 10.76% respectively, again significantly higher than the expected put costs. For a 0% floor and one-year life as shown in Section b of Table 8, the high volatility insurance costs are over 2% higher than the expected put costs in Scenario I and 5.6% higher using the volatility estimates including the Depression years.

Figure 3 details the empirically-based results for one-year volatilities and portfolio insurance costs. The empirical distribution of one-year volatilities is very similar to the derived normal distribution for the 1946–85 period. This similarity in probability levels is not characteristic of the empirical and normal distributions for the 1926–85 period. The median volatility of 13.1% is well below the 17% average; however, the positive skewness of the empirical distribution results in 95% probability levels of volatility of 34.4%, significantly higher than the 32% of the normal distribution.

These similarities and differences between the derived normal and empirical distribution results are carried over to the distribution of insurance

TABLE 8. *Analysis of Insurance Costs Based on Derived Normal Distribution.*

a. −5% Floor, 1-Year Term

Transaction Costs	Volatility Scenario I (Based on 1946–85)			Volatility Scenario II (Based on 1926–85)		
	.5%	1%	1.75%	.5%	1%	1.75%
Insurance cost						
Expected	2.870%	3.229%	3.799%	4.492%	4.857%	5.446%
Std. deviation	(1.30)	(1.34)	(1.41)	(3.10)	(3.16)	(3.26)
Extreme cost[a]	4.928	5.333	5.983	9.623	10.055	10.758
Volatility						
Revised expected[b]	14.5%	15.6%	17.3%	18.5%	19.7%	21.4%
Revised extreme	20.6	21.7	23.5	33.6	34.8	36.7

b. 0% Floor, 1-Year Term

Transaction Costs	Volatility Scenario I (Based on 1946–85)			Volatility Scenario II (Based on 1926–85)		
	.5%	1%	1.75%	.5%	1%	1.75%
Insurance cost						
Expected	4.773%	5.236%	5.860%	6.444%	6.910%	7.554%
Std. deviation	(1.15)	(1.50)	(1.54)	(3.38)	(3.42)	(3.50)
Extreme cost[a]	6.992	7.497	8.156	11.935	12.451	13.189
Volatility						
Revised expected[b]	14.4%	15.6%	17.3%	18.4%	19.7%	21.4%
Revised extreme	20.4	21.7	23.5	33.4	34.8	36.7

a. Extreme cost is defined as the cost for which there is only a 5% chance of higher costs or a 95% chance of the extreme cost or lower.

b. The unrevised expected volatility is 13% for Scenario I and 17% for Scenario II. The unrevised extreme value is 19% for Scenario I and 32% for Scenario II.

costs. The median put cost at the highest 1.75% trading cost level including extreme futures mispricing is 3.57% for the empirical distribution, compared to 3.80% for the derived normal distribution. The 95% probability level costs are very similar: 5.98% versus 6.05%. Major differences exist between the median cost for the 1926–85 base period of the expected value (normal distribution). The median insurance cost is 3.82%, compared to a 5.45% level for the expected put cost. The 95% probability level put cost is a high 13.45% for the empirical distribution versus 10.76% for the normal distribution.

The empirical distribution of volatilities, therefore, results in a much smaller difference between median insurance costs inclusive and exclusive of a Depression scenario. However, the differences in estimated costs at the extremes (high volatility levels) are greater based on the actual volatility expe-

FIGURE 3. *Analysis of Insurance Costs Based on Empirical Volatility Distribution.*

a. −5% Floor, 1-Year Term

Transaction Costs	Volatility Scenario I (Based on 1946–85)			Volatility Scenario II (Based on 1926–85)		
	.5%	1%	1.75%	.5%	1%	1.75%
Insurance cost						
Median	2.597%	2.962%	3.534%	2.867%	3.240%	3.823%
Extreme[a]	5.000	5.405	6.050	12.315	12.750	13.447
Volatility						
Median revised[b]	20.8%	21.9%	23.7%	41.0%	42.2%	44.2%
Minimum revised	5.2	6.0	7.3	5.2	6.0	7.3
Maximum revised	24.5	25.6	27.5	66.7	67.9	70.0

a. Extreme cost is defined as the cost for which there is only a 5% chance of higher costs or a 95% chance of the extreme cost or lower.
b. The unrevised median volatility is 12.3% for Scenario I and 13.1% for Scenario II. The unrevised extreme volatility is 19.2% for Scenario I and 39.4% for Scenario II.

b. 1-Year Volatility of Monthly S&P 500 Returns (frequency distribution)

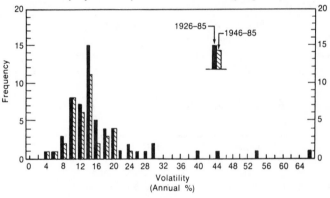

c. Distribution of Insurance Costs
(1-Year, −5% Floor, Annualized, 1.75% transaction cost)

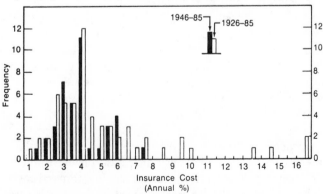

rienced over the last forty versus sixty years. The extreme volatility insurance cost is over three times that of the median value; the 95% probability cost from the normal distribution is just under two times the expected level.

V. Summary and Concluding Remarks

This study has addressed concerns regarding the magnitude of the impact of adverse volatility changes and extreme levels of futures mispricing on the costs associated with portfolio insurance. This issue has become prominent in assessments of downside protection programs using futures as feasible and cost-effective risk management strategies. The most important findings of the analysis of insurance costs were:

1. the impact of stock index futures mispricing (treated as an increment to trading cost) on portfolio insurance costs was relatively small in magnitude, less than a .5% incremental cost for a 3-year program, and a 1% incremental cost for a 1-year program;
2. the longer the life of the insurance program, the smaller the impact of both futures mispricing and volatility risk, holding the frequency of trading constant between the two (different term) programs;
3. the potential adverse impact on the cost of a portfolio insurance program of extreme levels of realized volatility was much larger in magnitude than that of futures mispricing, just under 1% (annualized) in a 3-year protection program and over 2% in a 1-year protection program for a scenario seen in equity markets in the last forty years.

The expected or median insurance cost can actually double or triple under extreme volatility conditions based on an analysis of the last sixty years of index volatility. An extreme volatility increase is defined as a move from the median or expected value to the 95% cumulative probability level. These extreme volatility conditions have a likelihood of only 1 in 20 of occurring. However, they are relevant in a discussion of the worst case scenario for those considering a portfolio insurance strategy. It is also important to point out that a much larger than expected insurance cost may be more easy to tolerate if it occurs in a steeply declining equity market. The benefit of having insurance in a −20% annualized return 3-year period or a −40% 1-year period should far outweigh the discomfort associated with higher than expected insurance costs. People are willing to pay somewhat more for flood insurance when rivers reach flood stage. Also, in a very positive equity return environment or a whipsaw market, increases in insurance cost associated with higher volatility and futures mispricing appear more burdensome.

Some supplementary insights were produced by the analysis of the relationship between S&P 500 futures mispricing and index returns. The standard deviation of these mispricing changes on the days of large index moves provided information for estimating the transaction cost impact of extreme futures mispricing. As expected, there was greater mispricing variability in more volatile index markets. The contemporaneous correlation between mispricing changes and the percentage index changes was significantly positive on days of large absolute index returns. Positive correlation was also observed between mispricing changes on day t and index returns on day $t+1$, perhaps arising from stock index arbitrage that is initiated by the futures mispricing. A more interesting result was the significant negative correlation between percentage index changes on day t and mispricing changes on the following day ($t+1$). This result was pervasive in the sample, regardless of the magnitude of the index return. This evidence supports a finding that the index movements may have a stronger lead than lag relationship to changes in stock index futures mispricing changes, and also that the lead relationship is opposite in sign to the lag relationship. The negative correlation between index returns and the subsequent day's mispricing change implies that insurers using futures to implement adjustments to stock index positions may benefit by waiting a day for adverse mispricing effects associated with the index change to diminish. It is important to note, however, that the beneficial effects of lower levels of mispricing may be accompanied by further changes in the index levels that eliminate or reduce the advantages of lower mispricing.

The evidence presented here suggests some guidelines for constructing portfolio insurance strategies using futures or option replication as the implementation vehicle. First, be especially conservative in selecting the volatility estimates on which anticipated insurance costs and allocations will be based. Evaluate results under extreme scenarios for volatility changes. The approach used here of adjusting the volatility estimate of the risky asset to assess the upper ranges of the cost of a protection program can provide valuable information regarding the magnitude and range of problems that may arise. If the investor is particularly cost-sensitive, taking steps to protect against increases in volatility may be advisable. Option strategies can be constructed so as to benefit from volatility increases. Also, the trading rule for determing changes in allocation can be adjusted to incorporate volatility changes inclusive of futures mispricing. Allocation models less sensitive to volatility changes can be utilized. These volatility hedging techniques are only available at a cost and would, therefore, increase the expected insurance cost. If futures mispricing is sizable at the time an allocation adjustment must be made, there may be a benefit in waiting until the subsequent day to transact in futures, given the evidence of a negative correlation between index returns and mispricing changes on the following day. This benefit must be balanced against the risk of a further index move in the same direction on the next day causing the allocation to be even further off-target.

Volatility uncertainty and futures mispricing do have an impact on portfolio insurance costs. This potential impact is measurable and to some extent avoidable at a cost. The important point is that these risks are not occasion to dismiss portfolio insurance, as implemented with stock inex futures, as a viable strategy or to necessarily encourage the selling of portfolio insurance. Sellers of portfolio insurance face the same type of volatility risk as buyers if they are engaging in option replication. However, they are affected adversely by declines rather than by increases in volatility. In making an informed and intelligent decision regarding the suitability of portfolio insurance, the risks and impact of futures mispricing and changing volatility should be weighed against the benefits of the protection program.

45

What's Wrong with Portfolio Insurance?*

Mark Kritzman
General Partner
Windham Capital Management

I. Introduction

Recent changes in pension accounting have formalized the notion that the asset mix decision should be driven by both pension assets and pension liabilities. Within this context, portfolio insurance, as it is typically applied, is *not* an appropriate strategy for pension funds:

- Portfolio insurance is economically meaningless, because it is insensitive to a pension fund's surplus value.
- Portfolio insurance may increase the volatility of a pension fund's surplus.
- Portfolio insurance is significantly overpriced relative to protection that is economically meaningful.

This article shows how the investor can adapt portfolio insurance to overcome these problems.

II. Portfolio Insurance

Portfolio insurance is an asset allocation strategy that continually rebalances a portfolio between a risky component and a riskless component so that the

---

*Reprinted from the Winter 1986 issue of *The Journal of Portfolio Management*.

total portfolio's return does not fall below some pre-specified minimum return. At the same time, the portfolio captures most of the risky component's return that may exceed the risk-free return.

The standard deviation of the risky component is a key determinant of the cost of portfolio insurance, in the sense that we can think of cost as lost opportunity should the risky component produce superior results. As the portfolio's value rises above the value associated with the minimum required return, the asset mix is shifted toward the risky component. As the portfolio's value falls, funds are shifted to the risk-free component to protect the portfolio's return from dropping below the minimum required return.

The cost of this protection equals the extent to which the portfolio fails to capture the favorable swing in the risky component's return. This cost will increase as the standard deviation of the risky component increases, because a greater percentage of the portfolio will be allocated, on average, to the risk-free component in order to satisfy the minimum required return.

III. The Portfolio Insurance Implications of Financial Accounting Standard No. 87

FAS No. 87 gives economic as well as accounting recognition to determination of a pension fund's health by the market value of both pension assets and pension liabilities. This standard recognizes the value of the pension fund surplus as the relevant measure of health, where surplus is defined as the difference between pension assets and liabilities. Moreover, the Financial Accounting Standards Board has instilled economic meaning into its definition of surplus by requiring companies to use market discount rates to value liabilities.

These changes affect both the balance sheet and the income statement. The balance sheet is affected because the FASB requires companies to enter a negative pension fund surplus as a liability. The income statement is affected because the pension fund surplus, whether it is negative or positive, is amortized over 10 to 20 years and reflected in reported earnings.

Including pension assets and liabilities in a company's financial statements, especially when liabilities are measured in an economically meaningful way, has important implications for portfolio insurance.

First, portfolio insurance protects only a pension fund's asset value. This insurance is completely insensitive to shifts in the present value of the pension liabilities, which, together with the pension assets, determine the value of the surplus. As it is surplus that affects a company's net worth and earnings, portfolio insurance is an economically meaningless exercise.

Second, although portfolio insurance is without economic meaning, it could have an economic consequence, by increasing the volatility of a company's net worth as well as its earnings. Consider a situation where the value of the pension assets declines. Because the FASB requires the pension liabilities to be valued at market, they could decline roughly in line with the pension assets, thus leaving the surplus value unchanged. If the assets were insured, however, some of the assets would be reallocated to the risk-free component, thereby changing the risk profile of the assets. This change in risk could lower the correlation between the pension assets and liabilities. Such a change in correlation would increase the volatility of the surplus, and, by extension, the volatility of the company's net worth and earnings. The same result might occur if the value of the pension assets increased.

Finally, portfolio insurance is unnecessarily expensive, given the alternative of insuring the *ratio* of pension assets to pension liabilities. This point invites elaboration.

Pension liabilities, when measured correctly, are partly correlated with pension assets. Conceptually, we can express the present value of pension assets as:

$$PVA = \frac{C}{k - g},$$

where:

PVA = present value of pension assets,
C = cash flows including dividends and interest payments,
k = discount rate, and
g = growth rate of cash flows.

Similarly, we can express the present value of pension liabilities as:

$$PVL = \frac{B}{k - g},$$

where:

PVL = present value of pension liabilities,
B = benefit payments,
k = discount rate, and
g = growth rate of benefit payments.

This conceptual model shows us that an increase in discount rates that causes the present value of dividend and interest payments to decline will, to the extent that benefit payments are of equal duration and risk, also cause the present value of the benefit payments to decline. Therefore, the net worth of the pension fund is naturally hedged, and the extent of this hedge is a function of the correlation between the pension assets and the pension liabilities. Portfolio insurance is unnecessarily expensive because it fails to exploit this natural hedge.

IV. Dynamic Asset/Liability Management

An alternative to portfolio insurance is dynamic asset/liability management. This strategy adapts the technology of portfolio insurance to incorporate pension liabilities. Portfolio insurance is designed only to protect pension assets, but dynamic asset/liability management is designed to protect the ratio of pension assets to pension liabilities. Specifically, the objective of dynamic strategies is to assure that a minimum asset/liability ratio is met or exceeded while capturing returns in excess of changes in pension liabilities.

We can accomplish this objective by substituting a "liability-mimicking portfolio" for the risk-free component in the portfolio insurance strategy. Such a portfolio would track precisely any changes in the present value of the pension liabilities. Although the portfolio would be risky in an absolute sense, it would be riskless relative to the liabilities. Within this context, any portfolio that was not perfectly correlated with the liabilities could serve as the risky component — even a portfolio that in an absolute sense was risk-free. The strategy would be executed by continually rebalancing the total portfolio between the risky component and the liability-mimicking component.

V. Benefits of Dynamic Asset/Liability Management

Dynamic asset/liability management is superior to portfolio insurance, because dynamic asset/liability management deals directly with pension fund surplus, which is what affects a company's net worth and earnings. Moreover, dynamic asset/liability management is significantly less expensive than portfolio insurance. The table shows the comparative cost of the two strategies.

Comparative Costs in Percentages

Minimum Required Return	One Year		Two Years		Three Years	
	PI	DALM	PI	DALM	PI	DALM
−1%	14.2	9.2	7.9	5.6	5.0	4.0
−2%	10.9	6.5	5.6	3.6	3.2	2.4
−3%	8.8	4.8	4.2	2.4	2.1	1.6
−4%	7.2	3.7	3.2	1.7	1.4	1.0
−5%	6.0	2.9	2.5	1.2	0.9	0.7

The column labeled PI shows the cost of portfolio insurance, assuming a return of 8% for the risk-free component and a standard deviation of 15% for the risky component.

The column labeled DALM shows the cost of dynamic asset/liability management, assuming a 15% standard deviation for the risky component, a 10% standard deviation for the liability-mimicking component, and a 75%

correlation between the two. The minimum required return is measured relative to the return of the risk-free component, and multiple-year results are annualized.

For example, consider alternative strategies with a one-year horizon and a −3% minimum required return. A $100 investment in a portfolio insurance strategy would assure a terminal value one year hence of no less than $104.76 (108 times 0.97). If the risky component generated a 20% return, however, the expected terminal value of the total portfolio is $120 times (1−0.088) or $109.44. A dynamic asset/liability management strategy that has an initial asset/liability ratio of 100% would be assured of a terminal asset/liability ratio of no less than 97%. If the risky component generated a net return of 20% relative to the liability-mimicking portfolio, however, the expected terminal asset/liability ratio is 120% times (1−0.048) or 114.24%.

Of course, the cost saving would increase if the liability-mimicking component behaves more like the risky component. For example, if both components had a standard deviation of 15% and were 90% correlated, the cost of a one-year strategy with a −3% minimum required return would equal 2.3% rather than 4.8%. The opportunity for gains in excess of changes in the present value of the liabilities, however, would be reduced commensurately.

VI. The Characteristics of a Liability-Mimicking Portfolio

What are the characteristics of a liability-mimicking portfolio? If we are interested in only the retired lives of a pension plan and if there were no anticipated changes in benefit policy, then an immunized or dedicated bond portfolio could serve as the liability-mimicking component. If, however, we are interested in total pension liabilities, including the accrued benefits of the current work force and the future benefits of employees yet to be hired, then we must consider potential changes in benefit policy as well as changes in the demographics of the work force. Within the latter context, the liability-mimicking portfolio should probably include an equity component to account for the growth characteristics of the liabilities. Factor analysis might be a useful tool to uncover the factor sensitivities of the liabilities and to structure a portfolio with similar sensitivities.

In any event, it is important to capture changes in the market value of the liabilities to take advantage of their correlation with the market value of the pension assets.

VII. Conclusion

This paper addresses the implications of FAS No. 87 on portfolio insurance and demonstrates that portfolio insurance, as it is typically applied, is economically irrational, because it ignores the surplus value of a pension fund. Moreover, portfolio insurance is unnecessarily expensive, because it fails to account for the correlation between pension assets and pension liabilities.

Nonetheless, investors can modify portfolio insurance to incorporate pension liabilities. The key modification is to substitute a portfolio that mimics the behavior of the pension liabilities and to use that portfolio as the risk-free component. With this modification, portfolio insurance can be adapted to protect a pension fund's surplus and can do so at a sharply reduced cost.

Appendix

The technical framework of dynamic asset/liability management is an adaptation of Margrabe's option model to exchange one asset for another.[1] After all, dynamic asset/liability management is tantamount to an option to exchange a risky portfolio for a liability-mimicking portfolio or, in other words, investment in a risky portfolio with a protective put option that has an exercise price indexed to the value of the liabilities.

Based on the Magrabe model, the value of such an option equals:

$$C = N(d_1)R - N(d_2)L$$

$$d_1 = \frac{\ln(R/L) + \frac{1}{2}(\sigma_R^2 + \sigma_L^2 - 2\alpha\sigma_R\sigma_L)T}{(\sigma_R^2 + \sigma_L^2 - 2\alpha\sigma_R\sigma_L)^{1/2}\sqrt{T}}$$

$$d_2 = d_1 - (\sigma_R^2 + \sigma_L^2 - 2\alpha\sigma_R\sigma_L)^{1/2}\sqrt{T}$$

where:

C = price of an option to exchange R for L,
R = price of risky portfolio,
L = price of liability-mimicking portfolio,
σ_R = standard deviation of risky portfolio,
σ_L = standard deviation of liability-mimicking portfolio,
α = correlation between risky portfolio and liability-mimicking portfolio,
T = investment horizon, and
$N(\ )$ = cumulative normal density function.

From put-call parity, we can determine the value of a put as:

$$P = C + L - R.$$

1. William Margrabe, "The Value of an Option to Exchange One Asset for Another," *Journal of Finance* 33, no. 1 (March 1978).

Since we are interested in replicating a strategy whereby we purchase as much of the risky portfolio as possible along with a protective put, we solve for the value of the put iteratively by changing the value of the risky portfolio so that its value, together with the value of the put, exactly matches the initial market value of the portfolio we are seeking to protect.

The initial allocation to the risky component equals $N(d_1)R$ divided by the market value of the total portfolio, and the cost of the protection equals one minus the market value of the risky portfolio as a percent of the total market value. Subsequent allocations will depend on the relative return of the two components as well as the passage of time.

The framework described above differs from the Black–Scholes framework, which is used for standard portfolio insurance.[2] In the model here, the risk-free return equals zero, because it represents the return of the liability-mimicking portfolio net of changes in the present value of liabilities, and risk is defined as the standard deviation of the risky portfolio net of the standard deviation of the liability-mimicking portfolio, recognizing, of course, their covariance.

---

2. Fischer Black and Myron Scholes, "The Pricing of Options and Corporate Liabilities," *Journal of Political Economy* 81 (May/June).

Name Index

Subject Index

The Institutional Investor Series in Finance

The Institutional Investor Series in Finance has been developed specifically to bring you—the finance professional—the latest thinking and developments in investments and corporate finance. As new challenges arise in this fast-paced arena, you can count on this series to provide you with the information you need to gain the competitive edge.

Institutional Investor is the leading communications company serving the global financial community and publisher of the magazine of the same name. Institutional Investor has won 36 major awards for distinguished financial journalism—including the prestigious National Magazine Award for the best reporting of any magazine in the United States. More than 560,000 financial executives in 170 countries read Institutional Investor publications each month. Thousands more attend Institutional Investor's worldwide conferences and seminars each year.